Learn FileMaker Pro 2024

The Comprehensive Guide
to Building Custom Databases

Third Edition

Mark Conway Munro

Apress®

Learn FileMaker Pro 2024: The Comprehensive Guide to Building Custom Databases, Third Edition

Mark Conway Munro
Lewisburg, PA, USA

ISBN-13 (pbk): 979-8-8688-0834-0   ISBN-13 (electronic): 979-8-8688-0835-7
https://doi.org/10.1007/979-8-8688-0835-7

Managing Director, Apress Media LLC: Welmoed Spahr
Acquisitions Editor: Miriam Haidara
Project Manager: Jessica Vakili

Cover image by Freepik (www.freepik.com)

Distributed to the book trade worldwide by Springer Science+Business Media New York, 1 New York Plaza, Suite 4600, New York, NY 10004-1562, USA. Phone 1-800-SPRINGER, fax (201) 348-4505, e-mail orders-ny@springer-sbm.com, or visit www.springeronline.com. Apress Media, LLC is a California LLC and the sole member (owner) is Springer Science + Business Media Finance Inc (SSBM Finance Inc). SSBM Finance Inc is a **Delaware** corporation.

For information on translations, please e-mail booktranslations@springernature.com; for reprint, paperback, or audio rights, please e-mail bookpermissions@springernature.com.

Apress titles may be purchased in bulk for academic, corporate, or promotional use. eBook versions and licenses are also available for most titles. For more information, reference our Print and eBook Bulk Sales web page at http://www.apress.com/bulk-sales.

Any source code or other supplementary material referenced by the author in this book is available to readers on GitHub. For more detailed information, please visit https://www.apress.com/gp/services/source-code.

If disposing of this product, please recycle the paper

Table of Contents

xvii

About the Author

Mark Conway Munro is an accomplished author and software developer with a career spanning over three decades. He began working with AppleScript and FileMaker in 1988, using these tools to manage information and automate digital workflows. In 1994, Mark channeled his expertise into founding Write Track Media, a computer consultancy firm dedicated to streamlining repetitive digital tasks and enhancing productivity. His innovative systems empower clients to achieve greater creativity by freeing them from routine work. Mark is also the author of several influential books, including *AppleScript: Developer Reference* (2010, Wiley) and the widely respected *Learn FileMaker Pro* series (2017, 2021, 2024, Apress).

About the Technical Reviewer

Brian Sanchez is a seasoned FileMaker developer, business workflow consultant, and founding member of aACE Software, which offers a world-class customizable ERP and Accounting solution. With over 25 years of experience, Brian has designed and implemented custom apps for inventory tracking, digital catalogs using FileMaker Go, as well as asset management and pricing tools. He has developed tailored solutions for dozens of SMBs, specializing in WebDirect systems, API integrations, and, more recently, artificial intelligence (AI) services. Brian holds multiple FileMaker certifications and is known for his development philosophy of creating robust systems that minimize the need for client support, focusing instead on long-term upgrades and enhancements. Additionally, he has served as the technical editor of the *Learn FileMaker Pro* series for the 2017, 2021, and 2024 editions (Apress).

Introduction

The first edition of *Learn FileMaker Pro* was released in 2017, covering version 16. While it was well-received, I believed there was room for improvement, particularly in terms of conciseness and the quality of examples. In 2021, I had the opportunity to update the book for its second edition, focusing on version 19. I took this chance to rewrite the manuscript, restructure the content, enhance the language, and integrate valuable reader feedback. The result was a slightly shorter book that delivered more information in a more accessible format. The response was overwhelmingly positive.

Now, three years later, I am pleased to introduce the third edition: *Learn FileMaker Pro 2024*. This edition has been retitled to align with Claris' new annualized product releases and includes updates for the many new features introduced in recent years. Since the last edition covered up to version 19.1, this includes updates for versions 19.2 through 19.6, the features introduced in version 2023 (20.1–20.3), and the newly released version 2024 (21.1). In my ongoing effort to improve, I have further refined the presentation. Many sections have been clarified and expanded, with advanced material moved to the back to make the early lessons more approachable for new developers. Example files have been recreated for each topic, making it even easier to follow along and experiment. Additionally, I've added new material on transactions, dynamic object references, machine learning, and artificial intelligence for more experienced readers.

With each edition, I've strived to address legitimate criticisms. Is this edition perfect? Perhaps not. But I believe it represents a significant improvement, offering plenty of new content for everyone. I hope you enjoy the book and find it helpful in your journey. If you do, please consider leaving a review on your favorite online bookseller's site and sharing it on social media. As always, I welcome your feedback and questions. Feel free to contact me at any of the following:

- *Facebook* – facebook.com/groups/LearnFileMaker/
- *LinkedIn* – linkedin.com/in/markconwaymunro
- *Website* – writetrackmedia.com

Mark Conway Munro, August 2024

PART I

Using FileMaker

FileMaker Pro is a document-based desktop application that merges an easy-to-use interface for data entry tasks with a robust environment for developers. This application is Claris' premier tool for developing custom database applications. Before diving into technical details, these first chapters focus on the user experience to introduce the software environment and familiarize users with how custom databases will be accessed. So we begin with an exploration of the following topics:

1. Introducing FileMaker

2. Launching the Application

3. Exploring a Database Window

4. Working with Records

5. Transferring Records

CHAPTER 1

Introducing FileMaker

FileMaker Pro is a software platform used to create relational database applications for modern workflows. Published by Apple subsidiary Claris International Inc., the software has matured into a uniquely accessible and powerful development tool. The platform is popular among novice programmers for its intuitive, low-code programming interface. Professionals appreciate access to advanced technologies, robust customization options, rich connectivity, and plug-in extensibility. An integrated architecture combines the data, logic, and interface layers into a seamless programming experience, known as a "full stack," which is especially welcoming for beginners. Using the flagship desktop application, developers can create a secure, multi-user, cross-platform solution and rapidly deploy it to mobile, cloud, and on-premise workflows. Solutions can range from simple spreadsheet-like worksheets to artfully designed, feature-rich, interface-driven applications. FileMaker is used by independent consultants, employees of small businesses, and members of teams working at medium to large businesses, nonprofits, and government agencies. Although it is easy to learn, business leaders who can't invest the time themselves and don't employ a development staff can easily find a professional consultant to develop a system tailored to meet their needs. Whatever the skill set, FileMaker is an excellent choice for building custom databases. This chapter introduces FileMaker and

- Discusses the history of FileMaker in a nutshell
- Reviews the product line

The History of FileMaker in a Nutshell

The early history of FileMaker is a zigzag between various names, publishers, platforms, and numbering systems before eventually settling into a stable, modern track.

© Mark Conway Munro 2024
M. C. Munro, *Learn FileMaker Pro 2024*, https://doi.org/10.1007/979-8-8688-0835-7_1

Nashoba Systems

FileMaker started its life in the early 1980s as Nutshell, an MS-DOS computer program developed by Nashoba Systems in Concord, Massachusetts, and distributed by electronics marketer Leading Edge. When the Macintosh computer was introduced in early 1984, Nashoba saw an opportunity and combined the Nutshell database engine with a graphic user interface to create a forms-based database product. Since Leading Edge wanted to remain a DOS-only vendor, Nashoba turned to a new distributor, Forethought, Inc. As a result, FileMaker version 1.0 was released in April 1985 for the Macintosh platform. In 1986, it was renamed FileMaker Plus to match the release of the Macintosh Plus. When Microsoft purchased Forethought in 1987, they tried to negotiate a purchase of FileMaker, which was outselling their own Microsoft File database application. However, Nashoba declined and began self-publishing the program, now named FileMaker 4. By today's standards, these early versions of FileMaker were incredibly primitive. However, it was very capable for its time, and the software filled an important need by providing an easy-to-use interface that became popular with the do-it-yourself crowd.

Claris International

In 1986, Apple formed Claris Corp. as a wholly owned subsidiary to develop and publish Macintosh software titles such as MacWrite and MacPaint. In 1988, Claris purchased Nashoba Systems to acquire FileMaker. By this time, Leading Edge and Nutshell had disappeared as other DOS and Windows database products dominated the market. In 1988, FileMaker II was released by Claris to match the naming scheme of their other products. After a few minor updates, the product was rebranded in 1990 under its modern naming and versioning format when FileMaker Pro 1.0 was released. Claris upgraded the product in 1992 with Windows support, making FileMaker Pro 2.0 the first cross-platform version. They began publishing a server application in 1994. It wasn't until 1995 with the release of version 3.0 that FileMaker became fully relational. By 1997, with version 4.0, FileMaker was a widely popular product and was outselling all other Claris products. Apple absorbed all the other products and bundled them into AppleWorks before it was discontinued in favor of their iWork suite. The Claris subsidiary was renamed after their only remaining product: FileMaker.

FileMaker

In 1998, the company changed its name to FileMaker Inc. to reflect the new singular focus on the database product line. Over the subsequent decades, they transitioned the product from an early relational database to a feature-rich development platform. The product gained native support for Mac OS X and later the modern macOS. Many features we take for granted today were added during this time, for example, a multi-table file architecture, the ability to open multiple windows in a single file, calculation variables, buttons, tabs, portals, web viewers, conditional formatting, built-in functions, and script steps. They continued improving the product by adding script triggers, integrated charts, filtered portals, themes, numerous new layout tools, recursive custom functions, and custom menus. More recent additions include support for JavaScript Object Notation (JSON), client URL (cURL), and Structured Query Language (SQL) – also features like add-on tables, self-lookup tables for list-detail layouts, automatic directory creation, FileMaker URL, and FileMaker API. This era witnessed various adjustments to the product line to include desktop, server, and mobile versions and saw the version numbering scheme shift to whole numbers based on a consistent annual upgrade schedule.

Claris International Reborn

In 2019, FileMaker announced a resurrection of the Claris brand name and a rebranding of the company as Claris International Inc. The name was changed to better reflect plans for expanded offerings, such as the evolving Claris Connect workflow integration service and Claris Studio web design platform.

Version 19 was released in May 2020 with a new updated user interface. During the span of six incremental upgrades, culminating with version 19.6, many new features were introduced and evolved. These included new functions to convert file paths to and from the FileMaker format, JavaScript integration in web viewers, and OAuth support for third-party authentication. It also introduced script transactions to queue data entry changes for save/revert all at once and Core Machine Learning (CoreML) support for image recognition and natural language processing.

The April 2023 update introduced a new annualized naming scheme as "FileMaker Pro 2023" with the actual version number of 20 displayed less prominently. This hinted at Claris' commitment to more frequent annual releases. This version added functions to access base tables in the schema, a new *Perform Script on Server with Callback* script step, an *OnWindowTransaction* script trigger, and the ability to send mail using OAuth. This version also saw the introduction of *layout calculations*, which enable a formula embedded directly on a layout to produce text.

In June 2024, Claris released FileMaker Pro 2024 (version 21), continuing the commitment to more frequent annual upgrades. This version included bug fixes, performance enhancements, and several new features. Notable new JSON functions make a JSON array from a value list and return live text from an image as JSON. The most prominent additions are new *artificial intelligence* (AI) functions and script steps, including the ability to connect to an AI account and to perform semantic finds in the database by a query phrase instead of field criteria.

Note   Many feature releases from 19.1 through 21 (2024) have been added throughout this updated addition!

Reviewing the Product Line

The entire FileMaker product line is summarized in Table 1-1. It is made up of five separate applications, each designed to address a specific function in developing, using, and sharing databases.

Table 1-1. *A summary of each product in the FileMaker product line*

Product Name	Platform(s)	Develop	Use	Share
FileMaker Pro	Mac, Windows	Yes	Yes	Limited
FileMaker Server	Mac, Windows, Linux	No	No	Yes
FileMaker Cloud	Linux on AWS	No	No	Yes
FileMaker Go	iOS devices	No	Yes	No
FileMaker WebDirect	Web browser	No	Yes	No

Creating with FileMaker Pro

At the forefront of the product line and the primary focus of this book is the flagship application; *FileMaker Pro*. This desktop application provides a multipurpose interface that can be used to create, share, and access database files on macOS and Windows computers. It is the only product that includes all the structural development tools required to define the data structure, design an interface, and build scripts and other resources in a single seamless low-code application programming interface.

The software provides front-end access to data through a familiar document-based desktop application that displays interface layouts (Chapter 3) and allows data entry (Chapter 4). Once a new database file is created (Chapter 6), a graphical schema editor makes it easy to define tables, fields, and relationships (Chapters 7–9). A layout editing mode facilities the design of rich interfaces that integrate table data content and interface objects (Chapters 17–22). A scripting workspace makes it easy to create reusable sequences of automated events by skillfully balancing object-driven assembly of steps with text-based coding (Chapters 24–27). Credential management features make it simple to create secure accounts that limit user access and activity within the file using a mix of internal and external authentication (Chapter 29).

Many advanced tools provide even more powerful control. Build a library of custom functions that can be reused anywhere in the file (Chapter 15). Override the entire menu bar with custom menus to take complete control of the user experience (Chapter 23). A script debugger helps identify problems and evaluate performance (Chapter 26). Save an entire database as XML, generate design reports with ease, and encrypt databases with AES 256-bit encryption to protect databases at rest (Chapter 30).

Data can be shared and integrated in a variety of ways. Users and scripts can easily import and export data between databases and text-based data formats (Chapter 5). Network sharing allows workgroups to access the same database in real time for simultaneous data entry and development tasks (Chapter 29). Numerous integration options are available to connect to external systems using AppleScript (macOS), Claris Connect, Dynamic Data Exchange (Windows), FileMaker API, JDBC, ODBC, SQL, and more.

Tip   Enable *Use advanced tools* under the *General* tab of application *Preferences* (Chapter 2) to enable access to all advanced features.

Sharing with FileMaker Server and Cloud

Two product offerings are used exclusively to host databases on a network for team sharing: FileMaker Server and FileMaker Cloud.

FileMaker Server is a database-hosting software package offering scalable, secure, and reliable round-the-clock access to databases for authorized users. Hosted files can be simultaneously accessed by multiple users of FileMaker Pro, FileMaker Go, and FileMaker WebDirect or through other systems using hosted databases as a back-end data source. The server manages event scheduling for running database backups, system-level scripts (shell script or batch file), and FileMaker scripts in a hosted database. Individual database scripts can be configured to run from the server rather than on a user's computer to offload tasks and save time. Administrators can access event and error logs to troubleshoot problems or view performance metrics to help optimize database performance. The server uses progressive downloading technology to begin streaming media content for immediate display without hesitation.

FileMaker Cloud is a Claris-managed cloud-hosting version of FileMaker Server with similar features plus full-time monitoring and support and the added ease of use for allowing remote access.

Note   Although this book focuses on using and creating databases, Chapter 32 introduces network sharing.

Accessing with FileMaker Go and WebDirect

Two offerings allow use of or access to databases developed with the desktop application: FileMaker Go and FileMaker WebDirect.

FileMaker Go is an iOS-only app available free of charge from Apple's App Store that allows iPhone and iPad users to access databases when away from their desktop computer. Users can open a database stored locally on their iOS devices or access one remotely from a FileMaker Server or FileMaker Cloud server over Wi-Fi or cellular networks. Optionally, databases built for the desktop can be designed with custom scripts to detect a user's mobile device and switch to layouts designed specifically for smaller screens and touch navigation. Calculations and scripts can take advantage of iOS technologies including media capture through the camera, signature capture through the touch screen, barcode scanning, touch/face identification, and more. A database can access information about the device's battery, location, attitude, air pressure, acceleration, magnetic heading, steps, and more.

FileMaker WebDirect is the easiest way to share a database on the Web. With a few settings, any database can allow access through a web browser without using coding tools like PHP, HTML5, CSS, or JavaScript. All the web programming required to present the database in a web front end is handled automatically by FileMaker Server or Cloud. Layouts are automatically rendered in the browser, and, except for certain incompatible script steps and the ability to work in multiple windows, most functionality is identical to that on a desktop or iOS device.

Summary

This chapter provided a brief historical overview of FileMaker and a summary of the present-day product line. Next, we begin our exploration of the desktop application.

CHAPTER 2

Launching the Application

FileMaker Pro is a desktop application for macOS and Windows with a dual-purpose interface for using and developing databases. It is the only application in the product line that can create a new database. This chapter introduces the default application user interface, covering these topics:

- Introducing the Launch Center

- Configuring application preferences

- Exploring menus (Browse mode)

Introducing the Launch Center

The *Launch Center* is a multi-tabbed window used to create new databases, access existing databases, convert databases, and link to educational resources. The window, shown in Figure 2-1, opens automatically when the application launches. Later, it can be accessed by selecting any of the following items under the *File* menu, each corresponding to a tab section of the window:

- *Create New* – Opens the *Create* tab, which contains options to create a database, convert Excel or text files into a database, and access educational resources

- *My Apps* ➤ *Show My Apps* – Opens the *My Apps* tab with access to databases from a FileMaker Cloud server

- *Favorites* ➤ *Show Favorites* – Opens the *Favorites* tab with access to local and hosted databases the user has saved as favorites from the local computer

- *Recent* ➤ *Show Recent* – Opens the *Recent* tab with access to databases recently opened on the local computer

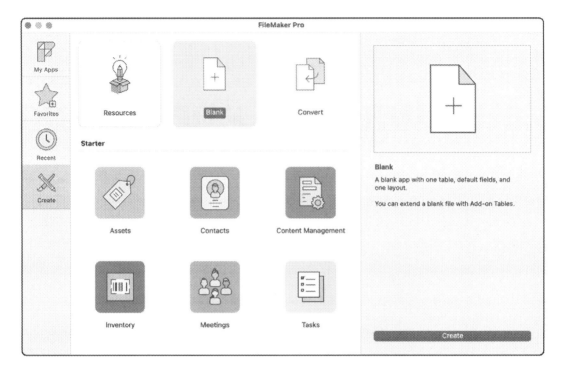

Figure 2-1. *The Launch Center is used to create, convert, and open databases*

Tip   Learn about creating new databases starting in Chapter 6.

Configuring Application Preferences

FileMaker's application preferences provide control and customization of key features of the local user environment, separated into six tabs: *General, Layout, Memory, Shortcuts, Plug-Ins,* and *Permitted.* To begin, open the *Preferences* window by selecting a platform-specific menu:

- *macOS – FileMaker Pro* ➤ *Settings*
- *Windows – Edit* ➤ *Preferences*

Preferences: General

The *General* Preferences tab, shown in Figure 2-2, controls options for the user interface, user name, notifications for software updates, enabling advanced tools, and choosing a startup file.

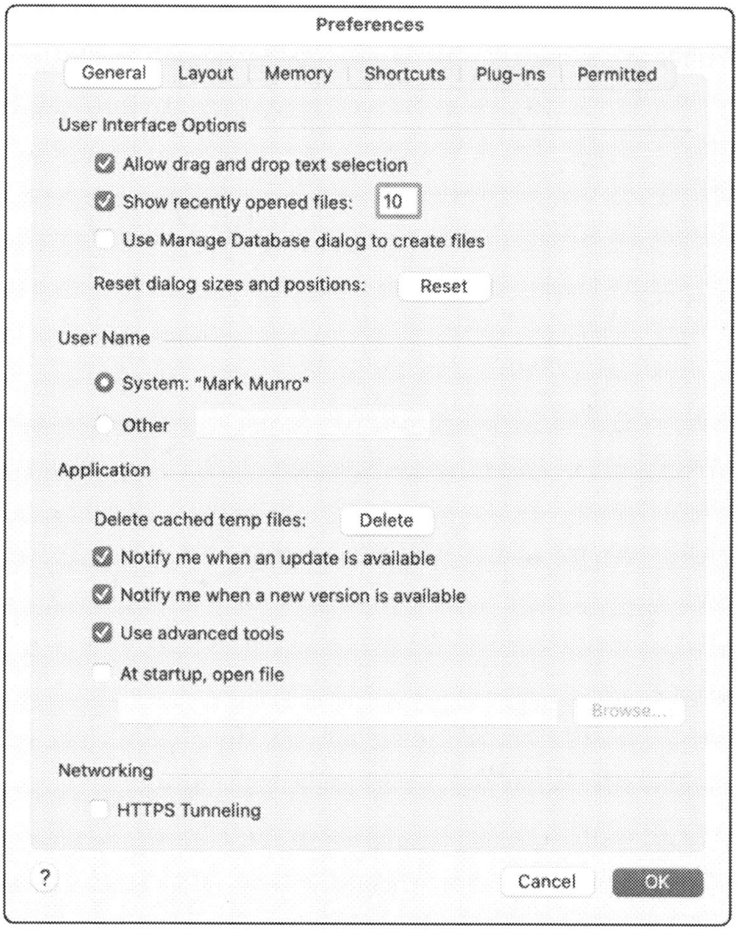

Figure 2-2. *The application's general preferences*

General: User Interface Options

The *User Interface Options* section of the *General* Preferences tab controls the following aspects of the application interface:

- *Allow drag and drop text selection* – Enable text selection dragging between fields, between layouts, and between fields and content from other applications.

- *Show recently opened files* – Control how many recent files appear in the *File* menu and *Launch Center*.

- *Use Manage Database dialog to create files* – Enable this option to automatically enter the schema editing interface when creating a new database file (Chapters 7–9).

- *Reset dialog sizes and positions* – Click to revert all application dialogs back to their default measurements.

There are a few Windows-only options, not shown in the image, including options to increase the size of layout objects for improved readability, selecting an interface language, and sharpening text. These features are controlled by the operating system on Macintosh computers.

General: User Name

The *User Name* setting of the *General* Preferences tab identifies how the name of a computer is identified. The behavior varies slightly by platform.

- On macOS, the user name defaults to "System" and uses the current user's computer account name. Choose "Other" to enter a static override for any user on the local computer.

- On Windows, a custom name must be manually entered here.

Note   The "user name" identifies the user associated with a computer where an "account name" identifies the user as logged into a database with specific credentials (Chapter 29).

General: Application

The *Application* section of the *General* Preferences tab controls the following application features:

- *Delete cached temp files* – Reset the application cache.

- *Notify me* – Enable one or both to control when FileMaker checks for and notifies the user when a software update is available.

- *Use advanced tools* – Enables a *Tools* menu and other developer abilities (recommended on any computer used for development).

- *At startup, open file* – Choose a database that will automatically open whenever the application is launched.

Tip   To have access to all development options, enable advanced tools and then quit and relaunch the application!

General: Networking

Added in version 20.3, the *HTTPS Tunneling* checkbox changes how the FileMaker Pro application communicates with FileMaker Server. For more information on this advanced topic, see the Claris Engineering Blog entry from November 16, 2023, titled "Using HTTPS tunneling between FileMaker Pro and FileMaker Server."

Note   See the "CH02-01 HTTPS Tunnelling.html" website shortcut in the example files.

Preferences: Layout

The *Layout* Preferences tab, shown in Figure 2-3, controls three options when designing interface layouts (Chapter 17).

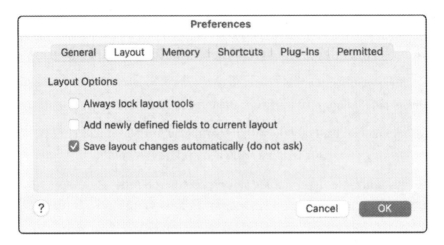

Figure 2-3. *The application's layout preferences*

- *Always lock layout tools* – Enable to lock a layout tool selection instead of automatically reverting to the cursor after applying a tool.

- *Add newly defined fields to current layout* – Enable to add newly defined fields at the bottom of the current layout. This can be annoying since a carefully sized layout suddenly increases in height to accommodate new fields with a default styling.

- *Save layout changes automatically* – Disable to receive a confirmation dialog when finishing work on a layout. Consider turning this off until you are confident in your skill designing layouts.

Tip   Choosing to always lock layout tools here may get annoying! Instead, double-click a tool to lock its selection when needed. Also, keep the *Add newly defined fields to current layout* option turned off to avoid layout resizing each time you add fields to a table!

Preferences: Memory

The *Memory* Preferences tab, shown in Figure 2-4, controls the file cache settings.

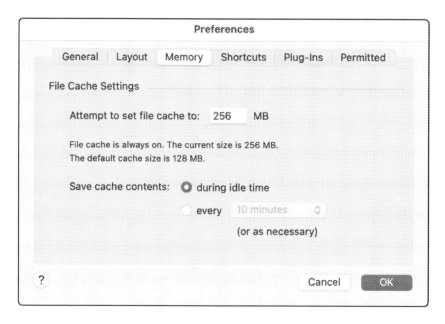

Figure 2-4. *The application's memory preferences*

As changes are made to a database's structure or content, FileMaker stores changes in the RAM cache and periodically writes the accumulated data to the hard disk. These settings control how often the cache is saved.

- *Attempt to set file cache to* – Allocates an amount of memory for the file cache. Use a higher value for improved performance and a lower value for less risk of data loss after a crash.

- *Save cache contents* – Choose when the cached data is written to disk: *during idle time* or at a specified interval.

Note   The default cache settings are usually fine for most solutions. Relaunch the application for cache setting changes to take effect.

Preferences: Shortcuts (macOS Only)

The *Shortcuts* Preferences tab, shown in Figure 2-5, displays a list of databases that have scripts with the *Enable Shortcuts Donation* option active (Chapter 24, "Scripts Menu (macOS)"). This is a macOS feature that allows the *Shortcuts* application,

Apple's system-level automation tool, to execute FileMaker scripts as part of a workflow or with voice commands through Siri. Since databases are automatically added here when opened, this provides the user the opportunity to disable files with shortcuts that they don't intend to use.

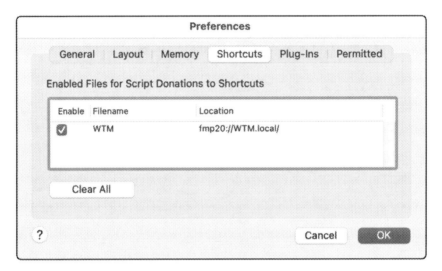

Figure 2-5. *The application's shortcuts preferences*

Preferences: Plug-Ins

The *Plug-Ins* Preferences tab contains a list of installed plug-ins (Chapter 28).

Preferences: Permitted Hosts

When a user attempts to open a database from an unsecured host, FileMaker presents the dialog warning shown in Figure 2-6. The user has the option to cancel the connection, allow a connect this one time, or authorize uncontested connections in the future by enabling the *Always permit connection to this host* checkbox before connecting. If they select that option, it adds the file to the application's list of permitted hosts.

Figure 2-6. *The warning when opening a database from an unsecured host*

The *Permitted* Preferences tab, shown in Figure 2-7, lists any host computers whose Secure Sockets Layer (SSL) certificates cannot be verified, which the user chose to authorize. Hosts can be removed from the list and will then require reapproval on the next connection. Enable the checkbox at the bottom to also receive a warning when a URL is about to open an unsecure file using a *FileMaker URL* (Chapter 33, "Accessing a Database with FileMaker URL").

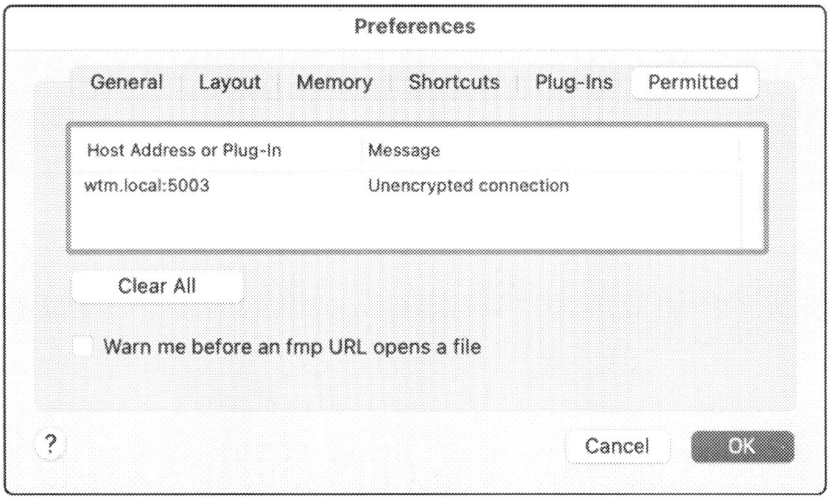

Figure 2-7. *The application's permitted hosts preferences*

Exploring Menus (Browse Mode)

The default menu bar, shown in Figure 2-8, contains commands for data entry, switching to other modes, and entering various development dialogs.

Figure 2-8. *The default Browse mode menu bar*

This section introduces the default Browse mode menus when a database file is open. It will appear different under various circumstances, such as the following:

- No database is open.

- The *Launch Center* is open.

- A development dialog is open.

- The window is in one of the other three non-Browse modes: *Find* (Chapter 4), *Preview* (Chapter 4), or *Layout* (Chapter 17).

- The Option key is held down.

- The database is using a custom menu set (Chapter 23).

- A script is running or paused.

- A modal window is open.

- A user's account doesn't grant them certain access (Chapter 29).

Note   Window modes are defined in Chapter 3.

Menu: FileMaker Pro (macOS Only)

The *FileMaker Pro* menu, shown in Figure 2-9, is a macOS-only menu that contains access to application metadata, settings, and some operating system features. These items are standards across all macOS applications. Go here to open *Settings* and to hide or quit FileMaker. On Windows, this menu doesn't exist, so *Preferences* is available under the *Edit* menu and *Exit* under the *File* menu is used to quit the application.

Figure 2-9. *The FileMaker Pro application menu*

File Menu

The *File* menu, shown in Figure 2-10, contains access to file and developer-related functions. The top portion contains functions for controlling files, including:

- *Create New* – Opens the corresponding tab of the *Launch Center* window, described earlier in this chapter.

- *Sign In/Out of Claris ID* – Used to log in or out of a Claris account to access databases hosted on a FileMaker Cloud server.

- *My Apps* – Open files hosted in a cloud account (when signed in).

- *Favorites* – Open files saved as favorite shortcuts.

- *Recent* – Open recently accessed files.

- *Hosts* – Open network-hosted databases with an option to open a *Hosts* window that summarizes servers by cloud, favorites, and local with an option to add, edit, or remove hosts (Chapter 32, "Opening a Hosted Database").

- *Open* – Select and open a database from a local folder directory.

- *Open Quickly* – Search favorites and recent files for quick access.

- *Close* – Closes the current database window.

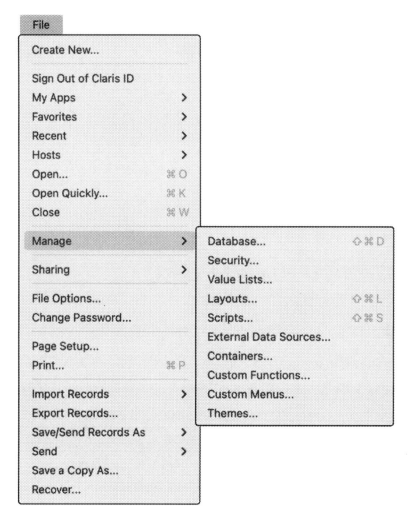

Figure 2-10. *The File menu and Manage submenu*

The next three items are developer related:

- *Manage* – A submenu of developer options (described later)

- *Sharing* – A submenu of options for uploading a file to a host or configuring over who can access the current database:

    - From a FileMaker application across a network (Chapter 32, "Configuring Network Settings")

    - From an ODBC/JDBC client (Chapter 33, "Setting Up FileMaker as an ODBC Data Source")

    - From a browser with WebDirect (Chapter 32, "Using WebDirect")

- *File Options* – Opens a dialog of settings for the current database (Chapter 6, "Configuring File Options")

Tip   Set up user accounts to limit access to developer functions (Chapter 29)!

The *Change Password* item allows a user to enter a new password if they have that capability enabled by their security privileges (Chapter 29, "Enabling Other Privilege Settings").

Below that, various menu items control output options:

- *Page Setup* (called *Print Setup* on Windows) and *Print* – Open standard operating system dialogs used to configure an open database window for printing.

- *Import Records* and *Export Records* – Transfer data in or out of the current database (Chapter 5).

- *Save/Send Record As* – Save a set of records as an Excel or PDF file or a snapshot link (Chapter 33, "Sharing Bookmarks with Snapshot Links).

- *Send* – Create an email manually or with a *FileMaker URL* link to the current database (Chapter 33, "Accessing a Database with FileMaker URL").

- *Save a Copy As* – Save the entire database as a copy, *compacted copy*, or *clone* (Chapter 31, "Saving a Copy As").

- *Recover* – Start to troubleshoot or salvage a damaged database (Chapter 31, "Recovering a File").

Menu: File ➤ Manage

The *Manage* submenu of the *File* menu, shown previously in Figure 2-10, contains access to the development interface for the current database file. Each of these is discussed in later chapters:

- *Database* – Define tables, fields, and relationships (Chapters 7–9).

- *Security* – Configure access credentials (Chapter 29).

- *Value Lists* – Define lists of values (Chapter 11), which can be used as the source for *field control styles* (Chapter 20).

- *Layouts* – Create and manage interface layouts (Chapter 18).

- *Scripts* – Create and manage macro-like action sequences (Chapter 24).

- *External Data Sources* – Manage connections to other FileMaker and ODBC databases (Chapter 33, "Connecting to an ODBC Database").

- *Containers* – Define locations for storing files and images (Chapter 10).

- *Custom Functions* – Create and edit custom formulas (Chapter 15).

- *Custom Menus* – Create and edit custom menus and menu items (Chapter 23).

- *Themes* – Create and edit collections of layout and layout object formatting styles (Chapter 22).

Edit Menu

The *Edit* menu provides standard features that are enabled when editing the contents of a field: *Undo, Cut, Copy, Paste, Clear,* and *Select All.* The *Find/Replace* submenu contains functions for doing text replacements within one or more fields for one or more records. The *Spelling* submenu options allow correcting text selected within a single field or stepping through every field on the layout (Chapter 4, "Spell-checking"). The *Export Field Contents* item presents the user a dialog to specify a name and location of a file in which to save the contents of the current field. This works with any field type but is intended for container fields (Chapter 10).

Tip   Holding down the Alt (Windows) or Option (macOS) key presents additional edit options.

View Menu

The *View* menu, shown in Figure 2-11, contains functions that control the view of the current database window. The first four items enable a Window mode (Chapter 3):

- *Browse Mode* – The default, used for data entry (Chapter 3–5).

- *Find Mode* – Begin a search process (Chapter 4).

- *Layout Mode* – Design interface layouts (Chapter 17).

- *Preview Mode* – Show a preview of the current layout and contents as it will print (Chapter 4).

The remaining menu items control other aspects of the view (most of these are discussed further in Chapter 3):

- *Go to Layout* – A list of accessible layouts, allowing manual navigation between them.

- *View as* – Choose one of three ways of looking at the current layout.

- *Status Toolbar* and *Customize Status Toolbar* – Control the visibility and content of the toolbar.

- *Formatting Bar* and *Ruler* – Toggle the visibility of an additional horizontal extension of the toolbar.

- *Zoom In* and *Zoom Out* – Increased or decreased magnification from 25% to 400%.

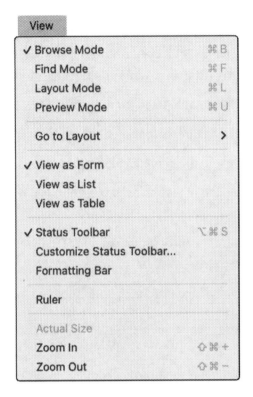

Figure 2-11. *The View menu*

Insert Menu

The *Insert* menu contains contextually sensitive functions for inserting files or text into a field (Chapter 4, "Modifying Field Content").

Format Menu

The *Format* menu contains submenus for standard text styling functions when editing field content: *Font, Size, Style, Alignment, Spacing,* and *Color.*

Records Menu

The *Records* menu, shown in Figure 2-12, contains all the functions for creating, duplicating, deleting, navigating, including, excluding, sorting, and manipulating records in the current database window (Chapter 4).

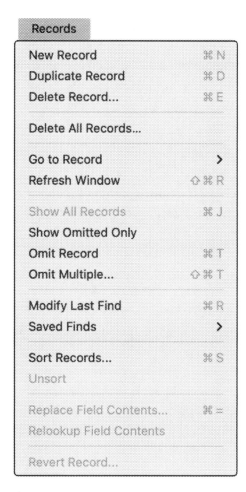

Figure 2-12. *The Records menu*

Scripts Menu

The *Scripts* menu provides access to the *Script Workspace* window and displays a list of individual scripts that have been configured to appear here as functions (Chapter 24).

Tools Menu

The *Tools* menu contains access to the *Script Debugger* (Chapter 26), *Custom Menus* (Chapter 23), and other tools (Chapter 30). It is only available when the *Use advanced tools* preference is enabled!

Window Menu

The *Window* menu contains many window-related functions used to create additional windows for a database or choosing among multiple windows for any open database (Chapter 3, "Managing Multiple Windows").

Help Menu

The *Help* menu provides access to online resources including a help guide, learning resources, upgrades, the community website, and other application-related functions.

Summary

This chapter introduced the FileMaker Pro desktop application's default windows, preferences, and menus. Next, we begin exploring a database window from the perspective of a user.

CHAPTER 3

Exploring a Database Window

A *database window* provides an interactive view into an open database file. When a database file is opened, a default window opens. Users and scripts can open and close additional windows, but, once the last of a file's windows closes, the file is closed. FileMaker's windows have different *window modes* for data entry and one for development. They also have several *content views* that determine how records are displayed. This chapter begins an exploration of a database window from a user perspective, covering these topics:

- Identifying window regions and modes
- Exploring the toolbar
- Managing multiple windows

Since creating a new database file isn't discussed until Chapter 6, to follow along with this exploration of the window interface, take a moment to download the *Learn FileMaker Pro 2024* sample files, by following the instructions posted here: `https://www.apress.com/gp/services/source-code`.

The "CH03-05 Sandbox" file contains a simple *Contacts* table with two layouts and a simple custom theme to render nice example pictures for the book. To follow along, open that file now.

© Mark Conway Munro 2024
M. C. Munro, *Learn FileMaker Pro 2024*, https://doi.org/10.1007/979-8-8688-0835-7_3

Identifying Window Regions and Modes

A database window, shown in Figure 3-1, is divided into two primary regions. The *status toolbar*, discussed later in this chapter, provides graphical controls that are uniform to all databases (with user-accessible local customization options). The *content area* includes the area below the toolbar that displays a custom user interface designed by a developer. In the Sandbox example, the content area is preconfigured with a few simple interface elements. When creating a new file (Chapter 6), this area would be completely blank and require a layout design (Chapters 17–23). In each window, the content area displays one layout at a time but can switch between any number of layouts created in the file. The rendering method of content varies by the selected *window mode* and *content view*.

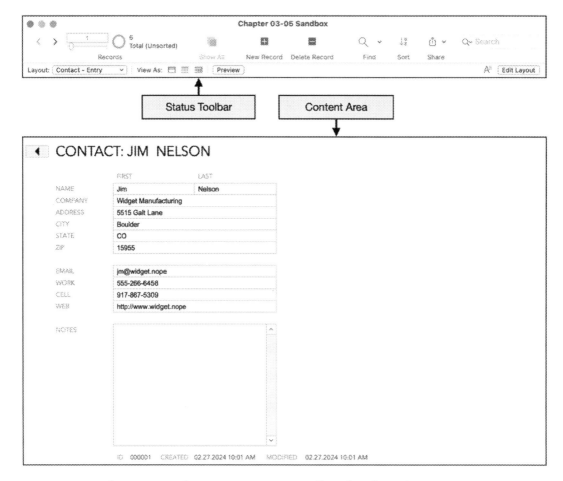

Figure 3-1. *The two window areas, status toolbar (top) and content area (bottom)*

Defining Window Modes

A *window mode* is a display state that converts a window's interface for a specific purpose. FileMaker has four modes: *Browse, Find, Preview*, and *Layout*.

Browse mode, the default window state, is used to display the content of a database and allow users to perform data entry–related tasks. In Browse mode, the content area of the window renders one or more records from one table assigned to the layout being viewed. Depending on the design of the layout and account permissions, a user can interact with the data to create, view, edit, delete, duplicate, search, sort, and omit records as well as interact with other layout objects such as buttons, panels, and web viewers.

Find mode is a window state used to enter search criteria. In Find mode, the layout transforms into a set of one or more blank record-like *find requests* into which the user enters criteria defining the desired set of records prior to performing a search (Chapter 4, "Searching for Records").

Preview mode is a window state that acts like a print preview, displaying the current layout and records as they would appear on a printed page. The layout will appear like Browse mode but is noninteractive. Fields will not be editable and buttons that aren't configured to hide during print appear as non-clickable art. Also, in the preview, objects may hide, slide, compress, summarize, and change formatting depending on how they are defined on the layout.

Layout mode is a window state used to create interface layouts (Chapters 17–22). Design tools to add and configure objects to the layout will appear in the toolbar and special sidebar panes when in this mode.

Each mode has a unique toolbar, menu bar, and content rendering methodology. Depending on their account privileges (Chapter 29, "Exploring Privilege Sets"), a user can change the mode of a window by clicking a mode button in the toolbar, selecting a mode from the *View* menu, or running a script that changes the mode.

Defining Content Views

A *content view* is an interface setting that determines how records are displayed in the content area of a window in Browse mode. Depending on restrictions enforced by the layout settings (Chapter 18, "Layout Settings: Views"), a user can control how they view records by choosing one of three options: *Form, List*, or *Table*. The current view of a layout can be changed by selecting from the *View* menu, clicking a *View As* icon in the toolbar, or running a script that changes the view.

Form view displays one record at a time rendered using the objects defined on the current layout. To see other records, use the navigation controls in the toolbar or custom interface elements configured to navigate to other records. This view is analogous to looking at one sheet of paper pulled out of a file cabinet or viewing a single page in a book.

List view displays a continuous list of records rendered by repeating all the objects defined on the current layout for each. In this view, the user can scroll up or down to see other records. This is analogous to looking across a sequence of tabs on folders in a file cabinet, glancing at a book's table of contents, or scrolling through a list of items on a web page.

Table view displays a set of records in a spreadsheet-style format of columns and rows while excluding other graphical elements that are present on the layout. The user can rearrange and resize columns by dragging their headings. They can sort the records by clicking a heading. New fields (columns) and new records (rows) can be created intuitively in a manner like a spreadsheet. An action pop-up menu is hidden within each field's heading and provides quick access to various features including sorting, summarization, field control, and view control. Table views aren't high on design and customizable functionality, but they provide a familiar environment for those used to working with spreadsheets and may be suitable for simple databases that don't require a polished interface.

Note   Although one layout can be switched to any view allowed by its settings, typically a layout is designed for a single view.

Exploring the Toolbar

There are three horizontal segments of the window's heading toolbar: *status toolbar, formatting bar,* and *ruler*. These can each be displayed or hidden depending on the user's access privileges, preferences, and the settings established by the developer.

Status Toolbar (Browse Mode)

The *status toolbar* is the entire area running along the top of the window containing controls pertinent to the current window mode. This is the only part of the window header that is visible by default. Unless hidden and locked by a script, users can toggle the visibility of the toolbar by selecting *View* ➤ *Status* from the menu.

Default Toolbar Items (Browse Mode)

The default toolbar configuration for Browse mode is shown in Figure 3-2. The controls in the top portion are customizable (discussed later in this section), and the bottom row is static.

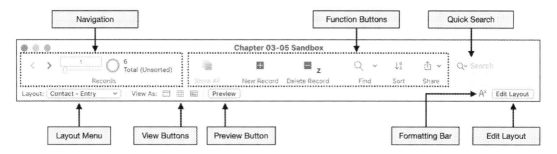

Figure 3-2. *The anatomy of the default Browse mode toolbar configuration*

Upper Toolbar: Navigation Controls

The *record navigation controls* in the toolbar, shown in Figure 3-3, display information about the set of records being viewed and allow movement between them.

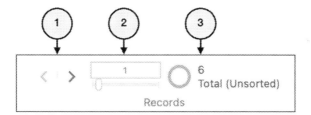

Figure 3-3. *The default Browse mode navigation controls*

The toolbar's navigation controls are

1. *Record navigation arrows* – Move to the previous or next record.

2. *Record number and slider* – The number of the current record. Move the slider or type a record number to jump to another record.

3. *Record count(s)* – The total record count, the found set count (if viewing a subset of the total), and the sort status. When viewing a subset, click the circle icon to toggle from the visible found records to the hidden omitted records.

Upper Toolbar: Function Buttons

The *function buttons* in the toolbar, shown in Figure 3-4, allow a user to perform various record functions (Chapter 4) and access a menu of sharing functions (Chapter 32, "Sharing Databases on a Network").

Figure 3-4. *The default toolbar buttons in Browse mode*

Upper Toolbar: Quick Find Search Field

At the top right of the toolbar is a search field used to perform a "Quick Find" (Chapter 4, "Searching with Quick Find").

Lower Toolbar: Layout Menu

The lower, non-customizable level of the toolbar starts with the *Layout* menu. In Browse mode, this displays a list of visible layouts (Chapter 18, "Layout Settings: General") and is used to manually navigate to another layout. This is also found in the *View ➤ Go to Layout* menu.

Lower Toolbar: Content View Buttons

Next in the lower bar are three content view buttons used to change the content as formatted in the window view as described earlier in this chapter. The view buttons enabled here are controlled by the current layout's settings (Chapter 18, "Layout Settings: Views").

Lower Toolbar: Preview Button

The toolbar's *Preview* button changes the window into Preview mode (Chapter 4, "Using Preview Mode").

Lower Toolbar: Formatting Bar Button

The *formatting bar* button toggles the visibility of a text-editing control bar between the status toolbar and the content area of the window (described later in this chapter).

Lower Toolbar: Edit Layout Button

The *Edit Layout* button changes the window to Layout mode (Chapter 17, "Using Layout Mode").

Customizing the Toolbar (Browse Mode)

The controls in the top portion of the toolbar are customizable at the user-computer level. This means that a user can control which functions are included and how they are arranged in the toolbar. These settings are application based and will apply locally for all databases. With a database open, select the *View ➤ Customize Status Toolbar* menu to open a customization panel. On macOS, this is a graphical panel attached to the window as shown in Figure 3-5. On the lower left of this dialog, a *Show* menu controls the button format in the toolbar: *Icon Only*, *Text Only*, or, the default, *Icon and Text*. On Windows, a less attractive list-based dialog appears with similar drag and drop options.

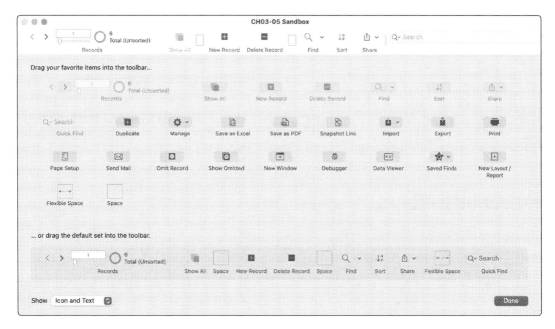

Figure 3-5. *The toolbar customization panel for Browse mode (macOS)*

Adding, Removing, and Rearranging Toolbar Items

To add an item to the toolbar, drag an icon from the customization panel up into the toolbar area and drop it. FileMaker will avoid duplication by automatically replacing an object already present in the toolbar when that same control is dropped elsewhere. To remove an item, drag it until it clears the toolbar area and release the mouse button. Items can be rearranged by dragging them within the toolbar.

Restoring the Default Toolbar Set

To restore the default control set, drag the group in the rectangle at the bottom of the panel and drop it in the toolbar.

Formatting Bar

The *formatting bar* is an optional set of text-formatting controls, shown in Figure 3-6. This appears between the bottom of the status toolbar and the top of the content area when the *View ➤ Formatting Bar* menu is selected or the button on the lower right of the toolbar is clicked. The controls for font, style, size, color, highlight, emphasis, and text alignment become enabled when the user clicks into a text field. The controls are also accessible through the *Format* menu in the menu bar.

Figure 3-6. *The formatting bar and toggle button*

Horizontal Ruler

A *horizontal ruler* appears below the other header bars. The *View ➤ Ruler* menu toggles the visibility of this ruler. The ruler's *measurement unit* can be changed using its contextual menu, with a choice of *centimeters*, *inches*, and *points*. The Browse mode ruler becomes useful when a text field is in focus, shrinking itself to the size of the field, and displaying tabs and margin controls, as shown in Figure 3-7. These field settings can also be modified with layout tools (Chapter 19, "Exploring the Inspector Pane"). In Layout mode, a horizontal and a vertical ruler are more useful by aiding the alignment and precise positioning of objects.

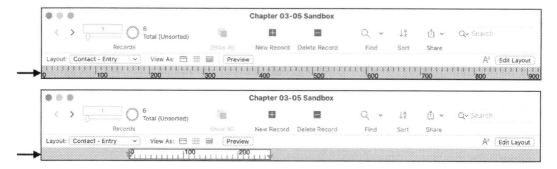

Figure 3-7. *The ruler visible (top) and when a field has focus (bottom)*

Managing Multiple Windows

When a database is opened, a window automatically appears. Users can navigate to records and other layouts within that window, or they can open additional windows to access multiple simultaneous, side-by-side views of the same file. For example, a single contact record can be viewed on a form layout in one window, a list of contacts in another, and a company record in a third. Both users and scripts can create and close windows as needed to view records and complete tasks.

Creating a New Window

Select the *Window* ➤ *New Window* menu to manually create a new window. The new window will open in front of and slightly offset from the current window. It will start as an exact duplicate of the current window, with identical properties: name (with suffix), window mode, content view, dimensions, toolbar visibility, current layout, found set, and current record. Once open, the new window can diverge from the original by searching, navigating, moving, and resizing.

Multiple windows are great for viewing records side by side or alternating between different work. However, conflict warnings will occur if a user tries to edit a record that is already being edited in another window. So it is a good idea to encourage users to use this feature sparingly, reminding them to close extra windows when finished with a task. Close a window by selecting the *File* ➤ *Close Window* menu or clicking the close icon on the window's heading.

Selecting a Window from the Menu

When a new window is created, it is added to the list at the bottom of the *Window* menu, as shown in Figure 3-8. This is a blended list of all visible windows for all open files. The list displays the current "stacking order" of windows from front to back. Select a window from the list to bring it to the front.

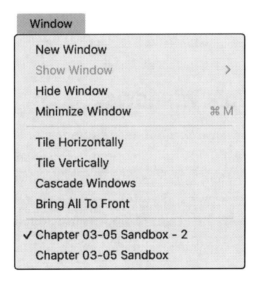

Figure 3-8. *The bottom of the Window menu lists all visible windows*

Hiding, Showing, and Ordering Windows

A window can be hidden from view while remaining open. A user can hide a window by selecting the *Window* ➤ *Hide Window* menu. Scripts can also hide windows. Some windows automatically open in a hidden state when one database opens another database to access records through a relationship. Every hidden window is listed under the *Window* ➤ *Show Window* submenu, as shown in Figure 3-9. Selecting a window from this list will make it visible and bring it to the front. The *Bring All To Front* item makes all hidden windows visible. Windows can be arranged with other windows using *Tile Horizontally*, *Tile Vertically*, and *Cascade Windows*. A window can be minimized to the macOS or Windows dock by selecting the *Minimize Window* menu item. When minimized, it is listed as an open window in the menu but must be selected to bring it back into view.

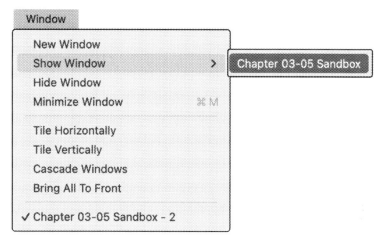

Figure 3-9. *The submenu containing hidden windows*

Summary

This chapter explored the anatomy of a window, toolbar controls, and managing multiple windows. Next, we begin working with records.

CHAPTER 4

Working with Records

A FileMaker database can be analogized to a spreadsheet: a *file* is like a spreadsheet document, a *table* is like a sheet or tab of that document, a *field* is like a column, and a *record* is like a row. A *table* represents a set of information that represents a particular kind of entity. A *record* is a primary unit of content in a table, one group of values that together represent a particular entity. For example, a record in a *Contacts* table represents a person, while a record in an *Inventory* table represents one product. When working in a database, users spend most of their time working with records. They create, edit, delete, omit, find, export, import, print, and view records. Although a database can contain many different tables each with its own collection of records, the examples from the *Chapter* 3-5 *Sandbox* file use a single *Contacts* table. This chapter explores user interactions with records, covering the following topics:

- Entering data
- Creating, deleting, and duplicating records
- Searching for records
- Working with a found set
- Printing

Note Open the "CH03-05 Sandbox" example file to experiment.

Entering Data

A data entry task involves *opening a record* by placing the cursor into a field, modifying content, moving from field to field, and then committing (closing) the record or reverting it.

© Mark Conway Munro 2024
M. C. Munro, *Learn FileMaker Pro 2024*, https://doi.org/10.1007/979-8-8688-0835-7_4

Opening a Record

A record is *open* when any field has focus and editing has begun. This transforms the fields to an editable state ready for data input. To open the current record for data entry, click into any editable field, or press the Tab key to enter the first editable field and begin typing.

Understanding Field Focus

A field has *focus* when it is currently ready to accept input. Only one field can have active focus at a time, and this fact is visually indicated by a text cursor blinking within the field. The visual appearance of the field can change depending on the layout settings applied to its "in focus" state (Chapter 22, "Editing an Object's Style Settings"). A layout can be designed to provide some visual change to make clear to users that the record is open and a field is ready to receive their input. For example, the field borders might become visible, change thickness, or change color. The field's fill color can also change. In the *CH03-05 Sandbox* file, focus is indicated by a simple darker border, as shown in Figure 4-1. Focus can be shifted to another field by either clicking it or pressing the Tab or other key(s) that are configured to go to the next object (Chapter 19, "Behavior"). The next field is determined by a "tab order" configured for the layout (Chapter 21, "Understanding Tab Order").

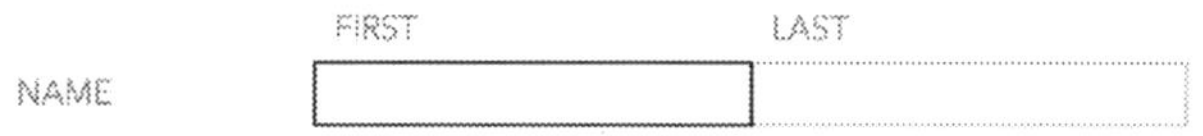

FIRST   LAST

NAME

Figure 4-1. *A field in focus in the Sandbox file*

Modifying Field Content

The content stored in a field is referred to as its "*value.*" Once a field has focus, a user can change its value in different ways depending on its defined data type (Chapter 8, "Introducing Field Types") or its configured layout behavior and formatting options (Chapters 19 and 20). Editing methods may include manual typing, cut, copy–paste, drag–drop, undo–redo, insert functions, or mouse clicks. The most common method of entering data into any data entry field is by simply typing on the keyboard. If a field is in focus, anything typed will flow in as its content.

Like most applications, FileMaker's *Edit* menu has commands for cut, copy, paste, undo, and redo. These functions only affect content stored in fields while they are in focus. For example, undo will step back text changes just made in the active field but does not reverse actions such as record creation or deletion and doesn't work after changes are committed when a record closes.

When drag and drop is enabled in the application preferences (Chapter 2), text can be dragged to rearrange it within a field. It can also be dragged from one field to another, between fields in different windows, and between fields and text in other applications.

The *Insert* menu and similarly named submenu of a field's contextual menu both contain functions for quickly inserting content into fields. Quickly insert the *Current Date*, *Current Time*, or *Current Username*. The *From Index* option is used to select and insert a value into the current field from an indexed list of values entered into that field on any record. The *From Last Visited Record* option inserts the value of the current field from the last record viewed. Inserting files into container fields (Chapter 10) is made possible by selecting the *Insert Picture, Insert Audio/Video, Insert PDF*, or *Insert File* function. Files can also be dragged and dropped into a container field.

Finally, fields can also be configured with a *control style* that allows data entry with mouse clicks. For example, a *checkbox* style allows selection of boxes to enter a value from a defined *value list* (Chapter 11), while a *calendar* style provides a graphical calendar for date entries (Chapter 20, "Configuring a Field's Control Style").

Closing a Record

After editing, a record must be closed to either *commit* or *revert* changes. Reverting changes closes a record and omits all changes made while the record was open. A record can be reverted by selecting the *Records* ➤ *Revert Record* menu. Committing a record closes the record and saves changes made during the session. During this process, FileMaker will perform any data entry validations defined by fields and report problems if any are detected (Chapter 8, "Field Options: Validation"). A record can be committed numerous ways. Manually commit a record by pressing the Enter key or clicking the layout's background, away from other objects. Other actions that will commit the current record include navigating to another record, creating a new record, closing the current window, closing the file, or running a script designed to perform these actions.

Tip   Layouts can be configured to automatically save changes or present a confirmation dialog when closing a record (Chapter 18, "Layout Settings: General").

Creating, Deleting, and Duplicating Records

Users can create, delete, delete all, and duplicate records. These commands are accessible to users through the *Records* menu. Some are also accessible through a toolbar icon or the record contextual menu on the background of a layout.

The *New Record* function creates a new blank record in the current layout's table of the front window and automatically opens it ready for input with focus in the first field.

The *Delete Record* function permanently deletes the current record in the window after presenting a warning dialog to confirm the user's intent. A user can bypass this warning dialog and instantly delete a record by holding Option (macOS) or Shift (Windows) while selecting the *Delete Record* option. While this may be a useful tip for power users, it can be dangerous and shouldn't be shared with new users. The *Delete All Records* function will delete every record being viewed in the found set after the user confirms the action in a warning dialog. These risky choices can be disabled using *custom menus* (Chapter 23) or with *custom privileges* in user accounts (Chapter 29).

The *Duplicate Record* function will create a duplicate of the current record with all local field values retained.

Tip   To reset the sandbox sample records back to their default starting point, choose *Reset Sample Records* under the *Scripts* menu.

Searching for Records

Although most tables will never reach FileMaker's 64 quadrillion total record limit, as the total record count increases, it becomes more difficult to find a specific record. Scrolling through even a few hundred records to find one is unnecessarily time-consuming. Instead, a *record search* can quickly isolate a smaller temporary subset of records based on user-specified criteria. Searching helps locate records for viewing or data entry work but also isolates a group of records for processes like printing or exporting. FileMaker offers several search methods:

- Perform fast searches using Quick Find or matching selected text in a field.

- Use Find mode to build complex searches.

- Formulas can perform SQL queries (Chapter 16).

- Scripts can automate the find methods available to users (Chapter 25, "Searching Records").

Caution   Except for SQL queries, all searches are context sensitive and executed from the perspective of a window's layout!

Performing Fast Searches

FileMaker offers two options for performing a fast, single-criterion search: *Quick Find* and *Find Matching Records*.

Searching with Quick Find

The *Quick Find* feature searches for records in the current layout's table where the specified criteria are found in any field on the layout that is configured specifically for Quick Find inclusion (Chapter 19, "Inspecting the Data Tab"). Enter a word or phrase into the search field located in the toolbar, shown in Figure 4-2, and then press the Enter key. The records visible in the window will be updated to only those with a matching value in any eligible field. The found/total record counts in the navigation area will reflect the difference. Click the magnifier icon in the Quick Find field to see a list of recent searches (from any table in the file). Select one to repeat it for the current layout's table.

Figure 4-2. *The Quick Find field in the toolbar*

Caution   After searching, the text remains in the search field but does not interact with the found set! If the user or a script changes the found set, that text becomes an obsolete reminder of the last search, but no longer relevant to the records actually displayed.

Searching with Find Matching Records

A *Find Matching Records* search uses the text selection within a field as the criteria to quickly search for any records containing that value in the same field. There are three functions available when highlighting some text in a field and right-clicking to access the contextual menu, shown in Figure 4-3. Each of these functions will perform a predefined type of search by matching the selected value in the current field. The *Find Matching Records* option performs a new find for records where the field contains the selected value. The other two will modify the current found set. *Constrain Found Set* performs a *narrowing find* that retains only those records in the current found set where the field contains the selected value. *Extend Found Set* performs an *expanding find* that adds to the found set any records in the total record count where the field contains the selected value.

Note   See "Manipulating a Previously Executed Find" later in this chapter for more on the topic of constraining and extending a find.

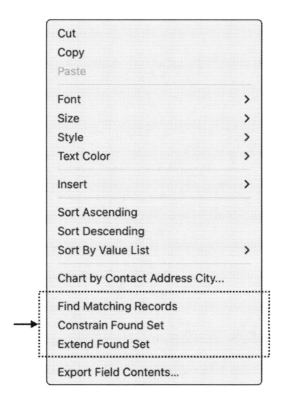

Figure 4-3. *The Find Matching Records functions of a field's contextual menu*

Using Find Mode

For more complex searches, Find mode is a transitional window state that transforms the menu, toolbar, and content area for entry of search criteria, as shown in Figure 4-4. To begin, enter Find mode by selecting *Find Mode* under the *View* menu or clicking the *Find* toolbar icon. The Find interface looks like a blank record and may startle first-time users into thinking the record they were viewing has been deleted. However, FileMaker makes it obvious by adding a magnifying glass icon on every field eligible for searching.

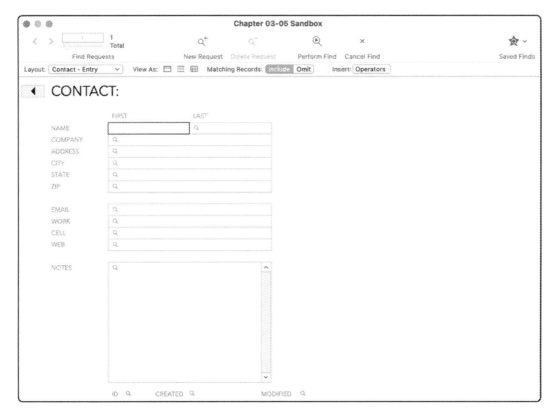

Figure 4-4. *A window transformed to Find mode shows find requests and search-related toolbar functions*

Status Toolbar (Find Mode)

The Find mode toolbar changes to search-specific buttons, either the default Find options or the user's customized set.

Default Toolbar Items (Find Mode)

The default toolbar for Find mode is shown in Figure 4-5. Like in Browse mode, the top portion can be customized by the user, and the bottom is static.

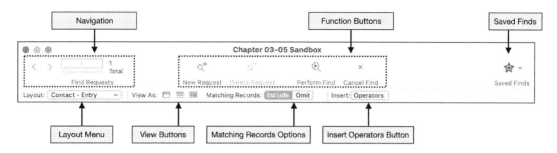

Figure 4-5. *The anatomy of the default Find mode toolbar*

Upper Toolbar: Navigation Controls

The *navigation controls* in Find mode are like those in Browse mode except that they display information and navigation options pertaining to *find requests* instead of records.

Upper Toolbar: Function Buttons

The *function buttons* in the Find mode toolbar are

- *New Request* – Create an additional find request to enter alternate criteria.

- *Delete Request* – Delete the current find request.

- *Perform Find* – Execute the find and show the results in Browse mode.

- *Cancel Find* – Return the window to Browse mode with the previous record set.

Upper Toolbar: Saved Finds Menu

The *Saved Finds* button on the far right of the toolbar provides access to a menu of past finds explicitly saved for the current table. These can be selected to instantly perform the find instead of entering custom criteria. See "Working with Saved Finds" later in this chapter.

Lower Toolbar: Layout Menu

The lower, non-customizable level of the Find mode toolbar starts with the *Layout* menu. This works the same as in Browse mode, allowing a user to switch layouts. In Find mode, this can be useful if the user wishes to create a find using multiple fields that are only visible on different layouts for the same table. However, since a find requires a single table as context, at the time a find is performed, only criteria entered on layouts for the same table as the current layout will be considered part of the request. Ideally, one should stay on a single layout for criteria entry.

Tip   Create a dedicated find layout in each table with all required fields and no non–search-related objects.

Lower Toolbar: Content View Buttons

The *content view* buttons work the same as in Browse mode (Chapter 3), rendering the find request(s) as a *list, form,* or *table* if the layout settings allow.

Lower Toolbar: Matching Records Options

The *Matching Records* buttons determine if records matching the current find request will be included or omitted from the resulting found set. See "Specifying a Matching Records Option" later in this chapter.

Lower Toolbar: Insert Operators Menu

The *Insert Operators* button opens a menu of search operators that can be inserted into a field with or without other criteria to enhance the search parameters. See "Using Search Operators" later in this chapter.

Customizing the Toolbar (Find Mode)

The Find mode toolbar is customizable at the user-computer level. Select the *View* ➤ *Customize Toolbar* menu to open the customization panel attached to the window as shown in Figure 4-6. Although the available buttons are different, they can be added or removed the same as in Browse mode (Chapter 3).

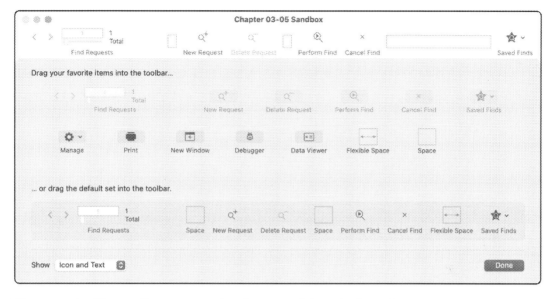

Figure 4-6. *The toolbar customization panel for Find mode*

Entering Criteria and Performing the Find

In Find mode, the window's content area is rendered as a blank version of the current layout, called a find request. This appears like a blank record but is used to enter search criteria as indicated by small magnifying glass icons in every field eligible for searching. Unlike with the *Quick Find* and *Find Matching Records* functions that search for one piece of information at a time, a find request allows criteria to be typed into more than one field. Users type criteria into specific fields to build more precise search requests. Criteria can be typed, pasted, or inserted into fields and can be combined with search operators. For records to qualify as a match, they must match all the values entered in a single request.

Once the desired criteria are entered into the appropriate fields, the search process can be performed by either pressing Enter, clicking the *Perform Find* toolbar button, or selecting the *Requests* ➤ *Perform Find* menu. FileMaker will search the current table for matching criteria in the fields indicated and display a found set of the results. If there are no results, a dialog will offer the user an option to return to Find mode and edit the criteria or cancel the process and return to Browse mode.

Try searching the *Contacts* table's sample records for records who work for a specific company, as shown in Figure 4-7, and follow these steps:

1. Navigate to the *Contact – List* layout.

2. Enter Find mode.

3. Click into the *Company* field.

4. Type the desired value, for example, "Widget."

5. Click the *Perform Find* button in the toolbar or press Enter.

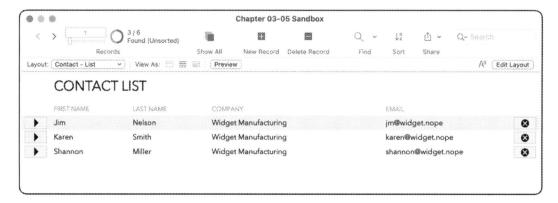

Figure 4-7. *The resulting found set of a search where Company contains "Widget"*

Experiment with different mixtures of criteria. For example, search for "Widget" in the *Company* field and "Karen" in the *First Name* field. Since the results must contain both values, only one record will be returned as a match.

Using Search Operators

A *search operator* is a character or set of characters that are used to narrow the focus of search criteria typed in a field. Without an operator, FileMaker defaults to an implied "begins with" type search, where matches are found at the beginning of words. So searching for "Widget" or "Wid Manu" or "W M" would all find records with "Widgets Manufacturing" in the field. Operators, described in Table 4-1, can be added to a field while in Find mode by typing them directly into a field, using the *Insert Operators* menu in the toolbar or selecting the *Operators* submenu from a field's contextual menu. To see operators in action, place an exclamation mark in the *Company* field to find all records with other records containing the same value, or search the *First Name* field for "*n" to find records with names ending with that character. Experiment with various operators to see the results.

Table 4-1. *A description of the available Find mode operators*

Operator	Description
=	By itself, finds records where that field is empty. In front of a value, matches a whole word within the field, excluding partial matches.
==	In front of a value, finds records with an exact match of the entire phrase within the field.
!	Finds records that have duplicate values in the field, that is, any record whose value in the field is also found in another record.
<	Finds numeric or text values that are less than the value entered after the symbol.
≤	Finds numeric or text values that are less than or equal to the value entered after the symbol.
>	Finds numeric or text values that are greater than the value entered after the symbol.
≥	Finds numeric or text values that are greater than or equal to the value entered after the symbol.
...	Finds a range of values based on text placed before and after the operator. For example, enter "1/15/2021...1/30/2021" (without the quotes) to find all records where the field contains a date including or between the two dates entered.
//	Finds records where the field contains today's date.
?	Finds records where the field contains an invalid value.
@	Finds records where the field contains a specific number of any character. For example, "@@" will find "He" or "It," while "@@@@" will find "Door" or "Test."
#	Finds records where the field contains a specific number of any number. For example, "#" will find "3" or "8" and "##" will find "33" or "81."
*	Use this in place of a character to create a search pattern indicating there must be some value present. For example, by itself, it will find every record with any value in that field (e.g., omitting empty), or typing "1/15/*" will find any records where the field contains a date of January 15 for any year.
\	Escapes the next character. This can be useful when searching for a literal operator by treating the operator as part of the search criteria and not as an operator. For example, to search for any records where the field contains a quote symbol, enter \".

(continued)

Table 4-1. (*continued*)

Operator	Description
""	Used to match the phrase exactly as typed between the quote marks.
*""	Used to match the phrase typed between the quote marks anywhere in a field containing a lot of text.
~	Used to perform a relaxed search in Japanese text.

Manipulating a Previously Executed Find

Once a find has been performed, there are three methods for further refining the results without having to start with a new request: *modifying*, *extending*, and *constraining* the last find.

Modifying the Last Find

The *Modify Last Find* function enters Find mode and recreates the find request(s) and criteria of the last find performed in the current table. This provides an opportunity to tweak the last criteria and perform a modified search. This command is available in the *Records* menu, in the menu under the toolbar's *Find* icon.

Extending the Last Find

The *Extend Found Set* function uses a new search to find and add matching records to the current found set. This can be accessed two ways. In Browse mode, highlight some text in a field, and select command from the contextual menu. The text selection is used to find records not in the found set and add them. In Find mode, enter criteria into one or more fields and select the *Requests* ➤ *Extend Found Set* menu instead of *Perform Find*. The new find will be performed, and the results will be added to the previous found set. To illustrate this, follow these steps:

1. On the "Contact – Entry" layout, enter Find mode.

2. Type "NY" into the *State* field.

3. Press Enter or click *Perform Find* to see a found set of contacts who live in New York.

4. Enter Find mode again.

5. Type "CO" into the *State* field.

6. Select "Extend Found Set" from the "Requests" menu to see a
    found set of contacts who live in New York or Colorado.

Constraining the Last Find

The *Constrain Found Set* function searches within the found set only, refining results further. This can be accessed two ways. While in Browse mode, highlight some text in a field, and select *Constrain Found Set* from the field contextual menu. The selection is used to find and retain only records from the found set with the matching value. In Find mode, enter criteria and select the *Requests ➤ Constrain Found Set* menu instead of *Perform Find*. Records in the previous found set that don't match the new criteria will be removed. To illustrate this, follow these steps:

1. On the "Contact – Entry" layout, enter Find mode.

2. Type "Widget" into the *Company* field.

3. Press Enter or click *Perform Find* to see a found set of contacts
    who work for Widgets Manufacturing.

4. Enter Find mode again.

5. Type "CO" into the *State* field.

6. Select "Constrain Found Set" from the "Requests" menu to see a
    found set of contacts who work for Widgets Manufacturing who
    live in Colorado.

Managing Multiple Find Requests

Entering Find mode creates a single default find request. Additional requests can be created to construct more complex searches. Each request provides one set of criteria defining values that indicate if a matching record should be *included* or *omitted* from the result. The results of all requests are combined into a new found set. If one request specifies records with a *State* of "NY" and another specifies records with a *State* of "CO," the result will be a combined list of everyone from those two states.

For requests that contain multiple field criteria, it helps to think of the difference between one or more requests using the following and/or terminology:

- A single request containing multiple field criteria acts as an "and" type search. A record must contain all the criteria of the request to be included in the result.

- A set of multiple requests act as an "or" type search. A record must match all the criteria of at least one request to be included in the results.

Users can create, delete, and duplicate find requests just like they can do with records. The only difference is that these functions are accessed through a *Requests* menu, which replaces the *Records* menu while in Find mode. Some of these are also accessible through a toolbar icon or the record contextual menu on the background of a layout.

Specifying a Matching Records Option

Every new find request has a default *Matching Records* option set to "Include." This means that records matching the request criteria will be included in the results. Changing this to "Omit" causes records matching the criteria to be excluded from the results of the previous request(s). In the example shown in Figure 4-8, the first request will *Include* every record with "Widget" in the *Company* field, while the second request will *Omit* any matches with a *First Name* of "Jim." The results will be all contacts working for Widgets Manufacturing except for people named Jim. Using this setting with multiple find requests makes it possible to construct and perform extremely complex include–omit multi-criteria searches.

Figure 4-8. *An example of a second find request set to omit results*

Tip   Multiple requests with different matching options perform the equivalent of multiple extend or constrain actions all at once!

Working with Saved Finds

Find requests can be saved for future reuse. In Browse mode, the *Saved Finds* menu is accessible from the *Find* toolbar button and the *Records* ➤ *Saved Finds* menu. In Find mode, it is available through the *Saved Finds* toolbar button. This menu is used to save and manage saved finds as well as perform saved or recent finds.

The *Save Current Find* option will open a dialog to start the save process. A name can be entered, and optionally, the criteria can be edited. In Browse mode, the last executed find will be saved. In Find mode, the current criteria entered will be saved.

The *Edit Saved Finds* option opens a dialog of the same name, shown in Figure 4-9, that is used to create, edit, duplicate, or delete saved finds.

Figure 4-9. *The dialog used to view and manage saved finds*

Managing a Saved Find Request

When saving a new find, a *Specify Options for the Saved Find* dialog opens with the name of the find. Clicking the *Advanced* button in this dialog (or selecting to edit a saved find) will open a *Specify Find Requests* dialog. Both dialogs are shown in Figure 4-10. Each line in the second dialog represents one find request of the saved find. Each request specifies a criteria summary and the action associated with it: *Find Records* or *Omit Records*. From here, requests can be *created*, *edited*, *duplicated*, or *deleted* using the buttons at the bottom. Double-click a request or select one and click *Edit* to open the editing dialog.

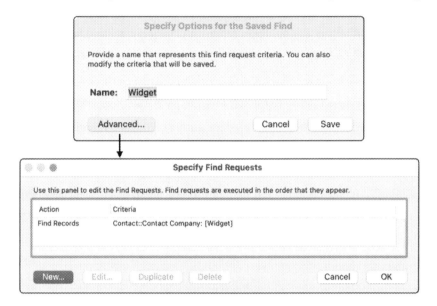

Figure 4-10. *The dialog used to view and manage find requests in a saved find*

Editing a Saved Find Request Criteria

The *Edit Find Request* dialog, shown in Figure 4-11, is used to edit a new or saved find request. This dialog can be opened by clicking *New* or *Edit* or double-clicking a find request in the *Specify Find Requests* dialog shown previously in Figure 4-10. This dialog is also used by script steps that create find requests or perform finds (Chapter 25, "Searching Records"). It shows a single find request, listing each field–criteria pair that makes up the request.

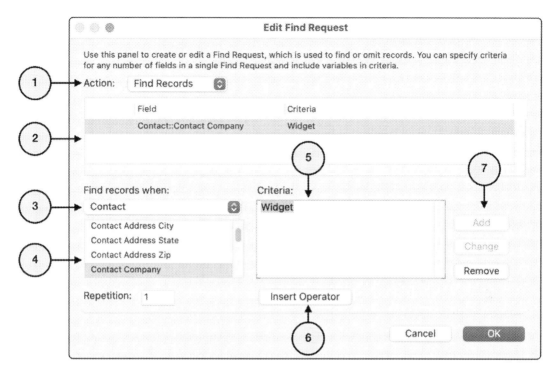

Figure 4-11. *The dialog used to edit a single request of a saved find*

In the dialog, you can edit the criteria of the request using the following controls:

1. *Action* – Choose "Find Records" or "Omit Records," indicating how matching records will be handled for this request.

2. *Criteria list* – List of the find request's field criteria. The selected row is editable below.

3. *Table* – Select a table containing the field to search.

4. *Field* – Select the search field.

5. *Criteria* – The value to search for in the selected field.

6. *Insert Operator* – Click to choose and insert an operator.

7. Buttons – Control how the current field–criteria will be handled in the list above: *Add* a new request, *Change* the currently selected request, or *Remove* the selected request.

Tip Building a complex find in Find mode is more intuitive than the dialogs. Use these only for making changes to a saved find.

Working with a Found Set

A *found set* is a group of records that are visible and navigable within the context of a window. While the found set may contain all records within a table, the term generally refers to a subset of records generated by a search or other actions. Records that are not part of the found set, those not actively visible or navigable, are called the *omitted set*. They still exist in the same table but are not included in the visible set. Within a single window, a found set for each table is retained when navigating to other layouts for the same table. When using multiple windows, the same layout for the same table can display a different found set, one in each window.

If the toolbar is hidden, it is impossible for a user to know if the found set consists of less than all records unless custom layout elements are created to display that information. Even with the toolbar visible, it's easy to miss. A new user might panic at first wondering where all their records have gone when looking at a small found set for a table they know contains a larger quantity of records. However, the difference is displayed in the record count in the navigation area of the toolbar, as shown in Figure 4-12. When all records are accessible, only the total count of records is displayed. When a subset is active, the first number indicates how many records make up the visible found set, while the second number indicates the total number of records including those that are omitted from the found set.

Figure 4-12. The record count when viewing all records (left) or a found set (right)

Changing the Records in the Found Set

The records in a found set can be changed by performing a find or one of several commands in the Records menu. The *Show All Records* command replaces the found set in the current window with all records in the current layout's table. The *Omit Record* command will move the current record from the found set to the omitted set. Use this to fine-tune results, omitting individual records instead of performing a new search. The *Omit Multiple* command allows the user to specify any number of records they wish to omit starting from the current record. For example, if the user is viewing the first record of a found set of 100 records and chooses to omit 10 records, the first 10 records will be omitted, leaving the remaining 90 records. However, if they are viewing record 50 of 100 and do the same thing, then records 50–59 will be omitted, leaving records 1–49 and 60–100. Finally, the *Show Omitted Only* command swaps the current found set with the omitted set. Alternatively, click the circle icon in the navigation area of the toolbar to toggle between the found or omitted records.

Sorting Records in the Found Set

The found set's sort status is always indicated in the record navigation area of the toolbar as shown in Figure 4-13. Records always default to creation order, which is considered an "unsorted" order. They can be sorted based on a selected list of *sort fields*, which can be defined using local or related fields in the *Sort Records* dialog, shown in Figure 4-14. The dialog can be opened by selecting the *Sort Records* command from the *Records* menu or from the record contextual menu. It is also available by clicking the *Sort* button in the toolbar or running a script configured to sort.

Figure 4-13. *The sort status is always displayed in the toolbar record count area*

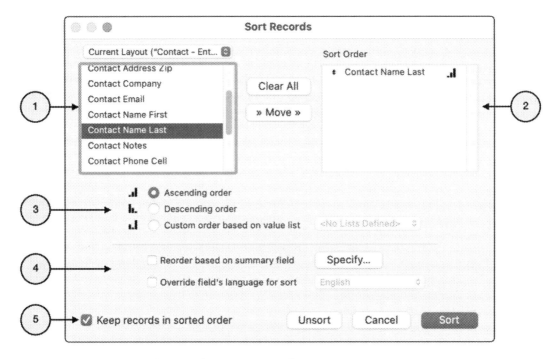

Figure 4-14. *The dialog used to sort records*

The *Sort Records* dialog contains following sort controls:

1. *Field selector* – Select a field from a list based on the table or layout selected in the pop-up menu.

2. *Sort Order* – The field order used to sort records. Add a field by double-clicking it in the field selector or with the *Move* button. Drag up or down to rearrange. Remove a field by double-clicking here or with the *Clear* button. To remove all fields, click *Clear All*.

3. *Sort field direction* – Choose the sort direction for the selected field: *ascending* (default), *descending*, or a *custom order* based on the content of a value list (Chapter 11).

4. *Advanced sort options*:

- *Reorder based on summary field* – Select a summary field (Chapter 8) to reorder records based on the position of the sort field's value as sub-summarized by another sort field. For example, a list of contacts can be summarized by a state (sort field) but sorted by the number of contacts living in each state (summary field).

- *Override field's language for sort* – Select a language used to index text fields when sorting.

5. *Keep records in sorted order* – Enable this to continuously re-sort whenever the contents of a sort field change. Deselect to have the records remain in order based on the last sort performed to avoid reshuffling during data entry tasks.

Modifying Field Values in a Found Set

Several commands allow modification of field values across an entire found set: *Replace Field Contents, Relookup Field Contents, Find and Replace*, and *Spell-checking*.

Replace Field Contents

The *Replace Field Contents* command under the *Records* menu opens the dialog shown in Figure 4-15. This is used to define a value that will be inserted into the current field on every record in the found set. The replacement value can be the literal value contained in the field of the current record, a serial number starting from a specified number on the first record and incremented a specified amount for each subsequent record, or the result of a calculation formula (Chapter 12).

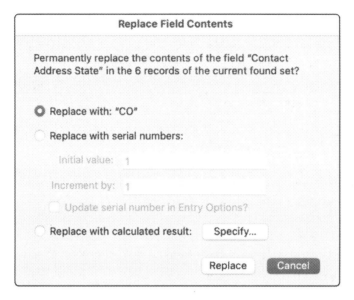

Figure 4-15. *The dialog used to define a replacement value to apply to every record in the found set*

Caution   Replace has no undo capability! Custom menus (Chapter 23) can hide this feature from users who don't require it.

Relookup Field Contents

When a field is defined to copy data from related records using a *looked-up value* (Chapter 8, "Configuring a Lookup Field"), the copied values can be manually forced to update for every record in the found set using the *Relookup Field Contents* command.

Caution   The lookup feature is a vestigial remnant from the days before better auto-enter options and relationships were available.

Find and Replace

FileMaker's *Find and Replace* function is like those found in text editors. It can locate text within one or all fields, for one or all records in the current found set, and optionally replace matches with alternate text. Select *Find/Replace* from the *Edit* menu to open the dialog shown in Figure 4-16.

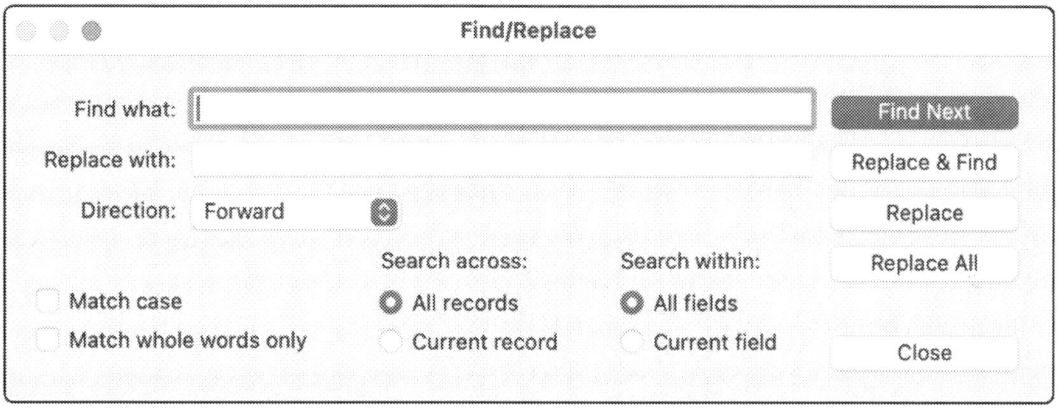

Figure 4-16. *The dialog used to find and replace text*

To begin, type text into the *Find what* field and optionally in the *Replace with* field. The *Direction* menu offers the choice of moving forward or backward through fields and/or records in a found set. Select the *Match case* checkbox for the find process to be case sensitive. Select *Match whole words only* to only consider a match when the text in a field contains the entire phrase typed into the *Find what* field. The *Search across* radio buttons instruct the function whether it should search all records in the found set or limit itself to the current record. The *Search within* option controls if it should search all fields on the layout or just the current field.

Once configured, the *Find Next* button locates and highlights the next instance of the text in the *Find what* field in the current field, next field, or next record, depending on the other settings in the dialog. The *Replace & Find* button will either locate the first instance of a match, if one has not yet been made, or replace the currently highlighted matched text with the replacement text and then locate the next instance of a match. The *Replace* button performs the replace function if a find has already selected a matching instance of the search text. Afterward, the cursor appears immediately after the replaced text. The *Replace All* button replaces all matching instances of the search text based on the settings in the dialog.

Spell-checking

FileMaker has an integrated spell-checker that can process a piece of selected text, the contents of a field, every field on the current record, or all records in the found set.

Exploring the Spelling Menu

The *Spelling* submenu of the *Edit* menu has several commands for standard spell-checking functionality. The *Check Selection* command quickly spell-checks selected text in the current field. *Check Record* checks the text in every field on the layout for the current record, and *Check All* checks every field on the current layout for every record in the found set. The *Correct Word* command checks the last word typed in a field but is only enabled when the *Check spelling as you type* setting is set to *Beep on questionable spellings* (Chapter 6, "File Options: Spelling"). You can *Select Dictionaries* to choose a language and *Edit User Directory* to add custom terms to the user dictionary.

Contextual Spelling Features

When the *Indicate questionable words with special underline* file option is enabled (Chapter 6, "File Options: Spelling"), any questionable words in the active field will be marked with a red underline. This option applies to an entire file but can be turned off for individual fields on a layout (Chapter 19, "Inspecting the Data Tab"). When on, a list of suggested spellings and alternate words are available at the top of the text contextual menu for the selected word, shown in Figure 4-17.

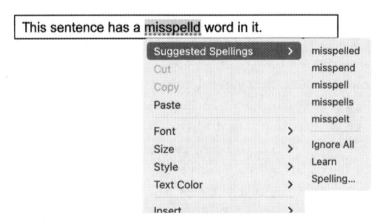

Figure 4-17. *A contextual menu shows alternative spellings for questionable words*

Printing

The content area of a window can be previewed and printed using familiar operating system *Page Setup* and *Print* dialogs.

Using Preview Mode

Preview mode is a transitional window state that changes the menu, toolbar, and content area for the purpose of viewing a layout in preparation for sending it to a printer or saving as a PDF file. To preview a layout, select *Preview Mode* from the *View* menu, or click the *Preview* toolbar icon. The toolbar options will change to print-related functionality, and the content area will become one or more noninteractive, non-editable pages rendered exactly as they will appear when printed. Any interactive objects such as buttons, tabs, slide controls, etc. will be displayed as a nonfunctional artwork. Depending on the settings of each layout object, some objects and data may be invisible, be reformatted, slide into a new position, or be cut off at the page margins.

Status Toolbar (Preview Mode)

The Preview mode toolbar will change to print-specific buttons, either default options or the user's customized set.

Default Status Toolbar Items (Preview Mode)

The default toolbar for Preview mode is shown in Figure 4-18. Like in Browse mode, the top portion can be customized, and the bottom is static.

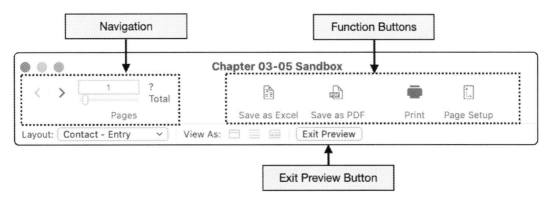

Figure 4-18. *The anatomy of the toolbar in Preview mode*

Upper Toolbar: Navigation Controls

The *navigation controls* in the Preview mode toolbar are like those in Browse and Find modes except that they display information about and allow movement between print pages instead of records or find requests. At first, the page count may be displayed as a question mark if the entire document has not yet been rendered. Click through pages or scroll to the end to update.

Upper Toolbar: Function Buttons

The function buttons included in the default Preview toolbar are

- *Save as Excel* – Export the records into an Excel file.

- *Save as PDF* – Save the preview as a PDF file.

- *Print* – Open the dialog to send the preview to a printer.

- *Page Setup* – Open the dialog to configure page setup to change the rendering.

Lower Toolbar: Exit Preview Button

The *Exit Preview* button will end the preview and return the window to Browse mode.

Customizing the Status Toolbar (Preview Mode)

The Preview mode toolbar is customizable at the user-computer level. Select the *View* ➤ *Customize Toolbar* menu to open the customization panel attached to the window as shown in Figure 4-19. Although the available buttons are different, they can be added or removed as described for Browse mode in Chapter 3.

Figure 4-19. *The toolbar customization panel for Preview mode*

Page Setup

The *Page Setup* dialog (*Print Setup* in Windows) is a standard operating system dialog used to configure how the current layout will behave when previewing or printing, shown in Figure 4-20. This can be accessed in Browse, Preview, or Layout mode by selecting *Page Setup* in the File menu. Here you can choose a printer, paper size, orientation, and scale percentage.

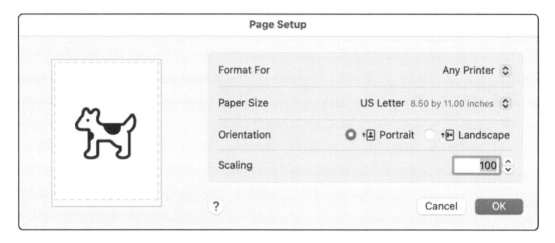

Figure 4-20. *The dialog to configure page settings*

Note   The *Layout Setup* dialog has some printing options for columns and page margins (Chapter 18, "Layout Settings: Printing").

Print Dialog Options

The *Print* dialog is a standard operating system dialog for configuring a print job, shown in Figure 4-21. This can be opened by selecting *Print* in the *File* menu or clicking *Print* in the Preview mode toolbar. While most of the options are identical to other applications, a few are specific to FileMaker. *Number pages from* accepts a page number that will be considered the first page for numbering purposes when using a dynamic page number placeholder on a report layout (Chapter 20, "Dynamic Placeholder Symbols"). Three print options determine how the content area of the window will be printed:

- *Records being browsed* – Include every record in the found set.

- *Current record* – Includes only the current record selected or in view when the *Print* dialog was opened.

- *Blank record, showing fields* – Print the layout without any record data. The adjacent menu controls how fields will be printed.

Figure 4-21. *The dialog for preparing a job to send to a printer*

Caution   FileMaker always recalls the last print option selected, even if you switch layouts or windows or have scripts generate a print. If this setting is not specified on each print job, it may appear as an error.

Summary

This chapter explored how users interact with records to enter data, perform searches, and print. In the next chapter, we focus on importing and exporting records.

CHAPTER 5

Transferring Records

FileMaker has *import* and *export* functions that transfer records between two locations. This allows repurposing data to avoid retyping, migrating data from other systems into FileMaker, migrating data between FileMaker databases, making a safe backup of key data outside of a database, duplicating commonly reused data from a template table into a content table, sending data to other systems, and more. FileMaker supports many standard file formats and allows the creation of new records or updates to existing records, with a granular selection of individual fields to be transferred. This chapter discusses the following data transfer topics:

- Supported file types
- Importing records
- Exporting records

Note   The *Import* and *Export* commands discussed in this chapter both have corresponding script steps, which are configured using the same dialogs shown here. Scripting is discussed in Chapters 24–28.

Supported File Types

FileMaker can import and export records in several formats, shown in Figure 5-1. In addition, content imports are supported from ODBC and XML sources or a folder containing picture, movie, or text files.

© Mark Conway Munro 2024
M. C. Munro, *Learn FileMaker Pro 2024*, https://doi.org/10.1007/979-8-8688-0835-7_5

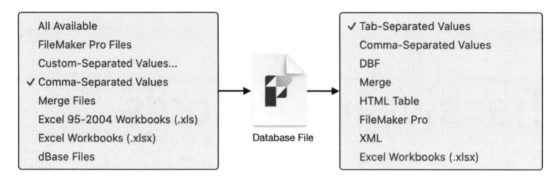

Figure 5-1. *The file types supported for record import (left) and export (right)*

Note   The new "*Custom-Separated Values…*" import option allows a selection of a delimiter and replaces the Tab-Separated Values import option found in older versions.

Importing Records

The *Import Records* function will create or update records in the table of the current window's layout. Records can be imported from various sources: a table within the same file, an external database, or one of various text-based external data files. To explore the feature, import some contact data into the *CH03-05 Sandbox* example file. Begin by downloading the free *us-500.csv* contacts sample file available from the Brian Dunning website.

Note   See the "CH05-01 Website Brian Dunning.html" shortcut in the example files.

To import, open the *CH03-05 Sandbox* example file, navigate to the *Contact – List* layout, and select the *File* ➤ *Import Records* ➤ *File* menu to open the *Choose File* dialog, as shown in Figure 5-2.

Figure 5-2. *The dialog used to choose a file to import*

The dialog allows a selection of a file to import from any directory. It can also access a database hosted on a FileMaker Server by clicking the *Hosts* button in the *Options* area at the bottom (Chapter 32, "Opening a Hosted Database"). This area also contains a *Show* pop-up menu of import-compatible file types that highlights files in the directory by type. The checkbox to create a recurring import provides a shortcut by skipping the manual import process and automatically creating a new table, layout, and script for repeated use in the future. For now, select the downloaded CSV file and click the *Open* button.

Note   Open the "CH03-05 Sandbox" example file to follow along.

Performing an Import

After selecting and opening the data file, a *Specify Import Order* dialog will appear, as shown in Figure 5-3. This dialog has regions for browsing source data, specifying an import type, selecting a target table, mapping fields between the source and target fields, and setting import options that vary depending on the type of import being performed. The default is an *Add* type import, where all records from the *Source* data will be added as new records in the *Target* table. Let's work through each of these areas to prepare our export.

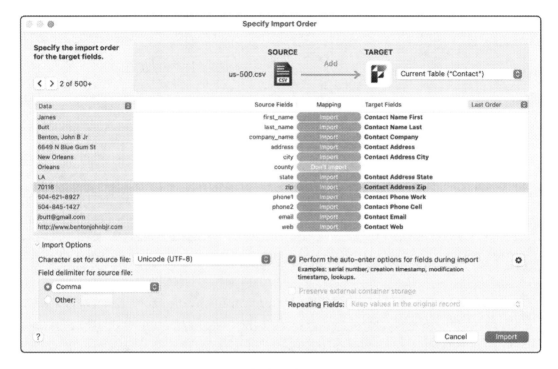

Figure 5-3. *The import dialog used for field mapping and specifying options*

Caution   This dialog design was introduced in FileMaker 18 and is completely different from earlier versions!

Browsing the Source Data

The *import source data* panel, shown in Figure 5-4, is displayed in a list on the leftmost column and is navigable using the arrow buttons above it. Note that the current record shown is "2 of 500+" and the pop-up menu above the list of data says "Data." If you click the back arrow to view the first record, the pop-up menu changes to "Use as Field Names." FileMaker has automatically assumed that the first record contains field names instead of actual data and preconfigured these two records so the first will be used as field names and the renaming will be treated as data and imported.

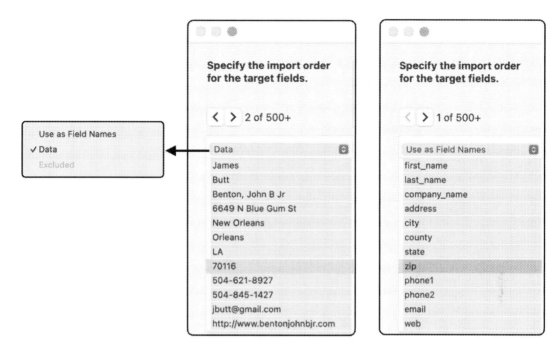

Figure 5-4. *The source side of the Specify Import Order dialog*

This menu is enabled for text-based data file imports and controls how incoming record will be handled. The three choices are

- *Use as Field Names* – Instructs the import to treat the selected incoming data as field names. This can be used when mapping fields, and it also indicates where the import should begin. If the record marked as field names isn't the first one, all preceding records will be marked as "Excluded" and not be imported.

- *Data* – Indicates that the selected data should be imported as a normal record. This is the choice made by default for all except the first record.

- *Excluded* – Indicates the record will be ignored and not imported. Any records preceding the one used for field names will be automatically excluded. But you can use this option to manually mark specific records that you don't want imported.

Moving to the right of the dialog, the *Source Fields* list shown in Figure 5-5, shows the field names from the source data if available. When importing from a text-based data file without a row flagged as providing field names, these will say "from source file." When importing from a FileMaker database, the actual field names will be displayed, and the only control over the source data side of the dialog is the ability to navigate and view source data records.

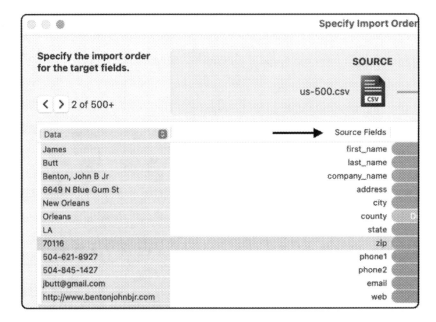

Figure 5-5. *The Source Fields column*

Selecting a Target Table

The *Target* is the destination table for incoming data and will default to the table of the layout displayed in the current window. The pop-up menu, shown in Figure 5-6, is a standard FileMaker table selection menu that lists the *Current Table, Related Tables, Unrelated Tables,* and a *Manage Database.* However, since an import must flow into the current layout's context, most of these options are disabled when importing. They are also irrelevant here because the *Sandbox* database has only one table. If you want to import into a different layout's table, you must cancel the import, switch to another table's layout, and start again. The only alternative to a target of the current table is to create a new table.

Figure 5-6. *The import target table pop-up menu*

Selecting the *New Table* option will configure the dialog to automatically create a new table during the import and flow the data into it. The *Target Fields* list will display new names as a numeric sequence with an "f" prefix unless a row has been assigned to *Use as Field Names.*

The *Manage Database* option is enabled and will open a dialog of the same name (Chapters 7–9) to create new fields in the target table so they can be included in the import without having to exit the import dialog.

Tip   To follow along, keep the target on "Current Table."

Mapping Fields from Source to Target

The import source file or target table may have more or less fields than the other, and they may be in a different order. It is necessary to indicate which source fields should be imported and to match them to an appropriate target field. This process of *mapping fields* is the primary purpose of the *Specify Import Order* dialog. Each selectable row of the central list shows columns for *Source Fields, Mapping,* and *Target Fields,* and these last two each open a menu of options.

The *Mapping* column displays the import status of the corresponding two fields: *Import* or *Don't Import*. To edit the mapping of a particular row, click the green icon to reveal the menu of options, as shown in Figure 5-7.

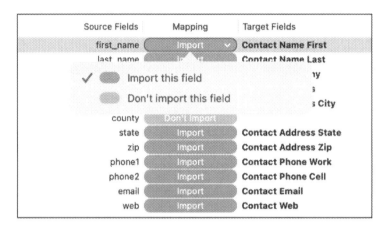

Figure 5-7. *The choice to import a selected field or not*

Each row in the *Target Fields* column opens a menu for selection of a target field that the corresponding source field should flow into, as shown in Figure 5-8. The current row's selection (if any) will be highlighted in the list. An icon indicates each field's current import status: an arrow means they are already configured elsewhere to receive input from the source, and a clear oval indicates they are not. Fields that don't accept data entry, like a calculation or summary field, will be grouped at the bottom under a "Not for Importing" folder (not shown). Click to select the appropriate target field for the corresponding source field. Once all input fields are mapped to targets, it's time to configure import options.

Figure 5-8. *The options available for arranging the list of target fields*

Setting Import Options

The *Import Options* section at the bottom of *the Specify Import Order* dialog controls various behaviors based on the type of import source. On the left, the text-parsing options, shown in Figure 5-9, are only visible when importing from a text-based file. Here you can choose a character set and field delimiter: *Comma, Tab, Semi-colon, Space,* or a *custom value.*

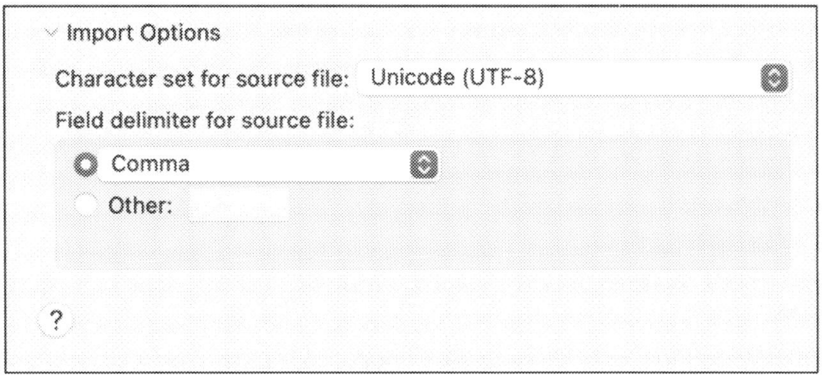

Figure 5-9. *The import options for text parsing*

The import options on the right, shown in Figure 5-10, affect behaviors when the new information is placed into database fields.

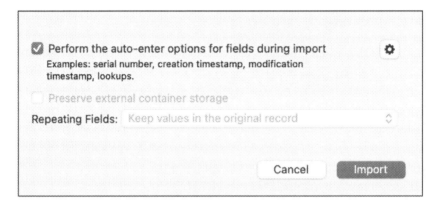

Figure 5-10. *The import options for performing auto-enter field options*

The *Perform the auto-enter options for fields during import* checkbox controls if fields defined with an auto-enter setting (Chapter 8) will update their values as part of the import. This allows serial numbers, creation/modification data, or other values to be preserved from the source file by unchecking the box or re-evaluated based on the target field definitions by checking them. Click the gear icon here to check which fields should or should not auto-enter. This can also be accessed by selecting the gear to the right of individual target fields in the mapping list above. When importing new records into the Sandbox file, turn this on for all fields by checking this box.

The *Preserve external container storage* checkbox suppresses container field content validation, allowing the target table to use existing external container contents. Select this when reimporting data back into an existing file or a copy of a file, to avoid decrypting and re-encrypting external files when the base directory of the source and target fields is the same. External storage for container fields is discussed in Chapter 10.

The *Repeating Fields* option offers a choice to keep repeating fields (Chapter 8, "Repeating") together in a single record or split them so each repetition becomes one new record when imported.

Finishing the Import

Once fields are mapped and options configured, click the *Import* button to perform the transfer process. An *Import Summary* dialog appears reporting the number of records added or updated, the number of skipped records and fields, and how many tables were created, if any. A text file named *Import.log* will be saved to the database file's folder containing details about the import process and noting any errors that may have occurred. After the import process, the *found set* in the window will be the imported records with any previously existing records hidden as an *omitted set* (Chapter 4, "Working with a Found Set").

Changing the Import Type

Besides the *Add*-style import described earlier, there are two other import types available: *Update* and *Replace*. Instead of creating records, these two are used to overwrite existing records. An import type selection panel is accessible by clicking in the space between the source and target icons, shown in Figure 5-11.

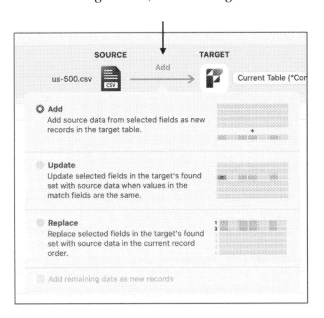

Figure 5-11. *The hidden panel to select a different import type*

Caution   When using an import that overwrites existing records, use extreme care and be sure you have a backup of your database!

Updating Matching Records in Found Set

An *Update*-style import is a nonlinear data transfer that will import each record of the source data into fields on an existing record in the target table based on match criteria. A *match field* is a new field mapping designation, shown in Figure 5-12, used to tag one or more fields as criteria for matching an incoming record to a record in the target table. During the *Update* import, each incoming source record will be matched to an existing record based on the selected match field(s). If a matching record is found, the remaining import fields will be updated in their mapped target fields for that record. If a matching record is not found, it will be skipped over unless the *Add remaining data as new records* checkbox is selected at the bottom of the selection panel, shown previously in Figure 5-11.

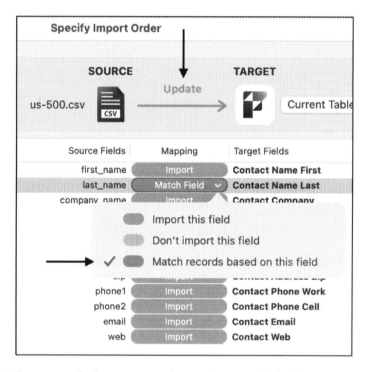

Figure 5-12. *The expanded mapping choice for match fields*

Replacing Records in Found Set

A *Replace* import will use the incoming record values to overwrite fields on existing records based on their linear position in the corresponding sets without any concern for matching records. In other words, the values from the first record in the source data will be used to replace values in the mapped fields of the first record in the target set – same for the second, third, etc. This can be useful in a situation where you need to export a set of data, manipulate it outside of FileMaker, and then immediately replace some or all field values of those same records. When using this import type, typically, the source data and the target table's current found set should contain the same number of records. If not, it will follow these two rules:

- If the source record count is less than the target found set, records in the found set beyond that source's count will not be modified.

- If the source record count is greater than the target found set, the import will stop after the number of records in that found set is finished, unless the Add remaining data as new records checkbox is selected.

Caution   It is far too easy to accidentally overwrite the wrong data using the *Replace* option! Consider using a *Match* import instead, which can replace information with more precision.

Setting Up an Automatic Recurring Import

The optional *Set up as automatic recurring import* checkbox is found in the *Choose File* dialog at the start of the import process, as shown previously in Figure 5-2. Selecting this will completely bypass the rest of the import process and create a new table, layout, and script that can be customized and used to automatically repeat the same import process in the future. When selected, it opens a *Recurring Import Setup* dialog shown in Figure 5-13. This dialog displays the path of the source data and has three configurable options. Select *Don't import first record* when the source file's first row contains field names. The other two fields on this dialog allow entry of a layout and a script name to override the default names shown based on the import file name.

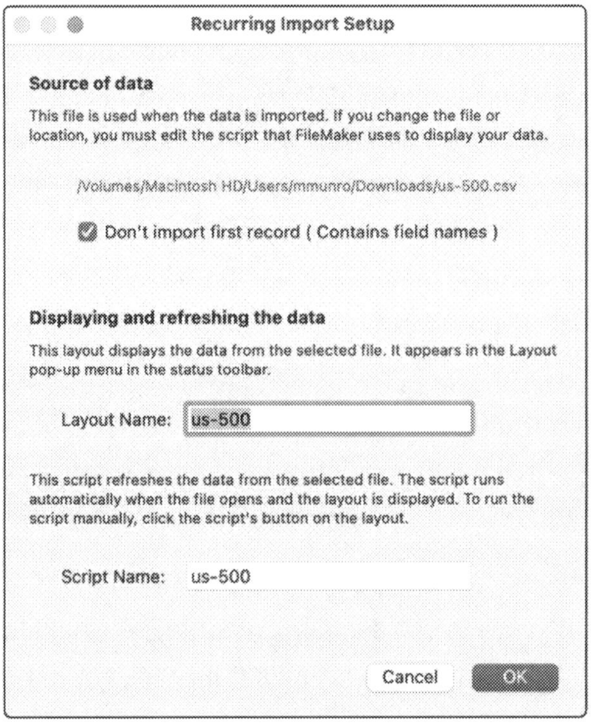

Figure 5-13. *The Recurring Import Setup dialog*

After configuring the options to your liking, click to continue. The following changes will be made to the database:

- A new table will be created with the same name as the source data file with a field for every column of data it contains.

- A new layout is created with the specified name and every field displayed.

- A script is created with the specified name that will navigate to the new layout, delete every record, and import the records from the file, thereby refreshing the data.

These resources can then be renamed and customized as needed to suit a specific workflow.

Caution   This is a clunky "training wheels" feature. For more precision, create a table, layout, and script yourself.

Exporting Records

The *Export Records* function will extract values from one or more selected fields from every record in the current window's found set and save them to a file of a specified type. To begin, open a database, navigate to a desired layout, and optionally perform a find to isolate a desired found set. Select the *File ➤ Export Records* menu to open a *Save As* dialog as shown in Figure 5-14. In addition to a standard selection of file name and folder location, a couple of FileMaker-specific options are available here. Select the *Type* of file for the export from the pop-up menu. The *After saving* checkboxes can be selected to initiate shortcuts for opening or emailing the new file after the export is finished. Click *Save* to continue the process and specify export fields.

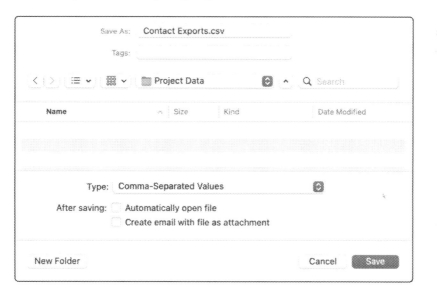

Figure 5-14. *A dialog used to specify an export location, file name, and type*

Specifying Export Fields

The *Specify Field Order for Export* dialog shown in Figure 5-15 is used to select the fields to include in an export, choose the order they will be saved in the output file, and configure formatting options.

Figure 5-15. *The dialog used to specify the export field order*

On the left, the pop-up menu is used to specify where to generate the field list below it. By default, this has the *Current Layout* selected, showing only the fields literally displayed on the current layout, both local and related. Select *Current Table* instead to show every field from the current layout's table occurrence, or choose a related table occurrence to include related fields in the export.

Note   Relationships and occurrences are discussed in Chapter 9.

Fields can be added to the export order by double-clicking in the list or using the *Move* or *Move All* button. The fields in the *Field export order* list will be saved to the output file in the order they appear and can be dragged into the desired order. Remove fields from the export list by double-clicking and clicking the *Clear* or *Clear All* button.

Once the field order is set, there are a few options available. The *Output file character set* menu specifies a character encoding for the export. The *Apply current layout's data formatting to exported data* checkbox will cause any number, date, or time field to be exported with the data formatted as it is on the current layout rather than the actual format of the data in the field (Chapter 19, "Data Formatting"). For example, if a number field contains "10" but is formatted on the current layout to display currency, for example, "$10.00," this box must be checked to export the number formatted as currency.

Summarizing Output into Groups

The *Group by* feature of the export dialog allows records to be summarized during the export, compressing individual records into groups, each with subtotals of key values.

Note   See the "*CH05-02 Summarizing Output*" example file.

Chapter 05 - Summarizing Output

COMPANY LIST (WITH REVENUE SUMMARY)

COMPANY	INDUSTRY	REVENUE	REVENUE SUMMARY
Online Tutor, LLC	Education	20	95
Mutual Investors Corp	Finance	5	95
Dividend Party, Inc.	Finance	10	95
Widget Books, Inc	Publishing	10	95
Learnign Resources	Education	15	95
Knowledge Bound Co.	Publishing	35	95

Figure 5-16. *The example file with a company list with revenue and revenue summary*

The example file contains one table of company records, each with an industry and revenue entered, shown in Figure 5-16. A *Revenue Summary* field summarizes revenue across records (Chapter 8, "Summary Fields"). In their current unsorted order, the only option is to export all four fields as regular fields, without summarization. Doing this to a tab- or comma-separated file results in data as shown in Table 5-1.

Table 5-1. *Hypothetical records showing how a non-grouped summary behaves*

Company	Industry	Revenue	Revenue Summary
Online Tutor, LLC	Education	20	95
Mutual Investors Corp	Finance	5	95
Dividend Party, Inc.	Finance	10	95
Widget Books, Inc.	Publishing	10	95
Learning Resources	Education	10	95
Knowledge Bound Co.	Publishing	35	95

The *Revenue Summary* field shows the same total revenue value for all records in both the List view and export because there is nothing defining a break that will put the records into summarized groups. To summarize unique industries, each with a total revenue, the records must be sorted by *Industry* and have a mechanism to summarize revenue by that sort field.

In a List view, records can be summarized into sub-groups by sorting and using a *sub-summary* layout part (Chapter 18, "Defining Summary Parts"). This allows report layouts to be created with one or more sorted sub-groupings of records showing summary totals (Chapter 34).

When exporting, a summary report can be generated by sorting and using the *Group by* option. Start by sorting the records by *Industry* and start an export to a comma-separated file named "Revenue Report.csv." When you reach the *Specify Field Order for Export* dialog, the *Group by* area will have a checkbox for the *Industry* field, shown in Figure 5-17. Select this box to inform the export that we are going to be summarizing records and add *Industry* to the export order.

Next, add the *Revenue Summary* field to the export list. An extra *Revenue Summary by Industry* field will be added automatically. It will be italicized to highlight the fact that it is not an actual field in the database, but a *summary group field* that will calculate values by industry.

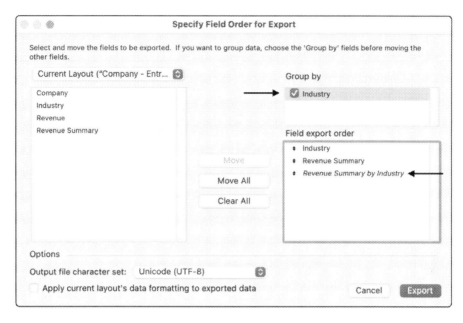

Figure 5-17. *The export dialog using the Group by feature to include a summary*

Finally, select and remove the *Revenue Summary* field from the export order. The *Revenue Summary by Industry* pseudo-field should remain in the list with *Industry*, as shown in Figure 5-18.

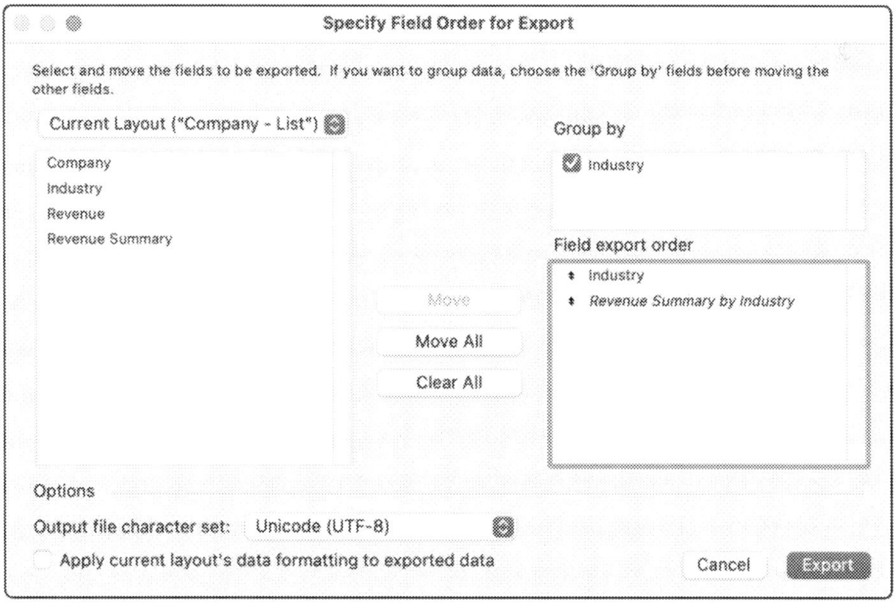

Figure 5-18. *An example of a field export order using the Group by feature*

With this configuration, the export file should contain one row for each industry with the total revenue of each in the second column, as shown in Table 5-2.

Table 5-2. *Data exported using the Group by option*

Education	35
Finance	15
Publishing	45

Summary

In this chapter, we explored the basics of importing and exporting records. In the next chapter, we shift from the user perspective to the developer perspective and begin defining data structures.

PART II

Defining Data Structures

The first step to building a custom database is to create a new file and begin defining the structure into which data will be stored. These chapters cover that process, exploring how to create files, tables, fields, relationships, containers, and value lists. Once finished, these will define the information to be stored and create a structural foundation that provides the relational context upon which interfaces will be constructed:

CHAPTER 6

Creating a Database File

In FileMaker, a *database file* is a document with a "fmp12" extension that contains a schema definition of structural elements and data entered by users. Files contain the "full stack" of a database, including presentation front end, process logic middleware, and data storage back end. Unlike the traditional approach where these components are physically separated and built with different languages, FileMaker folds all three into a familiar, document-based user experience with a built-in low-code development environment. Experienced software developers familiar with multitier architectures that employ command-line languages may find this arrangement initially disorienting. However, FileMaker expertly achieves the best of both worlds by uniting ease of use with powerful standards-based technologies. This chapter covers the basics of creating, configuring, and maintaining a database file, including

- Starting a custom project
- Creating a new database file
- Building a Sandbox table
- Configuring file options

Caution   Versions 12 thru 21 (2024) all share the same file extension and format. However, features introduced in newer versions are not backward compatible in older versions! A database's *File Options* can limit access to a minimum within that range of versions.

© Mark Conway Munro 2024
M. C. Munro, *Learn FileMaker Pro 2024*, https://doi.org/10.1007/979-8-8688-0835-7_6

Starting a Custom Project

A *database* is a structured collection of information stored in a generic format that is easily accessible for a wide variety of uses. The modern world is full of databases, and we interact with them constantly through apps and websites. Most of these are focused on one specific data type with predefined properties and procedures. For example, a calendar application allows a user to create and manage events with properties of date, time, attendees, notes, and alerts. Similarly, an email application allows management of messages with predefined properties of sender, recipients, subject, and body. These could each be thought of colloquially as an "event-base" and a "message-base" since, at their base, they store and provide access to information about events and messages. From a wider perspective, both events and messages are types of information; they are both forms of data. A calendar app accesses and manages an event database. A mail application does the same with a message database. Unlike these and countless other modern applications that provide front-end access to an out-of-sight database, an open-ended database application has no predefined data type; at its base is data, any kind of data. A database application like FileMaker allows a developer to create custom solutions that manage any data they define.

Applications such as a calendar or mail app provide a predefined database that is like a metaphorical filing cabinet, structurally locked and preconfigured by the vendor to accept a specific type of information. A user is free to enter information into this predefined framework but has little or no control over the framework itself. By contrast, a custom database is the metaphorical equivalent of that same filing drawer completely empty and unlocked so that you can define the content it accepts and decide how that information is stored, related, displayed, used, and shared. Every project starts fresh with the same blank slate waiting for you to define the framework and establish the capabilities that will be available to the user. So don't make the mistake of thinking of FileMaker as a system for only managing contacts or projects, and don't expect a new file to start out like an already defined database with a narrow focus. Although there are starter solutions and third-party templates available, creating a new file is like creating a new word processing document. Just as a word processing document can contain a wide variety of different content that you write, a new database created with FileMaker can store information about anything a developer defines it to manage: companies, contacts, inventory, invoices, messages, notes, people, products, tasks, and more. But it will start out as a blank document, waiting for your development based on your individual needs.

Creating a New Database File

There are several ways to create a new database file, all initiated from the *Create* tab of the *Launch Center* window, accessible by selecting *Create New* from the *File* menu:

- Using a *starter solution* template

- Starting from scratch with a blank file

- Converting a spreadsheet or other text-based files into a database

Creating a Database from a Starter Solution

A *starter solution* is a basic template provided by Claris as part of the FileMaker installation. Although this book is focused on creating your own databases by starting with a blank file, these templates can be used as a starting foundation upon which to build a custom solution. They can also serve as a decent learn-by-example tutorial. Try creating a database with the *Inventory* starter template by following the steps shown in Figure 6-1.

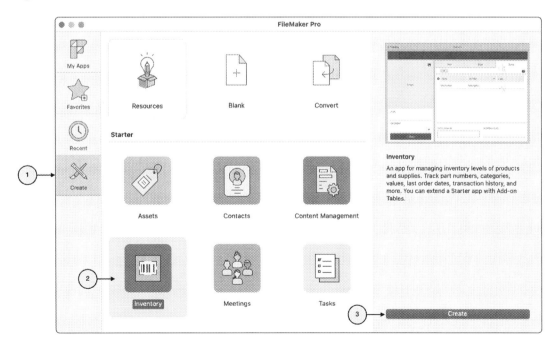

Figure 6-1. *The process of creating a new database from a starter solution*

1. Select the *Create* tab in the *Launch Center* window.

2. Click the *Inventory* icon under the *Starter* heading.

3. Click *Create* to specify a file name and location for the new file.

Caution   Starters are workable examples. However, like the examples throughout this book, any structural and design choices employed should not be taken as strict rules that must be unquestionably followed.

Creating a Database from a Blank Template

To create a new database from a blank template, follow the steps shown in Figure 6-2.

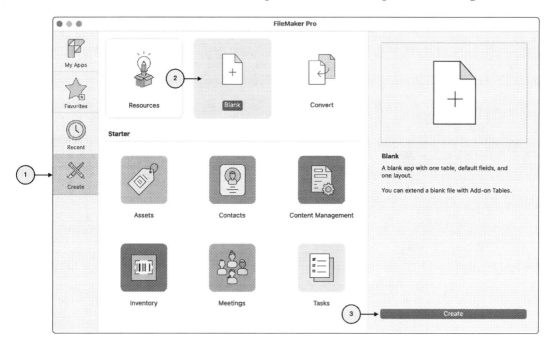

Figure 6-2. *The dialog used to create a new blank database file*

1. Select the *Create* tab in the *Launch Center* window.

2. Select the *Blank* icon.

3. Click *Create* to specify a file name and location for the new file.

Caution   New files will appear different from screenshots in this book because a custom theme (Chapter 22) was used for visual clarity. Download the sample files to follow the examples.

Converting an Existing File

FileMaker can automatically convert various file types into a database, including older FileMaker databases, spreadsheets, or other text-based data files. When importing these last two, it will automatically create a table and fields necessary to contain the information as part of the process. To begin, open the *Launch Center* and select the *Convert* option on the *Create* tab, and then select a source file.

Tip   Alternatively, you can drag and drop a compatible file onto the FileMaker application to start the conversion process.

A file dialog will open, allowing you to select a file. The *Show* option opens a menu of compatible file types, shown in Figure 6-3. Use this to limit the file selections to the selected type.

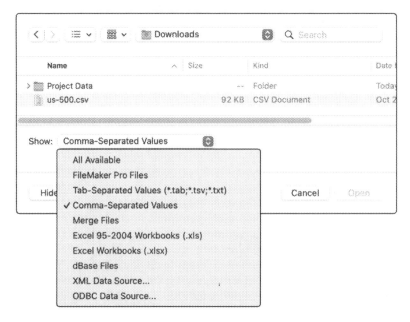

Figure 6-3. *The dialog used to create a new database file from a data file*

If the selected file is a FileMaker database with the "fmp12" extension, it will simply open since that is the current file format used by versions 12 through 21 (2024). If the file has the previous "fmp7" extension, FileMaker 2024 will recreate the file, saving a copy in the current file format. Any file with an extension prior to that must first be converted to the "fmp7" format using a copy of FileMaker 11 before FileMaker 2024 can convert it to the modern format.

If the source file is a structured data file, various conversion options will be presented across a sequence of dialogs. For example, if converting an Excel spreadsheet with multiple tabbed worksheets, a *Specify Excel Data* dialog will ask which worksheet should be used as the data source, and a dialog will prompt you to specify name and location for the new file. Then, a *Convert File* dialog similar to the *Specify Import Order* dialog (Chapter 5) opens allowing the target table name to be modified and choice to use field names from a selected source record. Once finished, the new database file will have one table with fields defined and two layouts: a form layout named "Layout #1" and a list layout named "Layout #2." The data structure and interface can then be customized to suit your purposes.

Building a Sandbox Table

To begin exploring the basics of a file and to provide a workspace to explore other lessons in future chapters, let's configure a rudimentary *Sandbox* database. This will provide a quick overview of building a table with fields and layouts, including a few steps that will be explained in more depth in later chapters. Start by creating a new database file named "CH06 Sandbox" from the blank template and open the file.

Tip   Performing these lessons will provide a crash course in setting up a database. However, these steps are already done in the "CH06 Sandbox" example file.

Changing the Default Table Name

A file created from the blank template automatically has one default table created with the same name as the file. So the example database should already have one table named "CH06 Sandbox" and one blank layout of the same name. In some situations, such as a database with a single table, having the table and file names matching is fine. However, in most cases, especially when building a database with multiple tables, the default table name will need to be modified. For example, a database with *Contact, Project,* and *Invoice* tables might have the file name of your company. For our purposes, and to gain a little practical experience, rename the default table to "Sandbox."

First, make sure the *Manage Database* dialog is open. Depending on application settings (Chapter 2, "General: User Interface Options"), the new file will either open in Layout mode (without opening the dialog) or in Browse mode (with the dialog open). If in Layout mode, open this dialog selecting the *File* ➤ *Manage* ➤ *Database* menu item. Then follow these steps, shown in Figure 6-4:

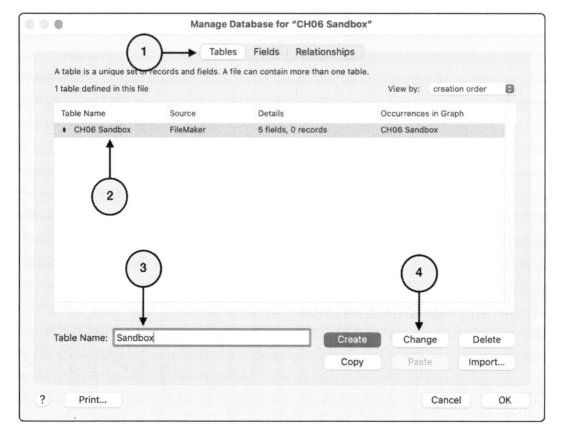

Figure 6-4. *Highlighting the process of renaming the default table*

1. Click the *Tables* tab.

2. Make sure the default table named "CH06 Sandbox" is selected.

3. Type "Sandbox" into the *Table Name* field.

4. Click the *Change* button.

Defining Fields

The renamed "Sandbox" table will already have five fields defined. Since version 17, FileMaker automatically creates default fields (Chapter 8, "Exploring Default Fields"). For now, we will ignore these and create one field of each available *data type* to serve as an example for experimentation on topics presented in forthcoming chapters.

Creating Data Entry Fields

First, we will create six *data entry fields* that can accept input from a user. To get started, open the *Manage Database* dialog. Then, follow the steps shown in Figure 6-5:

1. Click the *Fields* tab.

2. Click in the white space under the default fields so no field is selected.

3. Type "Example Text" into the *Field Name* text area.

4. Select "Text" from the *Type* menu.

5. Click the *Create* button or press *Enter*.

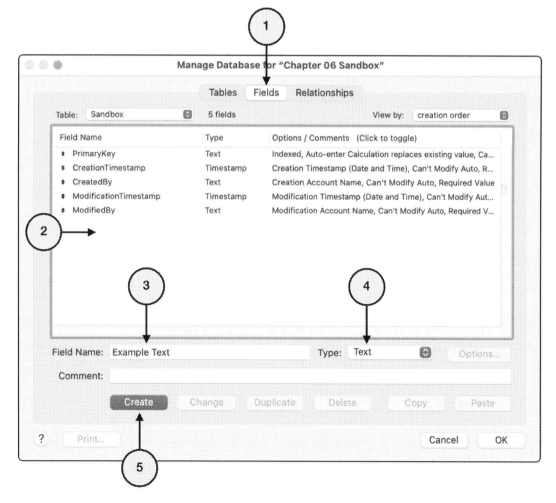

Figure 6-5. *The process of creating a text field in the Sandbox table*

Next, repeat this process for each of these field types:

1. Create a *Number* field named "Example Number."

2. Create a *Date* field named "Example Date."

3. Create a *Time* field named "Example Time."

4. Create a *Timestamp* field named "Example Timestamp."

5. Create a *Container* field named "Example Container."

Note   Field types and options are discussed in Chapter 8.

Creating a Calculation Field

Following the same process, create a *Calculation* field named "Example Calculation."
When the *Specify Calculation* dialog appears, follow the steps in Figure 6-6 to enter a
temporary placeholder calculation formula:

1. Type a zero as a placeholder formula in the text area.

2. Select "Number" for a result type.

3. Click OK to close and save.

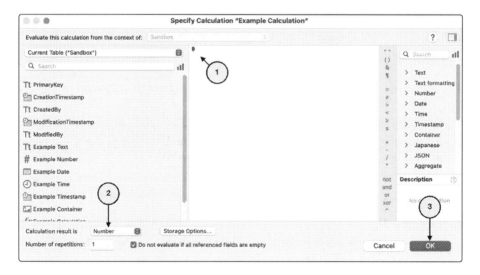

Figure 6-6. *The process of creating a placeholder calculation in the Sandbox*

Note   Calculation fields are discussed in Chapter 12.

Creating a Summary Field

Again, repeat the process to create a *Summary* field named "Example Summary." When the *Options for Summary Field* dialog appears, follow the steps in Figure 6-7 to select a default summary process:

1. Click the *Total of* radio button.

2. Select the *Example Number* field from the *Available Fields* list.

3. Click OK to close and save.

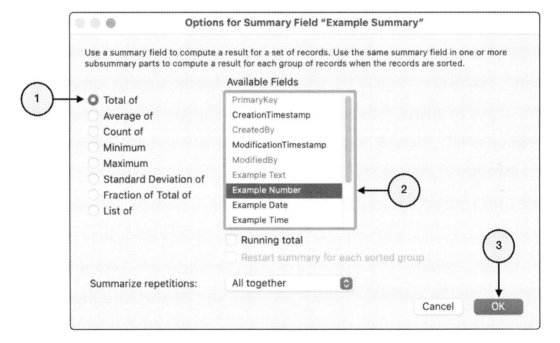

Figure 6-7. *The process of creating a summary field in the Sandbox*

Note   Summary fields are discussed in Chapter 8.

Reviewing the Sandbox Fields

Once finished creating data entry, calculation, and summary fields, the *Sandbox* table should contain five default fields and the eight example fields shown in Figure 6-8. If so, click to close the dialog, and save all changes.

Figure 6-8. *The complete list of fields in the Sandbox table*

Creating Layouts

Continuing with a rapid setup of a *Sandbox* example file, rename the default layout as a *Form view* for data entry and create a new a *List view* for scrolling through records.

Note   Content views were defined in Chapter 3.

Renaming the Default Layout as a Form View

A new database file will automatically have a default "form" layout with the same name as the file. Initially there would have been a single "CH06 Sandbox" layout. However, when the default table name was changed to "Sandbox," the layout should have changed as well. So, if following the instructions in this section, there should be a single blank layout named "Sandbox." Since we will have two layouts for the same table, we need to distinguish this one from the other by renaming it "Sandbox Form." To begin, select the *View ➤ Layout* menu item to enter Layout mode. Next, select the *Layout ➤ Layout Setup* menu to open the *Layout Setup* dialog, as shown in Figure 6-9. Then follow these steps:

1. Select the *General* tab.

2. Type "Sandbox Form" into the *Layout Name* field .

3. Click OK to close the window and save the change.

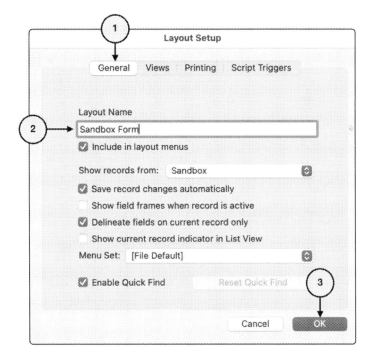

Figure 6-9. *The Layout Setup dialog with the layout name modified*

Note   Layout settings are discussed in depth in Chapter 18.

Adding Fields to a Layout

If *Layout* preferences (Chapter 2) are set to automatically add new fields to the current layout, then the eight example fields will already be present on the default layout. If not, enter Layout mode and follow these steps, as shown in Figure 6-10:

1. Confirm that the *Fields* tab is visible by selecting the *View* ➤ *Objects* ➤ *Fields* menu.

2. Select the entire list of fields by clicking in the field list and then selecting the *Edit* ➤ *Select All* menu.

3. Click, hold, and drag the list of fields onto the layout. The fields should appear on the layout, aligned and sized according to their data type.

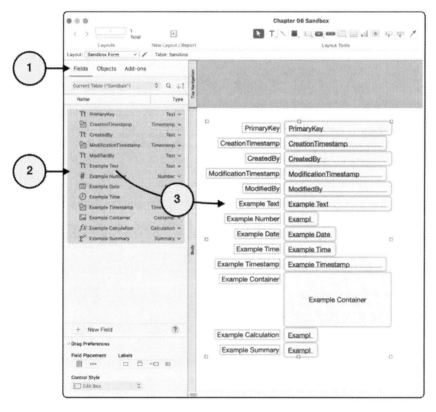

Figure 6-10. *Drag selected fields from the Fields tab to the layout*

Note   Learn about other ways to add fields to layouts in Chapter 20.

Adding a List Layout

While still in Layout mode, add a List view layout, by selecting the *Layout* ➤ *New Layout/Report* menu, and follow the steps in the dialog, shown in Figure 6-11:

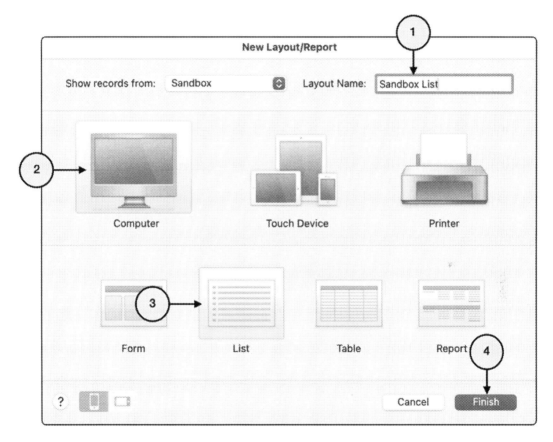

Figure 6-11.   *The dialog used to create a new layout or report*

1. Type "Sandbox List" into the *Layout Name* field.

2. Click a layout category of *Computer* in the first row of icons.

3. Click a layout type of *List* in the second row of icons.

4. Click *Finish* to close the dialog and complete the process.

Note   Other layout options are discussed in Chapter 18.

When finished, an empty List view layout will appear with three parts: *Header, Body,* and *Footer.* Because a List view has a horizontal orientation, the process of adding fields will change slightly, following the steps shown in Figure 6-12:

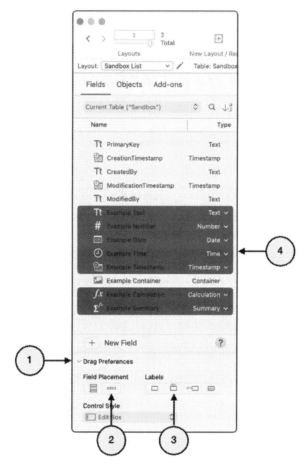

Figure 6-12. *Configure the Fields tab for dragging to a List view*

1. Confirm the *Drag Preferences* disclosure triangle is open and showing additional controls.

2. Select the *Horizontal* icon under *Field Placement.*

3. Select the *Labels* option to put labels above fields.

4. Select every example field except the container field by clicking each field while holding the Command (macOS) or Windows (Windows) key.

5. Next drag the selected fields onto the layout. Be sure to place them high enough so they land completely within the defined layout parts (horizontal white area).

6. Once placed, drag them down so that the fields are roughly centered in the Body part, as shown in Figure 6-13.

Figure 6-13. *The fields dropped into the Body part of the layout*

7. Reposition the labels squarely in the *Header* area by clicking them and using the mouse or arrow keys to move them around.

8. Remove the repetitive prefix from each field label by double-clicking each and deleting the extraneous "Example" portion.

9. Finally, adjust the size and position of the last two fields so nothing extends to the right in the gray area beyond the visible layout, as shown in Figure 6-14.

Figure 6-14. *The List view with cleaned-up labels and fields*

Note   Manipulating layout objects is discussed further in Chapter 21.

111

Configuring File Options

Like the application settings (Chapter 2), a database file has configurable settings. However, instead of being stored on a user's computer with the application, *file options* are stored in the database file and are accessible only when a database is open. Select the *File* ➤ *File Options* menu to open the *File Options* dialog, which is divided into five tabs: *Open, Icon, Spelling, Text,* and *Script Triggers.*

File Options: Open

The *Open* tab, shown in Figure 6-15, controls what happens when a database is opened.

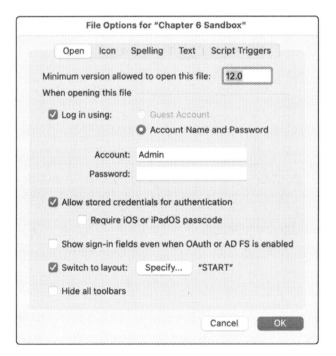

Figure 6-15. *The file options for open behavior*

The *Minimum version allowed to open this file* text field can restrict use of the file to only FileMaker versions at or above the version it is designed to support. Although all versions from 12.0 through 21.0 (2024) share the same file format, a database that uses features from newer versions should not be opened in an older version unless specifically designed with alternate functionality. To keep this file limited to the latest version, enter both a major and minor version number into the field (e.g., "21.0" instead of "21"). Below, five checkboxes control login and default interface functions:

- *Log in using* – Select this to enable automatic credential entry when a file opens. Do not use when a database requires tight security (Chapter 29)!

- *Allow stored credentials for authentication* – Enable to allow users to save credentials on their local device for automatic entry during future logins. The *Require iOS or iPadOS passcode* option requires entry of a passcode before storing credentials in their local keychain.

Caution   Do not allow automatic entry of credentials for databases in a shared computer environment or where tight security is important!

- *Show sign-in fields even when OAuth or AD FS is enabled* – Allows users to choose between OAuth and non-OAuth credentials when the former is used (Chapter 29).

  Switch to Layout – Specify a default layout at startup.

- *Hide all toolbars* – Select to start with the toolbar hidden.

File Options: Icon

The *Icon* tab, shown in Figure 6-16, allows customization of the icon that represents the database in the *Launch Center*, making it easier to visually locate a desired file. The default is the FileMaker 2024 icon. Choose an alternative from the built-in list of Claris-provided icons or specify a custom PNG or JPEG file by clicking *Custom*.

Figure 6-16. *The icon options control how a file appears in the Launch Center*

File Options: Spelling

The *Spelling* tab, shown in Figure 6-17, controls automatic spell-check settings. The *Indicate questionable words with special underline* checkbox will enable a red dotted line under any potentially misspelled words in a field with focus unless that field or object has been configured in the Inspector to explicitly disable the feature (Chapter 19, "Inspecting the Data Tab"). With the *Beep on questionable spellings* selected, a sound will be played anytime a user types a word that the dictionary flags as misspelled.

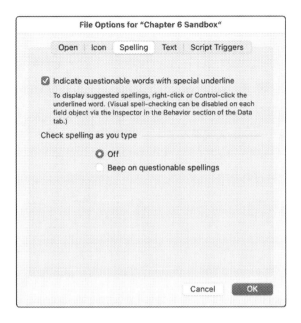

Figure 6-17. *The file options for spell-checking*

File Options: Text

The *Text* tab, shown in Figure 6-18, controls a few text entry options.

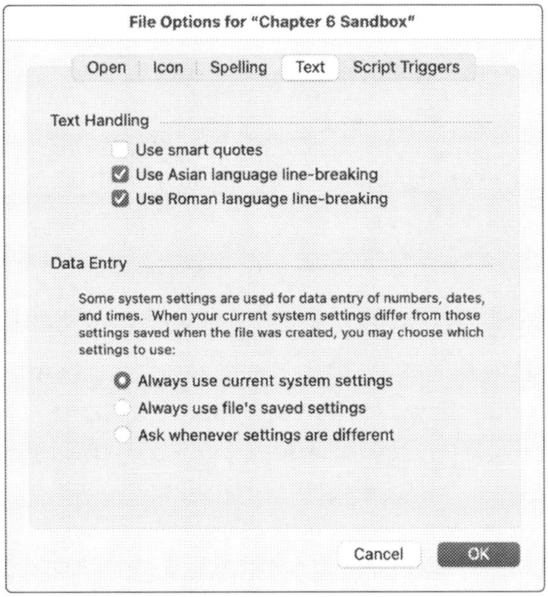

Figure 6-18. *The file options for text entry*

The *Text Handling* checkboxes control certain special data entry considerations. The *Data Entry* section handles formatting of various standard data like currency symbols, dates, and times. When FileMaker creates a new database, the file is automatically encoded with regional settings from the operating system of the local computer. On macOS, these can be found in the *System Preferences* ➤ *Language & Region* ➤ *Advanced* panel. Once the database file is created, these settings can't be modified. However, these settings give a choice of what happens when there is a difference between the user's operating system and the settings encoded in the database:

- *Always use current system settings* – Use the current system settings of the computer instead of those saved in the database file.

- *Always use file's saved settings* – Use the settings saved in the database file.

- *Ask whenever settings are different* – Ask the user at launch time which settings to use.

Note   Two new built-in functions allow access to information about the system and file's settings (Chapter 14, "Parsing Locale Elements").

File Options: Script Triggers

The *Script Triggers* tab is used to configure the database to automatically trigger scripts in response to interface events pertaining to the file (Chapter 27).

Summary

This chapter explored the basics of creating a file and configuring file options, and we created a *"Sandbox"* example file to provide a rapid sprint through the development interface and make a workspace to experiment in future lessons. In the next chapter, we will explore how to create tables and begin developing an object.

## CHAPTER 7

Building Tables

A *database schema* is like an architectural blueprint containing a structural definition for the information it will store and manage. A database application like FileMaker uses this information to create the digital structure into which data will be entered, viewed, and manipulated. A *table* is the fundamental unit of the schema that establishes a digital container for a class of entities whose information will be stored in the database. This chapter explores the following topics:

- Introducing object modeling
- Introducing the Manage Database window (Tables)
- Planning table names
- Managing tables
- Adding tables to the Sandbox database

Introducing Object Modeling

An *object model* or *data model* is an abstraction that defines elements of data for database entries, describing how they relate to properties of the real-world entities they represent and to other objects being modeled. A model is like an architectural blueprint that informs FileMaker about the structure of the information a database will store and manage. The term is used because the information is sometimes called a "virtual model" of the real objects represented by that structure. *Data modeling* is the process of creating a plan for the properties, relationships, and actions that control how a set of interconnected entity classes will be managed inside a database.

© Mark Conway Munro 2024
M. C. Munro, *Learn FileMaker Pro 2024*, https://doi.org/10.1007/979-8-8688-0835-7_7

Using a Spreadsheet as an Analogy

The primary elements of an object model are *tables*, *fields*, and *relationships*. Each is analogous to an element in a spreadsheet, as shown in Figure 7-1.

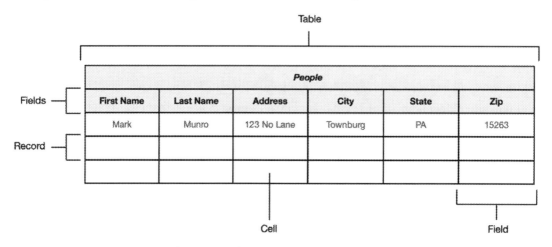

Figure 7-1. *Comparing elements of a database table to a spreadsheet*

Comparing a Table to a Spreadsheet Tab

A *table* allocates a space in the schema for a particular type of entity being modeled in the database. These are analogous to a tab in a spreadsheet. The term is used to refer both to the structural definition of a table as a storage model and to the content collected within that structure. So one may refer to both a table's fields (defined structure) and a table's records (content entered) as a "table."

The objects modeled as tables can be broad categories (people or products), narrow subcategories (employees or cars), properties of an entity (prices or components), actions (historical events or process steps), or any other type of information about a thing one needs to store and manage. In the early planning stages, a model may take the form of a simple list of table names, for example, Company, Person, and Project. Later, this expands into a field list for each table and shows how they interconnect to form a relational hierarchy. Complex systems can contain models defining dozens or hundreds of tables.

The spreadsheet metaphor for a table can continue for *fields*, *records*, and *cells*.

Comparing a Field to a Spreadsheet Column

A database *field* is like a column in a spreadsheet. It is a defined container in which one piece of information about an entity modeled by a table will be stored. In the example shown previously in Figure 7-1, each column heading names an individual field defining the column beneath it: *First Name*, *Last Name*, *Address*, etc. Like in a spreadsheet, the field is defined for a certain type of information.

Comparing a Record to a Spreadsheet Row

A database *record* is like a row in the spreadsheet. It represents one individual entry stored within the table for one instance of the object being modeled. While the table in the example represents people in general, a row or record represents one specific person. The record is one instance of the table's defined field set, created to store information about one specific person.

Comparing a Field Instance to a Spreadsheet Cell

A database *cell* is the formal name of an intersection of a field and record. In FileMaker, these are also referred to informally as "fields" with the implied understanding of the difference between an instance of a field definition for a specific record (cell) and the field definition itself (field).

Caution   Between the schema and interface design, there are four different ways the term "field" is used by FileMaker developers, which may be confusing at first (Chapter 20, "Working with Field Objects")!

Understanding the Limits of the Analogy

Other database concepts step further from the object model and don't have a direct spreadsheet analogy. However, these are worth at least mentioning here. A *relationship* defines a connection between two tables based on key fields. Although this is considered part of the schema, there is no method of connecting two spreadsheet tabs in a comparable way. A *layout* establishes an interface design into which the raw data stored in the data structure is displayed for users. Although spreadsheets sometimes have graphical interface features, this is also mostly incomparable. A *script* can be compared to a macro in that both store a sequence of steps that can be performed over and over with a click. Other database concepts in FileMaker may have some thread of similarities to features in a spreadsheet, but attempts to compare them become less and less productive. So the analogy is best left to a way of visualizing tables, fields, cells, and nothing more.

Introducing the Manage Database Dialog (Tables)

Tables are created and configured from the *Tables* tab of the *Manage Database* dialog, shown in Figure 7-2. Once a database file is open, this dialog can be opened by selecting the *File* ➤ *Manage* ➤ *Database* menu in Browse or Layout mode or selecting *Database* in the *Manage* toolbar menu in Layout mode. As we will see throughout the other chapters in the book, it is also accessible from various developer menus throughout the development interface in places where fields can be selected.

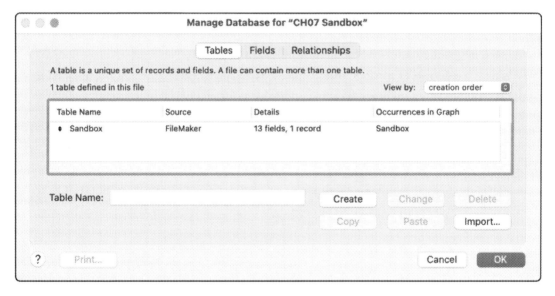

Figure 7-2. *The dialog used to manage tables*

The *Tables* tab displays a list of every table defined in the file. Each is made up of five properties listed in four columns:

- *Table Name* – Shows the assigned name, describing the entity class.

- *Source* – Indicates where the table resides, either "FileMaker" or the name of an ODBC data source.

- *Details* – Shows a count of fields defined as the table structure and records of data content stored.

- *Occurrences in Graph* – Displays a comma-separated list of every instance of the table in the relationship graph (Chapter 9).

Tables in the list can be selected to rename, delete, or copy and paste. A double-click switches to the *Fields* tab for that table. The *Table Name* field shows the name of the selected table (if any) and is used to change the name or to enter a name for a new table.

Caution   Closing with saving (OK) or without saving (Cancel) applies to all changes made in any tab while working in the dialog!

Planning Table Names

Once you have a list of the objects you wish to model in your database, the first step is picking a name for each table. During this process there are several things to consider, especially when your database will model numerous entities. There are technical considerations and other optional best naming practices.

Conforming to Technical Naming Rules

Every table name must at least follow these rules:

- Each table must be named with a unique word or phrase. No two tables in the same database file can have the same name.

- Names can include numbers but shouldn't start with a number or a period. Ideally, use only alphabetic characters.

- Names should not contain the name of built-in functions (Chapter 13), especially those that have no parameters such as *Random* or *Pi*. Also don't use the name of a custom function (Chapter 15).

- A name can include spaces. However, for some web integrations (other than FileMaker WebDirect, which doesn't care), you may need to avoid them completely.

- Although some reserved symbols and words can be used, they may conflict in calculation formulas and should be avoided (Chapter 12, "Avoiding Reserved Words").

Note   See the "CH07-01 Website Reserved Words.html" shortcut in the example files for a complete list of reserved words.

Exploring Best Naming Practices

Beyond technical considerations, you have the freedom to create any name. However, take a moment to consider what constitutes a good name. Every table name should describe the entity it stores using language that can exist harmoniously with other table names in the file. Here are a few suggestions to consider when developing a list of table names:

- Names should clearly indicate the entity class modeled by the table, concisely as possible without being cryptic. Use "Employees" instead of "People Who Work For Company" or "CompEmp."

- Use full words instead of abbreviations where possible. If a word is too long, consult a thesaurus for a shorter alternative.

- Avoid silly nicknames that require someone to be aware of an insider meaning or anything based on current events. Be professional and think long term.

- Consider the full context of all tables in the file. A table named "Stuff" can be fine in a database that manages only one kind of stuff. However, when modeling several kinds of stuff, use more descriptive names like *Inventory*, *Resources*, *Supplies*, etc.

- Use multiple words for clarity. When there are other tables for similarly named entities, make sure that their names are differentiated enough to avoid confusion, for example, *Company Resources*, *Vendor Resources*, etc.

- Be consistent, using the same format and keeping all names either singular or plural. For example, use either *Contact* and *Company* or *Contacts* and *Companies*.

- Also, be consistent when choosing word delimiters. Either use a space ("Project Budget"), underscore ("Project_Budget"), or, less readable but a valid option, no delimiter a.k.a. "camel case" ("ProjectBudget").

- Especially with large lists, consider using prefixes to organize tables into conceptual groups so they sort neatly in developer selection menus, as shown in Figure 7-3.

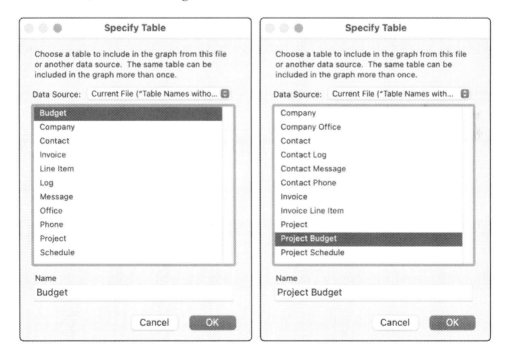

Figure 7-3. *A list of raw names (left) and the same with group prefixes (right)*

Caution   When starting with just a small number of tables, it is tempting to use simple names. However, most solutions will tend to grow over time, and you will thank yourself later for spending a little time now focusing on group naming.

Managing Tables

Tables can be added, renamed, and deleted using the buttons on the *Tables* tab of the *Manage Database* dialog.

Adding Tables

There are several different methods for adding tables:

- Create a new table.

- Duplicate an existing table.

- Import a table from another FileMaker database.

- Add a table from an external ODBC data source (Chapter 33).

- Create with record import (Chapter 5, "Selecting a Target Table").

Creating a New Table

Manually create a new table from the *Tables* tab of the *Manage Database* dialog by typing a name into the *Table Name* text area and clicking the *Create* button. The new table will appear in the list with five default fields (Chapter 8, "Exploring Default Fields").

Duplicating an Existing Table

If a new table is to be significantly like an existing one, consider duplicating to save time. The *Copy* and *Paste* buttons can be used to copy one or more tables selected in the *Manage Database* dialog and paste a duplicate of them into the list. This works between two different files providing a quick and simple way to exactly replicate a table from a past project into a new database. The duplicate table(s) will appear highlighted in the list, each with the same name as the original plus a unique numeric suffix (if pasting in the same file). Every field from the original table will be present in the new table, with the same names and settings. However, record content is not copied from the original; the duplicate table will contain no records.

Importing a Table

The *Import* button on the *Tables* tab of the *Manage Database* dialog begins the process of importing one or more tables from another FileMaker database. The source database can be a database in a folder directory or hosted by a FileMaker Server. After clicking the button, locate and open the database file containing the tables to be imported. FileMaker will present an *Import Tables* dialog listing all the tables available for import from the selected database, as shown in Figure 7-4. Check the desired table(s) and click OK to import. Here, too, only the structure will be imported so the tables will contain no records.

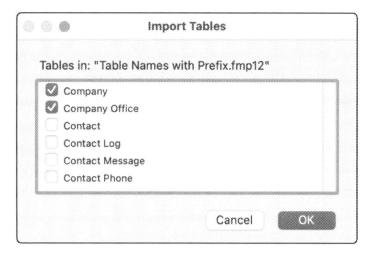

Figure 7-4. *The dialog used to import tables from another FileMaker database*

Renaming and Deleting Tables

A selected table in the *Tables* tab of the *Manage Database* dialog can be renamed or deleted.

To *rename*, select a table and enter a new name in the *Table Name* text area, and click the *Change* button. FileMaker will automatically disable this button if the new name is not unique.

To *delete*, select a table and click the *Delete* button. A *Delete Tables* warning dialog will appear to confirm you want to continue, as shown in Figure 7-5. The dialog includes a checkbox that, when selected, will also delete any occurrence of the table in the relationship graph (Chapter 9). If this option is disabled, any occurrences will become defunct "missing table" placeholders. A deleted table's field definitions and all records will also be deleted, while layouts will remain as broken resources until manually deleted or reassigned to another existing table.

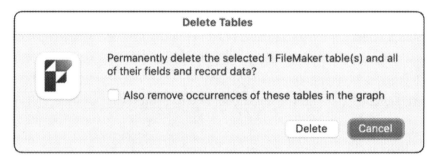

Figure 7-5. *The warning dialog when deleting tables*

Adding Tables to the Sandbox Database

If you are following along, add three tables to the Sandbox database: Company, Contact, and Project. For now, create the tables and leave the automatically created default fields, table occurrences, and layouts in place. Once finished, the dialog should appear as shown in Figure 7-6.

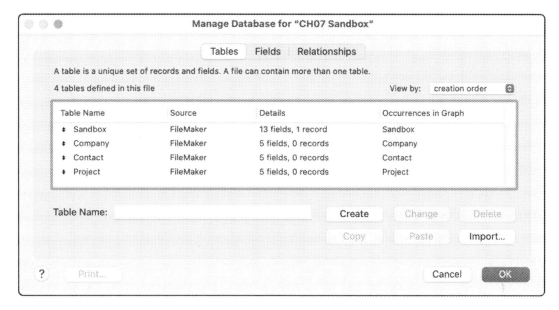

Figure 7-6. *The new tables added to the Sandbox with default fields only*

Note   See the "CH07 Sandbox" example file, where these have already been added.

Summary

This chapter explored the basics of creating and working with tables. In the next chapter, we learn how to add fields to tables and configure their various properties.

## CHAPTER 8

Defining Fields

Once a table is created, the next step to develop the schema is to define fields. Like a column in a spreadsheet, a *field* defines one named information space within a table, configured for a specific type of data. FileMaker will automatically create a few default metadata fields, but the rest must be defined. This chapter focuses on the following topics:

- Introducing field types
- Exploring default fields
- Creating your own standard fields
- Exploring best naming practices
- Introducing the Manage Database dialog (Fields)
- Setting field options
- Adding fields to the example database

Introducing Field Types

FileMaker supports eight different types of fields, which fall into one of two categories: *entry fields* and *display fields*.

Entry Fields

An *entry field* is a type of field capable of receiving data input by a user, script, or import process. FileMaker has six types of entry fields, each for a specific class of data: *text*, *number*, *date*, *time*, *timestamp*, and *container*.

© Mark Conway Munro 2024
M. C. Munro, *Learn FileMaker Pro 2024*, https://doi.org/10.1007/979-8-8688-0835-7_8

Note   An entry field's ability to accept data entry will depend on the field being present on a layout, configured to allow data entry, and the user's security settings must also allow editing!

Text Fields

A *text field* accepts entry of any combination of letters, symbols, or numbers as a string of any length up to ten million characters. Text fields can handle anything from a short single value or multiple paragraphs of verbose text.

By default, the content of a text field is plain, unformatted text. An instance of a field on a layout can have format settings imposed on its content when rendered in a window (Chapter 19, "Inspecting the Appearance Tab"). Also, a user can apply formatting to parts or all the contents (which overrides appearance settings). In this case, the format is embedded into the field's *content*.

When sorting records by a text field, the values will be sorted in alphabetical order. This means that numbers contained within the text will be sorted as text and evaluated one character at a time, for example, a value of "10" will sort before "2," since 1 comes before 2.

Number Fields

A *number field* accepts entry of any numeric value ranging from 10^{-400} to 10^{400} up to one billion characters per field.

Like a text field, the content in a number field starts without formatting, but layouts can impose style when rendering the field in a window, and users can embed styling onto the field's contents. In both cases, the *numeric value* of the field remains plain and unformatted when used in formulas.

A value in a number field can include non-numeric characters that are used to format numbers. For example, a number field can contain "5000" or "$5,000.00." While these additional characters don't adversely affect data entry, finding, or sorting, ideally only numerals should be physically entered into the field since currency formatting can be applied dynamically to an instance of the field on a layout (Chapter 19, "Data Formatting").

You can add non–currency-related text to a number field, but these will be ignored when used in calculations. For example, "Hello 10" will be accepted into a number field, but a calculation will treat it like "10" so that "Hello 10" added to 15 will produce a result of 25 by ignoring the non-numeric characters. This will have some unexpected implications. For example, typing "1 Fine 10" into a number field and then using it in a formula to add it plus 10 will produce a result of 120 since the numbers are extracted from the text and collapsed into a single value of 110. For your own sanity, it is best to keep number fields containing strictly numeric values.

When sorting records by a number field, the values in the field will be sorted in numeric order, so a value of 10 will sort properly after 2.

Tip   Use a text field to store numbers that require leading zeros. Formulas will still treat them like numeric values!

A good rule of thumb when choosing number as a field type over text is whether the field would ever be used in mathematical calculations. For example, a zip code, while it is a number, would be better assigned as a text field since you never perform mathematical calculations on zip codes. This avoids proceeding zeros from being truncated off, such as 07748, which would be correctly stored as 7748.

Date Fields

A *date field* accepts entry of a formal date within a range from January 1, 0001, through December 31, 4000. Dates must be typed using the *short date format* matching the database setting for dates and times that was inherited from the computer upon which the file was created (Chapter 6, "File Options: Text"). In the United States, the default format is typically "<month>/<day>/<year>." For example, January 15, 2017, would be entered into a date field as "1/15/2017." Although all dates must be entered as short dates, an instance of a date field on a layout can be configured to display the value a variety of formats (Chapter 19, "Data Formatting").

When sorting records by a date field, the values will be sorted chronologically.

Two-Digit Date Conversion

FileMaker requires all dates to have four-digit years, for example, "1992" or "2024." Any entry in a date field with a two-digit year will automatically be converted to a four-digit year using a formula based on the year in which the data entry action occurs. This includes all entry methods: manual typing, importing, auto-enter formulas, or script step entry. The conversion process assumes that a date with a two-digit year is more likely to refer to a time further in the past than the future. Therefore, automatic conversion of a date's year from two to four digits will adjust so the date falls within either the next 30 years or the preceding 70 years based on the current year when the data is entered. So, in 2024, typing "1/1/55" or earlier will be automatically converted to "1/1/1955," while "1/1/54" will convert to "1/1/2054." In a database managing dates that fall outside of that 100-year range, all dates must be

- Entered with four-digit years

- Entered in a text field instead of a date field where they can remain two-digit years

- Entered in a field with an auto-enter formula or script trigger that automatically converts the date to the desired four-digit equivalent before FileMaker imposes its automatic conversion

---

Caution   Prior to the year 2000, FileMaker allowed two-digit dates. When upgrading an old database, these automatically receive a century of 1900 unless manually converted before upgrading!

Time Fields

A *time field* accepts entry of a formal time string. Times must be typed using the *time format* matching the database setting for dates and times that was inherited from the computer upon which the file was created. In the United States, the default format is typically "<hour>:<min>:<sec> <am|pm>" or "10:30:00 am." Times can refer to a *time of day* or an *amount of time*, which can be used to denote things like time allotted or elapsed. For example, "0:15:00" refers to 15 minutes.

When sorting records by a time field, the values will be sorted chronologically by the amount of time.

Timestamp Fields

A *timestamp field* contains the unification a formal date and time in a single string. FileMaker allows timestamp values to range from January 1, 0001, 12:00 AM, through December 31, 4000, 11:59:59 PM. As with separate date and time values, a timestamp must be entered in a *short format* matching the database's settings for each component inherited from the computer upon which the file was created. The two components are entered with a space between them: "<date> <time>." For example, "1/1/2021 3:00 PM" or "8/1/2021 8:00 AM."

Tip   All dates, times, and timestamps are stored as numbers expressing time passed from a fixed point: the number of days passed since January 1, 0001, or the number of seconds passed since midnight. Formulas can calculate time/days elapsed or adjust dates and times by adding or subtracting a number (Chapter 13).

Container Fields

A *container field* accepts binary data in the form of a file that would be stored on a hard drive, including images, video, signatures, PDFs, etc. This allows files to be viewed, accessed, and optionally interacted with while looking at a corresponding record.

Storing files in containers keeps them connected to records so users don't have to navigate through a folder hierarchy looking for the appropriate file. There are numerous instances where it can be beneficial to attach a file to a record. For example, in a company resource management database, add a person's photo to their contact record or a packaging image to a product record. A photographer might connect image previews to an order and invoice. A PDF resume can be attached to a recruiter's candidate record.

Files are placed into container fields by a variety of functions including *Insert, Copy/Paste*, or *Drag/Drop*. A database running on an iOS device can use the *Insert from Device* script step to insert music, photo, camera, microphone, or signature data into a container.

Depending on the configuration of a database and field, the files displayed in containers can be embedded directly into the database structure or be linked to it from an external folder location (Chapter 10).

The default appearance of a file in a container field will depend on how it is inserted and the configuration of a field instance on a layout. Images tend to display the image in the file, while other types appear as a file like they would in a folder directory. Some file types have an *Interactive content layout* setting that allows for interactivity similar to their native applications (Chapter 19). For example, a PDF file can be stored in a field with a layout configuration that allows users to view and navigate through the pages of the document as if they were viewing it in Adobe Acrobat. Other file types with interactive options are photos, movies, and audio files.

FileMaker scripts (Chapter 24) can use a script step to generate PDFs based on records, save the PDF in a folder, and then import that file back into a container field. Some plug-ins can dynamically generate PDFs or other files and directly insert them into a field.

Caution   To edit a file in a container field, it must be exported and opened in its native application.

Display Fields

A *display field* is a non-editable field that automatically displays a value determined by its settings. FileMaker has two types of display fields: *calculation* and *summary*.

Calculation Fields

A *calculation field* is defined with a formula statement that is evaluated by FileMaker to produce a result (Chapter 12). Although calculations are like cells in a spreadsheet with a formula applied, there are two major differences.

First, in FileMaker, the formula is applied to the field definition itself, so it applies to the entire column. Each record's instance of the field uses the same formula to evaluate a result for the field. The result can vary depending on the formula since it draws fields relative to the context of the record, but the formula remains the same for all records.

Second, unlike in Excel, it is impossible for a user to type into the cell, wipe out the formula, and enter data instead. A calculation field is strictly non-editable except by developers who have access to edit the formula.

Summary Fields

A *summary field* is a field that automatically calculates a value based on another field's values across a set of records, based on the current user's context of a found set and sort order. For example, a summary field can calculate and display the total value of a field for every record in a found set or for subsets of records based on key sort fields. Summaries are configured with a combination of field options (explained later in this chapter) and layout part setup (Chapter 18). Summaries can also be used when exporting summarized data (Chapter 5).

Exploring Default Fields

Starting with FileMaker 17, every new table is created with the following *default fields* that are preconfigured to automatically enter standard metadata about a record:

- *PrimaryKey* – Enters a Universally Unique Identifier (UUID) for each record

- *CreationTimestamp* – Enters when a record is created

- *CreationBy* – Enters the name of the record creator

- *ModificationTimestamp* – Enters when a record was last modified

- *ModificationBy* – Enters the name of the last modifier

Once a table is created, these default fields can be edited, renamed, or removed as desired. The file that controls which fields are created for any future table is named *DefaultFields.xml* file and is in a language subfolder of the FileMaker Pro application. These can be renamed, removed, or expanded to fit your individual requirements.

However, these fields represent the minimum best practice for record metadata and are included by default because they have a long history of being overlooked by inexperienced developers. Take a moment to consider the merits of each of these standard fields.

Assigning a Primary Key

A record's *primary key* is a unique identifying value that represents a single record. The most common historical instance of this is the assignment of a customer or account number, which helps assist a customer service representative searching for a person's record. As we will see in the next chapter, a primary key is also critically important when formatting relationships between records in different tables where they allow records to be connected to each other using a permanent value guaranteed to never change over time.

Where traditionally developers would employ a sequential *serial number* as a primary key, the default field uses a more modern standard for generating unique values. A *UUID* can be either a 16-byte string or 24-byte number that is designed to guarantee uniqueness regardless of when or where it is generated, without any requirement of central authority or system coordination. So, while the traditional serial number provides adequate uniqueness for records being created in the same table in the same database file, a UUID can be assumed unique even when records are created in different tables and/or in different database files hosted separately, across all time. This is particularly useful for records created offline that later integrated with other records in a central system. With a UUID as a primary key, there is no need for resequencing to ensure uniqueness.

Tip   A traditional serial number is more human friendly as an account or customer ID. Consider using these for human interactions and UUIDs for primary keys in relationships.

Tracking Creation and Modification Values

The *creation* and *modification* metadata fields record the name and timestamp of each corresponding action, record creation and last modification. These provide a minimal level of tracking the user responsible for a change and can sometimes be helpful in sorting out a problem. Knowing who made the last change to a record can help direct the focus of user training to avoid similar mistakes in the future. Knowing when the last change was made can help in tracking down a backup copy of the database to retrieve data that was accidentally overwritten.

Caution   These fields provide a minimum level of audit tracking that may not be adequate for high-security systems. If required, an auditing system that tracks every change must be created manually.

Creating Your Own Standard Fields

In addition to the default fields, consider defining your own additional standard fields that could be useful in every table. A *standard field* is a field that can universally apply to all or almost any table. These don't need to be limited to auto-entered metadata values like the preceding default fields. Instead, they can be any field that stores content or provides some purpose that can apply generically no matter the table's entity or purpose. As you develop more, ideas for standard fields may become plentiful although not every standard field should be forced into every table. Some ideas might become *universal standards,* which are easily applicable to every table. Others may become *group standards,* which apply to only certain types of tables. Other *optional standards* may be applied sparingly to very specific types of tables. The most obvious standards are fields that contain information about the record rather than about the entity the record represents. Here are a few ideas for standardization across all tables:

- *Status* – A user-enterable status field that stores a progress value about the record, for example, new, active, hold, or done. The specific values may vary from one table to the next. For example, tables containing entity records may have values like "active or inactive," while tables used for transactional records with a lifespan could have values like "pending, open, closed."

- *Notes* – A freeform notes field used to store information about the record itself or the entity represented by the record. It can also be used to record a diary of user comments about the record.

- *Errors* – A calculation used to automatically compile and display data entry error notifications on layouts, providing instant feedback to users about problems with key fields. This can be an alternative to field validation warnings (discussed later in this chapter).

- *Title* – A calculation that combines key fields to create a heading for display at the top of entry layouts or in the body of a List view or portal rows to help users quickly identify a particular record.

- *Log* – A field used to store events that took place on the record, either entered by users or automatically.

Tip   As you begin developing your own tables, be on the lookout for opportunities to establish standard fields you find useful.

Naming Fields

Field names should follow the same general guidelines as tables, discussed in the last chapter. Names can have spaces, can include but not start with numbers, should avoid reserved terms, and should adequately describe the information they will contain without being excessively long. It is also a good idea to include a set of naming prefixes that denote field groups, organizing them when viewing them in a sorted list. However, when doing so, there are a couple things to consider.

Dealing with the Challenge of Group Prefixes

First, with fields, a group prefix will often result in a reversal of grammar that may be confusing for English-speaking users. This reversal tends to be more tolerable on tables than on fields. Changing "Budget" and "Schedule" to "Project Budget" and "Project Schedule" so they group with a corresponding "Project" table sounds fine. So do "Company Office" and "Invoice Line Item." However, grouping a contact table's first and last name fields by naming them "Name First" and "Name Last" is reversed from the common usage. Similarly, a home, cell, and work phone number would be group-named as "Phone Home," "Phone Cell," and "Phone Work" so they all sort together but are grammatically reversed from common usage.

Field names can be obscured from users by editing the name of a field label on a layout. As far as they see, the field "Name First" has a label of "First Name," and they don't know any different. However, the actual field names would be visible and confusing to users who perform a manual import, export, and sort. To resolve this, it may be necessary to further hide the schema resource naming from users by creating scripts to automatically perform these functions instead of requiring the user to know the actual names.

The more your skills develop, the more automation you'll perform with scripts anyway. For those situations where some users need to perform a task where they can see the field names, some additional training can resolve any confusion. In the end, it is worth considering name grouping for aiding you as a developer when navigating huge lists of hundreds of fields. It also assists in adding a second-level "super-group" field prefix.

Expanding to Second-Level Group Prefixes

When adding naming prefixes to tables, a single word is usually enough to create conceptual groups when seeing them in a sorted list. As shown in the last chapter, a "Project" prefix on "Project Budget" and "Project Schedule" tables forces these tables to sort together with "Project" in developer lists. When naming fields, consider adding an additional dimension, a "super-group" prefix that separates fields into two or more primary groups.

There are two primary groups of fields that will be present in every table, content fields and record metadata fields. A *content field* is any field that contains information about the record's subject, the specific object being modeled by the table's record. So a person's name, age, address, phone numbers, and more would all fall into this category because they contain the content about the person represented by the record. Unlike these, a *record metadata field* contains information about the record itself. This includes the default fields and other standard field ideas discussed in the last sections.

Since metadata fields will tend to be more standardized across tables, we can conceive of two top-level "super-groups," standard metadata fields and custom content fields. To force the fields into these two groups, choose a single word to represent each. The standard field prefix might be the word "Record" since the fields tend to contain metadata about the record. Keeping that the same in every table makes sense since the fields are uniform standards. For the custom fields, a unique prefix for the table makes more sense. The best choice is usually the single word that represents the objects modeled by the table. For example, a table of contact records can use "Contact" as a prefix, while a table of project budgets can use "Budget." This not only groups all content fields together, but it provides a developer an instant visual reminder of which table a field belongs when seeing it in various places in the development environment.

The example in Figure 8-1 shows lists with the same fields in three different naming formats. The first on the left is a list of fields named in a typical "raw" format, with one or two words describing their content, mixing content fields and record metadata fields together in an alphabetical sort. The second in the middle shows the same list but with a first-level group prefix assigned to most fields. This improves sort but still intermixes the two field sets. The third list on the right shows the addition of a second-level, super-group prefix that fully separates the content fields with a prefix of "Contact" from all the metadata fields with a prefix of "Record."

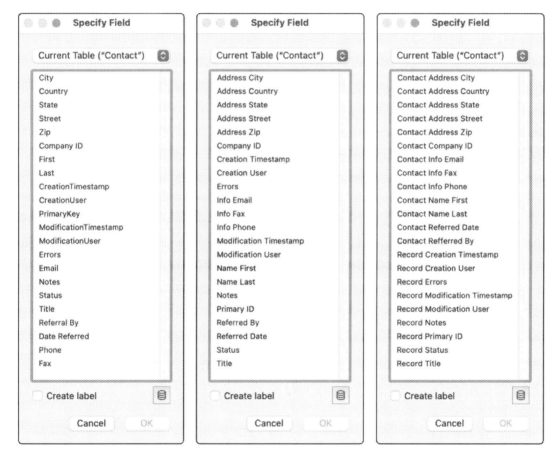

Figure 8-1. *Field names with no prefix (left), group prefix (middle), and super-group prefix (right)*

Although this approach may at first appear visually cluttered, as a list expands to include dozens or hundreds of fields, some kind of name-group organization will become more self-evidently beneficial to you and to future developers.

As a table's list of fields grow, you will find yourself identifying other potential super-group categories. For example, a table with records that link to several different related records might have a group for link fields used in relationships. Also, a table with lots of *control fields* used to accept relationship filtering choices or special selection fields might demand some other type of prefix to denote those as different from content and metadata and sort them together.

Tip   Don't worry about complex naming until you gain more experience. With FileMaker, you can rename fields later to change groupings unlike other database systems that don't feature dynamic object references.

Introducing the Manage Database Dialog (Fields)

Fields are defined in the *Fields* tab of the *Manage Database* dialog, shown in Figure 8-2. Select the *File* ➤ *Manage* ➤ *Database* menu and click the *Fields* tab.

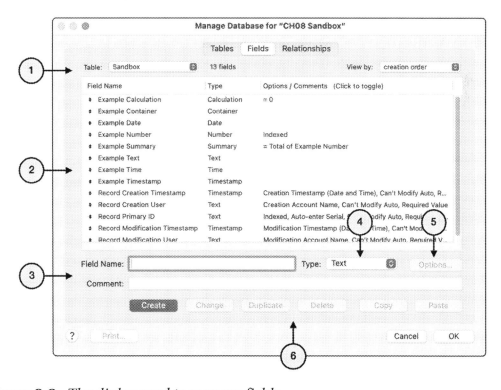

Figure 8-2. The dialog used to manage fields

The controls for field definitions include the following:

1. *Table menu* – Select a table to see its fields below.

2. *Field list* – Displays a list of fields defined for the selected table. Select one to configure options, change name, duplicate, or delete.

3. *Field Name and Comment* – Enter a new name for the selected field or a name for a new field. Enter a short developer comment about the selected field.

4. *Type* – Select a data type for a new field or to change the selected field's type.

5. *Options* – Click to edit field settings based on type.

6. *Buttons* – Used to create a new field or change, duplicate, delete, or copy–paste the selected field.

Creating a New Field

To create a new field, type a name into the *Field Name* text area of the *Fields* tab of the *Manage Database* dialog. Choose a data type for the field in the *Type* menu and click the *Create* button. The new field will appear selected in the list above, and the *Options* button will become enabled. When creating a new *Summary* or *Calculation* field, FileMaker will immediately open a dialog of options based on the selected type. Options for any existing field can be opened later clicking the *Options* button (described later in this chapter).

Duplicating an Existing Field

To save time when creating a batch of similar fields, consider creating one and then duplicating it any number of times. Select one or more fields and use the *Copy* and *Paste* buttons or click *Duplicate*. The duplicate field(s) will appear highlighted in the list, each with the same name as the original plus either a unique numeric suffix or a suffix of "Copy" depending on which method of duplication you use. All the settings of the original field(s) will be copied to the duplicate(s). Fields can be pasted in the same table, a different table in the file, or a table in a different database file.

> **Caution**   Any data entry–type fields added to a table will be empty for all existing records. Duplicating only replicates the field definition, not any content.

Modifying a Field Name or Comment

An existing field's name and comment can be changed by selecting it, entering a new value in the respective text area, and clicking the *Change* button. Any references to the field in formulas, layouts, and scripts will automatically be updated.

Modifying a Field's Type

Once a field is created and has data entered, changing its type should be a rare occurrence. If it becomes necessary due to a mistake or the need to structurally alter a database, select the field, choose a new value from the *Type* menu, and then click the *Change* button. Depending on the original and new type, a dialog may warn that existing content in the field will be converted to the new type across all existing records.

For example, changing from *text* to a *date* or *timestamp* will convert dates previously entered as text into formal dates and automatically convert years to four digits as needed (see "Two-Digit Date Conversion" earlier in this chapter). Also, changing a container to another data type will remove any non-textual data from the field. An embedded file or image would be deleted, leaving only the name and/or path of the file.

Changing any entry field into a *calculation* or *summary* will result in the permanent loss of any previously entered content since those two generate their own content automatically.

Deleting Fields

Fields can be deleted from a table by selecting them and clicking the *Delete* button. A warning dialog will confirm the deletion request. The selected field(s) will disappear from the list immediately; however, the actual deletion doesn't occur until you click *OK* to close the *Manage Database* dialog. Click *Cancel* instead if you made an error and don't want to save the deletion change. FileMaker does a pretty good job of cleaning up instances of the field on layouts. However, you may need to manually delete any lingering missing field references on layouts in other files that display a field through a relationship to the file you are deleting the field from. Any references to a deleted field in script steps or formulas will need to be manually removed or reassigned.

Tip   Consider first renaming a field to include the word "Deprecated" and then use a database design report (Chapter 31) to search for any instances of the field in use before deleting it!

Setting Field Options

In addition to a field's *name*, *type*, and *comment* properties, there are options that can be configured, which vary by field type. To edit these options, select the field in the *Fields* tab of the *Manage Database* dialog and click the *Options* button.

Options for Entry Fields

All entry fields have similar options that only vary slightly from one to the next. These are controlled through an *Options for Field* dialog with settings spread across four tabs: *Auto-Enter*, *Validation*, *Storage*, and *Furigana*.

Field Options: Auto-Enter

The *Auto-Enter* tab of the *Options for Field* dialog, shown in Figure 8-3, controls data that will be automatically entered into the field when a new record is created or when certain conditions are met.

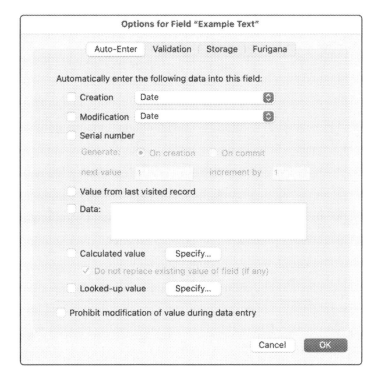

Figure 8-3. *The Auto-Enter tab of the options dialog for entry fields*

Caution   Although all the options here are checkbox controls, the first five operate as radio buttons, allowing only one to be selected since they would conflict and overwrite each other.

Automatically Enter the Following Data into This Field

Some of these settings are limited or disabled for certain entry fields depending on the specific data type they contain. The options include auto-entering:

- *Creation* – Select a metadata value to be entered at record creation: *Date, Time, Timestamp, Name,* or *Account Name.*

- *Modification* – Select a metadata value to be entered whenever a record is modified (same options as the preceding).

- *Serial number* – Enter a serial number at record creation or on first commit. The number is based on the value in the *next value* text area and automatically incremented each time by the value in *increment by* entry.

- *Value from last visited record* – Enters a value into a new record from the same field on the last record the user viewed.

- *Data* – Enters the static text value in the adjacent text area.

- *Calculated value* – Uses a formula to generate a result entered in the field (Chapter 12). The *Do not replace ...* checkbox will cause the field to not evaluate the calculation if the field contains previously entered data. Uncheck to allow the value to be updated.

- *Looked-up value* – Copies a value from a related field.

Tip   Uncheck the *Do not replace ...* checkbox when a calculated value needs to be re-evaluated after a record has been duplicated.

Configuring a Lookup Field

A *lookup field* automatically copies a value from a specific field from a related record immediately after a *key field* defining the relationship is updated. This is used to copy a value into a local field from a related record's field so that it will remain in place even if the related record is deleted. This feature is a vestigial remnant from the days before FileMaker was fully relational and before auto-enter calculations existed. It has been flagged as likely to be deprecated in future releases. Consider using either an auto-enter calculation or direct placement of a related field on a layout instead of a lookup.

Caution   This feature requires a relationship between two tables, which is discussed in Chapter 9.

To configure a lookup, click the *Looked-up value* checkbox on the *Auto-Enter* tab of the *Options for Field* dialog. This will open a *Lookup for Field* dialog, shown in Figure 8-4. This example is for the *Contact Company Name* field, which will be filled with a company name from a related *Company* table when a company ID is entered into the *Contact Company ID* field.

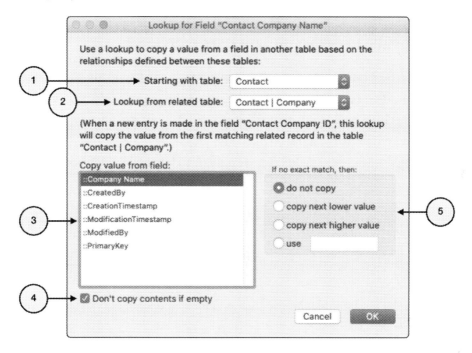

Figure 8-4. *The dialog for configuring lookup settings*

The dialog contains the following controls:

1. *Starting with table* – Select a table occurrence for the field being defined. This will be the *starting context* if multiple table occurrences exist for its table (Chapter 9).

2. *Lookup from related table* – Select a table related to the starting table to identify the relational conduit through which a field value will be copied.

3. *Copy value from field* – Choose a field from the lookup table whose value should be copied into the field being defined when the lookup happens.

4. *Don't copy contents if empty* – Select to halt the lookup if the selected field is empty, leaving any existing value in the target field.

5. *If no exact match, then* – Choose an action when no related record is found.

Prohibit Modification of Value During Data Entry

This checkbox at the bottom of the *Auto-Enter* tab of the *Options for Field* dialog makes the field non-editable at the data level regardless of a user's security settings or the field's edit settings on a layout. After any auto-enter option(s) have been performed, the field's value will be non-editable. This is useful for default fields such as the primary key or any other entry fields that you want to be read-only after an initial automatic entry.

Caution   This setting only prohibits a user from modifying the value. A script can modify it using various steps such as *Set Field* (Chapter 25, "Set Field")!

Field Options: Validation

The *Validation* tab of the *Options for Field* dialog, shown in Figure 8-5, allows the selection of one or more entry requirements for the field. These are used to automatically validate input and enforce the rules specified. When a field fails a validation check, the user is notified and given a choice for corrective action.

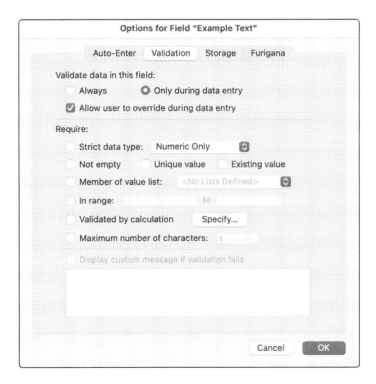

Figure 8-5. *The Validation tab of the options dialog for entry fields*

Controlling Validation Enforcement

The options at the top of the *Validation* tab control when input is validated and whether a user can override a validation warning. Select *Always* to cause the field to validate when data entry is performed and when importing into the field or *Only during data entry* to validate *only* during data entry and not during import.

Caution   Fields set to always validate will cause an entire record to be skipped over if validation fails when importing records. These will be reported with the total incidence of import errors without providing any additional detail!

Enable the *Allow user to override during data entry* box to change the validation warning options as shown in Figure 8-6. With the override option off, the warning dialog has two buttons. The *Revert Field* button will remove the current data entry changes and restore the previous saved value. The *OK* button returns the user to the uncommitted record where they can edit their entry to comply with the validation requirements before attempting to commit again. With the override option on, the *Revert Field* option remains and is joined by a new message offering to override the warning. Clicking the *No* button returns the user to edit the uncommitted record, while clicking *Yes* ignores the validation warning, accepts the changes as entered, and continues committing the record.

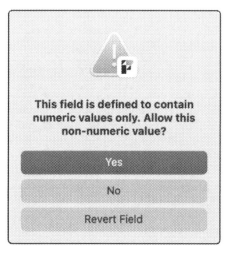

Figure 8-6. *The warning with allow override off (left) and on (right)*

Establishing Validation Rules

The following validation requirements can be imposed on the data entered:

- *Strict data type* – Restricts values to one of the following options: *Numeric Only, 4-Digit Year Date*, or *Time of Day*.

- *Not empty* – Requires a value in the record.

- *Unique value* – Requires a unique value in the field across all records.

- *Existing value* – Requires the input to already exist in the same field for at least one other record in the table.

- *Member of value list* – Requires the input to be present in the specified value list (Chapter 11).

- *In range* – Requires the input to be within a range specified, which can be text, date, time, or numeric values.

- *Validated by calculation* – Allows a custom validation formula (Chapter 12). The formula must evaluate to true (non-zero) for the entry to pass the validation test.

- *Maximum number of characters* – Requires input of a character length equal to or less than the number specified (for non-container fields only).

- *Maximum number of kilobytes* – This option replaces the preceding one for container fields, specifying an upper limit on the size of a file that can be placed into the field.

Tip   The *4-Digit Year Date* option here requires entry of a full year before FileMaker performs its automatic two-year date conversion. Use it to avoid unintended conversions for dates outside of that span.

Displaying a Custom Validation Failure Message

When a field fails the specified validation rules, FileMaker will generate a dialog message like those shown previously in Figure 8-6. The default message will include details about the specific validation failure, which can be helpful when multiple validation criteria are applied to a single field. However, the message is rather generic. Using the *Display custom message if validation fails* option allows the entry of an alternative custom static message for a field.

Exploring Advanced Validation Alternatives

Some developers use FileMaker's validation options sparingly and employ alternative methods. Many data entry errors can be anticipated and automatically corrected using an *auto-enter calculation* formula to clean up and replace the value entered. For example, the *GetAsNumber*, *Filter*, *Trim*, and *Substitute* functions can automatically remove undesirable characters that are typed in a field (Chapter 13). Keeping paragraph returns out of a field can be done by making the Return key move to the next field for

151

fields on layouts using *Behavior* settings in the *Inspector* pane (Chapter 19). When an error can be detected but not easily auto-corrected, an error-reporting calculation field can display a list of fields with errors. This removes an obtrusive dialog during entry and allows searching/sorting records with errors. However, then users can also ignore it. An *OnObjectValidate* script trigger (Chapter 27) assigned to a field can run a script that checks the field for detectable errors and stops the user from exiting the field until they are corrected. This allows a more elaborate, formula-driven dialog message to explain the problem. An *OnRecordCommit* script trigger can halt record commit until detected problems are corrected, providing a single dialog listing multiple validation problems instead of one on every field.

Field Options: Storage

The *Storage* tab of the *Options for Field* dialog, shown in Figure 8-7, controls how information is stored and indexed within a field.

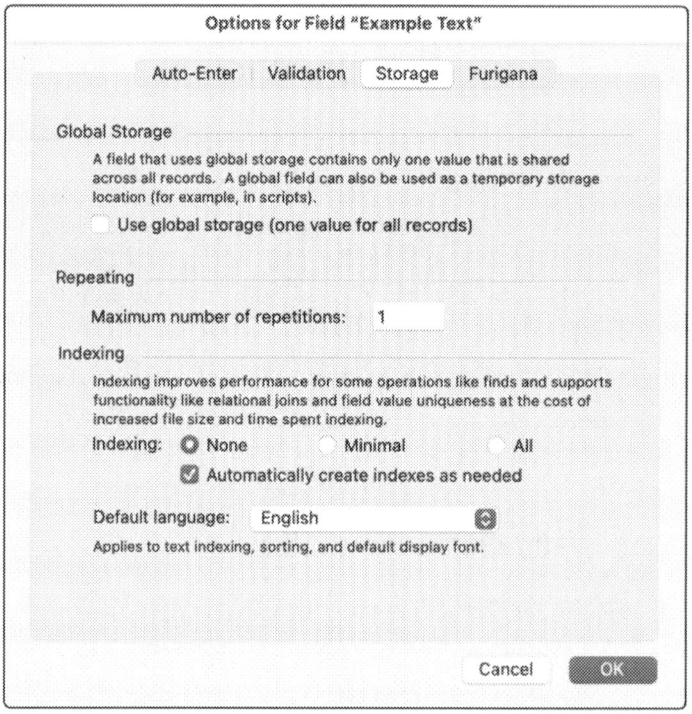

Figure 8-7. The Storage tab of the options dialog for entry fields

Global Storage

Fields can be configured to use local storage or global storage. They default to local storage but can be converted to global storage.

A *local field* is a unique instance for each record so every record can contain a different value. The value placed within the field is considered "local" to the record, which is separate from the same field on other records. Local fields can only be displayed and accessed from a layout context (Chapter 17) of their parent table or a table related to that table (Chapter 9).

A *global field* contains one value that will be shared across every record in the table and can be accessed from any layout context within the database. Using the spreadsheet analogy where a column represents a defined field and a row a record, a global field is like a column with the same value in every cell of that column for every row. A change to the value from the context of any one record automatically changes them all because there is only one value shared globally.

Tip   A global field's value is unique to each user and won't conflict with entries made by others. This makes it ideal for creating interface control menu fields.

In the *Storage* tab of the *Options for Field* dialog, the *Use global storage* checkbox converts a field to use global storage. FileMaker will present a warning dialog indicating that existing values within the field for existing records will be lost when the change occurs. Once a field is global, it can be used for a variety of special purposes, including the following:

- Storing a fixed value that is available to any calculation formula or layout regardless of context, for example, a tax rate that applies to all sales

- Creating a control field like a menu of options, for example, a pop-up menu of universal filtering or sorting options

- Providing temporary storage for scripts to place information that needs to interact with other calculation fields

- Storing static text or graphics that will be displayed on a multiple layout as iconography, branding, etc.

- Storing static print report headings, primary keys for temporary relationships, or other information

A *global variable* is preferable over a global field where possible because it doesn't clog up the field definition list. However, variables are limited to a single file. A global field in a table whose occurrence is added to other files becomes a universally shared value accessible from any file in a complex solution.

The value placed into a global field is only retained from one session to the next when entered on a non-hosted database that is open on a local copy of the FileMaker Pro desktop application. When opened across a network, values placed into a global field will not be saved between sessions and are not shared between users who access the file simultaneously. Each time the database is opened from a server host, the global field will contain the value entered when it was last opened locally by the desktop application. An *OnFirstWindowOpen* script trigger (Chapter 27) can perform a startup initialization to add a default value to a global field for the user's session.

Any type of field can be global, except for summaries, which are global by nature. This means that calculations and containers can also be global and used to store universal values and resources.

Tip   In the past, developers used global fields for a variety of functions that are now better managed with *variables* (Chapters 12 and 25), *custom functions* (Chapter 15), *merge variables* (Chapter 20), and *script parameters* (Chapter 24). Use global fields sparingly!

Repeating

A *repeating field* is a field defined to store multiple values for a single record. Instead of creating a separate field for each additional value of a certain type, a single field can be defined to repeat any number of times. For example, a single phone number field can be defined to store multiple numbers as if they were separate fields. Any type of field can be made to repeat. For an entry field, indicate the desired repetitions in the text area provided on the *Storage* tab of the *Options for Field* dialog. For a calculation field, enter the number of repetitions in the *Specify Formula* dialog (Chapter 12). A summary field becomes repeating when the field it summarizes is repeating and the option to summarize repetitions individually is selected (described later in this chapter).

The *Maximum number of repetitions* entered in the *Storage* tab of the *Options for Field* dialog defines the number of separate values the field can contain. To allow user entry into two or more of these repetitions, a field's instance on a layout must be configured to repeat (Chapter 19, "Inspecting the Data Tab"). There are a few implications to consider when using repeating fields, including the following:

- Repeating fields are never scrollable on a layout.

- You can add more repetitions later, but the number displayed on a layout must be manually adjusted to include them.

- The *Hide* function (Chapter 21, "Hiding Objects") hides the entire field, including all repetitions displayed on a layout.

- A *Find* process will search in all repetitions, including those not displayed on the current or any layout. It is not possible to limit a find to just a specific repetition.

- A *Sort* process will *only* look at the first repetition.

- Calculations that use a combination of repeating and non-repeating fields may not work together without the usage of the *Extend* function (Chapter 12, "Creating Repeating Calculation Fields").

- An *auto-enter calculation* only works on the first repetition.

- Repeating values might not work properly in sub-summary parts of reports (Chapter 18) and may need to be condensed into a single value with an aggregating function such as *List* (Chapter 13).

Tip   Repeating fields were historically used to achieve the function now better provided by portals (Chapter 20).

Indexing

A *field index* is a hidden list of words or values automatically generated from a non-global field's content. This list is used when performing searches, determining the uniqueness of a field value, and connecting records through relationships. A field's index serves a function like what a book index provides for humans, quickly separating the individual terms and allowing faster location of them without having to visually scan through every page. FileMaker uses two kinds of indexes, depending on the type of field and the option selected. A *value index* is created from every paragraph return–delimited line of text in a field. This is used to match related records and to search a field for matching values. Here, it helps to think of a "value" as a paragraph. This is used primarily for relationships, where each value is used to find a match in a related table. A *word index* is created from each unique word in a text field or a text calculation field. These are used for faster searching.

Caution   Indexing is required for some relational functions and improves search performance. However, it increases the file size of a database and should be used with conscious intent.

Indexing options in the *Storage* tab of the *Options for Field* dialog include

- *Indexing: None* – Prevents indexing completely. Use this for fields that don't require fast searching and won't be used to form relationships. Also, use to cause a calculation field to constantly re-evaluate a result.

- *Indexing: Minimal* – Create only a value index for the field.

- *Indexing: All* – Create a value index for non-text fields and both a word and value index for text fields.

- *Automatically create indexes as needed* – Allow FileMaker to create indexes as needed, for example, when a user performs a search on a previously unindexed field, this automatically switches *None* to *All* to generate and store an index for future use.

- *Default language* – Specify the language to use when indexing and sorting values in a text field. The default value will match the operating system of the computer upon which the file was created.

Tip   There may be situations where you want to customize the indexing settings to save file size. However, the default settings allow FileMaker to adjust them based on user and developer activity.

Container Storage Options

Container fields can't be indexed, so the *Storage* tab of the *Options for Field* dialog does not have the preceding options available when editing them and instead displays *container storage* options (Chapter 10).

Field Options: Furigana

The *Furigana* tab of the *Options for Field* dialog specifies a phonetic translation of Japanese text typed into the field. For more information on Japanese functions, see Claris' documentation website.

Options for Display Fields

Both *calculation* and *summary* fields only display an automatically generated value and have different options than entry fields. Clicking the *Options* button or double-clicking the field will open an alternative dialog of options specific to the field type.

For a *calculation* field, the *Options* button opens a *Specify Calculation* dialog where a formula can be entered and selection of the result data type, repetitions, storage options, and an evaluation context can be configured (Chapter 12).

For a *summary* field, the *Options* button opens an *Options for Summary Field* dialog for specifying the type of summarization, target field, and more. The summarization type selected determines what summary operation will be performed on the target field for a group of records to arrive at a value that will be placed into the summary field being defined. The available summary operations that can be performed for a field across a group of records are

- *Total of* – Calculates the total value

- *Average of* – Calculates the average value

- *Count of* – Counts how many records contain a value

- *Minimum* – Extracts the lowest available value

- *Maximum* – Extracts the highest available value

- *Standard Deviation of* – Calculates the standard deviation from the mean of all the values

- *Fraction of Total of* – Calculates the ratio of the value to the total of all the values in that field

- *List of* – Creates a carriage return–delimited list of every non-blank value

Options for Summary Field Dialog

The *Options for Summary Field* dialog is divided into five general sections, shown in Figure 8-8.

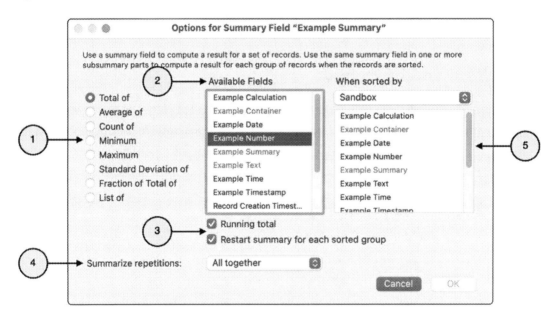

Figure 8-8. *The dialog of options for summary fields*

Caution   The options here provide an overview of summary settings but may seem too abstract. See practical summarization examples: building a complex report with sub-summary parts (Chapter 34) or performing a summary export (Chapter 5, "Summarizing Output into Groups").

The dialog contains the following controls:

1. *Summarization type* – Specify a summarization type (defined previously).

2. *Available Fields* – Choose from fields eligible for summarization. For example, choose a number field whose values should be totaled into the summary field.

3. *Conditional options* – This area will display either *one, two,* or *none* of the following options depending on which summarization type is selected: *Running total, Restart summary for each sorted group, Weighted average, Running count,* and *By population* or *Subtotaled.*

4. *Summarize repetitions* – When a repeating field is selected, identify how repetitions will be handled. Select *Individually* to display a separate summary for each repetition, making the summary field repeating. Choose *All together* to add all repetitions for a record and treat it as a single value for summarization.

5. *Conditional secondary field choice* – Depending on the preceding selected options, a field selection may be required for one of these secondary functions:

   a. *When sorted by* – Some operations allow a field to restart the summarization when a new sort value is detected. This creates summaries for multiple subgroups of records within a single found set. For example, you might want to summarize *sales per employee* or *revenue per client* using this feature. This option is available with the *Total of* or *Count of* summary type when the *Restart summary for each sorted group* option is selected or when the *Fraction of Total of* summary type is used with the *Subtotaled* option selected.

b. *Weighted by* – When using the *Average of* summary type with the *Weighted average* option selected, a field can be selected that will be used to weight the results.

Adding Fields to the Sandbox Database

At the end of the last chapter, we added three tables to the *Sandbox* database: *Company*, *Contact*, and *Project*. Now, using the lessons of this chapter, we can add a few fields to each of these. While these are not comprehensive lists of fields these tables would require in a real-world solution, they provide a few key examples to continue our exploration of building databases.

Note   See the "CH08 Sandbox" example file where these fields have already been added.

Defining Company Fields

In the *Company* table, create the following entry fields:

- Company Name (text)
- Company Description (text)
- Company Industry (text)
- Company Website (text)
- Company Status (text)

Defining Contact Fields

In the *Contact* table, create the following fields:

- Contact Name First (text)
- Contact Name Last (text)
- Contact Company ID (text)

- Contact Address Street (text)

- Contact Address City (text)

- Contact Address State (text)

- Contact Address Zip (number)

- Contact Address Country (text)

Defining Project Fields

In the *Project* table, create the following fields:

- Project Company ID (text)

- Project Contact ID (text)

- Project Name (text)

- Project Description (text)

- Project Budget (number)

- Project Budget Summary (summary as a Total of the Project Budget field)

Renaming and Modifying Default Fields

To follow along with the examples in the rest of the book and to gain some experience modifying field definitions, perform the following changes to the five default fields in all tables:

- Rename *PrimaryKey* to "Record Primary ID" and change it to auto-enter a serial number starting with "000001."

- Rename *CreationTimestamp* to "Record Creation Timestamp."

- Rename *CreatedBy* to "Record Creation User."

- Rename *ModificationTimestamp* to "Record Modification Timestamp."

- Rename *ModifiedBy* to "Record Modification User."

Note   Keeping the default field names is perfectly fine if you prefer.

Summary

This chapter explored the basics of defining fields. In the next chapter, we turn attention to forming relational links between tables.

CHAPTER 9

Forming Relationships

A *relational database* allows connections between two tables that automatically links individual records in each based on key field values. This chapter covers the following topics pertaining to relationships:

- Introducing relationships

- Managing data sources

- Introducing the Manage Database dialog (Relationships)

- Working with table occurrences

- Building relationships

- Adding notes to the graph

- Implementing a simple relational model

Introducing Relationships

A *relationship* defines a connection between tables forming a context of bidirectional conduits linking records in one table to one or more records in another. To serve as a digital model of real-world phenomenon, a database uses tables to represent entities and fields to store properties of entities. Similarly, relationships are used to digitally reflect how the entities connect or interact in the world.

Consider how the relationship between a company and employees would be modeled in a database. Each can be represented by a table: *Company* and *Contact*. Fields are created in each to store properties about the entities. As we have seen, a company's address, description, industry, name, and website would be fields. Similarly, a contact's email, name, phones, and title would be fields. Next, looking at how these two entities relate, we can identify the need for a connection between them in the database.

© Mark Conway Munro 2024
M. C. Munro, *Learn FileMaker Pro 2024*, https://doi.org/10.1007/979-8-8688-0835-7_9

Each company may employ one or more people, and conversely, each person is typically employed by a company. From this, we can define at least one relationship requirement in the database: each *Contact* record will require the option to be connected to a *Company* record. A person can be linked as an employee of a company, and conversely, a company can have one or more people linked as employees.

Every table created in a database adds a potential for more connections. For example, companies may need links to inventory, projects, budgets, assets, and procedures, while contacts may need links to contact information, correspondence, and more. Each of those implies more connections as the database grows. A project and budget may require links to tasks, timesheets, and invoices. The connections required will vary based on the database's purpose and the type of tables included in the object model. A relationship is defined when a developer decides a connection we see in reality should be rendered in the digital object model and explicitly specifies the field criteria used to compare and match values between records in each table.

Relationships make it possible to create *navigable links* between records in related tables. They also create a *relational context* between tables, which can be used by calculations, layouts, and scripts to access or display field values from various tables. Relationships transform a bunch of isolated tables into an interconnected network of information that can be dynamically accessed, displayed, and manipulated in numerous ways. Fields use a relationship when they pull related values to perform lookups, auto-enter calculations, or validation (Chapter 8). Formulas use them to access or manipulate related fields to calculate a result (Chapter 12). Layouts can display individual fields from related records or include a list of related records as a portal from another table (Chapter 20). Layout objects can use values from related fields in calculation formulas for conditional formatting, placeholder text, script parameters, tooltips, and hide functions (Chapter 21). Numerous script steps use relationships in formulas or when referencing a field (Chapters 24 and 25). Users can select fields from related tables in dialogs when manually exporting, importing, searching, and sorting. So understanding how relationships work is vital when planning and building a database.

Tip   While most relationships establish a connection between two different tables, it is possible to connect records to other records in the same table or to connect a record to itself, called a self-join.

Visualizing Relationships

A *match field* is any field used to form one side of the criteria for a relationship. Two match fields pair together with an operator to form a single criterion for defining a relationship. Any field can be used as a match field, although most relationships use keys. A *key field* is one that uniquely identifies a record in a table. While many fields are candidates, a good choice for a key is one that is both unique and unchanging.

For example, although a *Contact* record's email address field is unique to a person, it can change if the person's work changes, or they move to a new service provider. This makes it a poor candidate for a relational key because a change would sever the connection between previously linked records using the old key. Those old links can be manually updated but that requires work and can be prone to error. The result is a disconnect between important records.

To avoid this, we establish a *primary key* field that stores an automatically entered, anonymous, incremental, unique, and unchanging identification number as a standard in every table. This can be a simple auto-entered serial number (Chapter 8, "Field Options: Auto-Enter") or a more complex Universally Unique Identifier (Chapter 8, "Exploring Default Fields"). A *primary key* is a key field that contains a value that identifies a record in the same table in which the field is defined. For example, a *Record Primary ID* field in a *Company* table stores a primary key that identifies a specific company record, for example, "1105" for Widgets Manufacturing. Similarly, a *Record Primary ID* field in a *Contact* table stores a key value that identifies a specific person's record.

When a key value is placed in a field in one table that identifies a record from another table to form a relationship, it is called a *foreign key* because it identifies a record foreign to the table containing it.

Together, a primary key field and foreign key field form the basis for most relationships. Since these often create a hierarchical relationship, they are often referred to as a *parent–child connection*, as illustrated in Figure 9-1. In this example, the *Record Primary ID* is the primary key of a *Company*, and the *Contact Company ID* field in the *Contact* table contains a foreign key. When the values in both fields are equal, a relational link is formed between two records.

Figure 9-1. *An illustration of a single key field pair forming a relationship*

Each relationship must include at least one set of match fields but can include additional criteria. When more than one match field pair is defined, records will only link when all criteria match. The example illustrated in Figure 9-2 shows an additional set of fields, a *Company Contact Portal Filter* in Company and a *Contact Address State* in Contact. These second match fields would allow a user viewing a company record to select a state from a list, and that would be used to "filter" the list of contacts in a portal view, so it only displays those with an address in that state (Chapter 20, "Filtering Portal Records").

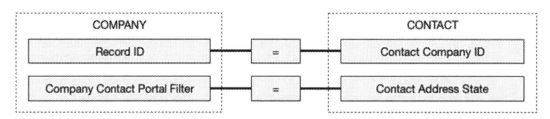

Figure 9-2. *An illustration of a relationship established by two match fields*

Relationships fall into one of the three general classifications named based on the number of matching records possible on each side: *one-to-one*, *one-to-many*, and *many-to-many*. FileMaker has a unique *multi-key option* that can be used to create one-to-many or many-to-many connections. These configurations can be enforced at the field validation level and/or through interface mechanisms that physically limit what can be selected or inserted into a key field. Another option is a *Cartesian join* that relates every record in one table to every record in another. These are set up at the relationship settings level with an operator.

One-to-One Relationship

A *one-to-one relationship* is a connection where a record in either table can only be matched to a single record in the other. The example in Figure 9-3 illustrates one set of matched records where a *Contact* record's *Record Primary ID* is entered as a foreign key in the *Cubicle* record's *Contact ID* field. The directionality of assignment is optional as there is no inherent requirement for which entity is primary and which secondary. As a developer, you can choose either a cubicle assigned to a person as shown or a person assigned to a cubicle, depending on your preference or other logistical considerations. The setup requires both key fields to be validated to contain a single value that is unique across all records within their respective tables. So, if applied to the example shown, each contact can only be assigned a single cubicle, and each cubicle can only be assigned one contact. If not restricted with a field validation rule, one contact could be attached to more than one cubicle, making this a one-to-many relationship instead.

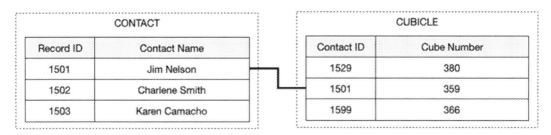

Figure 9-3. *Illustrating a one-to-one connection*

One-to-Many Relationship

A *one-to-many relationship* is a connection where a record in one table can be matched to one or more records in another. The example in Figure 9-4 illustrates one set of matched records where a *Company Record Primary ID* has been entered as a foreign key into the *Company ID* field of two records in a *Contact* table. This type of relationship is used often due to the number of real-world situations where an entity can relate to multiple entities. A company may have multiple offices, products, and employees. A person may have multiple phone numbers, email addresses, and web pages. A parent can have many children. This last example is why this arrangement is often referred to metaphorically as a *parent–child*-type relationship since, biologically, a child has only one father or one mother, but either one parent can have many children. The setup requires the primary key field to be validated to contain a single, unique value, while the foreign key field in the other table allows nonunique values. The directionality of assignment is dictated by the fact that the many side must contain the foreign key from the table containing the unique primary key.

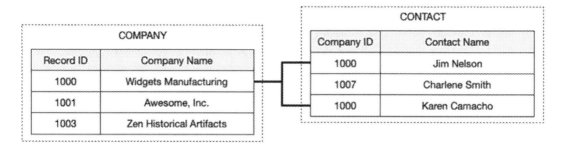

Figure 9-4. *Illustrating a one-to-many connection*

Many-to-Many Relationship

A *many-to-many relationship* is a connection where records on both tables can be connected to one or more records from the other. This is typically done by using an intermediary to join the two. A *join table* is a third table that exists primarily as a junction point, pivoting the connection between two related tables. Because of this, they are sometimes called *junction tables*. A join table has at least two foreign key fields, each containing a primary key from one of the two tables being joined. The example in Figure 9-5 illustrates such a relationship using a join table. The primary key from both Table 1 and Table 2 is each entered in a corresponding foreign key field on a single record in the join table, establishing a connection between the two tables.

Figure 9-5. *Illustrating a many-to-many connection through a join table*

An example of a many-to-many relationship is found connecting a company to contacts when there is a need to connect a person to their current employer while maintaining connections to their past employers, as illustrated in Figure 9-6. In this example, a *Company* table and a *Contact* table are connected through a join table named *Contact Employer*. The "Widgets Manufacturing" Company record has a connection to two join records that each connect to a contact record, one for Jim and one for Karen. While Jim's record has only a single connection to one join record, Karen's Contact record connects back to two companies: "Widgets Manufacturing" and "Zen Historical Artifacts." The use of the join table allows a record on either side to link to any number of records on the other.

Figure 9-6. *Illustrating connections with a many-to-many relationship*

Technically, a join table is not a single relationship since it really consists of two one-to-many relationships. However, it is often referred to as one relationship, especially when a join table exists only to facilitate the wider connection of two regular tables. In those cases, the join table contains only the two fields and is completely hidden from view and has no user-accessible interface. However, joins can include additional fields that are specific to the union of the two entities. For example, a phone number and email address for the contact at a particular company could be stored in a join table record. They can also have interfaces and even connections to other tables as needed.

FileMaker's Unique Multi-key Option

FileMaker has the unique ability to define a relationship using a key field containing multiple values. A *multi-key field* is a text or calculation field that contains a return-delimited list of keys used as a match field in a relationship. When a match field contains values separated by a return, each paragraph is treated as its own value and used to form a match, so the presence of any one value from one field found in the other will match and form a relational connection. Multi-key fields can be used to create a one-to-many relationship or a many-to-many relationship without the need for an intervening join table. The example in Figure 9-7 demonstrates this technique by showing a connection between two tables using a multi-key field as the match field on both sides. The field in the first record of *Table 1* finds three matching records in *Table 2* even though none of the fields contain all the same values. Matches are formed when at least one paragraph value is found on both sides. Setting up a multi-key, many-to-many relationship requires the match fields to be a text field (or a calculation field returning a text value) that allows multiple values and does not validate to require unique values. Although this example uses state names, any value, including serial numbers, can be used.

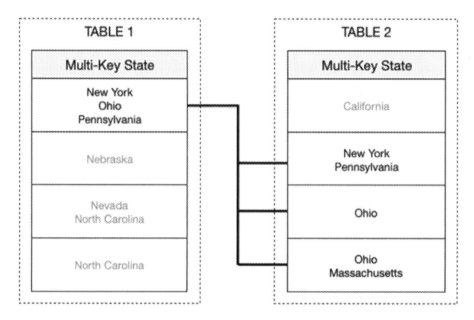

Figure 9-7. *An illustration of a multi-key field relational connection*

There are pros and cons to this technique. For example, there is no intersecting table in which to add fields or build layouts like with a join table, so this isn't a good choice if that is required. However, unlike with a join table, relational connections are retained when duplicating a record since the keys are contained locally instead of in a separate join table. So, if the first record in *Table 1* in Figure 9-7 were duplicated, it would retain all the same connections to records in the other table.

Indexing Match Fields

A relationship forms a bidirectional conduit that allows either table to act as the local starting context (parent) for formulas and layouts from which the other related table is targeted (child). However, for the connection to produce results, every match field used in the targeted (child) table must either be indexed or global. Since calculation fields can't be indexed when their formula contains related fields, a calculated match field on the targeted side must only include fields local to that table. Global fields can't be indexed but will still work on either side of the relationship. However, they are only practical on the local (parent) side since they produce a match to every record when used on the target (child) side.

Using Table Occurrences

Instead of directly connecting tables, relationships are connections between an abstraction of a table. In FileMaker, a *table occurrence* is a representative instance of a table placed into a graphical worksheet called the *relationship graph*. Although the tables are technically linked, it is done through a specific occurrence, one instance of the table. This avoids circular connections between tables and enables multiple connections between the same two tables based on different criteria. It even allows self-join connections between a table and itself.

Every table you create will be automatically represented in the relationship graph with a default table occurrence. Although this appears to be and can be thought of as synonymous to the table, it is only an occurrence of the table. As a database grows, multiple connections involving the same table become necessary but risk becoming circular, as illustrated in Figure 9-8 (left). Here, the connections between *company-to-contact* and *company-to-project* are standard one-to-many relationships and don't pose a problem. However, when a *contact-to-project* connection is required, it would create an overall circular connection between the three tables, which is forbidden. To resolve this, a new occurrence of the *Contact* table is created and used for the new relationship (right). Both instances of *Contact* represent the same table but from a different relational context.

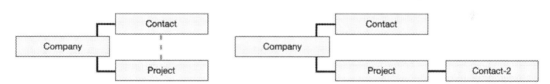

Figure 9-8. *A circular connection (left) is solved with a new occurrence (right)*

Context is a critically important concept in FileMaker. While a table is an isolated data structure defining and storing information in fields and records, a table occurrence specifies that data from a specific relational context and is used everywhere to control what tables are accessible from a given perspective. A calculation field's formula operates from a context that must be selected if there is more than one occurrence for the field's parent table. Value lists can be configured to filter values from a field to only those in an occurrence from a specific starting *interface context* (Chapter 11, "Using a Relationship"). Each layout requires an occurrence assignment that controls which fields can be displayed and establishes the context for object formulas. Numerous script steps automatically execute from the user context, based on the occurrence assigned to the layout active in the current window at the time they execute.

As more occurrences are added, they can be chained together in sequences. In the previous example, there is a connection from *Company* to *Project* to *Contact-2*. Each step between occurrences is often referred to as a "hop," referring to the number of occurrence steps to get from a starting occurrence to a target. A calculation, layout, or script step can access fields through any number of hops along a single relational chain, but reaching across too many can become problematic. In the preceding example, a formula in *Company* can access fields from *Contact-2* but only for the first related *Project* record because it must reach through that relational conduit. A more direct route to the other *Contact* occurrence directly connected to the *Company* occurrence provides access to all company contacts.

As the relational model grows in complexity, it can quickly become a monolithic mess that is both confusing and technically dangerous. Developers with less experience tend to rapidly connect more and more occurrences into one gigantic multipronged chain of occurrences, a single mass that is referred to as a *hub-and-spoke monolith*. Instead, the recommended approach is to build multiple separate *table occurrence groups*. Given the reliance on relational context everywhere in a database's development, a better understanding of these two approaches can make the difference between creating an efficient system and a colossal mess.

Tip   These discussions of relational models may be overwhelming to beginners, especially prior to creating layouts. However, it will be worth the effort to avoid mistakes later!

Avoiding Hub-and-Spoke Monoliths

A *hub-and-spoke monolith* is a relational model where table occurrences are linked into a massive, interconnected group, as illustrated in Figure 9-9. This structure tends to be adopted as an intuitive default by most new developers. They start by connecting a handful of default table occurrences. Then, as they attempt to add new relationships that would be circular, FileMaker prompts them to create new occurrences, and they leave the default name of the table with a numeric suffix. Soon, they have dozens or hundreds of poorly named occurrences interconnected in one massive group.

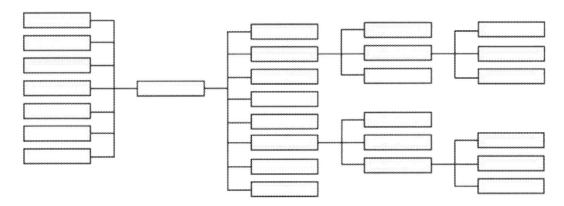

Figure 9-9. *Illustrating a hub-and-spoke monolithic relationship model*

Although this is not inherently problematic and can be a valid choice for simple databases, there are good reasons to avoid hub-and-spoke models completely. When each table has multiple occurrences in the mess, there is no easy way to tell which have been or should be used as a starting context. The result is hundreds or thousands of calculations, interfaces, and scripts zigzag around the complex structure, creating a conceptual gridlock. It quickly becomes confusing to keep track of which occurrence matches a certain context, for example, trying to choose between using *Contact-1*, *Contact-2*, *Contact-3*, and *Contact-4* in a formula requires time-consuming detective work. False starts and backtracking are necessary to correct a layout that is originally assigned the wrong context only discovered after placing dozens of objects on layouts that now need to be reconfigured. Adding new features begins to feel like a tedious chore, and the ability to conceptualize the whole structure requires an enormous effort. As the grip of the convoluted structure tightens, the mind-numbing confusion is just the beginning. A small oversight can result in the loss of data when a script performs a function from the wrong context or a user modifies a field through the wrong relationship because of an interface design error caused by developer confusion. Calculations reaching out in every direction across an excessive number of hops begin to make simple tasks dramatically slower and may return incorrect results. Eventually, technical problems appear as users struggle with unbearably slow performance and may even experience random application crashes. The temptation to blame the technology becomes overwhelming and some declare FileMaker to be an unreliable platform. But this is really the fault of a poor structural design chosen by an inexperienced developer!

The professional developer understands that a well-designed relational model is critically important for both technical reasons and the protection of their own sanity. A database is a complex integration of numerous components, and just as interface design is important to avoid user confusion, equal care should be taken in one's approach to structural design to avoid developer confusion and functional failure. Many of the problems with the hub-and-spoke model can be softened by conscientiously improving one's practices. For example, naming occurrences clearly and establishing a rule about which will be used as the starting context for calculations and layouts will help. Limiting formulas to reach out one or two hops from a given context helps too. But these techniques still require extra work to set up and a conscious effort to follow. In the end, the best solution is to avoid this model completely and instead use occurrence groups!

Embracing Table Occurrence Groups

The *table occurrence group* relationship model establishes a *primary table occurrence* for every table and a rule that these are never directly interconnected to each other. Any connection between two tables must be established by connection from a *primary occurrence* to a new *secondary occurrence* of a table to avoid any direct connections between primaries. This is also called an "anchor–buoy" model since each primary occurrence acts as an independent anchor to which related secondary occurrences can be attached where they are said to "float" away from it. In the setup illustrated in Figure 9-10, primary tables (gray) stand in a column on the left, not connected directly to each other. Each secondary table (clear) that connects to these is a duplicate copy of a primary table. Using this model and following a few rules can solve most of the confusion and potential for technical complications found with the hub-and-spoke method.

Tip   Use the auto-generated default table occurrences as primary tables, since all calculations will point to these table occurrences as their root by default (see "Context Indicator" in Chapter 12, "Exploring the Specify Calculation Interface").

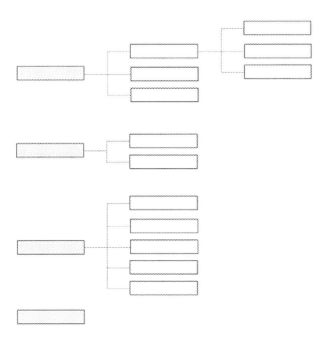

Figure 9-10. *Illustrating a table occurrence group relationship model*

Each primary occurrence on the left establishes the foundational anchor for an *occurrence context group*. These should be named with the actual table name to make clear that they represent the primary root occurrence, for example, Company, Contact, Project, etc. When building interfaces, only these primary occurrences should be used as the starting context for calculation fields, layouts, and value lists.

Each secondary occurrence "floats" off to the right from a primary. These should be named in a way that indicates the starting context group they connect to and include path information about how they relate back to the root primary occurrence of that group. This can take various forms but ideally starts with the name of the primary occurrence, with a delimiter indicating a hop to a new occurrence, and then the name of the secondary occurrence table. For example, a secondary *Contact* occurrence connected to the primary *Company* occurrence might be named "Company | Contact." The secondary part of the name could include additional information used to identify the nature of the relationship, for example, "Company | Contact Employees" indicating that this Contact occurrence is used from the company context and links to contacts that are a company's employees.

The physical separation between groups limits how far and in which direction a field or interface formula can reach out to access related fields since they are limited to related secondary occurrences related within their small "island" group.

Tip   Consider capitalizing the table name portion for emphasis. "Company | CONTACT" makes clear that the occurrence starts from Company but is an occurrence of the Contact table.

The "secondary" nomenclature here doesn't refer to the distance from the primary but indicates a classification status of occurrences that are not primary. So any occurrence existing at any number of "hops" away from the primary is called "secondary." For example, an occurrence of a *Phone* table might be connected to a secondary *Contact* occurrence, which is connected to the primary *Company* as shown in Figure 9-11. It is a third occurrence in a chain, two hops removed from the primary occurrence, but is still referred to as a "secondary" occurrence indicating the non-primary status of both.

Figure 9-11. *An example of two secondary occurrences extending from a primary Company table*

Tip   Although secondary occurrences can extend further, it's a good idea to limit each branch to about two or three hops if possible.

To illustrate the table occurrence group method, consider two groups of occurrences each anchored to *Company* and *Contact* tables respectively, as shown in Figure 9-12. The primary *Company* occurrence would be used as the context for every company calculation and layout. The three tables connected to it may be used within formulas (Chapter 12) and to define a portal on a layout (Chapter 20) accessing related *Contact*, *Project*, and *Invoice* records. The protruding *Phone* occurrence, two hops from *Company*, is added if the contact portal needs to display a phone number for a contact or if a calculation or script needs to access that information from the context of a *Company*. This assumes that phone numbers are stored in a separate table, unlike in our example file.

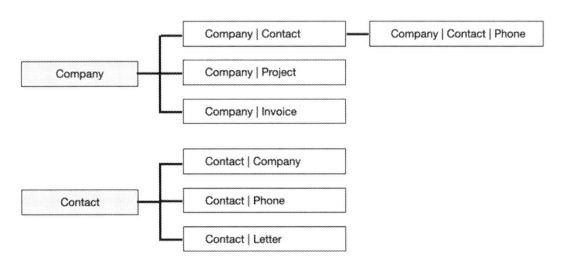

Figure 9-12. *An illustration of two hypothetical occurrence groups*

Similarly, the primary *Contact* occurrence would be used as the context for every contact calculation field and layout. The attached *Company* occurrence could be used to display the contact's employer name on a layout and used by scripts to navigate from a contact record to its related parent company. The *Phone* and *Letter* occurrences can provide the context for portals on contact layouts.

Using the occurrence group method will necessitate some redundancy in the relationship graph, and it may initially seem counterintuitive as unnecessarily increasing the number of occurrences. However, if implemented properly, eventually, the benefits prove themselves, and you will be thankful you took the time to implement it. The separation between groups streamlines performance and makes it easier to conceptually navigate the structure. Limiting all formulas and layouts to a primary occurrence starting context makes it easier to identify resources and avoids confusion. A naming scheme that includes the path from the primary keeps occurrence groups all sorted in the selection menus throughout the development interface, synchronizing the orderly relational structure in a list and making the selection of a target table even easier.

Planning a Relational Object Model

As we continue exploring the lessons in this and future chapters, we will be working with three simple occurrence groups in the *Sandbox* database, as shown in Figure 9-13. Each of the three primary occurrences on the left will be used as the context for every calculation formula and layout, while the secondary occurrences on the right can be used to create calculations, portals, and scripts.

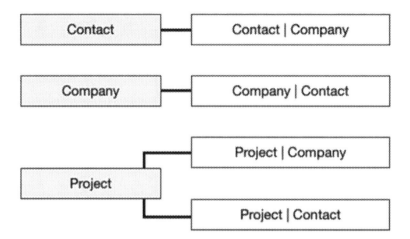

Figure 9-13. *The plan for table occurrences in the Sandbox database*

Managing Data Sources

A *data source* is a defined reference to a FileMaker or ODBC database from which individual tables may be accessed. By default, a FileMaker file is a self-contained database where all tables are contained within the same file. In this case, the implied data source of all tables you create is "Current File," and that will appear as an option in various table selection menus throughout the layout design interface. Our *Sandbox* file has several tables, so you don't need to worry about managing data sources for most of the forthcoming lessons. However, when creating a multi-file database or accessing ODBC tables (Chapter 33), additional data sources will be required. Before delving into relationships where we may refer to a data source and for situations where you need to access other sources, take a moment to see how these are defined.

Chapter 11 includes an example of a value list that "subscribes" to a list contained in an external FileMaker database file. So, as an example, let's prepare for that external data source now.

Introducing the Manage External Data Sources Dialog

External data sources are created, edited, and deleted from the *Manage External Data Sources* dialog, shown in Figure 9-14. This dialog can be accessed by selecting the *File ➤ Manage ➤ External Data Sources* menu. It is also accessible at the bottom of the *Data Source* pop-up menu found on the *Specify Table* dialogs that appear in various locations of the development interface. This dialog will list any existing external data sources and allow you to create, edit, and delete them. Click *New* to open the *Edit Data Source* dialog and define a new connection to an external data source.

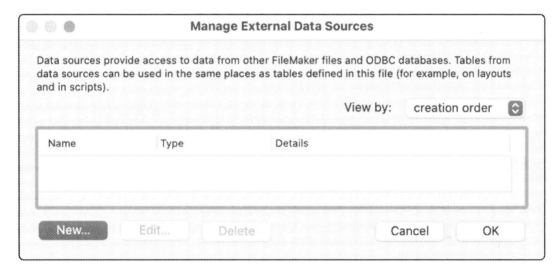

Figure 9-14. *The dialog used to manage external data sources*

Exploring the Edit Data Source Dialog

A data source is defined in an *Edit Data Source* dialog, shown in Figure 9-15. This is opened from the *Manage External Data Sources* dialog by clicking *New*, selecting a data source, and clicking *Edit*, or double-clicking directly on a data source in the list. A data source is defined with three values: *Name, Type,* and *File Path List.*

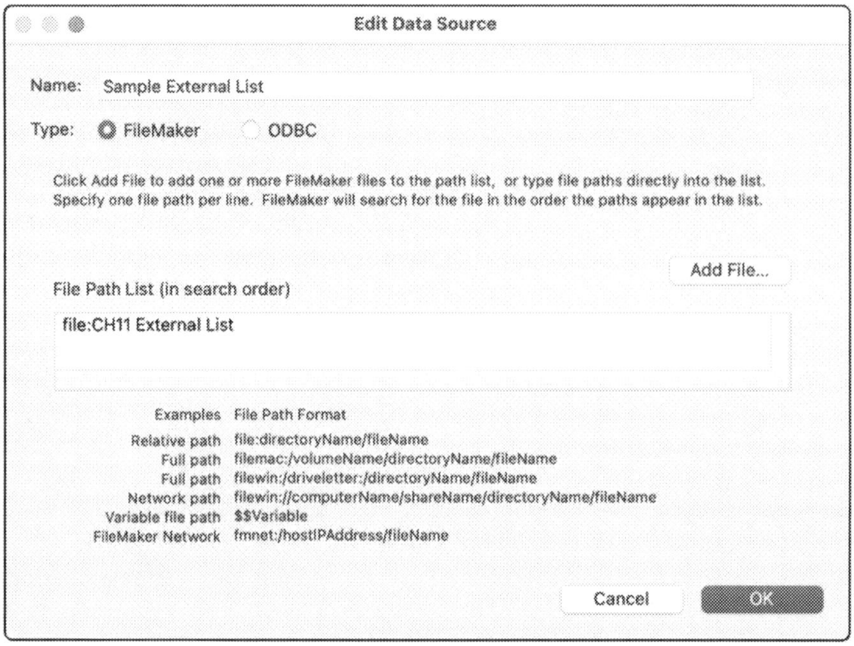

Figure 9-15. *The dialog used to edit a selected data source*

The *Name* you assign a data source will appear in menus throughout the development interface and should be something you will recognize. It can be the actual name of the external file being referenced or a version of that name edited for clarity. For example, connecting to the external FileMaker file called "CH11 External List" as shown, we enter a different name of "Sample External List." Although this isn't dramatically different, when external files are cryptically named, it's a good practice to rename them. For example, connecting to an inventory database named "PROD_INV," assigning a more recognizable name such as "Inventory" or "External Inventory" is prudent. A good rule is to make any new name shorter and clearer where needed.

The *Type* option offers two choices based on the data source being targeted and will change the interface depending on which is selected. The remainder of this section assumes a selection of "FileMaker."

Note   For details on configuring an ODBC-type data source, see Chapter 33, "Connecting to an ODBC Database."

The *File Path List* is used to specify one or more paths to the target data source (Chapter 24, "Specifying File Paths"). These can be a file in a directory on the local computer or network file paths. They can be literally inserted into the field here or be provided by a variable. The bottom of the dialog shows examples of each. Generally, you would use a single path here that you know points to an existing file. However, if more than one is specified, FileMaker will link to the first path that successfully finds a file. Click *Add File* to add a path automatically for a selected file, or type one manually.

In our example, shown in Figure 9-15, we typed "file:CH11 External List" indicating that the desired database will be located within the same folder as our Sandbox file. Once configured, click OK in both dialogs to save the data source for future use in Chapter 11.

Introducing the Manage Database Dialog (Relationships)

Like tables and fields, table occurrences and relationships are created in the *Manage Database* dialog. Select *File ➤ Manage ➤ Database* to open the dialog, and make sure the *Relationships* tab is selected, as shown in Figure 9-16. The scrollable white area is the relationship graph where table occurrences are added and interconnected to define relationships. Every table created in a file will automatically be added to the graph. So our four tables should already be present but with no relationships connecting them, as shown. The toolbar beneath the graph contains buttons that are used to perform various tasks.

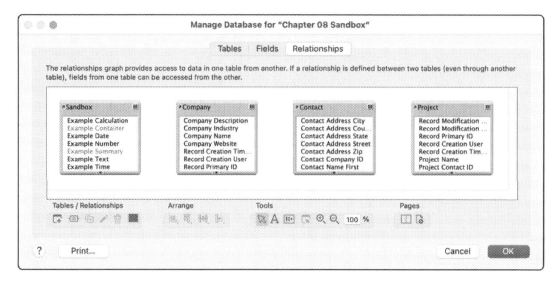

Figure 9-16. *The dialog used to manage relationships*

Working with Table Occurrences

A *table occurrence* is an instance of a table graphically represented in the relationship graph. Before defining relationships between occurrences, let's review the basics of selecting, interacting with, arranging, viewing, formatting, editing, adding, and deleting occurrences.

Selecting Table Occurrences

A selected occurrence will be highlighted with a shaded border, and its size, position, and formatting can be modified. Occurrences can be selected using a variety of different methods with the *Object Selection Cursor* in the *Tools* section activated, as shown in Figure 9-17. To select a single occurrence, click it directly in the graph. To select a group of non-clustered occurrences, hold the Shift key and click each desired occurrence. A second click on a previously selected occurrence while holding this key will deselect it. To select multiple occurrences clustered together in a group, click nearby on the white background, and then hold and drag until the selection rectangle encompasses the desired occurrences. Every occurrence touched by the selection box will be selected. Hold the Command (macOS) or Windows (Windows) key while dragging to only select items that are completely within the selection box's boundary.

Figure 9-17. *The cursor tool used to select and manipulate occurrences*

Later, when working with a large number of occurrences, it may become difficult to find and select specific instances within a complex graph. The menu under the *Select Tables* tool has two options to help, as shown in Figure 9-18. The *Select related tables 1-away* option automatically selects every occurrence that is directly related to the currently selected occurrence. The *Select tables with the same source table* option selects every occurrence that shares the same source table as the selected occurrence, which can be helpful trying to find other instances of a table in a complex graph.

Figure 9-18. *The tool for finding and selecting occurrences in complex graphs*

Interacting with Table Occurrences

With the cursor tool selected, an occurrence box can be moved, collapsed, expanded, resized, and scrolled from the points highlighted in Figure 9-19.

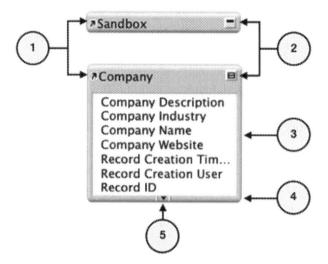

Figure 9-19. *Occurrence manipulation points when collapsed (top) and expanded (bottom)*

1. Click and hold the heading area of an occurrence to drag the box to a new location within the graph. Hover the cursor over the arrow icon to reveal an informative metadata popover.

2. On the right of the heading is an expansion toggle button icon. A single click will toggle the state of the occurrence between one of three states. Without any relational connections, one click collapses the box (top example), and another click expands it (bottom example). With relationship connections, an intermediate state collapses halfway showing only match fields used to form relationship(s) to other occurrences (not shown).

3. Drag the thin bar on the sides and bottom to resize the width or height, respectively.

4. Drag the bottom corners to resize the width and/or height depending on the direction.

5. When fully expanded, this arrow icon that appears at the top, bottom, or both is used to scroll up or down the list of fields. Individual clicks will move up or down one field at a time; holding will continuously scroll the list.

Practice in the *Sandbox* file by collapsing all the occurrences and moving them one above the other so they are roughly lined up in a vertical stack, as shown in Figure 9-20.

Figure 9-20. *The four table occurrences collapsed and arranged in a loose stack*

Arranging and Resizing Occurrences

The *Arrange* tools are used to align and resize groups of selected occurrences based on a selection from a hidden menu under these four icons, shown in Figure 9-21. Use these to align the left edges of the occurrences in the *Sandbox* file and distribute them vertically:

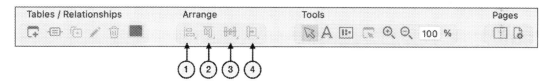

Figure 9-21. *Arrange tools contain menus for arranging and resizing occurrences*

1. Horizontally aligned by left, center, or right edges.

2. Vertically aligned by top, middle, or bottom edges.

3. Distribute horizontally or vertically.

4. Resize the width, height, or both, to smallest or largest.

Viewing Options

The *Tools* section includes four controls that modify the magnification of the relationship graph, shown in Figure 9-22:

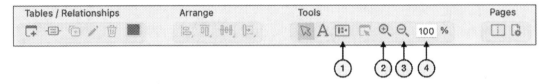

Figure 9-22. *The tools used to adjust the magnification of the relationship graph*

1. *Adjust Magnification* – Adjust the magnification to make every table occurrence fit in the view without scrolling.

2. *Magnification* – Click to activate, and then click in the graph to increase the zoom by 25%.

3. *Reduction* – Click to activate, and then click in the graph to decrease the zoom by 25%.

4. *Percentage* – Manually set the magnification percentage from 1 to 400.

Formatting Table Occurrences

The only formatting tool for table occurrences is a color menu accessible by clicking the *Color* tool located to the right of the *Delete* icon in the *Tables/Relationships* section. Color coding can be used in many ways to visually group table occurrences. For example, apply one color to all primary table occurrences and another to secondary or apply a color to each occurrence group. Colors can be used to indicate the type of operator used to connect a secondary occurrence to a primary one, or color can denote the function of the occurrence, for example, one color for those used as child portals, another for parent tables, etc. Colors can also be used to indicate the development status of each occurrence, for example, highlighting those being worked on or deprecated. Only developers see the graph, so use whatever formatting approach that helps you visually navigate a complex relationship graph.

Editing Table Occurrences

Table occurrences are edited by double-clicking an occurrence or by selecting one and clicking the *Edit Selection* button icon, shown in Figure 9-23.

Figure 9-23. *The tool used to edit an existing occurrence*

Introducing the Specify Table Dialog

From the *Specify Table* dialog, shown in Figure 9-24, the *data source, table*, and *name* of an occurrence can be modified. Typically, you don't need to change these for an occurrence unless undergoing significant restructuring or editing a duplicate of an existing table with a color or size you want to retain. When changing the selected table, the occurrence name will automatically update to that table unless the name has been edited since opening the dialog.

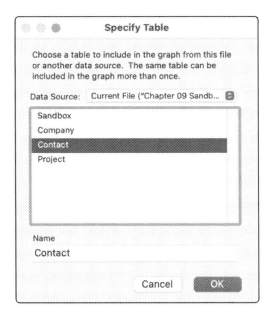

Figure 9-24. *The dialog used to specify which table is assigned to an occurrence*

Adding Table Occurrences

A table occurrence can be added to the graph for any table that exists in any data source defined in the current file. This can be done by creating a new table occurrence or duplicating an existing one.

Creating a New Occurrence

To create a new table occurrence, start by clicking the *Add Table* button icon, shown in Figure 9-25. This will open the *Specify Table* dialog. Choose a data source if the table you want to add is in a different file, select the table, and edit the name if desired. After the occurrence is created, it can be resized and positioned as needed.

Figure 9-25. *The tool used to add a new table occurrence*

Duplicating an Existing Occurrence

Sometimes duplicating an existing occurrence makes more sense than creating new. For example, if another occurrence for the desired table already exists in the graph, duplicating it saves the step of assigning the table manually. Also, a duplicate retains the size and formatting of the original, saving the time required to modify the default styling of a new one. Duplicating a group of related occurrences will even retain all relational connections between them. To duplicate the selected occurrence(s), click the *Duplicate Table* button icon, shown in Figure 9-26. Then reposition them in the graph.

Figure 9-26. *The tool used to duplicate an existing occurrence*

Deleting Occurrences

To delete an unwanted table occurrence, select it and either type Delete or click the *Delete* tool shown in Figure 9-27. Remember that this will only delete the *occurrence* of the table in the graph and not the *actual table*. However, any layout objects or script steps that use the occurrence as a context will be referencing a missing context and require an update.

Figure 9-27. *The tool used to delete an existing occurrence*

Printing the Relationship Graph

The entire relationship graph can be printed by clicking the *Print* button on the lower left of the *Manage Database* dialog. The *Pages* tools, shown in Figure 9-28, control page breaks and page setup.

Figure 9-28. *The tools used to prepare the graph for printing*

Building Relationships

Once occurrences are present in the graph, they can be linked together to define specific relationships. To follow along in the *Sandbox* file, create a duplicate of the *Contact* occurrence and name it "Company | Contact." Then position it to the right of the *Company* occurrence.

Adding Relationships

A relationship is formed when a connection between two occurrences is established. This can be done either by dragging a connection between two occurrences or using the *Add Relationship* button.

Dragging a Connection Between Occurrences

The most intuitive way of creating a connection between two occurrences is to use the cursor to drag a connection from a field in one occurrence to a field in another, thereby establishing a new relationship based on those two match fields. To begin, locate the two occurrences in the graph that will be connected, and click the icon in the upper-right corner of both until they are fully expanded so you can see their field list. Scroll until the desired match field for the relationship is in the visible region of each list. Click and hold on a match field from one occurrence. As you begin to drag the cursor toward the other occurrence, a line will appear connected to the first match field, shown in Figure 9-29. Once the cursor is on top of the desired match field in the other occurrence, release it. The line between the two fields should now remain in place and the new relationship will be established.

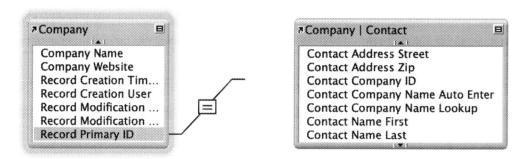

Figure 9-29. *Dragging a new relational connection between occurrences*

To continue with the example, connect the "Record Primary ID" field in Company to the "Contact Company ID" in Contact. This establishes a connection where the company can access a list of all the contacts assigned to it and the contact can access its assigned company.

Tip   Save time by quickly dragging a connection between any two fields currently visible and then edit the relationship (described later). It is easier to select the desired fields in the dialog's larger lists.

Using the Add Relationship Button

The other way to create a new relationship is by clicking the *Add Relationship* button in the toolbar, shown in Figure 9-30. Clicking this button opens an empty *Edit Relationship* dialog (discussed later in this chapter) with both tables set to an unknown occurrence. Since the connection is empty, occurrences and match fields must be selected before saving the relationship.

Figure 9-30.   *The tool used to create an empty relationship*

Manipulating Relationships

A relationship is represented in the graph by a line connecting two occurrences with a selector box in the middle, as shown in Figure 9-31. The box will display the operator used to form a match between the two fields, with the default being an equal sign.

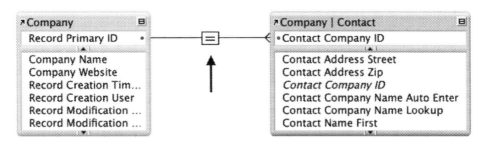

Figure 9-31.   *The relationship line with a selector box in the middle*

On each end of the line where it connects to an occurrence is an indication of the relationship type, shown enlarged in Figure 9-32. A straight line, like that on the left, indicates a *one* connection, and the "crow's feet" on the right side indicates a *many*.

Therefore, in this example, there is a *one-to-many relationship* connection from *Company* to *Contact*. FileMaker determines this by looking only at the auto-enter settings for the fields. Since the *Record Primary ID* field in *Company* is configured to auto-enter a unique serial ID for each record, it is displayed as a *one*. On the other side, the field has no restrictions, so it assumes a *many*.

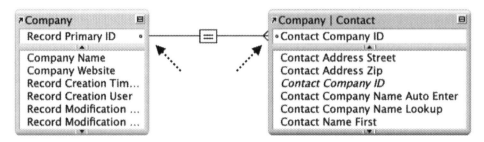

Figure 9-32. *End-of-line symbols indicate the type of connection on each side*

Caution   The end-of-line indicators only reflect field definition restrictions, not entry options on layouts or script functions.

When moving occurrences in the graph, the relationship lines will stay connected on both sides, regardless of one box's position relative to the other box. The line will split into three pivoting segments, as shown in Figure 9-33. Move one box far enough and the line will snap to the other side of the other box to maintain a connection.

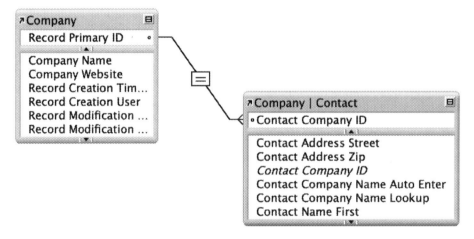

Figure 9-33. *The line splits into straight segments when an occurrence is moved*

Introducing the Edit Relationship Dialog

Relationships are edited in the *Edit Relationship* dialog, shown in Figure 9-34. This can be opened by either double-clicking the relationship connection box or by selecting it and clicking the *Edit Selection* tool, shown previously in Figure 9-23. This dialog shows each side of the relationship across the top, each table's fields with an operator between them. A list of match fields below it shows the relationship criteria, and there's a set of checkbox options below that. From here you have control over what constitutes the relationship and how records on each side behave in certain circumstances.

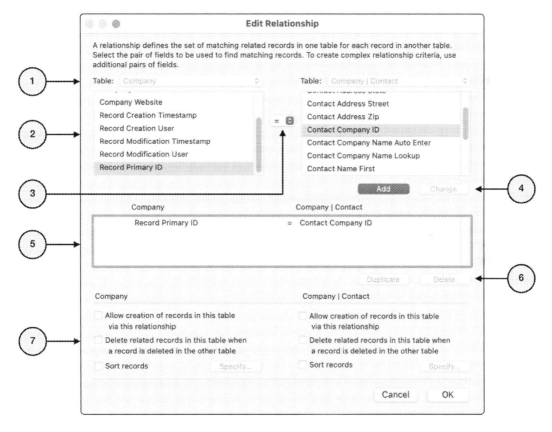

Figure 9-34. *The dialog used to edit a relationship's settings*

The controls on the dialog include the following:

1. *Table* – Select an occurrence for each side of the relationship when creating a new relationship. If editing an existing relationship, these are non-editable and can only be edited directly on the occurrence box in the graph.

2. *Selected a match field* – Select a pair of match fields to be added or changed in the list below.

3. *Comparative operator* – Select an operator to control how the selected match fields will be compared (described below).

4. *Selected match field buttons* – Click to add the selected fields as new criteria to the list below or change to update the fields in the selected combination below.

5. *Link field(s)* – Lists all the criteria defining the relationship.

6. *Link field buttons* – Click to duplicate or delete the selected link field.

7. *Relationship options* – Specify certain behaviors for each side of the relationship (described below).

Selecting a Comparative Operator

A *comparative operator* specifies how match field values will be compared to create a relational match. The available operators are shown in Table 9-1.

Table 9-1. *A list of comparative operators available for relationships*

Operator	Description
=	Match when values in both fields are equal to each other.
≠	Match when values in both fields are not equal to each other.
<	Match when the value in the left field is less than the value in the right field.
≤	Mach when the value in the left field is less than or equal to the value in the right field.

(*continued*)

Table 9-1. *(continued)*

Operator	Description
>	Match when the value in the left field is greater than the value in the right field.
≥	Match when the value in the left field is greater than or equal to the value in the right field.
X	Match every record on the left side of the relationship to all records on the right side, regardless of the actual values contained in the selected fields. This is often referred to as a Cartesian product, Cartesian join, or Cross join, where a connection between two tables is unrestricted by any criteria and every record will be a match no matter the criteria.

Relationship Options

The settings at the bottom of the *Edit Relationship* dialog, shown in Figure 9-35, control three functions for behavior on each side of the relationship.

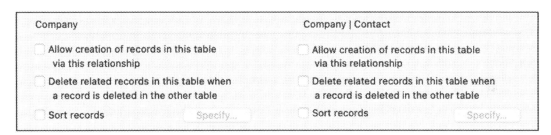

Figure 9-35. *Relationship options for each occurrence*

Allowing Creation of Related Records

The *Allow creation of records ...* option enables an easy way for users to create records in the table on one side of the relationship from a layout for the table on the other side. This is common in portals to allow an intuitive way to create new related records. In our example, if this checkbox is enabled on the *Contact* side of the relationship, a user viewing a *Company* record with a portal of contacts can easily create a new contact linked to that company by simply typing a person's name or another value into a field at the bottom of a portal showing related contacts. When enabled, any portal for that side of the relationship will automatically include a blank record at the bottom for this purpose.

Tip   See "Creating Records in a Portal Directly" in Chapter 20 for an example of this feature in action on an interface.

Automatically Delete Related Records

The *Delete related records …* option causes records in the table to be automatically deleted when a related record on the other side is deleted by a user or script. This is especially useful for cleaning up "child" records when their "parent" record is deleted. For example, when a company record is deleted, any related contact records can also be deleted if this feature is enabled on the *Company | Contact* side. Only use this when the lack of a parent record creates problematic "ghost records," detached records that aren't accessible or usable without a parent. To retain related records and allow them to later be attached to a new parent record, leave this option disabled.

Caution   Once configured, deletions will occur automatically and without additional warning! Once a user confirms the deletion of a record in a parent table, all child records related to that record will be instantly and permanently deleted.

Sorting Related Records

The *Sort records* option enables you to specify a record sort order at the relationship level to control how records appear when viewed through a relationship. This establishes the default record order for all layout portals and calculation formulas that access records through relationships. While a portal can be configured to sort records for display purposes (Chapter 20, "Exploring the Portal Setup Dialog"), which acts as an override, this feature sorts them at the relational root. This is important when using the *List* function (Chapter 13) when the order is important.

Adding Notes to the Graph

A *relationship note* is a free-floating colored text box added in the graph that can contain developer notes or other information. A note is created by selecting the *Text* tool, shown in Figure 9-36, and then clicking and dragging in the relationship graph. An *Edit Note* dialog, shown in Figure 9-37, allows entry and editing of the note text as well as specification of the font, size, text color, and background color of the note. This dialog will automatically open when creating a new note or when double-clicking an existing one. Once saved, a note can be moved, resized, minimized, aligned, or deleted in the same manner as a table occurrence.

Figure 9-36. *The tool used to create a new note*

Tip   A note can be created without selecting the Text tool by clicking and dragging the background while holding Option (macOS) or Alt (Windows).

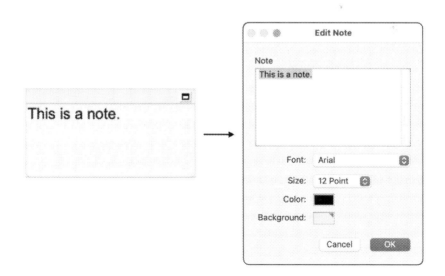

Figure 9-37. *A note (left) and the dialog used to edit it (right)*

Implementing a Simple Relational Model

Now the previously described relationship model can be implemented in the *Sandbox* database, as shown in in Figure 9-38.

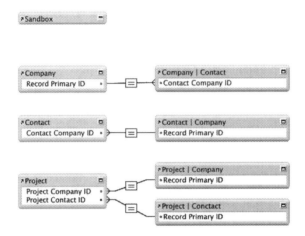

Figure 9-38. *The relational model for the Sandbox example file*

Note   See the "CH09 Sandbox" example file where these changes have already been made.

The following relationships should now exist in the file and can be used for the purposes listed here:

- *Company | Contact* – This can be used to display a portal on a *Company* layout for every contact assigned the Company's *Record Primary ID*.

- *Contact | Company* – This can be used to display the name of the company on a contact record and provide a navigable link from the latter to the former.

- *Project | Contact* – This will link a project to a contact record as the primary contact.

- *Project | Company* – This will link a project to a company record, allow displaying the name on a project record, and provide a navigable link between them.

Summary

This chapter introduced data sources, table occurrences, and relationships. In the next chapter, we will explore managing container fields and storage options.

CHAPTER 10

Managing Containers

A *container field* is a type of field that can store and display a single image or document file. Formally, the content of a container is referred to as a *binary large object* or *basic large object*, both commonly expressed as the acronym "BLOB," which is a collection of binary data representing an image, audio, or any file type (except folders) stored as a single data item in a database. In FileMaker, container fields have configuration options that influence how files are inserted into a field, where that material is actually stored (internally or externally), and how it is displayed when placed on a layout. This chapter provides an overview of the options for defining container fields, covering the following topics:

- Defining container storage options
- Using FileMaker managed external storage
- Using containers

Defining Container Storage Options

Unlike every other field type, there is a drastically reduced set of features to choose from in the *Options for Field* dialog when defining a container field. The *Auto-Enter* options are limited to a value from last visited record, a calculated value, or a looked-up value. The last two are limited to a container result or pulling from a container field, respectively. The *Validation* options allow requiring a value (not empty), setting a maximum number of kilobytes, and entering a custom validation formula. The *Storage* options are similar to regular fields, allowing global storage and repetitions. However, for containers, the indexing choices are replaced with *external storage options*. This last change requires some additional explanation.

© Mark Conway Munro 2024
M. C. Munro, *Learn FileMaker Pro 2024*, https://doi.org/10.1007/979-8-8688-0835-7_10

Explaining Container Storage Options

A container field can be configured to store files in one of two ways: storing the actual file inside of the database file or storing a reference to a file located outside the database file.

Storing Files Internally

When a new container field is defined, it defaults to store internally. Using *internal container storage* means that the entire content of a file is replicated and physically stored inside the database file. This has some advantages and disadvantages.

One advantage is that internal storage maintains portability of the database since all elements are stored in a single document file. If the database file is moved to a new directory or transferred to a different computer, all the information moves along with it, including container data. Although this isn't as much an issue for shared databases hosted on a server (Chapter 29), internal storage ensures that the files stored in container fields are accessible regardless of any user's lack of access to external files on an unmounted file server or an inaccessible coworker's computer. Since the file is literally copied into the database structure, if a user can access that, they can access the container content.

The downside to internal storage is that each file inserted into a field increases the size of the database file. This is not inherently a problem since a FileMaker database can be up to 8 terabytes in size. However, as the size of the file grows, performance may become degraded, especially when many users share access to a database over a network.

Generally, if the number or size of files stored in container fields is excessive, it's a good policy to insert file references into the fields and store the actual file externally. The user won't notice a difference in how they interface with the content if it is done correctly.

Storing a Reference to an External File

A *container field file reference* is a text string that stores an external file's location, type, and other information, which varies by type. For example, a *container image reference* includes the dimensions of the original image, a path to the file relative to the database, and an absolute path to the image. This example shows a reference to an image file located on a user's desktop:

```
size:731,960
image:../../../../../../../../Desktop/Flower Picture.jpg
imagemac:/Macintosh HD/Users/john_smith/Desktop/Flower Picture.jpg
```

Storing references in container fields maintains a lean, efficient database. Although the insertion process only stores the text-based reference in the field, that external file will still be rendered in the interface as if it were stored internally, based on the settings of an instance of the field on a layout. From the user's perspective, there is no difference when the field's content is displayed on a layout.

Caution   If a referenced file is missing, the field will display an error until it is restored.

There are two methods for using external files: *custom-managed* and *database-managed*.

Using Custom-Managed References in Any Directory

The traditional approach to external references in containers is *custom-managed external storage* where the external location of a referenced file can be any directory. The choice to use a *reference insertion* instead of *file insertion* is made when a document is inserted into a container. This is done by selecting a *Store only a reference to the file* checkbox option at the bottom of the *Insert* dialog, shown in Figure 10-1.

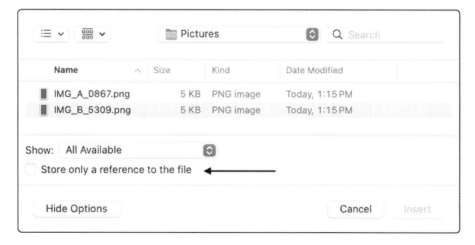

Figure 10-1. *The option to store a reference in the field instead of the file's content*

There are two problems with this approach. First, if the responsibility to check the box is left up to the user, the result is likely to be a mixture of some insertions as files and others as references. Second, the choice of directory from which to pull a file is wide open. Users can insert files or references from anywhere, including a well-organized network server volume accessible to everyone or a local disk accessible to no one else but the user performing the insertion. This results in some records having images that are missing for some users.

Concern about these issues ultimately depends on many factors. If a database is used by one person, it is less of an issue since they are responsible for managing external files in an accessible way to make them available through the database. A shared system is more complex and requires either training to ensure that everyone pulls images from sanctioned locations and always checks the box to store a reference. Scripts can be set up to manage the entire process and double-check to confirm the field contains a reference and remove any actual file added.

However, even with all of these techniques used, there is still a disadvantage. If the server volume, folder directories, or files are moved, renamed, or deleted, the reference links will be broken. For the best results, use reference storage with a managed directory on a FileMaker Server.

Using Database-Managed References in a Central Directory

The best choice for container field storage, especially for networked databases, is to use *database-managed external storage* where the database automatically saves an external copy of every inserted file into a managed folder and inserts a reference to it in the field. In this setup, no users have access to the actual folder directory that contains the files. Instead, FileMaker acts as a broker between the user and the stored material. This keeps documents safely stored and linked to records. Each field can be individually configured to control how managed files are stored. The user simply inserts files from anywhere, and they are copied through to a managed directory and a reference is inserted back into the field.

Using FileMaker Managed External Storage

To use *database-managed external storage,* you must define *base directories* and configure container fields to use them for external storage.

Defining Base Directories

A *base directory* is a developer-defined path to a folder directory that acts as the root location into which one or more container fields can store documents. The folder defined is fully managed by FileMaker, which will automatically create the folder and then manage an internal directory structure of subfolders and files depending on the settings defined for the base directory and individual fields. Every database file contains one default directory, automatically defined with the same name as the database and a formula prefix of [database location], meaning that the external container directory will be stored in the same folder as the database file.

Note   If a database file is renamed, the default base directory will not change but can be manually updated for consistency.

Exploring the Manage Containers Dialog

External container directories are defined in the *Manage Containers* dialog, which can be opened by selecting the *File* ➤ *Manage* ➤ *Containers* menu. This dialog has two tabs: *Storage* and *Thumbnails*.

Exploring the Storage Tab

The *Storage* tab of the *Manage Containers* dialog, shown in Figure 10-2, contains a list of defined base directories that are available for use when defining container fields. This dialog allows you to create new base directories or edit and delete existing ones. You can also initiate a transfer of documents using the *Transfer Data* button, which becomes highlighted after a field's assigned base directory is changed and documents are detected in the old location (see "Changing a Field Container Settings" later in this chapter).

The number of base directories in a given database file is completely up to the developer. The default directory can be shared by every container field in every table in the file. Alternatively, every table or even every field can be assigned a separate base directory. As we will see later in this chapter, the one default directory can still store each field's content into a dedicated subfolder. Although our example file shares the file's default base directory for two fields, let's review the process of creating and editing additional base directories.

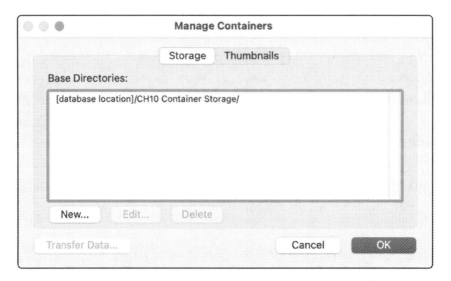

Figure 10-2. *The list of base directories used for managed containers*

Caution   Base directories can't be edited when a database is hosted on a FileMaker Server. Take the file offline and open with the FileMaker Pro desktop application to edit.

Creating and Editing Base Directories

To create a new base directory, click the *New* button. This will open a *New Base Directory* dialog, shown in Figure 10-3.

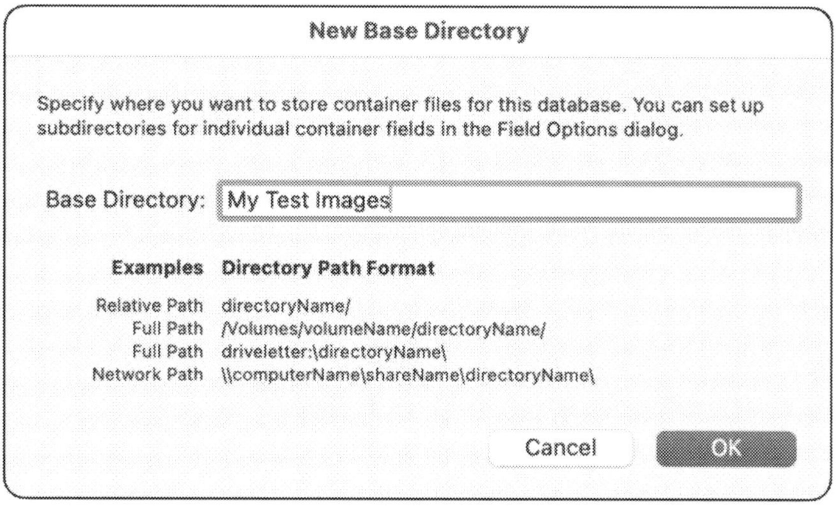

Figure 10-3. *The dialog used to specify a base directory's path*

This dialog contains a single text area into which you can either type a directory path or drop a folder to automatically insert its path. A path must be formatted as shown in the examples. If you place a full path to an existing folder directory, FileMaker will use that literal path as the base directory. If you enter a name or forward slash–delimited path segment, the [database location] prefix will automatically be entered after you save the new directory. Three examples showing each are shown at the bottom of the dialog in Figure 10-4.

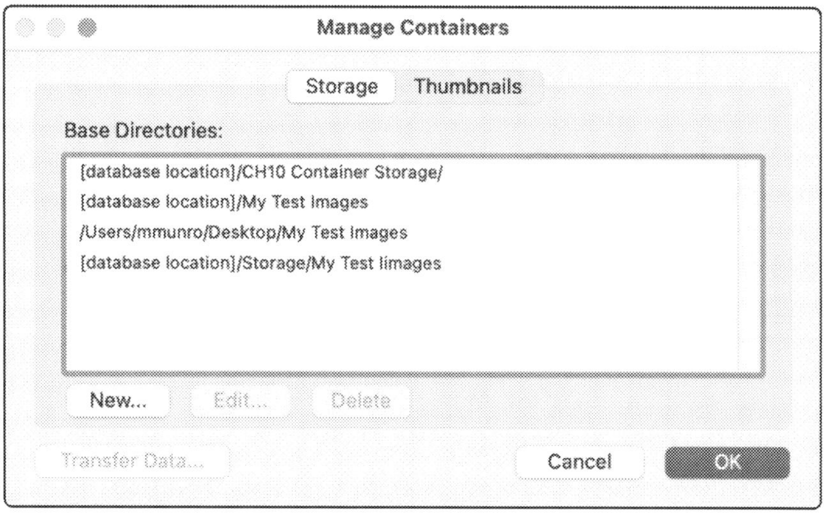

Figure 10-4. *Three new directories added, one name, one full path and one partial sub-path*

Caution   When using full paths to existing folder directories on a shared database, make sure all users have access to them! The best practice is to use a path relative to the database's location.

Once defined, a directory can be edited if it doesn't yet contain any managed files. If empty, double-click or click the *Edit* button in the *Manage Containers* dialog to open the selected base directory in the *Edit Base Directory* dialog (same as the *New Base Directory* dialog shown in Figure 10-3). If the directory does already contain files, create a new base directory, point any field using the old one to the new one, transfer the existing container documents, and then delete the old directory.

Note   FileMaker doesn't create the directory at its location until files are placed into a field using the directory for storage, but immediately removes the folder when the field in all records contains no files.

Deleting a Base Directory

When a base directory is no longer used, it can be deleted if it doesn't contain any managed files. Select it in the list and click the *Delete* button. FileMaker requires at least one base directory defined in a file, so a delete request will be rejected if there is only one in the list.

Exploring the Thumbnails Tab

The *Thumbnails* tab of the *Manage Containers* dialog, shown in Figure 10-5, controls automatic thumbnail generation, which can speed up interface rendering of containers, especially when transferred across a network. To activate thumbnails, select the *Generate and store thumbnails for images* checkbox to allow FileMaker to automatically generate and display a thumbnail for images when a layout attempts to display them. Then choose between the two storage options. The *Permanent storage* option will cause thumbnails to be cached both on disk and in memory, with the on-disk portion retained when the database is closed. Use this for the fastest performance. The *Temporary storage* option will cause thumbnails to be cached in memory only. When the database is closed, the cache is discarded. This will be slightly slower but save hard drive space.

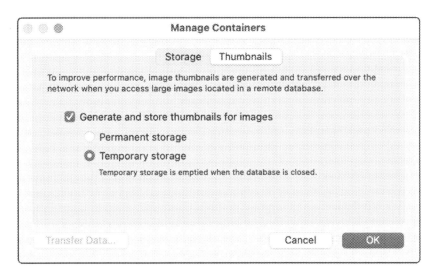

Figure 10-5. *The dialog used to specify a thumbnail generation*

Defining a Field's External Storage Directory

Once a base directory is defined, it can be assigned to individual container fields. Open the *Manage Database* dialog, select a container field, and click the *Options* button. Then select the *Storage* tab of the *Options for Field* dialog and enable *Container* options at the bottom, shown in Figure 10-6.

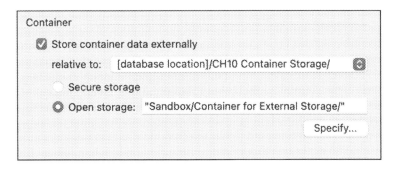

Figure 10-6. *The container field storage options*

Enable the *Store container data externally* checkbox and choose a base directory from the pop-up menu if more than one is defined. Next, choose a storage methodology. The *Secure storage* option will encrypt documents and automatically distribute the files randomly across automatically created subdirectories in a subdirectory within the base directory. This option automatically avoids conflicts between files with the same name stored in any field that is using the same base directory. It is also more secure since it divides a file into pieces and obscures them across a directory structure. The *Open storage* option keeps document data in the original file format and uses a developer-specified subdirectory, which is required to avoid conflicts between similarly named items stored for different tables and fields. The example previously shown in Figure 10-6 has automatically entered the table and field name as subdirectories of the base directory to help avoid conflicts. Click the *Specify* button to enter a custom subdirectory formula (Chapter 12) like the following example, which adds a folder to the hierarchy for the record serial number to ensure one container item per folder. This allows a record to have a file with the same name as another record without either overwriting the other:

```
"Sandbox/Container for External Storage/" & Record Primary ID & "/"
```

Caution   FileMaker Cloud Server requires all containers to use secure storage.

Changing a Field Container Settings

FileMaker automatically recognizes when a change is made to a container field's configuration. This includes changing between unmanaged internal and managed external storage, changing the field's base directory, or switching between secure and open storage. When a modified field definition is saved, a *Container Data Transfer* dialog will list any container fields modified during the session, as shown in Figure 10-7. To immediately transfer the external files to their new base directory, make sure the field has a check in the box and click *Transfer*. If you close instead, the unperformed transfer will be retained and can be performed later using the *Manage Containers* dialog's *Transfer Data* button.

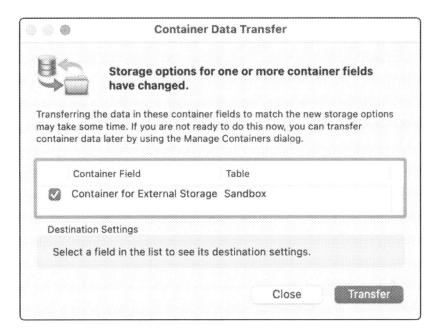

Figure 10-7. *The dialog indicating the need to transfer container field content*

Caution   Always transfer container data immediately after making a change to avoid problems!

Using Containers

Once a container field is defined and placed on a layout, it can be placed and configured on layouts (Chapter 19), and users can begin inserting and extracting files.

Inserting Files into Containers

When a container field is visible and accessible to a user on a layout, a document file can be inserted using a function from the *Insert* menu, by dragging and dropping, or by copying and pasting. Depending on the field definitions and layout settings for a container field, each method has different options and limitations that may impact how the document is inserted and the size of the database file.

Tip   To follow along with these examples, open the *Chapter* 10 *Container Storage* example database.

Using the Insert Menu

The *Insert* menu, shown in Figure 10-8, contains four options at the top for inserting a file into a container field with focus. These options will be enabled or disabled depending on the field's layout configuration. They are also available in the field's contextual menu and as script steps. Choosing any options will open a *Choose File* dialog, automatically optimized for the type of file corresponding to the menu item.

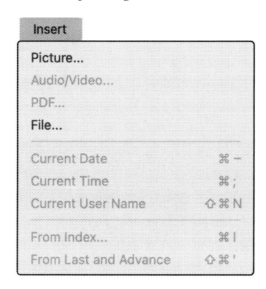

Figure 10-8.   *The options for inserting a file into a container field*

- *Picture* – Insert and display a picture's content.

- *Audio/Video* – Insert an audio or video file. This is only enabled when the field's layout settings allow *Interactive content*, which allows the file to be played directly from within the field without having to open the file in another application.

- *PDF* – Inserts a PDF file. This is only enabled when the field's layout settings allow *Interactive content*, which allows the file's pages to be viewed directly from within the field without having to open it in another application.

- *File* – Inserts any type of file into a field. The file will appear as it does in a directory folder, represented by an icon with no option to view or interact with its content.

Note   For more on layout settings, see Chapter 19, "Data Formatting Options for Containers."

Dragging and Dropping

Using *drag and drop* to insert a file from a directory into a container field on the current layout is the most intuitive method available. When dropping a file, FileMaker will automatically use the appropriate storage method based on dropped file's type and the configuration of the field. For example, if you drop an image, it will be inserted and displayed as if you selected the *Insert Picture* menu. If you drop a PDF or audio file into a field that has not been configured for *Interactive content*, the file will be placed into the field and displayed as a preview of the first page of the PDF or as a file icon. However, if the field is configured for interactivity, the file will be inserted as if you chose the menu corresponding to the file type and will be fully interactive. When dropping, there is no way for a user to manually specify external storage. Instead, the field's defined method of storage will be automatically applied.

Copying and Pasting

Using *copy and paste* to insert a file into a container is another convenient option. The clipboard can contain an actual file copied from a folder, the content of an image copied from a picture file opened in photo editing software, or a properly formatted text reference to a file. The result of pasting is identical to that of dragging and dropping, and there is no way to manually specify external storage (unless pasting a text reference).

Extracting Files from Containers

When a container field on a layout is editable, a user can save a copy of the contents from the record into a folder directory of their choosing using the *Export Field Contents* function. This is available under the *Edit* menu, in the field's contextual menu, and as a script step. When selected, a dialog of the same name will open, allowing the user to choose a folder in which to export the document. The file name will default to the name of the document in the container but can be renamed in this dialog. The dialog includes the option to automatically open the file and to create an email with the extracted file as an attachment.

Tip   This feature can also be used to save selected text from a field into a text file.

Summary

This chapter explored various methods of managing and using container fields. In the next chapter, we explore how to define value lists.

CHAPTER 11

Defining Value Lists

In FileMaker, a *value list* is generally any return-delimited sequence of alphanumeric content. Any list of companies, people, products, statuses, tax rates, zip codes, etc. are all examples of value lists. Lists can be created dynamically by formulas (Chapter 13, "Aggregating Data") and used for various purposes, including the technical formation of multi-key relationships (Chapter 9, "FileMaker's Unique Multi-key Option"). In the specific context of managing the database schema, a *value list* is a named structural resource that predefines a list of values that can be assigned as a *control style* to an instance of a field on a layout (Chapter 20, "Configuring a Field's Control Style"). This enables value-selection data entry used by *drop-down lists*, *pop-up menus*, *checkboxes*, and *radio buttons* to increase speed, ensure accuracy, and maintain consistency. The value list definition can be a simple batch of static values entered manually. Alternatively, it can be defined to dynamically compile a list of unique values from the actual contents of a field for all records in a table or for records viewed through a relationship from the context of a parent table. This chapter covers the following topics regarding defining value lists, including

- Introducing the Manage Value Lists dialog
- Using custom values
- Using a list from another file
- Using values from a field

© Mark Conway Munro 2024
M. C. Munro, *Learn FileMaker Pro 2024*, https://doi.org/10.1007/979-8-8688-0835-7_11

Introducing the Manage Value Lists Dialog

Value lists are defined using the *Manage Value Lists* dialog, shown in Figure 11-1. This dialog can be opened by selecting the *File* ➤ *Manage* ➤ *Value Lists* menu or clicking the pencil icon in the *Inspector* pane for fields assigned a list-based control style (Chapters 19 and 20). This dialog is used to create, edit, duplicate, and delete lists.

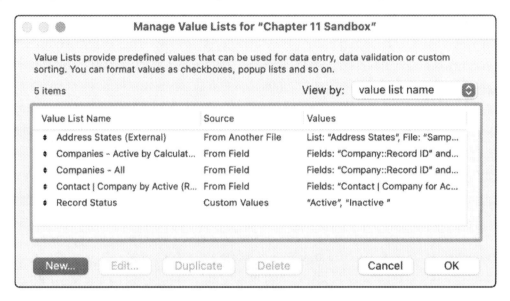

Figure 11-1. *The dialog used to manage value lists*

Tip   Selected value list(s) can be copied and pasted between files.

Each value list has three main properties shown in the list: *name, source* and *values.* The *name* is an identifier that you assign that will represent the list in interface controls when designing layouts. This can take any form but should generally follow the naming guidelines discussed for other resources. It should be descriptive of the values that will be generated by the list and as concise as possible without being cryptic. It is a good idea to include the name of the table used as the source of values or context where it will be used if applicable. A list's name can always be changed later and will automatically update everywhere it is used.

The *source* is one of three options that control how the list is defined to gather values. The choices, each described in more detail later in this chapter, are

- *Use custom values* – Manually define a static, return-delimited list of values.

- *Use value list from another file* – Select a value list from a different FileMaker database for use in this one. This allows a list to be defined once and then shared across numerous databases.

- *Use values from field* – Generate a list of unique values dynamically compiled from a field for every record in a table or from a subset of records through the context of a relationship.

Finally, the *Values* column of the dialog shows either the literal values of a custom list or the definition of how values are to be gathered.

To begin exploring the topic, let's create some value lists that we can use in our *Sandbox* example file.

Using Custom Values

A value list defined to *Use custom values* is ideal for a set of static values that will be entered into a field repeatedly. A country, product category, and record status are ideal candidates for a custom value list, giving the user an option to select the value instead of typing it. Whenever the values required for a list are not something that already exists anywhere in the database or should be fixed and not dynamically updated based on past data entry, this is the option to use.

To get started, create a simple value list that can be used to denote a record's status. For this example, we need a list with two choices: a record will be either active or inactive. In the *Manage Value Lists* dialog, click the *New* button to open the *Edit Value List* dialog. Then perform these steps, shown in Figure 11-2:

1. Enter a name for the value list, for example, "Record Status."

2. Select the *Use custom values* option.

3. Type values into the text area, for example, "Active" and "Inactive."

Figure 11-2. *A value list using custom values*

A carriage return separates each value. When this value list is assigned to a field as *radio buttons*, as shown in the *Company* layout of this chapter's *Sandbox* file, the user will be able to pick one value or the other, and it will be entered into the field automatically. Another example using the same field is shown there using the *pop-up menu* control style where the user can click to open a menu of values and make a selection. The values entered will be displayed in the order you enter them. They don't have to be alphabetical, but, if you want them to be in that order, you have to manually rearrange them.

Inserting Value Dividers

As the number of values grows, consider dividing items into groups. A *value divider* adds a non-selectable break between groups of list items, conceptually segmenting them into sections and avoiding visual clutter. Just type a hyphen by itself between values, as shown in Figure 11-3. The *Chapter 11 Grouping Values* example file shows this example and one for a checkbox style, which adds a blank space between groups of items.

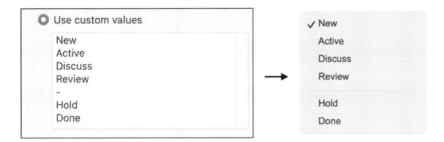

Figure 11-3. *A hyphen in the list definition (left) makes a non-selectable divider in a menu (right)*

Tip   Remember that field control styles are a layout configuration topic that is discussed in Chapter 20!

Using a List from Another File

The option to *Use value list from another file* allows the current database to use a value list defined in a separate file. This isn't necessary when building a single, self-contained database file. However, if a solution grows to include multiple files, each with an interface that uses the same value lists, subscribing to lists in other files allows an edit in one place to automatically update the lists in every other file. See the *Chapter 11 Sandbox* file for an example. The "Address States (External)" list uses the "Address States" list that actually exists in the *Chapter 11 External List* file. To create this list, open the *Manage Value Lists* dialog and click the *New* button to open the *Edit Value List* dialog. Enter a name for the list and then follow these steps to configure the list as shown in Figure 11-4:

1. Select the *Use value list from another file* option.

2. If the other database is already defined as an external data source, it will show up in the first pop-up menu. If not, it can be defined by selecting *Add FileMaker Data Source* from that menu and then locating and selecting the other database.

3. With the file selected, the *Value list* menu will be active and show lists in the external file. Select the desired list and close the dialog.

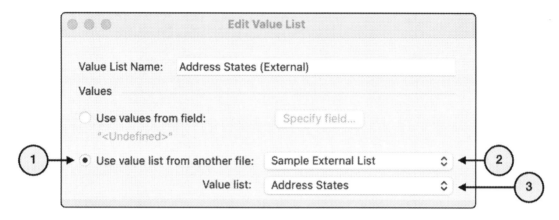

Figure 11-4. *A value list using a list from an external database file*

Tip   Managing data sources was introduced in Chapter 9.

Using Values from a Field

A list *Using values from field* will dynamically generate values from a target field's live data so the list content can change over time based on user input. Among other uses, this allows users to quickly connect records to other records by picking them from a list. There are countless examples of where this is useful. A product record can be attached to an invoice line item. An employee record can be connected to a company that employs them. A project record can be connected to a company, and a budget record can be connected to the project. A letter record can be connected to a letter template and then further customized. As a relational database, there are countless reasons to connect records. Value lists generated from fields for existing records help streamline this process.

Our *Sandbox* example file has a *Company* and *Contact* table. To manually connect a contact to a company without using a value list, we would have to follow this process:

1. Navigate to a layout for the *Company* table.

2. Enter Find mode.

3. Type the name of the company record and perform find.

4. Copy the company's *Record Primary ID* or remember it.

5. Navigate to a layout for the *Contact* table.

6. Enter Find mode.

7. Type the name of the contact record and perform find.

8. Paste or type the company ID into the contact's *Contact Company ID* field.

If the database is configured with a relationship that connects those two fields between those two tables, that data entry would establish a connection, and the contact layout could then display the name of the related *company* and navigate to it with a script.

But that process is far too laborious. Instead, we can create a value list that will automatically display the ID and name of every company entered in the database and assign that list to the field in contacts. Now a user viewing any contact record can simply click in the *Contact Company ID* field, see a list of every company record, select one, and have its ID entered into the field.

Let's create this value list three different ways to illustrate the options available.

Caution   To be used in a value list, the target field(s) must be at least minimally indexed! A calculation field using related values or a field configured to not index will not work as a value list source.

Creating an Unconditional Value List

Lists based on field values are *unconditional* by default and will include all unique values based on every record in the source field's table. This means that the list is *context insensitive* and can be used on fields from every layout without the need to establish a relationship to the source table. As new records are added, the list automatically updates everywhere it's assigned to a field.

To facilitate a *Contact* record assignment to a *Company* as previously described, create a value list named "Companies – All" like the one in the *Chapter* 11 *Sandbox*. The list will include all records sorted by name to allow the user to quickly identify and select the desired company. Once selected, the primary key for the company will be entered into the field to facilitate a solid relationship without concern for name changes in the future.

221

Tip   Every value list, conditional or unconditional, isn't aware of or affected by the current found set of records.

After creating a new value list and naming it, select the *Use values from field* source option. This will automatically open a *Specify Fields* dialog, shown in Figure 11-5.

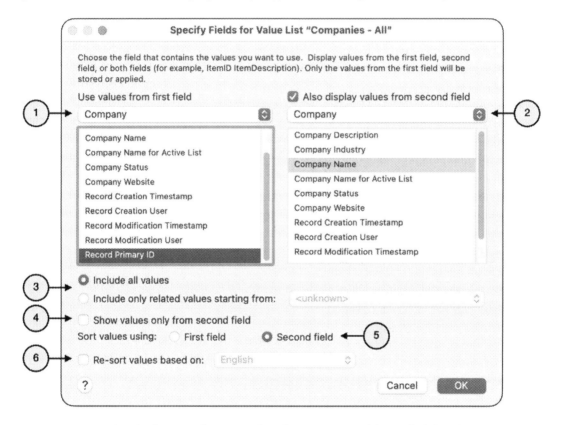

Figure 11-5. *The dialog used to specify a list generated from field values*

Use the following controls on this dialog to specify which field(s) will be used to generate values, indicate which values to include, and how they will be displayed:

1. *Use values from first field* – Choose a table occurrence and field to specify the first field that will be used in the list. This field's value will be inserted in a field when a selection is made.

2. *Also display values from second field* – Optionally, choose a second field from the same occurrence or one related to it. This value is displayed in lists for identification purposes but not inserted when

a selection is made. For example, if the first field uses a company identification number, the second field can display the human-readable company name.

3. *Include …* – Choosing *Include all values* generates a list of unique values from the selected field(s) for all records in the table. Choosing *Include only related values starting from* generates a list of values for only related records starting from the context of a table occurrence selected. This creates a contextual value list that changes depending on which record a user is viewing.

4. *Show values only from second field* – Limits to display values only from the second field but will still insert the first value when a selection is made.

5. *Sort values using* – Select which of the two fields to use to sort the list when displaying more than one field.

6. *Re-sort values based on* – Select a language to use when sorting values. This is useful when using languages where the dictionary sort order is different from the indexed sort order, for example, distinguishing between characters with and without diacritical marks.

In the "CH11 Sandbox" example file, you can see this value list assigned to a field, as shown in Figure 11-6.

Figure 11-6. *The Companies – All value list allowing quick entry of a company ID*

Note   See further discussion on implementing a two-field value list in Chapter 20, "Using Control Styles with a Two-Field Value List"

Creating Conditional Value Lists

A *conditional value list* contains a filtered set of values representing a subset of the available records. By offering a smaller list of only relevant values, users can more easily locate the value they need. As a database becomes more complex, you will encounter numerous instances where you need a conditional list. For example, after assigning a project record to a specific company, the list of contacts to add to an email list can be limited to only those working at that selected company. Similarly, adding a part to an invoice can be limited to a selected product already included.

Using our previous example of assigning a *Company* to a *Contact*, let's create a conditional list that limits the choices to only include company records with an active status. This can be done two ways: using a relationship and using a calculation field.

Using a Relationship

The first method for limiting the included values is to define it as a *relationship-driven conditional value list*. This automatically limits the values included in the list to those records that are accessible based on the context and criteria established by a selected relationship. The resulting list is *context sensitive* and can only be used on a layout whose assigned table (Chapter 17, "Understanding Contextual Access") is the same as that used in the relationship selected in the list definition process.

To create a conditional value list using a relationship, first select a *starting occurrence*, which will establish the layout(s) from where the list can be used. Usually, this is the occurrence assigned to the table of the layout where the list will be used. However, it can also be any occurrence that is related to the usage layout's occurrence. The relational criteria from the *starting occurrence* to the *list occurrence* control which matching records are included in the list and which are excluded.

As an example, build a value list in the *Sandbox* file that includes only *Company* records where the *Company Status* field contains a value of "Active." Since the value list requires a relationship to work, we will declare the *Contact* table as the starting occurrence. So the value list can be assigned to a field on any layout assigned to the *Contact* table. Before defining the list, a few preparatory steps are required.

A calculation field is required to establish the relationship that conditionally controls which records are included in the list. So first create a calculation field in the *Contact* table named "Contact Company Status Match" with a formula of "Active" and with a calculation result type of text (Chapter 12). Since the formula result will be the same for every record and since it will be a local key in the relationship (Chapter 9, "Indexing Match Fields"), it can be set to store a global value.

Next, in the relationship graph, create a new secondary occurrence of the *Company* table, and name it "Contact | Company for Active List," and position it to the right of the primary *Contact* table. This will be the list occurrence, from which the list will pull values.

Finally, connect this new occurrence to *Contact* with a relationship as shown in Figure 11-7. Once connected, from the perspective of the *Contact* table (the starting occurrence), the *Company* values pulled through the relationship from *Contact |Company for Active List* (the list occurrence) will be only those with a *Company Status* value of "Active."

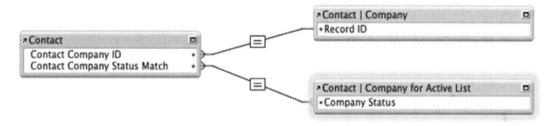

Figure 11-7. *The new relationship for the conditional value list*

Once finished setting up the relationship, create a new value list set to *Use values from field* and specify the fields as shown in Figure 11-8:

1. Choose fields from the new occurrence and choose to also display a second field.

2. Select the *Include only related values starting from* option.

3. Select *Contact* as the starting occurrence.

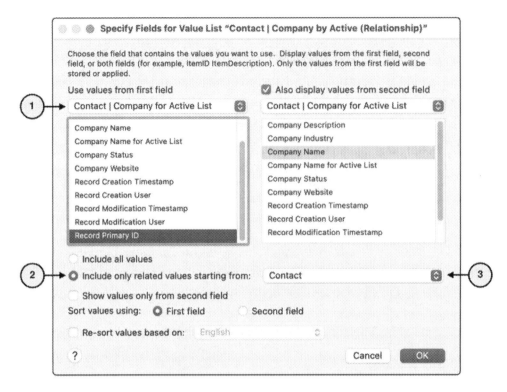

Figure 11-8. *The configuration of the value list made conditional with a relationship*

Once saved, assign the value list to the *Contact Company ID* field on a *Contact* layout as the source for a pop-up menu or drop-down list (Chapter 20, "Configuring a Field's Control Style") or see the preconfigured example in the *Sandbox* file. Click in that field to see a menu of active companies.

Caution   If the value list is empty, confirm that some company records have an "Active" status.

Although there are many valid uses for this technique, a relationship-driven value list is not always the best choice. As mentioned, the filtering mechanism is a relationship makes the list inherently context sensitive. To implement the same feature on layouts for other tables, it would require a duplicate set of resources. For example, to add the same list of active companies to a *Project* table would require a calculation match field created there, a new dedicated table occurrence connecting *Project* to *Company*, and an additional value list. To add it to Invoices requires yet another duplication of these resources. Implementing such a value list in six different tables would require one set of those four resources for each, giving you a total of 24 additional components. So using this technique for a widely used feature like an active company list would quickly clog up the relationship graph and value list definitions with extraneous resources to accommodate what should be a simple global value list. In cases like this, consider a *calculation-driven conditional list* instead.

Tip   Although FileMaker's limits on resources are high, it is a good practice to avoid multiple instances of similar resources that all achieve the same result where possible.

Using a Calculation Field

The second method of creating a conditional list is to base the list on a calculation field (Chapter 12). A *calculation-driven conditional value list* generates a subset of records using a calculation field in the source table whose formula result controls which records are included or excluded. Since FileMaker ignores empty values when building a list from a field, the only record values included in the list are those that are included in the calculation's result. When all the fields used in the formula are local and indexed, this is usually the best choice for creating a conditional value list that is both context neutral and resource efficient. The conditionality of the list is fully controlled in the schema at the field definition level instead of relying on the context of relationships and layouts.

In place of the last example, create a universal list of active companies that can be used anywhere in a database. To begin, create a calculation field in the *Company* table named *Company Name for Active List* that returns a text result and has a formula of

```
Case ( Company Status = "Active" ; Company Name ; "" )
```

Then create a value list that uses the *Record Primary ID* as the first field and the aforementioned calculation field as the second field, as shown in Figure 11-9. When creating a list this way, only the second field needs to be conditionally generated from a calculation. Once created, this list can be used from any layout context, regardless of the source table and without requiring a dedicated relationship:

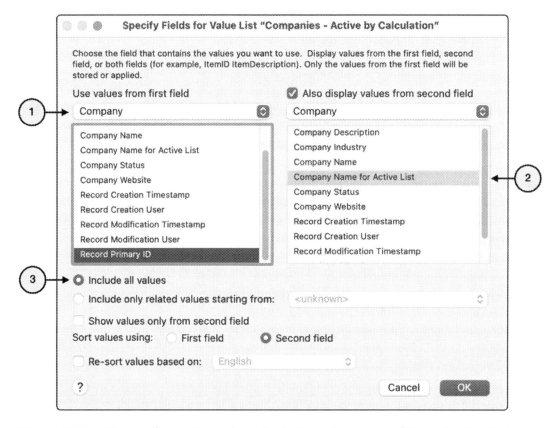

Figure 11-9. *The configuration of a calculation-driven conditional value list*

1. Select *Record Primary ID* from the *Company* table as the first field.

2. Select the *Company Name for Active List* calculation field as the second field.

3. Select the *Include all values* option.

Summary

This chapter explored how to create predefined value lists a variety of different ways. Assigning these to layout objects is discussed further in Chapters 19 and 20. But first, in the next chapter, we focus on writing formulas.

PART III

Writing Formulas and Using Functions

Formulas are used throughout the development environment to perform real-time calculations. They are used by field definitions to enter or display information. They control layout objects and determine a name, content, visibility, and more. Script steps use them to calculate values, control conditions, and more. A formula can be turned into a custom function, allowing you to amend the built-in function library. These chapters cover the basics of writing formulas:

## CHAPTER 12

Writing Formulas

A *calculation formula* is an equation made up of one or more statements expressing operations that can be executed to produce a result. Formulas can analyze, compare, concatenate, condense, convert, expand, format, parse, replace, or summarize any of FileMaker's supported data types. They can range in size from a simple mathematical equation to an extremely complex collection of interrelated expressions and nested logical clauses involving values of any data type. This chapter introduces the basics of writing formulas, covering the following topics:

- Introducing formulas
- How Formulas Work
- Defining formula components
- Writing formulas
- Adding simple calculations to the example file

Introducing Formulas

Formulas are used everywhere in the development interface. The *Replace Field Contents* dialog has an option to insert a formula result (Chapter 4). Many programming dialogs or panels have *Options*, *Specify*, *fx*, or *Pencil* icon buttons that access a formula dialog. The same applies to a *Specify* option in some pop-up menus. When defining a calculation field, a formula is entered. Regular fields have the option to accept formulas to generate an auto-enter value and/or to produce a validation result (Chapter 8). Custom functions are formulas that become global functions accessible from anywhere built-in functions are accessible (Chapter 15). The *Inspector* pane in Layout mode accepts formulas to hide objects and create placeholder text and tooltips (Chapter 19).

© Mark Conway Munro 2024
M. C. Munro, *Learn FileMaker Pro 2024*, https://doi.org/10.1007/979-8-8688-0835-7_12

Many layout objects accept formulas to determine their name or other criteria, including *button bars*, *buttons*, *popovers*, *tabs*, *portals*, *charts*, and *web viewers* (Chapter 20). Objects can have conditional formatting applied that can be controlled with a formula. Custom menus can use formulas to determine a name and visibility (Chapter 23). Script parameters can be generated with a formula (Chapter 24), and numerous script steps can or must be configured with formulas (Chapter 25). Security privileges can be configured to use formulas to determine access to schema resources (Chapter 29). The developer *Data Viewer* dialog has an *Edit Expression* dialog that accepts formulas to continuously monitor a result, which is useful for testing new code (Chapter 31). All of these open the *Specify Calculation* window, as shown in Figure 12-1. This dialog is where formulas are constructed.

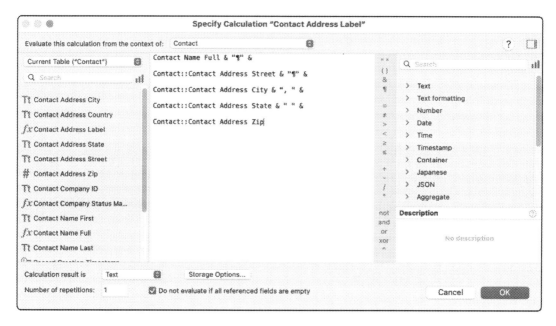

Figure 12-1. *A dialog used to define a calculation formula*

How Formulas Work

Before exploring the details of creating formulas, take a moment to review a broad overview of how formulas work. A *calculation formula* is created by writing a statement that expresses how a result should be produced. Formulas can include literal text and numbers, field references, variables, calls to functions, and more. After writing or editing a formula, it must be saved. During this process FileMaker scans the statement to check for syntax errors. This might include broken field references, missing functions, unterminated phrases (like missing closing quotes or parenthesis), or incorrectly structured statements. When a problem is detected, the save process is halted, the erroneous portion of the statement is highlighted, and a dialog message explains the details of the error. This process is repeated until there are no errors detected, and the code can be successfully compiled and saved. Once saved, a formula remains in an idle state, until it is *called* by any process that prompts it to *execute* and produce a *result*.

A formula can be called numerous ways. A field's auto-enter formula is called when a record is created or when fields used in the formula are altered. When a layout object is rendered, any formulas used by it will be called. This applies to objects that use formulas to generate a name, hide condition, contextual formatting, or other interface-related properties or conditions. A script step's calculation element is called when the step is executed as the script runs. A formula can be called by another formula, for example, a calculation field including another calculation field in its formula or a custom function calling another custom function or a calculation field.

When called, the formula's statement is *evaluated*, which means that the code is converted into a result by executing each operation in a specific order of precedence. Formulas are always evaluated from the context of a specific table occurrence. A formula used in a field definition requires a manually selected context of a table occurrence for the table in which the field exists. A formula associated with an interface element will use the context of the table occurrence of the layout upon which the object is being rendered. A formula used in a script step will use the context of the table occurrence of the layout displayed in the current window at the time it is executed. Formulas used in custom menus also use the current layout's table as a context.

The *result* of a formula is returned to the calling process, which handles it in a way appropriate to its function. For example, a calculation field will contain the result of its formula and display it when present on a layout. A layout object may change its displayed name, visibility, or appearance based on a calculation result. The *Set Variable* script step places the result of its formula into a variable, which can then be accessed by other formulas. The *Show Custom Message* script step will place a result into a dialog presented on screen. The type of object and the aspect of its configuration that called the formula determines the destination or use of the result. As you explore future chapters and begin working with layouts and scripts, you will discover the various ways in which formulas are used.

When a formula is unable to create a result due to an execution error, it will return a question mark. For example, if a formula is using a field that has been deleted or is inaccessible from the current context, the formula may return an error. A formula with an unterminated iterative process, like recursion or a *While* statement, will return an error after reaching its recursive limit. Again, these topics will be explored in future chapters. For now, let's explore the components that can make up a formula and then begin writing some formulas.

Defining Formula Components

A formula expression can be built using any combination of one or more *comments*, *constants, field references, functions, operators, reserved keywords*, and *variables*. In this section we define each component to prepare you for the practical lessons to follow.

Comments

A *comment* is a text string inserted into a formula that is ignored when the code is evaluated. Comments can be used to break code into sections or act as integrated documentation for developers. They can provide details of how the formula operates or how it works, store a record of changes, or include notes about unfinished work. Sections of formula code can be transformed into a comment to temporarily disable it without having to delete it. A comment may be placed at the top of the formula or anywhere between individual statements or sections of code. There are two styles of comment available: *end-of-line* and *multiline*.

Creating End-of-Line Comments

An *end-of-line* comment starts at any double forward slash and continues until the next paragraph return. Any text placed between the slashes and the end of line will be ignored by FileMaker when the formula is evaluated. The following example has several end-of-line comments. The first and second paragraphs are both comments and demonstrate that each line requires a new set of slashes to produce a comment. The third paragraph has a comment starting in the middle of the paragraph, after a formula adding two numbers. The formula portion of this line will be evaluated, while the comment portion will be ignored. The result of this entire formula will be the total of the two numbers: 4.

```
// This is a comment
// To continue on a second line you must use another set of symbols
2 + 2     // This comment starts in the middle of a line, after a formula
```

Creating Multiline Comments

A *multiline comment* uses an *initiating* and *terminating* symbol to indicate the start and end of a comment. These are used to transform an entire block of paragraphs into a comment. To start a multiline comment, use a forward slash and asterisk. To indicate the end of the comment, use the reverse, an asterisk and forward slash. Any text between these two will be ignored when the formula is evaluated. In the following example, the formula has two block comments that will be ignored with a formula between them that will be evaluated, again producing a result of the total of the two numbers: 4.

```
/*
This is a comment
The comment continues on additional lines
3 + 4 including this entire line
Until you terminate it here
*/
2 + 2
/*
This is another comment with returns as spaces
The comment continues on additional lines until terminated
*/
```

Tip   In addition to providing notes about a formula, you can "comment out" old code to retain it until replacement code is tested.

Constants

A *constant*, sometimes referred to as a *literal*, is a static, unchanging value literally typed into a formula. The value can be any of FileMaker's data types: *text*, *number*, *date*, *time*, or *timestamp*. A quantity, city name, event date, and start time are all examples of constants when typed literally into a formula. Numeric constants can be typed directly into a formula, while other text-based constants like dates, times, and strings must be contained within quotation marks so that they are interpreted as a literal value instead of as a field reference, function name, or variable. The following shows examples of each type of constant, as they might appear separately in a formula:

```
150
"New York"
"1/15/2024"
"10:15:00"
"1/15/2024 10:15:00"
```

A date and time constant entered as literal strings are seen as text and must be converted into actual date and time in order to be treated as such by the rest of a formula. This is done using a built-in function: *GetAsDate, GetAsTime,* and *GetAsTimestamp.*

```
GetAsDate ( "1/15/2024" )
GetAsTime ( "10:15:00" )
GetAsTimestamp ( "1/15/2024 10:15:00" )
```

Note   Learn more about built-in functions in Chapters 13–15.

Field References

A *field reference* is a pointer to a field that allows field values to be dynamically accessed by a calculation. A formula that contains only a reference to another field will cause the value in that field to be the value displayed in the calculation field. More complex formulas can use one or more field references in conjunction with other components to produce various results by combining, comparing, parsing, or otherwise manipulating the value contained in the field(s). You can create a calculation field that generates text for a mailing label by assembling a contact's name, address, city, state, and zip with paragraph returns, commas, and spaces. You can join a first and last name into one field for display purposes. You can parse an email address out of a field containing a name and address. A formula can draw on multiple field references and combine them with literal text passages to "write" the body of an email or letter.

References are typed or inserted into a formula without quotation marks. This is how a reference to the *Example Text* field from the *Sandbox* file could be inserted into a formula:

```
Example Text
```

Depending on the type of calculation and the location of the referenced field relative to the evaluation context, it is considered either *local* or *related*. A *local field* is a field that exists within the table of the current context. For a calculation field, the current context is that field's table, so any fields referenced that are also in that table are considered local to the calculation. For a formula used outside of a calculation field somewhere on a layout or in a script, the context will always be the table occurrence assigned to the window's layout at the time of evaluation. A *related field* is a reference to a field in a table outside the formula's operating context table.

When using a related field reference or when referring to a field in a script step, it must include a preceding table occurrence name to specify the relational context from which values should be pulled. This is done by combining an occurrence and field name with a double colon delimiter. For example, a reference to a *First Name* field in a *Contact* table occurrence would be formatted as shown here:

```
Contact::Contact First Name
```

When saving a formula, FileMaker will warn you that a "specified table can't be found" when a reference is missing the required table occurrence.

Caution   Field references should not be enclosed in quotes. There are circumstances where you might work with text-based field references. In that case, use techniques to keep them dynamic (Chapter 35).

Functions

A *function* is a predefined, named formula that is available for use in other formulas. Functions are like subroutines in other programming languages since they allow functionality to be stored outside of the current formula to help avoid redundancies. In FileMaker, there are two kinds of functions: *built-in functions* (Chapters 13, 14, and 16) and *custom functions* (Chapter 15). Here, we will introduce how to call a function in pattern to illustrate its use as a formula component. See those chapters for information on specific functions.

Calling a Function from a Formula

A *function call* is the use of a function in a formula. The call requests that the function execute and return a result back to the calling formula. A call is placed from a formula by typing its name or selecting it through the *Specify Calculation* interface. Generally, a function is named with two or more capitalized words together without spaces that concisely describe the process it performs. So a function call is simply a function name placed anywhere in a formula's statement, shown in pattern here:

```
FunctionName
```

Calling a Function with Parameters

A *function parameter* is an input value that can vary with each call to the function. When a function uses parameters, the calling formula must provide some input that is required. A parameter may contain material for the function to manipulate or specify instructions about how some process should be performed. Parameters are listed after the function name within a set of parentheses. If a function accepts more than one parameter, they are listed in order and separated with semicolons after the function name. Examples of both a single- and multi-parameter function call are shown in pattern here:

```
ExampleFunction ( parameter )
ExampleFunction ( parameter1 ; parameter2 ; parameter3 )
```

The *parameter value* of a function call can be a constant, field reference, literal, nested function, or variable expression as illustrated in these examples, each calling a hypothetical function that has a single parameter:

```
ExampleFunction ( "Hello, World" )
ExampleFunction ( 5000 )
ExampleFunction ( Invoice Tax Rate * Invoice Subtotal )
ExampleFunction ( AnotherFunction ( 15 ) )
```

FileMaker's built-in functions will define parameters with names that help indicate to a developer what information the parameter expects. Some parameters are named simply *text*, *number*, or *date*. When required, other parameters are named more specifically depending on the nature of the function, for example, *startingValue*, *numberOfValues*, *searchString*, *replaceString*, etc. A developer-created custom function should do the same.

Optional Parameters

Some built-in functions have parameters that are optional. An *optional parameter* can be included or ignored as needed when the function is called. When inserting a function call into a formula, FileMaker denotes optional parameters with braces. The *SortValues* function (Chapter 13) has two optional parameters as shown here:

```
SortValues ( values {; datatype ; locale} )
```

The curly braces indicate parameters that are optional. In the example above, the *values* parameter is required, while *datatype* and *locale* are optional. Before compiling the formula, the braces must be removed from the call along with any optional parameters that won't be used. The following examples show two calls to *SortValues*, one without optional parameters and a second with optional parameters included:

```
SortValues ( ContactNames )
SortValues ( ContactNames ; 2 ; "Korean" )
```

Nesting Expressions and Function Calls

A parameter can accept an expression as a value. This can be any formula statement, including calls to other functions. In this example, *ExampleFunction1* is called with a mathematical formula as a single parameter. This *parameter expression* will be evaluated into a result and that result sent to the function as the parameter value:

```
ExampleFunction1 ( ( 150 * 300 ) / 2 )
```

A *nested function call* is a parameter expression that includes a call to a function. In this example, the call to *ExampleFunction2* will be evaluated first, and its result will be used as the parameter sent to *ExampleFunction1*:

```
ExampleFunction1 ( ExampleFunction2 ( parameter ) )
```

Any number of function calls and other expression components can be included in the parameter statement. This example shows real built-in functions (Chapter 13) nested into a single call:

```
TextSize ( TextFormatRemove ( GetValue ( SortValues ( Report::NameList ) ;
1 ) ) ; 12 )
```

Although there are times where nesting is acceptable, the more function calls nested, the more difficult it is to read, edit, or troubleshoot a formula. A *Let* statement allows complex statements to be unnested (Chapter 13, "Using a Cascading Declaration Sequence").

Operators

An *operator* is a symbol used to express a type of operation within a formula. FileMaker has many different operators: *comparison, logical, mathematical,* and *textual.*

Caution   For clarity, examples in this section use simple formulas containing only constants. However, they can be used with any combination of components.

Comparison Operators

A *comparison operator* is a symbol used to compare two values, either a literal value or the evaluated result of two expressions made up of one or more components. These operators are similar to operations in mathematics but can be used to compare any values, not just numbers. The result of an expression comparing two expressions with a comparison operator will be a Boolean value, represented, respectively, by a 1 (true) or 0 (false).

Equal To

An *equal to* symbol is used to compare two values for similarity. The equation will evaluate true if the values are identical and false if they are not. These examples show various number comparisons, text comparisons, and function call result comparisons. The last example compares a field value to a literal text string and will be true or false depending on the value in the field:

```
100 = 100                  // result = 1
150 = 100                  // result = 0
"New York" = "New York"    // result = 1
"New York" = "NY"          // result = 0
GetAsDate ( "1/15/2021" ) = GetAsDate ( "1/15/2021" )      // result = 1
GetAsDate ( "1/15/2021" ) = GetAsDate ( "7/20/2021" )      // result = 0
GetAsTime ( "9:30:00" ) = GetAsTime ( "9:30:00" )          // result = 1
GetAsTime ( "9:30:00" ) = GetAsTime ( "12:15:00" )         // result = 0
Contact::Contact Address Zip Code = "44504"
```

Note   The *GetAsDate* and *GetAsTime* functions shown here are discussed in Chapter 13.

Not Equal To

Comparing two values for dissimilarity can be performed using either a *not equal to* symbol or a *less than* and *greater than* symbol side by side. An equation will evaluate false if the values are identical and true if they are not, as demonstrated in these examples:

```
100 ≠ 100                  // result = 0
150 ≠ 100                  // result = 1
"New York" <> "New York"   // result = 0
"New York" <> "NY"         // result = 1
GetAsDate ( "1/15/2021" ) ≠ GetAsDate ( "1/15/2021" )      // result = 0
GetAsDate ( "1/15/2021" ) ≠ GetAsDate ( "7/20/2021" )      // result = 1
GetAsTime ( "9:30:00" ) ≠ GetAsTime ( "9:30:00" )          // result = 0
GetAsTime ( "9:30:00" ) ≠ GetAsTime ( "12:15:00" )         // result = 1
```

Tip   The *not equal to* symbol can be created by typing an equal sign while holding the Option key on macOS.

Greater Than

A *greater than* symbol is used to compare the relative alphabetical, chronological, or numerical positions of two values. The equation will evaluate to true if the value on the left is greater compared with the value on the right:

```
150 > 100                       // result = 1
100 > 100                       // result = 0
"Bear" > "Automobile"      // result = 1
"Atlanta" > "New York"     // result = 0
GetAsDate ( "1/15/2021" ) > GetAsDate ( "1/10/2021" )        // result = 1
GetAsDate ( "1/15/2021" ) > GetAsDate ( "7/10/2021" )        // result = 0
GetAsTime ( "12:30:00" ) > GetAsTime ( "9:15:00" )           // result = 1
GetAsTime ( "9:30:00" ) > GetAsTime ( "10:45:00" )           // result = 0
```

Greater Than or Equal To

Comparing the relative positions of two values can be performed using either a *greater than or equal to* symbol or a *greater than* symbol followed by an *equal sign*. The equation will evaluate true if the value on the left is greater than or the same value compared to the value on the right, as shown in these examples:

```
100 ≥ 100                       // result = 1
100 ≥ 150                       // result = 0
"Bear" >= "Automobile"     // result = 1
"New York" >= "Ohio"       // result = 0
GetAsDate ( "1/15/2021" ) ≥ GetAsDate ( "7/20/2016" )        // result = 1
GetAsDate ( "1/15/2021" ) ≥ GetAsDate ( "7/10/2021" )        // result = 0
GetAsTime ( "12:30:00" ) ≥ GetAsTime ( "12:30:00" )          // result = 1
GetAsTime ( "9:30:00" ) ≥ GetAsTime ( "10:45:00" )           // result = 0
```

Tip   The ≥ symbol can be created by typing a *greater than* symbol while holding the Option key on macOS.

Less Than

A *less than* symbol is used to compare the relative positions of two values. The equation will evaluate true if the value on the right is greater than the value on the left:

```
100 < 350                  // result = 1
100 < 100                  // result = 0
"Automobile" < "Car"       // result = 1
"New York" < "New York" // result = 0
GetAsDate ( "7/20/2016" ) < GetAsDate ( "1/15/2021" )      // result = 1
GetAsDate ( "7/10/2021" ) < GetAsDate ( "1/15/2021" )      // result = 0
GetAsTime ( "9:15:00" ) < GetAsTime ( "12:30:00" )         // result = 1
GetAsTime ( "10:45:00" ) < GetAsTime ( "9:30:00" )         // result = 0
```

Less Than or Equal To

Comparing the relative positions of two values can be performed using either a *less than or equal to symbol* or a *less than* symbol followed by an *equal sign*. The equation will evaluate true if the value on the right is greater than or the same value compared to the value on the left, as shown in these examples:

```
100 ≤ 100                  // result = 1
100 ≤ 50                   // result = 0
"Automobile" <= "Bear"     // result = 1
"Ohio" <= "New York"       // result = 0
GetAsDate ( "7/20/2016" ) ≤ GetAsDate ( "1/15/2021" )      // result = 1
GetAsDate ( "7/10/2021" ) ≤ GetAsDate ( "1/15/2021" )      // result = 0
GetAsTime ( "12:30:00" ) ≤ GetAsTime ( "12:30:00" )        // result = 1
GetAsTime ( "10:45:00" ) ≤ GetAsTime ( "9:30:00" )         // result = 0
```

Tip   The ≤ symbol can be created by typing a *lesser than* symbol while holding the Option key on macOS.

Logical Operators

A *logical operator* is a keyword used to build compound conditions that join two or more separate expressions into a single expression or, in one case, to negate a single expression to reverse a Boolean result. The result of an expression using a logical operator will be a Boolean.

Tip   Parentheses are not required but advised to help visualize the separate expressions on either side of a logical operator and ensure proper execution order.

AND

The *AND* operator is used to combine two separate Boolean expressions into a combined equation that will evaluate true only if the result of both expressions are true:

```
( 150 > 100 ) AND ( "Bear" > "Automobile" )        // result = 1
( 150 > 100 ) AND ( "Bear" = "Automobile" )        // result = 0
```

OR

The *OR* operator is used to combine two separate Boolean expressions into a combined equation that will evaluate true if the result of at least one of the two expressions is true:

```
( 150 > 100 ) OR ( "Bear" < "Automobile" )        // result = 1
( 150 < 100 ) OR ( "Bear" = "Automobile" )        // result = 0
```

XOR

The *XOR* operator is used to combine two separate Boolean expressions into a combined equation that will evaluate true if the result of only one of the two equations is true. If both equations are true, it will return false:

```
( 150 > 100 ) XOR ( "Bear" < "Automobile" )        // result = 1
( 150 > 100 ) XOR ( "Bear" ≠ "Automobile" )        // result = 0
( 150 < 100 ) XOR ( "Bear" = "Automobile" )        // result = 0
```

NOT

The *NOT* operator is a unique logical operator that will negate the result of any expression to its right, thereby reversing the Boolean result of that expression. If the expression evaluates true, putting this operator in front of it will reverse it to return false and vice versa:

```
NOT ( 150 > 100 )                // result = 0
NOT ( "Tuesday" < "Monday" )     // result = 1
```

A reversal can also be achieved by comparing the Boolean result of an expression to 0. In this example, the false (0) result from the parenthesized expression is reversed by the subsequent comparison to 0. Notice that either 0 or the word False can be used to represent a not-true result:

```
( 150 < 100 ) = 0                // result = 1
( 150 < 100 ) = False            // result = 1
```

Mathematical Operators

A *mathematical operator* is a symbol used to perform or control arithmetic computations with one or more values or expressions. The mathematical operations can be performed not only on numbers but on other data types such as dates, times, and timestamps.

Note   For mathematical operations, a date or time value is automatically converted to a number (Chapter 8, "Introducing Field Types").

Addition

The *plus* symbol is used to add the value on the right to the value on the left:

```
100 + 50                          // result = 150
GetAsDate ( "1/5/2021" ) + 5      // result = 1/10/2021
GetasTime ( "1:15:00" ) + 300     // result = 1:20:00
```

Subtraction

The *minus* symbol is used to subtract the value on the right from the value on the left:

```
100 – 50                       // result = 50
GetAsDate ( "1/5/2021" ) - 2   // result = 1/3/2021
GetasTime ( "1:15:00" ) - 300  // result = 1:10:00
```

Multiplication

The *multiplication* symbol is used to multiply the value on the left by the value on the right:

```
100 * 50                       // result = 5000
GetAsDate ( "1/5/2021" ) * 2   // result = 1475590
```

Division

The *division* symbol is used to divide the value on the left by the value on the right:

```
100 / 50                       // result = 2
GetAsTime ( "1:15:00" ) / 2    // result = 2250
```

Raising to a Power

The *power of* symbol is used to raise the value on the left to the power of the value on the right:

```
100^2    // result = 10000
```

Precedence

A set of parentheses is used to change the order of *evaluative precedence* (discussed later in this chapter). FileMaker will evaluate formulas from left to right after first evaluating expressions that are enclosed within parentheses, working from the inside out and based on an order of precedence. Although these two equations perform the same mathematical operations on the same numbers in the same order, the results are drastically different due to the control of precedence imposed with parentheses:

```
100 * 2 + 50 / 25              // result = 202
( ( 100 * 2 ) + 50 ) / 25      // result = 10
```

Text Operators

A *text operator* is a symbol used to construct an equation that combines separate text items into a single item or performs other text-related functions. These include *quoting, concatenation, paragraph returns,* and *backslashes.*

Quoting Text

As we saw earlier in this chapter ("Constants"), a pair of *quotation marks* is used to indicate a literal text constant. Text entered into a formula without quotation marks will be interpreted as a *field, function,* or *variable.* Date and time constants must also be enclosed in quotation marks:

```
"John"
"1/15/2021"
```

Concatenation

A *concatenation operator* is used to join separate values into a single value. The *ampersand* symbol is the only such operator and can be used to join two text values together as shown in these examples:

```
"John" & "Smith"        //result = JohnSmith
"John" & " " & "Smith"  //result = John Smith
```

The symbol can be used to join any data types together, not just text. However, the values will be joined together as text and the result will be text. This shows results of joining numbers with other numbers and text with a date:

```
100 & 200 & 300              // result = 100200300
"Due Date: " & "10/15/2024" // result = Due Date: 10/15/2024
```

The results from function calls can be concatenated as well, as shown here where the results of two *Get* functions (Chapter 13) are joined with a space between them:

```
Get ( CurrentDate ) & " " & Get ( CurrentTime )
// result = 3/23/2024 10:56:43 AM
```

Caution   Although easy to confuse, the ampersand joins values together into a text result, while the AND operator logically unites the results of two expressions into a Boolean result.

Paragraph Return

The *paragraph return* symbol is used to insert a carriage return into a text value and can be placed in a calculation. Although a single return character can be placed outside of quotes as shown in the second example, putting multiple returns together outside quotes will produce an error and fail to compile. All three examples in the following return the same result:

```
"John Smith" & "¶" & "Jim Smith"
"John Smith" & ¶ & "Jim Smith"
"John Smith¶Jim Smith"
// result of all of these =
     John Smith
     Jim Smith
```

An easier way to concatenate values with paragraph returns is with the *List* function (Chapter 13). This example will produce the same result as those above:

```
List ( "John Smith" ; "Jim Smith" )
```

Tip   The paragraph return symbol can be created by typing a "7" while holding down the Option key on macOS.

Backslash

Quotes are operators and are not actually part of the value they contain. The *backslash* symbol is used to force a quote operator to be used literally instead. This is referred to as *escaping* a string since it allows operator use in a string without causing errors.

For example, a backslash preceding a quote symbol will force the quote symbol to be treated as text and become part of the result. Without the backslash, FileMaker will interpret a single quote as having a syntax error and not allow it to be saved:

```
5"                  // result = syntax error, will not compile
"5\""               // result = 5"
"Hello, World"      // result = Hello, World
"\"Hello, World\""  // result = "Hello, World"
```

Tip   FileMaker's built-in Quote() function will automatically enclose an parameter value into quoted text.

Understanding Operator Precedence

Operators in a calculation formula are evaluated in the following order of precedence:

1. Comments

2. Space, backslash, paragraph return, reserved name

3. Parentheses

4. NOT

5. Power of (^)

6. Multiplication, division

7. Addition, subtraction

8. Ampersand

9. Equal to, not equal to, greater than, lesser than, greater than or equal to, lesser than or equal to

10. OR, XOR

The best way to ensure that a formula will execute in the manner intended is to put parentheses around different expressions that should execute prior to preceding expressions.

Variables

A *variable* is a developer-defined container that stores a value that can be used in a calculation formula and other places in the development interface. Variables are named with a letter, word, or phrase you define. However, there are a few general naming considerations to keep in mind. Variable names should avoid reserved words and field names to avoid confusion and conflicts in formulas. Like table and field names, variable names should be concise but descriptively clear to indicate what data they contain. Although not an absolute requirement, consider staying consistent in format; choose either *"camel case"* (*variableNameExample*), *dot-delimited* (*variable.name.example*), *underscore-delimited* (*variable_name_example*), or some other standard of your choosing.

Once defined, the variable can be referred to by that name within a particular context depending on the variable's type. FileMaker has three different variable types, each with a different naming requirement and scope: *function*, *local*, and *global*.

Function Variables

A *function variable*, sometimes referred to as a *statement variable*, is a variable initialized within a *Let* or *While* function's statement (Chapter 13) that only exists when the statement is being executed that is only accessible from within its formula. Except for the normal restrictions, FileMaker imposes no special naming requirements to a statement variable. Names can be as short as a single character or a lengthy, multi-word phrase like any of the following examples:

```
X
data
firstName
first_Name
dateToProcess
table.name
```

Since function variables are limited to the statement in which they are defined, they can't conflict with similarly named variables in other formulas or within the same formula outside of the statement containing them. Therefore, standardized names can be reused from one formula to the next without concern for conflict.

> **Caution**   Sometimes called "local" because they apply within a statement's local formula, function variables should not be confused with actual local variables that extend beyond a single function's statement!

Local Variables

A *local variable* is a variable that persists during the evaluation of a formula or custom function or execution of a script. A local variable can be initialized within a *Let* or *While* statement (Chapter 13) and with the *Set Variable* script step (Chapter 25) and has a variety of uses: store information at one position in a script for use later in the same script, share information between a script and a custom function, or store information from one iteration to the next in a recursive custom function (Chapter 15). To declare a variable as local, FileMaker requires that it be named with a single dollar symbol prefix. Beyond that, the name can be as short as a single character or a lengthy, multi-word phrase and can use any of a variety of delimiters, as shown in the following examples. Since local variables are limited to the formula or script in which they are defined, they can't typically conflict with similarly named variables in other scripts. However, multiple calls to a custom function from the same script will retain any local variables used by that function:

```
$x
$data
$firstName
$recordNumber
$dateToProcess
$date.to.process
$date_to_process
```

> **Caution**   Although local variables can be used in field definition calculations, they aren't practical there and should be avoided.

Global Variable

A *global variable* is a variable that is accessible from any formula anywhere within a single database file and will persist until the file is closed or until it is reset to an empty value. Like local variables, a global variable can be initialized within a *Let* or *While* statement and the *Set Variable* script step (Chapter 13, "Using Logical Functions"). Global variables can be used to store custom preference settings that control custom functionality, to stage data being prepared for some purpose, or to log troubleshooting information to help track down problems with complex, multi-script processes or iterative formulas.

Caution   Limit global variable use to universal information required throughout the file! Avoid using them to exchange data between scripts; use parameters instead (Chapter 24).

FileMaker requires that global variables be named with a double dollar symbol prefix. Beyond that, names can be as short as a single character or a lengthy, multi-word phrase and can use any of a variety of delimiters, as shown in the following examples. Since they are global, they must each be uniquely and carefully named to avoid confusion and conflicts with other global variables used for different purposes in the same file. However, since they are not shared between files, standardized names can be reused from one file to the next without concern about them overwriting each other:

```
$$x
$$data
$$firstName
$$recordNumber
$$dateToProcess
$$date.to.process
$$date_to_process
```

Tip   The Data Viewer in the Tools menu (Chapter 26, "Exploring the Data Viewer") can be used to view and monitor global variables anytime and local variables during the execution of a script. It also provides a nice sandbox to create and test custom formulas.

Avoiding Reserved Words

A *reserved word* is a word, term, or symbol used by FileMaker for function names, predefined parameters, and operators. There are also words reserved for use when constructing SQL statements. These should not be used as the name of a table, field, custom function, variable, and other custom resources to avoid problems when writing formulas.

Note   See the "CH07-01 Website Reserved Words.html" shortcut in the example files for a complete list of reserved words.

FileMaker may allow a reserved keyword or function name to be used as a table name or field name. However, when referencing these in a formula, an error may occur because FileMaker has no way to distinguish between the reserved word as a *field reference* instead of an *operator* or *function call*. For example, you can name a field "AND," but when referring to it in a formula, it must be wrapped in curly brackets with a preceding dollar sign in order for it to be interpreted as a field and compile:

```
${AND}
```

The best practice is to never use reserved words as table or field names.

Writing Formulas

Let's start writing some formulas! A formula can contain any combination of components and can range from simple mathematics to complex logical statements.

Note   Examples in this chapter can be put in the *Example Calculation* field in the "CH12 Sandbox" example file and the results viewed on the Sandbox Form layout. Some are predefined in the "CH12- 01 Writing Formulas" example file.

Exploring the Specify Calculation Interface

To experiment with formulas, use the *Example Calculation* field of the *Sandbox* table in the *CH12 Sandbox* file. To begin, follow these steps:

1. Open the *Chapter 12 Sandbox* database.

2. Select the *File* ➤ *Manage* ➤ *Database* menu item.

3. Click the *Fields* tab.

4. Confirm *Sandbox* in the *Tables* pop-up on the upper left.

5. Click the *Example Calculation* field.

6. Click the *Options* button.

At the beginning of the chapter, we showed the *Specify Calculation* dialog where all formulas are written. Now we can delve into different areas of the dialog, as shown in Figure 12-2.

Note   Although shown here defining a calculation for a field definition, this interface is ubiquitous throughout the environment when designing layouts, building scripts, and more.

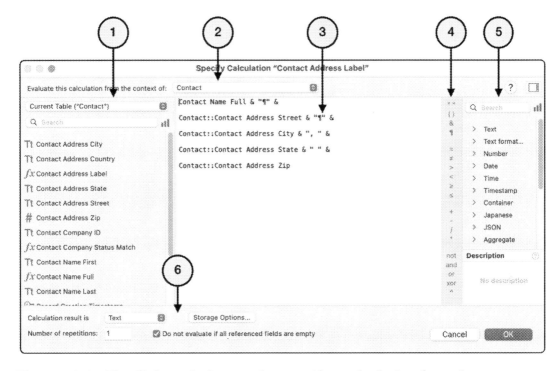

Figure 12-2. *The dialog window used to specify a calculation formula*

1. *Field selector pane* – Find and add fields to the formula. Select a table occurrence from the menu and double-click a field. You can also type field names directly into the formula text area.

2. *Context indicator* – For calculation fields only, choose an occurrence to serve as the context for the formula (when multiple relationship occurrences exist for the field's table).

3. *Formula text area* – This is the formula's code. Type, drag–drop, copy–paste, or insert content by clicking the panes to the left and right to build a formula.

4. *Operators* – Use these buttons to quickly insert an operator.

5. *Functions pane* – Access built-in, custom, and plug-in functions. Double-click to insert into the formula or type them manually. They can be organized hierarchically or alphabetically and searched.

6.   Settings for calculation fields only:

- *Calculation result is* – For field calculations, specify a data type for the result. Other formulas automatically specify by object or function type, for example, button names must be text.

- *Number of repetitions* – Specify the number of field repetitions (Chapter 8, "Repeating").

- *Do not evaluate ... checkbox* – Select this to return no value if every field referenced in the formula is empty.

- *Storage Options* – Open a dialog of indexing options (described in the next section).

Tip   Always use a primary table occurrence for a field's context (Chapter 9, "Embracing Table Occurrence Groups").

Getting Started with Formulas

Let's start exploring formulas with a few simple examples.

Constant-Only Formula

A *constant-only formula* is a formula that evaluates to a literal value without performing any actual operations. It is basically a statement containing a single value that will always evaluate to a result of the same value. Although rather basic, these have some practical use as a way of storing static information such as a current tax rate or value(s) used as a relationship match field to connect to a subset of related records of a certain type. For now, it will serve as a simple example to get us started writing formulas. Type "Hello World" into the formula area, and select a calculation result data type of text. The dialog should now look as shown in Figure 12-3. After saving the formula, the *Example Calculation* field on the layout should now display the text "Hello World" for every record. The result is the same on all records because the formula returns a static value. For it to vary from one record to the next, the formula would refer to components that vary from one record to the next, such as field references.

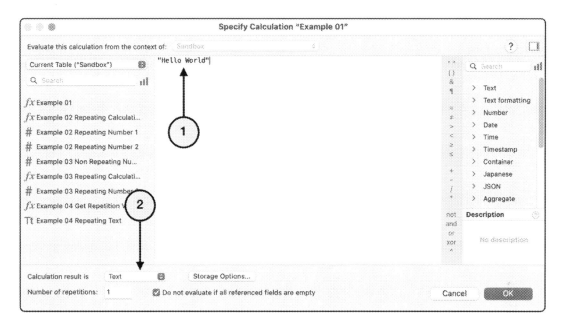

Figure 12-3. *A simple calculation formula with a static result*

Creating Intentional Errors

Before moving forward, it is important to understand the difference between a syntax error and a result error. A *syntax error* is an error with the format or language of the formula's code, which causes it to fail to compile. To illustrate this with the simple constant formula, remove the final quotation symbol from the previous formula. When you attempt to save the calculation, FileMaker will display the error dialog message shown in Figure 12-4. When a syntax error is detected, FileMaker will not allow you to save the formula until the problem is corrected.

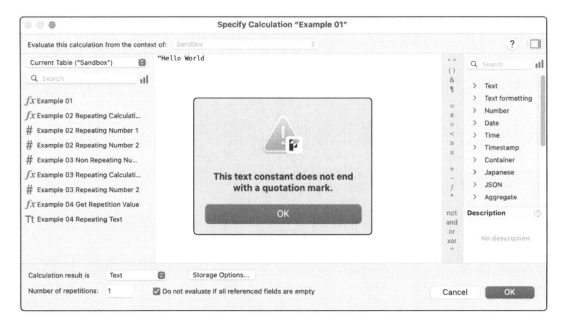

Figure 12-4. *An example error message for formula syntax errors*

Caution   Not every syntax error message will be this specific, but it usually gives you enough information to help find the error.

By contrast, a compiled and saved formula can produce a *result error* indicating a problem with the formula's settings or a component used within one or more of its operations. A result error will be displayed as a question mark. To illustrate this, restore the formula's closing quote mark to eliminate the syntax error. Then change the selection in the *Calculation result is* pop-up menu to date, time, or timestamp. FileMaker will allow saving because the formula's syntax is correct and it doesn't compare the result type setting (date) to the actual result data type (non-date text) because it assumes you have responsibly created a formula that produces the result you indicated. When you look at the field on a record, the result will now be displayed as a question mark. Not every mismatch result type produces a syntax error. Some, like number and container, will display a text result that looks normal but may not behave as expected when searching, sorting, or using the information in other formulas.

Experimenting with Storage Options

Like entry fields, calculation fields have *storage options* that control how the result of a formula is stored, as shown in Figure 12-5. The settings for *global storage* and *indexing* work similar to entry fields (Chapter 8, "Indexing") with an additional option for indexing. The *Do not store calculation results* checkbox forces a calculation to never index results and instead automatically recalculates anytime the field is accessed or displayed. If left unchecked, the field will evaluate once and store the results until something forces it to recalculate. If checked, it will recalculate a result every time it is displayed or accessed.

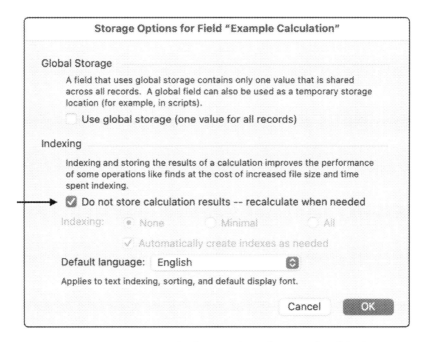

Figure 12-5. *The Storage Options dialog with indexing disabled*

To demonstrate the effect of storage, start with the `"Hello World"` formula configured to return a text result and the *Do not store ...* box unchecked. Save the formula and confirm that the field displays correctly in Browse mode. Then, open the formula again and type two forward slashes in front of the text to convert the entire formula into a comment, as shown below. This should cause the field to display an empty value because the only component, a literal text string, is commented out:

```
// "Hello World"
```

Without making other changes, save the formula and again view it in Browse mode. Don't be surprised if it still displays the value "Hello World" as if nothing changed. This is due to the existing records containing a stored result. If you select the Record ➤ New Record menu, the new record will correctly display a blank value in the field. This shows that, with the checkbox set to not recalculate the results, the previous value remains in older records and will remain until something triggers an update. To force the commented-out example to work correctly, check the *Do not store calculation results* checkbox, save, and view in Browse mode. The field will now be empty for all records, including old records.

Like other field types, calculations use index settings to pre-process results to speed up searches and sorts or to establish relationships. However, when set to store results, it may not recalculate when nothing explicitly triggers it to do so.

Although this simple example isn't a practical representation of the kinds of challenges you will face, it illustrates simply that there will be times when you need to adjust the storage settings. As a more practical example, a formula that uses built-in functions that count the records in a found set or get the current record number (Chapter 13) will not update properly when the result is stored! Unlike these, formulas that include references to fields will update automatically whenever those field values are modified.

Tip   Generally, don't allow calculations to store unless you have a clearly defined need to stop it from constantly recalculating.

Inserting Formula Components

The *Specify Calculation* dialog offers a lot of flexibility in how a formula is written. Any formula components can be manually typed, copy-pasted, or drag-dropped. Field references and function calls can also be inserted by double-clicking an item in the panes on either side of the dialog.

Using Auto-complete

The formula area of the dialog combines text-based entry with dynamic assistance that detects key phrasing and presents an auto-complete suggestion interface, as shown in Figure 12-6. As you type, the list of available components refreshes to include a mixture of every available function (built-in, custom, or plug-in) and field that starts with the letter or phrase typed. In the example shown, the letter "E" causes a list of three functions and a bunch of fields. As you continue typing – "Ex," "Exa," and "Exam" – the list continuously filters until you see only a list of our example fields.

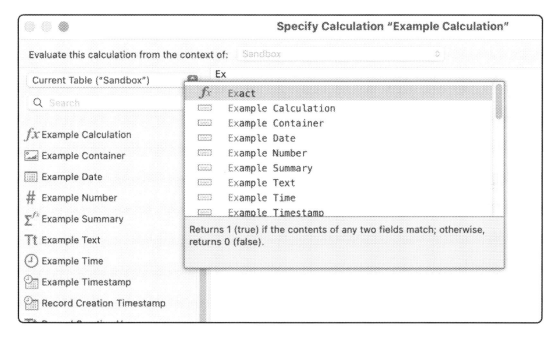

Figure 12-6. *An example of the auto-complete function when typing into formulas*

When the auto-complete list appears, you have the option to ignore it while continuing to type or to select an item for rapid insertion. An item can be located in the list by scrolling, vertically navigating with the arrow keys, or continuing to type enough text until the desired item is the default selection at the top of the list. Once located and selected, insert it into the formula by either double-clicking or pressing the Enter key.

Tip   Type the first capitalized letter of built-in functions (Chapter 13) to find a match. For example, type "Get(cd" to find *Get (CurrentDate)*.

Using the Field Selection Pane

The *field selection panel*, shown in Figure 12-7, is used to locate and insert a field reference. Although you can simply type a field name, this panel allows you to visually navigate the relational structure of the database to locate the desired field.

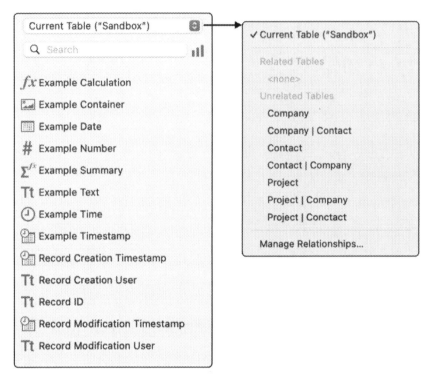

Figure 12-7. *The field selection pane on the left of the dialog*

The *table occurrence selection menu* at the top is used to select a table occurrence whose fields are displayed in the list below. Clicking this will open a menu displaying all table occurrences that have been defined in the file. When a *Specify Calculation* dialog is opened, the default selection in this menu will always be the *Current Table,* which is named to remind you of the context you are working. If editing a calculation field, the current table will be the table containing the field being defined, and the occurrence list will be separated into *related* and *unrelated* to help distinguish which relationships can be used in the formula and which cannot. If editing a formula for a layout object, script step, or other items, the default occurrence is the current layout's table and all occurrences are listed alphabetically leaving you responsible for safely selecting a valid relationship based on the appropriate context that will be active at the moment of execution (Chapter 17, "Understanding Contextual Access"). Once an occurrence is selected, the field list below updates and can be searched or sorted using the controls under the menu. To insert a field's reference into the formula, double-click it.

Using the Function Selection Pane

The *function selection pane*, shown in Figure 12-8, is used to locate and insert a function call into a formula. It provides access to a list of *built-in functions* (Chapter 13), *custom functions* (Chapter 15), and *plug-in functions* (Chapter 28). The list of functions can be listed alphabetically (shown) or grouped by category using a menu hidden under the sort icon. Search by keyword in the text area or by selecting one category from the sort menu. After locating a desired function, double-click it to insert its call into the formula. At the bottom of this pane is a short description of the selected function and a help button to open its online documentation.

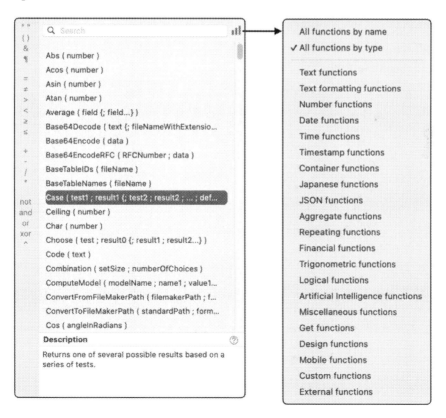

Figure 12-8. *The function pane on the right side of the dialog*

Creating Repeating Calculation Fields

A calculation field can be defined as repeating by entering a number in the *Number of repetitions* at the bottom of the *Specify Calculation* dialog. A *repeating calculation* works like a repeating entry field (Chapter 8, "Repeating"). However, there are a few techniques and built-in functions that may be necessary when working with repeating calculation fields.

Tip   Repeating fields were historically used to achieve the function now better provided by portals (Chapter 20).

Using Repeating Fields in a Repeating Calculation

Repeating calculations work as expected when all fields used in the formula are configured with the same number of repetitions as the calculation field. The example illustrated in Figure 12-9 shows two entry fields containing numbers that are added into a sum within a calculation field.

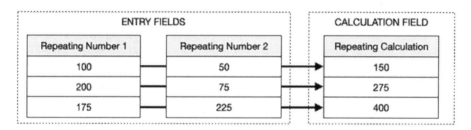

Figure 12-9. *An illustration of a calculation where all fields have the same number of repetitions*

In this example, each field is defined with three repetitions. Because of this, the repeating calculation field's formula can simply add the numbers together. The formula is automatically applied to each repetition of the two entry fields, and the resulting value for each is placed into the corresponding repetition in the calculation field:

```
Repeating Number 1 + Repeating Number 2
```

Note   See the "CH12- 01 Writing Formulas" example file.

Using Non-repeating Fields in a Repeating Calculation

When a non-repeating field is used in a repeating calculation field's formula, use the built-in *Extend* function to allow the non-repeating field to be virtually expanded to match the number of repetitions. The example illustrated in Figure 12-10 shows one single-repetition entry field, another entry field with three repetitions, and a calculation field with three repetitions.

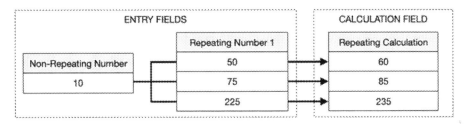

Figure 12-10. *An illustration of a mixture of repeating and non-repeating fields*

For the calculation field's formula to successfully apply the value in the non-repeating field to each value in the repeating field and to generate three results, the formula must extend the non-repeating field as shown in the following example. The single value will be treated as if it were three separate repetitions, each populated with the same value:

```
Extend ( Non-Repeating Number ) + Repeating Number 1
```

Other Repetition Functions

There are other built-in functions that are useful in both repeating and non-repeating calculations. The *Get (ActiveRepetitionNumber)* function returns a number indicating which repetition of the current field has the cursor focus. This can be used by interface-related calculations and script steps to determine where the cursor is located within a repeating field. This is a *Get* function and there are others that return active field name, contents, and table name (Chapter 13, "Discovering Active"). The *GetRepetition* function can be used to extract the value from a specific repetition of a specified repeating field. These functions are most useful in layout and interface formulas and not in field definitions.

The *Get (CalculationRepetitionNumber)* function returns a number indicating which repetition of a repeating calculation field is currently being evaluated. This is unique in that it allows a repeating calculation field's formula to know which repetition of its own field structure it is currently evaluating. That is useful when each repetition needs to perform slightly different functionality.

Including Space for Visual Formatting

When compiling a formula, FileMaker will ignore any extra spaces, tabs, and paragraph returns that are outside of quoted text. This means you can add white space throughout a formula to spread out the code and make it easier to read. When writing formulas, consider adopting a policy of adding space between items and to expand complex statements into an easier-to-read format.

Adding Horizontal Space Between Items

Space can be added between formula components to spread the text horizontally and making it easier to read. The following pairs of code show a cramped example without spaces and the same line repeated with space added. In each set, the two are functionally identical and will produce the same result:

```
(150+50)/25
( 150 + 50 ) / 25
```

```
$FirstName&$Space&$LastName
$FirstName & $Space & $LastName
```

```
Get(CurrentDate)
Get ( CurrentDate )
```

Expanding Statements with Vertical Space

Anytime a line of code extends far enough that it wraps to a new line, you might consider expanding it with paragraph returns. For example, a lengthy concatenation formula involving multiple fields can quickly grow and begin wrapping to multiple lines:

```
Contact::Contact Name Full & "¶" & Contact | Company::Company
Name & "¶" & Contact | Company::Company Industry & "¶" & Contact |
Company::Company Website
```

By adding a few paragraph returns, the expression can be forced onto multiple lines on our own terms, making it easier to read the fields:

```
Contact::Contact Name Full & "¶" &
Contact | Company::Company Name & "¶" &
Contact | Company::Company Industry & "¶" &
Contact | Company::Company Website
```

Nested function calls can also be treated in this manner. Consider the following example from earlier in this chapter:

```
TextSize ( TextFormatRemove ( GetValue ( SortValues ( Report::NameList ) ;
1 ) ) ; 12 )
```

Instead of having all four calls to built-in functions on a single line, adding paragraph returns and tabs allows us to see the nested structure in a more readable way. It still has two pairs of nested calls but is already easier to read:

```
TextSize ( TextFormatRemove (
    GetValue ( SortValues ( Report::NameList ) ; 1 )
) ; 12 )
```

Formulas involving complex *Case, Let, Substitute, While,* and certain JSON functions (Chapters 13 and 14) can also benefit from spaces, tabs, and carriage returns.

Managing Character Limits

FileMaker limits the overall text of each formula to 30,000 characters. When writing lengthy formulas, the natural tendency is to avoid adding spaces, tabs, and paragraph returns to save space and avoid hitting that limit. However, there are other techniques that can be employed to manage space without requiring code to become condensed and less readable. First, consider the reasons why the formula is so long. With some exceptions, lengthy formulas often have redundant elements and phrases. A lengthy field reference used repeatedly can be condensed into a shorter statement variable with a *Let* statement (Chapter 13). For example, a field reference of *Contact::Contact Name First* can be placed into a short variable called something like *nameFirst* and used repeatedly, with each subsequent instance using far less space. Also, renaming variables to shorten their length without losing clarity can save space. Some parts of a formula can be offloaded to a *custom function* (Chapter 25), especially when the functionality is generic and used elsewhere in the database. Another option is to break a complex calculation into separate fields or script steps, rather than trying to force a huge process into one. An efficient methodology when creating formulas should allow room for extra space to make things easier to read, edit, and troubleshoot.

Tip   Make a habit of paying attention to clarity and an efficient technical design regardless of formula length.

Adding Simple Calculations to the Example File

To experiment with formulas, add a couple of simple calculations to tables in the *Sandbox* database.

Company Contact Count

In the *Company* table, follow these steps to add a new calculation field called "Company Contact Count" with a formula that counts related contact records:

- Open the *Manage Database* dialog and select the *Fields* tab for the *Company* table.

- Create the new calculation field.

- Select the *Company | Contact* table occurrence from the pop-up menu in the field selection panel.

- In the formula area, begin typing "Count" and select the *Count* function from the auto-complete list.

- Double-click the *Record ID* field from the *Company | Contact* table occurrence. The formula should read

  ```
  Count ( Company | Contact::Record ID )
  ```

- Make sure the result type is *number*.

- Click to save and close the dialog.

- Place the new field on the *Company* layout to confirm that it accurately counts the related contacts for each company. Remember that the count will vary from one record to the next depending on company assignments to contacts.

Contact Full Name and Address Label

In the *Contact* table, add a new calculation field named "Contact Name Full" and define the formula to concatenate the first and last names. This can be used on layouts and in calculations instead of constantly using the two fields in formulas separately:

```
Contact Name First & " " & Contact Name Last
```

Then, add another field named "Contact Address Label" and define the formula to contain the address formatted as a single text value. The formula will look like this:

```
Contact::Contact Name Full & "¶" &
Contact::Contact Address Street & "¶" &
Contact::Contact Address City & ", " &
Contact::Contact Address State & " " &
Contact::Contact Address Zip
// result =
Karen Smith
521 Loft Street
San Francisco, CA 55555
```

Tip   Use the *Case* or *List* function (Chapter 13) to build a label without extra space when some fields are empty.

Summary

This chapter introduced the basics of writing formulas. In the next chapter, we will see many practical examples of formulas using a variety of useful built-in functions.

Exploring Built-in Functions

FileMaker includes a library of hundreds of *built-in functions* that can be used in formulas to perform common functionality and access information about the digital environment in which the database operates. This chapter explores many essential built-in functions, covering the following topics:

- Working with numbers, dates, and times

- Working with text

- Working with values

- Working with containers

- Introducing Get functions

- Accessing fields

- Aggregating data

- Using logical functions

- Nesting functions into complex statements

Note   Examples use literal values for parameters. However, these can also be variables, field references, expressions, and even nested calls to other functions!

© Mark Conway Munro 2024
M. C. Munro, *Learn FileMaker Pro 2024*, https://doi.org/10.1007/979-8-8688-0835-7_13

Working with Numbers, Dates, and Times

There are numerous functions available for getting, generating, parsing, and manipulating numbers, dates, and times.

Using Number Functions

FileMaker formulas can perform more than just basic mathematical operations. There are many built-in functions that provide more advanced numeric functionality: *Int*, *Random*, *Round*, *Mod*, *Set Precision*, and *Truncate*.

Note   See examples in the "CH13-01 Numbers" file.

Int

The *Int* function returns the integer part of a number by dropping any digits to the right of the decimal, without rounding. This is useful to quickly extract the whole number from a result.

```
Int ( 34.2653 )  // result = 34
Int ( -2.85 )    // result = -2
Int ( 10 / 3 )   // result = 3
```

Random

The *Random* function generates a pseudorandom number between 0 and .99999999999999999999. The result can be multiplied by any integer to generate a random number between 0 and that number, and the *Int* function can be used to extract the whole number.

```
Random               // result = .69521348632189605699
Random               // result = .49928041600104466902
10 * Random          // result = 8.16828354164749970145
Int ( 10 * Random )  // result = 8
Int ( 10 * Random )  // result = 3
```

Round

The *Round* function rounds a number to a chosen number of decimal places. It accepts a number and precision as parameter, with the latter being the number of decimal places that should be retained in the result generated from the former.

```
Round ( number ; precision )
Round ( 10.1564 ; 2 )    // result = 10.16
Round ( 10 / 3 ; 0 )     // result = 3
```

Mod

The *Mod* function calculates a remainder from the result of a number being divided by a divisor. It accepts a number and divisor as parameters. This is helpful in converting convert of measure, such as time increments.

```
Mod ( number ; divisor )
Mod ( 100 ; 60 )        // result = 40
Mod ( 410 ; 365 )       // result = 45
```

In this example, a field named "Time Passed" contains 310 as a number of minutes it can be converted into a text string displaying the hours and minutes elapsed using the formula shown. It uses *Int* to divide the minutes by 60 to extract the number of hours elapsed and *Mod* to determine the remaining minutes.

```
Int ( Time Passed / 60 ) & " hours, " & Mod ( Time Passed ; 60 ) &
" minutes"
// result = 5 hours, 10 minutes
```

SetPrecision

The *SetPrecision* function evaluates a math expression with a specified precision. This is not a rounding or truncating function but a way of expanding the decimal precision beyond the default of up to 16 digits returned by FileMaker. It accepts an expression and precision as parameters, with the latter being a number between 16 and 400 indicating the desired precision. Providing a precision value less than 16 will return the default of up to 16 digits.

```
SetPrecision ( expression ; precision )
22 / 7                              // result = 3.1428571428571429
SetPrecision ( 22 / 7 ; 20 )   // result = 3.14285714285714285714
SetPrecision ( 22 / 7 ; 30 )    // result = 3.142857142857142857142857142857
```

Truncate

The *Truncate* function shortens a number to a specified decimal precision without rounding. It accepts a number and precision as parameters.

```
Truncate ( number ; precision )
Truncate ( 10.246913 ; 2 )     // result = 10.24
Truncate ( 22 / 7 ; 4 )        // result = 3.1428
```

Working with Dates and Times

Built-in functions allow getting, creating, parsing, and calculating date- and time-related information.

Note   See examples in the "CH13-02 Dates & Times" file.

Getting Current Information

There are several *Get* functions that simply return the current date, time, or timestamp.

```
Get ( CurrentDate )            // result = 3/15/2024
Get ( CurrentTime )            // result = 2:05:10 PM
Get ( CurrentTimestamp )       // result = 3/15/2024 2:05:10 PM
```

Note   *Get* functions are discussed in more detail later in this chapter.

Getting Coordinated Universal Time (UTC)

This function returns the current time in *Coordinated Universal Time* (UTC) to the nearest millisecond without regard to the current time zone. UTC was previously known as *Greenwich Mean Time* (GMT) and is the primary time standard used to regulate clocks. The result represents the current time of the computer running the script in the form of the number of milliseconds since "1/1/0001 12:00 AM," without regard to the user's current time zone.

```
Get ( CurrentTimeUTCMilliseconds )    // result = 63846033798493
Get ( CurrentTimeUTCMicroseconds )    // result = 63846033779595296
```

To calculate the time for a specific time zone, factor in the UTC time zone adjustment for the region. For example, when New York City is 4 hours behind UTC, this formula will return the time adjusted for that region:

```
GetAsTimestamp (
   Round ( ( Get ( CurrentTimeUTCMilliseconds )  + ( -4 * 3600000 ) )
   / 1000 ; 0 )
)
```

Caution   Universal Time is not adjusted for daylight savings, so the preceding example will be off by an hour half of the year unless your formula adjusts for that change.

Creating Dates

The *Date* function accepts a numeric *month*, *day*, and *year* parameter and returns a date object. The following examples demonstrate how a date object is created. The first provides three values used to construct the date. The second shows that any of the parameters can be expressions which will be evaluated prior to the construction of the date. The third example shows how the function will automatically shift to a new month, day, or year if the month or day provided falls out of range. For example, a month value of 13 causes the function to automatically return a date for January of the next year. Similarly, setting a date to 2/30/2024 automatically adjusts to 3/2/2024.

```
Date ( month ; day ; year )
Date ( 3 ; 15 ; 2024 )          // result = 3/15/2024
Date ( 3 ; 15 ; 2024 + 10 )     // result = 3/15/2034
Date ( 13 ; 15 ; 2021 )         // result = 1/15/2022
```

The automatic date shift can be used to dynamically calculate the last day of any month regardless of the number of days in that month. Build a date for the following month with a zero for the day. The result will be one day before the first of the month specified, i.e., the last day of the previous month. These examples show how to get the last day of March and June.

```
Date ( 4 ; 0 ; 2024 )           // result = 3/31/2024
Date ( 7 ; 0 ; 2024 )           // result = 6/30/2024
```

Parsing Dates

Each of these parsing functions accepts a *date* parameter and returns a specific component indicated by the function name. The date provided can be a formal date from a date field or constructed with the *Date* function. It also accepts a literal text-based date. These show examples of each kind of date input being parsed.

```
Day ( Date ( 1 ; 15 ; 2024 ) )          // result = 15
Day ( "2/26/2024" )                     // result = 26
DayName ( Date ( 1 ; 15 ; 2024 ) )      // result = Monday
DayName ( "6/27/1758" )                 // result = Tuesday
DayOfWeek ( Date ( 1 ; 15 ; 2024 ) )    // result = 2
DayOfWeek ( "6/27/1758" )               // result = 3
DayOfYear ( Date ( 1 ; 15 ; 2024 ) )    // result = 15
DayOfYear ( "6/27/1758" )               // result = 178
Month ( Date ( 1 ; 15 ; 2024 ) )        // result = 1
Month ( "6/27/1758" )                   // result = 6
MonthName ( Date ( 1 ; 15 ; 2024 ) )    // result = "January"
MonthName ( "6/27/1758" )               // result = "June"
WeekOfYear ( Date ( 1 ; 15 ; 2024) )    // result = 3
WeekOfYear ( "6/27/1758" )              // result = 26
Year ( Date ( 1 ; 15 ; 2024 ) )         // result = 2024
Year ( "6/27/1758" )                    // result = 1758
```

The *WeekOfYearFiscal* function calculates a number representing the week of a year for a given date based on a specified starting date for a workweek. This is useful in accounting applications to calculate if a year has an extra pay period because a week is split across the calendar year boundary. These examples show how Friday, January 2, 2009, can be either the 1st week of 2009 or the 53rd week of 2008 depending on the day number provided as the start of the week, indicated by the second parameter.

```
WeekOfYearFiscal ( "1/2/2009" ; 1 )    // result = 53
WeekOfYearFiscal ( "1/2/2009" ; 2 )    // result = 1
WeekOfYearFiscal ( "1/2/2009" ; 3 )    // result = 1
WeekOfYearFiscal ( "1/2/2009" ; 4 )    // result = 1
WeekOfYearFiscal ( "1/2/2009" ; 5 )    // result = 1
WeekOfYearFiscal ( "1/2/2009" ; 6 )    // result = 1
WeekOfYearFiscal ( "1/2/2009" ; 7 )    // result = 53
```

Creating Times

The *Time* function accepts a numeric *hour*, *minute*, and *second* parameters and returns a time object.

```
Time ( Hour ; Minute ; Second )
Time ( 9 ; 15 ; 55 )    // result = 9:15:55
Time ( 2 ; 8 ; 19 )     // result = 2:08:19
```

Creating Timestamps

The *Timestamp* function accepts a *date* and *time* parameter and returns a timestamp object. These examples show that timestamps will automatically add the appropriate AM/PM suffix to the time portion.

```
Timestamp ( "1/15/2024" ; "9:15:55" )
// result = 1/15/2024 9:15:55 AM

Timestamp ( Date ( 5 ; 10 ; 1990 ) ; Time ( 10 ; 30 ; 00 ) )
// result = 5/10/1990 10:30:00 AM
```

If the hours are out of normal range, as in military time, the function will automatically convert to civilian time, also with the appropriate AM/PM suffix:

```
Timestamp ( "1/15/2024" ; "15:15:55" )
// result = 1/15/2024 3:15:55 PM
```

Parsing Times

The *Hour, Minute,* and *Seconds* functions each accepts a *time* or *timestamp* parameter and returns a number parsed from the input.

```
Hour ( "09:15:55 AM" )                    // result = 9
Hour ( "4/20/2024 03:30:00 PM" )          // result = 15

Minute ( "09:15:55 AM" )                  // result = 15
Minute ( "4/20/2024 03:30:00 PM" )        // result = 30

Seconds ( "09:15:55 AM" )                 // result = 55
Seconds ( "4/20/2024 03:30:00 PM" )       // result = 0
```

Calculating Time Elapsed

There are several ways to calculate the time elapsed from a start and end dates, times, and timestamps. The first example calculates the number of days elapsed by subtracting an end date from a start date. The others demonstrate the same with time. These produce a time result, representing the amount of time elapsed.

```
GetAsDate ( "1/30/2021" ) - GetAsDate ( "1/15/2021" )
// result = 15

Time ( 11 ; 15 ; 48 ) - Time ( 8 ; 10 ; 35 )
// result = 3:05:13

GetAsTime ( "4:15:00 pm" ) - GetAsTime ( "11:15:00 am" )
// result = 5:00:00
```

Although timestamps work the same, these will return the amount of time elapsed between the two date-time combinations. When these span across multiple days, the results may not be easily human-readable, as demonstrated by the following example.

The number of hours is summarized for all the days spanning between the two timestamps. See the "Converting Seconds into a Sentence" example at the end of this chapter to see how to convert time elapsed into a human-readable form.

```
GetAsTimestamp ( "8/1/2021 10:15 AM" ) - GetAsTimestamp ( "1/1/2021
10:00 AM" )
// result = 5088:15:00
```

Working with Text

There are numerous functions available for performing various operations on text values such as analyzing, changing data type, formatting, modifying, and parsing.

Analyzing Text

There are three functions available that are used to analyze the properties of a text string: *Length*, *PatternCount*, and *Position*.

Note   See examples in the "CH13-03 Analyzing Text" file.

Length

The *Length* function counts the total number of characters in the text provided, automatically converting non-text values to text before counting. For example, a number will be converted to text and the number of digits returned, e.g., 24 will return "2."

```
Length ( "Hello World" )        // result = 11
Length ( "Two¶Paragraphs" )     // result = 14
Length ( 359 )                  // result = 3
Length ( 359.0 )                // result = 3
Length ( 359.2 )                // result = 5
```

Note   When a decimal with a greater than zero value is included, the result will include the count of all characters, including the period.

Remembering that formal date objects are different than a date string, notice the difference in the following examples. The first example converts the date into a number and then to text and then counts the number of digits. A date string will simply count characters, producing a different value.

```
Length ( 1/15/2021 )          // result = 17
Length ( "1/15/2021" )        // result = 9
```

PatternCount

The *PatternCount* function counts the number of times a piece of text contains a particular string of characters. The first parameter specifies the text to be searched, and the second contains the string whose pattern will be counted. The result is a number indicating how many times the search string is detected inside the text.

```
PatternCount ( "Hello, World. How is your world today?" ; "world" )
// result = 2
PatternCount ( "15839" ; "4" )                          // result = 0
PatternCount ( "Jim¶John¶Jo" ; "Jo" )                   // result = 2
```

The function is not case-sensitive and searches for matches anywhere in the text, including as part of a word or paragraph.

```
PatternCount ( "The age of his page caused RAGE." ; "age" )   // result = 3
```

Tip   The *PatternCount* function finds partial matches in paragraphs. Use FilterValues to find full paragraph values instead (see "Manipulating Value Lists" later in this chapter).

Position

The *Position* function finds the numeric starting position of the first character of a specified occurrence of a string of text in a source text. The function accepts four parameters. The *text* parameter provides the text that will be searched, and the *searchString* indicates what pattern of text to locate. The *start* parameter is a number indicating the character position where the search will begin, counting from the left.

Finally, the *occurrence* parameter is a number indicating the desired occurrence of a match found in the search string after the starting position that should be used as the result. So, if a string exists multiple times in the text, the last two parameters can be used to specify where to start searching and/or which match of many should be returned.

```
Position ( text ; searchString ; start ; occurrence )

Position ( "Where is Waldo today?" ; "Waldo" ; 1 ; 1 )      // result = 10
Position ( "Where is Waldo today?" ; "Waldo" ; 1 ; 2 )      // result = 0
Position ( "Waldo is looking for Waldo?" ; "Waldo" ; 1 ; 2 ) // result = 22
```

Changing Data Types

There are several functions used to convert values into one of the following data types: *boolean*, *date*, *number*, *text*, *time*, and *timestamp*. Each accepts a single value of any data which it attempts to convert into the desired type indicated by the function name.

Note   See examples in the "CH13-04 Changing Data Type" file.

GetAsBoolean

The *GetAsBoolean* function will convert any value into a Boolean. The result will be 1 (true) when the data provided converts to a nonzero result or a container field contains a value. Otherwise, the result will be 0 (false). This function has a rather narrow usefulness and can be a little confusing to grasp. In these two examples, the first one returns 0 (false) because the data provided does not reduce to a number at all. The second example returns true because it does reduce to a number and is not zero. Here it is useful to look at number results and see if it is a zero which converts to false or a nonzero which converts to true.

```
GetAsBoolean ( "One Hundred" )        // result = 0
GetAsBoolean ( "100" )                // result = 1
```

The function can be used to see if a date, time, or timestamp value exists and is valid or not. Since each of these data times evaluates as a number, if they are empty, the result would be 0 (false) and if not empty it would be 1 (true).

```
GetAsBoolean ( Sandbox::Example Time )
```

It also provides another way to check to see if a container field has a value or not. Each of these three methods will return 1 (true) if the field contains data or 0 (false) if it does not.

```
Sandbox::Example Container = ""
IsEmpty ( Sandbox::Example Container)
GetAsBoolean ( Sandbox::Example Container) = 0
```

Note   Any comparison of two values produces a Boolean result, so there is generally no need for this function.

GetAsDate

The *GetAsDate* function will convert a text value containing date information into a formal date object. The data provided can contain leading zeros or not, as shown in these examples:

```
GetAsDate ( "1/5/2021" )              // result = 1/5/2021
GetAsDate ( "01/05/2021" )            // result = 1/5/2021
```

Text-based dates that include a two-digit year will be automatically converted with the assumption that the date falls within the next 30 years or the preceding 70 years from the current date (Chapter 8, "Two-Digit Date Conversion"). Dates intended to fall outside of that range will get incorrect results if you don't use four-digit years. These examples assume a current date of January 5, 2021:

```
GetAsDate ( "1/5/17" )                // result = 1/5/2017
GetAsDate ( "1/5/95" )                // result = 1/5/1995
GetAsDate ( "1/5/50" )                // result = 1/5/1950
```

When a number is provided, it will be used to calculate the number of days that have passed since January 1, 0001. For example,

```
GetAsDate ( 737805 )                  // result = 1/15/2021
```

Remember that this function only works on data providing date information. If there are additional contents in field or variable provided, it will return an error, as shown here:

```
GetAsDate ( "Birthdate 5/15/2015" )                    // result = ?
```

GetAsNumber

The *GetAsNumber* function will convert a value into a number. This can be useful to ensure proper results when a value is compared to or sorted with other numbers. Conversion to a number ensures that the value is treated as a numeric one instead of nonnumeric. When providing numbers as text, they are simply converted back into numbers. For example,

```
GetAsNumber ( "1234" )        // result = 1234
GetAsNumber ( "015" )         // result = 15
GetAsNumber ( "13.75" )       // result = 13.75
```

When converting text, any nonnumeric characters will be automatically ignored.

```
GetAsNumber ( "$25.09" )               // result = 25.09
GetAsNumber ( "He ran 9.75 miles." )   // result = 9.75
```

In some cases, relying on automatic filtering of nonnumeric characters might not provide a desirable result. Here the presence of two numbers separated by text is concatenated into a new number randomly when the text is removed.

```
GetAsNumber ( "3 men ran 9.75 miles." ) // result = 39.75
```

These examples assume a value of "03" is contained in a *Qty* text field and show the importance of converting text into a number prior to comparing it to other numeric values. Because of the leading zero on the text-based number in the field, the two values don't appear to be the same (in the first example) until the text is converted to a number (in the second example).

```
Qty = 3                                // result = 0
GetAsNumber ( Qty ) = 3                // result = 1
```

Similarly, comparisons will fail when a value isn't numeric. The following examples assume a value of "20" is contained in a *Qty* text field. Since it is a text value, 20 will appear as a smaller value than 3 because the text is compared character by character rather than the entire value compared as a number (2 is less than 3). Once converted to a number, as shown in the second example, it evaluates correctly.

```
Qty < 3                       // result = 1
GetAsNumber ( Qty ) < 3       // result = 0
```

GetAsText

The *GetAsText* function converts any value to a text string. This can be useful in allowing a numeric value to be evaluated and manipulated textually.

```
GetAsText ( 58.75 )                    // result = "58.75"
```

The function will even convert a container's content into one of two values depending on how the file is stored (Chapter 10, "Explaining Container Storage Options"). When stored internally, the name of the file will be returned. When a file is stored as a reference, the result will be a metadata string that varies by file type but includes the file's name and path.

```
GetAsText ( Contact::Image )
    // result = Sunset.jpg

GetAsText ( Contact::Image )
    // result =
          size:191,175
          image:Sunset.jpg
          imagemac:/Macintosh HD/Users/admin/Desktop/Sunset.jpg
```

GetAsTime

The *GetAsTime* function converts a text-based time or timestamp value into a time object to ensure proper results when compared to or sorted with other times. Non-time values will result in an error.

```
GetAsTime ( "5:15:00" )      // result = 5:15:00
GetAsTime ( "Hello, World" ) // result = ?
```

GetAsTimestamp

The *GetAsTimestamp* function converts a text-based value into a timestamp object to ensure proper results when compared to or sorted with other times. When the text provided does not contain information for a full timestamp but does include partial valid information, the function will fill in the missing information. For example, when a date is provided without time information, the function returns a timestamp for midnight on the specified date. When a number is provided, the function returns timestamp for that number of seconds since the first of January in the year 0001.

```
GetAsTimestamp ( "1/5/2017 5:15:00" )    // result = 1/5/2017 5:15:00
GetAsTimestamp ( "1/1/2017" )            // result = 1/1/2017 12:00 AM
GetAsTimestamp ( 100000 )                // result = 1/2/0001 3:46:40 AM
```

Converting Text Encoding

There are three functions that are useful when preparing text for web-related uses or other uses.

Note   See examples in the "CH13-05 Text Encoding" file.

Encoding Text for URLs

The *GetAsURLEncoded* function encodes text for use in a *Uniform Resource Locator* (URL). The function accepts a single text parameter, the value to be encoded for use as or in a URL. Any style information is removed from the text, and all characters are converted to UTF-8 format. Any non-letter or digit characters that are in the upper ASCII range are *percent encoded*, meaning they are converted to a percent symbol followed by the hexadecimal value of the character, e.g., spaces are converted to "%20."

```
GetAsURLEncoded ( "Hello World" )      // result = "Hello%20World"
GetAsURLEncoded ( "10% Surcharge" )    // result = "10%25%20Surcharge"
```

In this example, building a Facebook URL is constructed to search for a person by name. The function is used to quickly encode the name to convert spaces to "%20."

```
"https://www.facebook.com/search/top?q=" & GetAsURLEncoded ( "John Smith" )
// result = https://www.facebook.com/search/top?q=John%20Smith
```

Converting to CSS

The *GetAsCSS* function converts formatted text into the *Cascading Style Sheet* (CSS) format, preserving the font, size, color, and style attributes in a markup format. The following example assumes a record in a *Contact* table with a field named *Contact Notes* that contains the word "Hello" formatted so the font is "Arial," the size is 18, the style is bold, and the color is red.

```
GetAsCSS ( Contact::Contact Notes )
// result = <span style="font-family: 'Arial';font-size: 18px; color:
#FF2712;font-weight:bold;" >Hello</span>
```

Caution   Only styles applied directly to the text content is converted. This function doesn't look at style settings imposed on an instance of a field on a layout (Chapter 19, "Inspecting the Styles Tab").

Converting Text to SVG

The *GetAsSVG* function converts text to the *Scalable Vector Graphics* (SVG) format, which supports more text formats than HTML and may represent text more accurately in certain cases. This example assumes a record in a *Contact table* with a field named *Contact Notes* that contains the same styled text from the previous example.

```
GetAsSVG ( Contact::Contact Notes )
// result =
<stylelist>
<style#0>"font-family: 'Arial';font-size: 18px;color: #FF2712;font-weight:
bold;",begin: 1, end: 4</style>
</stylelist>
<data>
<span style="0">Hello</span>
</data>
```

Modifying Text

There are many functions available for performing text modifications, including changing case, filtering, and substituting characters.

Note   See examples in the "CH13-06 Modifying Text" file.

Changing Case

Three functions, each accepting a single text parameter, change the case of characters to *Upper, Lower,* and *Proper.*

```
Upper ( "Hello, World" )        // result = "HELLO, WORLD"
Upper ( "this is screaming" )   // result = "THIS IS SCREAMING"

Lower ( "Hello, World" )        // result = "hello, world"
Lower ( "THIS IS SCREAMING" )   // result = "this is screaming"

Proper ( "hello, world" )       // result = "Hello, World"
Proper ( "THIS IS SCREAMING" )  // result = "This Is Screaming"
```

Filter

The *Filter* function reduces a text value in the first parameter to only retain characters specified in the second. Any character not specified in the second parameter will be removed from the text provided in the first. These two examples show how to eliminate any nonnumeric values from some input. The first returns an empty string because every character was nonnumeric. The second converts a phone number to only the digits, by filtering out the human-display parenthesis, dashes, and white spaces.

```
Filter ( "Hello World" ; "1234567890" )        // result = ""
Filter ( "(212) 555-1234" ; "1234567890" )     // result = "2125551234"
```

This can quickly extract a number from text. However, the characters which are allowed to remain will be joined together when other characters are removed between them, so the result may not be useful. The first example below successfully extracts a zip code, but the next two return an unintended number result. For situations like this, consider other methods of parsing data out of text (discussed later in this chapter).

```
Filter ( "Las Vegas, NV 89101" ; "1234567890" )        // result = "89101"
Filter ( "1 Hello 2 World 3" ; "1234567890" )          // result = "123"
Filter ( "The price is $5,000.00" ; "1234567890" )     // result = "500000"
Filter ( "The price is $5,000.00" ; "1234567890." )    // result = "5000.00"
Filter ( "The price is $5,000.00" ; "1234567890.$" )   // result = "$5000.00"
```

Note   See *FilterValues* later in this chapter to perform a similar function with entire paragraphs instead of individual characters.

Substitute

The *Substitute* function replaces a search string within a piece of text with a replacement string without affecting the rest of the original text. When specifying one search-replace pair, the function is called with three parameters as shown here.

```
Substitute ( text ; searchString ; replacementString )
```

These examples demonstrate how to make simple replacements where one search value is replaced with one replacement value. In the first, the word "Four" is replaced in the source text with the word "Three." In the second, the question marks are replaced with exclamation points.

```
Substitute ( "One Two Four" ; "Four" ; "Three" )
// result = "One Two Three"

Substitute ( "Hello World? It is good to see you?" ; "?" ; "!" )
// result = "Hello World! It is good to see you!"
```

To specify multiple search-replace pairs in a single statement, each set of strings must be contained within square brackets and separated by a semicolon as shown in the following pattern:

```
Substitute ( text ;
    [ searchString1 ; replacementString1 ] ;
    [ searchString2 ; replacementString2 ] ;
    [ searchString3 ; replacementString3 ]
)
```

The following example demonstrates two search-replace pairs, first replacing "Four" with "Three" and then replacing "Six" with "Four":

```
Substitute (
  "One Two Four Six" ;
  [ "Four" ; "Three" ] ;
  [ "Six" ; "Four" ]
)
// result = "One Two Three Four"
```

These bracketed substitutions occur in series, which can be helpful when cleaning up complex values. To avoid unintentional substitutions, a value can be temporarily changed to preserve it during other substitutions and then be restored later. The example below shows the function replacing single paragraph returns with a space while preserving double paragraph returns. First, the double returns are converted into an arbitrary code and then converted back after the single paragraphs have been substituted with a space.

```
Substitute (
  "Paragraph 1¶¶Paragraph 2¶Paragraph 3" ;
  [ "¶¶" ; "%PP%" ] ;
  [ "¶" ; " " ] ;
  [ "%PP%" ; "¶¶" ]
)
// result =
Paragraph 1¶¶Paragraph 2 Paragraph 3
```

In this example, the result will be the text in the *Notes* field with all carriage returns and tabs removed:

```
Substitute ( Table::Notes ; [ "¶" ; "" ] ; [ "    " ; "" ] )
```

This example shows a quick but crude method of clearing extra space in a piece of text using three substitutions – replacing a quadruple space, triple space, and double space with a single space in succession to ensure that most extra spaces are removed.

This should capture most accidental extra spacing, but when cleaning up text pasted from external systems, like that pasted in from an email or web page, consider a more sophisticated method.

```
Substitute ( Table::Text Field ; [ "    " ; " " ] ; [ "    " ; " " ] ;
[ " " ; " " ] )
```

Tip   To guarantee all extra spaces are removed, repeatedly substitute double spaces with single spaces until none remain using the *While* function (described later in this chapter).

Parsing Text

Several text parsing functions can extract characters or words from the beginning, middle, or end of a text value. These include *Left*, *Right*, *Middle*, *LeftWords*, *RightWords*, and *MiddleWords*.

Note   See examples in the "CH13-07 Parsing Text" file.

Extracting Characters

The *Left* function extracts a specified number of characters from the provided text, starting from the first character on the left. If the number specified is greater than the number of characters in the text provided, the function simply returns the original value.

```
Left ( text ; numberOfCharacters )
Left ( "Hello, World" ; 8 )        // result = "Hello, W"
Left ( "Hello, World" ; 100 )      // result = "Hello, World"
```

The *Right* function extracts a specified number of characters starting from the last character on the right. It will also return the original value if the number specified exceeds the number of characters in the source.

```
Right ( text ; numberOfCharacters )
Right ( "Hello, World" ; 5 )    // result = "World"
Right ( "Hello, World" ; 100 )  // result = "Hello, World"
```

The *Middle* function extracts a specified number of characters from a specified position within a text string. Unlike the Left and Right functions, Middle requires a start parameter indicating where to begin pulling the specified number of characters.

```
Middle ( text ; start ; numberOfCharacters )
```

These examples extract the specified number of characters starting from a specific point.

```
Middle ( "Good Morning Everyone." ; 6 ; 7 )   // result = "Morning"
Middle ( 123456789 ; 4 ; 3 )                  // result = 456
```

Extracting Words

The *LeftWords* function extracts a specified number of words from the text provided, starting from the first word on the left. The words returned will include any space and punctuation that fall within the range specified.

```
LeftWords ( "Hello, World. How are you?" ; 3 )
// result = "Hello, World. How"

LeftWords ( "Hello, World. How are you?" ; 2 )
// result = "Hello, World"
```

The *RightWords* function extracts a specified number of words from the text provided, starting from the last word on the right.

```
RightWords ( "Hello, World. How are you?" ; 3 )  // result = "How are you"
```

The *MiddleWords* function extracts a specified number of words from the text provided, starting from a specified word anywhere in the text provided. The following example extracts two words starting from the third word:

```
MiddleWords ( "Hello World. How are you?" ; 3 ; 2 )   // result = "How are"
```

Working with Values

In FileMaker, a *value* is any single paragraph of return-delimited list of alphanumeric data. There are several functions available for counting, parsing, and manipulating lists of values.

Counting and Parsing Values

Several built-in functions can count and parse values in lists: *ValueCount*, *LeftValues*, *RightValues*, *MiddleValues*, and *GetValue*. Unlike text counting and parsing, these functions work with values, i.e., entire paragraphs.

Note   See examples in the "CH13-08 Count & Parse Values" file.

ValueCount

The *ValueCount* function counts the number of values in the text specified.

```
ValueCount ( "John¶Jane¶Jim¶Joe¶" )    // result = 4
```

LeftValues

The *LeftValues* function extracts a specified number of values from a list, starting from the first value.

```
LeftValues ( "John¶Jane¶Jim¶Joe¶" ; 2 )    // result = "John¶Jane¶"
LeftValues ( "159¶245¶396¶721¶" ; 3 )    // result = "159¶245¶396¶
LeftValues ( "John¶Jane¶Jim¶Joe¶" ; 10 )   // result =
                                   " John¶Jane¶Jim¶Joe¶"
```

RightValues

The *RightValues* function extracts a specified number of values from a list, starting from the last value.

```
RightValues ( "John¶Jane¶Jim¶Joe¶" ; 2 )    // result = "Jim¶Joe¶"
```

MiddleValues

The *MiddleValues* function extracts a number of values specified by the third parameter from a list of values in the first parameter starting from a value specified by the second parameter. In this example, one value is extracted, starting with the second.

```
MiddleValues ( "John¶Jane¶Jim¶Joe¶" ; 2 ; 1 )  // result = "Jane¶"
```

Caution   When extracting values from the left, right, or middle, a carriage return after the last value will be included and may need to be removed prior to using the result with other text functions!

GetValue

The *GetValue* function extracts a single value from a list by numeric position, without a trailing return character. If the number specified is greater than the number of values in the list provided, an empty string will be returned.

```
GetValue ( "John¶Jane¶Jim¶Joe¶" ; 3 )   // result = "Jim"
GetValue ( "159¶245¶396¶721¶" ; 2 )     // result = 245
GetValue ( "John¶Jane¶Jim¶Joe¶" ; 18 )  // result = ""
```

Manipulating Values

A few functions can manipulate values in a list, including *FilterValues*, *SortValues*, and *UniqueValues*.

FilterValues

The *FilterValues* function removes unwanted values from a list, working like *Filter* but for values rather than characters. The function accepts two parameters: *textToFilter* contains the values that will be manipulated, and *filterValues* indicates the desired values that are allowed to remain in the result. The result will be the original text with any values not specified in *filterValues* removed.

```
FilterValues ( textToFilter ; filterValues )
```

Any allowable values that exist more than once in the source will be included in the result in the same order and as many times as they originally appear. Notice how partial paragraph matches are not included in the results. For example, even though "NYC" includes "NY," it is filtered out because this function matches values (entire paragraphs) and not partial *strings*.

```
FilterValues ( "NY¶IN¶OH¶PA¶NY¶IN¶NYC" ; "PA¶NY" )  // result = "NY¶PA¶NY¶"
FilterValues ( "10¶100¶10¶1000" ; "10" )            // result = "10¶10¶"
```

Detecting Values Safely

The *FilterValues* function safely detects a full value match in situations where *PatternCount* would fail when it finds partial pattern matches. This is demonstrated in the two examples below, both checking to see if "age" exists in a list of values. In the first example, *PatternCount* finds three text pattern matches, so it returns a true value even though there is no complete paragraph value match. In the second example, *FilterValues* filters out all three values because none exactly match. So, the second example correctly returns a false result, indicating that a full value of "age" is not present in the list.

```
PatternCount ( "Rage¶Page¶Sage" ; "age" ) > 0     // result = 1
FilterValues ( "Rage¶Page¶Sage" ; "age"  ) ≠ ""   // result = 0
```

SortValues

The *SortValues* function rearranges the order of values in a list based on a specified data type. To sort values as text using the file's default locale, only a single parameter is required, the text to sort. Optional parameters allow specification of a datatype and/or locale. All three varieties are shown here:

```
SortValues ( values )
SortValues ( values ; datatype )
SortValues ( values ; datatype ; locale )
```

The *values* parameter is a list of return-delimited text values to be sorted. The *datatype* parameter is a number from 1 to 5 indicating the data type to use when sorting: 1, text; 2, numeric; 3, date; 4, time; and 5, timestamp. Here, a positive number indicates an ascending sort, while a negative number will sort in descending order. The *locale* parameter indicates one of several dozen locales to use when sorting, e.g., French, Norwegian, Ukrainian, etc. The result of the function will be the list provided rearranged.

```
SortValues ( "New York¶Illinois¶Pennsylvania¶California" )
// result =
    California
    Illinois
    New York
    Pennsylvania
```

These three examples sort the same list of numeric values different ways. The first sorts as text because no *datatype* is specified. The result puts 20 after 100 because "2" sorts alphabetically after "1," and the sort is performed one text character at a time. The second example specifies an ascending numeric sort and the third a descending numeric sort.

```
SortValues ( "100¶10¶200¶20" )        // result = "10¶100¶20¶200"
SortValues ( "100¶10¶200¶20" ; 2 )    // result = "10¶20¶100¶200"
SortValues ( "100¶10¶200¶20" ; -2 )   // result = "200¶100¶20¶10"
```

UniqueValues

The *UniqueValues* function returns a value list with any duplicate values removed. This function also accepts additional *datatype* and *locale* parameters that work the same as *SortValues*.

```
UniqueValues ( values )
UniqueValues ( values ; datatype )
UniqueValues ( values ; datatype ; locale )
```

These examples show the difference between results when treating the data as text (default) or specifying a numeric result. Notice that "10" and "10.0" are treated differently as text but the same when using a numeric datatype.

```
UniqueValues ( "15¶125¶10¶125¶10.0" )       // result = "15¶125¶10¶10.0"
UniqueValues ( "15¶125¶10¶125¶10.0" ; 2 )  // result = "15¶125¶10"
```

As always, functions can be combined by nesting one as the parameter for another. This example shows how to generate a list of results that are both unique and sorted.

```
SortValues ( UniqueValues ( "CA¶NY¶CA¶NY¶VT¶PA¶CA¶VT" ) )
// result = CA¶NY¶PA¶VT
```

Note   Values can be easily converted into a JSON Array (Chapter 14, "Using JSONMakeArray").

Working with Containers

Several built-in functions provide access to information about, extract text from, and read QR codes in a file stored in a container field.

Note   See examples in the "CH13-10 Containers" file.

GetContainerAttribute

The *GetContainerAttribute* function returns an attribute from the metadata of a file stored in a container field (Chapter 10). It accepts two parameters, a *field* and an *attributeName*. There are various attributes available which vary depending on the type of file in the field. Although not an exhaustive list, below are a couple examples of accessing general attributes about a file. See FileMaker's online documentation for a comprehensive list of all attributes available.

```
GetContainerAttribute ( Example Input Source ; "filename" )
// result = Img_1036.jpg

GetContainerAttribute ( Example Input Source ; "storageType" )
// result = Embedded
```

A group of attributes can be retrieved at once by specifying all, general, audio, image, photo, barcode, or signature as the *attributeName*. This example returns the attributes of an image.

```
GetContainerAttribute ( Example Input Source ; "image" )
// result =
Width: 1416
Height: 1930
DPI Width: 144
DPI Height: 144
Transparency: 1 (True)
```

When attributes are retrieved in groups, they always include a label with the value as shown above. Requesting an individual attributes only return the value. Also, some attributes will return a number that indicates a value when retrieved individually and the number with the text explanation of the value in parenthesis. For more details on the values returned, experiment with groups or consult FileMaker's help documentation.

GetLiveText

The *GetLiveText* function, introduced in version 19.5.1, recognizes and extracts any text found in an image stored in a container field. It accepts two parameters, a reference to a *container* and the *language* code to instruct the text-recognition algorithm how to identify the text. See FileMaker's online documentation for a complete list of language codes. The result of this will be a text string containing all the text that was recognized in the container field.

```
GetLiveText ( Example Input Source ; "en-US" )
```

GetLiveTextAsJSON

The *GetLiveTextAsJSON* function, introduced in version 21 (2024), extracts text found in an image stored in a container field like *GetLiveText* but includes the coordinate location of the text in an array as x/y values. This result separates different pieces of text by location making it possible to better discern the correct flow of information or to target by area, excluding text on the fringes.

```
GetLiveText ( Example Input Source ; "en-US" )
// result =
[
    {
        "x": 207,
        "y": 1467,
        "text": "Hello, World"
    }
]
```

Note   For more on the JSON format, see Chapter 14, "Using JSON."

ReadQRCode

The *ReadQRCode* function, introduced in version 19.5, reads a QR code in a container field's image and returns the text value.

```
ReadQRCode ( Example Input Source )
```

Note   FileMaker also provides a set of functions that encode/decode in Base64 and hexadecimal format and perform cryptographic tasks. See the online documentation for details on these.

Introducing Get Functions

Many *Get functions* provide a single piece of information about the computer's system, the user's environment, the current database context, the status of various processes, and more. These can be used to display key information, create conditional formulas that return different results, or perform a task based on some aspect of the current context or situation. They each require a single unchanging parameter, a keyword that indicates the desired information.

```
Get ( <StaticParameter> )
```

Tip   For a complete list of functions and fuller description of those listed here, see FileMaker's online documentation.

Credentials and User Information

These functions get information about the user and their database account credentials (Chapter 29).

```
Get ( UserName )                    // result = Karen Camacho
Get ( AccountName )                 // result = k.camacho
Get ( AccountExtendedPrivileges )   // result = fmapp
```

```
Get ( AccountPrivilegeSetName )        // result = [Full Access]
Get ( AccountGroupName )               // result = dbmarketing
```

OS, Computer, and App

These functions get information about the user's computer and application, or the host computer.

```
Get ( ApplicationArchitecture )  // result = x86_64
Get ( ApplicationLanguage )      // result = English
Get ( ApplicationVersion )       // result = Pro 20.3.2
Get ( HostApplicationVersion )   // result = Server 20.3.2
Get ( HostName )                 // result = DB-Server.local
Get ( HostIPAddress )            // result = 10.0.1.50
Get ( SystemDrive )              // result = Macintosh HD
Get ( SystemIPAddress )          // result = 10.0.1.27
Get ( SystemLanguage )           // result = "English"
Get ( SystemPlatform )           // result = 1
Get ( SystemVersion )            // result = 10.15.5
Get ( SystemLocaleElements )     // result = JSON of locale settings
Get ( FileLocaleElements )       // result = JSON of locale settings
```

Note   For examples of parsing the JSON results from the LocaleElements functions, see Chapter 14, "Parsing Locale Elements."

Records

These functions get information about the records in the table of the layout displayed in the current window. The results shown assume the current layout's table contains 500 records and the user is viewing the 15th record in a found set of 125.

```
Get ( FoundCount )         // result = 125
Get ( TotalRecordCount )   // result = 500
Get ( RecordNumber )       // result = 15
Get ( ActiveRecordNumber ) // result = 15
```

The difference between *RecordNumber* and *ActiveRecordNumber* is subtle and can be confusing but is useful when designing layouts (Chapters 17–21). Formulas used in custom functions, custom menus, and script steps all operate from the context of the current window and will always return the same value for both of these two functions. This is because, from that context, the record number will always be the same as the currently active record number. Alternatively, a formula used on a layout object operates from the context of a record. In that case, the *RecordNumber* will always be different for each record (based on the record's location in the found set), while the *ActiveRecordNumber* will always be the same for the entire found set (the one record in the found set the user has focus on). This can be useful with the *Hide* feature (Chapter 21, "Hiding Objects") where the following formula will hide an object on every record except the current one. To have a specific button or field appear only on the selected record in a list, use this as the object's hide condition.

```
Get ( RecordNumber ) = Get ( ActiveRecordNumber )
```

Layouts

Four functions can access information about the layout displayed in the front window. You can determine the name, number, table name, and view state of the current layout.

```
Get ( LayoutName )           // result = Sandbox - List
Get ( LayoutNumber )         // result = 2
Get ( LayoutTableName )      // result = Sandbox
Get ( LayoutViewState )      // result (Form View)  = 0
                             // result (List View) = 1
                             // result (Table View) = 2
```

Window

Many *Get* functions return window properties and dimensions.

Getting Window Properties

These functions provide information about the frontmost window's name, mode, style, or zoom level.

```
Get ( WindowName )        // result = "Sandbox"
Get ( WindowMode )        // result (Browse)  = 0
                          // result (Find)    = 1
                          // result (Preview) = 2
                          // result (Printing) = 3
                          // result (Layout)  = 4
Get ( WindowStyle )       // result (Document) = 0
                          // result (Floating) = 1
                          // result (Dialog)  = 2
                          // result (Card)    = 3
Get ( WindowZoomLevel )   // result = 100
```

Getting Window Dimensions

Several *Get functions* can access measurement from one of four dimensional domains, as shown in Figure 13-1. These are useful when accessing or changing a window's current position and size with script steps (Chapter 25).

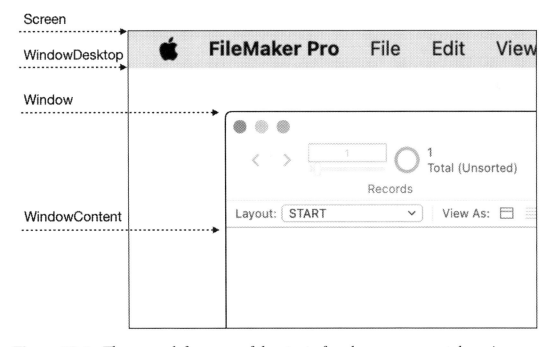

Figure 13-1. *The upper left corner of the start of each measurement domain accessible with Get functions*

Each of the four domains has a *Height* and *Width* function. Because a window can move around the desktop area, it has an additional *Top* and *Left* function.

```
Get ( ScreenHeight )              // result = 1440
Get ( ScreenWidth )               // result = 2560
Get ( WindowDesktopHeight )       // result = 1417
Get ( WindowDesktopWidth )        // result = 2560
Get ( WindowHeight )              // result = 613
Get ( WindowWidth )               // result = 840
Get ( WindowTop )                 // result = 75
Get ( WindowLeft )                // result = 100
Get ( WindowContentHeight )       // result = 492
Get ( WindowContentWidth )        // result = 825
```

Note   See examples in the "CH13-11 Window Dimensions" file.

These functions can be used with the *New Window* and *Move/Resize Window* script steps (Chapter 25, "Managing Windows") to center a window at a specific point on screen. Use them to calculate a new top and left position based on the height and width in relation to the screen dimensions. First, get the center point of the screen in each direction by dividing the height and width in half. Then subtract half of the window's corresponding dimension from those respective measurements. The following formulas calculate these two measurements to center an existing window. When creating a new window, the measurements for the window would need to be manually entered since the window doesn't exist yet.

```
( Get ( ScreenHeight ) / 2 ) - ( Get ( WindowHeight ) / 2 ) // Top
( Get ( ScreenWidth ) / 2 ) - ( Get ( WindowWidth ) / 2 )   // Left
```

Accessing Fields

Any calculation can include field references that directly access field content (Chapter 12, "Field References"). Several functions allow additional access to various meta-information about fields or advanced access to the data contained within.

Discovering Active

Three functions provide currently activity within the interface. Get the name, contents, or table name of whatever field is currently active. This is useful when creating functionality that needs to be aware of the current user's activity to provide responsive and adaptable features.

```
Get ( ActiveFieldName )             // result = Full Name
Get ( ActiveFieldContents )         // result = Mark Munro
Get ( ActiveFieldTableName )        // result = Contacts
```

Converting a Field Reference to Text

A dynamic field reference can be converted into a text reference. Then, you can parse the name of the field or its table.

GetFieldName

The *GetFieldName* function accepts a field reference and returns the entire reference as a string. Despite its name, it actually returns the entire reference as string, including the table occurrence.

```
GetFieldName ( Contact::Name First ) // result = "Contact::Name First"
```

With this result, you can parse the name of the table occurrence and/or field name with the *Substitute* function as shown in the example below.

```
GetValue (
     Substitute (
          GetFieldName ( Contact::Name First );
     "::" ; "¶" ) ;
1 )
// result = Contact
```

In the example above, the occurrence name is the same as the table name. If a related field is used, the result may not include the actual table name.

```
GetFieldName ( Contact | Company::Company Name )
// result "Contact | Company::Company Name"
```

To get the actual table name, use the new *GetBaseTableName* function instead.

Tip   Use this function to keep field references dynamic, especially when building SQL queries (Chapter 35, "Keeping Fields Dynamic in SQL Queries").

GetBaseTableName

The *GetBaseTableName* function, introduced in version 20.1, will return the name of the base table for a field. While the text-based reference returned by the *GetFieldName* function includes the table occurrence for the field, this function returns the actual table name of where the field is defined and requires no additional parsing.

```
GetBaseTableName ( Contact | Company::Company Name ) // result = "Company"
```

The function isn't parsing out some part of the field reference – it is looking at the actual table in which the field resides. This example shows a field in "Staff" which is an occurrence of a table named "Contact." The result isn't part of the field reference – it is the actual name of the table.

```
GetBaseTableName ( Staff::Name ) // result = "Contact"
```

Getting Field Content

There are two built-in functions that return the contents of a field in very specific ways. These are *GetField* and *GetNthRecord*.

GetField

As shown in the last chapter, to access a field's content from a calculation, simply place a dynamic field reference into the formula. However, when you have the name of a field as a text string, it won't be able to access that field's content without being converted into a dynamic reference. The *GetField* function returns the contents of a field based on a *text-based field reference* instead of a *dynamic field* reference (Chapter 35, "Keeping Field References Dynamic"). This is useful when building a field reference dynamically or using a field name stored in a text field or variable. The parameter can be either the name of the field or a full text-based reference to the table and field, with the latter required to access fields in a related table.

```
GetField ( "Contact Name Full" )              // result = Mark Munro
GetField ( "Contact::Contact Name Full" )     // result = Mark Munro
```

Since the function expects a text-based reference, providing a dynamic reference to a field will fail unless that field referenced happens to contain a text reference to another field. For example, if a field named "Referring Field" contains the text "Contact::Contact Name," then the function will accept a dynamic reference to the referring field and use its content to identify the target field and retrieve its content. This is the only instance where the function works as expected with a dynamic reference, as demonstrated in the following three examples. The first passes a text reference to the referring field which returns the actual contents of that field. The second passes a dynamic reference to the referring field so it uses the reference contained inside that field to identify and successfully return the value of the name field. Although the third also passes a dynamic reference, the field referenced contains the name "Mark Munro" which is not a field reference, so it returns an error.

```
GetField ( "Contact::Referring Field" ) // result = Contact::Contact Name
GetField ( Contact::Referring Field )   // result = Mark Munro
GetField ( Contact::Contact Name )      // result = ?
```

Caution   If this sounds confusing, remember that almost every scenario you encounter won't require text-based field references!

GetNthRecord

The *GetNthRecord* function returns the contents of a field from a specified record number within the current found set, even if it's not the current record in focus. The *fieldName* parameter must contain a dynamic reference to a field and the *recordNumber* parameter a numeric position of a record in the found set. This instructs the formula to fetch the value from *this field* for *that record*. This example would return the contents of the *Contact Name Full* field from the fifth record in the found set from the *Contact* table.

```
GetNthRecord ( Contact::Contact Name Full ; 5 )
```

This function can be used with an iterative process to gather information across numerous records in a found set much faster without having to actually navigate to each record one by one. It can also be used to access records through a relationship, scooping up a field value from any record in a portal. To use this on a batch of records in a loop, use the *While* function (this chapter), a recursive custom function (Chapter 15, "Building Recursive Functions"), or a looping script (Chapter 25, "Iterating with Repeating Statements").

Note   See "Compiling a Merged List of Related Records" later in this chapter for an example of *GetNthRecord*.

Getting Selected Text

Two *Get* functions extract the currently selected text within an active field.

- *Get (ActiveSelectionSize)* returns the number of characters selected.

- *Get (ActiveSelectionStart)* returns the character position at which a selection of text within a field begins.

Using these together, a calculation can extract the selection and replace it with another value. The following examples use functions discussed previously in this chapter to demonstrate how to access selection ranges. It assumes a *Contact Notes* field has focus and a portion of the text is currently highlighted. In three different steps, it parses the following:

- The text before the selection

- The selected text

- The text after the selection

Once these three are held in a variable as separate values, the selection can be modified and then reassembled for placement back into the field using a *Set Field* script step (Chapter 25) or further manipulated.

Note   See these examples in the "CH13-12 Selected Text" file.

The *Middle* function uses a reference to the field, the start of the selection, and its size. This example will extract whatever text is selected in the field.

```
Middle (
   Contact::Contact Notes ;
   Get ( ActiveSelectionStart ) ;
   Get ( ActiveSelectionSize )
)
```

The *Left* function can extract characters before the selection by subtracting 1 from the position the selection starts.

```
Left (
   Contact::Contact Notes ;
   Get ( ActiveSelectionStart ) - 1
)
```

The *Right* function extracts the text remaining after the selection by calculating the length of the field's contents and subtracting the position the selection starts, the size of the selection plus 1.

```
Right (
   Contact::Contact Notes ;
   Length ( Contact::Contact Notes ) - Get ( ActiveSelectionStart ) - Get
   ( ActiveSelectionSize) + 1
)
```

Once each of these are stored in *$before, $selection,* and *$after* variable, the data can be used in a variety of ways. For example, to replace the selection with "Hello, World," use the *Set Field* script step to change the contents of the field with the following formula:

```
$before & "Hello, World" & $after
```

Aggregating Data

Each of these Aggregate functions can perform summary and statistical computations on numbers, dates, and times: *Average, Count, List,* and *Sum.* Each function can accept any number parameter values that are literally typed in the formula, stored in variables, or contained in one or more fields. The examples in this section all focus on using fields for parameter input to compare the differences between using a single repeating field or a list of non-repeating, repeating, or related fields. Due to the similarity in behavior and the number of different combinations of input possible, all the examples in this section use the same data as shown in Figure 13-2.

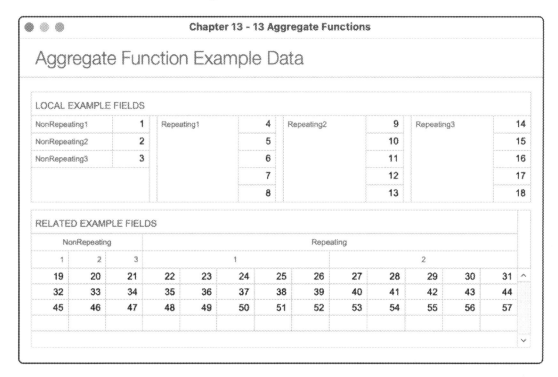

Figure 13-2. *A set of fields, local and related, with simple values that are used for all the examples in this section*

Note   See these examples in the "CH13-13 Aggregating Data" file.

Average

The *Average* function calculates the average of all values in one or more fields. It can accept a single repeating, a single related field, or multiple fields (repeating or not) with a semicolon delimiter.

```
Average ( field )
Average ( field1 ; field2 ; field3 ; etc. )
```

Using the Average Function with Local Fields

A list of *non-repeating local fields* returns the average based on all the values contained within the fields provided:

```
Average ( Example::NonRepeating1 ; Example::NonRepeating2 ;
Example::NonRepeating3 )
// result = 2
```

A *single repeating local field* returns the average based on all the values contained within that field:

```
Average ( Example::Repeating1 )
// result = 6
```

A *list of repeating local fields used in a non-repeating calculation* returns the average based on the first repetition from each field provided:

```
Average ( Example::Repeating1 ; Example::Repeating2 ; Example::Repeating3 )
// result = 9
```

A *list of repeating local fields used in a repeating calculation* returns the average for each repetition of the result based on the corresponding repetition from each field provided:

```
Average ( Example::Repeating1 ; Example::Repeating2 ; Example::Repeating3 )
// repetition 1 = 9
// repetition 2 = 10
// repetition 3 = 11
// repetition 4 = 12
// repetition 5 = 13
```

Using the Average Function with Related Fields

A *single related, non-repeating field* returns the average based on all the values from that field for each record related to the local record performing the calculation:

```
Average ( Related::NonRepeating1 )
// result = 32
```

A *list of related, non-repeating fields* returns the average based on the values from the fields provided for the first related record:

```
Average ( Related::NonRepeating1 ; Related::NonRepeating2 ;
Related::NonRepeating3 )
// result = 20
```

A *single related, repeating field* returns the average based on the values from every repetition from every record related to the local record performing the calculation:

```
Average ( Related::Repeating1 )
// result = 37
```

A *list of related, repeating fields used in a non-repeating calculation* returns the average based on the values from the first repetition of those fields from the first record related to the local record performing the calculation:

```
Average ( Related::Repeating1 ; Related::Repeating2 )
// result = 24.5
```

A *list of related, repeating fields used in a repeating calculation* returns the average based on the values from the corresponding repetition from each field provided from the first record related to the local record performing the calculation:

```
Average ( Related::Repeating1 ; Related::Repeating2 )
// repetition 1 = 24.5
// repetition 2 = 25.5
// repetition 3 = 26.5
// repetition 4 = 27.5
// repetition 5 = 28.5
```

Count

The *Count* function counts the number of values in one or more fields. Although the examples shown here count lists of numeric values, the function will count any type of data type. For example, both "8¶10¶2" and "Mon¶Tues¶Wed" contain three values.

```
Count ( field )
Count ( field1 ; field2 ; field3 ; etc. )
```

Using the Count Function with Local Fields

A *list of non-repeating local fields* returns the total non-blank value count based on all the values contained within the fields provided:

```
Count ( Example::NonRepeating1 ; Example::NonRepeating2 ;
Example::NonRepeating3 )
// result = 3
```

A *single repeating local field* returns the total non-blank value count based on all the values contained within that field:

```
Count ( Example::Repeating1 )
// result = 5
```

A *list of repeating local fields* used in a non-repeating calculation returns the total non-blank value count based on the first repetition from each field provided:

```
Count ( Example::Repeating1 ; Example::Repeating2 ; Example::Repeating3 )
// result = 3
```

A *list of repeating local fields* used in a repeating calculation returns the total non-blank value count for each repetition of the result based on the corresponding repetition from each field provided:

```
Count ( Example::Repeating1 ; Example::Repeating2 ; Example::Repeating3 )
// repetition 1 = 3
// repetition 2 = 3
// repetition 3 = 3
// repetition 4 = 3
// repetition 5 = 3
```

311

Using the Count Function with Related Fields

A single related, non-repeating field returns the total non-blank value count based on all the values from that field for each record related to the local record performing the calculation:

```
Count ( Related::NonRepeating1 )
// result = 3
```

A *list of related, non-repeating fields* returns the total non-blank value count based on the values from the fields provided for the first related record:

```
Count ( Related::NonRepeating1 ; Related::NonRepeating2 ;
Related::NonRepeating3 )
// result = 3
```

A *single related, repeating field* returns the total non-blank value count based on the values from every repetition from every record related to the local record performing the calculation:

```
Count ( Related::Repeating1 )
// result = 15
```

A *list of related, repeating fields used in a non-repeating calculation* returns the total non-blank value count based on the values from the first repetition of those fields from the first record related to the local record performing the calculation:

```
Count ( Related::Repeating1 ; Related::Repeating2 )
// result = 2
```

A *list of related, repeating fields used in a repeating calculation* returns the total non-blank value count based on the values from the corresponding repetition from each field provided from the first record related to the local record performing the calculation:

```
Count ( Related::Repeating1 ; Related::Repeating2 )
// repetition 1 = 2
// repetition 2 = 2
// repetition 3 = 2
// repetition 4 = 2
// repetition 5 = 2
```

List

The *List* function generates a return-delimited list of values for one or more fields, or other values.

```
List ( field )
List ( field1 ; field2 ; field3 ; etc. )
```

Using the List Function with Local Fields

A *list of non-repeating local fields* returns a carriage return-delimited list based on all the values contained within the fields provided:

```
List ( Example::NonRepeating1 ; Example::NonRepeating2 ;
Example::NonRepeating3 )
// result = 1¶2¶3
```

A *single repeating local field* returns a carriage return-delimited list based on all the values contained within that field:

```
List ( Example::Repeating1 )
// result = 4¶5¶6¶7¶8
```

A *list of repeating local fields used in a non-repeating calculation* returns a carriage return-delimited list based on the first repetition from each field provided:

```
List ( Example::Repeating1 ; Example::Repeating2 ; Example::Repeating3 )
// result = 4¶9¶14
```

A *list of repeating local fields used in a repeating calculation* returns a carriage return-delimited list for each repetition of the result based on the corresponding repetition from each field provided:

```
List ( Example::Repeating1 ; Example::Repeating2 ; Example::Repeating3 )
// repetition 1 = 4¶9¶14
// repetition 2 = 5¶10¶15
// repetition 3 = 6¶11¶16
// repetition 4 = 7¶12¶17
// repetition 5 = 8¶13¶18
```

Using the List Function with Related Fields

A *single related, non-repeating field* returns a carriage return-delimited list based on all the values from that field for each record related to the local record performing the calculation:

```
List ( Related::NonRepeating1 )
// result = 19¶32¶45
```

A *list of related, non-repeating fields* returns a carriage return-delimited list based on the values from the fields provided for the first related record:

```
List ( Related::NonRepeating1 ; Related::NonRepeating2 ;
Related::NonRepeating3 )
// result = 19¶20¶21
```

A *single related, repeating field* returns a carriage return-delimited list based on the values from every repetition from every record related to the local record performing the calculation:

```
List ( Related::Repeating1 )
// result = 22¶23¶24¶25¶26¶35¶36¶37¶38¶39¶48¶49¶50¶51¶52
```

A *list of related, repeating fields used in a non-repeating calculation* returns a carriage return-delimited list based on the values from the first repetition of those fields from the first record related to the local record performing the calculation:

```
List ( Related::Repeating1 ; Related::Repeating2 )
// result = 22¶27
```

A *list of related, repeating fields used in a repeating calculation* returns a carriage return-delimited list based on the values from the corresponding repetition from each field provided from the first record related to the local record performing the calculation:

```
List ( Related::Repeating1 ; Related::Repeating2 )
// repetition 1 = 22¶27
// repetition 2 = 23¶28
// repetition 3 = 24¶29
// repetition 4 = 25¶30
// repetition 5 = 26¶31
```

Sum

The *Sum* function adds a series of numbers into a total.

```
Sum ( field )
Sum ( field1 ; field2 ; field3 ; etc. )
```

Using the Sum Function with Local Fields

A *list of non-repeating local fields* returns the sum total based on all the values contained within the fields provided:

```
Sum ( Example::NonRepeating1 ; Example::NonRepeating2 ;
Example::NonRepeating3 )
// result = 6
```

A *single repeating local field* returns the sum total based on all the values contained within that field:

```
Sum ( Example::Repeating1 )
// result = 30
```

A *list of repeating local fields used in a non-repeating calculation* returns the sum total based on the first repetition from each field provided:

```
Sum ( Example::Repeating1 ; Example::Repeating2 ; Example::Repeating3 )
// result = 27
```

A *list of repeating local fields used in a repeating calculation* returns the sum total for each repetition of the result based on the corresponding repetition from each field provided:

```
Sum ( Example::Repeating1 ; Example::Repeating2 ; Example::Repeating3 )
// repetition 1 = 27
// repetition 2 = 30
// repetition 3 = 33
// repetition 4 = 36
// repetition 5 = 39
```

Using the Sum Function with Related Fields

A *single related, non-repeating field* returns the sum total based on all the values from that field for each record related to the local record performing the calculation:

```
Sum ( Related::NonRepeating1 )
// result = 96
```

A *list of related, non-repeating fields* returns the sum total based on the values from the fields provided for the first related record:

```
Sum ( Related::NonRepeating1 ; Related::NonRepeating2 ;
Related::NonRepeating3 )
// result = 60
```

A *single related, repeating field* returns the sum total based on the values from every repetition from every record related to the local record performing the calculation:

```
Sum ( Related::Repeating1 )
// result = 555
```

A *list of related, repeating fields used in a non-repeating calculation* returns the sum total based on the values from the first repetition of those fields from the first record related to the local record performing the calculation:

```
Sum ( Related::Repeating1 ; Related::Repeating2 )
// result = 49
```

A *list of related, repeating fields used in a repeating calculation* returns the sum total based on the values from the corresponding repetition from each field provided from the first record related to the local record performing the calculation:

```
Sum ( Related::Repeating1 ; Related::Repeating2 )
// repetition 1 = 49
// repetition 2 = 51
// repetition 3 = 53
// repetition 4 = 55
// repetition 5 = 57
```

Using Logical Functions

Logical functions use test conditions to produce variable results and perform other evaluative functions. These include four essential functions: *Case, Choose, Let,* and *While.*

Case

The *Case* function evaluates one or more expressions and returns a result corresponding to the first expression that returns a true result. If none of the expressions are true, an optional default result can be included. The function produces a conditional result like nested *if-else* type functions, but it handles multiple statements with less verbiage. At a minimum, the function requires parameters consisting of one *test-result* pair where the *result* is only evaluated and returned if the *test* portion is true. The *test* parameter must contain a text or numeric expression that evaluates to a Boolean. The *result* parameter can be a literal result or an expression that generates any result. This is the statement showing the two required parameters and a literal example that will return a text string if the value of x is greater than 10 or will return and empty value if it is not.

```
Case ( test ; result )
Case ( x > 10 ; "The answer is 10" )
```

Any number of additional test conditions can be added, and each will be evaluated in order until one evaluates true and causes the corresponding result to be returned. Think of this as follows: if *test* is true, then return *result*; otherwise, if *test2* is true, then return *result2*; otherwise if *test3* is true, then return *result3*; etc.

```
Case ( test ; result ; test2 ; result2 )
Case ( test ; result ; test2 ; result2 ; test3 ; result3 )
```

A final, untested default result can be included at the end to serve as the result when no prior test conditions produce a true result. If no default is provided, the result will be nothing when all tests are false. In this example, if the *test* and *test2* conditions are both false, the result will be whatever is produced by the *defaultResult* statement.

```
Case ( test ; result ; test2 ; result2 ; defaultResult )
```

As these statements grow, consider indenting and adding carriage returns to reformat them vertically, putting each test-result pair on its own line and making the statement easier to read and follow the logical execution of tests. Indentations can be achieved by typing spaces or inserting a tab character by holding Option key while typing a tab (macOS).

```
Case (
    test ; result ;
    test2 ; result2 ;
    test3 ; result3 ;
    test4 ; result4 ;
    defaultResult
)
```

Note   See examples in the "CH13-14 Case" file.

You will find countless uses for the *Case* statement. This example builds a sentence and uses it to optionally pluralize the word "widget" if the value in the Qty field is greater than 1.

```
"Enclosed find " & Qty & " widget" & Case ( Qty > 1 ; "s" ) & " for
inspection."
// result examples (varying by Qty) =
// Enclosed find 1 widget for inspection.
// Enclosed find 8 widgets for inspection.
```

In this example, a field named *Elapsed* contains the number of days an invoice is past due and generates one of four different text results indicating its status. If the value is 32, the result will be "Past Due" because the first two tests were false and the third was true. Similarly, a value of 64 will result in "Delinquent," while a value of 20 will receive the "On Time" default result.

```
Case (
    Elapsed > 90 ; "Severe" ;
    Elapsed > 60 ; "Delinquent" ;
    Elapsed > 30 ; "Past Due" ;
    "On Time"
)
```

Note   An *If* function is the same as *Case* except it requires nesting to handle more than one test-result pair and is considered obsolete.

Choose

The *Choose* function evaluates a single test condition to generate an integer and uses that number to select from a list of one or more result values. The *test* parameter must contain a text or numeric expression that evaluates to an integer. Any number of *result* parameters can be included and will be returned based on the number generated by the test. The results can be literal values or expressions that evaluate to any data result. The indexing of results is zero-based, so the first result listed will be returned if the test evaluates to a 0, the second result for a 1, etc.

```
Choose ( test ; result0 ; result1 ; result2 ; result3 )
```

Note   See examples in the "CH13-15 Choose" file.

In this example, a *Status* field contains a number from 0 to 4, and the *Choose* function is used to convert this into a textual status.

```
Choose ( Status ; "Low" ; "Guarded" ; "Elevated" ; "High" ; "Severe" )
```

This example uses a random number to pick one of four names. The test formula is first evaluated to select a random number between 0 and 4 which is then used to select one of the names.

```
Choose ( Random * 4 ; "Jim Thomas" ; "Shannon Miller" ; "Charlene Smith" ;
"Karen Camacho" )
```

Choose can be an alternative to *Case* when the result choices are selected by a variable numeric result from the same test.

Let

The *Let* function initializes one or more variables prior to performing a calculation statement to produce a result. It allows key information to be calculated and inserted into variables that are declared and initialized just prior to the evaluation of a calculation formula. The function accepts two expressions as parameters, a *variable declaration* and *calculation formula*. Think of this function as saying "Let *these variables* be initialized with *these values*, and then perform *this calculation*."

```
Let ( variables ; calculation )
```

The *variables* parameter is made up of one or more variable declarations. Each of these declares a variable name with a corresponding expression that produces the result to be inserted into the variable. The *variable expression* can include literal text, a field reference, or a formula of varying complexity. The formula can include calls to one or more built-in or custom functions. The variable name is declared on the left followed by an equal sign and the expression. Although the function is primarily used for declaring variables for use within the statement's calculation parameter, variables initialized here can be any type: *statement*, *local*, or *global* (Chapter 12, "Variable").

```
Let ( variable = expression ; calculation )
```

The *calculation* parameter can be any expression. This formula can use the variables declared before it and will produce the result of the overall statement. The example below shows the most basic form of the statement, with a single variable declared and initialized to the result of an expression prior to a calculation formula being evaluated.

```
Let ( variable = expression ; calculation )
```

When initializing more than one variable, square brackets must be added around the declaration parameter and a semicolon between each variable-expression pair. This shows the form of a statement declaring three variables.

```
Let ( [
   variable1 = expression1 ;
   variable2 = expression2 ;
   variable3 = expression3
] ;
   calculation
)
```

Note   See examples in the "CH13-16 Let" file.

This simple example shows a *Let* statement that sets three variables and then uses them all in the calculation formula. It sets a *taxRate* variable to a static amount and then pulls a *quantity* and *unitPrice* from corresponding fields. The three are used to create a total price for the current line item by multiplying the quantity times the unit price and then multiplying that result times the tax rate.

```
Let ( [
    taxRate = .0875 ;
    quantity = Invoice Line Item::Quantity ;
    unitPrice = Invoice Line Item::Price ;
    total = quantity * unitPrice
] ;
    total + Round ( total * taxRate ; 2 )
)
```

The *Let* function is arguably the most useful function in FileMaker. Beyond the ability to declare variables immediately prior to using them, it is incredibly useful when constructing complex formulas. It can eliminate redundancy and make the formula's logical steps easier to read, troubleshoot, and edit. For example, a field reference can be compressed into short variable name and used multiple times in a formula. Also, a lengthy formula can be broken down into a sequence of smaller steps, each producing a part of a final value and making it available for the next step. In the example below which does not use a *Let* statement, a reference to a *Contact::Contact Last Name* field is used in a *Case* statement several times, each time repeating the full field reference. The name is first checked and returns a missing name result if empty. Then, as a default condition, the name is parsed into a folder path suffix where the first character is a folder, the first three characters is a folder, and finally the last name is a folder. So the result if a name is found will be "M:Mun:Munro:" if the last name field contains "Munro."

```
Case (
    Contact::Contact Last Name = "" ; "Missing Name:" ;
    Left ( Contact::Contact Last Name ; 1 ) & ":" &
    Left ( Contact::Contact Last Name ; 3 ) & ":" &
    Contact::Contact Last Name & ":"
)
```

A *Let* statement can place the field's value into a short variable name which can then be used in its place throughout the formula. This example only accesses the field's value one time by placing its content into the *last* variable. The *Case* statement remains the same except all field references have been replaced with the variable.

```
Let (
   last = Contact::Contact Last Name
;
   Case (
      last = "" ; "Missing Name:" ;
      Left ( last ; 1 ) & ":" &
      Left ( last; 3 ) & ":" &
      last & ":"
   )
)
```

Using a Cascading Declaration Sequence

Another use for *Let* is to break down a complex nested statement into a more readable format. Do this with a "cascading declaration" which uses the same variable several times to gradually establish a value over a sequence of steps. In the following example, four functions are nested in a single line making even this short formula difficult to read. Working from the inside out, this example does the following:

- Get content from a *Notes* field.

- Extract the first paragraph from this using the *GetValue* function.

- Eliminate all formatting with the *TextFormatRemove* function.

- Replace dashes with periods using the *Substitute* function.

  ```
  Substitute ( TextFormatRemove ( GetValue ( Contact::
  Notes ; 1 ) ) ; "-" ; "." )
  ```

Instead of vertically nesting all of these functions in a single line, this example separates each step into a separate variable declaration in a *Let* statement. Since it is building a single result in steps, the same variable name can be used, with each step making a small change and replacing the previous value in a downward cascading flow.

```
Let ( [
    note = Contact::Notes ;
    note = GetValue ( note ; 1 ) ;
    note = TextFormatRemove ( note ) ;
    note = Substitute ( note ; "-" ; "." )
] ;
    note
)
```

This technique isn't necessarily the best for every situation. Sometimes adding returns and tabs to spread out a nested formula would be a simpler solution. However, with more complex statements, this technique becomes more obviously superior. The next example below performs a longer sequence of text cleanup and assembly steps. Observe how easy it is to read step by step compared to what this would look like in a single nested statement.

```
Let ( [
    tab = "      " ;
    line = "-------------------------" ;
    intro = "The following summarizes our last conversation:" ;
    name = Contact::Contact Name ;
    note = Contact::Contact Notes ;
    note = TextSizeRemove ( note ) ;
    note = TextFontRemove ( note ) ;
    note = TextColorRemove ( note ) ;
    note = Substitute ( note ;
        [ tab & "•" & tab ; "• " ] ;
        [ tab & "•" ; "• " ] ;
        [ "•" & tab ; "• " ] ;
        [ tab & "○" & tab ; "• " ] ;
        [ tab & "○" ; "• " ] ;
        [ "○" & tab ; "• " ] ;
        [ "¶¶" ; "¶" ]
    ) ;
```

```
  note = Case ( note ≠ "" ; List ( line ; note ; line ) ) ;
  note = List ( name & "," ; intro ; note )
] ;
  note
)
```

While

The *While* function is a complex statement that repeats a sequence of logic variables, while a specified condition is true. This shows the form of the statement and its four parameters.

```
While (
[
   initialVariable
] ;
   condition ;
[
   logicVariables
] ;
   result
)
```

Tip   Think of this function as a *Let* statement that repeats.

The *initialVariable* parameter allows one or more variables to be declared and initialized for the statement, the same as in a *Let* statement. These are enclosed in brackets and have variable name-expression pairs, separated by an equal sign. A semicolon separates each variable-expression set from others. This shows the expanded form of the statement with three variables declared.

```
While (
[
   variable1 = expression1 ;
   variable2 = expression2 ;
```

```
    variable3 = expression3
] ;
    condition ;
[
    logicVariables
] ;
    result
)
```

The *condition* parameter is a Boolean expression that controls the looping action. If the result is *true* and the maximum number of allowable iterations hasn't been reached, the function will repeat the logical steps. The default iteration limit is 50,000 loops, but this can be controlled with the *SetRecursion* function (Chapter 15, "Controlling Recursion Limits"). The conditioning formula can be as simple as checking a counter variable that increments once per loop or a more sophisticated formula that checks several different properties of one or more variables.

The *logicVariables* parameter is another set of variable declarations that will be repeated until the function terminates. These are structured like the *initialVariables*, as shown in the example below with one logic variable joined by an example counter increment. This will repeat ten times, adding a random number to the *result* variable each time until returning the list at the end.

```
While (
[
    result = "" ;
    counter = 0
] ;
    counter < 10 ;
[
    result = List ( result ; Random * 10 ) ;
    counter = counter + 1
] ;
    result
)
```

The *result* parameter is an expression that generates the result of the statement. The formula here can include values set in any of the *initial variables* or *logic variables*.

Any of the expressions in the initial variables, condition formula, logic variables, and result formula can include field repetitions, literal text, function calls, and more. Let's work through a few examples to further illustrate this powerful function.

Removing Double Spaces with a While Statement

To demonstrate the basic structure of a *While* statement, create an example that will remove every extra space between words in a piece of text. Using a repeating function ensures that all extra spaces are removed without the need to specify double, triple, quadruple, etc. spaces. While a double space remains in the text, the function will repeat and remove it. Since we only focus on replacing a double space with a single space, a triple space will require two loops to correct and a quadruple three. This code will clean all the double spaces out of text from an example input field.

```
While (
   [
      data = Example 01 Input
   ] ;
      PatternCount ( data ; "  " ) > 0 ;
   [
      data = Substitute ( data ; "  " ; " " )
   ] ;
      data
)
```

Note   See the "CH13-17 Clean Double Space" example file.

First, a *data* variable is initialized to the contents of a field. Next, a *condition* is established that will cause the function to repeat if *data* contains any double spaces. It uses the *PatternCount* function to determine if the number of double spaces in *data* is greater than zero. One logic variable reinitializes the *data* variable, using the *Substitute* function to replace double spaces with a single space. This will continue looping until there are no double spaces remaining and then the *data* variable becomes the result. When finished, the statement returns the original field contents without any extra spaces.

Place this formula into an auto-enter calculation (Chapter 8, "Field Options: Auto-Enter") that uses the *replace an existing value* option to have any double spaces typed into the field automatically removed when the user exits the field.

Alternatively, create a custom function (Chapter 15) to automatically clean text from any field. A function parameter accepts any field and will return the cleaned text. The field's auto-enter calculation calls the function instead of having its own copy of the formula. This allows the same formula to be reused efficiently throughout your database.

Compiling a Merged List of Related Records

To continue exploring the function, this example will create a merged list of two fields extracted from any number of related records. If run from a *Company* record that has a relationship to *Contacts*, it pulls a list of names and titles from the related records and merges these values together to form a single contact list. In other words, a list of return-delimited *names* and a list of return-delimited *titles* become a return-delimited list of "name title" for all related records. First, we setup the *initial variables*.

```
While (
[
    names = List ( Company | Contact::Contact Name Full ) ;
    titles = List ( Company | Contact::Contact Title ) ;
    total = ValueCount ( names ) ;
    current = 1 ;
    result = ""
] ;
```

Note   See the "CH13-18 Compile Related" example file.

The *List* function is used to initialize two variables, one with a list of related contact names and the other with a list of related contact titles. The *ValueCount* function counts the number of names and puts that into a *total* variable. A *current* variable is initialized to 1 and will be compared to *total* as the condition that controls how many loops to perform. Then a *result* variable is initialized to an empty string. This is where we will build the output result.

Now, the *condition* is set to repeat while the *current* value is less than or equal to the *total* of values – the logical variables will be repeated.

```
total ≥ current ;
```

The *logic variables* begin with an *entry* variable set to the current name and title with a space between them. This uses the *GetValue* function and the *current* variable to pull the next name from each list. The *result* variable is reinitialized with the *List* function to add the *current* entry value to the list of previous results that have been compiled on past iterations. Finally, the *current* variable has 1 added to itself to indicate which iteration we are on and help control when the loop terminates.

```
[
  entry =
    GetValue ( names ; current ) & " " &
    GetValue ( titles; current ) ;
  result = List ( result ; entry ) ;
  current = current + 1
] ;
```

Finally, the result formula is simply returning the *result* variable which contains the accumulated values. Putting all these pieces together gives us the following formula.

```
While (
 [
   names = List ( Company | Contact::Contact Name ) ;
   titles = List ( Company | Contact::Contact Title ) ;
   total = ValueCount ( names ) ;
   current = 1 ;
   result = ""
] ;
   total ≥ current ;
[
   entry =
     GetValue ( names ; current ) & " " &
     GetValue ( titles; current ) ;
   result = List ( result ; entry ) ;
```

```
    current = current + 1
] ;
    result
)
```

Remember that the *List* function always excludes blank values! If one related record in the preceding example is missing a value in one of the two fields, the merged results will be mismatched for every subsequent record. Only use this method if certain both fields always have a value. Instead, consider using *GetNthRecord* to pull values one by one as shown in this example.

```
While (
 [
   total = Count ( Company | Contact::Record Primary ID ) ;
   current = 1 ;
   result = ""
] ;
   total ≥ current ;
[
   entry =
     GetNthRecord ( Company | Contact::Contact Name ; current ) & " " &
     GetNthRecord ( Company | Contact::Contact Title ; current );
   result = List ( result ; entry ) ;
   current = current + 1
] ;
   result
)
```

In this example, the *Count* function is used to count the number of related records. Then, when initializing the *entry* variable, the *GetNthRecord* will pull fields from the next related record, controlled by the *current* variable.

Compiling a List from Local Records

The *GetNthRecord* function can also be used in a *While* statement to gather a list of values in a field from every record in the local found set. Instead of pulling fields through a relationship, this example gets the *Record Primary ID* from every record in the current found set. A *fieldID* variable is set to contain a reference to the *Record Primary ID* field. The *Get (FoundCount)* function sets the *number* variable to the count of records the user is viewing. A *Case* statement is used to adjust the number to 50,000 if the number of records in the found set is greater than that. With the *result* initialized to an empty string, the *condition* takes over and begins to process records, starting from the bottom of the list, working to the top, stopping at record 1. Each iteration will get the record in the found set indicated by the *number* variable using the *GetNthRecord* function and add it to the result with the *List* function.

```
While (
[
   fieldID = Sandbox::Record Primary ID ;
   number = Get ( FoundCount ) ;
   number =
      Case (
          number > 50000 ; 50000 ;
          number
      ) ;
   result = ""
] ;
   number > 0 ;
[
   result = List ( GetNthRecord ( fieldID; number ) ; result ) ;
   number = number - 1
] ;
   result
)
```

Note   See the "CH13-18 Compile Local" example file.

The next example below expands on the last but also pulls the company name. The results will be the company name followed by a space and the ID in parenthesis.

```
While (
[
   fieldID = Record Primary ID ;
```

```
    fieldName = Company Name ;
    number = Get ( FoundCount ) ;
    number =
        Case (
        number > 50000 ; 50000 ;
        number
    ) ;
    result = ""
] ;
    number > 0 ;
[
    entry =
        GetNthRecord ( fieldName ; number ) &
        " (" & GetNthRecord ( fieldID ; number ) & ")" ;
    result = List ( entry ; result ) ;
    number = number - 1
] ;
    result
)
```

Introducing Iterative Reduction

Take a moment to consider how the last two examples are different from previous examples. They both use an *iterative reduction* to track the current record and control the loop condition with a single variable. Instead of using a *total* and *current* variable, the *number* variable controls both the *condition* and identifies the current record we are extracting. It starts as the number of records in the found set which is reduced by 1 after each iteration until it reaches 0 and the condition stops the function. This is a great technique to lower the number of control variables required to manage the loop. Because this technique works backward through the found set from the last record to the first, the method for adding the current value to the *result* variable must be reversed. The other examples used *List* to add the current value after the previous result – this uses it to add the result after the new value.

Nesting Functions into Complex Statements

Built-in functions can be combined and nested to create statements as complex as necessary to produce a desired result. The examples in this section demonstrate the move from simple statements to more complex by combining various functions and statements into a single calculation formula.

Creating a Record Metadata String

This example uses a record's ID, creation, and modification fields to construct a string summarizing the metadata for a record. For now, we will create a calculation field in each table of the *Sandbox* file named *Record Metadata* which can be placed on the bottom of layouts.

Note   See the "CH13-20 Record Metadata" example file.

The formula is made up of one *Let* statement which pulls values from five metadata fields. The creation and modification timestamps are converted into a short date format with leading zeros for the month and day ("02.15.2024") and each placed into a variable. Finally, the result concatenates all this together into the final string that shows the record ID, as well as the date and user who created and modified the record.

```
Let ( [
  id = Record ID ;
  creator = Record Creation User ;
  created = Record Creation Timestamp ;
  modifier = Record Modification User ;
  modified = Record Modification Timestamp ;
  creation =
    Right ( "0" & Month ( created ) ; 2 ) & "." &
    Right ( "0" & Day ( created ) ; 2 ) & "." &
    Year ( created ) ;
  modification =
    Right ( "0" & Month ( modified) ; 2 ) & "." &
    Right ( "0" & Day ( modified) ; 2 ) & "." &
    Year ( modified)
```

```
] ;
   "ID " & id & " | " &
   "Created on " & creation & " by " & creator & " | " &
   "Modified on " & modification & " by " & modifier
)
// result = ID 55326 | Created on 07.01.2020 by Admin | Modified on
07.01.2020 by Admin
```

This formula can be displayed on a layout as a field, a *layout calculation,* a *formula-named object* like a *button bar,* or a *merge field* (Chapter 20).

Creating a Record Count String

For some solutions, you may want to automatically hide and lock the window toolbar with a script (Chapter 25) and employ custom menus (Chapter 23) to exert tighter control over what features a user can access. However, then your interface must provide custom access to information and features you want them to have that are now hidden. If your interface provides custom navigation buttons, it will need to also display information about the found set and current record.

Although not excessively complex, the example below creates a record string with a *Let* and *Case* statement combined with a few *Get* functions. It accesses at the record counts (total and found) and active record number and builds a text string that displays the information in a displayable format. The result is a sentence that shows the record number they are viewing, the total record count, and, if not viewing all records, the number of records in the current found set.

Note   See the "CH13-21 Record Count" example file.

```
Let ( [
   total = Get ( TotalRecordCount ) ;
   found = Get ( FoundCount ) ;
   current = Get ( ActiveRecordNumber )
] ;
```

```
  "Record " & current & " of " & found &
  Case ( found ≠ total ; " Found ( " & total & " Total )" )
)
// result (viewing all)        = Record 2 of 6
// result (viewing found set)  = Record 2 of 4 Found ( 6 Total )
```

The *Let* statement first places the total record count, found count, and active record number into three variables. These are then used to construct a short sentence by concatenating some elements of literal text with those variables. The *Case* statement handles alternative text depending on if the user is viewing all records or not. If viewing a found set, it states the record viewed out of the found count and then includes the total count in parenthesis.

Like the record metadata string example that preceded it, this formula can be displayed on a layout various ways, including as a field, a *layout calculation,* a *formula-named object* like a *button bar*, or a *merge field* (Chapter 20).

Caution   When using the preceding example as a calculation field formula, turn indexing off under *Storage Options* to ensure it refreshes properly!

Creating a Time Elapsed Sentence

The next example creates a sentence that expressed an amount of time elapsed. When provided a start and end timestamp from a field, variable, or other source, this formula converts the time difference between the two into a sentence staying the days, hours, minutes, and seconds elapsed. It uses *Let, Substitute, Case,* and a few other built-in functions.

Note   See this example in the "CH13-22 Time Elapsed" file.

The *Let* statement starts by initializing a *start* and *end* timestamp. These are shown as static text converted to timestamps; however, one or both values could be extracted from fields, variables, or another source. These two are subtracted from each other, and the resulting number of seconds is placed into the *elapsed* variable. Then, it begins a sequence of steps that repeat a similar patter to determine the number of *days, hours, minutes,* and *seconds* elapsed. Each step first divides the elapsed time by the divisor appropriate, e.g., dividing seconds by 86400 and extracting the integer determine the number of days elapsed. Then, the number of days is multiplied by this same number, and that is subtracted from the elapsed time to prepare for the next step in the sequence.

```
Let ( [
 start = GetAsTimestamp ( "8/1/2021 10:00 AM" ) ;
 end = GetAsTimestamp ( "8/2/2021 11:15:10 AM" ) ;
 elapsed = GetAsNumber ( end - start ) ;
 days = Int ( elapsed / 86400 ) ;
 elapsed = elapsed - ( days * 86400 ) ;
 hours = Int ( elapsed / 3600 ) ;
 elapsed = elapsed - ( hours * 3600 ) ;
 minutes = Int ( elapsed / 60 );
 elapsed = elapsed - ( minutes * 60 ) ;
 seconds = Int ( elapsed ) ;
 result =
  List (
   Case ( days ≠ 0 ; days & " day" & Case ( days > 1 ; "s" ) ) ;
   Case ( hours ≠ 0 ; hours & " hour" & Case ( hours > 1 ; "s" ) ) ;
   Case ( minutes ≠ 0 ; minutes & " minute" & Case ( minutes > 1 ; "s" ) ) ;
   Case ( seconds ≠ 0 ; seconds & " second" & Case ( seconds > 1 ; "s" ) )
  )
] ;
   Substitute ( result ; "¶" ; ", ")
))
// result = 1 day, 1 hour, 15 minutes, 10 seconds
```

Once the *days, hours, minutes,* and *seconds* variables are calculated, a *result* variable is initialized to contain a list of each segment in text form. Four *Case* statements check if each variable is not zero and creates one portion of the result. If *days* is not zero, the number of days is concatenated with a literal text string, a space, and the word "day." A second *Case* statement concatenates an "s" at the end to pluralize the result if the number in *days* is greater than 1. This can be read "if *days* is not zero, then display the number, a space, the word 'day' and, if days is greater than one, also an 's'." If included, it constructs a sentence segment with a conditional suffix, e.g., "1 day" or "10 days."

After each of the four *Case* statements are evaluated, one for one time element, the values are placed into the *result* variable using the *List* function. This creates a return-delimited list of segments like the following:

```
1 day
1 hour
15 minutes
10 seconds
```

Since *List* automatically excludes any empty values, if one or more of these segments are empty because of a zero value, it will be excluded without leaving an extra, empty paragraph in the list. For example, if the *start* and *end* times are exactly 1 hour and 10 seconds apart, the *result* variable will only include two paragraphs.

```
1 hour
10 seconds
```

Finally, in the calculation portion of the *Let* statement, the *result* variable is converted from a return-delimited value list to a comma-space-delimited sentence using *Substitute.*

Converting a Number to a Sentence

The next example converts a number representing a number of years into a sentence, e.g., it will convert "124" into "One Hundred Twenty Four Years." This is done in a *Let* statement that uses *Case, Choose,* and a few other functions.

Note   See this example in the "CH13-23 Number Sentence" file.

The *Let* statement declares four variables. A number is pulled from a field and placed into an *n* variable. This number is then split into three digits using the *Mod* and *Int* functions. So, if the input number is 156, then *a* is set to 6, *b* set to 5, and *c* set to 1. These numbers will be used in the calculation with *Case* and *Choose* statements to select the appropriate text components which are concatenated together to build the words representing the number.

```
Let ( [
 n = Sandbox::Example 01 Input ;
```

```
 a = Mod ( n ; 10 ) ;
 b = Int ( Mod ( n ; 100 ) / 10 ) ;
 c = Int ( n / 100 )
] ;
 Case ( c > 0 ; Choose( c ; ""; "One"; "Two"; "Three"; "Four"; "Five";
"Six"; "Seven"; "Eight"; "Nine" ) & " Hundred " ) &

 Case ( b > 1 ; Choose( b ; ""; ""; "Twenty "; "Thirty "; "Forty ";
"Fifty "; "Sixty "; "Seventy "; "Eighty "; "Ninety ") ) &

 Case ( a > 0 and b ≠ 1 ; Choose( a ; ""; "One "; "Two "; "Three ";
"Four "; "Five "; "Six "; "Seven "; "Eight "; "Nine ") ) &

 Case ( b = 1 ; Choose( a ; "Ten "; "Eleven "; "Twelve "; "Thirteen
"; "Fourteen "; "Fifteen "; "Sixteen "; "Seventeen "; "Eighteen ";
"Nineteen ") ) &

 "Year" & Case ( n > 1 ; "s" )
)
// result = "One Hundred Fifty Six Years"
```

Summary

This chapter discussed many useful built-in functions and how they can be used together to form complex formulas. Remember that FileMaker has over 300 built-in functions that are useful when writing formulas. More of these will be mentioned in the forthcoming chapters, and all are described in the online help guide accessible from the hint at the bottom of the *Functions* pane in the *Specify Calculation* dialog. In the next chapter, we will continue our exploration of built-in functions looking at the *JavaScript Object Notation* (JSON) functions.

CHAPTER 14

Using JSON

JavaScript Object Notation (JSON) is an open-standard, lightweight, data-interchange format originally specified by Douglas Crockford in 2000, standardized in 2013, and finalized to its current version in 2017. It was derived from the JavaScript programming language to fulfil a need for a language-independent, real-time, server-to-browser exchange protocol that didn't require plug-ins. In JSON, objects are formatted using a relatively simple key/value pair structure that is easy for humans and machines to read and write. As a result, it has become popular with *Representational State Transfer* (REST) web services as an indispensable tool for a variety of data exchanges. In version 16, FileMaker introduced a set of built-in functions that are used to create and manipulate JSON data. Developers quickly adopted these as a means of exchanging data with external systems and facilitating a more efficient method of exchanging data between scripts. Today, JSON is an indispensable tool for sending, receiving, manipulating, and storing complex data. This chapter introduces JSON, covering the following topics:

- Defining the JSON format
- Creating JSON
- Parsing JSON
- Manipulating JSON
- Handling errors

Introducing the JSON Format

The JSON format involves two primary types: *JSONObject* and *JSONArray*.

Defining a JSONObject

A *JSONObject* is a bracketed list of data elements. An *element* is a combination of an identifying *key* and an associated *value*. Similar structures are referred to by many terms in other programming languages, including *array*, *dictionary*, hash *table*, keyed *list*, *record*, and *struct*.

```
{"key":value}
```

The *key* is a text string that acts like a label, naming and identifying the element. An element's *value* contains some data content that is one of the following types:

1. *JSONString* – A text string

2. *JSONNumber* – A numeric value

3. *JSONBoolean* – A true or false value

4. *JSONArray* – An ordered list of comma-separated values contained within square brackets

5. *JSONObject* – A JSON object nested in the element of a parent object (or the parent object itself)

6. *JSONNull* – A null value

0. *JSONRaw* – A value that will be determined by the JSON parser

---

Note   A JSON value type can be specified by name or the associated number in the list above.

A JSONObject with a single element containing an identification number is formatted with a label in quotes, a colon followed by the value, enclosed in curly brackets. Here the key's value is a *JSONNumber*:

```
{"id":5103}
```

In this example, the value contains *JSONText*, a person's first name:

```
{"First":"John"}
```

A *multielement object* uses a comma to separate each uniquely named element. For example, this object contains data about a person with elements for *id*, *first name*, *last name*, and *title*:

```
{"id":5103,"First":"John","Last":"Smith","Title":"Chief Technology
Officer"}
```

Any extra spaces around the elements will be ignored, so the preceding example is considered identical to this multiline format example:

```
{
   "id" : 5103,
   "First" : "John",
   "Last" : "Smith",
   "Title" : "Chief Technology Officer"
}
```

The value of an element can be another object, creating a nested hierarchy of objects. This example shows an object with two product elements (*Product1*, *Product2*) each containing a nested *JSONObject* of product metadata:

```
{
   "Product1":{"name":"Widget 1","price":39.99,"vendor":15},
   "Product2":{"name":"Widget 2","price":55.48,"vendor":38}
}
```

Defining a JSONArray

A *JSONArray* is a type of object that contains a list of unlabeled values separated by commas and enclosed in square brackets. Arrays don't have explicit key labels, relying instead on an implied *zero-based numeric index* indicating each value's position starting with 0 as the first position. The following example is of an array of numbers:

```
[1,2,3,4,5]
```

An array can contain other data types, including text as shown in this example:

```
["Karen","Charlene","Jeff","Susan","Howard"]
```

An array can be the value of a JSONObject, as shown here where the *friends* and *colleagues* elements are an array containing a list of names.

```
{
    "friends":["Dan","Brian","Carolyn","Karen","Walker"],
    "colleagues":["Brian","Michael","Mary","Nadya"]
}
```

Similarly, arrays can contain objects. This example shows an array of two items, one object with two *Product* elements and another object with two *Employee* elements:

```
[
    {"Product1":"Widget 1","Product2":"Widget 2"},
    {"Employee1":"William"," Employee2":"Janice"}
]
```

External systems will provide data in a JSON format defined by them, which you will have to learn in order to manipulate. However, when creating JSON in FileMaker, the structure of an object can be whatever you define. Any number of objects, arrays, and data types can be mixed and matched, joined, or nested, using custom labels to create a unique structure based on the requirements of your database.

Setting Elements

FileMaker provides two built-in functions that can create JSON: *JSONSetElement* and *JSONMakeArray*.

Using JSONSetElement

The *JSONSetElement* function will set the value of one or more elements in a new or existing object. The function call has four parameters, defined here:

```
JSONSetElement ( json ; keyOrIndexOrPath ; value ; type )
```

- *json* – Can contain an existing object or array. It can be left an empty string when creating JSON.

- *keyOrIndexOrPath* – A *name, array index,* or *path* that identifies
  the element to be set. If the element already exists, its value will be
  replaced. If not, it will be created.

- *value* – The new value for the element being set.

- *type* – An optional specification of a data type for the value. If it is
  an empty string, FileMaker will use the first character of the value to
  determine a type which may not be accurate.

The results will be either a new or modified JSON object or JSON array. Let's explore
the difference between setting an element by *key, array index,* or *path*.

Note   See the "CH14-01 JSONSetElement" example file.

Setting an Element by Key

To set an element by key, provide a name for the key and a corresponding value. The
following example creates a simple object with a *name* element:

```
JSONSetElement ( "" ; "name" ; "First Class Widgets"; "" )
// Result = {"name":"First Class Widgets"}
```

Tip   Instead of an empty string, set the *json* parameter to "{}" or "[]" to ensure the
result is an object or array.

In the *Let* statement below, the preceding result is placed into a variable named
data, and that value is provided as the *json* parameter for a subsequent *JSONSetElement*
call. This provides an example of adding a new element to an existing object, in this case
a *category* element:

```
Let ( [
   data = JSONSetElement ( "" ; "name" ; "First Class Widgets"; "" )
] ;
   JSONSetElement ( data ; "category" ; "Manufacturing"; "" )
)
// Result = {"name":"First Class Widgets","category":"Manufacturing"}
```

Setting the value of an element that already exists in the object provided will replace the existing value with the new value.

```
JSONSetElement ( {"name":"Honda"} ; "name" ; "Ford"; "" )
// Result = {"name":"Ford"}
```

Setting an Element by Array Index

To set a value in an array position, the *keyOrIndexOrPath* parameter must be a number in square brackets indicating the zero-based position of the desired element. To create an array with one value in the first position, use 0 as the index.

```
JSONSetElement ( "" ; "[0]" ; "Claris" ; "" )
// Result = ["Claris"]
```

Because the result is an array instead of an object, the brackets are square and there is no explicit label for the position of the value. In contrast, if you fail to include the square brackets around the index position on the second parameter, the results will be an object instead of an array.

```
JSONSetElement ( "" ; "0" ; "Claris" ; "" )
// Result = {"0":"Claris"}
```

To set an element in an existing array, the value at the index position specified will be replaced with the new value, even if it is a different data type. This example replaces the *number* in the third array position with some *text*:

```
JSONSetElement ( "[1,2,3,4]" ; "[2]" ; "Claris" ; "" )
// Result = [1,2,"Claris",4]
```

If an index position specified is beyond the range of existing values, FileMaker will insert one or more *null* placeholders to target the desired position.

```
JSONSetElement ( "" ; "[3]" ; "Claris" ; "" )
// Result = [null,null,null,"Claris"]
```

```
JSONSetElement ( "[1,2,3,4]" ; "[6]" ; "Claris" ; "" )
// Result = [1,2,3,4,null,null,"Claris"]
```

Note   See "Dynamically Calculating the Next Array Position" later in this chapter to learn how to programmatically determine the next array position.

Setting an Element by Path

When working with complex JSON, where elements must contain nested objects and arrays, a *path* can be used to refer to elements deeper than the first level. A *path* is specified by denoting a sequence of keys that define a hierarchical structure down to a nested element location, each separated by a period. Any elements in the path that don't exist in the JSON provided will be automatically created. For example, the following path will create an object with a first-level element key named "contact" that contains a second-level element that is an object with a key named "name" containing the *value* specified.

```
JSONSetElement ( "" ; "contact.name" ; "Karen C"; "" )
// Result = {"contact":{"name":"Karen C"}}
```

A path can be as long as necessary based on the structural requirements and can combine keys and array index positions. This example creates a *name* element at the first position inside of an array inside of a *contacts* element inside of a *company* element.

```
JSONSetElement ( "" ; "company.contacts.[0].name" ; "Karen C"; "" )
// Result = {"company":{"contacts":[{"name":"Karen C"}]}}
```

Specifying a Data Type

The previous examples all leave the *type* parameter blank because the data provided is obviously text, and we can rely on FileMaker to automatically choose the correct format. However, sometimes a type must be specified to ensure the correct result. For example, if the *value* starts with a numeric digit and no type is specified, FileMaker will automatically treat it like a number. This means that text with leading zeros or other formats like dates and phone numbers will be converted and truncated into a number. These two examples illustrate the importance of specifying a type for text-based text strings. In each, the value is the same but only the second one specifies that it should be treated as a text string.

```
JSONSetElement ( "" ; "phone" ; "555-867-5309" ; "" )
// Result = {"phone":555}

JSONSetElement ( "" ; "phone" ; "555-867-5309" ; JSONString )
// Result = {"phone":"555-867-5309"}
```

Caution   The type should be specified as a keyword and not a text string. Enclosing it in quotes will cause it to be ignored or to produce undesirable results. Use *JSONString* instead of "JSONString."

Types can be specified by the keyword or number for the desired type, presented at the start of this chapter. The following examples demonstrate setting a string or number using both methods.

```
JSONSetElement ( "" ; "phone" ; "555-867-5309" ; JSONString )
JSONSetElement ( "" ; "phone" ; "555-867-5309" ; 1 )
// Result = {"phone":"555-867-5309"}

JSONSetElement ( "" ; "quantity" ; "$5,000" ; JSONNumber )
JSONSetElement ( "" ; "quantity" ; "$5,000" ; 2 )
// Result = {"quantity":"5000"}
```

Setting Multiple Values at Once

To set multiple keys with a single function call, use semicolon-delimited, square-bracketed sets of the *keyOrIndexOrPath*, *value*, and *type* parameters. The example below sets two first-level elements (*name* and *category*) in one call to the function:

```
JSONSetElement ( "" ;
   [ "name" ; "First Class Widgets"; "" ] ;
   [ "category" ; "Manufacturing"; "" ]
)
// Result =
   {
      "name":"First Class Widgets",
      "category":"Manufacturing"
   }
```

Building Complex Objects and Arrays

Building complex JSON, either your own structural design or one dictated by an external system, can feel overwhelming. Let's work through writing a formula to build the vendor JSON result shown below. The object is made up of one numeric element (*id*), two text elements (*name, category*), an object element (*contact*) which contains three text elements (*phone, email, web*), and an array element (*products*) which contains objects containing four elements (*aisles, id, name, price*).

```
{
    "category":"Manufacturing",
    "contact":
        {
            "phone":"555-867-5309",
            "email":"sales@widgets.nope",
            "web":"www.widgets.nope"
        },
    "id":350,
    "name":"First Class Widgets",
    "products":
        [
            {
            "aisles":[3,8]
            "id":1000,
            "name":"Widget 1",
            "price":39.99,
            },
            {
            "aisles":[2,4]
            "id":1001,
            "name":"Widget 2",
            "price":59.99,
            }
        ]
}
```

Note   See the "CH14-02 Building Complex Objects" example file.

The example below will build the structure shown above with a single call to the *JSONSetElement* function with 16 individual *key, value,* and *type* combinations. The first three set first-level key/value combinations with the *id, name,* and *category*. Then, a first-level *contact* element is created, and three elements were added to it: *phone, email,* and *web*. Finally, a first-level *products* element is created with two array elements, each with several nested elements. Study this formula and compare to the result above to see how easy it is to build complex structures.

```
JSONSetElement ( "" ;
    [ "id" ; "350" ; "" ] ;
    [ "name" ; "First Class Widgets" ; "" ] ;
    [ "category" ; "Manufacturing" ; "" ] ;

    [ "contact.phone" ; "555-867-5309" ; JSONString ] ;
    [ "contact.email" ; "sales@widgets.nope" ; "" ] ;
    [ "contact.web" ; "www.widgets.nope" ; "" ] ;

    [ "products.[0].aisles.[0]" ; 3 ; "" ] ;
    [ "products.[0].aisles.[1]" ; 8 ; "" ] ;
    [ "products.[0].id" ; 1000 ; "" ] ;
    [ "products.[0].name" ; "Widget 1" ; "" ] ;
    [ "products.[0].price" ; 39.99 ; "" ] ;

    [ "products.[1].aisles.[0]" ; 2 ; "" ] ;
    [ "products.[1].aisles.[1]" ; 4 ; "" ] ;
    [ "products.[1].id" ; 1001 ; "" ] ;
    [ "products.[1].name" ; "Widget 2" ; "" ] ;
    [ "products.[1].price" ; 59.99 ; "" ]
)
```

Building Objects Dynamically

To generate the *products* array portion of the above example dynamically, based on records related to the current *Company* record, a *While* statement can incrementally read and add each product to the result. Instead of a fixed, hard-coded number of products, the statement can build it based on the found set of records or number of related records.

The example below starts by initializing a *json* variable with six elements from fields on the current *Company* record and then gets a *count* of the related *Product* records and initializes a *current* variable to 1. These two will be used as the condition for how long the statement should execute, incrementing once for each related *Product* record until the *current* is greater than the *count*.

The logic portion uses the *GetNthRecord* function to place field values for the current *Product* record (as viewed through a relationship from Company) into variables. These are then inserted into the *json* as an additional element in the *products* array. Finally, the *current* variable is incremented by 1 for the next loop until it exceeds the *count*. The result will be the same as the previous example but with a quantity of records dictated by the records present in the related table.

```
While (
[
   json = JSONSetElement ( "" ;
       [ "id" ; Company::Record Primary ID ; JSONString ] ;
       [ "name" ; Company::Name ; "" ] ;
       [ "category" ; Company::Category ; "" ] ;
       [ "contact.phone" ; Company::Phone ; JSONString ] ;
       [ "contact.email" ; Company::Email ; "" ] ;
       [ "contact.web" ; Company::Web ; "" ]
      ) ;
   total = Count ( Products::Record Primary ID ) ;
   current = 1
] ;
   current ≤ total ;
[
   aisle1 = GetNthRecord ( Products::Aisle1 ; current ) ;
   aisle2 = GetNthRecord ( Products::Aisle2 ; current )  ;
```

```
    id = GetNthRecord ( Products::Record Primary ID ; current ) ;
    name = GetNthRecord ( Products::Name ; current ) ;
    price = GetNthRecord ( Products::Price ; current ) ;
    prefix = "products.[" & current - 1 & "]." ;
    json = JSONSetElement ( json ;
        [ prefix & "aisles.[0]" ; aisle1 ; "" ] ;
        [ prefix & "aisles.[1]" ; aisle2 ; "" ] ;
        [ prefix & "id" ; id ; JSONString ] ;
        [ prefix & "name" ; name ; "" ] ;
        [ prefix & "price" ; price ; "" ]
        ) ;
    current = current + 1
] ;
    JSONFormatElements ( json )
)
```

Using JSONMakeArray

The *JSONMakeArray* function, introduced in version 21 (2024), will convert a list of
values into a JSON Array. The function call has three parameters, defined here:

```
JSONMakeArray ( listOfValues ; separator ; type )
```

- *listOfValues* – Any text containing multiple values delimited by a
  separator that will be converted into a JSONArray. This can be literal
  text, a field value, or the result of a function.

- *separator* – The text string that determines how the values will be
  parsed into separate values. Leave as an empty string to indicate a
  paragraph return as the value separator.

- *type* – A JSON data type that should be used for the values in the
  array. Use *JSONRaw* if the values are mixed types that should be
  retained in the array.

Before the *JSONMakeArray* function, converting list of values into an array required
a *While* loop extracting each value and inserting it into the next array position. The
function greatly simplifies the process.

Converting a Return-Delimited List

Text-based value lists are common in FileMaker. A defined *value list* (Chapter 11) is either a static list of return-delimited text values or one derived from fields. The result of the *List* function (Chapter 13, "List") is the same. To convert a standard return-delimited list of text values to an array, pass them to the function as shown in the example below.

```
JSONMakeArray ( "Dog¶Cat¶Horse" ; "" ; "" )
// result = [ "Dog" , "Cat" , "Horse" ]
```

Specifying a Data Type

Since the *type* parameter was left as an empty string in the previous example, the data type of the array values is automatically determined based on the content. Sending a list of numbers instead changes the output format as shown in this example.

```
JSONMakeArray ( "359¶124¶1837" ; "" ; "" )
// result = [ 359 , 124 , 1837 ]
```

Similarly, a mixture of value types will be automatically converted to their respective data types.

```
JSONMakeArray ( "Dog¶Cat¶Horse359¶124¶1837" ; "" ; "" )
// result = [ "Dog" , "Cat" , "Horse" , 359 , 124 , 1837 ]
```

To conform the results to a desired type, specify it in the *type* parameter. For example, this forces all values to be a text string.

```
JSONMakeArray ( "Dog¶Cat¶Horse359¶124¶1837" ; "" ; JSONString )
// result = [ "Dog" , "Cat" , "Horse" , "359" , "124" , "1837" ]
```

Specifying Other Delimiters

The *value delimiter* can be any text value used to separate values in the list being converted. So, the *listOfValues* can contain values separated by a comma, tab, space, or any other string with any number of characters. In this example, a list of animals is separated by a comma+space. When that string is entered as the *separator*, the results will be correctly parsed.

```
JSONMakeArray ( "Dog, Cat, Horse" ; ", " ; "" )
// result = [ "Dog" , "Cat" , "Horse" ]
```

Converting Mixed Data Types

A value in the list sent to the function can be any data type. This includes a *JSONObject* and *JSONArray*. To have these formats correctly retained in the output, be sure to specify either and empty string as the *type* or, to be safe, use *JSONRaw*. For example, assume a field named "Input Values" contains these four values, each of a different type:

```
{ "name" : "Widget", "price": 59.99 }
[ "product 1" , "product 2" ]
359
"Hello, World"
```

In this case, the following formula will produce an array where the first item is a *JSONObject*, the second a *JSONArray*, the third *JSONNumber,* and the fourth a *JSONString.*

```
JSONMakeArray ( Input Values ; "" ; JSONRaw ) )
```

When converting values with JSON objects or arrays embedded, be sure to not use a character as a separator that is found within the JSON formatting. For example, a comma or colon shouldn't be a separator in the example above!

Using JSONFormatElements

FileMaker's JSON functions all remove spaces and paragraph returns from around the elements in an object or array, returning it in a compressed format. This is both efficient and difficult to read. For example, when creating an object with four elements, the results will look like this:

```
{"id":5103,"First":"John","Last":"Smith","Title":"Chief Technology
Officer"}
```

The *JSONFormatElements* function reformats an object or array by inserting extra space and paragraph returns strategically to render it in an easier to read format. If the object above was processed with this function, it produces the following result.

```
JSONFormatElements( json )
// Result
   {
      "id":5103,
      "First":"John",
      "Last":"Smith",
      "Title":"Chief Technology Officer"
   }
```

Tip   Use this function to reformat results you intend to read, especially when troubleshooting!

Deleting Elements

The *JSONDeleteElement* function will delete an element from an object or array. The function call has two parameters. The element at the specified key, index, or path will be completely removed from the json provided.

```
JSONDeleteElement ( json ; keyOrIndexOrPath )
```

Note   See the "CH14-04 Deleting Elements" example file.

Deleting an Object Element by Key

An element of a *JSONObject* can be deleted by specifying the identifying key. The following example removes the *name* element, leaving only the *id* remaining:

```
JSONDeleteElement ( {"name":"Honda", "id":350} ; "name" )
// Result = {"id":350}
```

Deleting an Array Element by Index Position

An element of a *JSONArray* can be deleted by specifying its index position, the zero-based position in the list of values enclosed in square brackets. Deleting an index position in an array will automatically shift values to avoid an empty position. In this example, the third value in the array is specified at index position "[2]" and is removed in the result.

```
JSONDeleteElement ( "[1,2,3,4,5]" ; "[2]" )
// Result = [1,2,4,5]
```

Deleting an Element by Path

An element deep in the structure can also be deleted by specifying the key path required to locate it. This example will completely remove the first price from the first product of the vendor example, shifting the second price into the position of the first:

```
JSONDeleteElement ( Sandbox::JSON ; "products.[0].price" )
```

Caution   Deleting an element will delete all data contained within it, including nested objects and arrays!

Parsing Elements

Several built-in functions can parse or analyze objects and arrays: *JSONGetElement,
JSONGetElementType, JSONListKeys, JSONListValues.* Each of these requires the following two parameters:

- *json* – An object or array from which information will be parsed

- *keyOrIndexOrPath* – An optional parameter that references a specific element key, array index position, or a path to a nested element. This can be left blank when accessing the first level.

The examples in this section assume that a field named "JSON" in a *Sandbox* table contains the complex vendor JSON built previously in this chapter.

Note   See the "CH14-05 Parsing Elements" example file.

Using JSONGetElement

The *JSONGetElement* function will return the value of a specified element from the *JSON* provided.

```
JSONGetElement ( json ; keyOrIndexOrPath )
```

Referring to an Element by Key

To refer to an element by key, use its label name in the *keyOrIndexOrPath* parameter. This example shows a request for the *name* element which results in a text string containing the vendor's name.

```
JSONGetElement ( Sandbox::JSON ; "name" )
// Result = "First Class Widgets"
```

This example requests the *contact* element, so the result is a *JSONObject* containing three elements.

```
JSONGetElement ( Sandbox::JSON ; "contact" )
// Result =
    {
        "phone":"555-867-5309",
        "email":"sales@widgets.nope",
        "web":www.widgets.nope
    }
```

Referring to an Element by Array Index

When the object is an array, the *keyOrIndexOrPath* parameter should be a number in square brackets indicating the zero-based position of the desired element. By using an index position of 2, this example extracts the third value from an array of names. This example assumes the following array is in a variable named *JSON*:

```
["Michael","Mary","Walker","Karen"]
```

Using index position 2, we will extract the third name from the array:

```
JSONGetElement ( json ; "[2]" )
// Result = "Walker"
```

Referring to an Element by Path

When working with complex JSON, where elements must contain nested objects and arrays, a *path* can be used to refer to elements deeper than the first level. A *path* is specified by denoting a sequence of keys that define a hierarchical structure down to a nested element location, each separated by a period. To extract the *phone* element from the vendor example, we must specify that it is contained within the *contact* element as shown in the example below.

```
JSONGetElement ( Sandbox::JSON ; "contact.phone" )
// Result = 555-867-5309
```

A path can be as long as necessary based on the structure of the object and can combine keys and array index positions. This example extracts the *price* from the second item in the *products* element.

```
JSONGetElement ( Sandbox::JSON ; "products.[1].price" )
// Result = 59.99
```

Similarly, this example will extract the second array position of the *aisle* element from the first array position of the *products* element:

```
JSONGetElement ( Sandbox::JSON ; "products.[0].aisles.[1]" )
// Result = 8
```

Using JSONGetElementType

The *JSONGetElementType*, introduced in version 19.5, returns the type of an element stored in an object. The result will be the object type represented by a number.

```
JSONGetElementType ( json ; keyOrIndexOrPath )
```

Since no key is specified here, this example returns the type of the entire object:

```
JSONGetElementType ( Sandbox::JSON ; "" )
// result = 3 (JSONObject)
```

This example checks the type of a specific element:

```
JSONGetElementType ( Sandbox::JSON ; "name" )
// result = 3 (JSONString)
```

These examples check if the *products* element is a specific type or not:

```
JSONGetElementType ( Sandbox::JSON ; "products" ) = JSONArray
// result = 1 (true)
```

```
JSONGetElementType ( Sandbox::JSON ; "products" ) = JSONObject
// result = 0 (false)
```

Caution   Object types are keywords not text strings! Enclosing them in quotation marks will return an incorrect result.

Using JSONListKeys

The *JSONListKeys* function returns a return-delimited list of the name of every *key* in the object or in a specified element.

```
JSONListKeys ( json ; keyOrIndexOrPath )
```

This example shows how to get a list of the keys from the vendor JSON example:

```
JSONListKeys ( Sandbox::JSON ; "" )
// Result =
    category
    contact
    id
    name
    products
```

The *keyOrIndexOrPath* parameter can be used to specify a nested element containing an object or array. This example will return a list of keys for the *contact* element:

```
JSONListKeys ( Sandbox::JSON ; "contact" )
// Result =
    phone
    email
    web
```

Since an array has no key labels, the keys returned will be a list of the zero-based index positions of items, as shown here specifying the *product* element:

```
JSONListKeys ( Sandbox::JSON ; "products" )
// Result =
    0
    1
```

Using JSONListValues

The *JSONListValues* function generates a return-delimited list of the *value* of every *key* of an object or array.

```
JSONListValues ( json ; keyOrIndexOrPath )
```

This works like *JSONListKeys* except it returns the *values* instead of the *keys*. This example returns the values of every element in a *contact* element:

```
JSONListValues ( Sandbox::JSON ; "contact" )
// Result =
    555-867-5309
    sales@widgets.nope
    www.widgets.nope
```

Caution   Since results are a list of paragraphs, a value that contained multiple paragraphs of text may cause some values to not be aligned with the right key at the corresponding position in a list of keys!

Parsing Locale Elements

Two *Get* functions introduced in version 19.1.2 provide access to *locale elements*, which are a JSON object containing various information about regionally specific settings. These allow you to create calculations, interfaces, and scripts that vary by a user's region. Although support for multiple regions might not be a popular requirement among your users, it can't hurt to be aware of these functions, and they are useful as examples of parsing JSON.

Note   See the "CH14-06 Parsing Locale Elements" example file.

The *Get (SystemLocaleElements)* function provides information about the locale of the client's system. The *Get (FileLocaleElements)* function provides information about the file's locale which is the location of the system the file was originally created on. The latter function can be either the system or file depending on the *Data Entry* settings in *File Options* (Chapter 6). The results of these can be parsed using the *JSONGetElement* function.

To see all the values returned from these functions,

```
JSONFormatElements ( Get ( SystemLocaleElements ) )
JSONFormatElements ( Get ( FileLocaleElements ) )
```

To determine the currency symbol in use on the client's computer,

```
JSONGetElement ( Get ( SystemLocaleElements ) ; "Currency.Symbol" )
// result = "$"
```

To determine the file's expectation of the metric system,

```
JSONGetElement ( Get ( FileLocaleElements ) ; "Misc.Metric" )
// result = 1 (true) or 0 (false), dpending on the file's settings
```

This example shows how to extract a list of month names and abbreviations from the system locale elements and pull the value for the third month and returns the month with its abbreviation in parenthesis, i.e., "March (Mar)."

```
Let ( [
    json = Get ( SystemLocaleElements ) ;
    full = JSONGetElement ( json ; "Date.DMQ.Months.NameList" ) ;
```

```
    abbrev = JSONGetElement ( json ; "Date.DMQ.Months.AbbrvList" )
] ;
    JSONGetElement  ( full ; "[2]" ) &
    " (" &
    JSONGetElement  ( abbrev ; "[2]" ) & ")"
)
```

Caution   Remember that a *JSONArray* is zero-based. Therefore, in the example above, the "[2]" key is used to extract the *third* value from the arrays containing month names and abbreviations.

We can also determine if time is being returned as 12-hour or 24-hour (military) format:

```
JSONGetElement ( Get ( FileLocaleElements ) ; "Time.12h" )
// result = 0 (using 24 hour military time format)
```

The value in a field containing a length measurement taken in feet can be converted into meters whenever the local system is configured for the metric system. This example assumes a *Measurement* table has a field named *Length* which contains a value always entered in feet. The *Let* statement places that value into a variable named *valueFeet*. Next, the system's locale elements are placed into a *json* variable, and the metric setting is parsed from it into a *useMetric* variable. This value will be a 1 (true) or 0 (false) indicating if we should convert to metric or not. Finally, a result is calculated using a *Case* statement. If the system's locale indicates local use of the metric system, the value from the field is converted to meters. Then the appropriate suffix of "meters" or "feet" is added to the text result.

```
Let ( [
    valueFeet = Measurement::Length ;
    json = Get ( SystemLocaleElements ) ;
    useMetric = JSONGetElement ( json ; "Misc.Metric" )
] ;
```

```
  Case (
    useMetric ; ( valueFeet * .3048 ) & " meters" ;
    valueFeet & " feet"
  )
)
```

Note   Since the JSON structure of the data from the locale functions may change in future software upgrades, the *APIVers* key indicates the structural version of the result. This can be used to determine the appropriate way to parse specific information.

Overcoming Parsing Challenges

When receiving JSON from other systems, you don't have any control over the structure of the object. Sometimes, these systems will return data in perplexing formats that fall short of an ideal key/value methodology. For example, an ideal format for contact information would be a simple key/value relationship as a *JSONObject* as shown here:

```
{
    "address" : "123 Back Avenue",
    "city" : "Somewhereville",
    "first" : "John",
    "last" : "Smith",
    "state" : "New York",
    "zip" : "10101"
}
```

Values from the above can be simply extracted by referring to the key and getting the corresponding value:

```
JSONGetElement ( json ; "first" )
```

But what happens when a system doesn't conform to this kind of simple format? The real-life example below was contact information returned from a system as an array where each element was an object and the identifying "key" was itself a value under a *label* key.

```
[
  { "label" : "first" , "value" : "John" , "id" : 1 },
  { "label" : "last" , "value" : "Smith " , "id" : 3 },
  { "label" : "address" , "value" : "123 Back Avenue " , "id" : 2 },
  { "label" : "city" , "value" : "Somewhereville" , "id" : 6 },
  { "label" : "state" , "value" : "New York" , "id" : 4 },
  { "label" : "zip" , "value" : "10101" , "id" : 5 }
]
```

If the above result is always structured the same way, where each label is always in the array position shown, you can parse it by referring to the array value and then the "value" label, here getting the *first* value by referencing its array position.

```
JSONGetElement ( json ; "[0].value" )
// result = "John"
```

However, there is no guarantee this data will always conform to this order. In fact, the *id* values not being in order are a hint at the unreliability of that assumption! Further, if this information can be mixed with other data that may or may not be present from one data pull to the next, it is highly dubious to trust the array order as permanent. If a future data pull includes a *company* and *market* value mixed into the order, parsing code using the technique above will fail to perform as expected.

There are two ways to parse this data without knowing which array position will contain the desired value. One option is to create a formula to search the array's objects and find one with a specific value in the *label* element and then extract the value from the corresponding *value* element. The other option is to write code to first convert the entire thing into a proper key/value structure.

Note   See the "CH14-07 Parsing Challenges" example file.

Searching for a Single Element by Label

This example targets a single *value* based on its *label*, performing the equivalent of a search within an array. The *While* statement loads the array from a field into an *input* variable and initializes a *searchFor* variable with the label value we are looking for. Then it uses a reductive iteration to check each item in the array until it finds one where the *label* element contains the desired value and returns the contents of the corresponding *value* element. On each iteration, the first array object is extracted, and two values parsed. The value of the *label* element is put into a *current.key* variable and the value in the *value* element into a *current.value*. If the *current.key* contains the field name in the *searchFor* variable, the *current.value* is placed into the *result*. If not, the first element is deleted from the *input,* and the statement iterates to the next element. Using this method allows us to step through each element without having to count the number of array positions and track which is the current one.

```
While (
 [
   input = Sandbox::JSON ;
   searchFor = "state" ;
   result = ""
 ] ;
   result  = "" and input ≠ "[]" and input ≠ "" ;
 [
   current.key = JSONGetElement ( input ; "[0].label" ) ;
   current.value = JSONGetElement ( input ; "[0].value" ) ;
   result = Case ( current.key = searchFor ; current.value) ;
   input = JSONDeleteElement ( input ; "[0]" )
 ] ;
   result // = "New York"
)
```

Converting to a Proper Key/Value Format

The second option for dealing with the odd array formatting of the array of contact information is to outright convert the entire thing to a proper key/value object format. Here we also use a *While* statement with a reductive iteration. At the start, the array value is placed into an *input* variable. A *result* variable is also initialized as an empty string.

The *condition* portion allows the statement to keep looping as long as the *input* variable is not an empty array or an empty string.

In the *logic* section of the statement, the *key* and *value* are extracted from the first array position and placed into a variable. Next, a new element is created in the *result* using *JSONSetElement* and the extracted key/value combination. Finally, the first array object is deleted from *input* and the statement repeats.

```
While (
[
    input = Sandbox::JSON ;
    result = ""
] ;
    input ≠ "[]" and input ≠ "" ;
[
    key = JSONGetElement ( input ; "[0].label" ) ;
    value = JSONGetElement ( input ; "[0].value" ) ;
    result = JSONSetElement ( result ; key ; value ; JSONString ) ;
    input = JSONDeleteElement ( input ; "[0]" )
] ;
    JSONFormatElements ( result )
)
```

In the end, the *result* variable will contain the original *label* and *value* data in the simple and easily parsed key/value format shown here:

```
{
    "address" : "123 Back Avenue ",
    "city" : "Somewhereville",
    "first" : "John",
    "last" : "Smith ",
    "state" : "New York",
    "zip" : "10101"
}
```

Encoding Special Characters

FileMaker makes it easy to work with JSON by automatically encoding and decoding special characters. For example, if a value contains a paragraph return, these will be encoded as a backslash and a lowercase "r" as shown here:

```
JSONSetElement ( "" ; "states" ; "NY¶PA¶OH" ; "" )
{"states":"NY\rPA\rOH"}
```

When parsing out an element's value, these characters will be decoded back to normal paragraph returns. In this example, if the above result is in a *json* variable, the result will be a return-delimited list of state abbreviations:

```
JSONGetElement ( json ; "states" )
// Result =
    NY
    PA
    OH
```

If paragraph symbols are manually encoded when setting an element, they will be "escape-encoded" and treated as literal text rather than converted to paragraphs.

```
JSONSetElement ( "" ; "states" ; "NY\rPA\rOH" ; "" )
{"states":"NY\\rPA\\rOH"}

JSONGetElement ( json ; "states" )
// Result = "NY\rPA\rOH"
```

In that case, use *Substitute* to convert the encoded returns into actual paragraph returns.

```
Substitute ( JSONGetElement ( json ; "states" ) ; "\r" ; "¶" )
// Result =
    NY
    PA
    OH
```

Manipulating Elements

Let's work through two examples demonstrating how to calculate the next position in an array and how to merge one *JSONObject* into another.

Note   See the "CH14-08 Manipulating Elements" example file.

Calculating the Next Array Position

To successfully add a value at the end of an existing array, a formula must correctly specify the next index position. When that number isn't known, the next position must be dynamically calculated. Use *JSONListKeys* to get a list of the current array positions, and then use *ValueCount* to count how many keys are present. Because array indexes are zero-based, the number of values present can be used as the next index position. The example below illustrates this within a *Let* statement. The number of keys in the *currentArray* variable is listed and counted. The result will be 3 since the array currently has three values (10, 15, 30) at three index positions (0, 1, 2). This count is then used as the *nextKey* by placing it in square brackets and creating a *newArray* with the *newValue* inserted. The result is the original array with a new value inserted at the end.

```
Let ( [
    currentArray = "[10,15,30]" ;
    keys = JSONListKeys ( currentArray ; "" ) ;
    total = ValueCount ( keys ) ;
    nextKey = "[" & total & "]"  ;
    newValue = "Claris" ;
    newArray = JSONSetElement ( currentArray ; nextKey ; newValue ; "" )
] ;
    newArray
)
// Result = [10,15,30,"Claris"]
```

Merging JSON

FileMaker doesn't provide a built-in function to merge two objects into a one. However, a formula using a *While* statement can extract the value of each key from one object and add it to another. To begin, these examples assume we have two fields named "JSON 1" and "JSON 2" containing the following data:

```
Sandbox::JSON 1 =
{
   "Company" : "Widgets, Inc.",
   "First Name" : "Jim",
   "Last Name" : "Smith"
}

Sandbox::JSON 2 =
{
   "Address" : 123,
   "Company" : "Widgets, Inc.",
   "State" : "New York",
   "Zip" : 10001
}
```

A *While* statement can merge these two into a single object. To begin, two variables will be initialized to load the field data into variables: *json1* and *json2*. Another variable *allowReplace* will be initialized to a 1 to indicate we will allow a value from a key in the second object to replace one with the same name in the first. Changing this to 0 will cause the code to ignore elements in the second object with matching names. Next, a list of keys for each object is placed into a *json1Keys* and *json2Keys* variable. Finally, a *result* variable is set to contain *json1*.

The *condition* portion of the statement will allow the *While* to keep looping as long as *json2Keys* is not an empty string.

During each iteration, the next key from the *json2Keys* list will be used to extract a value from *json2* and insert it into *json1* if the current key is either 1) not present in json1 or 2) *allowReplace* is set to true. Since we are using a reductive iteration method here, once the current key is processed, it is removed from the *json2Keys* variable using the *RightValues* and *ValueCount* functions. This will repeat until the *json2Keys* variable is empty.

```
While (
  [
    json1 = Sandbox::JSON 1 ;
    json2 = Sandbox::JSON 2 ;
    allowReplace = 1 ;

    json1Keys = JSONListKeys ( json1 ; "" ) ;
    json2Keys = JSONListKeys ( json2 ; "" ) ;
    result = json1
  ] ;
    json2Keys ≠ "" ;
  [
    name = GetValue ( json2Keys ; 1 ) ;
    value = JSONGetElement ( json2 ; name ) ;
    result = Case (
        FilterValues ( json1Keys ; name ) = "" or
        allowReplace = 1 ; JSONSetElement ( result ; name ; value ; "" ) ;
        result ) ;
    json2Keys = RightValues ( json2Keys ; ValueCount ( json2Keys ) - 1 )
  ] ;
    JSONFormatElements ( result )
)
```

Caution   The example assumes both inputs are JSONObjects and are not empty! If one or both are anything other than an object or empty, it will result in an error. A *Case* statement can check and return an empty string instead to avoid this.

Handling Errors

Parsing a correctly formatted JSON is very forgiving. If you attempt to extract a value for a key that doesn't exist, the result will simply be an empty string. The same is true when requesting an array position outside of the number of array elements currently present or when using a path that doesn't exist.

However, when a source value provided isn't valid JSON, an attempt to set or get a value or format it will result in an error. In that case, the result will be a text value starting with a "?" followed with details about the error. The example below shows a mistyped object with the comma delimiter between the first key/value pair instead of a colon.

```
{ "Name" , "Karen" , "State" : "NC"}
```

Formatting errors like this can occur when manually typing an object into a text string instead of using the *JSONSetElement* function. For example, when manually typing JSON for insertion into a *Let* statement variable as shown below, the key and value quotes must be escaped with a backslash. This lends itself to error.

```
Let ( [
        json = "{\"Name\",\"Karen\",\"State\":\"NC\"}"
] ;
        JSONFormatElements ( json )
)
```

When executed, the result will be the following error:

```
? * Line 1, Column 8
  Missing ':' after object member name
```

In this example, the alleged JSON source is a text string instead of an object or array.

```
JSONGetElement ( "Hello World" ; "city" )
```

The result here includes two errors, with the first being the primary cause:

```
? * Line 1, Column 1
  Syntax error: value, object or array expected.
* Line 1, Column 2
  Extra non-whitespace after JSON value.
```

The inconvenience of a JSON error can range from an annoyance to a catastrophe. A calculation field value displaying an error instead of an extracted value is frustrating to users and interrupts the workflow. A complex scripted process that creates thousands of records and generates hundreds of emails automatically sent to customers with errors can have a negative financial impact on a business. It is critical that code be written to avoid errors as much as possible and include safety checks to avoid embarrassing disaster.

Note   See the "CH14-09 Handling Errors" example file.

Detecting an Error Result

To detect an error, check if the result has a question mark as the first character using the *Left* function, as shown in the example below. A Let statement begins by attempting to parse a *city* element from some JSON and place the result into a *jsonResult* variable. Next, it checks to see if that result starts with a question mark. The *errorDetected* variable will be 1 (true) if the result contains an error message and 0 (false) if it does not. The calculation portion of the *Let* statement can then handle results differently depending on the validity of the JSON parsing result.

```
Let ( [
  jsonResult = JSONGetElement ( json ; "city" ) ;
  errorDetected = Left ( jsonResult ; 1 ) = "?"
] ;
   // handle valid or invalid results differently
)
```

While the above example looks at a single parse attempt, the one below checks an entire JSON prior to attempting to extract any values. To confirm valid JSON, it runs the whole value through the *JSONFormatElements* function. This will return an error if any part of it is malformed.

```
Left ( JSONFormatElements ( json ; 1 ) = "?"
```

Similarly, this example confirms the type of the object using *JSONGetElementType*. This example will produce a 1 (true) result if the value in *json* is properly formatted object or array.

```
JSONGetElementType ( json ; "" ) = JSONObject or
JSONGetElementType ( json ; "" ) = JSONArray
```

Tip   Manually created JSON can be validated at `www.jsonlint.com`. However, to ensure properly formatted elements and avoid errors, use the *JSONSetElement* function to generate new JSON.

Detecting Missing Keys

Although not a *technical error*, in some situations, a missing key may be considered a *workflow error* and need to be detected and handled. If, under normal circumstances, a specific key will always have a value, it is easy to detect when they are missing by parsing it and check if the result is empty:

```
JSONGetElement ( json ; "city" ) = ""
```

However, if a value is sometimes allowed to be empty but should be present as an empty key, the above will not be adequate. When building your own JSON, it is easy to ensure that all required keys are present. When parsing JSON from external systems, it may be properly formatted and pass the above error tests but still have missing keys that you expect to be there. This can happen for several reasons. As systems evolve, the data structure may change. If you are not up to date with the specifications of the systems your database interacts with, the data received may not have essential keys that your code expects, or they may be present but residing at a different path within the object. The same may be true if there is a bug in your request or in the external system. When unexpected structural changes would adversely affect the outcome of your processing code, consider building in some protective measures. In this example, a *Company* key is required but renamed "Employer." If your code is looking for the former, the result will always be an empty text value.

```
{
    "Name" : "Karen",
    "Employer" : "Widgets, Inc.",
    "State" : "NC"
}
```

Checking for Missing Keys

As a preventative measure, this example uses the *JSONListKeys* and *FilterValues* functions to confirm the presence of three specific keys and return a number indicating the number missing. Then a formula or script can take some other course of action and/ or warn a developer that something has changed with the JSON structure.

```
Let ( [
   keys = JSONListKeys ( Sandbox::JSON ; "" ) ;
   missing.company = FilterValues ( keys ; "Company" ) = "" ;
   missing.name = FilterValues ( keys ; "Name" ) = "" ;
   missing.state = FilterValues ( keys ; "State" ) = ""
] ;
   missing.company + missing.name + missing.state
)
// Result = 1 (indicating that one key was missing)
```

Listing Missing Keys

Alternatively, this example uses a similar approach, but instead of returning a count of missing keys, it produces a list of missing key names.

```
Let ( [
   keys = JSONListKeys ( Sandbox::JSON ; "" ) ;
   missing = "" ;

   key = "Company" ;
   missing.1 = Case ( FilterValues ( keys ; key ) = "" ; key ) ;

   key = "Name" ;
   missing.2 = Case ( FilterValues ( keys ; key ) = "" ; key ) ;

   key = "State" ;
   missing.3 = Case ( FilterValues ( keys ; key ) = "" ; key )

] ;
   List ( missing.1 ; missing.2 ; missing.3 )
)
// Result = Company (indiciating that key is misisng)
```

Checking an Array of Objects for Missing Keys

This more complex example checks an array where each object is expected to have the same three keys. For this example, assume a field named "Contact List" contains the array below. First, notice the problems. The first and second array element are both an object, but the first has a *company* key while the second has an *employer* key. Further, the last two array items are text values instead of objects.

```
[
  {
    "Company" : "Widgets, Inc.",
    "Name" : "Karen",
    "State" : "NC"
  },
  {
    "Employer" : "Write Track Media",
    "Name" : "Mark",
    "State" : "PA"
  },
  "Brian",
  "NJ"
]
```

The technique in the previous example can be wrapped into a While statement to confirm that 1) there is an array and that 2) each item within it is an object and has the three expected fields. Any errors found should be returned.

This *Let* statement loads the field value into an *input* variable which is checked to see if it is an empty as a string, object, or array. In the result portion of the statement, a *Case* statement first checks to see if the empty variable is 1 (true) and, if so, returns the string "empty json." Next, it checks to see if the input variable contains an array and, if not, returns the string "not an array." Finally, if those two tests pass, it performs a *While* statement that loads the *input* into a *json* variable and steps through each array element and writes to a result variable if the element is 1) not an object or 2) missing one or more fields.

```
Let ( [
  input = Sandbox::JSON ;
```

```
    empty = input = "" or input = "{}" or input = "[]"
] ;
  Case (
  empty ; "empty json" ;
  JSONGetElementType ( input ; "" ) ≠ JSONArray ; "not an array" ;

  While (
  [
    json = input ;
    keyCount = 0 ;
    result = ""
  ] ;
    json ≠ "[]" ;
  [
    current.element = JSONGetElement ( json ; "[0]" ) ;
    wrong.type = JSONGetElementType ( current.element ; "" ) ≠
    JSONObject ;
    keys = JSONListKeys ( current.element ; "" ) ;
    key = "Company" ;
    missing.1 = Case ( FilterValues ( keys ; key ) = "" ; key ) ;
    key = "Name" ;
    missing.2 = Case ( FilterValues ( keys ; key ) = "" ; key ) ;
    key = "State" ;
    missing.3 = Case ( FilterValues ( keys ; key ) = "" ; key ) ;
    missing =
        Substitute (
          List ( missing.1 ; missing.2 ; missing.3 ) ; "¶" ; ", " );
    result =
        List ( result ;
        Case (
          wrong.type ; "Index [" & keyCount & "] is not an object" ;
          missing ≠ "" ; "Index [" & keyCount & "] missing " & missing
        ) ) ;
    json = JSONDeleteElement ( json ; "[0]" ) ;
    keyCount = keyCount + 1
  ] ;
```

```
    result
  )
  )
)
```

Using the example shown previously, the above code returns the following text result:

```
Index [1] missing Company
Index [2] is not an object
Index [3] is not an object
```

Summary

This chapter introduced JSON and explored how to create, parse, and manipulate JSON objects and arrays using several built-in functions. We also covered some examples of how to overcome parsing challenges, how to merge two JSON objects, and how to handle errors. In the next chapter, we will learn how to create custom functions.

## CHAPTER 15

Creating Custom Functions

A *custom function* is a developer-defined formula that is added to the library of available functions within the database it is installed. They add custom code alongside built-in functions, acting like extensions to the file's calculation resources. Once defined, the function is globally accessible from the formula for any field definition, interface element, or script step. Unlike regular calculation formulas, custom functions can be defined to accept parameters and can be recursive. A well-designed, open-ended, reusable custom function can reduce redundancies in formulas, simplify calculations, and save enormous amounts of development time. In this chapter, we discuss the process of creating and using custom functions, covering topics such as the following:

- Introducing custom functions dialogs
- Creating a custom function
- Adding parameters to a custom function
- Building recursive functions

Note Custom functions can only be created and edited with advanced tools enabled (Chapter 2).

© Mark Conway Munro 2024
M. C. Munro, *Learn FileMaker Pro 2024*, https://doi.org/10.1007/979-8-8688-0835-7_15

Introducing Custom Function Dialogs

Custom functions are created and managed from the *Manage Custom Functions* dialog, shown in Figure 15-1. To open it, select the *File ➤ Manage ➤ Custom Functions* menu. This dialog is used to create, edit, duplicate, delete, and import custom functions.

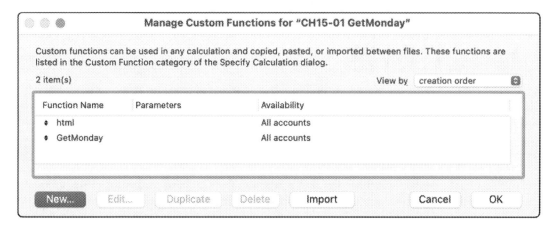

Figure 15-1. *The dialog used to manage custom functions*

Tip   Custom functions can be copied and pasted between two files or imported.

Creating a new function or editing an existing one will open the *Edit Custom Function* dialog, shown in Figure 15-2. This dialog is used to define a custom function and is similar to a *Specify Calculation* dialog but with a few important differences.

The *Function Name* field allows the function to be assigned a named so it can be called by other formulas in the same way built-in functions are called.

Several tools are used to define optional parameters. A *Function Parameter* is a positional input variable that is assigned a value when another formula calls the function being defined here. These work like parameters on built-in functions except you define them. After entering a new parameter name, clicking the plus icon will create it in the list below. Select an existing parameter, change the name, and click the pencil icon to rename it. A selected parameter can be deleted by clicking the minus icon. Once in the list, they can be drag-arranged to specify their order. Since parameters are positional, values passed when the function is called are inserted into the variable at the corresponding position in the list. Changing the order of an existing function's parameters will require rearranging the values in any existing call. Once created, double-click a parameter in the list to insert it into the formula below.

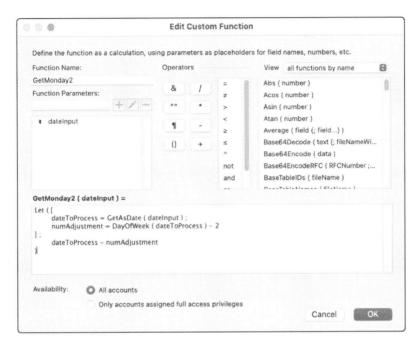

Figure 15-2. *The dialog used to define a custom function*

The function's formula is entered into the formula text area. Unlike in the *Specify Calculation* dialog, there is no auto-complete suggestion interface, so everything must be typed manually or inserted using the buttons and lists in the top half of the dialog. Although functions will always execute in the current window's context and can include field references, these must be manually entered because there is no selection pane for fields on this dialog. This exclusion is a subtle reminder that functions are accessible from any context and it is safer to push field values into the formula as a parameter to avoid making the function unnecessarily context sensitive. There are times where you want to include a field reference in the function, but that limits its ability to provide global functionality.

The top-right area contains controls for inserting operators and function calls into the formula. The *Availability* option at the bottom allows a choice to make a function accessible to only accounts with full access (Chapter 29).

Beyond these differences, custom functions are written just like other formulas and must adhere to the same 30,000-character limit.

Creating a Custom Function

To begin, create a simple custom function without parameters named *GetMonday* that calculates the date for the Monday of the current week using the following formula:

```
Let ( [
    dateToday = Get ( CurrentDate ) ;
    numAdjustment = DayOfWeek (dateToday) - 2
] ;
    dateToday - numAdjustment
)
```

The formula uses a *Let* statement to put today's date into a variable called *dateToday*. To determine the number of days today's date needs to be adjusted to land on a Monday, it converts *dateToday* using the built-in *DayOfWeek* function. Then, since we know Monday is always the second day of a calendar week, we subtract 2 from that number and put the result into a variable named *numAdjustment*. Finally, that adjustment number will be subtracted from today's date to arrive at the date for this week's Monday. For example, if today is a Friday, that is the sixth day of the week. Since we want to determine the corresponding Monday, which is the second day of the week, we subtract 2 from that number to arrive at the number of days we need to subtract from the current day in order to arrive at a Monday in the current week. No matter what day of the week it is when the formula runs, the result of this formula will always be the corresponding Monday's date. It even works when running it on Sunday since the adjustment number will be negative 1 (the result of 1 minus 2). When that negative number of days is subtracted from Sunday, the result will be adding one day (today's date minus negative 1 days) which will be Monday's date.

To create this custom function, open the *Manage Custom Functions* dialog, and click the *New* button to open the *Edit Custom Function* dialog. Then follow the steps shown in Figure 15-3, first entering a name of "GetMonday" and then entering the formula. Click the OK button to save the function and then click OK in the *Manage Custom Functions* dialog. Now we can use this function to calculate the date on Monday of the current week no matter what day of the week it is.

Note   See the "CH15-01 GetMonday" example file.

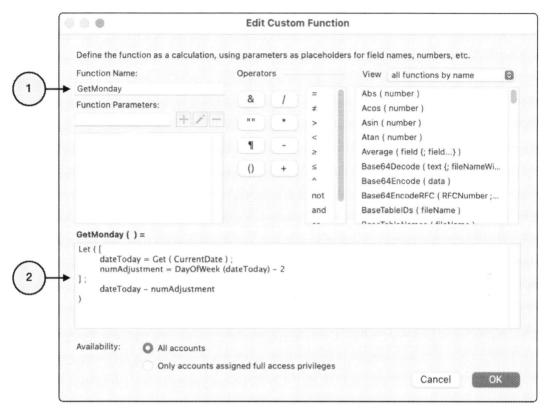

Figure 15-3. *The steps required to create the example custom function*

Using the Function

To see this in action, either check out the "CH15-01 GetMonday" example file or insert the function call into any formula using the same process used to insert a built-in function. Test this in a *Sandbox* file from a previous chapter by following these steps:

1. Open the *Fields* tab for the *Sandbox* table in the *Manage Database* dialog.

2. Double-click the *Example Calculation* field or select it and click the Options button.

3. Change the field's formula to *GetMonday*.

4. Change the calculation result type to date.

5. Click OK to save the calculation formula and close the *Specify Calculation* dialog.

6. Click OK to save and close the *Manage Database* dialog.

Now view the result on the *Sandbox Form* layout for any record. If the calculation containing this function call were evaluated on March 14, 2024, a Thursday, the result should be the preceding Monday: March 11, 2024.

Adding Parameters to a Custom Function

The previous example demonstrates how to construct a simple custom function. However, it lacks usefulness due to limited flexibility. Although its use of the current date does offer some flexibility and will continue to work in the future, it is locked to only return the Monday relative to today. With parameters and modifications to the formula, the function can be expanded to calculate any specified weekday from any starting date.

As previously introduced (Chapter 12, "Calling a Function with Parameters"), a *function parameter* is a value that can vary with each call to the function allowing formulas to push specific values into an open-ended function. Parameters provide variable input and/or instructions for what processing should be performed and allow a function to adapt to different situations. When defining a custom function, any number of parameters can be created for any functional purpose required and named to descriptively convey that purpose. Since there is no way to control the type of data a formula passes to your function as a parameter, be sure to choose a name that describes the intended data type(s) it is intended to receive. For example, a parameter named "input" is too vague, while "dateInput" or "startDate" clearly states what type of data is expected. For our example, we want to add two parameters to our function: an input date named "dateInput" and a desired result weekday named "dayRequested." Let's work through several examples to expand the flexibility of the function.

Adding an Input Date Parameter

First, create a duplicate of the previous function that we will expand to calculate the corresponding Monday from any starting date provided in a parameter named "dateInput." Open the *Manage Custom Functions* dialog, select the *GetMonday* function, and click the *Duplicate* button. Then click the *Edit* button to open the function in the *Edit Custom Function* dialog, and make the changes shown in Figure 15-4.

Note   See the "CH15-02 GetMonday2" example file.

Figure 15-4. *The steps required to modify the duplicate function*

1. Change the name of the function to "GetMonday2."

2. Type the parameter name "dateInput," and then click the + button
    to create the parameter in the list below.

3. Modify the code so that the *dateInput* parameter is used in place
    of the current date and is converted to a date using the *GetAsDate*
    function. Also, rename the *dateToday* variable to *dateToProcess*:

```
Let ( [
    dateToProcess = GetAsDate ( dateInput ) ;
    numAdjustment = DayOfWeek ( dateToProcess ) - 2
```

```
] ;
    dateToProcess - numAdjustment
)
```

Tip   Create new functions in the *Data Viewer* (Chapter 26, "Exploring the Data Viewer") with parameters temporarily declared as *Let* variables, so you can see the result as you work.

Save the function and modify the formula in the *Example Calculation* field to call the new function. Since it converts the input to a date automatically, the parameter can be either a text field containing a date value, a date field, a literal text string containing a date, or a date value built with a function. An example of each option of these is shown below. After choosing your formula, save it, and view the results in Browse mode. The result should be the Monday relative to whatever date you specified as input:

```
GetMonday2 ( Sandbox::Example Text )
GetMonday2 ( Sandbox::Example Date )
GetMonday2 ( "8/7/2024" )
GetMonday2 ( Date ( 8 ; 7 ; 2024 ) )
```

Adding a Day Requested Parameter

To continue the evolution of the function, add an additional parameter called *dayRequested* that accepts a weekday name and returns a date for that weekday relative to the *dateInput* provided. First, create a duplicate of the *GetMonday2* function. Since the new, expanded function will no longer be locked to a Monday result, the new function's name should change to "GetDay." Add a second parameter named "dayRequested." Finally, change the code as shown here:

```
Let ( [
 dateToProcess = GetAsDate ( dateInput ) ;
 list = "Sunday¶Monday¶Tuesday¶Wednesday¶Thursday¶Friday¶Saturday" ;
 list = Left ( list ; Position ( list ; dayRequested ; 1; 1 ) ) ;
 dayNumber = ValueCount ( list ) ;
 numAdjustment = DayOfWeek ( dateToProcess ) - dayNumber
```

```
] ;
 dateToProcess - numAdjustment
)
```

Note   See the "CH15-03 GetDay" example file.

The code will accept a day name (e.g., "Wednesday") in the *dayReqeusted* parameter and convert that into a day number (4) by finding that day's position in a list of day names. This is done by adding three steps to the formula. A new *list* variable is initialized to contain a paragraph return-delimited list of weekday names. In the next line, the *list* variable is modified using the *Left* and *Position* functions to reduce the list to only the day names prior to the one requested. So, if "Wednesday" was the day requested, *list* would contain "Sunday¶Monday¶Tuesday¶W." Finally, the ValueCount function is used to convert that list into the weekday number (4), which is placed into the *dayNumber* variable. This determines the *numAdjustment* value which is used to adjust the input date as in previous versions. Once the new function is saved, modify the formula in the *Example Calculation* to call the new function. In this example, the result will be the date of Friday for the week of January 4, 2021:

```
GetDay ( "3/4/2021" ; "Friday" )      // result = 3/4/2021
GetDay ( "1/4/2021" ; "Wednesday" )   // result = 1/6/2021
```

Tip   This formula could be simplified if the day requested parameter was modified to accept a weekday number instead of a day name!

Adding a Default Date Option

As a further refinement, modify the function to automatically use a default date when one is not specified in the *dateInput* parameter. This provides a shortcut for any formula calling the function that wants to use the current date. Currently, if the function were used to calculate the Friday for the current date, right now, a calling formula would be required it to explicitly include today's date in the call as shown here:

```
GetDay ( Get ( CurrentDate ) ; "Friday" )
```

Modifying the first line of the *Let* statement from the last example, a *Case* statement can automatically default to the current date when none is provided in the parameter. When a call passes an empty string instead of a date, this condition will allow the function to produce a result. Modify the first line of the Let statement as shown here:

```
dateToProcess = Case ( dateInput = "" ; Get ( CurrentDate ) ; GetAsDate
( dateInput ) ) ;
```

Now, a formula can request a day relative to the current date by passing in an empty string in the first parameter or for a specific date by providing one, as shown in the following two examples:

```
GetDay ( "" ; "Friday" )
GetDay ( "1/4/2021" ; "Friday" )
```

Note   See the "CH15-04 GetDay with Default" example file.

Stressing the Importance of Thorough Testing

Every formula should be carefully tested prior to live production use. Being accessible from anywhere in the database, a custom function requires even greater care. This is especially true for complex functions that accept parameter input. A single test showing a function working may not be adequate since different input may cause conditions not anticipated by the formula. Instead, perform as many tests as possible with a variety of input to confirm that it will handle a full range of possible values in various combinations.

The testing requirements of each custom function will be different. Start by asking what variety of input might be received. There are many questions we might ask regarding the previous example. What if the date provided is at the start of the week: a Sunday or a Monday? What if the date is at the end of the week: a Friday or a Saturday? What if the day requested is the same day of the date provided? Will the function work under each of these circumstances? Will it operate correctly when requesting any day of the week relative to any date? Do all the anticipated data types – date, timestamp, and text string with a date – return an accurate result? To confirm this, we can devise a set of tests for each condition and confirm the results.

Note   See the "CH15-05 GetDay Test" example file.

To begin, convert the list of questions into a list of test scenarios that will adequately confirm the desired functionality with a large enough sampling of input. In our example, at the minimum, the following tests should be performed:

- *dateInput* – Run seven tests, one test for each day of the week as input, in addition to at least one test of each accepted data type.

- *dayRequested* – Run seven tests, one test for each day of the week.

This indicates the need for at least 16 tests. Rather than performing these tests manually, one by one, the following single calculation formula, entered in the *Example Calculation* field, covers them all at once by producing a single text result that lists all the various results:

```
Let ( [
   dateInput = Date ( 3 ; 10 ; 2024 )
] ;
  List (
   "Input = " & dateInput & " (" & DayName (dateInput) & ")" ;
   "+1 Sunday=" & GetDay ( dateInput + 1  ; "Sunday" ) ;
   "+2 Sunday=" & GetDay ( dateInput + 2  ; "Sunday" ) ;
   "+3 Sunday=" & GetDay ( dateInput + 3  ; "Sunday" ) ;
   "+4 Sunday=" & GetDay ( dateInput + 4  ; "Sunday" ) ;
   "+5 Sunday=" & GetDay ( dateInput + 5  ; "Sunday" ) ;
   "Sunday=" & GetDay ( dateInput; "Sunday" ) ;
   "Monday=" & GetDay ( dateInput ; "Monday" ) ;
   "Tuesday=" & GetDay (dateInput; "Tuesday" ) ;
   "Wednesday=" & GetDay ( dateInput; "Wednesday" ) ;
   "Thursday=" & GetDay ( dateInput; "Thursday" ) ;
   "Friday=" & GetDay ( dateInput; "Friday" ) ;
   "Saturday=" & GetDay ( dateInput; "Saturday" ) ;
   "Timestamp=" & GetDay ( GetAsTimestamp (dateInput); "Sunday" ) ;
   "Text Date=" & GetDay ( GetAsText (dateInput)  ; "Sunday" ) ;
   "Text TS=" & GetDay ( GetAsText (GetAsTimestamp (dateInput))  ;
   "Sunday" )
```

```
    )
)
// result =
Input = 3/10/2024 (Sunday)
+1 Sunday=3/10/2024
+2 Sunday=3/10/2024
+3 Sunday=3/10/2024
+4 Sunday=3/10/2024
+5 Sunday=3/10/2024
Sunday=3/10/2024
Monday=3/11/2024
Tuesday=3/12/2024
Wednesday=3/13/2024
Thursday=3/14/2024
Friday=3/15/2024
Saturday=3/16/2024
Timestamp=3/10/2024
Text Date=3/10/2024
Text TS=3/10/2024
```

Caution   Be sure to change the Example Calculation result data type to "text" since this test formula returns text instead of a date.

This formula uses a *Let* statement to place a start date into a variable and uses that to perform repeated calls to the function and concatenates the individual results into a block of text. The first six results show that, as the *dateInput* is incremented to cover each day of an entire week, the result for the requested Sunday remains the same. This assumes a start date of a Sunday. The next seven results show that using the same *dateInput* while requesting a different day of the week works since the results span a 7-day period. Finally, the last three results show that when the *dateInput* is a timestamp, text-based date, or text-based timestamp, the result remains the same. With this test completed and confirmed, it should now be safe to use this custom function.

Building Recursive Functions

A *recursive function* is a formula that is capable of generating self-referencing calls, i.e., calling and executing itself from within itself. In FileMaker, custom functions are the only formulas that can be recursive. Recursion is often confused with the iterative functionality found in looping scripts or in the new *While* function (Chapter 13, "While"). Although there are similarities and many tasks can be accomplished using either, recursion is actually very different. In a repeating process, a piece of code is executed numerous times in succession; each iteration is completed before the next begins. By contrast, a recursive process creates and runs successive new instances of the same code during execution of the preceding instance, a difference illustrated in Figure 15-5. Each instance queues up in memory forming what is known as a *call stack* until it reaches a termination point known as a *base case* where it stops calling itself and produces a result that cascades back up the stack, collapsing it to produce the final result.

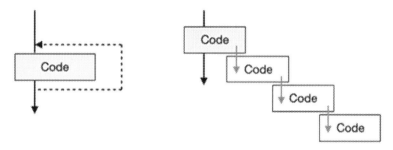

Figure 15-5. *The difference between looping (left) and recursion (right)*

Both the iterative loop and recursive options are superior to hard-coded statements that restrict the number of iterations. For example, using *If* or *Case* statements requires each possible iteration to be explicitly stated in a fixed sequence. You have to write out each condition and are limited to only the number you explicate. Similarly, a *Let* statement can perform a fixed number of cascading variable declarations. Again, this is limited in number to what you actually write. While these are fine for small numbers of static choices that never change and don't vary in number, often a more dynamic approach is warranted.

A *looping script* is easy to set up and runs quickly (Chapter 25, "Iterating with Repeating Statements"). However, scripts can't be triggered from within a formula, so they are limited to interface-related actions and events.

For an exclusively formula-based solution, the choices are the iterative *While* function or a recursive custom function. There are pros and cons of each. The *While* function has the advantage of working in any formula, while recursion is strictly limited to custom functions. The nested hierarchy of the recursive stack can be more difficult to conceptualize, but using the *While* function is not without its own confusion. Both can feel overly wordy in simple examples and mind-boggling in more complex ones, but recursion really pushes the boundaries of one's conceptualization. Using *While* may be a little faster and doesn't have the same memory impact. Although many programming challenges can be handled with either approach, when performing a complex, repeated process through hierarchical data, recursion is sometimes the only practical choice.

Building Simple Recursive Functions

To grasp the basic structure of a recursive function, start with some simple examples.

Creating a Range of Dates

First, create a new function named "DateRange" that accepts *startDate* and *endDate* parameters and uses these to return a list of every date in the range using the formula here:

```
startDate &
Case (  endDate = startDate ; "" ; "¶"  & DateRange ( startDate + 1 ;
endDate ) )
```

Note   See the "CH15-06 DateRange" example file.

The formula concatenates the start date and the result of a *Case* statement. The statement determines if a recursive call should be issued to increment the date forward by one day or not. On each iteration, if the end date equals the start date, the formula returns an empty string, thereby providing a terminating base case that collapses the results back up the recursive chain. If the two dates are different, a paragraph return is included, and then the function calls itself with the start date incremented by one. Each recursive call repeats this process until the start date equals the end date, creating a result as shown in the following example:

```
DateRange ( GetAsDate ( "1/1/2021" ) ; GetAsDate ( "1/5/2021" ) )
// result =
    1/1/2021
    1/2/2021
    1/3/2021
    1/4/2021
    1/5/2021
```

Merging Two Lists

Create another function named "MergeValues" that accepts two return-delimited text value lists and returns a blended list. The code for this function shown in the following assumes two parameters, *column1* and *column2*:

```
Let ( [
    current =
        GetValue ( column1 ; 1 ) & " " &
        GetValue ( column2 ; 1 ) ;
    column1 = RightValues ( column1 ; ValueCount ( column1 ) - 1 ) ;
    column2 = RightValues ( column2 ; ValueCount ( column2 ) - 1 )
] ;
    current &
    Case ( column1 ≠ "" ; "¶" & MergeValues ( column1 ; column2 ) )
)
```

Note   See the "CH15-07 MergeValues" example file.

In the above example, the *Let* statement is used to break the task into steps. The *GetValue* function extracts the first value from both inputs and concatenates it into a current variable with a space between them. Then, the two column input parameters are reduced by one value using the *ValueCount* and *RightValues* functions to remove the first value. The result is the value in the *current* variable and the result of a Case statement that either terminates the recursion (if no values remain in *column1*) or calls itself to continue to the next iteration. This example call has three labels and phone numbers as input and shows the corresponding result:

```
MergeValues ( "Work¶Home¶Cell" ; "555-2121¶555-3421¶867-5309" )
// result =
    Work 555-2121
    Home 555-3421
    Cell 867-5309
```

Controlling Recursion Limits

An *infinite regress* occurs when a recursive or looping function fails to terminate and continues running without end in an endless loop. To avoid this, FileMaker imposes a limit on the number of iterations a recursive stack can include. Any formula that exceeds this limit will stop executing and return an error expressed as a question mark. Prior to FileMaker 18, the limit varied depending on the type of recursion used. Functions using *tail recursion*, where the recursive call is the final step at the end of the function's formula leaving no processing unfinished, had a limit of 50,000 total recursive calls. Functions using *head recursion*, where the placement of a recursive call anywhere within the formula, was previously limited to 10,000 total calls. However, in version 18, both tail- and head-recursive calls and the *While* function have a default limit of 50,000 iterations. Also introduced in that version is the *setRecursion* function which allows a developer to set the maximum number of iterations allowed higher or lower than this default limit and vary that amount from one formula to another.

```
setRecursion ( expression ; maxIterations )
```

This is a *conditioning function* which sets the iterative terms for processing the expression it encloses. Any recursive function calls or *While* statements included in the first parameter's statement (the *expression*) will be limited to the number specified by the *maxIterations* parameter. Use this to increase or decrease the maximum number of iterations allowed. For example, try calling the previous *DateRange* function with a start and end date more than 30 days apart from within a *setRecursion* statement limited to 30 iterations. This example fails because the recursive calls necessary to finish the task exceed the limit of 30.

```
setRecursion ( DateRange ( "1/1/2021" ; "2/10/2021" ) ; 30 )
// result = ?
```

Next, increase the limit to an amount greater than the range of dates to see if it functions properly. If the preceding example were modified with a limit of 60, it is more than enough to cover the range of dates specified, and a proper result will be delivered.

Note   See the "CH15-08 DateRange with Limit" example file.

The following example shows the function increasing the limit to 250,000 in order to execute a simple *While* statement that increments a counter up to 200,000. This example serves no practical function but simply illustrates the ability of the function to far exceed the default recursion limit.

```
SetRecursion (
    While (
        counter = 0 ;
        counter < 200000 ;
        counter = counter + 1 ;
        counter
    ) ; 250000
)
```

Embedding Test Code Inside a Function

Earlier we discussed writing test code to quickly perform multiple tests of the *GetDay* custom function with a variety of different input. Recursion opens the possibility of storing that test code inside of the custom function it tests. While it may seem unnecessary to save test code at all, it can be prudent to retest a function anytime it is modified in the future. A *Case* statement can be used to detect a test request and perform an alternate set of code. In this example, the *dateInput* parameter will be used to determine if the call to the function was asking for test results or normal operations and run one or the other accordingly as shown in the following pattern:

```
Case ( dateInput = "Test" ; <<test code>> ; <<normal code>> )
```

Note   See the "CH15-09 DateRange Test Embedded" example file.

Using this format, we can combine the previous example's test code with the original function code to convert the formula into the following combined statement. To demonstrate this technique, create a new function called *GetDay2* with this new capability. In this example, if the *dateInput* receives a value of "Test," it will perform the test routine; otherwise, it will assume the parameter contains a date and will perform its normal function.

```
Case ( dateInput = "Test" ;
//    Test Code
   Let ( [
      dateInput = Date ( 1 ; 17 ; 2021 )
   ] ;
      "Input = " & dateInput & " (" & DayName (dateInput) & ")¶" &
      "1 Sunday=" & GetDay2 ( dateInput + 1  ; "Sunday" ) & "¶" &
      "+2 Sunday=" & GetDay2 ( dateInput + 2  ; "Sunday" ) & "¶"
      "+3 Sunday=" & GetDay2 ( dateInput + 3  ; "Sunday" ) & "¶" &
      "+4 Sunday=" & GetDay2 ( dateInput + 4  ; "Sunday" ) & "¶"
      "+5 Sunday=" & GetDay2 ( dateInput + 5  ; "Sunday" ) & "¶" &
      "+6 Sunday=" & GetDay2 ( dateInput + 6  ; "Sunday" ) & "¶" &
      "Sunday=" & GetDay2 ( dateInput; "Sunday" ) & "¶" &
      "Monday=" & GetDay2 ( dateInput ; "Monday" ) & "¶" &
      "Tuesday=" & GetDay2 (dateInput; "Tuesday" ) & "¶" &
      "Wednesday=" & GetDay2 ( dateInput; "Wednesday" ) & "¶"
      "Thursday=" & GetDay2 ( dateInput; "Thursday" ) & "¶"
      "Friday=" & GetDay2 ( dateInput; "Friday" ) & "¶" &
      "Saturday=" & GetDay2 ( dateInput; "Saturday" ) & "¶" &
      "Timestamp=" & GetDay2 ( GetAsTimestamp ( dateInput ) ;
      "Sunday" ) & "¶"
      "Text Date=" & GetDay2 ( GetAsText ( dateInput )  ;
      "Sunday" ) & "¶" &
      "Text TS=" & GetDay2 ( GetAsText ( GetAsTimestamp ( dateInput ) )  ;
      "Sunday" ) &
   )
```

```
;
//    Regular Code
   Let ( [
      dateToProcess  = GetAsDate ( dateInput ) ;
      list = "Sunday¶Monday¶Tuesday¶Wednesday¶Thursday¶Friday¶Saturday" ;
      list = Left ( list ; Position ( list ; dayRequested ; 1; 1 ) ) ;
      dayNumber = ValueCount ( list ) ;
      numAdjustment = DayOfWeek ( dateToProcess ) – dayNumber
 ] ;
      dateToProcess  - numAdjustment
   )
)
```

Summary

This chapter covered the basics of developing your own custom functions and the possibility of making them recursive. In the next chapter, we explore using the *Structured Query Language* (SQL) with the *ExecuteSQL* function.

CHAPTER 16

Introducing ExecuteSQL

The *structured query language* (SQL) is a standardized programming language used in relational databases to perform operational functions. Created in the 1970s, it became the standard language for relational databases. The American National Standards Institute (ANSI) and the International Organization for Standardization (ISO) adopted an official SQL standard in 1986 and 1987, respectively. Since then, updates have been released, and numerous companies now have proprietary and open source SQL-compliant systems. While FileMaker is not built on the standard, it has some support for internal and external SQL queries. In version 9 (2007), FileMaker introduced the ability to create live connections to external ODBC data sources (Chapter 33). In version 12 (2012), the *ExecuteSQL* function was added to perform queries against FileMaker tables from any calculation formula. A *SQL Query* is a text-based instruction for an action. The most frequently used type of query and the only one supported by the *ExecuteSQL* function in FileMaker is the SELECT query, which retrieves a desired result set. Experienced SQL programmers will appreciate the direct back-end access but may find the limitation constraining. Others may find the divergence from FileMaker's low code, context-centric access confusing. But the ability to perform a search, sort, and summarization of data directly within a calculation formula from any context is enormously useful. This chapter explores this function, covering the following topics:

- Defining the ExecuteSQL function
- Creating SQL queries
- Accessing the database schema
- Exploring other SQL features

© Mark Conway Munro 2024
M. C. Munro, *Learn FileMaker Pro 2024*, https://doi.org/10.1007/979-8-8688-0835-7_16

Defining the ExecuteSQL Function

The *ExecuteSQL* function allows a formula to retrieve data directly from any table occurrence within the file's relationship graph completely independent of any relationship between it and the current interface context. A call to the function must include three parameters: *sqlQuery*, *fieldSeparator*, and *rowSeparator*. It can also accept one or more optional arguments.

```
ExecuteSQL ( sqlQuery ; fieldSeparator; rowSeparator )
ExecuteSQL ( sqlQuery ; fieldSeparator; rowSeparator ; arguments )
```

The parameters in the statement are defined as follows:

- *sqlQuery* – A text expression or reference to a field that contains a SELECT statement specifying the location and criteria for fetching a desired data result.

- *fieldSeparator* – A text string containing the character(s) that should be used as a separator between fields in the result. If left empty, a comma is the default.

- *rowSeparator* – A text string containing the character(s) that should be used as a separator between records in the result. If left empty, a paragraph return is the default.

- *arguments* – One or more text values that are used as dynamic parameters in the query, replacing question marks typically in a WHERE clause.

The results of the function will be a text string with the value for each specified field, for every matching record, delimited by the specified or default separators. For example, using default separators, the result will be paragraphs representing records made up of comma-separated field values.

Caution   This calculation function should not be confused with the similarly named script step used to access external systems!

Understanding the Limits of ExecuteSQL

Before exploring how to write queries for use in this function, take a moment to consider a few limitations. These are especially important for experienced SQL programmers who might expect functionality that is not supported by *ExecuteSQL*. For those new to SQL, it is still worth reviewing, but don't worry too much about any unfamiliar functions.

- As mentioned in the introduction, the function is currently limited to the SELECT command only. It does not support any other common functions that perform record changes or modify schema such as DELETE, INSERT, UPDATE, INSERT INTO, CREATE TABLE, DELETE TABLE, etc.

- FileMaker's relational connections are not recognized or required by the function. If a relationship is required, the SELECT statement must use a JOIN clause to dynamically create temporary relationships for use within the query.

- The function does not recognize the current layout context. Instead, it directly accesses a table based on the occurrence specified.

- Values must be sent to the function with SQL-92 compliant date and time formats with no braces. To apply the correct formatting in a query, use a DATE, TIME, or TIMESTAMP conditioning operator, or the value may be evaluated as a literal string. It will not accept the ODBC/JDBC formats for date, time, and timestamp constants contained in braces.

- The function will return date, time, and number data using the Unicode/SQL format rather than the date and time settings of the database file or operating system. So, these must be converted for use as dates in FileMaker.

- Sorting performed by the function uses the Unicode binary sort order.

Creating SQL Queries

At a minimum, the *sqlQuery* portion of the *ExecuteSQL* function requires a SELECT statement, which can include numerous optional clauses, and these can be used to perform numerous different data retrieval tasks. First, we will define the statement and then explore examples of using these statements within the *ExecuteSQL* function.

Defining SELECT Statements

When calling the *ExecuteSQL* function, the *sqlQuery* parameter must contain a properly formatted SELECT statement. Minimally, this defines what to find and from where, following the pattern shown here:

```
SELECT <what> FROM <where>
```

Usually, the *what* is the name of one or more fields, and the *where* is the name of the table occurrence from which to extract them. For example, the following example would return the contents of a *Name* field from every record in a *Contact* table occurrence:

```
SELECT Name FROM Contact
```

The preceding code shows an example of the simplest statement, requesting one field from all records. However, SELECT statements can be much more complex and include many optional clauses. An exploration of each of these will follow. For now, they are all shown here and briefly defined in Table 16-1:

```
SELECT/SELECT DISTINCT <fields>
FROM <tables>
JOIN <table> ON <formula>
WHERE <formula>
GROUP BY <fields>
HAVING <formula>
UNION <select>
ORDER BY <fields>
OFFSET <number> ROW/ROWS
FETCH FIRST <number> PERCENT/ROWS/ROW/ONLY/WITH TIES
```

Table 16-1. *The definitions of each available clause of a SELECT statement*

Keyword	Clause description
SELECT	Specifies one or more fields to select. Can include fields, constants, calculations, and functions. Use an asterisk to select all fields
SELECT DISTINCT	Adding the DISTINCT operator will remove any duplicates from the result
FROM	Specifies one or more tables from which to select the fields
JOIN	Defines a table and relational formula to allow the results to include fields through a temporary relationship
WHERE	Defines one or more criteria formulas that specify qualifications for records included in the result
GROUP BY	Identifies one or more selected fields used to summarize the results
HAVING	Defines one or more formulas that specify the criteria for the inclusion of a grouped result. HAVING is to a GROUP BY what a WHERE is to a SELECT
UNION	Used to combine two or more SELECT statements into a single result
ORDER BY	Identifies one or more selected fields to use to sort the results
OFFSET	Specifies a starting point within the selected set for the records that will be included in the result
FETCH FIRST	Specifies the number of records that should be retrieved from the starting point, either the first record or a record specified by OFFSET
AS	Creates a shorter alias for a table name that can be used elsewhere in the statement as a prefix to identify a field's table, especially when there is more than one table involved, like when using a JOIN clause

Formatting Requirements

There are a few formatting requirements to keep in mind when writing SELECT statements. These include the following:

- The names of tables, fields, and statement commands within a query are not case sensitive. However, typing SQL commands and operators in uppercase helps to visually differentiate them from field and criteria values.

- Literal criteria, such as that used within a JOIN, WHERE, and HAVING clause, are case sensitive and will fail to locate matching values of a different case. Also, all literal textual criteria must be enclosed in single quotations.

- When listing multiple tables and fields, always use a comma-space delimiter between them.

- Table and field names don't need to be enclosed in double quotes unless they contain spaces or begin with nonalphabetic characters. Since the SELECT statement is itself contained in quotations, quotes used within must be escaped with a preceding backslash.

Using the SELECT Statement

Although the SELECT statement is the only one supported by the *ExecuteSQL* function, it is very capable. Before delving into the many different optional clauses, let's explore the basic statement and discuss techniques for using it effectively.

Selecting an Entire Table

The most basic query is one in which *every field* will be selected for *every record*. This can be performed with a simple statement.

```
SELECT * FROM <TableName>
```

The statement must always begin with the word SELECT followed by an indication of which fields to select and from which table. In this case, the asterisk informs FileMaker to select all fields. The <TableName> placeholder shown above is replaced with the name of an actual table occurrence whose base table the function should access. The SELECT statement shown in the following example will fetch every field from the Contact table:

```
SELECT * FROM Contact
```

Put this in quotes and use it as the first parameter of an *ExecuteSQL* statement as shown in this example:

```
ExecuteSQL ( "SELECT * FROM Contact" ; "" ; "" )
```

Note   See the "CH16-01 Select All Fields" example file.

Enter the formula in a calculation field to produce a result similar to the one displayed in Figure 16-1 that should appear in the field in Browse mode. Each paragraph of the result is extracted from a single record and contains a comma-separated list of every field value, both in creation order (therefore field order may appear different than this example).

```
000001,15:30:14,2016-11-04,2016-11-04,3:30:14 PM,Mark Munro,Mark Munro,,James,Butt,,,6649 N Blue Gum St,New Orleans,70116,Orleans,LA
000002,15:30:14,2016-11-04,2016-11-04,3:30:14 PM,Mark Munro,Mark Munro,,Josephine,Darakjy,,,4 B Blue Ridge Blvd,Brighton,48116,Livingston,MI
000003,15:30:14,2016-11-04,2016-11-04,3:30:14 PM,Mark Munro,Mark Munro,,Art,Venere,,,8 W Cerritos Ave #54,Bridgeport,08014,Gloucester,NJ
000004,15:30:14,2016-11-04,2016-11-04,3:30:14 PM,Mark Munro,Mark Munro,,Lenna,Paprocki,,,639 Main St,Anchorage,99501,Anchorage,AK
000005,15:30:14,2016-11-04,2016-11-04,3:30:14 PM,Mark Munro,Mark Munro,,Donette,Foller,,,34 Center St,Hamilton,45011,Butler,OH
000006,15:30:14,2016-11-04,2016-11-04,3:30:14 PM,Mark Munro,Mark Munro,,Simona,Morasca,,,3 Mcauley Dr,Ashland,44805,Ashland,OH
000007,15:30:14,2016-11-04,2016-11-04,3:30:14 PM,Mark Munro,Mark Munro,,Mitsue,Tollner,,,7 Eads St,Chicago,60632,Cook,IL
```

Figure 16-1.   *An example of the result of a SQL query*

Note   Although the examples in this chapter assume the formula is used in a calculation field, these can be used in any formula including those attached to layout objects (Chapter 20) and script steps (Chapter 25).

Selecting Individual Fields

For situations where you don't need every field from the table, the SELECT statement can specify individual fields.

Caution   The examples here use the common practice of typing table and field names as literal text. However, these will break if the field name changes! Use techniques to keep field references dynamic (Chapter 35, "Keeping Fields Dynamic in SQL Queries").

Specifying a Single Field

To select a single field from a *Contact* table, change the asterisk to the name of the field, remembering to enclose it in escaped quotes if it contains spaces. The following formula selects the *Contact Address City* field from every record of the *Contact* table. This will result in a return-delimited list of city names. Notice that the list includes the field value for every record, so it will include many duplicates.

```
ExecuteSQL ( "SELECT \"Contact Address City\" FROM Contact" ; "" ; "" )
// result =
   Hamilton
   Ashland
   Chicago
   San Jose
   Sioux Falls
   San Jose
   Ashland
   ...etc...
```

Note   See this in the "CH16-02 Select Single Field" example file.

Specifying Multiple Fields

To select multiple fields, list each in a comma-space separated string:

```
SELECT <Field1>, <Field2> FROM <Table>
```

For example, to select the *Contact Address City* and *Contact Address State* fields from the *Contact* table, use the following formula. The result of this statement will be a comma-delimited list of city and state names.

```
ExecuteSQL (
"SELECT \"Contact Address City\", \"Contact Address State\" FROM Contact" ;
"" ; "" )
```

```
// result =
  Hamilton,OH
  Ashland,OH
  Chicago,IL
  San Jose,CA
  Sioux Falls,SD
  San Jose,CA
  Ashland,OH
  ...etc...
```

Note   See this in the "CH16-03 Select Multiple Fields" example file.

Getting Unique Values with SELECT DISTINCT

To automatically alphabetize results and remove duplicates, use the SELECT DISTINCT command. The following example will generate a list of alphabetically sorted, unique values from *the Contact Address City* field of the *Contact* table:

```
"SELECT DISTINCT \"Contact Address City\" FROM Contact"
```

Note   See this in the "CH16-04 Select Distinct" example file.

The uniqueness of the result is based on the entire record value, not individual fields within it. For example, when selecting only the city, the results will include only one entry for "San Jose." However, if multiple fields are selected, like a street address and city shown in the following example, the results will include multiple entries for San Jose since the full record now includes other values. For example, "123 First Street,San Jose" is not fully equal to "1837 Fifth Ave,San Jose," so both would be included in the result.

```
"SELECT DISTINCT \"Contact Address Street\", \"Contact Address City\"
FROM Contact"
```

Reformatting SELECT Statements for Clarity

Unlike the preceding examples that are short and easy to read, SELECT statements can grow in complexity and wrap to multiple lines. There are two techniques that can be used to reformat statements and avoid visual clutter: adding extra space and using a *Let* statement to construct the statement step by step.

Adding Extra Space with Tabs and Paragraph Returns

FileMaker will ignore extra white space in the *sqlQuery* text string so paragraph returns and tabs can be used to separate the statement into readable blocks, as shown in the following pattern. A combination of a tab and paragraph return separates each clause of the statement onto its own line, where it is indented to stand out from the enclosing statement. Following this pattern will make the statement easier to read:

```
ExecuteSQL ( "
    SELECT <field>
    FROM <table>
    JOIN <table> ON <formula>
    WHERE <formula>
    ORDER BY <field>
" ; "" ; "" )
```

When using multiple fields, find conditions, or other components, those can be pushed onto their own line, further indented for additional clarity as shown here in this pattern:

```
ExecuteSQL ( "
    SELECT
        <field1>,
        <field2>,
        <field3>
    FROM <table>
    JOIN <table> ON <formula>
    WHERE
        <condition1> and
        <condition2> and
        <condition3>
```

```
    ORDER BY
        <field1>,
        <field2>
" ; "" ; "" )
```

Using a LET Statement

Another method of eliminating the visual confusion with a complex query is the use of a *Let* statement. The entire SELECT query can be built in pieces using separate variables that are later combined into a single variable and inserted into the *ExecuteSQL* statement, as shown in this example:

```
Let ( [
        sFields = "SELECT <Fields>" ;
        sTable = "FROM <Table> " ;
        sJoin = "JOIN <table> ON <formula> " ;
        sWhere = "WHERE <formula> " ;
        sGroup = "GROUP BY <fields> " ;
        SQL = sFields & sTable & sJoin & sWhere & sGroup
] ;
        ExecuteSQL ( SQL ; "" ; "" )
)
```

Tip   Create a custom function to accept a field reference and other criteria and return a fully assembled query statement.

Exploring the Benefits of Aliases

An *alias* is a short text string that can act as a proxy for a table name elsewhere in a SELECT statement. When a SELECT statement contains repeated references to more than one table, as in a JOIN clause (discussed later in this chapter), aliases are used to identify the table containing a field. Although an alias can be made up of any number of characters, a space-saving mechanism shorter is always better. To establish an alias, use the AS clause after the identification of a table, and follow it with a text alias, as shown in the following pattern:

```
SELECT <field> FROM <table> AS <alias>
```

For example, to create an alias "c" for the *Contact* table, format it like this:

```
SELECT <field> FROM Contact AS c
```

Once the alias is established, it can be used as a prefix on any field name, in any clause, to identify the table to which a field belongs. While aliases are not required when selecting fields from a single table or with a simple query, the following example demonstrates how aliases work. Notice that the alias is defined at the end of the statement but can be used in previous clauses.

```
SELECT c.Notes FROM Contact AS c
```

When a field with spaces in its name is enclosed in double quotations, the alias prefix should precede the name outside of the quotes.

```
SELECT c.\"Contact First Name\" FROM Contact AS c
```

Although an alias is unnecessary in all the following short examples, as a demonstration of the formatting with or without an alias, each of these will generate the same result:

```
SELECT Notes FROM Contact
SELECT Contact.Notes FROM Contact
SELECT c.Notes FROM Contact AS c
```

Note   Aliases will be shown more useful in more complex examples later in this chapter.

Inserting Literal Text in the Field List

Literal text strings can be inserted before, between, and after field names within the SELECT statement and will be repeated in the results for each record. Literals must be enclosed in single quotation marks and separated from fields by a comma. This example demonstrates a `'Name:'` label inserted into the field results. Also, here the *fieldSeparator* of the *ExecuteSQL* statement is a space instead of an empty string. This overrides the default comma shown in previous examples.

```
ExecuteSQL ( "
     SELECT
         'Name:',
         \"Contact Name First\",
         \"Contact Name Last\"
     FROM Contact"
; " " ; "" )
// Result
Name: Joe Sample
Name: Karen Smith
Name: Sam Camacho
Name: Theodore Kyle
```

Note See this in the "CH16-05 Inserting Literal Text" example file.

Concatenating Results

A query can include instructions for preprocessing separate field values into combined results using concatenation, the action of linking things together in a chain or series. Instead of receiving a result of raw comma-delimited set of field names which would require further parsing and manipulating, concatenation provides more useful results. This can be achieved using either the + or ‖ operators, although the latter is both more reliable and less likely to be confused with the same operator used in mathematical calculations. The following example query shows first and last names being concatenated into a single string, with a space inserted between them:

```
ExecuteSQL ( "
     SELECT \"Contact Name First\" ‖ ' ' ‖ \"Contact Name Last\"
     FROM Contact
" ; "" ; "" )
// Result
Cynthia Johnson
Karen Camacho
Sandy Robinson
Thomas Smithfield
```

Alternatively, the plus-sign delimiter would produce the same results.

```
SELECT \"Contact Name First\" + ' ' + \"Contact Name Last\"
```

In the preceding two examples, the same result could also have been achieved by placing a space in the *fieldDelimiter* parameter. However, when a larger group of fields is selected, concatenation allows a different delimiter to be specified between every field. Both the default and override field delimiter are the same between every field – concatenation allows granular control between individual field pairs. The following shows a more realistic example of using concatenation with a custom field delimiter (single paragraph return) and a custom record delimiter (double paragraph return) to generate a contact's full name and mailing address as a three-paragraph result. The first-last name and city-state-zip are each concatenated, and then a custom field and record delimiter format the results into a list of mailing addresses. In this example, we also switched from the + concatenator to the double pipe characters since the city and state would disappear from results when joined with the zip code which is a number and apparently confuses FileMaker.

```
ExecuteSQL ( "
    SELECT
        \"Contact Name First\" || ' ' || \"Contact Name Last\",
        \"Contact Address Street\",
        \"Contact Address City\" || ', ' ||
        \"Contact Address State\" || ' ' ||
        \"Contact Address Zip\"
        FROM Contact" ; "¶" ; "¶¶" )
// Result
Joe Sample
555 Nowhere Lane
Brooklyn, NY 11215

Karen Smith
521 Loft Street
Los Angeles, CA 55555
```

Note   See this in the "CH16-06 Concatenation" example file.

Using the WHERE Clause

Adding a WHERE clause to a SELECT statement allows the query to target specific records based on search criteria. The *formula* portion can contain one or more expressions that define the criteria used to match records, typically including a field, an operator, and a search value.

```
SELECT <field> FROM <table> WHERE <formula>
```

Note   See the "CH16-07 Select Where" example file.

Creating a WHERE Clause with a Single Expression

To limit the results to contacts from California, a WHERE formula would be composed of the field name (in quotes if required), an equal sign as the operator, and "CA" in single quotes. The following example demonstrates this by requesting the first and last name of every contact within that state. Remember, when this is inserted into the *ExecuteSQL* function call (not shown), the entire statement would be enclosed in quotes, and the quotes around field names would need to be escaped with a backslash.

```
SELECT
    "Contact Name First",
    "Contact Name Last"
FROM Contact
WHERE "Contact Address State" = 'CA'
```

Creating a WHERE Clause with Multiple Expressions

For complex criteria, a WHERE clause can contain multiple search expressions separated by a comparison operator of AND or OR. For example, when searching for contacts living in a city that is common to many states, such as "Milford," use two expressions to specify both the city and the state. To do this, use the AND operator between the two expressions, requiring results to match both criteria.

```
WHERE "Contact Address City" = 'Milford' AND "Contact Address State" = 'PA'
```

Similarly, to find contacts from two different states, for example, from Pennsylvania or Ohio, use an OR operator to include results from either expression.

```
WHERE "Contact Address State" = 'PA' OR "Contact Address State" = 'OH'
```

Using the ORDER BY Clause

The ORDER BY clause can be added to specify result sorting.

```
SELECT <field> FROM <table> ORDER BY <fields>
```

The following example returns a list of the last name of every contact sorted by state.

```
SELECT "Contact Name Last" FROM Contact ORDER BY "Contact Address State"
```

Combining the ORDER BY with a WHERE clause, the following example will return the last name of every contact living in a city named "Milford" sorted by state.

```
SELECT "Contact Name Last"
FROM Contact
WHERE "Contact Address City" = 'Milford'
ORDER BY "Contact Address State"
```

Note   See the "CH16-08 Order By" example file.

Using the JOIN Clause

Adding a JOIN clause creates a temporary relationship between two table occurrences that exist only during the execution of the SQL query. These are used to select fields from records in different tables and return a blended result based on a relationship specified in the query. A JOIN allows other clauses like WHERE or ORDER BY to refer to fields from either table or both. For example, fields from *Contact* records can be selected, include the name of a related *Company* record, and be sorted by company name. The JOIN clause contains the name of a table that should be related to the FROM table with a formula expressing the criteria that should be used to form the temporary relationship. The full formula pattern is shown here:

```
SELECT <field> FROM <table1> JOIN <table2> ON <formula>
```

The following example connects *Contact* and *Company* tables to select every contact's first name and their related company's name based on a match between the *Contact Company ID* field in *Contacts* (aliased *con*) equals the *Record Primary ID* field in *Company* (aliased *com*). By assigning an alias to both tables, it can use these as shorter prefix in the SELECT field list, the JOIN clause and the ORDER BY clause.

```
SELECT
    con."Contact Name First",
    com."Company Name"
FROM Contact AS con
JOIN Company AS com ON
    con."Contact Company ID" = com."Record Primary ID"
ORDER By com."Company Name"
```

Note   See the "CH16-09 Join" example file.

Using the GROUP BY Clause

Adding a GROUP BY clause generates an aggregate value based on one or more fields. This is a SQL equivalent of a native FileMaker summary field (Chapter 8, "Summary Fields") or a grouping summary when exporting (Chapter 5, "Summarizing Output into Groups"), generating a summarization of data based on a sort-group field. For example, if an *Invoice* table had a field named *Company* and another named *Amount*, the following example without grouping will return a list of the company and amount of each invoice separately, sorted by company:

```
SELECT Company, Amount FROM Invoice GROUP BY Company
// Result =
    Pretend Printer Corp. - 38000
    Pretend Printer Corp. - 867
    Widgets Manufacturing - 520
    Write Track Media - 10000
    Write Track Media - 2500
```

```
Write Track Media - 7500
Zen Historical Artifacts - 4785
Etc.
```

Two changes are required to create a result that shows the total for company invoices summarized by state. First, add the SQL *Sum* function on the *Amount* field to prompt a summarization of the field instead of individual results. Second, change the ORDER BY clause to a GROUP BY clause to cause the results to be both sorted by company name and collapsed to show the total of all invoice amounts as a summary, once for each company.

```
SELECT Company, Sum ( Amount ) FROM Invoice GROUP BY Company
// Result =
    Pretend Printer Corp. - 38867
    Widgets Manufacturing - 520
    Write Track Media - 20000
    Zen Historical Artifacts - 4785
```

Note   See the "CH16-10 Group By" example file.

Adding a HAVING Clause

Combining a HAVING and GROUP BY clause allows the statement to define which grouped results will be included, acting like a WHERE clause but for summarized results. Building on the previous example, the following example uses a HAVING clause to only include results for companies where the summary of invoice amounts is greater than a certain dollar amount, in this case $5,000. The results of this example exclude two companies because their total invoice amount was less than the limit set by the HAVING clause.

```
SELECT Company, Sum ( Amount ) FROM Invoice GROUP BY Company HAVING Sum (
Amount ) > 5000
// Result =
    Pretend Printer Corp. - 38867
    Write Track Media - 20000
```

Note   See the "CH16-11 Group By Having" example file.

Using the UNION Clause

Adding a UNION clause can combine the results of two or more SELECT statements, whether from the same table with the same or different criteria or from different tables, as long as each selects the same number of fields and each field position is the same data type across them all. For example, if the first SELECT statement returns three fields with the data types of text, number, and text, a second SELECT statement can pull data from a different table to be merged with the results of the first as long as it also returns three fields with the same data types in the same order. The following is a simplified pattern of adding UNION between two SELECT statements that doesn't show other clauses which can be included in either or both statements.

```
SELECT <fields1> FROM <table1> UNION SELECT <fields2> FROM <table2>
```

In this example, a database has two tables, one for *Client* and one for *Vendor*. A UNION clause allows us to generate a list of all company names, including records from both tables. The result is a blended, alphabetized list of company names from both tables.

```
SELECT \"Client Name\" FROM Client UNION SELECT \"Vendor Name\" FROM Vendor
// Result =
Perpetual Motion Dreams, Inc.
Pretend Printer Corp.
Skyline Industries
Thrift Ventures, LLC
Widgets Manufacturing
Write Track Media
Zen Historical Artifacts
```

By default, this clause automatically excludes duplicate entries from the merged result. Use UNION ALL to include all results, even duplicates.

Note   See the "CH16-12 Union" example file.

Limiting the Results of a Query

The OFFSET and FETCH FIRST clauses can be used separately or in unison to limit results to a specific number starting from a specific location.

Using the OFFSET Clause

The OFFSET clause is used to specify the number of records to exclude from the top of the result. This example will exclude the first 20 records and return the remaining records starting from record 21:

```
SELECT "Name First" FROM Contact OFFSET 20 ROWS
```

Using the FETCH FIRST Clause

The FETCH FIRST clause limits the number of rows returned. This example will return only the first ten results:

```
SELECT "Name First" FROM Contact FETCH FIRST 10 ROWS ONLY
```

Combining the OFFSET and FETCH FIRST Clauses

A combination of the OFFSET and FETCH FIRST clauses can fetch specific groups of records from the result. This allows subsets of results to be extracted in a sequence of small batches, often referred to as *paging results*, where each query returns one "page" of results at a time, as was common in the early days of websites. The OFFSET portion indicates where the desired group begins, and the FETCH FIRST portion limits the number of records accessed from that starting point. This code shows several examples of accessing batches of records, ten at a time.

```
SELECT "Name First" FROM Contact FETCH FIRST 10 ROWS ONLY
SELECT "Name First" FROM Contact OFFSET 10 ROWS FETCH FIRST 10 ROWS ONLY
SELECT "Name First" FROM Contact OFFSET 20 ROWS FETCH FIRST 10 ROWS ONLY
SELECT "Name First" FROM Contact OFFSET 30 ROWS FETCH FIRST 10 ROWS ONLY
SELECT "Name First" FROM Contact OFFSET 40 ROWS FETCH FIRST 10 ROWS ONLY
```

The first statement returns records 1 through 10, the second records 11 through 20, the third records 21 through 30, and so on. Using this technique, an interface can be designed to allow a user to step back and forth through groups of results one "page" at a time.

Accessing FileMaker's System Tables

The *ExecuteSQL* function has the ability to access four system tables which provide meta-information about the database's schema:

- *FileMaker_Tables*

- *FileMaker_BaseTables*

- *FileMaker_Fields*

- *FileMaker_BaseTableFields*

These tables are inherent in every FileMaker database file. They can be used in a SELECT statement as if they were custom table occurrences to access information about the tables and fields that make up the database structure. This allows your database to become aware of its own internal structure and opens up the possibility for designing interfaces leveraging this information.

Caution   These tables are not visible anywhere in the development environment and are only accessible using the ExecuteSQL function.

Selecting the System's Tables

The *FileMaker_Tables* system table automatically contains one virtual record for every *table occurrence* defined in the relationship graph. It contains the following fields:

- *TableName* – The name of the table occurrence

- *TableID* – An identification number automatically assigned to the table occurrence

- *BaseTableName* – The name of the *base table* for the table occurrence, which will be different than the *TableName* if the occurrence is renamed in the relationship graph

- *BaseFileName* – The name of the file in which the occurrence's base table exists (not the data source name but the actual file name)

- *ModCount* – The number of modifications made to the table structure since its creation

---

Note   See the "CH16-13 System Tables" example file.

To select all five fields for every table occurrence in the database, use the following query formula in the *ExecuteSQL* function.

```
"SELECT * FROM FileMaker_Tables"
// Result =
    Company,1065090,Company,Chapter 16 Sandbox,8
    Company | Contact,1065093,Contact,Chapter 16 Sandbox,12
    Contact,1065091,Contact,Chapter 16 Sandbox,12
    Contact | Company,1065094,Company,Chapter 16 Sandbox,8
    Project,1065092,Project,Chapter 16 Sandbox,5
    Project | Company,1065095,Company,Chapter 16 Sandbox,8
    Project | Conctact,1065096,Contact,Chapter 16 Sandbox,12
    Sandbox,1065089,Sandbox,Chapter 16 Sandbox,58
```

To select individual fields, replace the asterisk with a comma separate list of field names. This example returns the list of every table occurrence name by specifying the *TableName* field.

```
"SELECT TableName FROM FileMaker_Tables"
// Result =
    Company
    Company | Contact
    Contact
    Contact | Company
    Project
    Project | Company
    Sandbox
```

To select the actual table name, use BaseTableName instead. To eliminate duplication when more than one table occurrence exists for some tables, use SELECT DISTINCT. This example does both, to get a unique list of the actual table names represented by all the table occurrences in the file.

```
"SELECT DISTINCT BaseTableName FROM FileMaker_Tables"
//Result =
```

```
Company
Contact
Project
Sandbox
```

Selecting the System's BaseTables

The *FileMaker_BaseTables* system table, added in version 20.1.1, automatically contains one virtual record for every table defined in the current database file. In a large file, this may be faster since it doesn't contain a record for every instance of a table, just one for each base table. It contains the following fields:

- *BaseTableName* – The name of the table.

- *BaseTableID* – An identification number automatically assigned to the table occurrence.

- *Source* – The name of the file in which the occurrence's table resides. Tables local to the current file will contain "<Internal>" here, while those external will contain the data source from which it is pulled. A table with a broken reference will return "<Missing>."

- *ModCount* – The number of modifications made to the table structure since its creation.

Note See the "CH16-14 System BaseTables" example file.

To select all four fields for every table occurrence in the database, use the following query formula in the *ExecuteSQL* function.

```
"SELECT * FROM FileMaker_BaseTables"
// Result =
    Company,1065090,Company,Chapter 16 Sandbox,8
    Company | Contact,1065093,Contact,Chapter 16 Sandbox,12
    Contact,1065091,Contact,Chapter 16 Sandbox,12
    Contact | Company,1065094,Company,Chapter 16 Sandbox,8
    Project,1065092,Project,Chapter 16 Sandbox,5
```

419

```
Project | Company,1065095,Company,Chapter 16 Sandbox,8
Project | Conctact,1065096,Contact,Chapter 16 Sandbox,12
Sandbox,1065089,Sandbox,Chapter 16 Sandbox,58
```

To select individual fields, replace the asterisk with a comma separate list of field names. This example returns the list of every table occurrence name by specifying the *BaseTableName* field.

```
"SELECT BaseTableName FROM FileMaker_BaseTables"
// Result =
    Company
    Contact
    Project
    Sandbox
```

Selecting the System's Fields

The *FileMaker_Fields* system table automatically contains one virtual record for every field defined in every table occurrence in the database. It contains the following fields:

- *TableName* – The name of the field's table occurrence

- *FieldName* – The name of the field

- *FieldType* – The SQL data type of the file, e.g., *varchar, timestamp, decimal*, etc.

- *FieldID* – An identification number for the field

- *FieldClass* – The class of the field: Normal, Summary, or Calculated

- *FieldReps* – The number of maximum repetitions defined

- *ModCount* – The number of modifications made to the field since it was created

Note   See the "CH16-15 System Fields" example file.

This example returns all seven values for every field for every table in the database:

```
"SELECT * FROM FileMaker_Fields"
// Results =
Company,Company Description,varchar,6,Normal,1,1
Company,Company Industry,varchar,7,Normal,1,1
Company,Company Name,varchar,8,Normal,1,1
Etc.
```

To select the table and field names, replace the asterisks with the desired fields, separated by a comma-space, as shown here:

```
"SELECT TableName, FieldName FROM FileMaker_Fields"
// Results =
Company,Company Description
Company,Company Industry
Company,Company Name
Etc.
```

Remember that these SELECT statements are like any you use against a custom table and can include other clauses. For example, add a WHERE clause to pull only the field names for a specific table, as this example demonstrates:

```
"SELECT FieldName FROM FileMaker_Fields WHERE TableName = 'Contact'"
// Results =
Contact Address City
Contact Address Country
Contact Address State
Etc.
```

Since this system table contains fields based on table occurrences, the results will include duplicates if there is more than one occurrence for a given base table. An iterative process like a *While* function (Chapter 13), a recursive custom function (Chapter 15), or a looping script (Chapter 25, "Iterating with Repeating Statements") can get the name of every base table and then step through these to retrieve the fields for each, thereby avoiding any duplicates. However, a new function allows direct access of fields for base tables only eliminating the need for these complex techniques to acquire a list of base table fields only.

Selecting the System's BaseTableFields

The *FileMaker_BaseTableFields* system table, added in version 20.1.1, automatically contains one virtual record for every field defined in the current database file. In a large file, this may be faster since it doesn't contain a record for every instance of a table, just one for each basic table. It contains the same fields of information as the *TableFields* system table except that the *TableName* field is called *BaseTableName*.

Exploring Other SQL Features

FileMaker includes additional SQL functionality beyond the material covered in this chapter. Numerous functions can be embedded into a SELECT statement to manipulate the results, many providing functionality like FileMaker's own functions. There are commands available to manipulate dates, times, and strings. Numeric values can be aggregated or used in mathematical computations. Conditional actions can be embedded, and numerous operators can be used with field values and SQL functions to manipulate results.

The *Execute SQL* script step, not to be confused with the similarly named built-in function discussed throughout this chapter, allows more robust manipulation of external ODBC/JDBC data sources from external databases.

Also, a FileMaker database can be used as an ODBC/JDBC data source and supports incoming SQL queries from external databases.

For more information about these topics, visit `www.claris.com` and search for the *FileMaker ODBC and JDBC Guide* and *FileMaker SQL Reference* documents.

Summary

This chapter introduced the basics of using the *ExecuteSQL* function and provided examples of many features of the SELECT statement. In the next chapter, we begin to explore layout design, giving users an interface through which to access your data structure.

PART IV

Designing User Interfaces

An interface provides an access point for users and scripts to interact with the data stored in tables. As the visual representation of a database, it is arguably one of the most important and should be carefully crafted to ensure a delicate balance of a technically sound structure and an intuitively usable appearance. These chapters explore the basics and the tools available for designing the layouts that are the front end of a solution:

CHAPTER 17

Introducing Layouts

A *layout* is a developer-designed graphical template that defines how records, fields, and objects will be rendered as an interactive experience for users to interact with database content. A database file's window(s) can display any layout defined that is visible to the current user by layout settings (Chapter 18) and accessible by their account settings (Chapter 29). Each window can only display one layout at a time which is referred to as the *current layout*. When a database first opens, the current layout will be a default layout selected based on how the database is configured. This can be a layout selected in *File Options* (Chapter 6), one opened by a *Script Trigger* (Chapter 27), or the last layout that was open when the file was closed while running on a local computer. While Claris starter solutions begin with predefined layouts, a custom database begins with a single empty layout. This provides a clean palette for a developer to begin designing a custom interface. The table occurrence assigned through a layout's settings establishes the relational context for which database fields can be displayed. This chapter begins exploring interface design by introducing layout basics, including the following:

- Visualizing layout architecture
- Understanding contextual access
- Planning layouts
- Using Layout mode

Visualizing Layout Architecture

A *layout* is a configurable space that contains a stack of one or more horizontal regions that together create a single screen or page, as illustrated in Figure 17-1. A *layout part* is one of a handful of different types, each with inherent and configurable properties that determine their rendered appearance and behavior (Chapter 18, "Working with Parts").

© Mark Conway Munro 2024
M. C. Munro, *Learn FileMaker Pro 2024*, https://doi.org/10.1007/979-8-8688-0835-7_17

Interface objects like buttons, fields, text, and more can be placed into a part. Each of these have their own inherent and configurable properties (Chapter 20) that together define a layout's structure. This work is performed while in Layout mode.

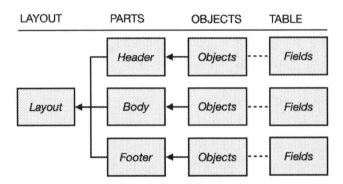

Figure 17-1. *A visualization of layout's anatomy*

The exact rendering of the layout in a window for users varies depending on the selected Window mode and Content view. Browse, Find, and Preview mode will render the layout for entry, searching or printing, respectively, with the exact appearance varying when a user or script chooses from the developer-enabled content views or changes the window mode (Chapter 3). The illustration in Figure 17-2 shows how records from an assigned table are merged with a layout design based on the mode and view and rendered in a window for the user.

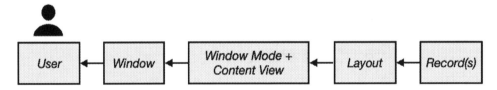

Figure 17-2. *A visualization of the layout rendering process*

Understanding Contextual Access

Previously, we introduced how relationships between tables are established with representative table occurrences (Chapter 9, "Using Table Occurrences"). This allows multiple different connections between the same tables, each placing a table within a specific *relational context* which is used by field calculations and value lists.

When designing layouts, the subject of context becomes even more important. Users view and modify table data through a window that displays an interface rendered by merging of a layout design with table data. However, as shown in Figure 17-3, instead of accessing table data directly, a layout is assigned a table occurrence. This means that a layout establishes an *interface context* corresponding to the *relational context* of that assignment. Here we see (from left to right) a user viewing a window which is displaying a layout for a *Contacts* table occurrence of a *Contacts* table.

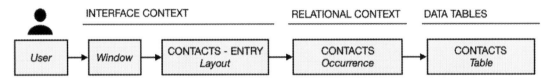

Figure 17-3. *An illustration of how a user looking at a window views a layout assigned to an occurrence which represents a table in a relational context*

A layout extends a specific relational perspective from the back-end data to the front-end interface. It creates an intersecting context point where users and scripts can create, delete, edit, find, print, and view records stored in the occurrence's underlying table or tables relationally connected to it. The layout's occurrence assignment determines which records and fields are accessible when the layout is rendered. Any field that is local to a layout's assigned table occurrence or is in a related occurrence's table can be placed on the layout by a developer, viewed by the user, and used in calculations embedded into layout objects, custom functions, scripts, and custom menu items.

To further illustrate this point, consider a table setup shown in Figure 17-4. On the relationship side, we see three table occurrence groups starting with a primary occurrence of *Company*, *Contact*, and *Project*. Each of these is connected to secondary table occurrences, keeping a clean separation between the primary occurrences (Chapter 9, "Embracing Table Occurrence Groups"). This means that from the context of the *Contact* occurrence, field calculations and interfaces can access records from that table and from *Company, Phone,* and *Letter* through a secondary occurrence. The user is viewing a *Contacts-Entry* layout in the current window, and that layout is assigned the *Contact* occurrence, so that layout shares the same relational access to those other tables, through the secondary occurrences.

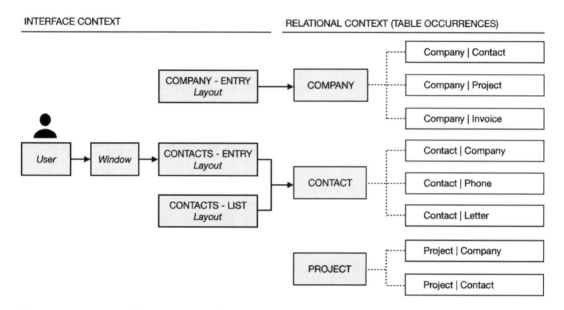

Figure 17-4. *An illustration of how tables, occurrences, layouts, and windows interconnect to present an interface*

The *Contacts-Entry* layout displays records from the *Contacts* table through the relational context of the primary *Contacts* table occurrence. Any field from the *Contacts* table placed on that layout will render the value stored for the current record being viewed. Additionally, fields from the *Company* table can be placed on the layout but only by way of the *Contacts | Company* occurrence. This will automatically display record(s) based on the relationship criteria between the two occurrences and only display matching records. The *Contact-List* layout is assigned the same occurrence, so it displays records from the same relational context. Switching between the two *Contacts* layouts (Entry or List) within the same window will retain the *current record* and *current found set* until they are changed by the user or a script.

Planning Layouts

Layouts will vary in complexity based on their purpose, the needs of a given workflow, budgetary restrictions, and the skills of the developer-designer. A quickly constructed spreadsheet-like table view can provide the ad hoc simplicity that adequately serves a specific need. In a modern workplace, populated with sophisticated professional users, an elaborate design is usually more appropriate and may even be expected.

Poorly designed layouts become a cluttered, confusing, visual nightmare that frustrates a user's ability to work. Such "solutions" tend to cause more problems than they solve. A well-designed layout can range from a modest but practical design up through an artistically expressed, robustly featured, efficiently visualized, graphical masterpiece that anticipates a user's needs and extends powerful, time-saving tools for manipulating and repurposing data in a convenient and intuitive way. Whatever the approach, layout design and planning is important. The entire experience a user has with a database is through a layout. The appearance and functionality of that layout design will greatly influence their evaluation of the database and of you as its developer.

Caution   When learning or building a proof of concept, design can be temporarily less important. Many examples in this book are created for demonstration and not intended as examples of good design!

When designing an interface, start by making a list of the layouts you envision for each table. Typically, every table requires at least one list and one form/entry layout to allow users to perform basic functions. A *list layout* is suitable for scrolling through a found set to locate a desired record and then navigating to an expanded layout. A *form layout*, also called an *entry layout*, is ideal for viewing and performing data entry tasks. Beyond that, layouts can vary based on the nature of the information, the company workflow, and other considerations. Some tables require layouts for printing envelopes, labels, or financial reports. Others require layouts for special data entry tasks or for interactions with the smaller screens of mobile devices. Layouts can be created to act as dialogs that inform and guide users or to provide workspaces optimized for specific tasks. Sometimes layouts are created by developers to troubleshoot or confirm data. Additional layouts can be added at any time during development and even after deployment, so it isn't necessary to plan every layout upfront. But a good starting plan is important.

Start planning by creating a list of desired layouts. Then connect them into a navigational flowchart to help visualize how the user will move around the interface. Even a rough sketch can be helpful, like the one shown in Figure 17-5. The diagram shows a rough representation of *the Chapter 17 Sandbox* database with an added menu layout and various placeholders for hypothetical future layouts not currently included. The navigational arrows are illustrating a general interface connection between layouts. The user should be able to navigate back and forth between a menu and each primary list view. They should also be able to go back and forth between a list and form/entry view for each table. A sandbox is not linked navigationally because it is for developer experimentation and not for daily tasks performed by users. In the actual interface, navigation functions may be much more complex depending on the number of tables, the relationships between them, the style of the navigational controls you develop, and other factors. For example, from a *Company* form layout, a portal might list related *Contacts* and allow navigation directly to them. So, technically, there will be navigational connections between *Company* and *Contact*, *Company*, and *Project*. For now, the diagram simply gives you a "big picture" overview of the flow. It shows you which layouts you need to build now and the starting navigational functions you must provide.

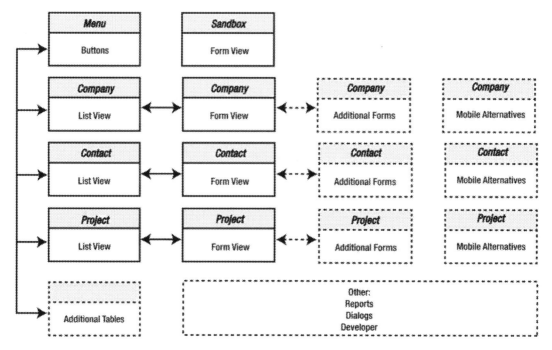

Figure 17-5. *A rough sketch of a simple layout flow with expansion placeholders*

A layout's name can take whatever form you want. Ideally, they include the name of the table they represent and something to describe their general function. Although FileMaker allows layouts with the same name, keep the names unique to avoid confusion. The *Chapters 17–23 Sandbox* demo file uses the name of the primary table for the main Form layout and the same plus a descriptor for other layouts, e.g., *Invoice*, *Invoice List*, and *Invoice Report*.

Once you have at least a rough plan prepared, enter Layout mode and begin exploring the environment used to design interfaces.

Using Layout Mode

Layout mode is an alternate window state in which the entire application environment is transformed to accommodate layout design work. In this mode, the toolbar buttons and menu items change to provide control over interface-related functions. Each side of the window has optional layout panes that provide access to fields, objects, add-ons, and configuration settings (Chapter 19). The entire content area becomes an editable workspace where you can add, configure, and style objects to control how things will be rendered in other modes (Chapters 20 and 21). To enter Layout mode, select the *View* ➤ *Layout Mode* menu or click the *Edit Layout* button in the toolbar.

Status Toolbar (Layout Mode)

When a window is placed into Layout mode, the options available in the toolbar will change dramatically. The Browse mode controls for managing records, and performing data entry tasks will be replaced with tools for adding objects to the layout and performing other design-related functions. The controls available will be either the default Layout mode items or the user's customized set.

Default Status Toolbar Items (Layout Mode)

The default status toolbar for Layout mode is shown in Figure 17-6.

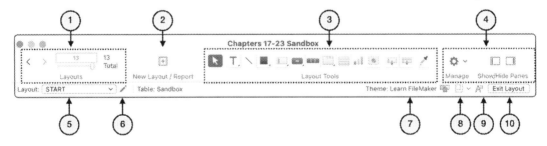

Figure 17-6. *The status toolbar for Layout mode*

- Navigation controls
- New Layout/Report button
- Layout tools

- Developer menu and pane toggling

- Layout menu

- Layout Settings button

- Theme Selection

- Screen and Device Dimension menu

- Formatting Bar button

- Exit Layout button

Upper Toolbar: Navigation Controls

At the top left of the toolbar are navigation controls that appear and function similar to Browse mode (Chapter 3) except they refer to and control navigation through layouts rather than records. The total refers to the total number of layouts that exist in the file, and the number in the text box indicates which layout is being viewed.

Caution   Although included here, recent versions of FileMaker exclude navigation controls from the default Layout mode toolbar. Customize the toolbar to add these essential tools.

Upper Toolbar: New Layout/Report Button

The only function button present in the default toolbar is *New Layout/Report* which starts the process of creating a new layout (Chapter 18). Other function buttons can be added by customizing the toolbar.

Upper Toolbar: Layout Tools

The central row of icons are layout object tools, which are defined in Table 17-1. Most are *object-creation tools* that are used to insert a new instance of a specific type of object (Chapter 20). The majority of those are *draw-mode activation tools* that, once selected, allow object creation by clicking and dragging within the layout creation area. Each of these is a transitory selection which deactivates and reverts to the selection tool after an object is created. Double-click one of these to lock it, and allow rapid creation of multiple objects of the same type one after another without having to reselect the tool. The tool will then remain active until another tool is selected. Many tools have dual modes: click to create a default object type or click-hold to reveal a menu of similar object types. Two of the object-creation tools are *drag-insertion tools* which are click-dragged from the toolbar onto the content area to initiate the creation of a field or layout part. Finally, two tools are *object manipulation tools* which are used to select an object or apply formatting. Each of these are briefly defined here and will be revisited as we explore layout design in the next several chapters.

Table 17-1. *Each layout tool defined*

Icon	Tool description
![selection]	*Selection tool* – Select objects on the layout to move or configure them
T	*Text tool* – Add or edit text on a layout or in object types like buttons, tabs, etc.
\	*Line tool* – Draw a line on a layout. Hold the Shift key to lock for a straight horizontally or vertically line. Hold Option to lock to a 45-degree angle.
▪	*Shape menu* – Click to select the *Rectangle* shape tool or click-hold to choose from a menu of *Rectangle*, *Rounded Rectangle*, or *Oval*. Hold the Shift or Option key to maintain a uniform height and width while dragging its boundaries.
▫	*Field menu* – Click to select an *Edit box* mode or click-hold to choose a specific control style. Drag in the content area to create a field object and select a field assignment. Once created, the control style can be modified (Chapter 20, "Configuring a Field's Control Style").
▭	*Button menu* – Click to select the Button tool or click-hold to choose from a menu of *Button* or *Popover Button*.
▦	*Button bar tool* – Draw a segmented bar that can contain multiple *Buttons* and/or *Popover Buttons*.
▭	*Multi-panel Object menu* – Click to select the *Tab Control* tool or click-hold to choose from a menu of *Tab Control* or *Slide Control*.
▤	*Portal tool* – Draw a portal, for viewing a list of records from a related table.

(*continued*)

Table 17-1. (*continued*)

Icon	Tool description
	Chart tool – Draw a graphical chart object.
	Web Viewer tool – Draw a web viewer object.
	Field tool – Drag a new field down onto a layout.
	Part tool – Drag a new layout part onto a layout (Chapter 18).
	Format Painter tool – Select to copy and apply format settings from one object to another.

Upper Toolbar: Developer Menu and Pane Toggling

The *Manage Database* icon reveals a shortcut menu of developer options that are also accessible through the *File* ➤ *Manage* menu (Chapter 2). The two *Show/Hide Panes* buttons toggle a pane on each side of the window in Layout mode (Chapter 19).

Lower Toolbar: Layout Menu

The lower, non-customizable level of the Layout mode toolbar starts with the *Layout* menu. Similar to the same menu in Browse mode (Chapter 3), this menu always lists *every layout* in the file and adds access to the *Manage Layouts* dialog (Chapter 18). It is used to quickly switch to edit another layout the same as selecting a layout from the *View* ➤ *Go To Layout* submenu.

Lower Toolbar: Layout Settings Button

Next to the *Layout* menu, a button opens the *Layout Settings* dialog where options and behaviors can be set for the current layout (Chapter 18, "Configuring Layout Settings").

Lower Toolbar: Theme Selection

The *Theme Selector* displays the name of the theme assigned to the layout with a button that will open a theme selection dialog. A *layout theme* is a collection of stylistic settings that, once assigned to the layout, can be quickly applied to objects and allows changes to be synchronized across the entire database (Chapter 22).

Lower Toolbar: Screen and Device Dimension Menu

The *Screen and Device Dimension* menu allows a choice of dimensional guide overlays that show an orange border in the layout design area visually denoting the boundaries of specific screen dimensions. Click the box portion of the icon to toggle the visibility of all the overlay boxes for selected dimensions.

Lower Toolbar: Formatting Bar Button

The *Formatting Bar* button toggles the visibility of a text-formatting control bar between the status toolbar and the design area of the window (Chapter 3, "Formatting Bar").

Lower Toolbar: Exit Layout Button

The *Exit Layout* button will switch the window back to Browse mode with an optional dialog asking if you want to save changes depending on preference settings (Chapter 2, "Layout Settings").

Customizing the Status Toolbar (Layout Mode)

The toolbar in Layout mode is customizable at the user-computer level exactly as it is in Browse mode (Chapter 3, "Customizing the Status Toolbar") except that the buttons available are Layout mode specific. To begin customizing, enter Layout mode and then select the *View* ➤ *Customize Toolbar* menu to open the customization panel attached to the window as shown in Figure 17-7. Once open, items can be added, removed, or rearranged in the same manner as in Browse mode.

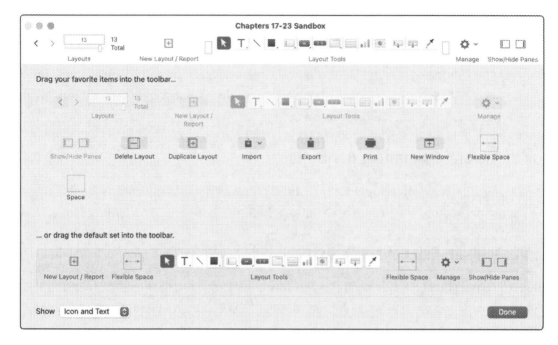

Figure 17-7. *The toolbar customization panel for Layout mode (macOS)*

Exploring Menus (Layout Mode)

The menus in Layout mode are like Browse mode but with a few notable changes. In addition to the *Records* menu being completely removed, the *Edit, View, Insert,* and *Format* menus are changed. Also, a *Layouts* and *Arrange* menu are added.

Edit Menu

The *Edit* menu options change in Layout mode, as shown in Figure 17-8. Among the notable differences are as follows:

- *Copy object style* – Copies style information of a selected object.

- *Paste object style* – Applies previously copied style information to the selected object.

- *Revert changes to style* – Reverts any formatting changes applied to the selected object back to the style assigned (Chapter 22).

- *Duplicate* – Duplicates the selected layout object(s).

- *Export field contents* – This function is removed in Layout mode.

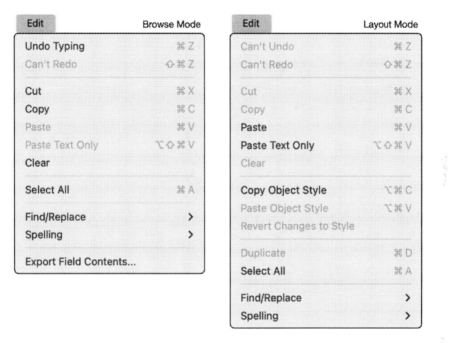

Figure 17-8. *The Edit menu in Browse mode (left) and Layout mode (right)*

View Menu

The *View* menu options change in Layout mode, as shown in Figure 17-9. Among the notable differences are as follows:

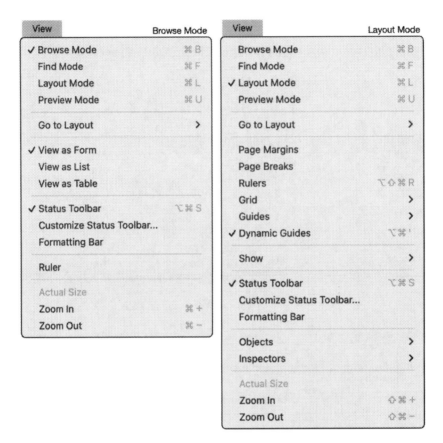

Figure 17-9. *The View menu in Browse mode (left) and Layout mode (right)*

- *Go to Layout* – Like the Layout menu in the toolbar, in Layout mode, this submenu allows navigation to any layout including layouts that are designated to not appear in the Browse mode equivalent menu.

- *View as* – These three Browse mode view functions are removed.

- *Rulers* – Pluralized in Layout mode, toggles the visibility of both the horizontal and vertical rulers.

- *Page margins* – Select to activate page border guides superimposed on the layout background based on the current print settings.

- *Page breaks* – Select to activate page breaks superimposed on the layout background.

- *Grid* – A submenu of two choices: *Show Grid* toggles the visibility of a grid of major and minor lines, reminiscent of graph paper superimposed on the background, and *Snap to Grid* toggles the magnetic attraction of objects to the grid.

- *Guides* – A submenu of two choices: *Show Guides* toggles the visibility of manually placed blue guidelines, and *Snap to Guides* toggles the magnetic attraction of objects to those.

- *Dynamic guides* – Select to activate automatic guides that appear around and between an object when it is dragged around a layout.

Note   See further discussion of rulers, grids, guides, and dynamic guides in Chapter 21, "Layout Positioning Helpers."

- *Show* – A submenu listing special iconography and display options in Layout mode, including the following:

  - *Show Sample Data* in place of field names.

  - *Show Text Boundaries and Field Boundaries* will make an object's dimension visible regardless of styling.

  - The remaining options toggle the visibility of a small icon called an object badge superimposed over objects indicating key features, each defined in Table 17-2.

- *Objects* – A submenu with an option to open an *Objects pane* tab: *Fields*, *Objects*, and *Add-ons*.

- *Inspectors* – A submenu with options to toggle the visibility of the Inspector pane and to create new floating Inspector windows.

Note   See further discussion of *Objects* and *Inspector* panes in Chapter 19.

Table 17-2. *A list of layout object badges*

Icon	Description
	The object is formatted as a button
	The object has conditional formatting features applied
	The object will not be visible when printing
	The object has placeholder text applied
	The object is a popover button
	The object has a Hide formula (Chapter 21)
	The object is searchable with Quick Find
	The object is searchable with Quick Find but will be slower due to lack of indexing or other considerations
	The object or layout responds to script triggers (Chapter 27)
	The object will slide left when printing
	The object will slide up when printing
	The object has a tooltip text assignment

Note   See more detail on using Quick Find in Chapter 4, "Searching with Quick Find," and configuring fields for Quick Find in Chapter 19, "Behavior."

Insert Menu

The *Insert* menu opens change radically in Layout mode, as shown in Figure 17-10.

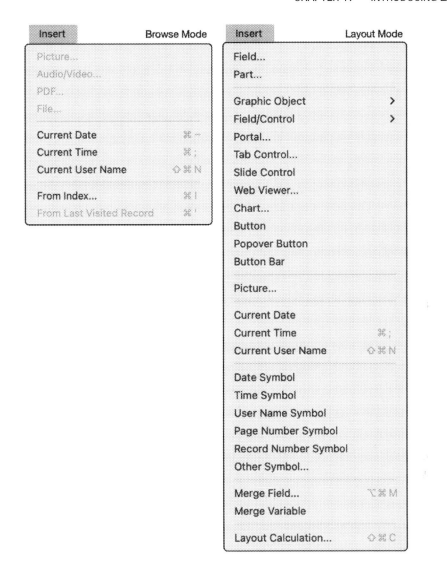

Figure 17-10. *The Insert menu in Browse mode (left) and Layout mode (right)*

The first two sections mirror the tools of the Layout mode toolbar, providing an alternate method of inserting any type of layout objects. In the middle are functions for inserting a *Picture* or placing static text of the *Current Date, Current Time,* and *Current Username.* Below these are functions used to insert *dynamic placeholder symbols,* specially formatted text that is automatically replaced with current values at the time a layout is rendered in non-layout modes. These symbols include the following:

- *Date symbol* – The current date; {{CurrentDate}}.

- *Time symbol* – The current time; {{CurrentTime}}.

- *User name symbol* – The user's computer name; {{UserName}}.

- *Page number symbol* – The current page number when a page is printed or previewed; {{PageNumber}}.

- *Record number symbol* – The current record's number within the found set; {{RecordNumber}}.

- *Other symbol* – Opens a dialog listing over a hundred symbols.

- *Merge field* – Opens a Specify Field dialog and inserts a selected field as a merge field; <<FieldName>>.

- *Merge variable* – Inserts a starter tag which can be edited to a specific variable; <<$$VariableName>>.

- *Layout calculation* – New in FileMaker 20.2, opens a *Specify Calculation* dialog which accepts a formula that will be added directly on the layout as a text object; <<f:Formula>>.

Note   Dynamic placeholder symbols, merge fields, merge variables, and layout calculations are discussed in Chapter 20, "Working with Text."

Format Menu

The Format menu options change in Layout mode, as shown in Figure 17-11. New items are enabled based on the current selection.

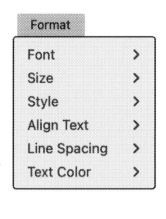
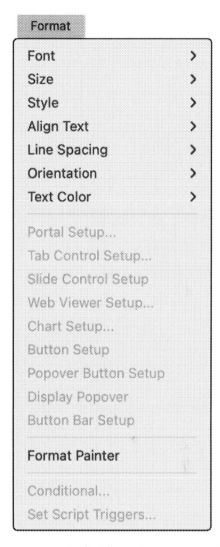

Figure 17-11. *The Format menu in Browse mode (left) and Layout mode (right)*

- *Orientation* – A submenu with two options: *Horizontal* is the default and *Sideways* (Asian text only).

- *Setup options* – This section of the menu contains nine setup menu items that are enabled based on the type of a selected object. They open the corresponding setup dialog, the same as double-clicking the object (Chapter 20).

- *Format painter* – Performs the same function as the tool in the toolbar, copying and applying format settings from one object to another.

- *Conditional* – Opens a dialog for defining special format rules (Chapter 21).

- *Set script triggers* – Opens a dialog for connecting an object action to a script (Chapter 27).

Layouts Menu

The *Layouts* menu replaces the Browse mode *Records* menu and provides access to functions related to managing, designing, and configuring layouts, as shown in Figure 17-12.

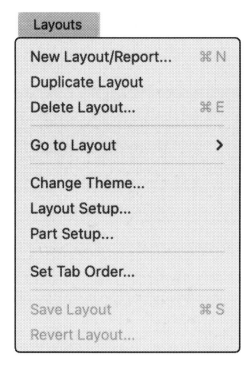

Figure 17-12. *The Layouts menu is unique to Layout mode*

The following functions are available in this menu:

- *New Layout/Report* – Starts the process of creating a new layout

- *Duplicate Layout* – Duplicates the current layout

- *Delete Layout* – Deletes the current layout after a warning

- *Go To Layout* – A submenu of options to go to another layout: *Next,*
  Previous, or by number

- *Change Theme* – Opens a dialog to assign a different theme to the
  layout (Chapter 22)

- *Layout Setup* – Opens a dialog for configuring layout settings
  (Chapter 18)

- *Part Setup* – Opens a dialog for part settings (Chapter 18)

- *Set Tab Order* – Opens a dialog to configure the Browse mode object
  tabbing order (Chapter 21)

- *Save Layout* – Saves any unsaved changes while remaining in
  Layout mode

- *Revert Layout* – Discards any unsaved changes and reverts the layout
  to its previously saved state while remaining in Layout mode

---

Note   See further discussion of managing layouts in Chapter 18.

Arrange Menu

The *Arrange* menu is unique to Layout mode and provides access to object arrangement functions, as shown in Figure 17-13. This includes functions *grouping, locking, stacking order, rotation, alignment, distributions,* and *resizing* (Chapter 21).

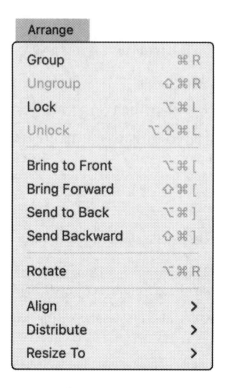

Figure 17-13. *The Arrange menu items*

Summary

This chapter introduced Layout mode, discussed a few key concepts, and identified changes to the window, toolbar, and menu. In the next chapter, we go deeper and define layout parts and get started creating layouts.

Getting Started with Layouts

Before designing the objects and fields that a user will interact with, there are a few things to consider as you start creating layouts. A layout can be composed of one or more parts, and various settings are available that control basics of how the layout operates. Understanding these will be important as you create layouts for different purposes. Also, take a moment to consider a few basic rules for optimizing a layout's performance to ensure that you aren't designing an interface that lags and causes user frustration. This chapter covers the following topics:

- Adding and deleting layouts
- Configuring layout settings
- Using the Manage Layouts dialog
- Working with layout parts

Adding and Deleting Layouts

There are two ways to add layouts to a database file: creating a new layout and duplicating an existing layout. Enter Layout mode to get started.

Creating a New Layout

To create a new layout, select the *New Layout/Report* function from the *Layout* menu, or click the toolbar icon of the same name. This opens the dialog, shown in Figure 18-1, which may step through additional screens based on the selected target device type and function selected. The configuration of a new layout can be modified after creating

M. C. Munro, *Learn FileMaker Pro 2024*, https://doi.org/10.1007/979-8-8688-0835-7_18

it, and some find it easier to choose *Computer* and click *Finish* to bypass the rest of the setup assistant and manually finish the process. However, for new developers and for initial configuration of complex report layouts, this dialog can be an enormous time saver.

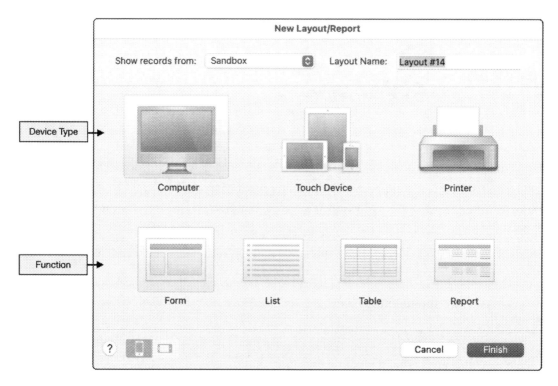

Figure 18-1. *The dialog used to create a new layout*

To begin, choose a table occurrence from the *Show records from* menu at the top. This establishes the relational context that will be used as the interface context for the new layout. Then replace the default numerically sequenced *Layout Name* with a custom name that adequately describes its function.

Select a device type for the layout by clicking one of three icons: *Computer, Touch Device*, or *Printer*. The *Touch Device* icon opens a pop-up menu with a list of device choices based on screen size: *iPad Pro 9.7", iPad mini 6, iPhone 14, iPhone 13 mini, iPhone SE3*, and *Custom Device*. While any layout can be used on a combination of devices, these choices help determine default size and configuration options for the new layout to save a little time later. Also, when creating a layout for a touch device, an orientation option at the bottom of the dialog allows selection of portrait or landscape. It also includes width and height dimension fields when the touch device selection is a *Custom Device.*

Select a primary function to further control default settings. These choices vary depending on the target device selection. The choices for *Computer* and *Touch Device* are shown in Figure 18-1. These roughly correspond to *Content Views* (Chapter 3) and optimize the default layout setup to accommodate a particular type of view choice. The choices for a *Printer* change the function options, as shown in Figure 18-2.

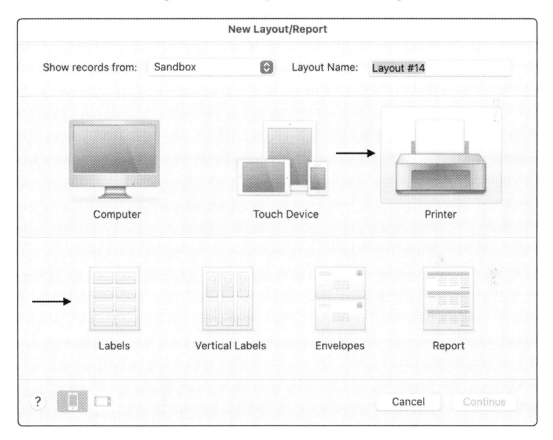

Figure 18-2. *The function options change when Printer is selected*

A *Form* layout is generally used to view a single record for data entry tasks or entering find criteria. They can also be used for creating custom dialogs or print layouts. A *List* layout is used to display a list of multiple records in a found set. A *Table* layout is a low-design list view that displays records and fields in a format resembling a spreadsheet.

A *Report* is the only layout function that is common to all device types. It is a type of List layout that is optimized for either viewing or printing summarized lists of data using sub-summaries and a grand summary. A *Label* layout is a type of List layout that is optimized for printing directly onto labels. These can be created *vertically* or *horizontally* and can be sized in the next dialog based on a preconfigured Avery or Dymo label template or custom measurements. An *Envelope* layout is a type of Form layout optimized for printing directly onto envelopes.

Tip   Remember that any layout can be viewed as a Form, List, or Table. These choices here only influence default setup options which can be modified and viewed differently later.

With options selected, click the Finish button. For *List* or *Form* layouts, the process ends with the new layout open and ready for customization. However, *Labels, Envelopes, Report*, and *Table* layouts have additional dialogs that open with further customization options.

Note   See more advanced report constructions in Chapter 34.

Duplicating an Existing Layout

To save time and maintain uniformity between layouts, consider designing a template for a typical List and Form layout that can be duplicated and customized for other tables or uses. The current layout can be duplicated by selecting the *Layouts* ➤ *Duplicate Layouts* menu. Also, open the *Manage Layouts* dialog, and use the duplicate feature there (see "Using the Manage Layouts Dialog" later in this chapter). The new layout will have the same name as the original with the word "Copy" appended to it. Everything else about the layout will be the same as the original including all parts, objects, formatting, settings, selected theme, and the assigned table occurrence. Once duplicated, the new layout can be renamed, assigned to a new table occurrence if necessary, and further customized as needed.

Deleting a Layout

To delete a layout, navigate to it and select the *Layouts* ➤ *Delete Layouts* menu. Alternatively, select the layout in the *Manage Layouts* dialog and click the *Delete* button. These options will present a warning before deleting the layout. However, once approved, the action is permanent and not reversable!

Configuring Layout Settings

The *Layout Setup* dialog controls the behaviors, appearance, and functions of a layout. To open this dialog, enter Layout mode, and select Layout Setup from the Layouts menu or click the pencil icon next to the *Layout* menu in the lower level of the toolbar. The dialog is divided into four tabs: *General, Views, Printing*, and *Script Triggers*.

Layout Settings: General

The *General* tab of the *Layout Setup* dialog contains general settings, as shown in Figure 18-3.

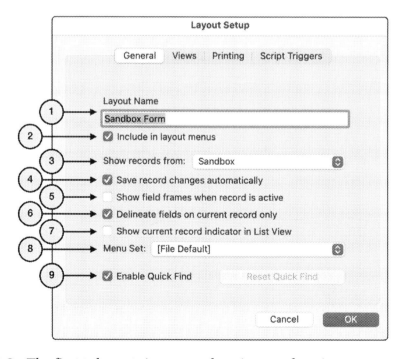

Figure 18-3. *The first tab contains general settings and options*

1. *Layout name* – Edit the layout's name.

2. *Include in Layout menus* – Enable for the layout to be a navigable option for users in the *View* menu and toolbar. Click to make the layout only navigable in Layout mode.

3. *Show records from* – Select a table occurrence to establish the layout's context.

4. *Save record changes automatically* – Control how field changes are saved when a user or script commits a record. If unchecked, a dialog will be presented with a *Save, Don't Save,* and *Cancel* option. If not, changes will save automatically.

5. *Show field frames when record is active* – Enable to show special borders on every field when a record is active.

6. *Delineate fields on current record only* – Enable to cause only fields on the current record to have a border. Consider using style-driven controls instead (Chapter 22).

7. *Show current record indicator in List view* – Enable a black bar on the left of the current record in a List view. Consider the *Use active row state* for the Body part (described later in this chapter) which allows style-driven control of objects for an active record (Chapter 22).

8. *Menu set* – Select a custom menu set for the layout (Chapter 23).

9. *Enable quick find* – Enable the *Quick Find* feature (Chapter 4) for the layout. The button is used to reset all fields to their default Quick Find setting.

Layout Settings: Views

The *Views* tab of the *Layout Setup* dialog, shown in Figure 18-4, contains three checkboxes controlling which content view types are available to a user (Chapter 3, "Defining Content Views"). The *Properties* button opens the *Table View Properties* dialog that controls how a layout appears in Browse mode when viewed in Table view.

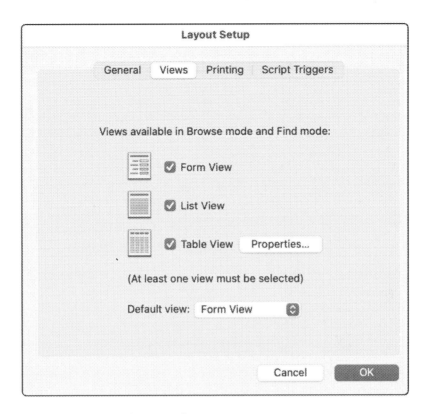

Figure 18-4. *The second tab controls view options*

Layout Settings: Printing

The *Printing* tab of the *Layout Setup* dialog, shown in Figure 18-5, controls columns and page margins when printing the layout. Not to be confused with print and paper size settings accessible through the *Page Setup* and *Print* options in the *File* menu, these focus on spacing and columns of the layout, controlling the available printable area in which to place objects.

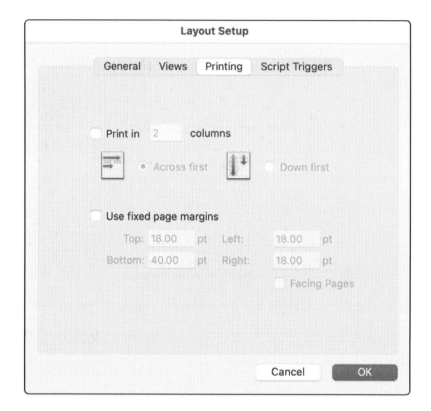

Figure 18-5. *The third tab controls specific layout print options*

Layout Settings: Script Triggers

The *Script* Triggers tab of the *Layout Setup* dialog is used to connect layout events to scripts (Chapter 27) to automatically carry out a sequence of actions when the user performs certain actions.

Using the Manage Layouts Dialog

The *Manage Layouts* dialog, shown in Figure 18-6, is used to reorder layouts, add separator lines for the *Layouts* menu, and group layouts into folders. It also integrates all management features used to *create, view, edit, duplicate, delete,* and *open* layouts. Open this dialog using the *Manage Layouts* option from the *Layouts* pop-up menu in the toolbar or choosing the *File* ➤ *Manage* ➤ *Layouts* menu.

Every layout in the file will be listed in a table view in this dialog with columns for layout name, associated table, and menu set. Layouts can be dragged to reorder in the list or moved into folders, which are created using the menu attached to the *New* button. The checkbox next to a layout corresponds to the *Include in Layouts* menu of the *General* tab of the *Layout Settings* dialog (previously discussed). This option indicates if it will be a navigable option for users in Browse or Find modes.

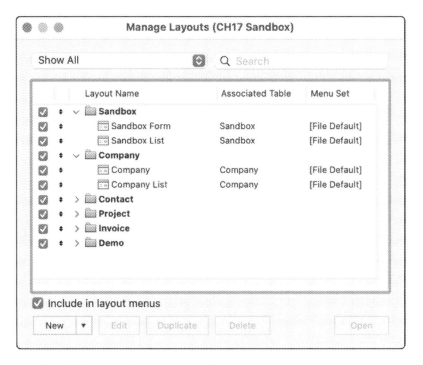

Figure 18-6. *The dialog used to manage layouts*

Above the list of layouts, a pop-up menu that defaults to *Show All* will quickly filter the list to only those layouts contained within a specific folder. The adjacent *Search* field filters the list by keyword helping you locate one in a long list of layouts. The New button at the bottom allows the creation of a *layout*, *folder*, or *separator line*. There are also buttons to *Edit*, *Duplicate*, *Delete,* and *Open* a selected layout.

Tip   Folders can be nested hierarchically. A folder structure defined here forms submenus in the *Layouts* menus, making it easier for users to manually navigate a complex database.

Working with Layout Parts

A *layout part* is a horizontal slice of the layout design area that contains objects which together are rendered into an interface. Every layout must have at least one part but can be made up of a combination of parts necessary for your design. There are several *part types* available, and each of them influences how components contained within will be rendered in non-Layout modes. Although it varies depending on which options are used when creating a layout, each new layout generally has at least three default parts: *Header*, *Body*, and *Footer*. But others can be added or removed as needed.

Defining Layout Regions and Controls

There are several important regions and controls in Layout mode, highlighted in Figure 18-7.

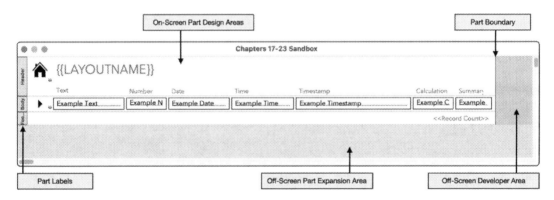

Figure 18-7. *The basic anatomy of a layout*

A *part label* is a small box attached to the left side of each part. These contain the name of the part type and are multipurpose buttons providing access to three functions. To open a configuration dialog, double-click a part label. A single click while holding the Command (macOS) or Windows (Windows) key will toggle the label to a vertical or horizontal orientation. A right-click on a label opens a contextual menu with options to open the part configuration dialog, choose a fill color for the part, or apply a style to the part (Chapter 22).

The *on-screen part design areas* are delimited horizontal slices of the layout space that runs from the left side of the window to the part boundary. This "part stack" makes up the layout design area and represents what will become the content area of the window when rendered in non-Layout modes. New parts can be inserted below or between existing parts, expanding the part stack further down into the *off-screen part expansion area* below. Unused parts can be deleted from the layout by clicking its label and typing Delete, until reaching the last part.

The *part boundary* is a vertical line that separates the visible part stack on its left from the *off-screen developer area* on its right. When viewed in other modes, everything on the left of this boundary will be rendered as the content area filling the window, while everything to the right will remain hidden off-screen. The off-screen area on the right can be used to store developer notes and other layout elements that are not accessible to users but provide special functionality.

Tip   Fields configured for Quick Find (Chapter 4) placed in the off-screen area will still produce results.

Resizing a Part Area

Parts can be resized vertically and horizontally to any dimension that does not exceed the maximum limit of 32,000 x 32,000 points (about 444 inches).

To *vertically resize* a part, position the cursor at the line below the part area until the cursor changes into a short horizontal black line with two arrows on either side, pointing up and down. Then click and drag the cursor up or down to contract or expand the height of the part above the line. When the part labels are viewed horizontally, you can grab the label and drag up or down to resize the part.

To *horizontally resize* the entire part stack, position the cursor anywhere at the part boundary line until it changes into a short vertical black line with two arrows, pointing left and right. Then click and drag the cursor left or right to contract or expand the width of the part stack as needed.

Alternatively, select a part label and adjust the width and height values in the *Position* settings of the *Inspector* pane (Chapter 19, "Inspecting the Position Tab").

Defining Part Types

There are ten different part types available, each with specific inherent properties. Double-click any part in Layout mode to open the *Part Definition* dialog, shown in Figure 18-8. The radio button list at the top of the dialog shows the type of the selected part. The list of parts is displayed in the order that they can appear on screen and can be conceptually divided into two categories: *standard parts* and *summary parts*.

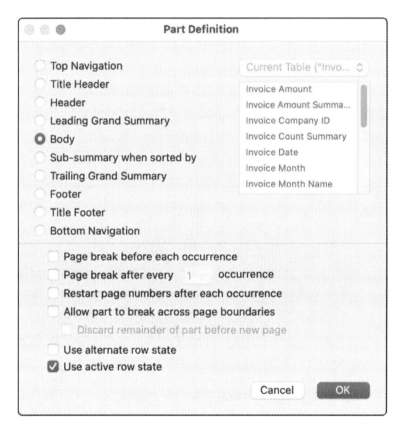

Figure 18-8. *The list of available layout part types at the top of the Parts Definition dialog*

Defining Standard Parts

A *standard part* displays objects without any summarization function. Each layout is limited to a single instance of each standard part, and they must fall within an automatically enforced stacking order. There are seven different standard part types (shown here in order):

- *Top navigation* – Intended for on-screen navigation buttons and other controls. This will not print, and it will not zoom in or out when the window view settings are changed.

- *Title header* – Appears at the top when printing, replacing a *Header* on the first page. This is not displayed in Browse mode.

- *Header* – Appears at the top, except when printing the first page if a Title Header is present.

- *Body* – Represents a single instance of a record. In List view, this part and every object placed within it will be repeated once for every record in the found set. In Form view, it renders once for the current record only.

- *Footer* – Appears at the bottom, except when printing the first page if a Title Footer is present.

- *Title footer* – Appears at the bottom of the first page when printing, replacing a Footer. This is not displayed in Browse mode.

- *Bottom navigation* – Intended for on-screen navigation buttons and other controls. This will not print or resize.

Tip   Don't worry too much about changing parts until you have more experience and need to create more complex interfaces.

Defining Summary Parts

A *summary part* is used to insert summarization values for groups of records and is especially useful when creating layouts where subcategorization of records is desired in print or when browsing records. A summary field placed in a summary part will display a value based on a group of records specified by the part type and its own summary field settings. There are two types of summary parts, each with a *leading* and *trailing* variety indicating a position relative to the Body (above or below it).

- *Grand Summary* – A summary field here will display a summarized value for all records in the current found set. It can be placed at the beginning (*Leading Grand Summary*) or end (*Trailing Grand Summary*) of the layout part stack.

- *Sub-summary When Sorted by* – A summary field placed here will display summarized values for one sorted subgrouping of records within the found set. It is used to calculate subtotals based on a specified break field and separates records into sorted groups. Any number of sub-summary parts can be placed both above and below the Body, and they will only appear if records are sorted by the specified break field. A single sub-summary part will be repeated once for every group of records that result from the break field's sort.

Note   See Chapter 34 for an example of a complex report with sub-summary parts.

Managing Parts

In Layout mode, parts can be added, deleted, and reordered to create a custom layout.

Adding a Part Using the Toolbar Button

The *Part* tool, shown in Figure 18-9, can be clicked and dragged down into the layout area to add to the part stack. The cursor will turn into a clenched fist dragging a black horizontal line. Move this into a position above or below an existing part that approximates the location within the stack to insert the new part and then release. The *Part Definition* dialog will open and allow the selection and configuration of a new part. Once finished and the dialog is closed, you can resize the part and begin adding objects.

Figure 18-9. *The tool used to drag a new part into the layout part stack*

Tip   Dragging a new part this way is imprecise and changes the size of an existing part. To avoid this, use the *Part Setup* dialog described later in this chapter.

Configuring a Part

Parts are defined using the *Part Definition* dialog, shown in Figure 18-10. When a new part is created, this dialog automatically opens. For an existing part, double-click a part label, select the *Layout* ➤ *Part Setup* menu, or choose *Part Definition* from the part label's contextual menu.

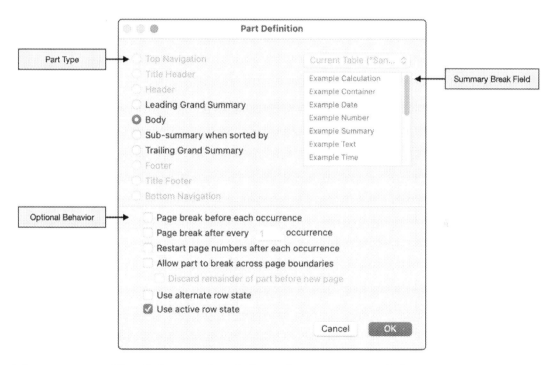

Figure 18-10. *The dialog used to define a layout part and choose various options*

The *Part Type* choices are automatically enabled or disabled based on the location within the stack of the part being defined. For example, a *Body* part can't change into a Header if there is already one defined, nor can you change it to a *Title Header* if it is in a stack below an existing *Header*. However, as shown, a body can be changed into one of three summary types.

The *Summary Break Field* on the right only becomes enabled when defining a *Sub-summary* part. The field selection here indicates that the sub-summary part should be visible as a break between groups of records when those records are sorted by that field. These are often used to insert subtotals in financial reports (Chapter 34). For example, a sub-summary part can be used with a *Company Name* break field and an *Invoice Total Summary* field to display a sorted list of companies with a summarized total of all their invoices within the found set.

The first four option checkboxes control how the part will be handled when printing or viewing in Preview mode. Select *Page break before each occurrence* to automatically insert a page break before each instance of the *Trailing Grand Summary, Body*, or *Sub-summary* part being defined. The *Page break after every X occurrence* will insert a page break after the part has been displayed a specified number of times. This allows limits placed on the number of times a *Body* or a *Sub-summary* part can be repeated on a single page. Use *Restart page numbers after each occurrence* to reset the page numbering after each instance of the part. Use this with a *Title Header* to create a title page that is not included in the numbering sequence or with a *Sub-summary* to restart numbering after each section. Finally, the *Allow part to break across page boundaries* allows a part to be split by a page boundary. Without this option selected, a part will never be split between pages unless its contents won't fit on a single page. Instead, a blank space is left at the bottom of the current page, and the part begins on the next page. Enable this option to override this default behavior and split at a page break to eliminate empty space. The adjacent *Discard remainder of part before new page* checkbox will truncate any remaining content for the part instead of displaying it on the next page, thereby clipping the content at the page break.

The two options at the bottom control the visual appearance of the part. The *Use alternate row state* checkbox enables the *Body* to be alternatively styled to visually delineate records. Enable *Use active row state* to have the *Body* visually indicate the current record with special styling.

Tip   The appearance of the alternate and active row states can be edited by selecting these in the *Object State* menu of the *Inspector* pane (Chapter 22).

Deleting a Part

To delete a part and all the objects it contains, select the part label and type Delete.

Using the Part Setup Dialog

Parts can be managed with greater precision using the *Part Setup* dialog, shown in Figure 18-11. To open this dialog, select *Part Setup* from the *Layouts* menu or from the contextual menu available by right-clicking anywhere on the layout. The list displays every part defined on the current layout and is the only place where summary parts can be repositioned above or below the body. To add a part, click the Create button. This inserts the part in the list and on the layout without resizing other parts as occurs when dragging a new part from the toolbar. To edit a part, select it and click the Change button to open the *Part Definition* dialog. Use the Delete button to delete the selected part. There is no cancel or undo option available in this dialog, so, if a mistake is made, click the Done button, and then select the *Edit* ➤ *Undo* menu to immediately reverse any changes made.

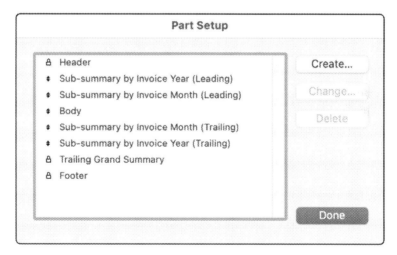

Figure 18-11. *The dialog allows more precise control over the part stack*

Summary

This chapter introduced the basics of creating and configuring layouts. In the next chapter, we begin exploring the controls used to set up layout objects.

CHAPTER 19

Surveying Layout Panes

Configuration tools for fields and objects are available in two panes, one integrated on either side of the window in Layout mode. The *Objects* pane and the *Inspector* pane are both visible by default in Layout mode but can be hidden when not required. In this chapter, we explore the controls available on these two panes:

- Exploring the Objects pane
- Exploring the Inspector pane

Exploring the Objects Pane

The *Objects pane* is an integrated region on the left side of a window in Layout mode that contains three tabs: *Fields*, *Objects*, and *Add-ons*. The visibility of this pane can be toggled by either clicking the *Show/Hide Pane* button in the toolbar or selecting an item from the *View ➤ Objects* menu.

Defining the Fields Tab

The *Fields* tab of the *Objects* pane, shown in Figure 19-1, was added in version 17 and replaced the previously detached *Field Picker* palette. This panel consolidates some schema function shortcuts with some layout design functions. It provides access to directly create fields, modify their data type, and access the *Field Options* dialog (Chapter 8, "Setting Field Options"). Controls at the bottom allow preconfiguration settings that are applied when adding a field to a layout.

© Mark Conway Munro 2024
M. C. Munro, *Learn FileMaker Pro 2024*, https://doi.org/10.1007/979-8-8688-0835-7_19

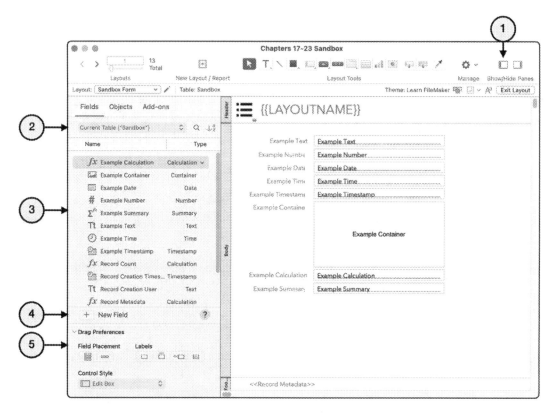

Figure 19-1. *The Fields tab of the Objects pane*

1. *Toggle button* – Click here to show and hide the *Fields* pane.

2. *Table occurrence* – Choose a table occurrence to access a field list other than the current layout's assigned occurrence. Click the adjacent search icon to reveal a filter text area to show fields by keyword.

3. *Fields* – Lists fields in the selected occurrence. Drag one or more to the layout to add an instance. Use the *Type* menu as a shortcut to change the schema type. Right-click to open a contextual menu to delete, rename, or open the *Field Options* dialog (Chapter 8).

4. *New field* – A shortcut to create a field directly in the selected occurrence's table.

5. *Drag preferences* – Controls how fields are configured when dragged to the layout:

- *Field placement* – Stack new fields vertically or aligned horizontally in a row.

- *Labels* – Include a label at a selected relative position.

- *Control style* – Set a default data control style (Chapter 20).

Defining the Objects Tab

The *Objects* tab of the *Objects* pane, shown in Figure 19-2, was added in version 17 and replaced the previously detached *Layout Objects* palette. This provides a view of every object currently on the layout, including but not limited to fields. This allows the rapid location and selection of items, including those in groups or hidden behind other objects. It also has a search field and filter control for quickly locating an object by name or type.

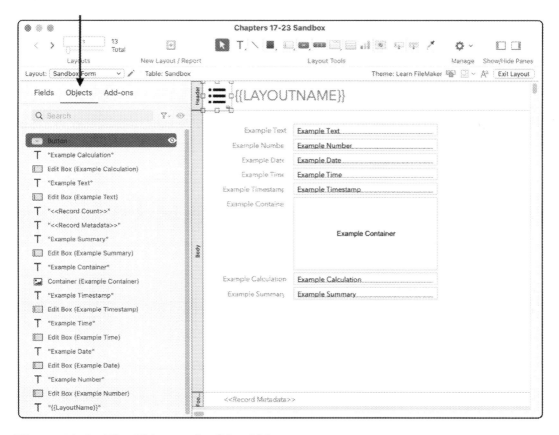

Figure 19-2. *The Objects tab of the Objects pane*

Objects in the list are ordered vertically based on their layout stacking order, akin to layers in a graphics program. So, items listed from top to bottom represents their front to back layering on the layout.

Each object is displayed with a default name unless a custom name has been assigned. The default name displayed will vary by object type. For example, a label displays its text value, a field shows its control style and field name, and a button will be named by object type.

There is a lot of functionality built into the object list that isn't immediately obvious. An object selected in the list will cause the corresponding object on the layout to be selected and vice versa. Grouped objects and multilayered objects like portals, tab controls, and slide controls show in the list with their nested hierarchy which can be expanded or collapsed in the list. A *Hide* icon next to an item's name can be toggled to temporarily make an item invisible in Layout mode to help declutter the design area for focused work. Finally, a contextual menu contains additional functionality, shown in Figure 19-3.

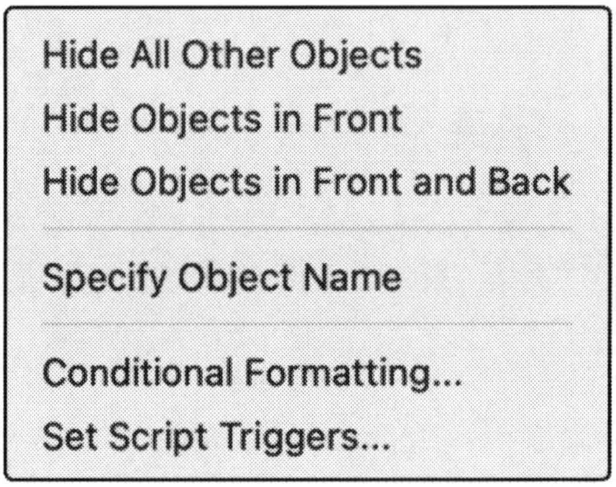

Figure 19-3. *The contextual menu for items listed in the Objects tab*

The first three commands in the contextual menu will hide objects relative to a selected object. These are useful when trying to manipulate an object that is layered behind other objects or in cluttered groups.

- *Hide all other objects* – Hides every object on the layout except for the selected object(s)

- *Hide objects in front* – Hides every object that is layered in front of the selected object(s)

- *Hide objects in front and back* – Hides every object that is layered in front of and behind the selected object(s)

Note   Objects are only temporarily hidden in Layout mode but continue to render normally in other modes. To restore all objects visibility, click the eye icon at the top of the object list to the right of the object search field.

The other commands allow manipulation of object properties directly from the list. These functions are also accessible from the Inspector panes or the contextual menu of the object on the layout.

- *Specify object name* – Reveals a field for entering a custom name (Chapter 21, "Naming Objects"). Names can also be set in the Inspector pane.

- *Conditional formatting* – Opens a dialog for defining conditionally applied styles (Chapter 21).

- *Set script triggers* – Opens the dialog for connecting layout object events to scripts (Chapter 27).

Defining the Add-ons Tab

The *Add-ons* tab of the *Objects* pane, shown in Figure 19-4, was added in version 19 that allows drag and drop insertion of preconfigured resource components. An *add-on module* is a collection of XML, JSON, and graphic elements that automate the insertion of specialty resources into a FileMaker database to instantly add an advanced feature.

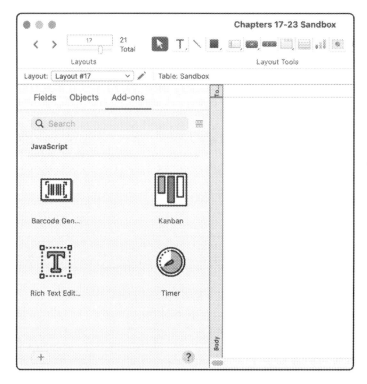

Figure 19-4. *The Add-ons tab of the Objects pane with some add-ons added*

Caution   Add-ons are appealing because they promise the instantaneous addition of advanced features. However, they add a lot of schema and interface resources to your file and might be confusing to new users at first. Experiment carefully.

Click the *add* (+) icon to open a panel containing a library of available modules. Select one and click *Choose* to add it to your file. The module will appear as an icon in the pane and, depending on the selection, may add some combination of tables, fields, relationships, scripts, and value lists to the database. Once added, drag the icon to any layout to instantly create a set of functional objects, pre-wired into the schema. The resources can be further customized to adjust to the formatting and functional needs of the database. To remove, right-click an add-on icon, and choose the *Uninstall Add-on* option. A warning dialog includes a checkbox option that can also automatically delete all the resources that were added to the database.

Caution   Some add-ons require a detectable primary key field in the current layout's table and will refuse to work if one can't be found.

Exploring the Inspector Pane

The *Inspector pane* is an integrated region on the right of a window in Layout mode, as shown in Figure 19-5. The visibility of this pane can be toggled by either clicking the Show/Hide Inspector Pane button on the far-right side of the toolbar or by selecting an item from the *View* ➤ *Inspectors* menu. Unlike the *Objects* pane, the *Inspector* can also be opened into one or more floating palettes using the *View* ➤ *New Inspector* menu. This pane is loaded with controls used to edit the format and behavior settings for any selected part or object on the layout. The controls are organized into four icon-labeled tabs: *Position*, *Style*, *Appearance*, and *Data*. Each of these has various sets of controls grouped into collapsible regions.

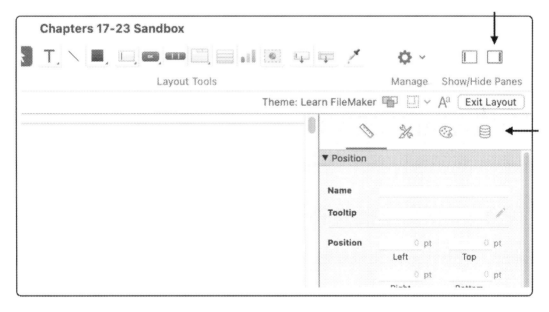

Figure 19-5. *The Inspector pane is divided into four icon-labeled "tabs"*

Inspecting the Position Tab

The Inspector pane's *Position tab* is divided into five collapsible regions: *Position,* *Autosizing, Arrange & Align, Sliding & Visibility,* and *Grid.* The settings in these are used to control the positions of objects when designing in Layout mode and when viewing in Browse mode relative to a resizing window.

Caution   Some position settings move objects when designing in Layout mode, while others dynamically affect behavior when viewed in Browse mode or when printing.

Position

The *Position group,* shown in Figure 19-6, contains options for naming an object, defining a tooltip, establishing a fixed position on a layout, and resizing.

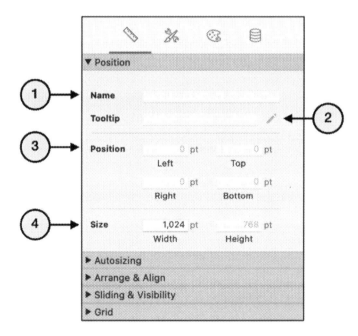

Figure 19-6. *The first group of settings on the Position tab of the Inspector pane*

1. *Name* – Specify an object's name (Chapter 21, "Naming Objects"). This is generally optional but is required for targeting objects with some built-in functions and script steps. Also, it helps for identifying the item in the *Objects* pane.

2. *Tooltip* – Specify text to be displayed as a floating tooltip when the user holds the cursor over the object in Browse mode. The icon opens a *Specify Calculation* dialog for formula-generated tips.

3. *Position* – Control positioning of a selected object within the design area precisely than dragging. These are proportionally locked, so changing one will automatically adjust the opposing value to maintain the width or height.

4. *Size* – Resize an object more precisely than dragging.

Tip   The unit of measurement for the position and size will match the current ruler's settings but can be changed by clicking the labels, which cycle through the options *centimeters*, *points*, and *inches*.

Autosizing

The *Autosizing group*, shown in Figure 19-7, contains *anchoring control* over how an object moves or grows when a window is resized. Objects can be anchored to the left, top, right, or bottom by toggling the lock icon at the respective side of the box. A lock on any side means that the current distance between that side of the object and the corresponding edge of the layout/window will remain fixed as the window is resized in non-Layout modes.

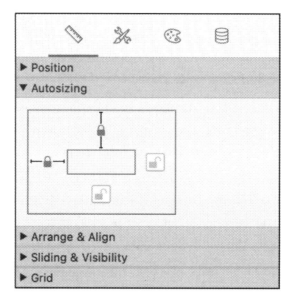

Figure 19-7. *The Autosizing settings on the Position tab of the Inspector pane*

Using these locks in different combinations can create many different positioning and sizing effects.

- Lock the top and left to cause an object to retain its size and remain stationary as the window is resized.

- To retain an object's size but stick to the bottom right of the layout, anchor only the bottom and right sides.

- Objects will expand their size when two opposing anchors are active.

  - To expand an object's width as the window is resized, lock the left and right anchors.

  - To expand an object's height as the window is resized, lock the top and bottom anchors.

- An object with no anchoring will remain the same size and float in both dimensions, staying in place relative to the moving center of the resizing window.

Note   When the top and bottom anchors are locked, a portal object (Chapter 20, "Working with Portals") will dynamically increase its row count.

Arrange & Align

The *Arrange & Align group*, shown in Figure 19-8, contains six groups of buttons that are used to adjust object alignment, distributed space, relative size, group status, arrangement, and locked status. These are not object properties but are tools used to arrange selected objects neatly to tighten an interface design when in Layout mode. To activate these buttons, select two or more objects in the layout. All these settings can also be found under the *Arrange* menu.

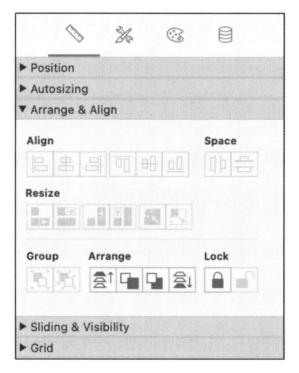

Figure 19-8. *The Arrangement controls on the Position tab of the Inspector pane*

1. *Align* – Align two or more objects by side: *Left, Center, Right, Top, Middle,* or *Bottom.*

2. *Space* – Evenly distribute groups of objects relative to each other *Horizontally* or *Vertically.*

3. *Resize* – Sync the height and/or width of a group of objects based on the smallest or largest among them.

4. *Group* – Convert individual objects into a single group or ungroup them. Grouped items can be moved as one, assigned a group name or tooltip, and resized together (with mixed results).

5. *Arrange* – Change the stack position of selected objects using *Bring to Front, Bring Forward, Send Backward,* and *Send to Back.* This is useful when items are positioned to overlap other objects.

6. *Lock* – Change the locked status of objects. Locking protects from accidental modification when designing layouts. Items can't be moved or otherwise modified until they are unlocked.

Sliding & Visibility

The *Sliding & Visibility group,* shown in Figure 19-9, controls how objects behave when printing, saving as a PDF file, or viewing in preview mode. There are three primary checkbox options: *Sliding left, Sliding up based on,* and *Hide when printing.*

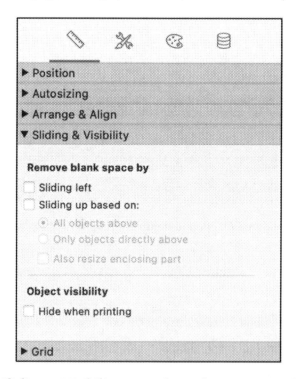

Figure 19-9. *The Sliding & Visibility controls on the Position tab of the Inspector pane*

The *Sliding left* option causes an object to shrink its width to the minimum required to display its content. Any fields on the same horizontal plane with this setting will also slide to the left to maintain the relative distance between the fields.

The *Sliding up based on* option causes an object to shrink its height to the minimum required to display its content and to slide up as far as possible based on the other objects in the same vertical plane. When this object is selected, other options below will become enabled. Select the *All objects above* option to cause objects in a common horizontal plane to slide up together relative to objects resizing above them. Select the *Only objects directly above* option to cause objects in a common horizontal plane to slide up independent of each other relative to resizing objects directly above them. Select the *Also resize enclosing part* checkbox to cause the layout part enclosing the object to shrink vertically relative to the lowest object after all resizing is complete. For example, a notes field expanded on a large layout part accommodates the potential for lengthy content, but can be configured to shrink to only the space necessary to display the actual content.

The *Hide when printing* checkbox causes an object to be invisible when printing.

Sliding and visibility settings can be used to tighten up a view for printing. This is especially useful when you aren't sure of the space necessary to display a field's content. You can expand the height or width of the field to ensure all its content will be displayed. However, when the content requires less space, the printout will look funny with text floating all over the place. Consider an example where you have each element of a mailing address in a separate field. The street address portion might be one, two, or three lines in height depending on the record. The city might be a short name like "Ajo" in Arizona or longer like "Mooselookmeguntic" in Maine.

Note   See the "CH19-01 Sliding" example file.

Placing the fields on a layout expanded to accommodate the maximum anticipated content can be balanced with slide settings, as shown in Figure 19-10. The name, address, and city fields are extra wide to accommodate longer content, but every field is set to slide left. The address field is triple the height of the others to allow extra information like a suite number or department name. This field and those below are set to slide up. The result in Preview mode or when printing is a collapsed address with all extra space removed.

Name			John Smith
Address			125 East Avenue
			Apt 2B
City	State	Zip	New York NY 101020

Figure 19-10. *An example of address fields collapsing using slide left and up*

Tip   You can also use field or layout calculation to achieve the same result. See an example formula in Chapter 12, "Contact Full Name and Mailing Label."

Grid

The *Layout Grid* is a sequence of evenly spaced horizontal and vertical lines overlaid on a layout background to form a regular grid of minor and major areas, shown in Figure 19-11. The grid is only visible in Layout mode and used to assist with precision manual placement and spacing of objects.

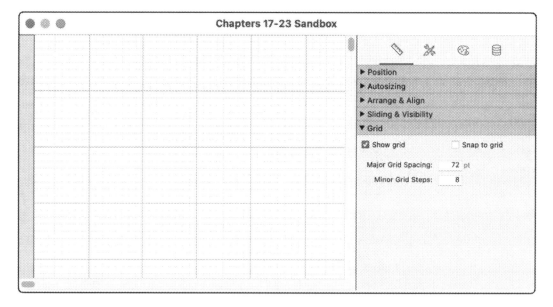

Figure 19-11. *The grid visible on the background of a layout and controls on the Position tab of the Inspector pane*

The *Grid group* in the Inspector pane contains settings that control the layout grid. Unlike other settings, these apply universally to every layout in the current file. The *Show grid* checkbox enables or disables the visibility of the grid. Selecting *Snap to grid* forces objects to fall on grid lines when manually dragged to a new position. The major and minor grid spacing can be customized in the two fields, with the default being 72pt spacing and 8 minor steps.

Tip   You can also use manual and dynamic guides to visually align objects in Layout mode (Chapter 21).

Inspecting the Styles Tab

The Inspector pane's *Style tab* displays and controls the theme and style assigned to the layout and selected object (Chapter 22).

Inspecting the Appearance Tab

The Inspector pane's *Appearance tab* is divided into six regions: *Theme and Style, Graphic, Advanced Graphic, Text, Paragraph,* and *Tabs.* All but the first of these can be collapsed or expanded.

Theme and Style

The *Theme and Style group* is a non-collapsible section of the tab that displays the theme and style assigned to the layout or selected object with adjacent icon menus for updating these when changes are made. The pop-up menus below these allow selection of an *object part type* and *object part state,* and each combination of these has a different set of format settings in the rest of the panel (Chapter 22, "Editing an Object's Style Settings"). For the exploration of appearance settings in this chapter, we will assume editing the options for the object itself (vs. a component part) in its default Normal state.

Graphic

The *Graphic group,* shown in Figure 19-12, controls graphic settings of the chosen part type and state of selected objects.

The *Fill* menu contains four choices that conditionally change the options available below it: *None, Solid Color, Gradient,* or *Image*. The default option is *None* meaning the object will be transparent. Select *Solid Color* to have the option to choose a fill color or *Gradient* to access more advanced fill settings, both using controls like standards found in graphics applications. The *Image* option allows selection of an image file that will be displayed as a background. A pop-up menu here allows control over how the image is handled with the following options: *Original Size, Scale to Fit, Scale to Fill, Slice,* and *Tile*.

The *Line* options control an object's border type: *None, Solid, Dashed,* and *Dotted*. The size of thickness and a color can be specified. The border icons allow selection of which dimensions of an object have a border: *All, Left, Top, Right, Bottom,* and *Between repetitions* in repeating fields. Finally, the *Corner Radius* number indicates the rounding points (pixels) for border corners that will be applied to the corners selected in the adjacent clickable quadrant selector.

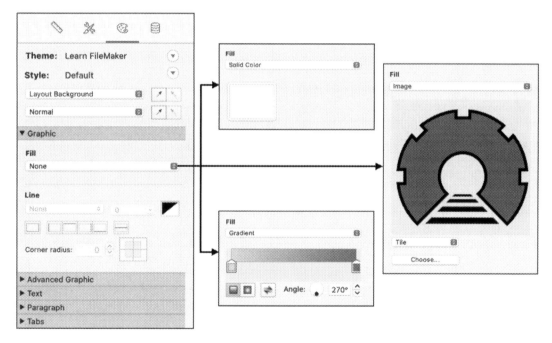

Figure 19-12. *The Graphic group of the Appearance tab of the Inspector pane*

Advanced Graphic

The *Advanced Graphic group,* shown in Figure 19-13, controls effects and padding of an object.

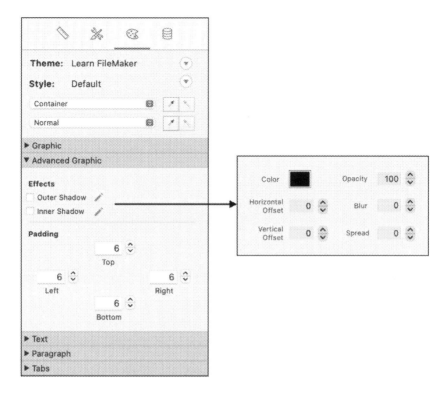

Figure 19-13. *The Advanced Graphic group of the Appearance panel of the Inspector pane*

The *Effects* checkboxes enable an outer and inner shadow on the object using the adjacent pencil icon buttons to open a panel with specific settings for *Color, Offsets, Opacity, Blur,* and *Spread.*

The *Padding* numbers control the amount of distance between the *Left, Top, Right,* and *Bottom* borders of an object and its content. These settings may compete with the paragraph settings for control over indentation and spacing, causing confusion if used simultaneously.

Text

The *Text group,* shown in Figure 19-14, controls standard text and style settings for the chosen part and state of the selected object. These include a selection of font family, style, and size, text settings for color and style, as well as baseline settings for type, thickness, color, and offset. All of these are also accessible from the *Format* menu in Layout mode.

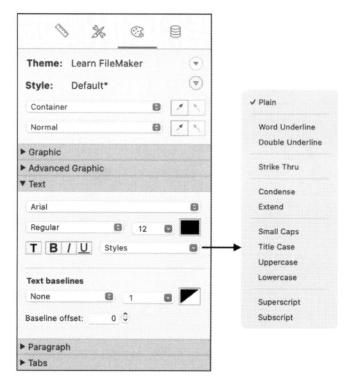

Figure 19-14. *The Text group of the Appearance panel of the Inspector pane*

Paragraph

The *Paragraph group*, shown in Figure 19-15, controls alignment and spacing settings for text.

Figure 19-15. *The Paragraph group of the Appearance tab of the Inspector pane*

The *Alignment* icons control the horizontal and vertical alignment of text within the object, e.g., a field's content, button's name, etc. The *Line spacing* options adjust the spacing of paragraphs, controlling height, space above, and space below, based on a selected unit of measure. The *Indents* settings insert space for text on the first line of a paragraph and the entire left and right indent, all based on a selected unit of measure.

Caution   Some paragraph settings may compete with padding settings!

Tabs

The *Tabs group*, shown in Figure 19-16, controls the tabbed spacing of the text in an object. Click the buttons to add or remove *Tab positions* in the list. Click into a position to edit the measurement, and choose an *Alignment* and *Leader* character.

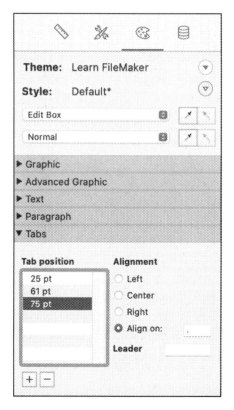

Figure 19-16. *The Tab group of the Appearance panel of the Inspector pane*

Inspecting the Data Tab

The Inspector pane's *Data tab* is divided into three collapsible regions: *Field, Behavior,* and *Data Formatting.*

Field

The *Field group*, shown in Figure 19-17, controls settings of a selected field.

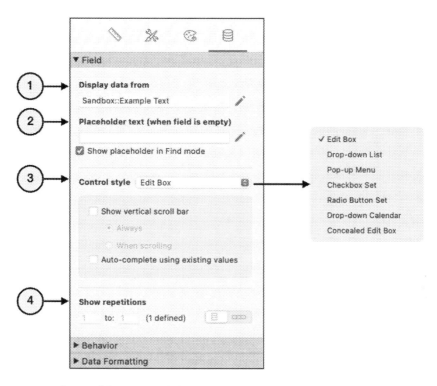

Figure 19-17. *The Field group of the Data tab of the Inspector pane*

1. *Display data from* – Specifies the table::field assigned to the selected field object on the layout by clicking the adjacent pencil button to open a *Specify Field* dialog (Chapter 20, "Exploring the Specify Field Dialog").

2. *Placeholder text* – Enter text or click the icon to define a formula that will be displayed in a field when it is empty (Chapter 20, "Prompting Input with Field Placeholders").

3. *Control style* – Select an input style for the field. The settings in the shaded area below will vary depending on the selection (Chapter 20, "Configuring a Field's Control Style").

4. *Show repetitions* – Controls which repetitions of a field are displayed on the layout and their orientation. Repetitions are an option when defining a field (Chapter 8, "Field Options: Storage").

485

Behavior

The *Behavior group*, shown in Figure 19-18, controls various object behaviors.

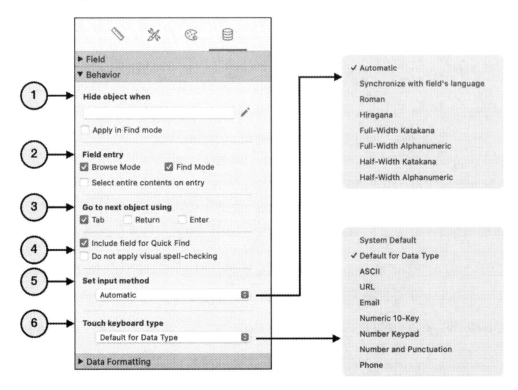

Figure 19-18. *The Behavior group of the Data tab of the Inspector pane*

1. *Hide object when* – Enter a formula to control when an object should be hidden. The hide condition will *Apply in Find mode* only when that checkbox is selected.

2. *Field entry* – Control when a user can enter the field in Browse and/or Find modes. The checkbox below causes the entire contents of the field to be selected when entering the field.

3. *Go to next object using* – Select which key(s) jump to the next field/object. By default, FileMaker uses a Tab to jump fields and Enter to commit a record. Enabling Return here prevents the user from typing a return character in the field.

4. *Quick find and spell-checking* – Control if a field is included in
   a Quick Find (Chapter 4, "Searching with Quick Find") and will
   visually highlight spelling errors.

5. *Select input method* – Choose a language for a field input if
   necessary.

6. *Touch keyboard type* – Choose an iOS device keyboard type for the
   field from the menu of options (for FileMaker Go users only).

Data Formatting

The *Data Formatting group* includes control over how a *number, date, time,* or *container*
field's content will be displayed onscreen. Each data type has a group of controls that are
conditionally enabled depending on the data type of the selected field.

Caution   These settings control how field values are displayed on screen but do
not affect the contents of the field. For example, a number field can be formatted
to display its content as currency ($1,543.00), while the field still contains just the
number (1543).

Data Formatting Options for Numbers

The *Format* menu options for *numbers* are shown in Figure 19-19 with the conditional
controls displaying controls for currency formatting.

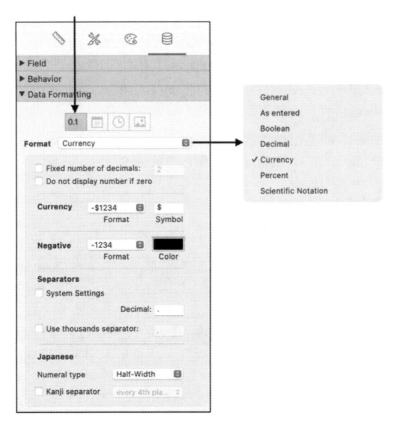

Figure 19-19. *The Data Formatting options for number fields*

- *General* – Displays a numeric value as entered with no special formatting but may round or express it in scientific notation to fit within the boundaries of the field.

- *As entered* – Displays a numeric value exactly as it was entered with no changes for any reason, displaying a question mark if the number extends beyond the boundaries of the field.

- *Boolean* – Transforms zero and nonzero values into a Boolean format. The default is Yes and No, but these can be replaced with other words or symbols, e.g., True and False, 1 and 0, etc.

- *Decimal* – Includes options for number of decimal places, notation, negative value formatting, choice of separators, and more. For example, 1003.7568 can be displayed as 1,003.75 or #1003.

- *Currency* – Includes options for displaying monetary formats, e.g., 5.7534 can be displayed as $5.75, €5, etc.

- *Percent* – Includes option for displaying percentages, e.g., .62 can be displayed as 62% or 62.00%.

- *Scientific notation* – Specify a fixed number of decimal places.

Data Formatting Options for Dates

The *Format menu options for dates* are shown in Figure 19-20.

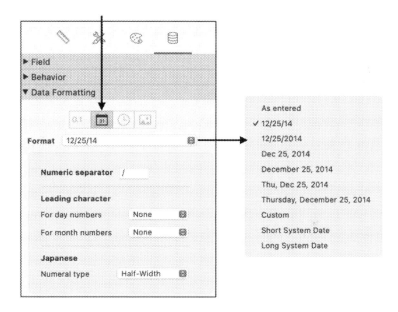

Figure 19-20. *The Data Formatting options for date fields*

The choices for dates include a variety of preconfigured date formatting options. Once a choice is made, the control area below presents any applicable options. In the example shown, a short date format is selected with control over the *Numeric separator*, *Leading character* for days and months, and a *Numeral type* for Japanese text. When *Custom* is selected as the date format, this area provides more granular control, as shown in Figure 19-21. You can then build your own date format using up to four date components, in any order, with any delimiter and with leading zero options for day and month numbers.

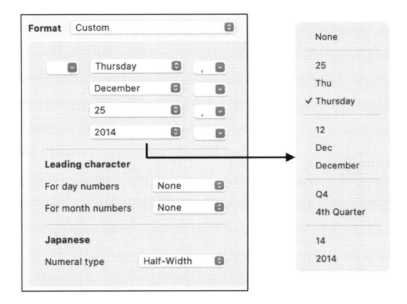

Figure 19-21. *The options for building your own date format*

Data Formatting Options for Times

The *Format* menu options for *times* are shown in Figure 19-22.

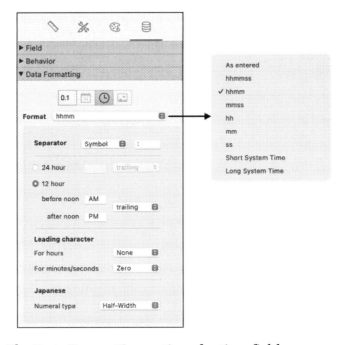

Figure 19-22. *The Data Formatting options for time fields*

The options for time formatting are like those for dates. Choose from a variety of preconfigured time formats or enter a custom format. Other options include military vs. civilian time and leading zeros.

Data Formatting Options for Containers

The *Format* menu options for *containers* are shown in Figure 19-23.

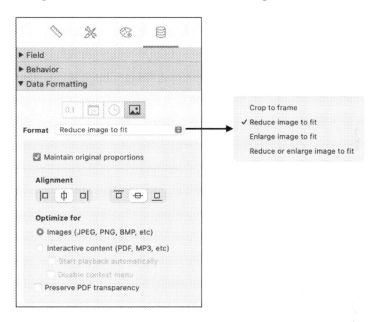

Figure 19-23. *The Data Formatting options for container fields*

The options control how an image should resize, relative to the field object: *Crop to frame, Reduce image to fit, Enlarge image to fit,* or *Reduce or enlarge image to fit.* Several additional settings are available below the menu. There is an option to M*aintain original proportions,* which keeps the image's aspect ratio fixed when it is reduced or enlarged to fit in a field. The *Alignment* controls provide positioning within the field. Other options control image optimization or enable interactive control over PDF, audio, and video files embedded in a field.

Summary

This chapter introduced the *Object* and *Inspector* panes. We explored the various tools and settings they make available. In the next chapter, we can finally begin creating objects.

CHAPTER 20

Creating Layout Objects

A *layout object* is an interface element used to display information, accept data entry, and/or initiate a scripted process. In FileMaker, there are eight basic object types: *field, text, button, panel, portal, web viewer, chart,* or *shape*. This chapter introduces every type of layout object, covering the following topics:

- Inserting an object onto a layout

- Working with field objects

- Working with text

- Working with button controls

- Working with panel controls

- Working with portals

- Working with web viewers

- Working with charts

Inserting Objects on Layouts

Objects can be added to a layout using any of the following methods in Layout mode:

- Using a toolbar icon, shown in Figure 20-1. For most, select the tool, and then click and drag on the layout design area to define the dimensions of the object. A couple must be dragged from the icon to the layout.

- Select object type from the *Insert* menu to quickly place a new instance at a default size and position on the layout.

493

© Mark Conway Munro 2024
M. C. Munro, *Learn FileMaker Pro 2024*, https://doi.org/10.1007/979-8-8688-0835-7_20

- Duplicate an existing object to a new instance by selecting it and choosing the *Edit* ➤ *Duplicate* menu.

- Select an existing object and use the Copy and Paste functions to make a duplicate on the same layout or another layout.

- Select an existing object and drag while holding Option (macOS) or Windows (Windows) to create a new copy of an existing object on the same layout or a layout in another window.

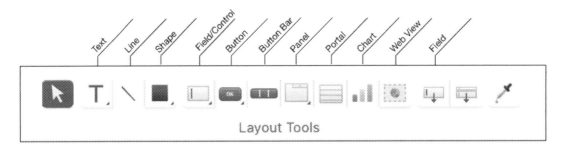

Figure 20-1. *The toolbar icons used to add objects to layouts*

When an object is first added to a layout, it will be in a raw state waiting to be configured. Depending on the type, an object can be configured using different methods. Double-clicking most object types will open a type-specific configuration dialog, usually focused on data configuration options rather than formatting or other behavior control. A selected object can also be manipulated using options in the toolbar's lower *Formatting Bar* (Chapter 3), menus such as *Format* and *Arrange*, and all the options in the *Inspector* pane (Chapter 19). Some configuration dialogs can also be accessed through a contextual menu, accessed by a right-click on the object.

Caution   The actual appearance of any object on a layout in Browse mode will vary depending on the object state, custom format settings, conditional format settings (all in Chapter 21), and the theme assigned to the layout (Chapter 22).

Working with Field Objects

In FileMaker, the meaning of the term *field* will vary greatly depending on the context of discussion. Take a moment to acknowledge the difference between four things that are usually blurred together under this single term, as illustrated in Figure 20-2:

- A *field definition* in a table's schema, its underlying data structure

- A *field cell*, an instance of the definition for a specific record of content

- A *field object* on a layout being designed

- A *field display* rendered on a layout in Browse mode

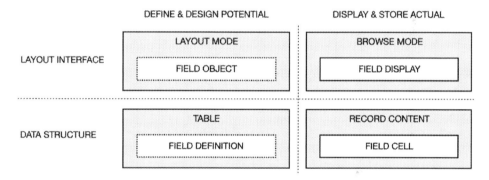

Figure 20-2. *An illustration of the various uses of the term "field"*

There is no inherent problem with referring to all of these as a "field," and one shouldn't feel obligated to use the formal terms shown. In fact, even this book will sometimes refer to these interchangeably as a field. However, it is important to acknowledge the differences to avoid confusion.

A table's *field definition* is an individual unit of storage potential that establishes the data type and settings in the underlying database schema. This definition is replicated as a *field cell* for each record created in the table's data content, transforming the potential of the definition into an actual unit of storage that will contain information. This is the spreadsheet metaphor: a field definition is like a column, a record is a row, and each instance of the field for a record is a cell. In FileMaker, since a user interacts with the data structure through a layout, the metaphorical spreadsheet is entirely hidden from view, and the distinction is less important to them. To them a field is a place where they can enter some data.

When designing a layout, a *field object* is a graphical element that defines the position, behavior, and appearance of where and how a field cell should be displayed. In Layout mode, the field object is assigned a *field reference* which is a pointer to a *field definition*. When viewed in Browse mode, that layout object is rendered as a *field display* showing information stored in the field cell for the record currently in focus – formatted and behaving in accordance with the settings of both the table's field definition and the layout's field object.

Adding Fields to a Layout

A field can be added to a layout by one of numerous methods. Some of these will place the field object and then ask you to specify a field reference. Others require a reference to be specified prior to creating the object. One method works either way depending on the circumstances. Let's briefly look at all the ways to add a field to a layout.

Specifying the Field Reference After Adding

Each of the following methods will first add an *undefined field object* to the layout and then immediately present a *Specify Field* dialog (described in the next section) asking for the selection of a field reference:

- Drag the *Field* tool from the toolbar down onto the layout.

- Select the *Field/Control* toolbar menu to set the cursor into a *field drawing mode,* and then click and drag to create the field object. Click the tool once to auto-select the default Edit box control type. Click and hold to select a control type from the menu.

- Select the *Insert* ➤ *Field* menu.

- Duplicate one selected field using the *Edit* ➤ *Duplicate* menu.

Specifying the Field Reference While Adding

Each of these methods adds a field with a reference already specified as part of the process:

- Drag one or more fields to the layout from the *Fields* tab of the *Objects* pane (Chapter 19).

- Copy and paste an existing field.

- Add fields in a dialog when creating a new layout (Chapter 18, "Creating a New Layout").

- Duplicate multiple selected fields using the *Edit* ➤ *Duplicate* menu.

- Drag and drop an existing field while holding Option (macOS) or Windows (Windows) to create a new duplicate of the field object. This works within a single layout or between layouts in two windows.

When drag-duplicating fields between windows from two different files, the field assignment varies. If the receiving file has a field defined with the same name as the field being dragged in a table with the same name, it will be placed already referencing that field. If the receiving file does not have a matching field but does have a matching table name, the field will be placed with a <Field Missing> reference. If the receiving file has neither a matching field nor table name, the field will be placed as a blank field object, waiting for you to specify a field reference.

Exploring the Specify Field Dialog

Adding a field using any method that requires the selection of a reference will tentatively place a blank field object and open a *Specify Field* dialog, shown in Figure 20-3. At the top, select a table occurrence from the menu. The current layout's assigned table occurrence will always be at the top of the menu with every other occurrence in the file included in one of two lists below it: *related* and *unrelated*. Any field can be added to a layout, but only those from the current table or a related table will display as expected. Once a field is located and selected, check the box to optionally create a label, and click OK to add the field to the layout.

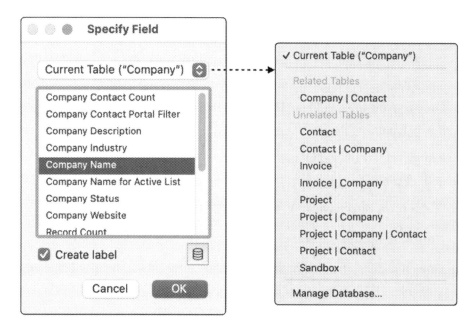

Figure 20-3. *The dialog used to select a field reference*

Editing the Reference of an Existing Field

To reassign the reference for an existing field object, open the *Specify Field* dialog by double-clicking the field, choosing *Specify Field* from its contextual menu, or clicking the pencil icon next to the *Display data from* settings in the *Field* group of the *Data* panel in the *Inspector* pane (Chapter 19, "Inspecting the Data Tab").

Working with Field Labels

A *field label* is a text object placed adjacent to a field to help users identify its content. Labels can be created manually by inserting a text object or automatically using the *Create label* option in the *Specify Field* dialog. Once created, these can be edited, moved, formatted, and manipulated like any other text object. Labels created automatically remain dynamically linked to the field name. If the label hasn't been manually edited, the field's defined name is modified in the schema, and the label automatically updates to reflect the new name. A label for an existing field can be added later by double-clicking the field to reopen the *Specify Field* dialog and selecting *Create label* box and clicking OK. The label will reappear as a dynamically linked value next to the existing field object.

Configuring a Field's Control Style

A *field control style* is a layout setting that modifies the appearance and entry options for a field to streamline data entry. A field can be assigned one of seven types available in the *Control style* menu in the *Field* group on the *Data* tab of the *Inspector* pane, shown in Figure 20-4.

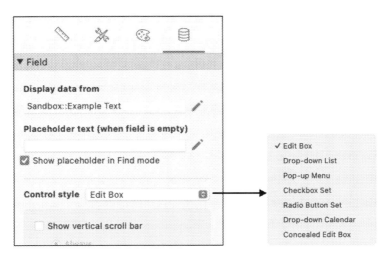

Figure 20-4. *The menu of available field control styles*

Edit Box

An *Edit box* is the default control style that renders a field as a box into which the user can perform freeform data entry tasks. These can vary in size from a single line of text to multiple paragraphs and can include a scroll bar to allow entries longer than the size of the field's frame, all shown in Figure 20-5. All container fields are automatically locked to an Edit Box control style.

Figure 20-5. *Edit boxes; single line (top), multiline (bottom left), and with a scroll option (bottom right)*

Note   See the "CH20-01 Edit Box" example file.

Once this style is selected, settings are enabled, as shown in Figure 20-6. From here, choose to *Show a vertical scroll bar* that appears *Always* or only *When scrolling*. Selecting the *Auto-complete using existing values* option will cause the field to make content suggestions while the user types, based on past entries. To complete a suggestion, the user types Enter.

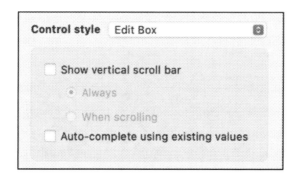

Figure 20-6. *Examples of various edit box control options*

Pop-up Menu

The *pop-up menu* control style opens a menu of choices when the user clicks a field, as shown in Figure 20-7. This allows data entry to be performed by simply clicking a predefined value instead of typing.

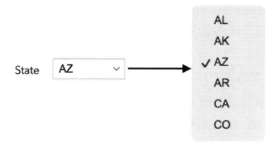

Figure 20-7. *A pop-up menu at rest (left) and open (right)*

Note   See the "CH20-01 Pop-up Menu" example file.

The settings for pop-up menus include the selection of a developer-defined value list (Chapter 11) and a few optional features, shown in Figure 20-8.

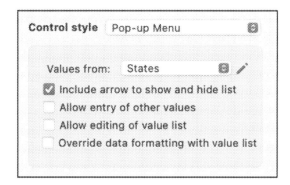

Figure 20-8. *The pop-up menu control options*

Select the *Include arrow to show and hide list* checkbox to cause an arrow to be drawn on the field that visually indicates that it will open a menu. The menu will spring open no matter where the user clicks on the field, so this is simply a way of informing the user.

The middle two checkboxes give the user the ability to bypass or modify the value list. Select the *Allow entry of other values* checkbox to allow users to enter custom values into a dialog by selecting an "Other" option automatically added at the bottom of the list of values. Select the *Allow editing of values* checkbox to allow users to edit a static value list in a dialog by selecting an "Edit" option automatically added to the list of values.

The *Override data formatting with value list* checkbox is useful when a value list is generated from fields (Chapter 11, "Using Values from a Field"). If a field uses a list generated from a *Record ID* and *Company Name*, selecting will always enter the *Record ID* into the field and display that as the current value. Selecting this checkbox option causes the field to display the Company Name as if it were the entry. This allows the value list to be defined to *Show Values Only from Second Field* and display that as the entry even though the actual entry is the ID. See "Using Pop-up Menus for Two-Field Value List" later in this chapter for an example.

Drop-Down List

The *drop-down list* control style opens a list of values when the user clicks a field but displays it as an addition to regular entry. This makes it a combination edit box with an attached menu of value list items, as shown in Figure 20-9. This allows a user a choice of either typing a custom value or choosing a preexisting value from a list.

Figure 20-9. *A drop-down list at rest without an arrow (left), with an arrow (middle), and open (right)*

Note   See the "CH20-03 Drop-down List" example file.

The settings for drop-down lists include the selection of a developer-defined value list (Chapter 11) and a few optional features, as shown in Figure 20-10.

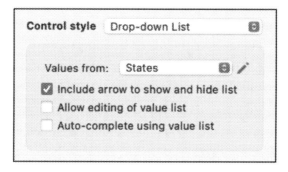

Figure 20-10. *The drop-down list control options*

Select the *Include arrow to show and hide list* checkbox to cause an arrow to be drawn on the field that visually indicates that it will open a menu. Unlike a pop-up menu, when the arrow icon is included, the user must click it to open the menu.

The *Allow editing of values* checkbox works like the same option on a pop-up menu. It allows users to edit a static value list in a dialog by selecting an "Edit" option automatically added to the list of values.

Enable the *Auto-complete using value list* checkbox to cause the field to make content suggestions while the user types, based on values in the assigned list. To complete a suggestion, the user types Enter.

Checkbox Set

The *checkbox set* control style transforms a field into a series of checkboxes, each with a text label, as shown in Figure 20-11. This style allows a user to select one or more individual values from the assigned list. Intended to facilitate the entry of multiple values into a single field, selected values are inserted into the field as a carriage return-delimited list of values, e.g., if "Banking" and "Retail" are checked, the actual value in the field will be "Banking¶Retail." Checkboxes automatically run horizontally, vertically, or both depending on the width of the field.

Industry

☐ Aerospace ☒ Banking   ☐ Education ☒ Retail
☐ Agriculture ☐ Communications ☐ Health

Figure 20-11. *A checkbox set control style*

Note   See the "CH20-04 Checkbox Set" example file.

The settings for a checkbox set include the selection of a value list, as shown in Figure 20-12. Select the *Allow entry of other values* checkbox to allow users to enter custom values into a dialog by selecting an "Other" option automatically added to the list of checkboxes. The Icon menu allows control over the selection symbology: switching from the default X to a fancy checkmark.

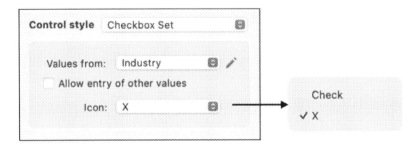

Figure 20-12. *The checkbox set control options*

Radio Button Set

The *radio button* set control style renders a field as a set of selection circles, each with a text label, as shown in Figure 20-13. This style works like checkboxes but encourages the selection of a single value from the list. When a selection is made, the corresponding value replaces the previous value in the field maintaining a single selection. The radio button format doesn't provide an intuitive method for removing a selection and leaving the field empty. However, to clear the selection, a user can click the current selection while holding the Shift key or click anywhere in the field and typing Delete.

Industry

◯ Aerospace   ◯ Banking   ● Education   ◯ Retail
◯ Agriculture ◯ Communications ◯ Health

Figure 20-13. *A radio button set*

Note   See the "CH20-05 Radio Button Set" example file.

The settings for a radio button set includes a selection of a value list and option to *Allow entry of other values*, as shown in Figure 20-14.

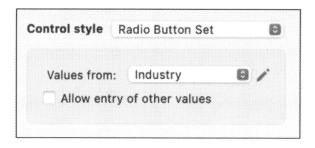

Figure 20-14. *The radio button set control options*

Note   The number of columns in checkboxes and radio button is automatically set by the width and height of the field on the layout.

Drop-Down Calendar

The *drop-down calendar* control style opens a graphical calendar widget attached to the bottom of the field when the user clicks a field but displays it as an addition to regular entry. This makes it a combination of an edit box and graphical entry tool, as shown in Figure 20-15.

Figure 20-15. *A drop-down calendar at rest without optional icon (left), at rest with icon (middle), and open with active focus (right)*

The calendar panel includes several controls that assist the user to quickly navigate to a specific date, including a few subtly hidden. Click the month and year at the top to reveal a hidden pop-up menu that allows quick navigation to any month. The up/down arrow to the right moves back or forward 1 year for the selected month. The left/right arrows move back and forward 1 month for the selected year. Click a date in the calendar to select it, or click *Today* in the footer to select the current date. Once a selection is made, the date is inserted into the field and the calendar closes.

Note   See the "CH20-06 Drop-down Calendar" example file.

The settings for a calendar includes an option to include an icon to show and hide the calendar, as shown in Figure 20-16. Select the *Include arrow to show and hide calendar* checkbox to cause an arrow to be drawn on the field that visually indicates that it will open a menu. Like a drop-down list, when selected, the user must click the icon to open the menu. The auto-complete option will suggest dates based on past entries as the user types.

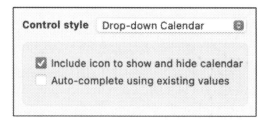

Figure 20-16. *The options for a drop-down calendar*

Tip   The calendar control style can be used with non-date fields. The selection will be entered into text fields as a text string and into timestamp fields as the date selected with the current time.

Concealed Edit Box

A *concealed edit box* control style renders the field as an edit box with each character displayed as a bullet. When the field has focus, it displays one bullet for every character entered but reverts to displaying eight bullets once focus shifts to another field or the record is committed, as shown in Figure 20-17. This control style has no options.

Figure 20-17. *A concealed edit box without focus (left) and with focus (right)*

Caution   Concealed edit boxes are intended to provide *minimal security only.* The data stored in the field is *not* encrypted. It is obscured from view on layouts where the control style is applied but continues to be accessible to scripts and calculations, which can access and manipulate the data as they would any other field.

Using Control Styles with a Two-Field Value List

There are challenges to consider when designing an interface that uses a drop-down list or pop-up menu control style with a two-field value list. These are commonly used to facilitate the entry of a foreign key record identifier to establish a relationship to a record in another table (Chapter 9, "Visualizing Relationships"). For example, to establish a relationship to a *Company* record from a *Contact, Project,* or *Invoice* record, the *Record Primary ID* of the company must be entered in these tables. However, a value list of just IDs requires the user to know the ID associated with the desired company which is not an intuitive interface design. By contrast, a two-field value list, like the one shown in Figure 20-18, can include the company name in the list for the user identification while still inserting the ID once a selection is made.

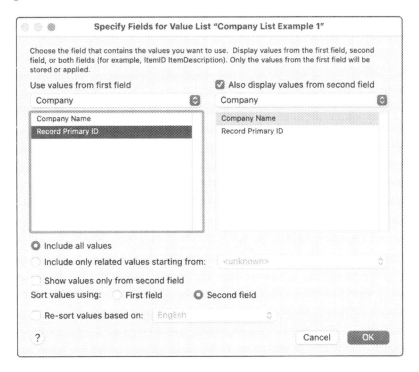

Figure 20-18. *An example of a two-field value list sorting by the second field*

Although it seems straightforward when defining the list, complexity arises when implementing this into a layout design. Let's explore the options and issues involved by working through a few examples.

Note   See the "CH20-07 Two Field Value Lists" example file.

Using a List and Relationship to Display Second Field

First, create a *Company ID* field in another table and apply the value list with the drop-down list control style, as shown in Figure 20-19. With the list opens, the user can look at the alphabetically sorted list of company names and select the one they want and have the corresponding ID inserted into the field. In terms of data entry, this works great. However, after the selection is made and the list closes, only the ID is displayed in the field, so it is no longer clear which company is assigned to the record being viewed.

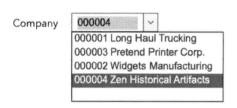
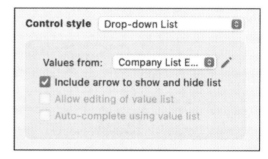

Figure 20-19. *The value list assigned to a field (left), configured as a drop-down list (right)*

One approach to resolving this is to add a relationship between the *Company ID* field in the Contact table to the Company table's *Record Primary ID* as shown in Figure 20-20.

Figure 20-20. *A relationship to a Company occurrence through which the Company Name can be displayed in a Contact table*

Now the *Company Name* field can be added to the layout by specifying it through this relationship, as shown in Figure 20-21.

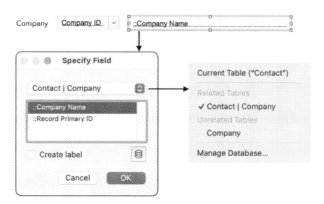

Figure 20-21. *Adding the Company Name field to the Contact layout through the new relationship*

Now, in Browse mode, the company name will be displayed next to the ID after a selection is made and the list closes, as shown in Figure 20-22.

Figure 20-22. *Now the Company Name displays after the selection is made*

The preceding example has a long tradition as a method for displaying the name with an ID when assigning a foreign key and is a valid technique. However, it has some drawbacks that cause developer to seek other options. First, it makes the entry feel a little unnatural since the click is on the ID field, but you select a value by name, and then the ID is entered in the field you clicked while the name appears in the field off to the side. It also clutters the layout showing both the ID and the name. Since IDs are often not something a user needs to see, some developers opt for a creative stacking the two fields so the name field sits on top, overlapping the ID field. By configuring the name field on top to not allow data entry (Chapter 19, "Behavior: Field Entry"), a click will pass through it to the ID field, as shown in Figure 20-23. If the ID field is a drop-down list without the arrow icon, a click will immediately open the menu. When a selection was made, the ID field will be hidden by the name field.

Figure 20-23. *The ID field is hidden behind the name (left) until the user clicks the fields (right)*

This creates the illusion of a single field, always displaying the name until editing. However, it is still not ideal. The list still shows ID numbers, so they aren't really hidden. Configuring the value list to *Show Values Only from Second Field* causes the ID to disappear from the list of options, but then you see a list of names with the ID in the field above. Further, although there are valid uses to stacking fields and other objects on top of each other, it's clunky to overlay fields for this purpose, especially when there is a better option.

Using a Menu with Override Data Formatting Option

The more modern alternative to the preceding approach is to use a pop-up menu control style with the *Override data formatting with value list* option selected. Combined with a value list configured to *Show Values Only from Second Field*, the result is a single field on the layout that displays a list of company names but enters the corresponding ID into the field while keeping the ID completely hidden from the user. This also drops the requirement of a relationship to displaying the name, although the relationship can be used for navigation scripts and other functions.

To implement this technique, the *Company ID* is widened to accommodate a company name. After confirming that the value list is set to only show the second field, configure the field to display as a pop-up menu, and with the override option selected, as shown in Figure 20-24. Now the list will only show company names, and the field, while still containing an id, will override that with layout formatting to display the selected value from the value list, the company name. This works without overlapping fields or requiring extra table occurrences and relationships.

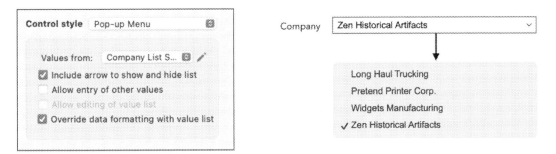

Figure 20-24. *The pop-up menu configuration (left) allows one field and its menu to display names only even though it contains an ID (right)*

Although this approach is modern and far superior to the previous ones, it is not without its own drawbacks. If the list of company records is configured to only show those with a status value of "active" (Chapter 11, "Creating Conditional Value Lists"), then any older records linked to inactive companies will show a blank value in the field since the company vanishes from the list showing active only. So, the technique is most useful when the value list will always show all records and may not work when the list is conditional. This illustrates a principle in FileMaker that there are several ways to approach every problem and choosing the right approach for a given context requires some serious consideration.

Bypassing Value List Entry Restrictions

The four control styles that use value lists will implicitly encourage user compliance with certain data entry restrictions, as shown in Table 20-1. The *drop-down menu, pop-up menu,* and *radio button* control styles are intended to facilitate the entry of a single value. The *pop-up menu, checkbox set,* and *radio button set* are intended for entry of value list items only, while drop-down list allows direct typing of alternative values. However, these "rules" are not strictly enforced rules, and they can be bypassed by crafty users. For example, users can click into a field and paste values from the clipboard to bypass both restrictions. Also, holding the Shift key while clicking radio buttons allows multiple selections. Most users will never realize these abilities exist so it may never be a problem. But some will and others may click or paste to bypass the restrictions by accident. For situations where it is important to restrict data entry to options made available with a control style, it may be necessary to take explicit steps to make it impossible for users to bypass the value list.

Table 20-1. *The implied restrictions for entry into fields using value list driven control styles*

Control style	Single item	Value list items only
Pop-up menu	Yes	Yes
Drop-down list	Yes	–
Checkbox set	–	Yes
Radio button	Yes	Yes

Halting Entry of Custom Values

Even with the *Allow entry of other values* checkbox disabled on control styles, the entry of values not present on a field's assigned value list can be done several ways. For example, when the field has focus, text in the clipboard can be pasted. Any of the text-entering functions from the *Insert* menu can be used to insert values. Users can also drag a text selection from another field or even another application and drop it into the field. Importing records can bypass the interface as can many script steps. There are several ways to tighten up data entry, making it impossible to bypass the assigned value list.

Using Field Validation

A simple method to stop users from bypassing the assigned value list is to use the validation feature at the schema level, where nothing can get past it (Chapter 8, "Field Options: Validation"). Select the *Member of value list* checkbox and pick the value list from the adjacent menu as shown in Figure 20-25. By deselecting *Allow user to override during data entry* checkbox, there will be no choice for the user but to revert the field and start over. This will apply to every use of the field on any layout (including those where a value list control style is not used) and will warn the user about the error. This is a good option for situations where universal coverage is desired.

Note   See the "CH20-08 Halting Bypass with Validation" example file.

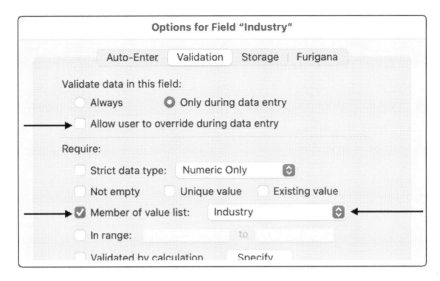

Figure 20-25. *Using the Validation options to restrict entry to only items on a specific value list*

Caution   Using the *Always* option for field validation can disrupt importing.

When using any field validation option, you can always specify a custom warning dialog message (Chapter 8, "Controlling Validation Enforcement").

Filtering Out Bad Values with a Calculation

Alternatively, an *auto-enter calculation* at the field definition level (Chapter 8, "Field Options: Auto-Enter") can automatically preprocesses data input to confirm that any entries made are appropriate and automatically remove any that are not. This provides the advantage of removing erroneous values without an error dialog, so it is great for a nondisruptive correction and won't slow down a user's data entry. It can even auto-clean during imports as long as the *Perform the auto-enter options* checkbox option is selected for the field (Chapter 5, "Setting Import Options").

Note   See the "CH20-09 Filtering out Bad Values" example file.

The formula below will automatically filter out any value entered that is not in the list. It uses a *Let* statement and the built-in *ValueListItems* function to place the items in a value list named "Industry" into a variable named *itemsAllowed*. Then, the built-in *FilterValues* function (Chapter 13, "Manipulating Values") removes every item entered that isn't found in the list of items allowed. Since this formula is used as part of the field definition, it can use the *Self* function to access the value of the field itself.

```
Let (
    itemsAllowed = ValueListItems ( Get ( FileName ) ; "Industry" )
;
    FilterValues ( itemsAllowed ; Self )
)
```

This approach is ideal because it just fixes problems without requiring a distracting intervention from the user. However, it may cause confusion and appear like a bug to an inexperienced user who would have no idea what error they committed to make their pasted value disappear. They may not even be aware that the values were automatically removed.

Using a Script Trigger

Finally, the *OnObjectValidate* script trigger (Chapter 27) can be used to run a script that validates the user's entry and takes corrective action. The script can be created to automatically clean up and/or inform the user about their error. It can even abort the validation process and force them to correct it before continuing. This is a good option for a layout-specific intervention that can autocorrect with a custom notification or inform and require a user change but not necessarily apply to every instance of the field on other layouts.

Halting Entry of Multiple Values

By design, a *checkbox set* is the only value list-driven control style that intuitively allows the selection of multiple items from a value list. When used as intended, all other control styles replace an existing value when a new value is selected, essentially restricting entry to a single selection. However, users can select more than one item, using any of the following methods:

- Hold the Shift key while clicking additional options.

- Use the Paste command to enter a return-delimited list.

- Drag a return-delimited list from another field or application.

- When the *Allow entry of other values option* is enabled on the field, a user can choose "Other" and manually enter multiple values in the dialog.

- Use a script step such as *Set Field, Insert Text, Replace Field Contents, Import Records*, and more (assuming they have access to edit scripts).

There are a few ways to stop multiple values from being entered in a field.

Note   See the "CH20-10 Halting Multiple Values" example file.

Using Field Validation with a Calculation

A simple method to stop users from entering multiple values into a field is using the validation feature at the field definition level. Select the *Validated by calculation* checkbox, as shown in Figure 20-26. Then enter this formula in the *Specify Calculation* dialog. If the number of values in the field is more than 1, a validation error dialog will appear, forcing the user to revert the record and try again. Be sure to disable the *Allow user to override during data entry* checkbox.

```
ValueCount ( Self ) ≤ 1
```

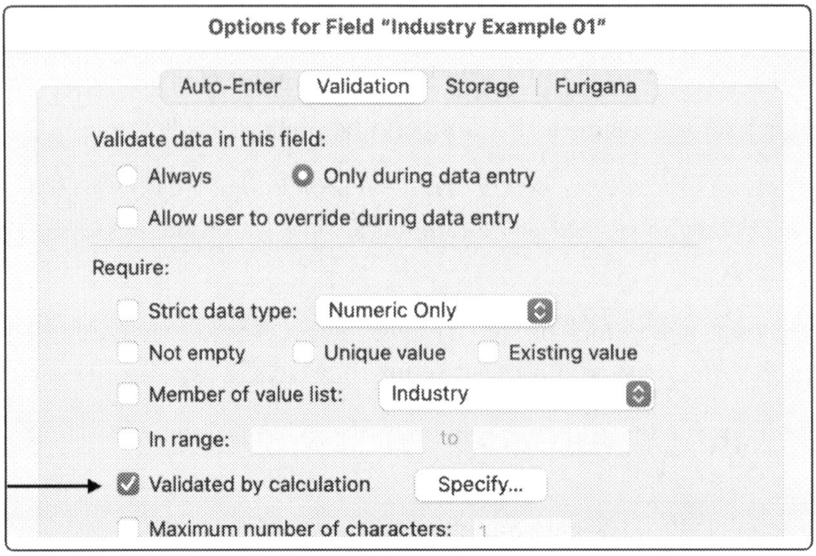

Figure 20-26. *Using the Validation options to restrict entry of multiple values*

Using Auto-Enter to Limit Field to a Single Value

An auto-enter calculation can automatically remove extra values, leaving behind the first or last value entered. This quietly enforces the rules by autocorrecting the entry. Use one of the following two code examples as the *auto-enter calculation* in field definitions (Chapter 8, "Field Options: Auto-Enter"). The first example uses *GetValue* function to automatically remove any values selected after the first. The second adds the *ValueCount* function to retain the last value entered instead.

```
GetValue ( Self ; 1 )
GetValue ( Self ; ValueCount ( Self ) )
```

Using a Script Trigger to Limit Field to a Single Value

Use an *OnObjectValidate* Script Trigger (Chapter 27) to run a script that detects the presence of multiple values in the field, and either automatically remove excess values or warn the user and halt the validation process until they correct the problem.

Prompting Input with Field Placeholders

A *field placeholder* is a text value that will be displayed in a field when empty. This can be used in lieu of a field label or to provide users a short instructional call to action. Since the placeholder is applied to the field as a layout object and not to the field definition, each instance on a new layout must be configured separately. To avoid confusion, the placeholder value has its own *part style state* (Chapter 22) which allows a formatting variation to distinguish a placeholder from actual field content, which defaults to grayed out text.

Note   See the "CH20-11 Field Placeholders" example file.

The example in Figure 20-27 shows three instances of the same *Company Name* field. The first shows the default state of a new field added to a layout without a placeholder. The second shows an example of a placeholder used instead of a label, displaying the field name as a prompt inside the field. While this technique saves space, once actual data is entered into the field, the placeholder text vanishes, and no label will be shown. That may be confusing in cases where the content isn't easily identifiable. The third example shows the field with a permanent label and a descriptive prompt as a placeholder.

Figure 20-27. *An example without placeholder (top), with field name as placeholder (middle), and with a placeholder prompt (bottom)*

Note   A field formatted as checkbox or radio button can't have a placeholder text value.

Entering Placeholder Text

To define a placeholder, select a field in Layout mode, and open the *Field* group on the *Data* tab of the *Inspector* pane. A static value can be typed directly into the Placeholder text box, shown in Figure 20-28. To generate a placeholder with a calculation, click the pencil icon next to the *Placeholder text* field. The placeholder text will be displayed when the window is in Browse mode. Enable the *Show placeholder in Find mode* checkbox to also show it in Find mode.

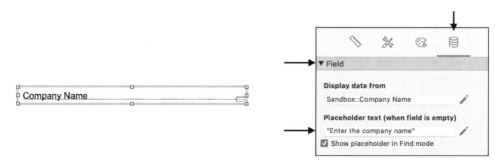

Figure 20-28. *The controls for defining a field's placeholder text*

When a placeholder is enabled in Find mode, a formula can display a different placeholder than what is shown in Browse mode. Using a *Case* statement, this formula checks the *WindowMode* and alters the text accordingly:

```
Case (
    Get ( WindowMode ) = 0 ; "Enter a Company name" ;
    "Search for a Company name"
)
```

Showing Field Repetitions

When a field is added to a layout, it will automatically be configured to show a single repetition. A field defined to be repeating (Chapter 8) can be displayed on a layout with some or all defined repetitions, oriented vertically or horizontally. Select the field, and use the *Show Repetitions* settings on the *Field* group of the *Data* tab of the *Inspector* pane, shown in Figure 20-29. The maximum number of defined repetitions available for the field is displayed in parentheses. Enter the starting and ending repetition in the two fields to control which and how many repetitions are visible on the layout. The adjacent buttons toggle the orientation. This shows all five potential repetitions of a *Hobbies* field shown arranged both vertically and horizontally using the orientation icon buttons.

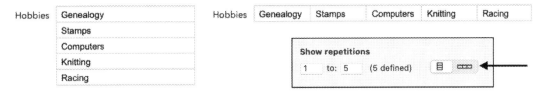

Figure 20-29. *The controls for defining how many repetitions appear on a layout*

Note   See the "CH20-12 Repeating Fields" example file.

Working with Text

A *text object* is any element of literal text placed directly on a layout as opposed to a text property of an object or a text field. There are five different types of text objects: *static text, dynamic symbols, merge fields, merge variables,* and *layout calculations.*

Static Text

A *static text object* is a piece of literal text that contains an unchanging string of characters used for labeling or conveying a message to users. This can contain rich formatting and multiple paragraphs if necessary. In Layout mode, create a static text object by choosing the *Text* tool in the toolbar and then click-dragging in the layout design area to define the object boundaries. When you release the cursor, begin typing. Once created, text can be edited and formatted by selecting the tool and clicking the object or by double-clicking it. Due to its nature as an unchanging value, static text isn't very useful. However, by using symbol coding within the text, the text object can be made to include dynamically updating content.

Note   See the "CH20-13 Text Objects" example file.

Dynamic Placeholder Symbols

A *dynamic placeholder symbol* is a special string in a text object that is automatically replaced with a predetermined value whose content may vary over time. This can include a date, time, or any one of the dozens of symbols available, each corresponding to a *Get function* (Chapter 13, "Introducing Get Functions"). Symbols are made up of a keyword enclosed in double braces. These can be manually typed into a static text object or added to a layout by selecting one from the *Insert* menu. Toward the bottom, the menu includes an item for common placeholders like *Date Symbol*, *Time Symbol*, etc. After these, an *Other Symbol* item will open a dialog showing all the available symbols. Selecting an item from the menu adds the corresponding symbol into the current text object with edit focus. If no text has focus, it will add a new object. To have the current date rendered on a layout, create a text object with the value shown here:

```
{{CurrentDate}}
```

Since symbols are text strings, they can be combined with other symbols and static text components to create compound strings. The following example can be placed in the footer of a print layout to automatically display the date, time, and user account at the time the report was printed:

```
Report printed on {{CurrentDate}} at {{CurrentTime}} by {{AccountName}}
```

Merge Fields

A *merge field* is a symbolic tagging format that allows a field's content to appear on a layout within a text object. Use the *Insert ➤ Merge Field* menu to add one into the current text object with edit focus or as a new object. Merge fields are made up of a field name enclosed in two left/right angle bracket symbols and can also be typed manually.

```
<<FieldName>>
```

When referencing a field local to the current layout's table, only the field name is required. A related field must include the name of the table occurrence to provide a contextual reference.

```
<<TableName::FieldName>>
```

Tip   For tight spaces, try shrinking the font size of a lengthy merge field (except the first character). In Browse mode, the entire value will render with formatting based on the first character.

Merge fields can also be combined with other text. The following text placed on a *Contact* layout will display the full name of a contact and the name of the related Company assigned to them:

```
Contact <<Contact Name First>> <<Contact Name Last>> at <<Contact |
Company::Company Name>>
// Result = Contact Karen Smith at Atlas Shoulder Pads LLC.
```

Caution   Empty fields used in a compound merge field string will show up blank in a string with other static text surrounding it to form a sentence that doesn't make sense! Consider using a Layout Calculation for more complex strings.

Merge Variables

A *merge variable* is a symbolic tagging format that allows a global variable (Chapter 12, "Variables") to be rendered as a text object on a layout. Like merge fields and dynamic symbols, merge variables can be used in any combination with other merge variables, text, symbols, and merge fields. Use the *Insert ➤ Merge Variable* menu to add one into the current text object with edit focus or as a new object. Merge variables are made up of a variable name enclosed in two left-shift and two right-shift symbols, following the pattern shown here:

```
<<$$VariableName>>
```

Layout Calculations

In version 20.2.1, FileMaker introduced the ability to embed formulas directly on a layout in a text object. This adds a new dimension to creating dynamic interfaces and eliminates the need to use old fashion techniques for displaying calculated results on a layout such as display calculation fields or button bars. A *layout calculation* is a tagging format that indicates that a text object contains a formula. These are indicated by two less than symbols, an *f:* prefix, a formula followed by two greater than symbols, as shown in this example. The formula contains a *Case* statement that will either display the company name if one is entered or a text indicating that the entry is still pending.

```
<<ƒ:Case ( Company Name = "" ; "<No Company Entered>" ; Company Name )>>
```

To insert a new layout calculation, you can type the formula with tags into a text object or select the *Insert ➤ Layout Calculation* menu. When using the menu option, the formula will be created inside of a text object with cursor focus. Otherwise, a new text object will be created. A standard *Specify Calculation* dialog will automatically open to accept the formula text.

Caution   You only need to type the formula tags if you are manually typing the formula in a text object! If using the *Specify Calculation* dialog, type only the formula and the tags are inserted automatically.

To edit an existing layout calculation, select it and then choose *Edit Layout Calculation* from the object's contextual menu or from the *Insert* menu. This will reopen the formula in the *Specify Calculation* dialog and allow editing.

A layout calculation formula can be combined in a text object with any combination of other static text, placeholders, merge fields, and merge variables. You can even place two or more formulas inside of a single text object. However, since a formula result can include static text, field values, data storied in variables, and the results of built-in functions that correspond to dynamic placeholders, consider using one calculation per text object, and return the entire text result from the formula.

Working with Button Controls

A *button control* is a layout object that provides the user with the means to initiate an action in Browse and Find mode. FileMaker has four options for buttons: three native button types – *buttons*, *popover buttons*, and *button bars* – and the ability to transform any other object type into a button. Depending on the type of configuration, a button can run a script (Chapter 24), perform a single script step, or open a popover interface element. Buttons allow a developer to embed active controls into the interface for initiating all kinds of activity. They can aid a user in navigating, creating, deleting, or searching records. They can perform any number of built-in or custom scripted functions, providing shortcuts for users that relieve the burden of manually repeating complex tasks.

Note   See the "CH20-14 Buttons" example file.

Working with Buttons

A *button* is a layout object that provides the functionality of a traditional graphical push button. A button can be formatted with a text title, icon, or both, as shown in Figure 20-30. The object style settings can also be modified with full control over background, border, text formatting, and icon style. Buttons can be added to a layout using the toolbar icon or selecting the *Insert ➤ Button* menu. When a button is created, a *Button Setup* dialog opens which allows configuration of the button's label and action. This dialog can be opened for an existing button by double-clicking it or selecting the *Button Setup* command from the *Format* menu or the button's contextual menu.

Figure 20-30. *Examples of different button formats*

Configuring a Button's Label

A *button label* is the identifying text and/or icon displayed within the boundary of the button that communicates to users what functionality it will perform. The label is defined in the top portion of the *Button Setup* dialog. A button label can be text, icon, or a combination of the two.

Using a Text Label

To define a button with a text label, choose the *label* option at the top of the *Button Setup* dialog, and enter the text for the label, as shown in Figure 20-31:

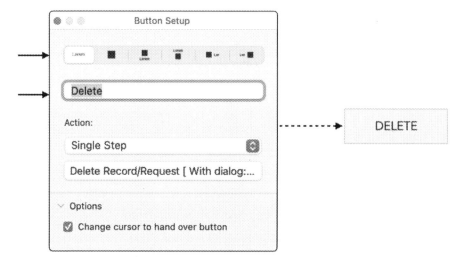

Figure 20-31. *A button configuration (dialog) rendering a named button (right)*

Tip   A button label can include a merge field typed into the text area to create dynamic names. For more dynamic naming control, use a single segment button bar instead of a button.

Using an Icon Label

When defining a button with an icon label, the *Button Setup* dialog controls transform to allow selection and configuration of an image, as shown in Figure 20-32. After choosing the icon only option at the top of the dialog, select an icon from the list of standard icons. This icon library can be expanded by clicking the plus icon below and choosing a PNG or SVG image file to import. New images added here will be available from any layout within the database file. Type in a size for the icon or use the slider below the icon list to shrink or enlarge.

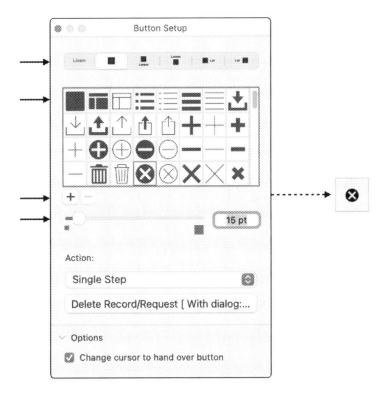

Figure 20-32. *A button configuration (dialog) rendering an icon button (right)*

Note   Unlike other controls, the size setting for buttons will always be displayed in points regardless of units currently selected for the ruler.

Using a Text Label and Icon

The remaining options across the top of the Button Setup dialog allow specifying one of four combinations of text label and icon. The difference between them is the location of the text label relative to the icon: below, above, right, or left.

Configuring a Button's Action

The bottom portion of the *Button Setup* dialog controls the function that will be performed when the user clicks the button in Browse or Find modes. This can be configured to perform one of two actions: *Single Step* or *Perform a Script*.

Performing a Single Step

For buttons that need to perform one specific function, the *Single Step* action can be selected, as shown in Figure 20-33. Choosing this option opens a *Button Action* dialog which is a limited version of the *Script Workspace* dialog (Chapter 24). Instead of creating a full script, you can choose one of a list of available *Steps* (Chapter 25-26) and configure it as the button's action. In this example, the *Delete Record/Request* step has been assigned with default configuration options. Once a step has been located and assigned, clicking OK closes the dialog.

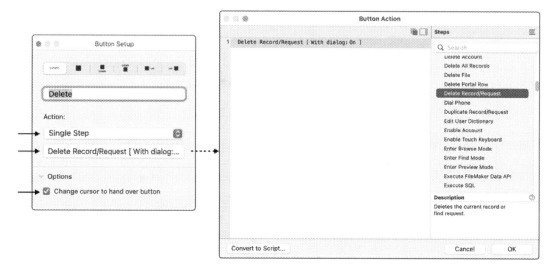

Figure 20-33. *A button configured to perform a Delete Record/Request script step*

Once a step has been assigned and configured, the *Action* area at the bottom of the setup dialog will display it. To change the command assigned, click it. Enable the *Change cursor to hand over button* checkbox to cause the cursor to change when placed over the button, providing a visual indication to the user that it is an active button.

There is a natural limit to the usefulness of using the *Single Step* option. Since only one command can be assigned, there is no way to perform other required actions. For example, sometimes a window requires a follow-up refresh to register other changes based on the step performed by the button. In some cases, this can be handled by assigning a *Script Trigger* to the button to run another script. However, in that and many other cases, it really makes more sense to configure the button to *Perform a Script* instead of a *Single Step*.

Performing a Script

To configure a button to run a script when the user clicks, change the button's action to *Perform a Script*. This will immediately open a *Specify Script* dialog (Chapter 24, "Exploring the Specify Script Dialog"), allowing the selection of an existing script and entry of other options. After choosing the script, the *Action* area at the bottom of the *Button Setup* dialog will display the script, parameter, and options, as shown in Figure 20-34. Click the assigned script to open and directly edit the script steps. Click the adjacent script icon to choose a different script for the button. The *Optional Script Parameter* text area will open a *Specify Calculation* dialog allowing entry of a formula that will generate data to be sent to the script as a parameter (Chapter 24, "Sending Parameters").

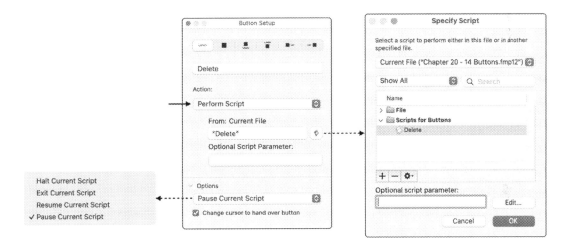

Figure 20-34. *The dialog configured to perform a script*

The *Options* area beneath includes a checkbox to *Change cursor to hand over button* like the Single Step option previously discussed. The menu above allows one of four choices for how to handle a currently paused script after the button's script runs. The choices are as follows:

- *Halt current script* – Any other paused scripts will be halted after the button's script runs.

- *Exit current script* – The current paused script will stop, but control reverts to and resumes any other scripts that called it prior to its pausing.

- *Resume current script* – The paused script will resume running after the button's script runs.

- *Pause current script* – The current script will remain paused after the button's script runs.

These options become important in situations where a script opens a layout and pauses for user input before continuing. A *Continue* and *Cancel* button on that layout would each be configured differently with respect to the paused script. The *Continue* button would resume it while the *Cancel* might exit or halt the paused script.

Popover Button

A *popover button* is a type of button control that opens a floating interface panel when clicked. The popover interface area can contain any number of additional layout objects (except other popover buttons) to reduce visual clutter by hiding a group of elements until needed. Popovers can be used for a variety of different purposes such as expanding fields for input, presenting documentation tips for users, or opening a menu of actions, like the example shown in Figure 20-35.

Figure 20-35. *A popover button, with its panel open showing a few objects for sending reports*

To begin, choose the *Insert* ➤ *Popover Button* menu, or click-hold the *Button* toolbar icon, and choose *Popover Button* from the menu, shown in Figure 20-36.

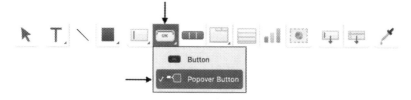

Figure 20-36. *The tool to create a new popover*

Once the tool is selected, the cursor will turn into crosshairs prompting a click and drag in the layout's content area to draw the boundaries for the button component. When finished, the button will appear on the layout with an attached popover interface open to a default size and an adjacent *Popover Button Setup* dialog. Now you can define the interface and configure the options to customize the new popover button.

Defining the Basic Popover Interface

A new popover appears as a button with an attached blank popover interface open, as shown in Figure 20-37.

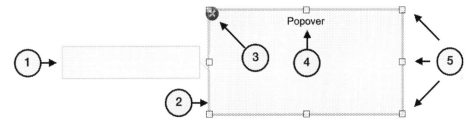

Figure 20-37. *A new popover button ready for editing*

The following elements make up the popover button interface:

1. *Button* – The button the user clicks to open the popover, blank until you specify a label and/or icon like a standard button.

2. *Interface/design area* – This area pops open when the user clicks the button. In Layout mode, add elements to design the interface.

3. *Close button* – This button, only visible when editing the popover in Layout mode, will close the interface.

4. *Title* – An optional title for the popover.

5. *Resizing handles* – These "handles" can be pulled to decrease or increase the size of the interface area in any direction.

Tip   Click the popover design area to show resize handles.

Exploring the Popover Button Setup Options

A popover's label and behavior are configured using the *Popover Button Setup* dialog, shown in Figure 20-38. This automatically opens when a popover button is created but can be opened later one of three ways. Click the popover button and select the *Format* ➤ *Popover Button Setup* menu or select *Popover Button Setup* from the *Format* menu or the button's contextual menu. Alternatively, double-click directly on the button.

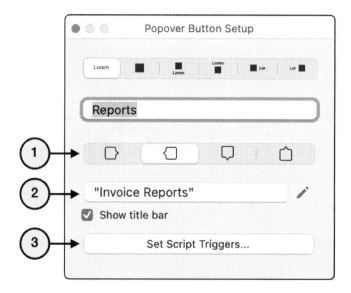

Figure 20-38. *The dialog used to configure a popover's label and behavior settings*

The top portion of the setup dialog is identical to setup dialog for standard buttons, allowing control over the button's label and/or icon. The bottom portion contains settings specifically for the popover interface panel:

1. *Directional control* – Choose a preferred direction for the popover interface to open relative to the button. FileMaker will override the choice to ensure that the interface never goes off-screen.

2. *Title* – Enter a title for the heading of the interface area, or click the pencil icon use a formula. The *Show title bar* checkbox controls if the title shows up at the top of the panel when open.

3. *Set script triggers* – Opens a dialog to configure script triggers (Chapter 27) to perform automatic actions when a popover opens, closes, etc.

Button Bar

A *button bar* is a layout object that defines a group of interconnected button segments, as shown in Figure 20-39. Create a bar by choosing the *Insert* ➤ *Button Bar* menu or using the corresponding tool in the toolbar. Each segment of the bar can be defined independently as a standard *button* or as a *popover button*. The segments each have their own label and icon, but the choice of label type (text only, icon only, or both) applies to all segments in the bar.

Figure 20-39. *An example of a three-segment button bar*

Button bars appear to have been originally conceived as a mode indicator since the last segment a user clicks on stays formatted as a current selection. This makes sense if treating them like tabs where you click to view an associated panel or if clicking one puts the record in a certain mode, like editing or viewing. However, they are more likely used as a group of normal buttons, and this behavior can be a little confusing. This behavior of locking the selection can be overridden by configuring the *Active segment* (discussed in the next section) to 0 and refreshing the window after a segment's script action has been performed. This ensures that no segment is active by default which is reset after a click.

Tip   When designing groups of buttons, use button bars instead of individual buttons to visually unite them for users and to make them easier to move around when designing a layout.

Exploring the Button Bar Setup Options

Button bars are configured using the *Button Bar Setup* dialog, shown in Figure 20-40. This dialog automatically opens when a new bar is created and can be opened later by double-clicking a button segment. It can also be opened by selecting *Button Bar Setup* from the Format menu or the button's contextual menu. This dialog is a hybrid of settings for a *button* and a *popover button* with a few controls specific to button bars.

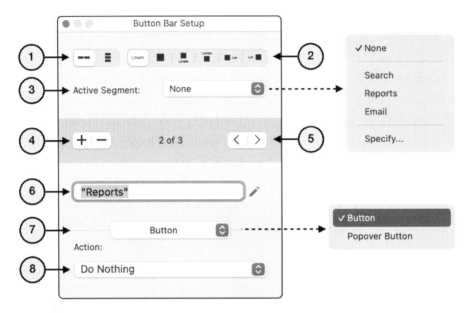

Figure 20-40. *The dialog used to configure a button bar*

The top portion contains controls for the overall bar.

1. *Bar orientation control* – Select the direction for segments: horizontally or vertically.

2. *Button labeling options* – Select a labeling option (identical to buttons and popovers).

3. *Active segment* – Choose the segment, if any, to be selected by default. Choose one by name or *specify* a formula-driven choice.

4. *Segment control* – Add or remove segments from the bar starting from the currently selected.

5. *Segment navigation* – Select a specific segment whose settings will be displayed for configuration below.

The bottom portion of the dialog applies to the currently selected segment:

1. *Button labeling specification* – Like standard buttons, enter a name and/or select an icon for the button segment's label depending on the option selected at the top.

2. *Segment type* – Select a type for the current segment: *Button* or *Popover Button*.

3. *Action menu and specification* – This area provides action controls depending on the type selected. The options are identical to those for a button or popover button.

Making Any Object a Button

In addition to formal button controls, any layout object or group of objects can be converted into a simple push button. Select one or more objects, and click the *Format ➤ Button Setup* menu or the contextual menu option of the same name. This automatically groups the object(s) together with a button object and then opens a simplified *Button Setup* dialog, as shown in Figure 20-41. Because the object is not a native button, the only configuration choices are a choice of *Action* and the option to change the cursor. Once converted into a button, the objects will no longer be receptive to input native to their type, e.g., fields will no longer accept data entry. If the new button group is ever ungrouped, FileMaker will warn that doing so will delete the button definition.

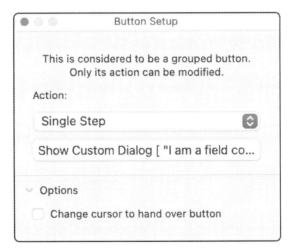

Figure 20-41.   *The dialog used to assign an action to an object button*

Tip   An object or group of objects will appear in the *Objects* pane under a hierarchical heading of "Grouped Button."

Working with Panel Controls

A *panel control* is a layout object that contains multiple object groups, organized in separate panels, which can be alternately displayed within the area of the object. These save space by allowing part of a layout to be used for multiple purposes, one at a time. FileMaker has two such object types: *tab controls* and *slide controls*.

Note   See the "CH20-15 Panels" example file.

Tab Control

A *tab control* is a multi-panel layout object with labeled tabs reminiscent of file folders, as shown in Figure 20-42. When a user clicks one tab, a corresponding panel becomes active, displaying one group of layout elements. Simultaneously, all other tabs are then inactive and their panels are hidden from view. Each panel can be designed with any number and different layout objects.

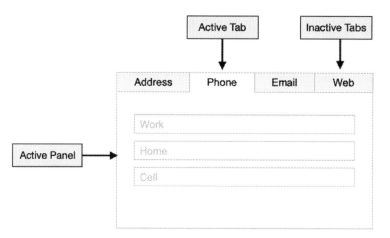

Figure 20-42. *An example of a tab control with four tabbed panels*

Tip   A tab panel can contain any layout elements including other tab controls! However, try to avoid cluttering your design with too many nested tab controls.

To create a new tab control, select the *Insert ➤ Tab Control* menu item or click the toolbar icon, and choose Tab Control from the menu, as shown in Figure 20-43.

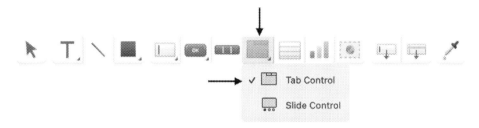

Figure 20-43. *Selecting the tab control tool from the toolbar*

Exploring the Tab Control Setup Dialog

Tabs are configured using the *Tab Control Setup* dialog, as shown in Figure 20-44. This will automatically open when a new tab control is created. It can be opened later by double-clicking anywhere on a panel of a tab control. It can also be opened by selecting the *Tab Control Setup* item from the *Format* menu or the tab control's contextual menu.

Figure 20-44. *The dialog used to define a tab control*

The controls available on the dialog are as follows:

1. *Tabs* – Lists each tab defined for the object. Drag to reorder.

2. *Tab Name* – Type a name when creating a new tab or edit the name of the selected tab. Click *Specify* to generate a name with a formula. The buttons below will create, rename, or delete the tab named.

3. *Default Front Tab* – Select the default tab that is selected when the window is refreshed.

4. *Tab Justification* – Select the justification of the tab's labels: *Left*, *Center*, *Right*, or *Full*.

5. *Tab Width* – Select the width of the tabs (described below).

6. *Tabs Share Single Style* – Select this checkbox to uniformly share one theme style on all tabs of the control (Chapter 22).

The *Tab Width* menu provides several options that control the size of tab labels.

-   *Label Width* – The width varies based on each label name.

-   *Label Width + a Margin of* – The width varies based on each label name plus the specified "padding" margin in pixels.

-   *Width of Widest Label* – Use uniform widths based on the longest label name.

-   *Minimum of* – The width based on each label name above a specified minimum.

-   *Fixed Width of* – Use uniform widths based on a specified width.

Slide Control

A *slide control* is a multi-panel layout object where panels are accessed by swiping left or right on an iOS device or by clicking a navigation dot, as shown in Figure 20-45. These function like tab controls but without visible labels and are reminiscent of image viewers used by websites. Create a new slide control by choosing the *Insert* ➤ *Slide Control* menu or clicking the toolbar's panel icon, and choose *Slide Control*.

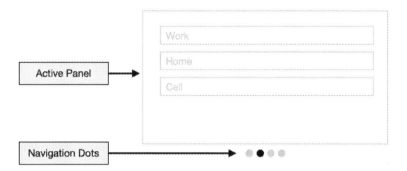

Figure 20-45. *An example of a four-panel slide control*

A slide panel can be styled in a way to make its border and dots invisible. Then, if the panel background is the same color as the layout, it will appear as if the objects in the panel are on the layout. This allows an interface design that has groups of objects that appear, disappear, or switch with other objects without the user being aware of the panel structure. If each panel is assigned an object name in the *Inspector* pane (Chapter 21, "Naming Objects"), they can be activated with the *Go To Object* script step.

Exploring the Slide Control Setup Dialog

Slide controls are configured using the *Slide Control Setup* dialog, shown in Figure 20-46. This will automatically open when a new control is created. It can be opened later by double-clicking the background of a slide control. It can also be opened by choosing *Slide Control Setup* from the *Format* menu or the slide control contextual menu.

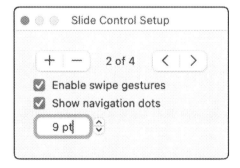

Figure 20-46. *The dialog used to configure a slide control*

Across the top, the setup dialog has controls used to add, remove, or navigate back and forth to a specific panel using the buttons. The *Enable swipe gestures* checkbox allows users to slide from one panel to another by swiping back or forth on iOS. The *Show navigation dots* checkbox controls the visibility of navigation dots so users on a macOS or Windows computer can click to other panels when swiping isn't an option. Disable both to make manual navigation impossible for users when you build scripts to control which panel is visible at a given moment in time.

Tip   The order of panels in the Slide Control can be reordered in Layout mode by dragging the navigation dots.

Finding Objects on Panel Controls

Both tab and slide panels will display the hierarchical structure in the Objects pane, as shown in Figure 20-47. The *Tab Control* (shown on the left) expands to show each panel by name, each of which expand to list of all the elements placed in the panel. Similarly, the *Slide Control* (shown on the right) expands to show each panel and their items, but the panels will show up with a generic name of "Panel" unless they are explicitly assigned an *Object* name in the *Inspector* pane. This makes it much easier to select items nested in the object hierarchy when designing layouts.

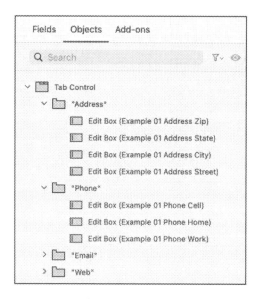
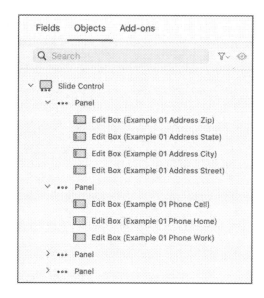

Figure 20-47.   *The panel controls display their object hierarchy in the Objects pane*

Working with Portals

A *portal* is a layout object that displays a list of records from a table occurrence related to the current layout's occurrence. Portals are one of the primary reasons to create relationships, so you can display and interact with related records in a child table from a parent table (Chapter 9, "Visualizing Relationships"). Figure 20-48 shows an example of a *Contact* portal as it would appear on a *Company* layout. The context provided by the relationship determines which contacts are displayed from a given company record. A *portal row* represents one related record and can include fields and other layout objects. Depending on the portal setup, users can add, delete, edit, view, or navigate to a specific contact record represented in the portal as a row.

Note   See the "CH20-16 Portals" example file.

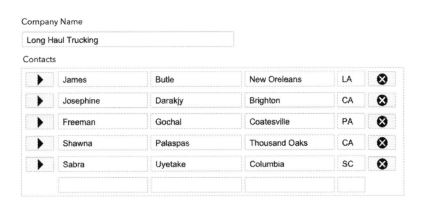

Figure 20-48. *An example of a portal showing contacts as viewed from a company record*

Note   Remember that portals are layout objects and have an array of custom formatting options. The examples here are basic, showing the essentials.

Exploring the Portal Setup Dialog

To create a new portal, choose the *Insert ➤ Portal* menu or select the tool in the toolbar.
Portals are configured using the *Portal Setup* dialog, shown in Figure 20-49. This opens
automatically when a new portal is created. It can be opened later by double-clicking
anywhere on the background of a portal. It can also be opened by selecting *Portal Setup*
from the Format menu or the portal's contextual menu.

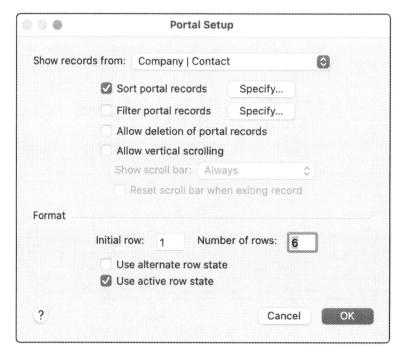

Figure 20-49. *The dialog used to configure a portal*

Configuring Portal Content and Behavior

The table occurrence selected from the *Show records from* pop-up menu acts as the data
source for the portal. For the portal to work, the selection here must be an occurrence
related to the table of the current layout upon which the portal is placed. The menu
assists in this selection by showing the layout's table at the top and separates other
occurrences into *Related Tables* and *Unrelated Tables*.

The *Sort portal records* checkbox enables a portal sort order imposed on the records
displayed. This will take precedence over a sort at the relationship level (Chapter 9,
"Sorting Related Records"). Checking the box will open a *Sort Records* dialog (Chapter 4,

"Sorting Records in the Found Set"), but instead of sorting now, it captures and stores criteria for sorting when rendering an interface Browse or Find modes. The dialog can be reopened later using the adjacent *Specify* button.

The *Filter portal records* checkbox enables a formula to determine which related records should appear at a given moment (see "Filtering Portal Records" later in this section).

The *Allow deletion of portal records* checkbox allows users to delete a selected portal row with the Delete key. The *Allow vertical scrolling* checkbox enables scrolling up and down when the number of related records exceeds the number of visible rows. Selecting this enables a *Show scroll bar* choice between *Always* or only *When scrolling*. The *Reset scroll bar when exiting record* option will automatically scroll back to the first row when a record is committed instead of retaining the user's current scroll position.

Configuring Portal Format Options

The *Format* settings at the bottom of the *Portal Setup* dialog allow control over which related records appear in the portal and which style options apply. The *Initial row* accepts a number indicating the first row that should be displayed. Any related records preceding that number will be omitted from the view. The *Number of rows* indicates how many portal rows should be displayed on the layout. Any related records after that number will still be included in the portal but are only accessible by scrolling if enabled. The *Use alternate row state* and *Use active row state* checkboxes will apply style settings (Chapter 22) to differently format every other row and the currently selected row to provide the user visual cues.

Tip   Configure the portal's settings in the *Inspector* pane (Chapter 19, "Autosizing") to lock to the bottom of the window to automatically show more rows on larger screens.

Designing Portal Rows

In Layout mode, a portal's first row is the design area where fields, buttons, and other objects can be placed to define the template for how each row will be rendered in Browse mode, as shown in Figure 20-50. This is like the Body portion of a List layout – here the top row design is repeated for each record.

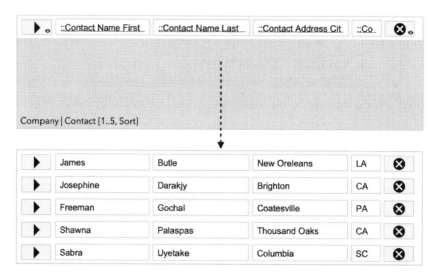

Figure 20-50. *A portal in Layout mode (top) rendered in Browse mode (bottom)*

Objects placed in the portal are rendered from the context of the layout's occurrence in relation to the portal's occurrence. This is important to remember when choosing what objects to place inside a portal and how to configure them. Any fields added into the portal must be either from the portal's assigned occurrence or occurrences that are related to it in a direct line away from the layout's occurrence. In the example above, any field from the *Company | Contact* occurrence can be included in the portal, but nothing from *Company* or directly from *Contact* can. Fields from tables beyond the portal's table can be put in the portal but will only display a value from the first matching record through the relationship conduit from the context of the record for each portal row. So, the contact portal can include a field that hops across multiple relationships to show a field from an invoice line item from an invoice related to the contact, but it will only show the value from the first line item for the first invoice for the contact based on the relational connections along that chain. If this sounds confusing, that's because it is. Generally, it's best to keep fields in portals limited to the assigned table occurrence or no more than one step further.

Any object in a portal must be thought of in the context of the portal's occurrence. When writing formulas for hide, tooltips, conditional formatting, script parameters, etc., the formula must be restrained to include fields based on the portal's occurrence context rather than the layout's. For example, a button added to the portal that performs the *Set Field* step will change a field value in the related record for the row it appears on, while the same button placed on the layout outside of the portal will change the field value in the first related record.

Creating Records in a Portal Directly

In Browse mode, portals automatically update anytime new matching records are created in the portal's source table. If viewing a *Company* record on a layout with a *Contact* portal, any new contact record that is created to that company will appear in the portal. For example, if the user viewing the company record wants to create a new related contact record, they would have to switch layouts, create a new *Contact* record, enter the ID to link it to the company, and then return to the original *Company* layout to see it in the portal. A script created to perform those steps in sequence can be assigned to a button on the Company layout.

Alternatively, a portal can be configured with a shortcut that allows users to create a new record directly in the portal by typing into any field on an empty portal row at the bottom of the record list. This ability is configured at the relationship level instead of the layout object. Open the *Manage Database* dialog and enable the *Allow creation of records* checkbox in the *Edit Relationship* dialog (Chapter 9) on the side of the relationship used as the portal's data source, in this case, *Company | Contact*. Once done, any portal assigned that occurrence would display one blank row at the bottom, as shown in Figure 20-51.

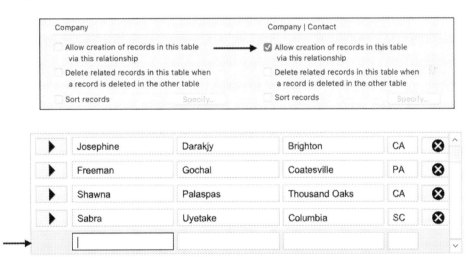

Figure 20-51. *The setting (top) that enables a blank portal row for creating new records (bottom)*

Note   The blank row isn't a record and will be programmatically ignored by functions that summarize related records such as *Count*, *List*, *Max*, *Min*, *Sum*, etc. (Chapter 13).

When the user types into any editable field in that blank row and then moves focus to another field or commits the record, a new record will be instantly created in the remote table. The new record will automatically populate each match field with the appropriate value required to relate it to the currently viewed parent record. In the example presented, the new *Contact* record will be created with the current *Company* record's *Record Primary ID* in its *Contact Company ID* field. Although the new record remains in the portal, it may sort to a new position based on the values in any sort field defined at the relationship level and/or specified in the portal's settings. Once finished, a new blank row will appear for the creation of additional new records.

This feature may confuse users since the empty row appears like an actual record with no field values. If a user thinks it is a mistakenly created empty record, they may try to delete it. Use a *Hide* formula (Chapter 21) to make the buttons invisible when the related *Record Primary ID* is empty (which would be the case when it's not yet a record). Also, consider using *Placeholder text* in the first field that makes it clear that this is a space for creating a new record. These techniques make it less conspicuous. However, some developers disable the feature entirely and use a custom script to perform the sequence required to create related records.

Deleting Portal Rows

Portal rows are a representation of records from another table, and they will disappear from the portal whenever the related record is deleted. A portal can be configured to allow users to delete a record directly within the portal. Open the *Portal Setup* dialog and select the *Allow deletion of portal records* option. Once enabled, a user can select a portal row and type the Delete key to delete the related record and remove it from the portal display. FileMaker will present a somewhat vague confirmation dialog asking if the user wants to continue with the deletion. If they confirm, the related record will be permanently deleted completely. The delete row confirmation dialog's vagueness may confuse users who don't realize which row they have selected and accidentally delete the wrong record. Instead, a button that handles the process always affects the row clicked. It can also optionally run a script with a custom dialog that provides a more informative confirmation message.

Filtering Portal Records

The relationship between the layout's occurrence and portal's occurrence automatically provides a baseline filter controlling the records displayed in a portal. Only records with a relational match of the current record's occurrence will be included. By contrast, the filtering option in the *Portal Setup* dialog allows a formula to further control which of those records will be displayed in the portal. The *portal filter formula* is evaluated once for each available related record, and they are only displayed if the result is true (1).

The filter formula can be as simple or as complex as needed to determine if a record should be included. For example, if the *Contact* table has a *Contact Status* field that contains "Active" or "Inactive," the Company | Contact portal can use the following formula to only display active contacts:

```
Company | Contact::Contact Status = "Active"
```

Since the formula operates within the list of related records, *it already assumes the record matching criteria of the relationship itself.* As a result, the filter formula does not need to re-specify that criteria, nor can it work to extend the results beyond that criteria to include non-related records.

Filtering formulas can be as complex as necessary to determine if a record should be included or filtered out. It can include field comparisons and can be based on a user's entry in one or more *control fields* exclusively for soliciting filtering preferences. For example, a field positioned near the portal can allow users to choose to show contacts that are active, inactive, or both. In the example shown in Figure 20-52, the *Company | Contact* portal will show a set of records based on the user's selection in the *Portal Filter* field.

Figure 20-52. *An example of a portal filtering field giving the user a choice of viewing all, active, or inactive records*

The portal's filter formula uses a *Case* statement to first force all records to return a true (1) value if the user chooses to show "All." If not, the *Contact Status* field of the related records must match the *Portal Filter* to be included.

```
Case (
    Company::Portal Filter = "All" ; 1 ;
    Company | Contact::Contact Status = Company::Contact Filter Choice
)
```

The records that show up after filtering can be referred to as the *filtered set*. This is like a found set after a search is performed but refers here to the limited set within the found set of related records based on the filter criteria. It is important to remember that **filtering** only affects the *display* of related records and does not affect the actual relationship. Any calculation that accesses records through the relationship will continue to see all related records even when the portal displays a filtered set! Optionally, the filtering criteria can be added to the relationship's match field setup to resolve this issue.

The portal won't refresh until the user commits the record. To update automatically, use the *ObjectModify* script trigger (Chapter 27) that performs script steps to commit the record.

Note See a more advanced filter example on the Company layout of the "Chapters 17-23 Sandbox" example file!

Creating Portals Based on the Current Table

Traditionally, portals are used to display records from a table related to the current layout's table (Chapter 9, "Building Relationships"). In version 17, portals became capable of using the layout's table as a data source to automatically display records from the current found set. This is used to create an integrated List view and Form view side by side on the same layout. The user sees a list of available records next to one record selected for viewing/editing, as shown in Figure 20-53. This setup is called a *master-detail layout* or *list-detail layout* and has the benefit of reducing the number of layouts and making it easier for users to move from a list to a specific record and back again.

Note   See the "Chapter 20-17 Master-Detail Portal" example file.

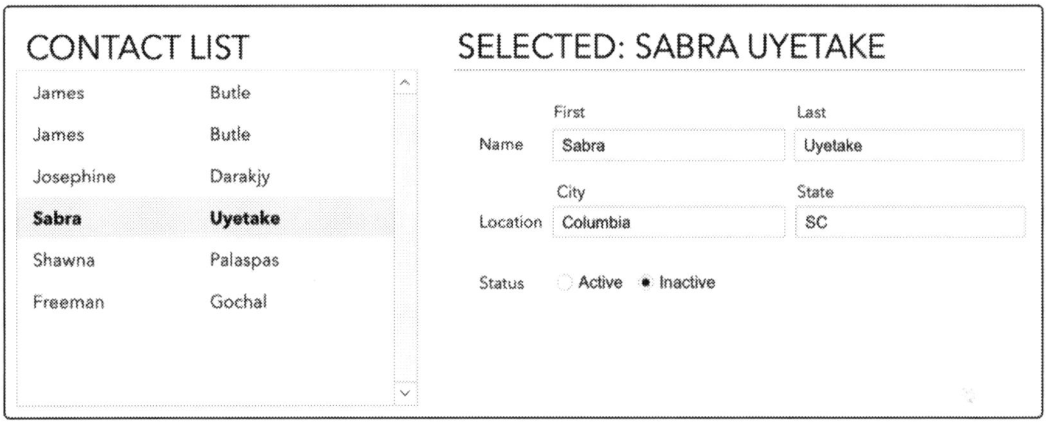

Figure 20-53. *An example of a master-detail portal*

The *Portal Setup* options for a portal based on the current table are greatly reduced, as shown in Figure 20-54. This highlights key differences in how functionally different one configures and uses such a portal compared to one based on a related table.

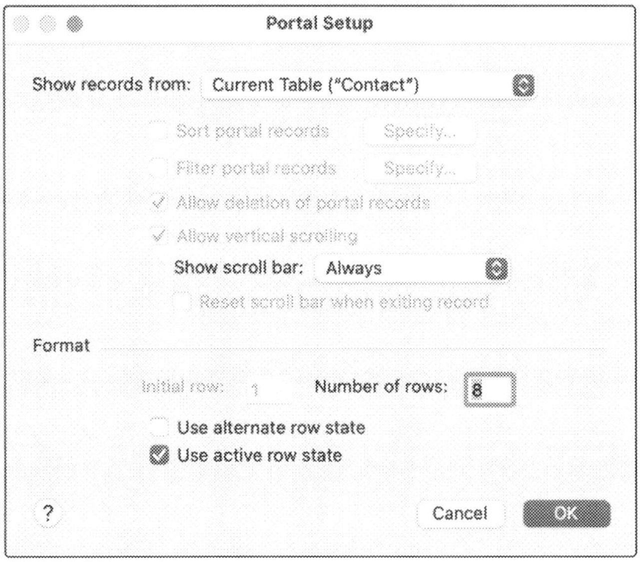

Figure 20-54. *An example of the options for a portal based on the current table*

The options for sorting, filtering, and deleting are all disabled as these functions are automatically controlled by the found set of records in the window. To sort the list of portal records, select *Sort Records* from the *Records* menu. To change the list in the portal, perform a find in the window. When the current record is deleted, it vanishes from the portal. Similarly, creating a new record can be achieved by selecting *New Record* from the *Records* menu. The records in the current found set will appear in the portal in the order they are sorted in the window.

When configuring the portal on a layout, there is no need to setup navigation button or script functions. When the user clicks a portal row, the window automatically moves to that record. A button can be added to be visually consistent with a list view, but it doesn't require any scripting since the row selection performs the navigation without a script. If the *Use active row state* option is enabled in the *Portal Setup* dialog, the portal row style will automatically change to highlight the background of the row for the current record.

When writing a formula for conditional formatting or hiding items (Chapter 21) on a portal row for the selected record, use two *Get* functions to check if the *RecordNumber* and *ActiveRecordNumber* are the same, as shown below. For example, use this to apply a conditional bold style to fields in the portal. If the formula returns a true (1) result, that means that the portal row represents the record the user is actively viewing.

```
Get ( RecordNumber ) = Get ( ActiveRecordNumber )
```

Working with Web Viewers

A *web viewer* is a layout object that displays a web page or custom HTML directly on a layout. Viewers can be configured as display only or have user interaction enabled. The content displayed can be generated by any of the following:

- A static web address pointing to a specific website

- A web address pulled from a database field or dynamically generated from a formula

- A Claris-provided address formula that merges fields with predefined URL formats for Google search, Google maps, FedEx, or Wikipedia

- Custom HTML code from a field or formula, which can include hard-code elements, field data, and even images in fields

- A web address or custom HTML code provided by a script

Caution   Custom web addresses must begin with a correct URL scheme such as http://, https://, ftp://, or file://.

Exploring the Web Viewer Setup Dialog

To add a web page to a layout, select the *Insert ➤ Web Viewer* menu, or use the tool in the toolbar. The viewer appears on the layout as a square/rectangle with a globe inside of it. The *Web Viewer Setup* dialog will automatically open, shown in Figure 20-55. This can be opened later by double-clicking a web viewer. It can also be opened by selecting the *Web Viewer Setup* from the *Format* menu or the viewer's contextual menu.

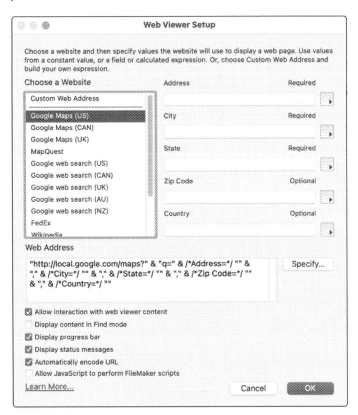

Figure 20-55. *The dialog used to configure a web viewer*

The *Choose a Website* list on the top left specifies a source URL. Choose from a list of data-driven templates or select *Custom Web Address* to enter your own URL or HTML. When using a template, the *component generators* on the right accept values that will be inserted into the URL. These can be literal text, a reference to a field, or a formula that generates the value. The values are then automatically entered into the URL below depending on the template selected. Since the templates are reasonably intuitive to figure out, our focus will be on creating custom web content.

The *Web Address* area allows entry of a URL or HTML code, either typed as literal text or generated with a formula. Click the *Specify* button to enter a custom formula.

The checkbox options at the bottom control various viewer features. The *Allow interaction with web viewer content* option allows the rendered web page to respond to user clicks and typing. Enable the *Display content in Find mode* checkbox to also render the page in Find mode. The *Display progress bar* and *Display status message* options add information to the viewer when a page is loading. The *Automatically encode URL* option will *percent-encode* special characters in the address to ensure proper web safe formatting. For example, spaces are converted to %20 if this box is checked. Alternatively, the built in *GetAsURLEncoded* function can be used in a formula to handle encoding (Chapter 13, "Encoding Text for URLs"). The *Allow JavaScript to perform FileMaker scripts* option was added in version 19 to enable the HTML code to directly call native FileMaker scripts using a *FileMaker.PerformScript* JavaScript function (described later in this section).

With the *Allow interaction with web viewer content* option enabled, users can interact with a web page as with any standard browser. They can click links to navigate to other pages and interact with rich content such as movies. Although very capable, viewers aren't intended to act as a full-featured web browser, and there may be some limitations. The *Open Link in New Window* function in the viewer's contextual menu in Browse mode will redirect the page out of FileMaker to the user's default browser application and allow a fuller web experience.

Note   See the "CH20-17 Web Viewer" example file.

Building a Web Page Using Data from Fields

As an alternative to displaying a published web page using a URL, a viewer can be provided HTML code that generates a custom page. FileMaker uses the *data universal resource identifier* scheme, which is a standard method of including data within the code of a web page instead of accessing external resources. This format is expressed with the following formula, with square brackets indicating optional elements:

```
data:[<media type>][;base64],<data>
```

This formula contains the following elements:

- *data:* – This prefix indicates the scheme being used and is required when sending html instead of a URL.

- *media type* – Optionally indicates the type of material contained in the data. A web page would use *text/html*, while an image would use *image/<type>*, for example, *image/png*. If no media type is specified, the data will be assumed to be *text/plain*.

- *base64* – This optional extension, delimited from the media type with a semicolon, is used to indicate that the data content is binary data, which is encoded in ASCII format using the *Base64 binary-to-text encoding* scheme.

- *data* – Preceded with a comma, this would be replaced with a sequence of characters containing the content being described, either HTML code or Base64 image data.

Note   Since version 15, the data and media type are optional. The text can begin with <html> or <!DOCTYPE html> and render as expected in a web viewer.

Creating a Hello World Web Page

This code defines a simple example web page formula for a web viewer:

```
"data:text/html,
<html>
<head>
```

```
</head>
<body>
<h1>Hello, World</h1>
</body>"
```

The HTML for a custom page can be as elaborate as required to display the desired information. Add a *style tag* to control text formatting with *Cascading Style Sheets* (CSS). This example modifies the color of the h1 style to display the text in green:

```
"data:text/html,
<html>
<head>
<style>
h1 {
color: green;
}
</style>
</head>
<body>
<h1>Hello, World</h1>
</body>"
```

Add a *script tag* to include JavaScript functions as demonstrated by the following example that opens an alert dialog when the page loads:

```
"data:text/html,
<html>
<head>
</head>
<body>
<script>
alert('Hello, World!')
</script>
<h1>Hello, World</h1>
</body>"
```

Caution   When calculating content for a web viewer in a formula, all text must be enclosed in quotation marks. Any quotes within that text must be escaped with a preceding backslash.

Including Text Fields in a Web Page

When building a web page with a calculation, inserting fields is done the same as in any formula (Chapter 12). Simply insert a field reference into the formula outside of the quoted text. This example will display the Company Name field of the current record.

```
"data:text/html,
<html>
<head>
</head>
<body>
<h1>" & Company::Company Name & "</h1>
</body>"
```

Including a Container Field Image in a Web Page

Images from the Web can be included by inserting the URL in an *image tag*. However, to include an image stored in a database field, use FileMaker's built-in *Base64Decode* function to convert the image into text.

```
"data:text/html,
<html>
<head>
</head>
<body>
<h1>" & Company::Company Name & "</h1>
<img src='data:image/imagemac;base64," & Base64Encode ( Company::Company
Logo ) & "'>
</body>"
```

Calling a FileMaker Script with JavaScript

In version 19, FileMaker added the ability for JavaScript in a web viewer to call a native FileMaker script. If the *Allow interaction* and *Allow JavaScript* options in the *Web Viewer Setup* dialog is enabled, buttons and URLs in HTML code can call a *FileMaker. PerformScript* function with two parameters: a script name and parameter. The following simple example assumes a script named "Test Script" exists that will generate a dialog using the *Show Custom Dialog* script step that displays the script parameter (Chapters 24 and 25). The code renders a button that calls a JavaScript function named *runScript()* that runs the FileMaker script. If configured correctly, clicking the button should cause FileMaker to open a dialog with a message of "Hello, World!"

```
"data:text/html,
<html>
<head>
</head>
<body>
<h1>Test FMP Script</h1>
<button onclick=\"runScript()\">Test FMP Script</button>
<script>
   function runScript() {
      FileMaker.PerformScript ( \"Test Script\", \"Hello, World!\" );
   }
</script>
</body>
</html>"
```

Alternatively, the *FileMaker.PerformScriptWithOption* function adds a numeric parameter for specifying how to handle an actively running or paused FileMaker script.

```
FileMaker.PerformScriptWithOption ( \"Test Script\", \"Hello!\" ; 1 );
```

The *option* parameter can be a number from 0 to 5, indicating that any active script should Continue (0), Halt (1), Exit (2), Resume (3), Pause (4), or suspend+resume (5).

Caution   JavaScript calls only work on pages rendered in a FileMaker web viewer. To enable calls from a standard browser, use the FileMaker URL (Chapter 33).

Working with Charts

A *chart* is a layout object that draws a graphical representation of data in one of several popular charting formats: *column, stacked column, positive negative column, bar, stacked bar, pie, line, area, scatter,* or *bubble.* The data source for a chart can access data from the current found set, a group of related records, or data generated by a calculation formula. Charts are configured in a *Chart Setup* dialog, shown in Figure 20-56. This automatically opens whenever a new chart object is inserted onto a layout. This dialog can be reopened for an existing chart object by double-clicking. It can also be opened by selecting *Chart Setup* from the *Format* menu or its contextual menu. The dialog is divided into two main sections: a chart preview area continuously updates a drawing of the chart as it is configured and a settings sidebar of togglable sections for various settings – *Chart, Styles,* and *Data Source.*

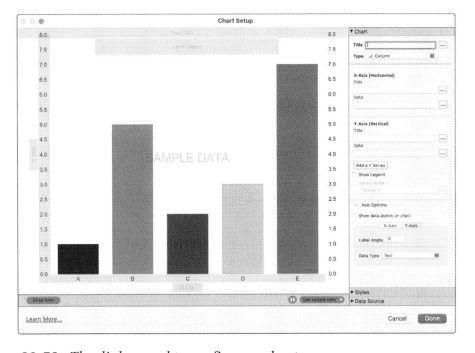

Figure 20-56. *The dialog used to configure a chart*

Creating a Chart Using Calculated Data

A chart generated with calculated data can pull information from either static values or fields from the current record. Insert a chart object onto a layout, and then configure the settings as shown in Figure 20-57 to generate the pie chart shown in Figure 20-58.

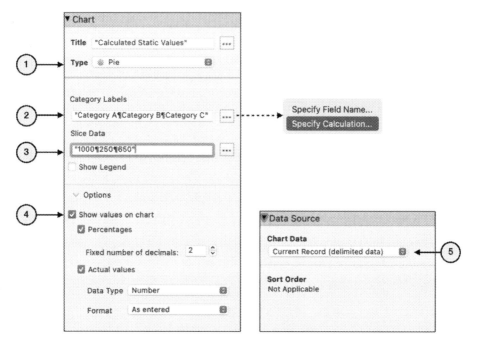

Figure 20-57. *The settings for a simple pie chart based on calculated data*

1. *Type* – Starting in the *Chart* settings section, select "Pie" as the type and optionally enter a title.

2. *Category labels* – Enter a return-delimited list of categories for the chart, e.g., "Category A¶Category B¶Category C."

3. *Slice data* – Enter a return-delimited list of numbers for each category slice of the pie, e.g., "1000¶250¶650."

4. *Options* – Configure settings as shown.

5. *Chart data* – From the *Data Source* settings group, select *Current Record (delimited data)* to instruct the chart engine to use data from the context of the current record only.

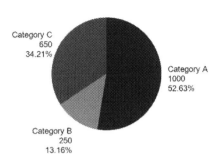

Figure 20-58. *The chart generated by the example data*

The labels and/or data for the preceding chart could be generated using field values by clicking the icon with three dots to open the *Specify Formula* dialog. Also, there are numerous configuration options that allow control over the *Data Type, Format,* and other elements of how data is presented in the chart.

Note   See the "CH20-18 Charts from Calculated Data" example file.

Creating a Chart Using the Found Set

More complex charts can be generated from a found set of records using summarized data. For example, an *Invoice* table can have a layout with a bar chart showing sales per year for whatever found set the user is viewing. This example assumes these fields are present in the table:

- *Invoice date* – A date field containing the date of the invoice

- *Invoice amount* – A number field containing the total amount of the invoice

- *Invoice year* – A calculation (or auto-enter calculations) that uses the *Year* function to contain a number representing the year of the current invoice's date

- *Invoice amount summary* – A summary field that is configured to contain a *Total* of *the Invoice Amount* field

557

Note   See the "CH20-18 Charts from Found Set" example file.

Create a chart on a layout assigned the *Invoice* table occurrence, with settings configured as shown in Figure 20-59, to generate the chart shown in Figure 20-60.

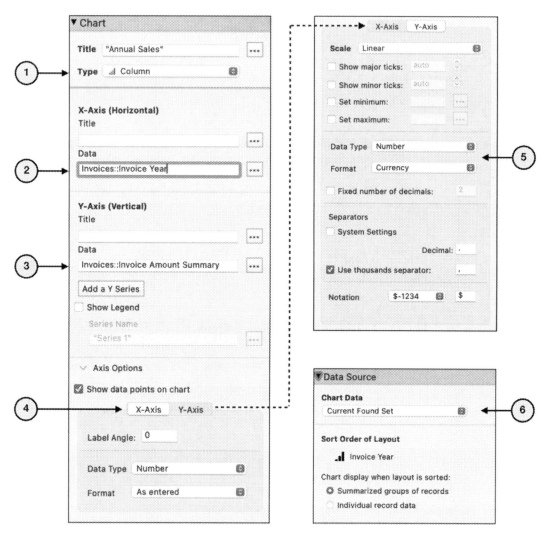

Figure 20-59. *Configuring a bar chart using data from the found set*

1. *Type* – Select "Column" as the type.

2. *X-axis (horizontal): Data* – Select a field containing text that will act as the labels for the bars. To avoid duplicate values, FileMaker will automatically summarize these if the found set is sorted by the field specified. In our example, select the *Invoice Year* field.

3. *Y-axis (vertical): Data* – Select a summary field containing the numeric values for the bar height. In our example, select the *Invoice Amount Summary* field.

4. *X-axis* – Select a *Data Type* of "Number" and set *Format* to "As Entered."

5. *Y-axis* – Select a *Data Type* of "Number" and set *Format* to "Currency." Then set currency options: select *Use thousands separator* and choose a *Notation* symbol.

6. *Data source: Chart data* – Switch to the *Data Source* section of the settings. Select *Current Found Set* to instruct the chart engine to summarize data from across all the records.

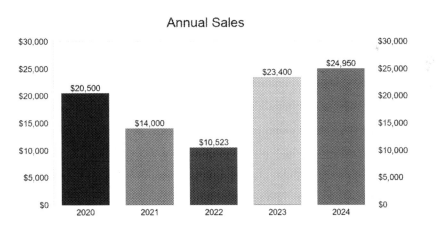

Figure 20-60. *An example of the chart summarizing annual invoice sales*

Caution   For the chart to summarize correctly, records must be sorted by the x-axis field (*Invoice Year*), and the y-axis field must be a summary field (*Invoice Amount Summary*).

Summary

This chapter explored how to create and configure every type of layout object. In the next chapter, we learn how to manipulate, arrange, and configure objects.

CHAPTER 21

Manipulating Objects

Layout objects can be manipulated and configured in a variety of ways. This chapter covers these topics:

- Selecting, resizing, and moving objects
- Arranging and aligning objects
- Hiding objects
- Conditional formatting
- Understanding tab order
- Naming objects

Selecting, Resizing, and Moving Objects

An object can be selected, resized, and moved in the same manner as most drawing programs.

Selecting Objects

To select an object, click it with the cursor or click the layout near the object, and drag the cursor over or around it. The object will become highlighted with an outline that includes eight *sizing handles*, as shown in Figure 21-1.

Figure 21-1. *An object at rest (left) vs. a selected object (right)*

To select more than one object at a time, either click them one by one while holding down the Shift key or click the background and drag the cursor so that the focal rectangle touches all the desired objects. Hold the Command (macOS) or Windows (Windows) key while dragging to require that an item be completely within the boundaries of the focal rectangle before it will be selected. When multiple objects are selected, they share one set of sizing handles, outlining the overall space of the group, as shown in Figure 21-2. Objects can be deselected by clicking the layout background or by selecting another object. To deselect one of a group of selected objects, click the object while holding the Shift key.

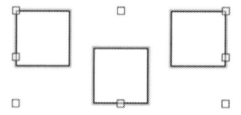

Figure 21-2. *Objects selected together will share sizing handles*

Caution   Shape objects with no fill can only be selected by clicking their borders. Clicking the center of an object will click through the object onto objects behind it or the background of the layout.

Resizing Objects

To resize an object, drag one of the eight sizing handles in or out from the center of the object, as shown in Figure 21-3. Alternatively, specific *Width* and *Height* measurements can be typed into the *Position* tab of the *Inspector* pane controls for precision resizing of objects. To uniformly resize groups of objects, use the *Resize To* functions, described later in this chapter.

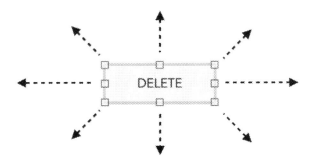

Figure 21-3. *Resize an object in any direction using the size handles*

Moving Objects

One or more selected objects can be moved to a new location by dragging them around the layout or using one of three other methods. The arrow keys will nudge a selection one pixel at a time in one directional plane. The settings on the *Position* tab of the *Inspector* pane allow objects to be precisely placed by typing a new measurement for *Left*, *Right*, *Top*, or *Bottom*. To move groups of objects relative to each other, use the *Arrange* and *Align* functions, described later in this chapter.

Layout Positioning Helpers

There are four features that are helpful when positioning objects manually: the *ruler*, *grid*, *guides*, and *dynamic guides*. These can be used individually or together to guide an object to a new location.

Ruler

The *ruler* is a horizontal and vertical strip running along the entire left and top of a window's content area that displays incremental markings based on a chosen unit of measurement: inch, centimeter, or point. The full ruler, as shown in Figure 21-4, is only visible in Layout mode when the *View* ➤ *Rulers* menu is active.

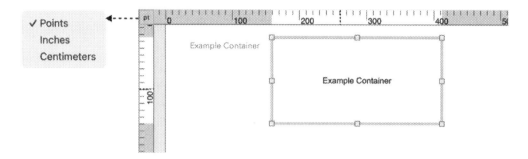

Figure 21-4. *The Layout mode ruler assists for precise positioning*

The ruler has several nonobvious features. At the corner where the horizontal and vertical rulers intersect, a button displays the current unit of measure. Click this to cycle through the available units for the ruler. The selected unit can also be changed from the ruler's contextual menu. The cursor's current position is marked in each ruler with a dotted line, and, when dragging an object, the rulers denote the boundaries of object with a white highlight.

When editing the content of a text object, the top ruler transforms into a gray bar with a text ruler overlay that only spans the width of object, as shown in Figure 21-5. This focused ruler controls indentation, margins, and tabs within the text object using controls like the text ruler accessible in Browse mode when editing a field.

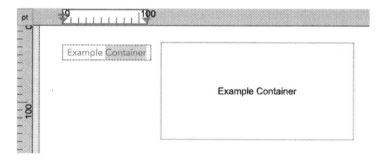

Figure 21-5. *The top ruler transforms when editing a text object in Layout mode*

Grid

The *layout grid* is a sequence of evenly spaced horizontal and vertical lines overlaid on a layout background that denotes minor and major areas. These lines, resembling graph paper, are only visible in Layout mode when the *View* ➤ *Grid* ➤ *Show Grid* menu item is active or the corresponding check box in the *Inspector* pane is enabled (Chapter 19, "Grid"). When visible, the lines can visually assist in uniform alignment of objects. Activating the *View* ➤ *Grid* ➤ *Snap to Grid* menu setting in the Inspector will cause an object being dragged to be magnetically attracted to the next grid line in the direction of travel.

Tip   FileMaker's guides and dynamic guides are a modern alternative to the antiquated grid.

Guides

A *layout guide* is a movable blue line used to align objects and define regions of a layout design. Multiple guides can be placed horizontally or vertically on the layout, as shown in Figure 21-6. Guides don't print and are only visible in Layout mode when the *View* ➤ *Guides* ➤ *Show Guides* menu is active. Click anywhere on the left or top ruler and then drag right or down, respectively, and release a new guide at the desired position on the content area. Guides can be repositioned by dragging them to a new position or removed completely by dragging them back to the ruler. When visible, guides can visually assist in uniform alignment of objects. Activating the *View* ➤ *Guides* ➤ *Snap to Guides* menu will cause a dragged object to be drawn to the next available guide in the direction of travel.

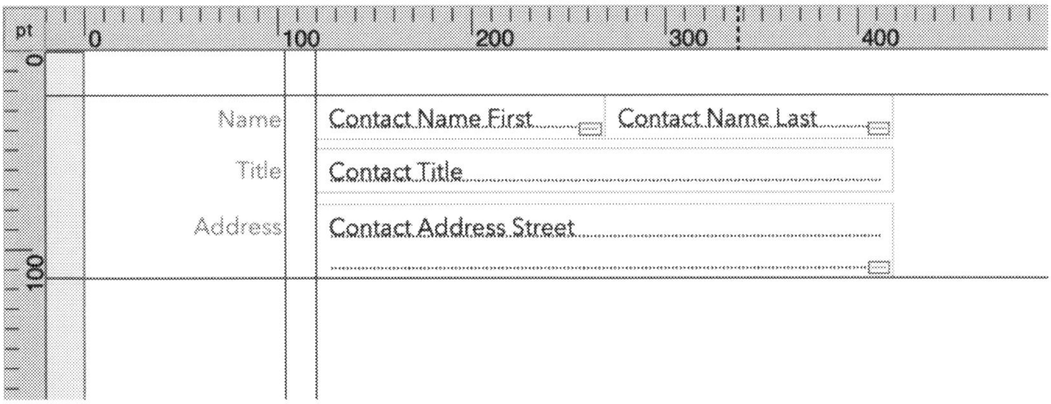

Figure 21-6. *A layout with several guides defining regions*

Dynamic Guides

A *dynamic guide* is one of a set of blue indicators that appear and disappear as an object is moved around a layout showing alignment and arrangement relationships based on proximity to other objects. Dynamic guides are activated or deactivated with the *View* ➤ *Dynamic Guides* menu. Once active, the guides are completely automatic and encourage a uniform arrangement of items on a layout. Like the grid and guides, objects will be magnetically drawn to dynamically guided positioning.

When first moving an object, no guides will appear when the current position does not align to any other objects on the layout. As the object is dragged or nudged with arrow keys and begins to align with other objects, one or more dynamic guides will appear, as shown in Figure 21-7. Alignments are shown for *left, right, horizontal center, top, bottom,* and *vertical center,* connecting to one or more other objects.

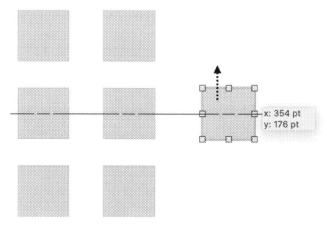

Figure 21-7. *As an object aligns with one or more objects, a guide will appear*

When an object is dragged into a position that creates a consistent spacing pattern, those are highlighted as well, as shown in Figure 21-8. These appear for horizontal and vertical distribution and are displayed simultaneously with alignment guides.

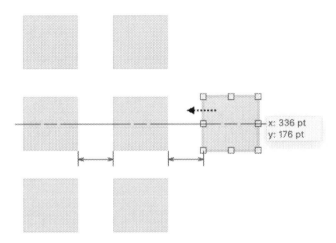

Figure 21-8. *Multiple guides can show alignment and distribution spacing*

Note   Examples in this chapter are shown with uniform square shapes for illustrative purposes only. All features work with any object type, in any nonuniform size or arrangement.

Arranging and Aligning Objects

When working on complex layouts with dozens or hundreds of items, moving, sizing, and spacing groups of objects can be a tediously repetitive manual chore. FileMaker has tools that assist in the task of *aligning, distributing, resizing, rotating, grouping,* and *locking* objects. These are all accessible from the Layout mode in the *Arrange* menu in the menu bar, a submenu of an object's contextual menu, and in the *Arrange & Align* group of tools on the *Position* tab of the *Inspector* pane (Chapter 19). Except for *Rotate*, these functions work with any combination of object type.

Align

The *Align functions* automatically align groups of selected objects horizontally or vertically. For example, with several misaligned objects selected, choose the *Arrange* ➤ *Align* ➤ *Left* menu item or corresponding tool in the *Inspector* pane to instantly align them along their left border, as shown in Figure 21-9. Objects can be aligned *Left, Center, Right, Top, Middle,* or *Bottom*.

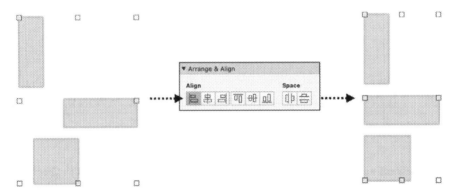

Figure 21-9. *Transforming misaligned objects (before) to aligned (after)*

Resize

The *Resize To functions* automatically resizes a group of selected objects to *Smallest Width, Smallest Height, Smallest Width and Height, Largest Width, Largest Height,* or *Largest Width and Height*. For example, with several nonuniformly sized objects selected, choose the *Arrange* ➤ *Resize To* ➤ *Smallest Width* menu or corresponding tool in the *Inspector* pane to instantly resize every object to a uniform size and height based on the object with the smallest of each, as shown in Figure 21-10.

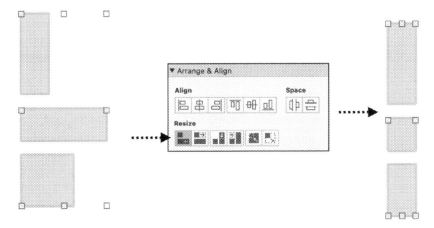

Figure 21-10. *Transforming nonuniform objects (before) to a uniform size (after)*

Distribute

The *Distribute functions* will reposition a group of objects so that they are uniformly spaced horizontally or vertically within the outside measurements of the entire group along the respective axis. For example, with several nonuniformly spaced objects selected, choose the *Arrange* ➤ *Distribute* ➤ *Vertical* menu or corresponding tool in the *Inspector* pane to instantly reposition every object uniformly spaced apart from one another from top to bottom.

Rotate

Many objects can be rotated in a clockwise direction in 90-degree increments by selecting the *Arrange* ➤ *Rotate* menu item. The exceptions are button bars, charts, popovers, portals, slide controls, tab controls, and web viewers.

Group

A set of selected objects can be transformed into a single *group object* by selecting the *Arrange* ➤ *Group* menu. Once joined together, the grouped objects can be moved or resized as a single unit but still manipulated individually within the group by clicking once on the group and a second time on an item within it. Objects such as buttons, button bars, charts, fields, web viewers, and more can be functionally edited while grouped by double-clicking directly on them. To ungroup formerly grouped objects, select the *Arrange* ➤ *Ungroup* menu.

Lock

Locking an object causes it to become non-editable in Layout mode. This helps avoid accidental deletion or movement of objects on complex layouts. A locked object can't be moved, resized, reassigned, reconfigured, or changed in any way until it is unlocked. Lock a selected object or group of objects by selecting the *Arrange* ➤ *Lock* menu. Once locked, the item will not respond to any editing attempts. Attempting to change some settings through the *Inspector* will produce a dialog stating that the change can't be made because of the object's locked status. However, in many cases, the command will just be silently ignored. An object can be unlocked with the *Arrange* ➤ *Unlock* menu. When selected, locked objects display an "x" icon in place of each sizing handle, as shown in Figure 21-11.

Figure 21-11. *A locked object indicated by its sizing handles*

Object Stacking

Objects exist within a front to back stacking order. When two objects are moved together, the one created more recently will appear on top of the other. There are four commands that change an object's position within the stack, as illustrated in Figure 21-12: *Bring to Front, Bring Forward, Send Backward,* and *Send to Back*. Each of this will move the selected object(s) within the object stack.

Note   The object stacking order is also reflected in the *Objects* tab of the *Objects* pane, where objects on top of the list are in front of those below. They can be dragged up and down the stack here as well.

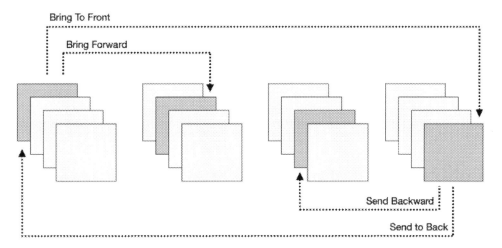

Figure 21-12. *An illustration of commands that affect an object's stack position*

Hiding Objects

A *hide formula* will cause an object to be hidden from view in Browse, Find, and Preview modes. Select the object and enter a formula in the *Hide objects when* area of the *Behavior* section of the *Data* tab of the *Inspector* pane. When that formula returns a true (1) result, the object will be hidden in non-Layout modes. The formula entered can be based on various criteria: the values in fields, conditions of the window, and details about the user's environment. For example,

- A button can be hidden until data is entered in specific fields, like a print button hiding until fields required for the report have a value.

- A field configured as a pop-up menu can be hidden if the assigned field-driven value list is currently empty.

- Data entry-specific buttons and objects can be hidden when the window is in Find mode.

- A chart can be hidden until enough information has been entered into fields to draw something useful.

- A set of portals can be toggled depending on the type of record, like showing a purchase order portal for vendor contacts while switching to a project portal for customer contacts.

- Items a user's access privilege (Chapter 29) doesn't allow them to see can be hidden so they don't see blocked out fields saying "no access" and can't click buttons that produce access denied errors.

- A multi-segment button bar can toggle so only one segment shows at a time as a technique to toggle a button's icon and function.

Using Hide to Toggle a Button Bar

One practical example of using a Hide formula is the use of a button bar as a combinations of field label and toggle-function button. Using a button bar as a field label is a great way to save space by allowing one object to identify the field and provide a function button. This is especially useful for a label on a field containing a foreign key since it can be used to navigate to the related record, create a new related record, and more. With the ability to hide objects, we can create a two-segment button bar that changes icon and functionality depending on a corresponding field's value. For example, consider a field label next to a *Contact Company ID* pop-up menu field in a *Contact* table. Instead of a simple text label that identifies the field, use a toggling label with two functions. One segment will open a selected company if one is selected. The other will allow the user to create a new company if one is not selected yet.

Note   See the "CH21-01 Hide Toggle" example file.

Start by creating a two-segment button bar, both with a label that contains text (the word "Company") and an icon. The first segment will have a plus icon and will run a script that creates a new Company record and assigns it to the contact record. That segment will be hidden after the user selects a company. The second segment will have an arrow and will run a script that navigates to the selected company. That segment will be hidden if no company has been selected. So, each segment receives a different hide formula, as shown in Figure 21-13, so that only one will appear at a time depending on if a selection has been made yet.

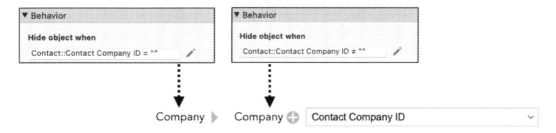

Figure 21-13. *A two-segment bar as a field label that always hides one segment*

The formula on the navigation segment below will hide the first segment if no company has been selected from the menu.

```
Contact::Contact Company ID = ""
```

The formula on the navigation segment below will hide the second segment if a company has been selected from the menu.

```
Contact::Contact Company ID ≠ ""
```

Tip   A third segment could be added with a search icon and no script as an inactive label in Find mode. The hide formulas would check the window mode and adjust the hide action accordingly.

Based on the preceding configuration, the label with a plus icon will only appear when no company is selected, and the label with the navigation icon will only appear when one is selected, both shown in Figure 21-14.

Figure 21-14. *The label button when a company is empty (top) or selected (bottom)*

Tip   Use a hide formula that always return true (1) to embed developer notes on a layout that are only visible in Layout mode.

Reversing Complex Hide Conditions

When faced with a complex hide formula, it can be confusing to juggle all the criteria to yield a negative result. In these cases, consider reversing the formula to produce a true/false value for when to *show* the object and then reverse it with the *Not* function (Chapter 12, "Logical Operators"). In this example, the formula looks at a *Record Status* field to determine when an object should be hidden. A value that is not "New" and not "Active" should cause the object to hide. Even a simple example like this can be confusing because we are specifying not equal to multiple values.

```
MyTable:: Record Status ≠ "New" and
MyTable:: Record Status ≠ "Active"
```

We can simplify the formula and make it easier to think about by reversing the logic. Here, we list the values that show the object as a sequence of what should cause it to show and then reverse it for hide.

```
Not (
     MyTable:: Record Status = "New" or
     MyTable:: Record Status = "Active"
)
```

Conditional Formatting

A layout object has static formatting applied with the tools in the *Style* tab of the *Inspector* pane (Chapters 19 and 22). *Conditional formatting* is the application of dynamic styling overrides to this layout styling based on one or more conditions. A *formatting condition* determines one set of style changes. These are defined with either a custom formula or a selection of 20 predetermined content values. This allows the application of a baseline format to the object itself and a series of style changes that are triggered by different circumstances. An object's conditions are defined in the *Conditional Formatting* dialog, shown in Figure 21-15. To open this dialog, select the target object(s), and choose the *Format ➤ Conditional* menu, or choose the *Conditional Formatting* option from the object's contextual menu.

Note   See the "CH21-02 Conditional Formatting" example file.

At the top of the dialog, the *condition list* will show all the defined conditions for the object. These will be evaluated in order from top to bottom. The checkbox indicates an active condition. Use the *Add* and *Delete* buttons to create or remove conditions. The selected condition's criteria and format settings are displayed and edited below.

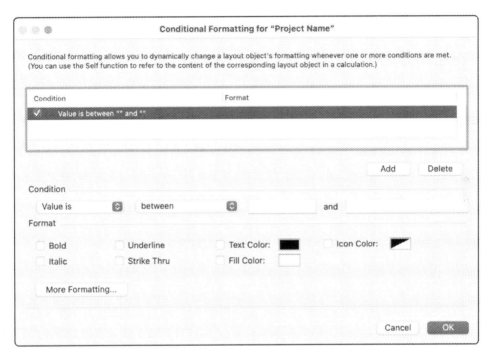

Figure 21-15. *The dialog used to define format overrides based on conditional criteria*

Defining Conditions

A *conditional formatting condition* defines the circumstances under which a set of format settings will be applied to an object. The condition can be either a selection of a *predefined value-based condition* or a *custom formula-based condition*.

Caution   Conditional formatting will override layout formatting but will *not* override formatting applied directly to text within a field!

Using Value-Based Conditions

A *value-based condition* determines when formatting should be applied by comparing the value of the object to static criteria using a selected *conditional operator*, as shown in Figure 21-16. Select *Value Is* in the first menu and select an operator from the second menu. Depending on your choice, one or more text boxes will appear to the right into which static values can be inserted to form the conditional criteria. In the example, if the value of the *Project Status* field is *equal to* "Urgent," the field text will be colored red and made bold.

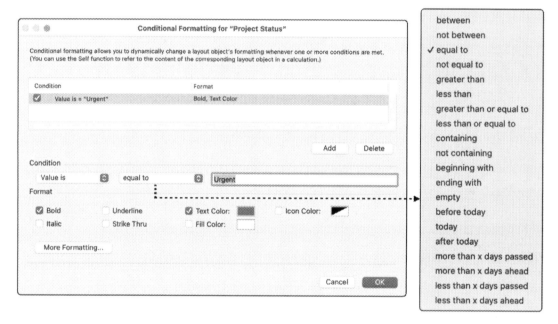

Figure 21-16. *The options for a value-driven condition*

Using Formula-Based Conditions

A *formula-based condition* uses a custom formula's true (1) or false (0) result to determine if formatting should be applied. Because formulas can include any number of fields or functions, this provides broader control and allows multiple criteria to determine the result. Even some simple criteria require a formula, for example, when the value of one field will affect the formatting of many other fields, not just itself.

In the *Condition* section of the *Conditional Formatting* dialog, select *Formula Is* in the first menu, as shown in Figure 21-17. A formula directly into the field or click the *Specify* button to open the *Specify Calculation* dialog. The example will format the *Project Status* field bold and red if its value equals "Urgent" and a *Project Overdue* field equals "Yes."

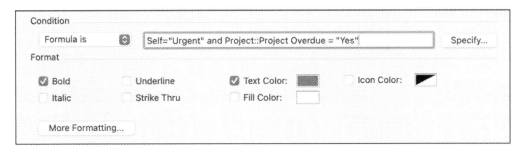

Figure 21-17. *The interface for a formula-driven condition*

Conditionally Formatting a Project List

To illustrate a use of conditional formatting, consider an example of a *Project Status* field's value controlling the formatting of itself and other fields in a list, as shown in Figure 18. In this example, we define two conditions and apply them to every field in the portal so they are conditionally formatted bold when the status is "Active" or gray when it is "Hold." Records with a status of "Pending" are left unchanged with default layout formatting. The result is three format tiers that visually emphasize the urgency of records. Remember, these format changes are imposed on top of the default formatting for the fields set through the Inspector pane.

Number	Project Name	Status	
1001	Creative Musings Artwork	Urgent	^
1005	Convention Display	Urgent	
1007	Marketing Plan Development	Urgent	
1002	Shoe Design Proposal	Pending	
1004	Media Development	Pending	
1003	Widget Sales Pitch	Hold	
1006	Photo Shoot	Hold	v

Figure 21-18. *An example of conditionally formatted fields in a portal based on record status*

The *Project Status* field's menu has three values: *Urgent, Pending,* and *Hold.* Because this field will be formatted based on its own value, it can be configured with the value-based conditions, shown in Figure 21-19. When its value is equal to "Urgent," it applies bold and red formatting, and when it equals "Hold," it applies a light gray color.

Condition	Format
☑ Value is = "Urgent"	Bold, Text Color
☑ Value is = "Hold"	Text Color

Figure 21-19. *The defined status field uses value-based conditions*

The other two fields are configured with formula-based conditions because they need to look at the status field to determine their formatting. The conditions and format settings are essentially the same but expressed in a formula, as shown for the *Project Name* field in Figure 21-20. Here the formula looks for "Urgent" or "Hold" in the *Project Status* field and then applies formatting.

Condition	Format
☑ Formula is Project::Project Status = "Urgent"	Bold, Text Color
☑ Formula is Project::Project Status = "Hold"	Text Color

Figure 21-20. *The formula-driven conditions for other fields in the list view*

When multiple conditions are defined for an object, they are evaluated from top to bottom, and each true result appends its formatting rule to the previous, overriding it if necessary. Drag the conditions up or down in the list to order them as needed to produce the desired hierarchy.

Tip   Select multiple fields to apply the same conditional formatting rules to them all at once.

Understanding Tab Order

The *tab order* is a layout setting that defines the sequence of how the user moves focus from one object to another (Chapter 4, "Understanding Field Focus") using the keyboard. The Tab key is the default of the three *Go to next object using* keys in the *Behavior* group of the *Data* tab of the *Inspector* pane (Chapter 19, "Behavior"). This is where the feature got its name as did the action of "tabbing" through fields when using the keyboard. The default tab order is generally left to right and top to bottom through every object that can accept focus. However, as objects are moved around on a layout or are added later, the tab order will need to be reset to avoid bouncing focus back and forth haphazardly. When setting a custom order, objects that don't require data entry, like calculation fields or buttons, can be excluded and will be skipped over as the user tabs.

Changing the Tab Order

In Layout mode, select the *Layout* ➤ *Set Tab Order* menu to place the layout into a tab order editing mode, shown in Figure 21-21. Each object capable of receiving focus will have an arrow icon attached to one side. These contain the object's current tab order number and are editable. Delete an object's number to remove it from the tab order. Click inside a blank arrow to automatically assign the next available number in the tab order, and/or edit the number by typing over it. FileMaker enforces a unique number sequence by automatically changing an object's value when its assigned number is typed elsewhere. You can change a tab order number midstream, as it will automatically cascade the rest of the tab values beyond that number.

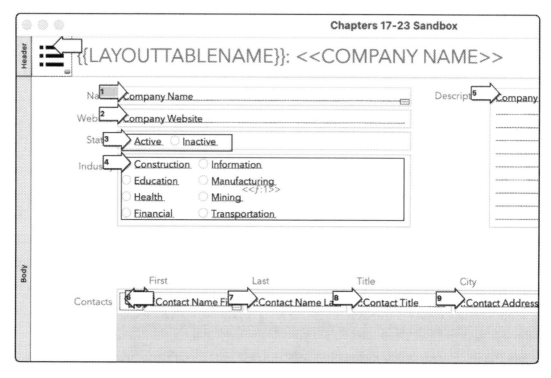

Figure 21-21. *A window in tab-editing mode has customizable order arrow fields*

Using the Set Tab Order Dialog

The *Set Tab Order* dialog shown in Figure 21-22 opens automatically when a layout is placed into tab-editing mode. This dialog is used to perform batch tab order functions and to exit back to regular Layout mode.

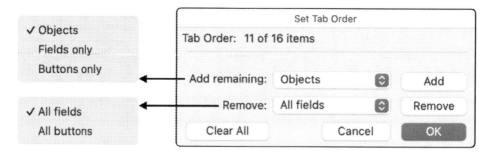

Figure 21-22. *The dialog used to control batch tab order functions*

The following batch actions are available on the Set Tab Order dialog:

- The *Add Remaining* menu applies a default order to any objects of the selected type that are not yet assigned. Choose *Objects*, *Fields only*, and *Buttons only*, and then click Add.

- The *Remove* menu will remove the tab order from either *All fields* or *All buttons*. Choose an option, and then click the Remove button.

- The *Clear All* button will delete the tab order from every object on the layout, providing a clean slate for reassignment.

Tip   After adding or moving any object, return to Browse mode and tab through the fields to confirm a desirable order. The order will usually need resetting, so make it a habit in your design process.

Naming Objects

The *object name* property is an optional static text identifier that can be manually assigned to a layout object or group of objects in layout mode. While names are not strictly required, they will be helpful when looking for objects in the *Objects* pane and necessary for certain functions and script steps that can refer to non-field objects like portals, tab control, slide control, and web viewers. For example, the *GetLayoutObjectAttribute* function can only refer to an object by the name property. Similarly, scripts steps like *Go To Object*, *Refresh Portal*, and *Set Web Viewer* require an object name as a target reference.

An object name for a field should not be confused with the field definition's name. These are two separate things. A *field definition name* is a universal definition of a specific data container that will be common to the field anywhere it is placed or referenced. It is part of a field reference. By contrast, an object name (for a field or any object) is a text based identifying property unique to a single layout instance of the object. So, a specific instance of a field can be assigned an object name different from its defined name. Also, each instance of the same field on any layout can have a different object name.

To assign an object name, enter Layout mode and select an object. In the *Position* group of the *Position* tab of the *Inspector* pane, click into the *Name* text area and type a name for the object. Names are not case sensitive, and they must be unique among all objects on the same layout.

Tip   A named object pasted on a layout with an object of the same name will be renamed to ensure unique naming between all objects on the layout. Always review names after pasting!

Summary

This chapter explored various options for manipulating layout objects, including selecting, resizing, moving, arranging, aligning, hiding, conditionally formatting, tabbing, and naming. In the next chapter, we will explore the themes and styles feature.

Using Themes and Styles

Format settings are applied directly to objects in Layout mode using the controls found in the *Format* menu or in the *Appearance* tab of the *Inspector* pane (Chapter 19). Although first appearing basic, there is a very sophisticated formatting system hiding among these unassuming controls. Every object is made up of one or more *parts* and several *operational states*, each of which can be individually styled using the appearance settings. The collection of format settings assigned to one object can be saved to a custom named *style* to act as a template. Styles can be applied to other objects of the same type so that a change to the settings of one can be saved back to the style template and automatically update all the others. All the styles defined for every object type are stored in a collection called a *theme* which is assigned to one or more layouts. When style changes to objects on one layout are saved back to the theme, those changes are automatically applied to all the objects on every layout using the theme. This facilitates consistency in object design across multiple objects and layouts, keeping format settings synchronized throughout an entire file. It is also recommended as a best practice for improved system performance. This chapter covers the basics of using themes and styles, including the following:

- Introducing styles
- Using themes
- Using styles

Introducing Styles

A *style* is a saved collection of appearance settings for a specific object type that can be applied to objects of the same type with a single action. Styles are powerful tools in FileMaker, but they are limited to one aspect of a layout object's design and differ

583

somewhat from what developers may be used to in other applications. They are also far more complex that they may seem at first glance. Before getting started building a theme, take a moment to review some details about styles.

Understanding the Limits of Styles

A style only holds settings found on the *Appearance* tab of the *Inspector* pane. These include *fill*, *border*, *corner radius*, *shadows*, *padding*, *font*, *size*, *style*, *alignment*, *line spacing*, *indents*, and *tabs*. Other non-format related object properties like *position*, *size*, *auto-sizing*, *sliding*, *hiding*, *repetitions*, and all *behavior* settings are not part of the style and must be set on each object separately. Even properties that affect an object's appearance like *control style and data formatting* are also not part of the style. Other limitations will come to light as we compare FileMaker's styles to those in other applications. However, some of these are what make styles so powerful when designing an interactively engaging user interface.

Tip   Styles only store object properties that can be configured on the *Appearance* tab of the *Inspector* pane in Layout mode. They don't affect the actual content of fields or store other behavioral properties.

Comparing to Styles in Other Applications

In many ways, styles in FileMaker are similar to those found in word processing, desktop publishing applications, and cascading style sheets (CSS) since they enable the rapid application of formatting to new objects and facilitating global style updates to existing objects throughout an entire database file. However, they are also different in a couple important ways. First, they are *layout object styles* used by developers to facilitate efficient layout design and are not available to users when editing the text contents of a field in Browse mode. FileMaker has no user accessible mechanism for storing and reusing *content styles*. Users can apply individual formatting changes to text inside of fields, but there is no method to apply these in batches from a library of styles like found in other applications. Second, unlike CSS and desktop publishing, styles in FileMaker are discretely nonhierarchical and cannot inherit attributes from other styles. Third, because they are applied to dynamic objects in an interactive interface, styles in FileMaker have more dimension than those found in text-based applications. A style stores one group of every *format setting* for every possible combination of *object state* and *object part*, forming a complexity that isn't immediately obvious to a casual observer. However, those who take the time to leverage the power offered by styles are far better for it!

Exploring Style Components

All style controls are in the *Appearance* tab of the *Inspector* pane, as illustrated in Figure 22-1 for a hypothetical *Sort* button selected in Layout mode.

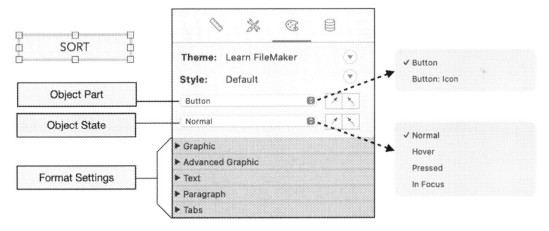

Figure 22-1. *An illustration of the complexity of an object style*

At the top of the pane, the theme and style are listed.

A *theme* is a collection of one or more styles for every object type that can be assigned to one or more layouts. FileMaker ships with dozens of built-in themes. Any of these can be used without modification or duplicated and customized to meet your needs. A *custom theme* with a larger and more practical selection of styles can be custom-tailored to your design sensibilities and technical requirements (more on themes later in this chapter).

Below the theme, the *style* assigned to the selected object is listed. All objects start assigned to the default style based on the type of object. Styles can be assigned, redefined, updated, and saved as new.

Note   Assigning styles to objects and customizing them are discussed later in this chapter.

Beneath the theme and style assignments at the top of the *Appearance* tab of the *Inspector* pane are two menus that are used together to define multiple different format settings for an object. Although unlabeled in the pane, these are the *object part* and *object state* menus. This is where the power of FileMaker's object formatting multiplies.

An *object part* is either the object itself or a component of it. Each part can be separately formatted. For example, a button is made up of two parts: a *button* and an *icon*. A portal is also composed of two parts: a *portal* and a *portal row*. A more complex object like a button bar has four parts: a *button bar, divider, segment,* and *icon.*

An *object state* is the status of an object relative to a user's interaction with it. Most objects have at least four states. A *Normal* state means the object is visible but not actively engaged. This is every object's default state. An *In Focus* state indicates the object has active focus, e.g., a field with the cursor in it or the currently active segment of a button bar. The other two common states indicate the cursor's interaction with the object: *Hover* and *Pressed.* Some objects have additional states available based on their nature, e.g., fields have a *Placeholder Text* state when no content is entered, and a button bar segment has an *Inactive* state.

Tip   The eyedropper icons next to the part and state menus allow format settings to be copied and pasted between states or between objects.

Every *part-state combination* is configured with all object-applicable format settings. This enables a dynamic interface design where the overall appearance of an object changes based on the user's action. For example, when the user moves their cursor over a button, its border, shading, or text color can change to indicate that it is an active element that accepts a mouse click. When the user clicks the button, a new format is applied which can deepen in color to visually indicate the pushing activity. This combination of parts and states creates an exponential number of format settings that can be defined for a given object. For example, a button has eight different groups of format settings, one for each of the four states for each of the two parts, as illustrated in Figure 22-2. Remember, this illustrates one style defined that can be saved and then applied to any number of additional buttons on the same layout or on any layout using the same theme. A theme can contain dozens or hundreds of separate styles for buttons and for any other object type.

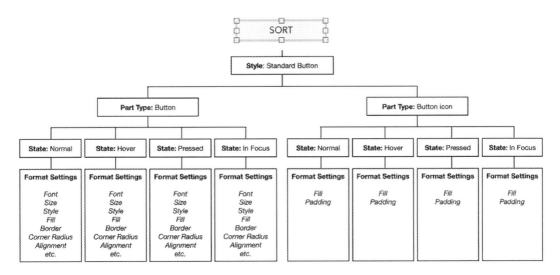

Figure 22-2. *Visualizing the number of format setting groups available for a button*

Using Themes

A new database will have 17 default themes to choose from. The default layout of a new database will always be assigned the *Apex Blue* theme. In past versions, FileMaker would automatically try to determine the best option for the new layout type following a few basic rules. For example, if the current layout's theme was *Luminous* and a new *Touch Device* layout was created, it would assign the corresponding touch theme, in this case *Luminous Touch*. However, that behavior has been removed in favor of the new layout having the same theme as the current layout being viewed at creation time. Once the new layout is created, you can assign another theme to the layout.

Changing a Layout's Theme

After a layout is created, the default theme assigned can be changed using the *Change Theme* dialog, shown in Figure 22-3. In Layout mode, this dialog can be opened by clicking the icon next to the theme name listed in the second row of the toolbar. It can also be opened by selecting *Change Theme* from the *Layout* menu or the contextual menu on the layout's background.

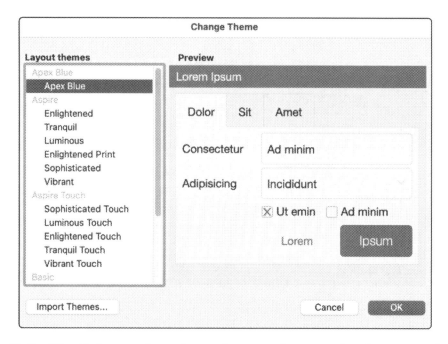

Figure 22-3. *The dialog used to select a theme assignment for the current layout*

The dialog categorizes a list of the available themes with the theme assigned to the current layout selected. Nothing is directly editable in the dialog. You can only select a theme or import themes from another file. After selecting a different theme and closing the dialog, every object on the layout will be affected, depending on the styles available in the new theme compared to those assigned to objects from the old. If the new theme has a style with the same name as the one assigned an object, the object will retain that assignment and change the format settings to the corresponding style from the new theme. Style names are not case sensitive, so any name match will work. An object assigned a style name not found in the new theme will be assigned the Default style for the object's type from the new theme.

Most formatting changes not saved to styles and back to the old theme will be lost during the theme transition. Some unsaved text formatting changes will be retained when the theme is changed, e.g., text size. To retain unsaved formatting changes, FileMaker has a rather clever two-stage undo process after a layout's theme is changed. Immediately after assigning a new theme to a layout, the first use of the *Undo* command will retain the new theme assignment but restore any object attributes that were lost due to being unsaved in the old theme. A second use of *Undo* will fully restore the layout to the previous theme. This allows you to assign a new theme on a trial basis, go back a half step, and have an opportunity either to save previously unsaved changes into new or existing styles within the newly assigned theme or to revert completely to the old theme.

Tip   For the best experience, avoid changing themes after designing layout elements! Choose a theme and use it consistently throughout your database, constantly updating style changes.

Managing Themes

Themes are managed from the *Manage Themes* dialog, shown in Figure 22-4, which can be opened by selecting the *File* ➤ *Manage* ➤ *Themes* menu item. This dialog lists every theme that is in use or has been used on a layout within the database file. Anytime a theme is assigned to a layout, it is automatically added to this dialog's list.

Figure 22-4.   The dialog used to manage themes

The dialog lists every theme used and shows how many layouts it is currently assigned. Built-in theme names will always be contained within square brackets. The *Import* button begins the process of bringing custom themes in from another database. The *Rename* button allows the assignment of a new name to a custom theme. Built-in themes can't be renamed, but they can be duplicated to create a new custom named theme. Themes can be deleted here if they aren't in use in the file.

Note   This dialog deletes unused custom themes completely. Unused assignments for built-in themes can be deleted from here too, but the actual built-in theme is still available to be added to future layouts.

Importing a Theme

Once you have designed a custom theme or have access to one from an example file, it can be imported into a new file. Try creating a new file and then click the *Import* button on the *Manage Themes* dialog. When the file selection dialog opens, point it to the *CH22–01 Styles* file. Next you should see an *Import Themes* dialog like the one shown in Figure 22-5. Select the checkbox next to the *Learn FileMaker* theme and click to finish the import.

Figure 22-5.   *The dialog used to select which theme to import from another file*

When finished, the list of themes in both the *Manage Themes* and *Change Themes* dialogs will include the imported theme, as shown in Figure 22-6. Close the dialog and assign the theme to a layout.

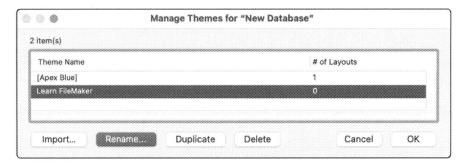

Figure 22-6.   *The imported theme is now available for use*

590

Caution   The *Learn FileMaker* theme has many examples for demonstration purposes but is not intended to be a comprehensive theme.

Using Styles

Each object added to a layout is automatically assigned the type-appropriate *Default* style from the layout's theme. Default styles can't be renamed or deleted, but they can be saved with modified settings or saved as a new custom style. Styles are assigned to a selected object by choosing it from the *Object Style* menu in the object's contextual menu or selecting a style from the *Styles* pane of the *Inspector* pane, both shown in Figure 22-7.

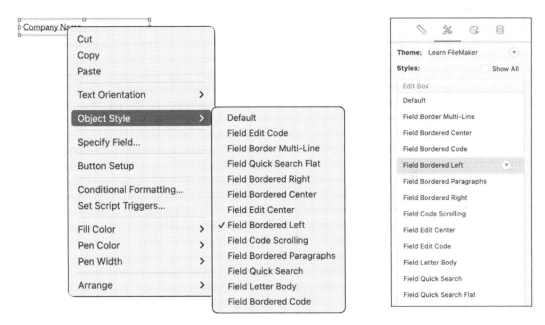

Figure 22-7. *Select a style from the object contextual menu (left) or the Inspector (right)*

Note   See the "CH22–01 Styles" example file.

Editing an Object's Style Settings

Styles are created and modified through a selected layout object. To modify an object's formatting and save it to the style and theme, follow the steps shown in Figure 22-8.

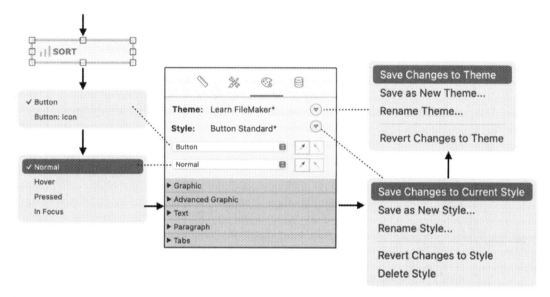

Figure 22-8. *The process for modifying an object's formatting and saving to a style*

First, select an object and then click the *Appearance* tab of the *Inspector* pane, and then follow these steps starting at the top and left and moving counterclockwise:

- Select an object part, e.g., Button.

- Select an object state, e.g., Normal.

- Edit any of the format settings.

- Select *Save Changes to Current Style* from the Style arrow icon menu.

- Select *Save Changes to Theme* from the *Theme* arrow icon menu.

To better understand this process, step through the example in more detail.

After selecting the object on the layout, begin by selecting an *object part* from the pop-up menu. The default selection here will be the object type itself. All components of an object made up of a hierarchy of components will be listed beneath that. For example, when editing a button, the parts will be the *button* itself and the *button icon*, since each of these can have different formatting. Select the part that will have its formatting edited.

Now, choose an *object state*. The default selection will always be the *Normal* state, representing the selected part when the object being acted on by a user. Selecting a different state will cause the object's appearance on the layout to change, previewing how it will appear in the selected state based on the current format settings.

Once the desired part and state are selected, begin modifying format settings using the formatting controls in the *Inspector* pane or the *Format* menu. Then repeat this for other parts or states as needed.

Caution   To avoid styles and themes getting out of sync, make a habit of updating everything *immediately* after every format change!

Keeping Object Styles in Sync

When an object's format settings are modified, the changes are applied only to that object and do not change the assigned style. Instead, changes are held as *unsaved style changes*. To properly use styles, these changes must be explicitly saved, either back to the assigned style or as a new style. When changes are saved back to an object's existing style, the formatting will be automatically updated to all other objects assigned the same style on the same layout, as illustrated in Figure 22-9. In this example, a *Sort* button's format settings are modified, and the changes are saved back to the style updating the *Search* and *Actions* buttons, keeping everything in sync.

Figure 22-9. *Format changes must be saved to the style to update other objects*

When an object has unsaved style changes, the icon next to the *Style* at the top of the *Appearance* tab of the *Inspector* pane will turn red, previously shown in Figure 22-8. Click this icon to reveal the menu of action options. The *Revert Changes to Style* option will eliminate all unsaved changes and restore the object to previously saved settings. The *Save as New Style* option saves the object's current format settings as a new style which is then assigned to the object, leaving the previously assigned style unchanged. Finally, the *Save Changes to Current Style* option will update the assigned style based on the unsaved format settings and then automatically update the format settings of all objects on the layout that share the same style. The menu also includes options to *Rename Style* and *Delete Style*.

Keeping Layout Themes in Sync

When changes to a style are saved, the changes are synchronized to objects on the current layout but do not update other layouts. Like how formatting changes must be saved back to the style, changes to styles are held as *unsaved theme changes* which require saving back to the theme, as illustrated in Figure 22-10.

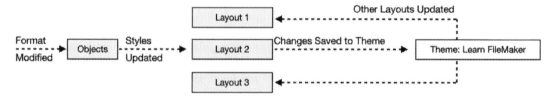

Figure 22-10. *Style changes must be saved to the theme to update other layouts*

When a theme has unsaved changes, the icon next to the *Theme* at the top of the *Appearance* tab of the *Inspector* pane will turn red, previously shown in Figure 22-8. Click this to reveal a menu of action options. The *Revert Changes to Theme* option eliminates all unsaved changes made to any style on the current layout, restoring every style for every object to those last saved to the theme. The *Save as New Theme* option saves a copy of all styles into a new theme. Finally, *the Save Changes to Theme* updates the current theme with all the style updates made and updates the format settings of all objects on every layout that shares the same theme.

Caution   Once Style changes are synced to the Theme, reverting the layout (Chapter 17, "Layouts Menu: Revert Layout") will revert the Layout's object formatting and styles, but not the Theme's styles!

Summary

This chapter introduced the basics of using themes and styles to improve the efficiency of interface design. In the next chapter, we will explore customizing the application menus to create a unique user experience.

Customizing Menus

The default menus are designed to accommodate tasks performed by developers or users and may be adequate for many deployment situations. However, the default menu bar can be completely overridden with custom menus. Doing so elevates a solution from being a database running like a document in the FileMaker application to being a fully *custom application*. The level of customization can vary based on the needs of the database. A simple database may benefit from key changes that intercept and alter a few functions. A more sophisticated interface design might be professionally complimented with a unique menu system tailored to specific functionality. Customizing menus gives you total control over which functions a user can access, how they are named, and the organizational structure of their presentation. If a single custom menu doesn't suffice, a group of menus can dynamically change based on a variety of conditions. This chapter explores the basics of custom menus, covering the following topics:

- Exploring custom menu basics
- Introducing the Manage Custom Menus dialog
- Creating a custom menu set
- Customizing menu items
- Installing a menu set
- Explaining the link between commands and menus
- Creating status-based custom menu

Exploring Custom Menu Basics

Like any modern application, the *menu bar* in FileMaker is a horizontal strip running along the top of the screen (macOS) or the top of a database window (Windows). A *menu set* is a collection of menus that can be installed into the menu bar to become the

597

© Mark Conway Munro 2024
M. C. Munro, *Learn FileMaker Pro 2024*, https://doi.org/10.1007/979-8-8688-0835-7_23

active menu set. A new database will default to a non-modifiable set named "[Standard FileMaker Menus]," as shown in Figure 23-1. The components of a menu set can be included or excluded programmatically, so one set provides the menus for all four window modes, Browse, Find, Layout, and Preview.

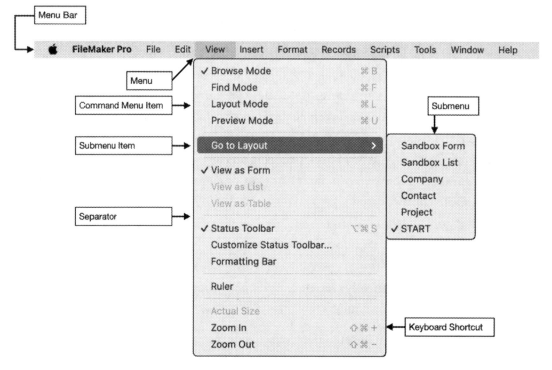

Figure 23-1. *A terminology overview of menu components showing the default menu set*

A *menu* is a primary item of a menu set that adds a named collection of items to the menu bar. A *menu item* is a single item under a menu. Items can be one of three types: *command, submenu,* or *separator.* A *command menu item* adds a specific function to a menu. All the default menu items trigger a standard FileMaker command. A *submenu item* is an item that springs open a secondary menu of options subsumed under it. Submenus can form a nested hierarchy where one menu item opens a submenu with an item that opens another submenu. Every submenu is defined first as a menu which is then connected to the menu item that will open it. Like with standard menu commands, FileMaker has a bunch of default submenus defined and used by standard menu commands. A *menu separator* is a nonfunctional horizontal line used to separate groups of menu items to create a more visually pleasing organization of items. A *keyboard shortcut* provides an alternative way for a user to trigger the menu item.

As a developer, you can create any number of custom menus with any combination of items that each performs a built-in function or custom script. Once defined, a custom menu can be added to one or more custom menu sets or used as a submenu by any custom menu item. A custom menu set can be created using any of the following:

- A totally custom menu created and built from scratch.

- Any of three non-customizable standard FileMaker menus added with all their standard menu items: Format, Scripts, and Window.

- Any of eight standard FileMaker menus that can be duplicated and mostly customized as needed: FileMaker Pro, File, Edit, View, Insert, Records, Request, and Help.

- A choice of about two dozen standard submenus that can be attached to the menu set as a stand-alone menu or added as a submenu attached to a custom menu item. These include submenus such as Open Recent, Import Records, Go to Layout, Manage, Sharing, Show Window, and more.

Some menus can never be completely removed from the application and are not customizable in any way. On a macOS computer, the *Apple menu* contains standard operating system functions and is completely unaffected by the custom menu set and can't be modified in any way. A *FileMaker Pro* menu and a *Help* menu are always at opposite sides of the menu bar regardless of their presence in a custom menu set. The *Tools* menu is visible when the *Use Advanced Tools* option is enabled in preferences (Chapter 2, "General: User Interface Options"). Even with an empty custom menu set installed, these will be present.

Introducing the Manage Custom Menus Dialog

Custom menus and sets are defined in the *Manage Custom Menus* dialog, shown in Figure 23-2. This dialog can be opened by selecting the *Manage Custom Menus* option available in three places: the *File* ➤ *Manage* menu, the *Tools* ➤ *Custom Menus* menu, and the *Menu Set* pop-up menu in the *General* tab of the *Layout Setup* dialog.

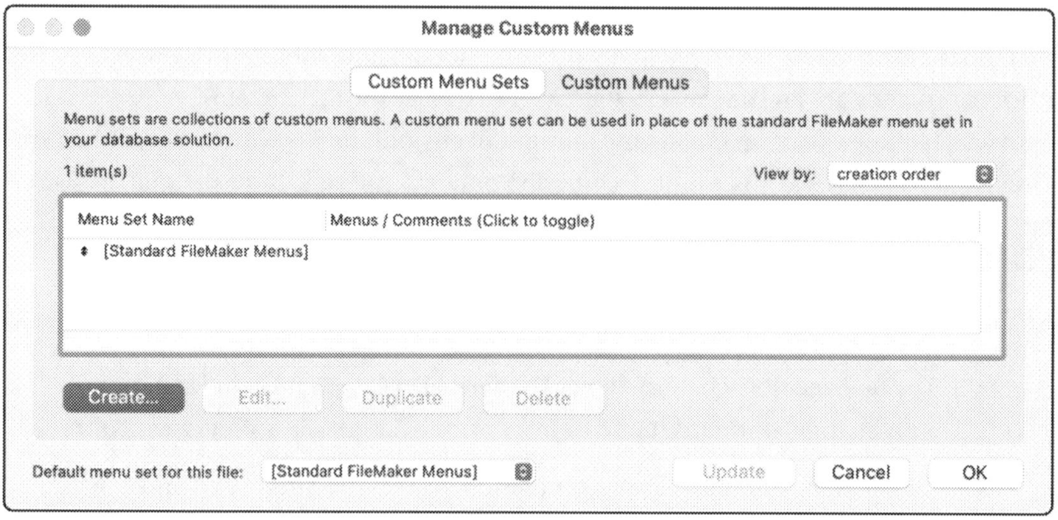

Figure 23-2. *The dialog used to define custom menus and sets*

The dialog has two tabs and both will be essentially empty when first opened. The *Custom Menu Sets* tab lists all the menu sets defined in the file, including the default standard set which is always included and can't be removed. The *Custom Menus* tab lists every defined custom menu. The *Create, Edit, Duplicate,* and *Delete* buttons act on either menu sets or menus, depending on which tab is active. Also available at the bottom of the dialog is a pop-up menu for selecting and updating the *Default menu set for this file.*

Before starting to create sets and menus, take a moment to grasp the complex intersection of features between these two tabs and the dialogs used to create and edit menus, as illustrated in Figure 23-3. Although confusing at first, this illustration presents an overview of the dialogs and functions that will be described later in this chapter.

From the *Custom Menus* tab (right), clicking *Create* opens the *Create Custom Menu* dialog which offers a choice of creating a menu based on a standard menu or starting with an empty one. Once that choice is made, the *Edit Custom Menu* dialog opens where menu items are defined.

From the *Custom Menu Sets* tab (left), you can end up at the same dialogs. When clicking to create or edit a menu set, the *Edit Custom Menu Set* dialog opens listing the menus that have been assigned to the set. From there, selecting a menu and clicking *Edit* will open the *Edit Custom Menu* dialog while clicking the Add button which opens a *Select Menu* dialog. This latter dialog lists all the standard FileMaker submenus and any custom menus that have been created. Select one to add it to the menu set, or click the plus (+) button to open the *Create Custom Menu* dialog to create and edit a new menu the same as from the other tab.

As we work through the examples in the next sections, refer to this illustration to help orient yourself. Although it doesn't matter which path you take when creating menus, if it helps keep you focused, create menus from the Custom Menu tabs and then return to the *Custom Menu Sets* tab to add them to a set.

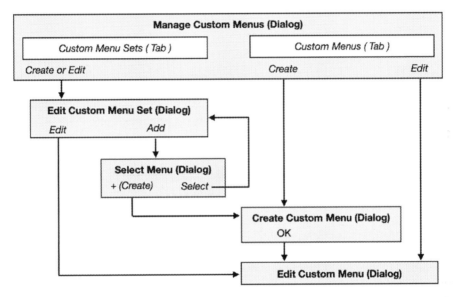

Figure 23-3. *The somewhat confusing intersection of dialogs for custom menus*

Creating a Custom Menu Set

Start a new menu set by opening the *Manage Custom Menus* dialog and clicking the *Custom Menu Sets* tab. Click the *Create* button to open a new empty menu set in an Edit *Custom Menu Set* dialog, shown in Figure 23-4. Enter a *Menu Set Name* and an optional developer *Comment* in the two fields at the top. Now we are ready to begin adding menus to the set.

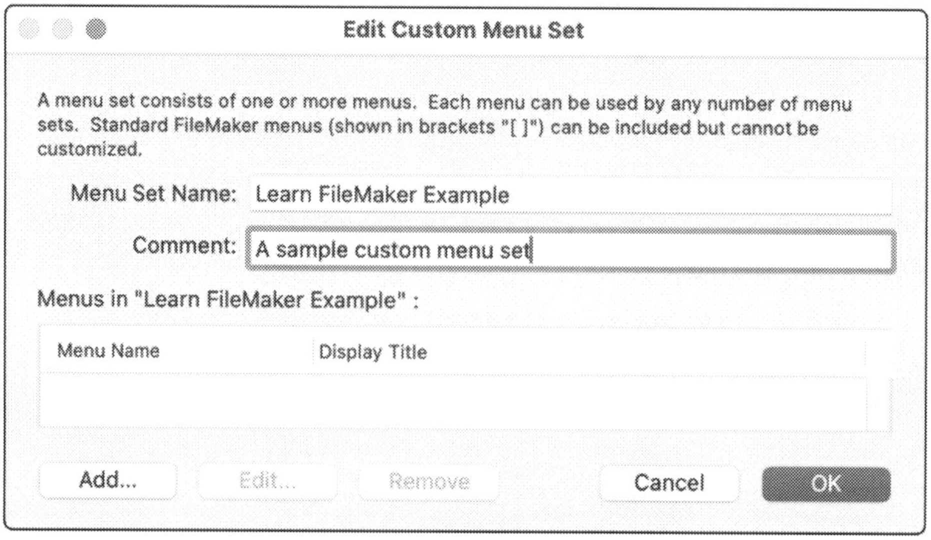

Figure 23-4. *The start of creating a new custom menu set*

Adding Copies of Standard FileMaker Menus

Although a new menu set can be completely designed from new blank menus, creating a duplicate of the standard menu set is a good place to start for basic customization. This is the most likely scenario you will encounter and is ideal for experimenting. To do this, we need to add two sets of menus. The three non-customizable standard FileMaker menus are added one way, and the remaining "duplicate-to-customize" menus are added another way.

To begin, click the *Add* button to open the *Select Menu* dialog, shown in Figure 23-5. This dialog lists all available menus that can be added to a custom set. Until custom menus are created, this dialog will only list standard submenus which are denoted by square brackets around the menu names. Hold down the Command (macOS) or Windows (Windows) key to allow for multiple selections, and click the three standard menus at the top of the list: *Format*, *Scripts*, and *Window*. Once selected, click the *Select* button to add the three selected menus to the custom set.

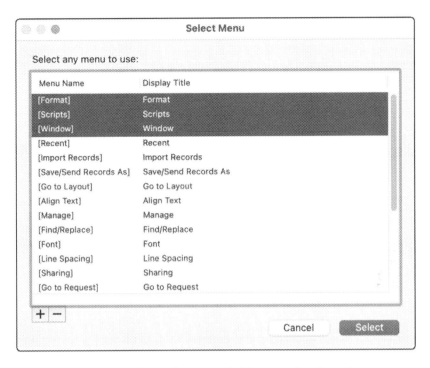

Figure 23-5. *The dialog used to select available standard and custom menus*

Now back on the *Edit Custom Menu Set* dialog, click the *Add* button again to open the *Select Menu* dialog again. This time, click the plus (+) icon to open the *Create Custom Menu* dialog, shown in Figure 23-6.

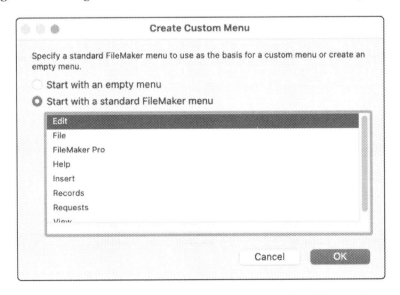

Figure 23-6. *The dialog used to create a new menu and add it to the set*

This dialog offers the choice of two options for the new menu. The *Start with an empty menu* option creates a new unnamed menu with no menu items. The *Start with a standard FileMaker menu* option will create a copy of a selected standard FileMaker menu, which can later be customized. For now, add each of the eight standard menus listed, one at a time. Select *File* and click *OK* to open the duplicate menu in the *Edit Custom Menu* dialog. For now, just click OK in that dialog to leave the copy in its default state. Then click the plus (+) icon in the *Select menu* and repeat for each of the menus. Once finished, the *Select Menu* dialog should contain a list of all eight copies of the standard menus, shown in Figure 23-7.

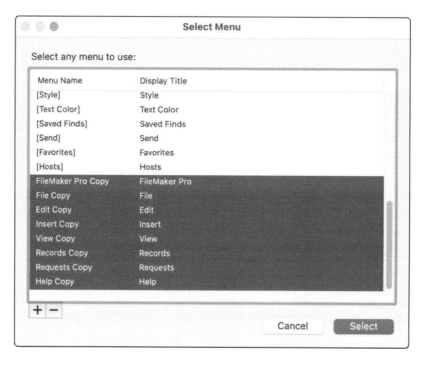

Figure 23-7. *The dialog after creating a copy of every standard FileMaker menu*

These copies of standard menus have now been added to the database as custom menus but still need to be added to the custom menu set. Hold the Command (macOS) or Windows (Windows) key, select all eight of the standard menu copies, and then click the *Select* button. This will return to the *Edit Custom Menu Set* dialog, showing a list of all 11 menus we have added, shown in Figure 23-8.

Figure 23-8. *The new custom menu set with copies of all standard menus in place*

Menus can be drag-arranged in the list with two exceptions: the *FileMaker Pro* menu will remain locked as the first in the list, and the *Help* menu will remain locked as the last menu in the list. Once the menus are in the desired order, click OK to save the changes and close the dialog. Then click OK to close the *Manage Custom Menus* dialog. Now you can manually install the custom menu set for the current layout by selecting it from the *Tools ➤ Custom Menus* menu (see more on installing later in this chapter). When the custom menu set has a check mark next to its name in this menu, it is installed. Since the custom set we created is simply a copy of the standard menu set, you should notice no differences between the current menus compared to the standard FileMaker menus. Next, we can begin customizing the new menu set.

Customizing Menu Items

Whether editing standard menu items or configuring new empty menu items, the process of customizing a menu is essentially the same; open it in the *Edit Custom Menu* dialog, then modify settings, edit menu items, or add new items.

Exploring the Edit Custom Menu Dialog

Configuring a menu and defining the items it contains are both done from the *Edit Custom Menu* dialog, shown in Figure 23-9. This dialog is opened automatically when creating a new custom menu and can be opened later from either tab of the *Manage Custom Menus* dialog. From the *Custom Menus* tab, select a menu, and click the *Edit* button or double-click directly on the menu. From the *Custom Menu Sets* tab, select a menu set and click the *Edit* button or double-click directly on the menu set. Then select a menu and click *Edit* button or double-click directly on the menu.

The top of the *Edit Custom Menu* dialog includes configuration controls for the menu itself. The bottom section includes a list of the menu's items. From here, items can be created, duplicated, or deleted or have their properties and behavior defined.

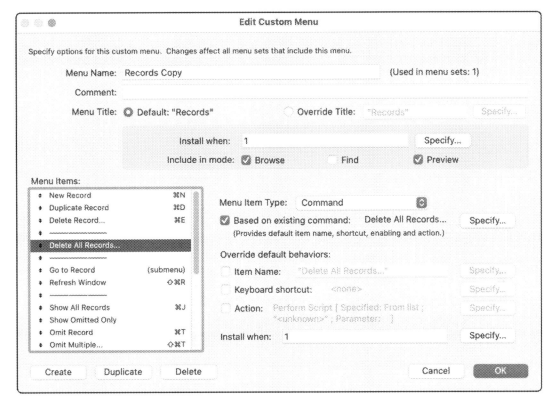

Figure 23-9. *The dialog used to configure a menu and define its items*

Configuring Menu Settings

At the top of the *Edit Custom Menu* dialog, the *Menu Name* field accepts a custom name for the menu up to 100 characters. This name is only visible within the programming interface and is not necessarily the title that will appear in the menu bar. In the example, rename the custom menus, removing the "Copy" suffix that was added to each when copied from the standard menus into our custom set. Below that, the *Comment* field is used to store an optional description of the menu for developers, up to 30,000 characters.

The *Menu Title* controls the name of the menu when it appears in the menu bar. If the menu is a copy of a standard menu, a Default option will be available. This will be the standard name, e.g., "Records." To override this or to enter a name for a custom blank menu, the *Override Title* option includes a field and a *Specify* button allowing entry of a literal name or a formula that calculates a name. Custom menu names can be up to 30,000 characters in length; however, due to the dimensional limitation of screens and the nature of human perception, it is best to limit each menu name to a single word.

To control when a menu is installed in the menu bar, use one of the two controls that work in concert. The *Install when* setting allows a formula to control when a menu is installed by returning a Boolean value, with a static default entry of true (1). The *Include in mode* checkboxes apply that formula based on the Window mode. For example, uncheck Find to hide the menu in Find mode.

Tip   The menu name and title are defined separately for situations where you have two versions of the same menu. They can have the same title for the user but a different name for developers!

Configuring Menu Items

At the bottom of the *Edit Custom Menu* dialog is a list of menu items and controls used to define their properties. The controls on the right vary depending on the type of menu item selected: *command, submenu,* and *separator*. Each of these has one common setting: an *Install when* text area that works the same as described earlier for the menu, allowing a formula that returns a Boolean that controls when the menu item will appear within the menu. For separators, this is the only option available.

Defining a Command Menu Item

The settings available for a *command menu item* are shown in Figure 23-10.

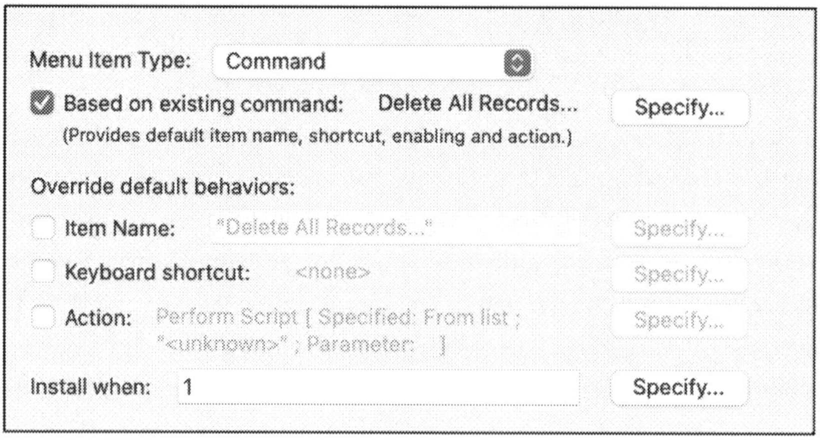

Figure 23-10.   *The settings for defining a command menu item*

The *Based on existing command* can be enabled if the item's function will be an existing FileMaker command (with or without overrides). A *Specify FileMaker Command* dialog will open the first time the checkbox is enabled but can be opened later using the *Specify* button. The dialog presents a list of all available commands that can be selected to assign it to the menu item. For information about the benefits of basing an item on a command even when the menu item will perform a custom script, see "Exploring the Link Between Commands and Menus" section later in this chapter.

Below this there are three *Override default behaviors* checkboxes. These provide override for default behavior when based on a menu or defining custom settings when starting from an empty item.

The *Item Name* checkbox can be enabled to activate an override for the default command name or to enter a name for a custom item. Names should be short action-oriented statements that clearly describe the function performed. For example, "Print Sales Report" and "Send Proposal Request" may be good names, while "Send to Accounting" doesn't make clear what is being sent, and "Get Approval" doesn't make clear the action being taken.

The *Keyboard shortcut* checkbox will override a default keyboard shortcut for a standard menu item or establish one for a custom item. A *Specify Shortcut* dialog appears the first time this box is checked or when the adjacent *Specify* button is clicked. While open, any key combination typed will be captured as the shortcut for the menu item. Be sure to avoid any keyboard combinations that are reserved for operating system functions or standard FileMaker menus that will remain in use!

Finally, the *Action* checkbox allows a custom script or single script step to be assigned as the menu item's function using the same interface as a layout button (Chapter 20, "Configuring a Button's Action").

Defining a Submenu Item

The settings available for a *submenu item* are shown in Figure 23-11. The *Specify* button opens a *Select Menu* dialog allowing the assignment of any standard menu or custom menu as the submenu for the menu item being edited. The *Item Name* checkbox and field allow entry of a custom name for the submenu, overriding the name of the menu selected above.

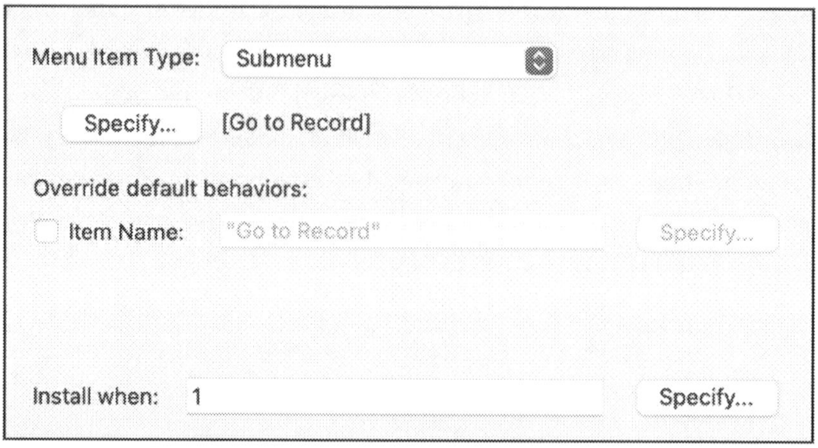

Figure 23-11. *The settings for defining a submenu item*

Modifying a Standard Menu Item

Let's work through a few examples of customizing standard menu items: renaming, overriding functionality, and conditional removal. This section assumes a custom menu set was created with copies of all the standard FileMaker menus, as previously described.

Note   See the "CH23–01 Sandbox" example file.

Renaming a Menu Item

Menu items, including those based on standard commands, can be assigned any name, including one dynamically generated with a formula. An example of such a need can be found with standard items that are intended to provide a generic functionality from any layout. Because of this, they are named to be descriptive of function without specifying context. Regardless of the layout a user is viewing, the default menus are always named *New Record*, *Delete Record*, or *Duplicate Record*. This can become confusing when users are moving between different layouts, especially with multiple windows open. When they select *New Record*, it may result in a record created in a different table than the one they intended. With custom menus, the name can be set with a formula that uses a built-in function to look at the current layout context to include the table name in the menu item, e.g., "New Contact Record" or "New Project Record."

To begin, open the *Manage Custom Menus* dialog and click the *Custom Menus* tab. Double-click the *Records* menu to open the *Edit Custom Menu* dialog, as shown in Figure 23-12. Select the *New Record* menu item in the list, and enable the *Item Name* checkbox to override the default name. Click *Specify* to open the *Specify Calculation* dialog if it didn't automatically open. Then enter a formula for the name.

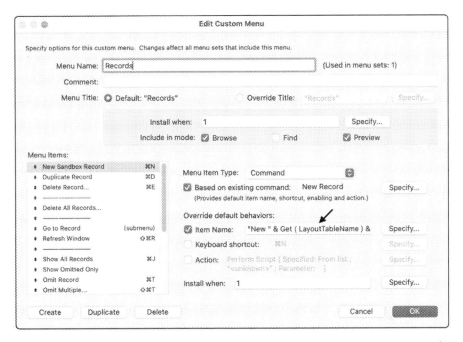

Figure 23-12. *The custom naming formula for the New Records menu item*

The exact formula will vary depending on how the tables are named. If named like the examples we have used previously – *Contact*, *Company*, and *Project* – then the following formula should produce the conditional menu items shown in Figure 23-13.

```
"New " & Get ( LayoutTableName ) & " Record"
```

Figure 23-13. *Examples of a conditionally named New Record menu*

If any table names are not phrased in a way that won't work as a menu, a more complex statement might be required to convert the raw table name for the layout to something more suitable. This example uses a *Let* and *Case* statement to convert two table names and allow the rest to use the actual table names.

```
Let ( [
  tableName = Get ( LayoutTableName ) ;
  menuName =
   Case (
    tableName = "Sales2024" ; "Sales Report" ;
    tableName = "Convention Event" ; "Event" ;
    tableName
   )
] ;
  "New " & menuName  & " Record"
)
```

This process can be repeated for many items in the Records menu, such as the duplicate and delete items. However, the first item in the menu specifying the table should provide a solid contextual orientation for the remaining items and may be sufficient. Adding the table name to each item will clutter up the menu and make it visually difficult to parse.

Tip   Naming tables more carefully from the start avoids having to manually translate them for uses such as a menu name.

Overriding a Menu Item Function

A custom script can be used to override the function of a standard menu command or to provide a function for a custom item. As an example of changing a standard command function, consider the *Delete Record* and *Delete All Record* menu items. Both present rather vague, generic warning messages to confirm the deletion process, but neither makes clear exactly what will be deleted. The *Delete Records* process asks the user if they want to "Permanently delete this ENTIRE record?" with the assumption that the user is explicitly aware of which record they are about to delete. However, if the user is looking at a list view or when using multiple windows, it is possible they might become disoriented and accidentally confirm deletion of the wrong record. Renaming the menu item as discussed in the last section can avoid this confusion about which table they are looking at. However, using a custom script with a more articulate custom dialog provides additional protection. A script using a *Show Custom Dialog* step (Chapter 25) can present a more specific prompt. For example, a message can include the table name and the contents of a field representing the record (e.g., a contact or project name) and/ or a reminder that related material will also be automatically deleted. This formula will include the table name:

```
"Permanently delete this " & Upper ( Get ( LayoutTableName ) ) & " record?"
```

Once the desired message formula is established, it can be used in a script that performs steps to ask the user, evaluate their response, and continue with the deletion process or not. The button the user clicks in the dialog is placed into a $button variable which is used in an *If* statement to *Exit Script* if they click *Cancel*. If they didn't cancel, the script continues, performing a *Delete Record/Request* step with the default dialog turned off.

```
Set Variable [ $message ; "Permanently delete this " & Upper ( Get (
LayoutTableName ) ) & " record?" ]
Show Custom Dialog [ "Confirm Deletion Request" ; $message ]
Set Variable [ $button ; Get ( LastMessageChoice ) ]
If [ $button = 1 ] // Cancel Button
  Exit Script
End If
Delete Record/Request [ with dialog:Off ]
```

Caution   Scripts and script steps are introduced starting in Chapter 24.

Once written and tested, override the *Delete Record* menu item's *Action* to point to the custom script. The default message should now be replaced with the custom script dialog, as shown in Figure 23-14.

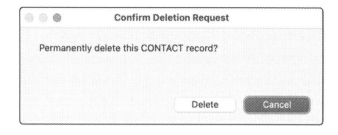

Figure 23-14. *The default delete dialog (left) and a custom example (right)*

A more complex formula can be even more specific. This example builds a dialog message that includes the table name and a record identifying title that varies for each table. The result is the dialog shown in Figure 23-15.

```
Let ( [
  tableName = Get ( LayoutTableName ) ;
  recordTitle =
    Case (
      tableName = "Contact" ; Contact::Contact Name Full ;
      tableName = "Company" ; Company::Company Name ;
      tableName = "Project" ; Project::Project Name ;
      tableName = "Invoice" ;
        Invoice::Invoice Number & " for " &
        Invoice I Company::Company Name ) ;
      recordTitle =
        Case ( recordTitle = "" ; "Unitled" ; recordTitle )
] ;
  "Permanently delete this " &
  Upper ( Get ( LayoutTableName ) ) &
  " record for " &
  recordTitle &
  " any related records?"
)
```

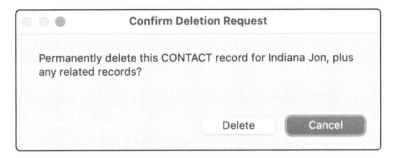

Figure 23-15. *An example of a more robust confirmation delete dialog message*

Tip   Although these examples use table names as text strings, consider techniques for keeping these dynamic (Chapter 35).

Removing a Menu Item Conditionally

A menu can be conditionally hidden under specific conditions. For example, the *Delete All Records* menu item is useful for developers and knowledgeable users but potentially dangerous for some. There is a real possibility that a user thinks they are deleting a small found set of records or a single record and inadvertently delete every record in the table. To avoid this, hide the menu item for this command by modifying the formula controlling when it is installed.

In the *Edit Custom Menu* dialog, select the menu item and click *Specify* button next to the *Install when* setting. Enter a formula that evaluates to 1 (true) only for users who are allowed to use the function and 0 (false) for everyone else. For example, the following formula will install the menu item only for users with a developer's *full access privileges* to the file (Chapter 29, "Exploring Privilege Sets"):

```
Case (
   Get ( AcccountPrivilegeSetName ) = "[Full Access]" ; 1 ;
   0
)
```

Hiding menus or items is a good idea when conditions would make a function cause an error or be otherwise confusing for the user. For example, certain custom menu items should be hidden in Find mode to avoid performing functions that only apply to Browse mode. Similarly, some custom menus should be hidden when viewing an empty found set, when a script is paused, or when a card-style window is open (Chapter 25, "Creating a New Window").

Adding a Custom Menu

Adding a completely new menu creates a space where you can provide users convenient access to custom scripts without cluttering a layout with dozens of buttons or clogging up standard menus with dozens of new items. For example, a *Reports* menu can present a list of menu items that run various report scripts, while an *Action* menu can provide access to scripts that perform repeated actions. The *Scripts* menu (Chapter 24) can be used for this purpose since it allows scripts to be selectively included in a hierarchical folder-based arrangement of submenus. However, sometimes, it is beneficial or desirable to hide that menu and create one or more fully custom menus to provide a more professionally branded interface. This is necessary when the menu needs any kind of programmatic variability since the default *Scripts* menu items can't use formulas to dynamically change names or be conditionally hidden. Scripts displayed there also can't be assigned custom keyboard shortcuts. Adding one or more completely new menus solves these problems.

The setup will vary based on the number and variety of functions requiring a presence in the menu. For example, when faced with a large quantity of search and report scripts, a developer may add two menus: *Search* and *Report*. However, if the number of items in each is sparse or these are two among dozens of required custom menus, one might consider adding a single menu called *Actions* and having each category be a submenu. Alternatively, a single custom menu with a client's name is a great way to adding a personalized collection of custom actions.

Creating an Actions Menu

To create a new *Actions* menu, open the *Manage Custom Menus* dialog, click the *Custom Menus* tab, and click the *Create* button. Then follow these steps:

1. Select *Start with an empty menu* and click OK.

2. In the *Edit Custom Menu* dialog, enter a custom name (e.g., "Actions"), an override title of the same name, and only include the menu in Browse mode. Then click OK.

3. Click the *Custom Menu Sets* tab of the *Manage Custom Menus* dialog.

4. Select the *Learn FileMaker* menu set and click Edit.

5. In the *Edit Custom Menu Set* dialog, click Add.

6. In the *Select Menu* dialog that opens, scroll to the bottom and select the *Actions* menu, and then click the *Select* button.

7. In the *Edit Custom Menu Set* dialog, drag the *Actions* menu to the desired location within the list of menus.

8. Click OK to close the *Edit Custom Menu Set* dialog and then OK to close the *Manage Custom Menus* dialog. If the custom menu set is active, the menu bar should have a new *Actions* menu, as shown in Figure 23-16.

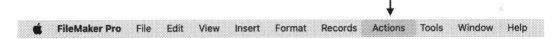

Figure 23-16. *The new menu appearing in the menu bar*

Adding Items to the Actions Menu

With the new menu added to the menu set, add menu items as needed.

Adding a Command Menu Item

To add a command item, return to the *Custom Menus* tab of the *Manage Custom Menus* dialog, and open the custom *Actions* menu. Then click the *Create* button to add a new menu item. To get started with a simple example, make an "About This Menu" item that displays a dialog by following these steps:

1. Enable the *Item Name* checkbox and enter a name of "About This Menu" into the adjacent text area.

2. Enable the *Action* checkbox.

3. In the *Specify Script Step* dialog that opens, select the *Show Custom Dialog* step (Chapter 25), and configure it to display a message describing the menu's purpose and function.

4. Click OK to save back through all the dialogs.

Now the *Actions* menu should have a single menu item that displays a dialog describing its function.

Adding a Submenu Item

As menus become more crowded, organize groups of items. Using separators can help divide a long list of items into separate groups. For more complex situations, use submenus to organize items into subcategories and make it easier for users to locate a specific function. For example, a *Searches* submenu can list all the available search functions, while a *Reports* submenu can list all the reports, moving both groups of items from the main list of an *Actions* menu while keeping them accessible there.

Tip   Consider using the "rule of seven" to determine when to divide menu items into groups using separators or submenus. As a group of items approaches or exceeds seven items, consider separating them into category groups using an appropriate criterion.

To add a *Reports* submenu to the *Action* menu, start by creating a new custom menu named "Actions > Reports" with an *Override Title* of "Reports," as shown in Figure 23-17. Create a few menu items with custom names but don't worry about assigning a script yet. For now, these can be placeholders. Then click OK to return to the *Manage Custom Menus* dialog.

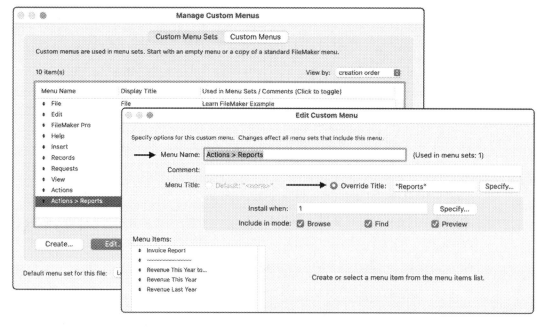

Figure 23-17. *The new menu appearing in the menu bar*

This new menu will not be added directly to the custom menu set as a menu! Instead, open the *Actions* menu and create a new item named "Reports," and configure it as a submenu pointing to the new submenu, as shown in Figure 23-18.

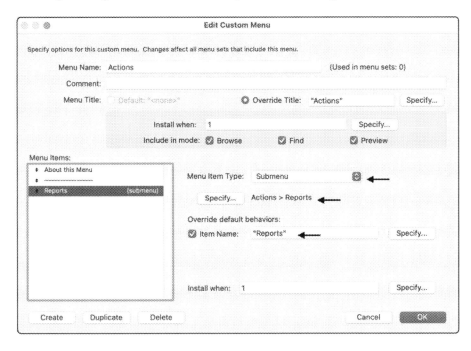

Figure 23-18. *An example of a submenu attached to an item in the Actions menu*

After saving your way out of the dialogs, the *Actions* menu should now display a *Reports* submenu, as shown in Figure 23-19.

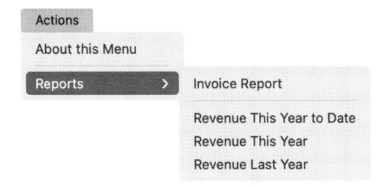

Figure 23-19. *An example of the submenu as it appears to users*

Installing a Menu Set

Once configured, a custom menu set can be made active by installing it numerous ways, including the following:

- Select it as a file default in the *Manage Custom Menus* dialog.

- Select it as a default for individual layouts in the *Layout Options* dialog (Chapter 18, "Layout Settings: General").

- Select it temporarily for a layout by users with full access (Chapter 29, "Exploring Privilege Sets"), by selecting it in the *Tools* ➤ *Custom Menus* menu. This resets when they navigate away from the layout.

- Set by a script using the *Install Menu Set* script step (Chapter 24, "Writing Scripts"). This can be temporary for the current layout or set as the file's default.

Using a script to install a menu set as active for a layout allows formula-driven variation in the decision about which set to install. A set of *If* and *Else If* script steps (Chapter 25, "Using Conditional Statements") can use information about the user, the window, the layout, conditions of records being viewed, etc. to decide which menu set should be installed.

Explaining the Link Between Commands and Menus

When using custom menus, certain functions may be disabled in FileMaker's application interface. For example, the *New Record* command is accessible through a menu item, a toolbar icon, record contextual menu item, and two controls embedded in Table view (an icon and contextual menu). If the default "New Record" command is deleted from the installed custom menu set, these will become disabled. However, simply adding a new menu item named "New Record" back into the custom menu will not cause them to be re-enabled! This is because of how FileMaker links commands and menus to each other, which in turn controls the name, enabled status, and action of these default contextual menus and toolbar icons. The functionality of these elements is only customizable through the active menu set by means of a menu item that is configured to be *Based on existing command* the command the element is intended to access. To begin to unravel how this works, let's review how FileMaker links interface elements together, as illustrated in Figure 23-20. All five of these standard interface elements are based on the same command, which makes them interrelated.

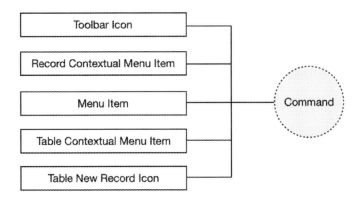

Figure 23-20. *All interface elements for New Record are based on the same command*

However, the association of being based on the command doesn't mean all elements run the command directly. They also don't get their name or enabled status directly from the command. Instead, FileMaker connects four of them to their "based on" command *through the menu item in the active menu set* that is based on the same command, as illustrated in Figure 23-21. The menu item based on the *New Record* command becomes the conduit between the other elements also based on that command. The other four elements pull their name, tooltip, and enabled status from the menu item. A click is also routed through the menu item's action to the command.

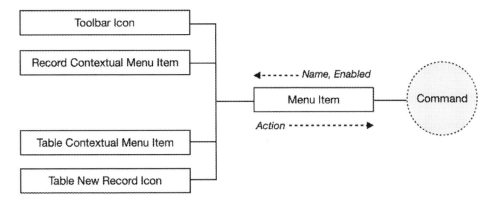

Figure 23-21. *Other elements draw their name, enabled status, and action through the menu item based on the same command*

This eloquent setup allows *indirect customization* of the other standard interface elements when using custom menus. A custom menu can be linked to a command through its *Based on existing command* setting and configured with a custom *Item Name, Action,* and *Include when* that overrides the defaults for the command. These override settings automatically apply to the other instances of the command in the interface! This explains why using custom menus suddenly disabled all the other interface elements. FileMaker doesn't look at the *name* or *title* of a custom menu item to enable these elements – it looks for one that is *based on* the same command.

Use the example of the *New Record* command to illustrate this technique. It is present in the *Records* menu and the other non-editable locations mentioned, e.g., the toolbar icon. The default menu item is based on the command and is automatically enabled unless the user's credentials forbid it (Chapter 29, "Exploring Privilege Sets"). Other access points like the toolbar icon look to the menu set for the item also based on the *New Record* command to determine their own name, tooltip, and enabled status. They also use the menu item's action – routing a click on any of those other interface elements is the equivalent of selecting the menu item directly. A command-based custom item will represent that command the same way, as shown in Figure 23-22.

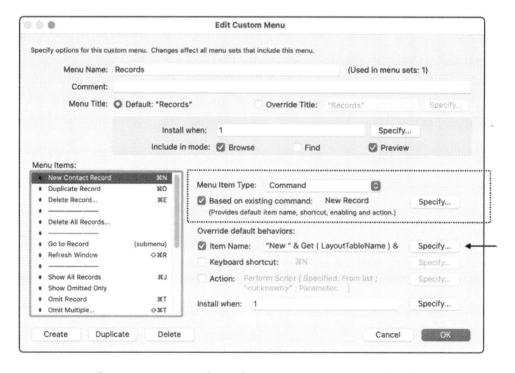

Figure 23-22. *The custom menu based on existing command with an overridden name*

Since the menu item is given an *Item Name* override, that name will show up in all the other places the *New Record* command is present. This includes the toolbar icon and record context menu, both shown in Figure 23-23. If a custom script is assigned to the menu item, the toolbar icon runs that instead of the default command. If the menu item's *Install when* formula returns false, these items will all be disabled.

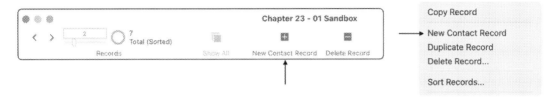

Figure 23-23. *The modified icon (left) and contextual menu (right)*

Caution   Unlike standard interface elements, buttons on a layout aren't based on commands this way. The configuration of these is responsible for their name, enabled status, visibility, and action.

Creating a Status-Based Custom Menu

A *status-based menu item* visually indicates the state of a mode of operation with a checkmark next to its name. A few standard menu items are status based, like the examples found in the *View* menu, as shown in Figure 23-24. The *Status Toolbar* menu item is an example of a *single status menu item* that toggles between an on or off status. It will display a check mark when the toolbar is visible and no check mark when it is not visible. That one menu item can be selected to toggle this choice back and forth. When a status isn't binary, a set of more than two menus can combine into a group where one is active at a time. One of the four available Window modes at the top of the *View* menu will always have a check mark next to it indicating it as active. Similarly, one of the three *View as* options will be marked indicating the current Content view selected for the active window.

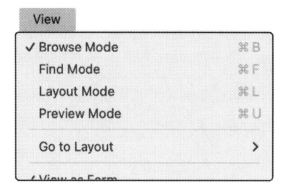

Figure 23-24. *Status-based menus are denoted with a check mark when active*

When menu items are based on commands, they will continue to function this way. Beyond that, there is no built-in method to make one or a set of custom menu items status based, and there is no way to include a check mark in the proper position to simulate such a state. However, since an item's name can be the result of a calculation, it is possible to have a single menu item's name changed to indicate a current state and create a similar toggle effect each time a user selects the item. For example, a menu item can be configured to alternate between two names, e.g., "Enable Tooltips" and "Disable Tooltips," by creating a global variable that stores a status value and using that to generate the menu item's name. The menu's action can look at the variable's current value to determine how to toggle to the opposite state, which then changes the menu item's name.

To illustrate this, create a custom menu item under the *Actions* menu (created earlier in this chapter) that will have an *Item name* formula shown in the following example. First, it uses a *Let* statement to initialize a *$$Mode_Tooltips* variable if it doesn't yet contain a value. This is done with a *Case* statement that checks the variable and sets it to 0 if it is empty or uses the current value if not. Then, another *Case* statement builds a menu name that reflects the action that will be taken depending on the current value. If the variable has a value of 0, indicating tooltips are off, the name will be "Enable Tooltips." If the variable has a value of 1, indicating tooltips are on, its name will be "Disable Tooltips."

```
Let ( [
        $$Mode_Tooltips = Case ( $$Mode_Tooltips = "" ; 0 ; $$Mode_Tooltips )
] ;
        Case ( $$Mode_Tooltips = 1 ; "Disable Tooltips" ; "Enable Tooltips" )
)
```

The menu item's *Action* should be configured to run a script that performs two steps. First, the *Set Variable* script step (Chapter 25, "Setting Variables") will toggle the value in the variable using the following *Case* statement. Then, to refresh the menu name for the current layout, the script will also need to perform the *Install Menu Set* step to reinstall the custom set.

```
Case ( $$Mode_Tooltips = 1 ; 0 ; 1 )
```

Once the menu item is saved, layout objects can be assigned a tooltip formula in the *Position* tab of the *Inspector* pane to conditionally determine if a tooltip should be displayed:

```
Case ( $$Mode_Tooltips = 1 ; "<tooltip text>" ; "" )
```

Now, when the user selects the *Enable Tooltips menu item*, the global variable is assigned a value of 1, tooltips begin appearing when the cursor hovers on objects, and the custom menu item's name changes to *Disable Tooltips* which will hide the appearance of tooltips.

Note   See the "(Menu) Toggle Tooltips" script, "Example Text" field, and custom "Action" menu in the "CH23-01 Sandbox" example file.

Summary

This chapter introduced the options for creating custom menus. In the next chapters, we begin creating scripts that can be assigned to menus, buttons, and event triggers to automatically perform a sequence of actions.

PART V

Automating with Scripts

Scripts automate repetitive actions to assist users in navigating an interface and performing complex data entry tasks. They execute a sequence of functions that can be triggered by a user's choice, an interface event, an external system, or a FileMaker Server schedule. Scripts can improve data entry efficiency, reduce human errors, and free staff from having to perform frequent manual work in a system. These chapters explore the basics of creating and debugging scripts:

CHAPTER 24

Introduction to Scripting

A *script* is a developer-defined action sequence stored for later execution. By compressing a series of tasks into a saved item that can be executed with a click, scripts can save users an enormous amount of time while improving consistency, reducing errors, and increasing productivity. Scripting liberates users from having to manually perform mundane data entry chores and allows them to focus more attention on creative endeavors and customer engagement. Scripts are constructed by choosing from the numerous built-in steps that can navigate, search, sort, print, export, communicate, and more. Additional steps are added to this library by plug-ins (Chapter 28). This chapter introduces scripting, covering the following topics:

- Surveying places to run a script
- Introducing the script workspace
- Writing scripts
- Setting variables
- Specifying file paths
- Performing other scripts
- Emphasizing the importance of context
- Managing script errors

M. C. Munro, *Learn FileMaker Pro 2024*, https://doi.org/10.1007/979-8-8688-0835-7_24

Surveying Places to Run a Script

In FileMaker, scripts are the "heartbeat" of a database. They keep users in action, make interfaces responsive, free users from mundane repetitive chores so they can focus on more productive work, and communicate with external systems. They can be executed many ways, by enabling or attaching them to interface points including the following:

- The *Script Workspace* window allows developers to run scripts from the editing interface.

- The *Scripts* menu provides access to scripts enabled to be there.

- An interface object can be connected to a script as a button action. These include buttons, button bars, or any object converted to act as a button (Chapter 20, "Working with Button Controls").

- A custom menu item can be connected to a script (Chapter 23, "Configuring Menu Items").

- An interface event can run a script (Chapter 27).

- Scripts can be run by other scripts.

- External scripting languages like AppleScript (macOS) or ActiveX (Windows) can run scripts (Chapter 33, "Automating FileMaker with AppleScript").

- A script can be run with a URL (Chapter 33, "Accessing a Database with FileMaker URL")

- JavaScript code in a web viewer's HTML can run a script (Chapter 20, "Calling a FileMaker Script with JavaScript").

- A FileMaker Server schedule can run a script.

- The Data API can run scripts from web services (Chapter 33, "Connecting with the FileMaker Data API").

Caution   Some script running capabilities, especially from external systems, depend on a user's account privileges (Chapter 29).

Introducing the Script Workspace

The *Script Workspace* is a window where all scripts are written and managed, as shown in Figure 24-1. This can be opened by selecting the *File* ➤ *Manage* ➤ *Scripts* menu item or the *Scripts* ➤ *Script Workspace* menu item. The workspace is divided into four sections: *toolbar, scripts pane, script content area,* and *steps pane*.

Caution   The workspace in a new database will appear completely empty until the first script is created! Click the + button to get started.

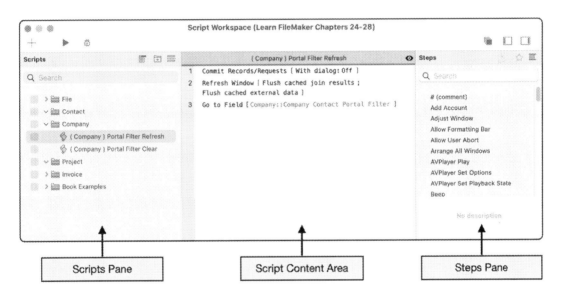

Figure 24-1.   *The workspace for defining scripts*

Exploring the Workspace Toolbar

The *toolbar* of the *Script Workspace* window, shown in Figure 24-2, is a static toolbar of controls focused on script design and troubleshooting.

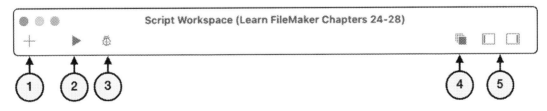

Figure 24-2.   *The workspace toolbar contains several static buttons*

The following function buttons are available in the toolbar:

1. *Create Script* – Create a new script and open it for editing.

2. *Run Script* – Run a selected script directly from the *Script Workspace* using the context of the frontmost window behind it.

3. *Debug the current script* – Opens the *Script Debugger* window and runs the selected script (Chapter 26).

4. *Compatibility* – Dims steps in the selection pane and the content area based on compatibility with the software platforms selected from this menu.

5. *Pane toggling* – Two toggle buttons control the visibility of the *Scripts pane* on the left side of the window and the *Steps pane* on the right.

Exploring the Scripts Pane

The *scripts pane* on the left side of the *Script Workspace* window displays a list of every script defined in the file. Scripts are displayed with a checkbox, icon, and name, as shown in Figure 24-3.

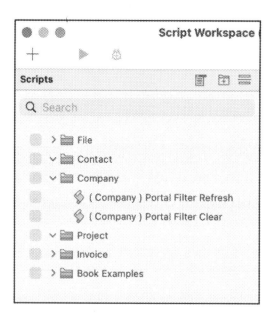

Figure 24-3. *The scripts pane on the left side of the workspace window*

In the pane, each script is an interactive region that hides an assortment of functionality.

- *Single click* on a script name will open it in the content area where it can be viewed and edited. When unmodified, a script closes when another is selected.

- *Single click* on a selected script will cause the name to become editable directly in the list. Edit the name and type Enter.

- *Double-click* on a script will open it in a "locked tab" where it remains open until explicitly closed.

- *Right-click* on a script will open a contextual menu containing functions also present in the *Scripts* menu (described later in this chapter).

A *script folder* can be used to organize groups of scripts. Click the middle icon at the top of the pane to create a new folder. Then type a name and type Enter. Once created, scripts can be dragged from anywhere in the list into a folder. Folders can be dragged into other folders to create a nested hierarchy which can be collapsed or expanded to hide or show each folder's content. Like scripts, two successive single clicks on a folder make its name editable. Folders don't just organize scripts in the workspace window; they form submenus when included in the *Scripts* menu.

A *separator line* can be inserted anywhere in the list to create visual space between long lists of folders or scripts. Just click the line icon on the right at the top of the pane.

The *checkbox* makes a script, folder, or separator appear in the *Scripts* menu. The row of checkboxes is visible by default. If the checkbox is not visible, click the first icon at the top of the pane.

Scripts, separators, and folders in the list can be deleted, duplicated, and more using keyboard shortcuts. The commands in the contextual menu and in the *Scripts* menu are visible only when the *Script Workspace* is open.

Exploring the Script Content Area

The *script content area* at the center of the *Script Workspace* window is used to view or edit the action steps that define a script, as shown in Figure 24-4.

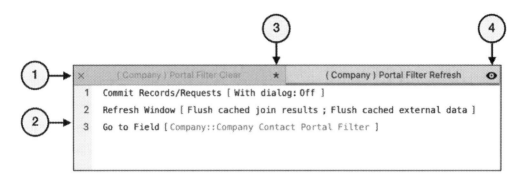

Figure 24-4. *The script content area of the workspace window where scripts are viewed and edited*

1. *Script tabs* – Hover the cursor over a tab to reveal and click to close icon. Right-click a tab to open a contextual menu of functions. Drag horizontally to rearrange tab order.

2. *Script steps* – A numbered list of interactive lines, each representing one step in the scripted process.

3. *Unsaved change indicator* – An asterisk icon indicates the script has been modified since opening. It will remain open when another script is opened.

4. *Preview mode indicator* – Indicates the script is open in a temporary state and will be replaced if another script is opened. Click to remove the icon and it will remain open when another script is opened.

Steps Pane

The *steps pane* on the right of the *Script Workspace* window contains a list of every available command a script can execute in either alphabetical or categorical order, as shown in Figure 24-5. This includes built-in steps (Chapter 25) and steps installed by plug-ins (Chapter 28). The pane's visibility requires a selected script.

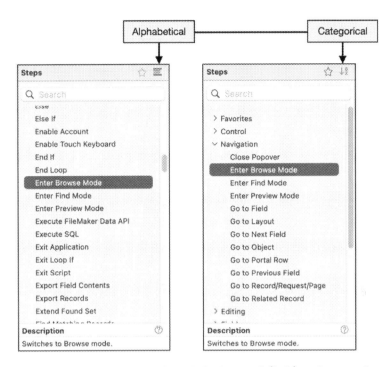

Figure 24-5. *The pane of steps can be alphabetical (left) or hierarchical (right)*

A step can be inserted into the active open script by double-clicking it or by right-clicking and choosing *Insert Into Script* from the contextual menu. That menu includes options to add or remove the step from the *Favorites* category (only available when steps are viewed in a categorical hierarchy) or to open the step in the online help guide. The description pane at the bottom provides a brief description of the selected step, and the help icon button opens the online documentation.

Exploring Menus (Script Workspace)

The menu bar is radically transformed when working in the *Script Workspace*. Any active menu set (standard or custom) is temporarily replaced by a standard menu bar designed for working with scripts. Many inapplicable standard menus are removed completely, while the *Edit, View,* and *Scripts* menus are radically transformed.

Edit Menu

The *Edit* menu of the workspace contains a modified set of functions, as shown in Figure 24-6. Below standard functions for undo, redo, and clipboard content, new items have been added for *Duplicate Step*, Select All steps, and a toggling item to *Disable* or *Enable* a selected script steps.

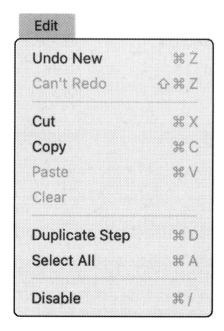

Figure 24-6. *The Edit menu when working in the Script Workspace*

View Menu

The *View* menu of the workspace contains a completely unique set of functions, as shown in Figure 24-7. This menu provides basic workspace functions for hiding and showing various panes, managing tabs, and other functions. Many of these are accessible through various buttons and contextual menus within the workspace.

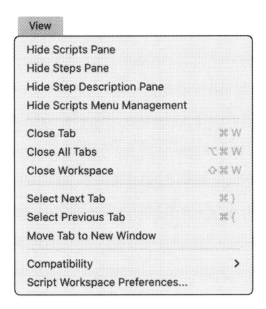

Figure 24-7. *The View menu when working in the Script Workspace*

Scripts Menu (macOS)

The *Scripts* menu when working in the *Script Workspace* is completely transformed, as shown in Figure 24-8. It contains functions for creating, importing, opening, renaming, duplicating, deleting, saving, reverting, and running the current script. Many are also available in the toolbar or contextual menus. One notable function, *Grant/Revoke Full Access Privileges*, configures a selected script to run with full access privileges even when the current user does not have full access (Chapter 29). When a script has been granted full access, a small icon of a person appears next to its name in the list. Another recent addition is the *Enable Shortcuts Donation*, which makes the script available to be executed by macros created in the macOS *Shortcuts* application.

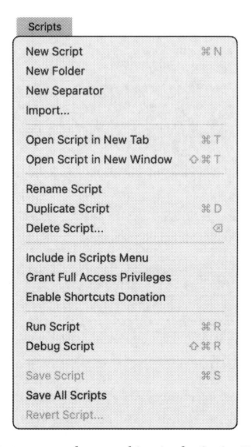

Figure 24-8. *The Scripts menu when working in the Script Workspace*

Caution   The *Scripts* menu is macOS only! In Windows, these functions can be found in a modified File and Edit menus.

Writing Scripts

To create a script, click the + button in the toolbar or select the *Scripts* ➤ *New Script* menu item. The new script will appear in the scripts pane and open as a tab with editing focus on the label awaiting entry of a custom name. Enter a name and type Enter or click away from the tab to commit it. Then, steps can be added to build the script.

Exploring Script Step Basics

A *script step* is a command instruction inserted into a script workflow that defines a specific action to be executed as one in a sequence of events. Although steps can be inserted into the workflow by typing their name into a blank line of the content area, they are really object-based, not text-based. Unlike command-line based scripting environments, once a step is inserted, it can be selected, dragged, duplicated, copied, pasted, or deleted but is no longer editable by typing. Some steps have active regions that allow typing a formula or selecting menu options directly in line. However, most configurable options are modified by clicking to open a pane or dialog.

Inserting Script Steps

Steps can be added to a script using auto-complete in a blank line of the content area or using the *Steps* pane.

Inserting Steps Using Auto-Complete

A new script will have one blank row. To activate an auto-complete suggestion interface, click the row and begin typing a step name. A list of available steps appears and is filtered as you type additional characters, as shown in Figure 24-9. To select a step, either click directly a step, use the keyboard arrows, or keep typing until the desired step is at the top of the list. Once selected, insert the step by typing Enter or double-clicking it. The step will be transformed from editable text into an interactive object.

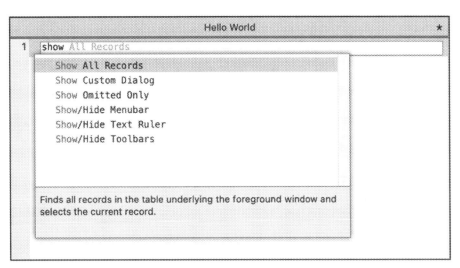

Figure 24-9. *The script step options available for auto-complete*

Inserting Steps from the Steps Pane

To insert using the *Steps* pane, locate the desired step in the list by scrolling, using the arrow keys, typing a few characters of the step's name to scroll down the list or using the *Search* field to filter the list. Once selected, insert the step into the script workflow by typing the Enter key, double-clicking it or right-clicking it and selecting the *Insert into Script* item from the contextual menu.

Configuring Script Steps

Script steps can be divided into two fundamental categories, with and without configurable options.

The *steps without configurable options* will perform a predetermined function without any variability. These appear in the script workflow by name only without any interactive options. Some examples include *New Record/Request, Go to Next Field, Show All Records*, and *Beep*. They can be dragged around to position them in the workflow but offer no optional functionality.

By contrast, *steps with configurable options* appear in the workflow with square brackets after the command name. When added to the script, these steps may contain default settings, value labels, or nothing between the brackets, as shown in the following examples:

```
Allow User Abort [ Off ]
Enter Browse Mode [ Pause: Off ]
Set Variable [ ]
Perform Script [ <unknown> ]
```

Once configured, they will display all or some of the selected settings between the brackets. The configuration options vary by step, but they can be roughly divided into two groups: those configurable directly inline and those configured with an options dialog or panel. Some combine both configuration approaches in a single step.

Configuring Settings Directly Inline

The *steps with inline option configuration* have one or more interface components that are accessible and editable directly between the bracketed area of the step statement without opening a separate panel or dialog. There are three different types of inline options you will encounter: *formula text, toggle buttons*, and *menus*.

Inline Editing with Formula Text

The *steps with inline formula editing* allow a calculation to be typed directly into the script step. These include steps like *If, Exit Loop If,* and *Exit Script.* When inline editing is available, a red box appears between the square brackets. With the cursor over this, the box deepens in color and has a red outline. Click it to reveal an expanded formula text area, as shown in Figure 24-10.

Figure 24-10. *A formula step at rest (top), with hover (middle) and with active focus (bottom)*

Note   Inline formula editing is a convenience for entering a short formula but is impractical for longer formulas. Click the *fx* icon to open a full-sized *Specify Calculation* dialog.

The inline formula editor is fully featured like the *Specify Calculation* dialog (Chapter 12, "Exploring the Specify Calculation Interface"). It includes auto-complete suggestions and allows for multiline formula entry and editing, both shown in Figure 24-11. After typing a formula, compile and save by clicking outside of the formula area or by typing the Return or Enter key. If a syntax error is detected in the formula, the full *Specify Calculation* dialog will automatically open with an error notification dialog, forcing you to remedy the problem before saving.

Figure 24-11. *An inline multiline formula showing the auto-complete interface*

Tip   To insert a carriage return in an inline formula, type Return while holding down the Option key (macOS) or Alt key (Windows).

Inline Editing with a Toggle Button

The *steps with an inline toggle button* allow a choice between two possible options. These can be identified by a labeled value between the brackets that would logically offer a binary choice with a blue border outlining the current value when the cursor hovers over it, as shown in Figure 24-12. To toggle the current value for the opposite, click it or press the space bar with the step selected.

Enter Browse Mode [Pause: Off]

Enter Browse Mode [Pause: Off]

Enter Browse Mode [Pause: On]

Figure 24-12. *A toggle button at rest (top), with hover (middle) and with after click (bottom)*

Tip   When available in combination with a dialog or popover of configuration options, the toggle setting is generally only accessible inline and not included on a dialog with other options.

Inline Editing with Pop-up Menu

The *steps with an inline pop-up menu* allow a choice between several possible options. These can be identified by a value between the square brackets and the appearance of a blue border outlining the current value when the cursor hovers over it. Click it to reveal a pop-up menu of other values, as shown in Figure 24-13.

Figure 24-13. *A pop-up menu at rest (top), with hover (middle) and with active focus (bottom)*

Configuring Steps with an Options Dialog

More complex combinations of configuration options are presented in a dialog or panel interface. Some dialogs are unique to the step, while others open standard dialogs. For example, many different steps open a *Specify Field* or *Specify Calculation* dialog. Some dialogs present a few simple options, while others summarize settings alongside buttons that open additional dialogs. Some open an independent dialog window, while others open a popover panel that remains connected to the step as a kind of middle ground between inline editing and dialog editing. The method of opening an options interface also varies between steps. A step that has a configuration dialog will display a gear icon to the right of its statement when selected. Clicking this icon will open the options interface, like with the *Set Variable* step, as shown in Figure 24-14.

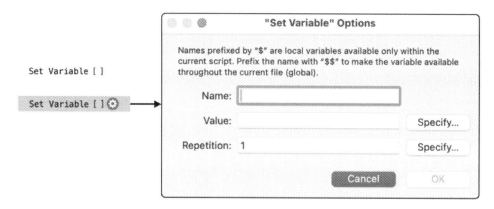

Figure 24-14. *A step not selected (left, top), selected (left, bottom), and the options dialog opened by clicking the gear icon (right)*

Note   See "Setting Variables" later in this chapter for more about this step.

Instead of a full dialog, some steps open a popover panel of options. Like dialogs, panels may include directly editable settings and buttons that open other dialogs. For example, the *Enter Find Mode* step opens a simple configuration panel, as shown in Figure 24-15. This panel contains a checkbox and *Specify* button which enables storing criteria and opens the standard *Find Request* dialog (Chapter 4, "Editing a Saved Find Request Criteria"). Unlike dialogs, which typically have buttons to save changes or cancel, any changes made in these panels are saved immediately. A popover can be closed by clicking the script workspace outside of the panel's boundaries or typing the Return or Enter key.

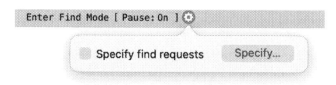

Figure 24-15. *A popover streamlines the selection of options for some steps*

Tip   Many steps have multiple active regions using a combination of configuration styles.

Specifying Targets

Many script steps present dialogs to allow you to specify a target. Some steps require a variable and present a version of the *Set Variable Options* dialog, described previously. A handful require a field selection using the *Specify Field* dialog (Chapter 20, "Exploring the Specify Field Dialog"). Many present a *Specify Path* dialog (described later in this chapter). In addition to these, many steps use the *Specify Target* dialog, shown in Figure 24-16. This dialog allows the specification of a field or variable as the target for some information. For example, most of the available *Insert* steps have been converted to this dialog, and many of the newer *Data File* steps use it as well. This dialog allows the selection of either a field or entry of a variable name. Other steps provide access to a *Specify Calculation* dialog used to determine the value to be inserted.

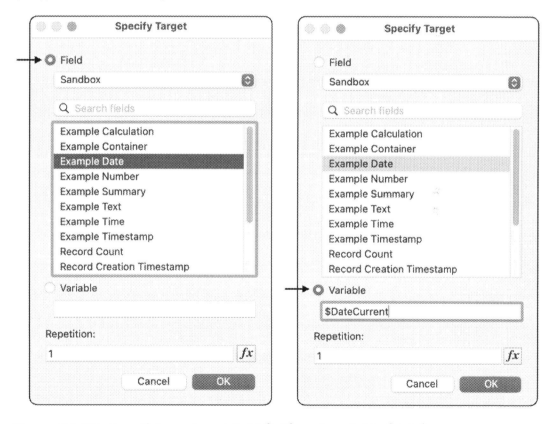

Figure 24-16. *Specifying a target field (left) and variable (right)*

Caution   The *Specify Target* dialog has replaced the former *Specify Field* option from older versions for many script steps!

Script Comments

A *script comment* is a text note placed into a script as a nonfunctional step. Comments appear as a line of text with a preceding pound or hash symbol, as shown in Figure 24-17. These are used to provide inline documentation, describing the function of a script or of a group of steps. When combined with empty comments, they help to separate sections of a script and avoid visual clutter. When a comment is added to a script without any content, it becomes a blank line.

```
# This script will demonstrate good commenting practices

# Setup & Declarations
Freeze Window
Allow User Abort [ Off ]
Set Error Capture [ On ]
Set Variable [ $To ; Value: "Joe@FakeCompany.com" ]
Set Variable [ $Subject ; Value: "Example Database Report" ]

# Find open projects
Go to Layout [ "Project" (Project) ]
Enter Find Mode [ Pause: Off ]
Set Field [ Project::Project Status ; "Active" ]
Perform Find [ ]

# Compile the report information
Go to Record/Request/Page [ First ]
Loop
    Set Variable [ $Result ; Value: $Result & Project | Company::Company Name & ": " & Project::Project Name & "¶" ]
    Go to Record/Request/Page [ Next ; Exit after last ]
End Loop

# Email the result
Send Mail [ Send via E-mail Client ; With dialog: Off ; To: $To ; Subject: $Subject ; Message: $Result ]
Go to Layout [ original layout ]
```

Figure 24-17. *A script with several comments and steps*

Tip   Multiline comment can be created by typing Return while holding down the Option key (macOS).

Setting Variables

The *Set Variable* step sets the value of a local or global variable (Chapter 12, "Variables") at a specific point in a script's workflow. Variables can be used within a script to "park" values at one step for use by another. They can store a value for use later in the script, assemble data from multiple contexts, track iterations that control looping behavior, and more. They will be one of the most used steps in any database. Insert the step into a script, and then open the *Set Variable Options* dialog, shown in Figure 24-18, by either double-clicking the step or clicking the gear icon next to it.

Note   See the "Chapter 24 – 01 Set Variable" example file.

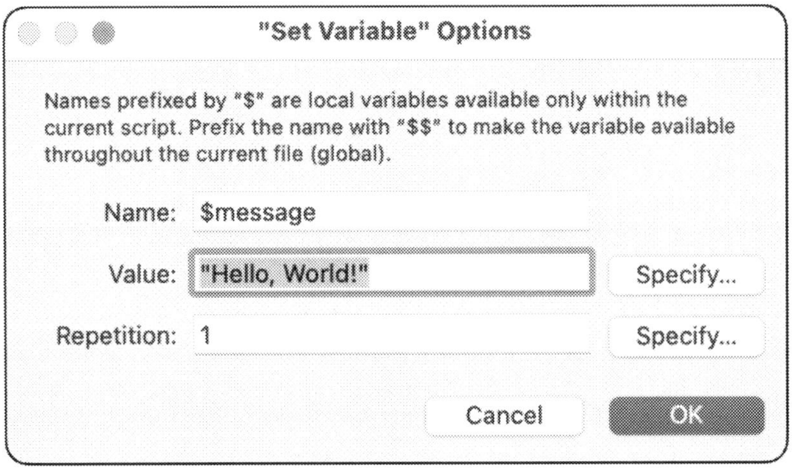

Figure 24-18.   *The dialog used to set a variable*

The *Set Variable Options* dialog is where a variable is named, and value determined for the selected *Set Variable* step. In this example, a variable named *$message* is set to a value of "Hello, World!"

The *Name* field is used to specify the name of the target variable. This can be a new variable or an existing one. The name is how the variable will be used in subsequent formulas within the script, so choose something clear and descriptive. A single dollar sign prefix denotes a *local variable,* and a double dollar sign prefix denotes a *global variable.* If no prefix is entered, a single sign will be added automatically. No spaces or reserved words should be used here.

The *Value* field is where you enter the information to be stored in the variable when the step executes. This can be a literal text value, a field reference, or a formula entered by opening a *Specify Calculation* dialog using the adjacent *Specify* button.

The *Repetition* field specifies the repetition number of the named variable that should receive the specified value. This allows a single variable to contain multiple separate values, like a repeating field (Chapter 8).

Tip   Since numerous variables with different names can be created, the repetition feature should be reserved only for special situations where you need an expandable number of programmatically determined values.

Specifying File Paths

There are many instances in the development interface where file paths must be specified. This can be found when managing data sources (Chapter 9) and many script steps like *Import Records, Export Records, Save Records as Excel, Save Records as PDF, New File, Open File, Read from Data File,* and more (Chapter 25). Paths are entered into a *Specify File* dialog, as shown in Figure 24-19. The *File Path List* text area can contain one or more return-delimited paths. If more than one is entered, FileMaker will check each one, in the order entered, until it finds a valid path pointing to an existing file.

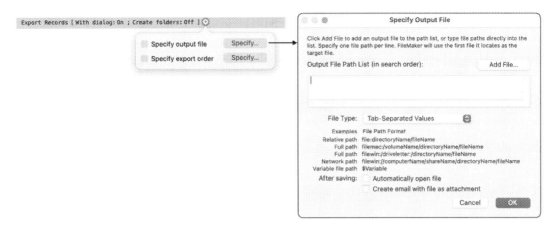

Figure 24-19. *The dialog used to specify a file path for the Export Records step*

Formatting Paths

The *Specify File* dialog includes a list of example paths showing how these can be entered using various formats to point to a file in a local directory or server folder directory or at a FileMaker Server network address. Properly formatting a path can be tricky, especially when addressing files in a local directory relative to the database running locally. There are various prefixes that can be mixed and matched with different path format types. If a path is incorrectly entered or the target file is moved after a path has been defined, a file missing error will occur when FileMaker attempts to access it.

Defining File Path Prefixes

A *file path prefix* indicates a specific type and/or operating system of the file being specified.

- *file, image,* or *movie* – A generic, cross-platform file path.

- filelinux, *imagelinux, movielinux* – A path to an item on a Linux computer.

- *filemac, imagemac, moviemac* – A path to an item on a macOS computer.

- *filewin, imagewin, moviewin* – A path to an item on a Windows computer.

- *filenet* – A path to a database hosted on a FileMaker Server, regardless of the host's platform. If both the source and the target database are located on the same server, the file prefix will suffice, regardless of the folder structure on the server.

Tip   If uncertain which prefix to use or how to format a path, use the *Add Files* button to manually select a file in an *Open File* dialog, and allow FileMaker to formulate the best path option automatically. Then edit as needed.

Identifying Path Types

FileMaker paths can be created as a *relative path, full path, network path* (Windows), and *network address path* (FileMaker Server).

Relative Path

A *relative path* specifies a target file from the context of the current database location. This format assumes the source and target database are both not hosted and have a portion of their directory location in common. In other words, they are running locally from a folder on the same hard drive. Although sometimes confusing, these paths have the benefit of allowing the location of the two files to move with a parent folder structure if the relative location between the two remains the same. The formula for a relative path is composed of three elements: a *prefix*, an optional *path differential,* and *file name*.

```
file:[pathDifferential]fileName
```

The prefix and file name are always required, while the path differential can be included when there is a difference between the two folders containing the source and target databases. The following examples assume two files: an open database named "Test Source" that requires a path to a database named "Test Target." If these two files are sitting in the same directory folder, there is no need to include any information about the difference between their locations, so the path will be simply the prefix and the name of the target file.

```
file:Test Target
```

However, if the source file is moved to the macOS Desktop and the target to the user's Documents folder, the two files will have only part of their path in common, as shown here:

```
Macintosh HD/Users/john_doe/Desktop/Test Source
Macintosh HD/Users/john_doe/Documents/Test Target
```

In this case, for the source file to point to the target file, it would need a differential of two periods and a forward slash indicating that we must move up the directory hierarchy one folder and then down into the Documents folder to locate the file as shown in the following path:

```
file:../Documents/Test Target
```

If the source file remains on the Desktop but the target is again moved into a Documents subfolder named "Target Subfolder," the file path would need to include the additional subfolder as shown here:

```
file:../Documents/Target Subfolder/Test Target
```

If the source is now moved into a folder on the Desktop named "Source Subfolder," the differential must change again to indicate the need to move up the two levels before navigating downward into the target file's folder. For example, assume the two files are in the following folders:

```
Macintosh HD/Users/john_doe/Desktop/Source Subfolder/Test Source
Macintosh HD/Users/john_doe/Documents/Target Subfolder/Test Target
```

For this setup, the file path would require two sets of double-period, forward slash path differentials that indicate we must move up two folder levels to reach the common parent folder before heading back down into the folder structure to find the target, as shown in the following path:

```
file:../../Documents/Target Subfolder/Test Target
```

Tip   When linking two databases, try to keep them in the same folder, host them on a server, or use a full path where possible to avoid confusion.

Full Path

A *full path* is a path to a target file in a folder that is specified from the context of the disk volume containing it. If the target file stays in the same location, the path will continue to work regardless of where the source database is located. Full paths can be used for macOS directories on the local startup hard drive, an external disk, and for Windows local directories. The formula of a full path varies slightly depending on the operating system of the user computer but must include a *prefix, volume, directory,* and *file name,* as shown here:

```
filemac:/volume/directoryName/fileName
filewin:/driveLetter:/directoryName/fileName
```

If a file is in the user's Documents folder on a macOS computer, the path would be formatted like this:

```
filemac:/Macintosh HD/Users/alex_smith/Documents/Test Target
```

The generic *file* prefix will also work and be completely cross-platform.

```
file:/Macintosh HD/Users/alex_smith/Documents/Test Target
```

Network Path (Windows Shared Directory Only)

A *network path* is a path to a target file stored in a server directory in a Windows environment. The formula of a network path must include a prefix, computer, *share point, directory,* and *file name,* as shown here:

```
filewin:/computerName/shareName/directoryName/fileName
```

On a macOS computer, a full path can point to a local or network directory.

Caution   Don't store a FileMaker database on a network directory where multiple users can access it simultaneously as this will cause file corruption! Use network paths primarily to link to images or other non-database files.

FileMaker Server Network Path

A *FileMaker network path* is a path to a target database file hosted on a FileMaker Server computer (not any form of file sharing). The formula of a network path must include a *prefix, server address,* and *file name,* as shown here:

```
fmnet:/addressOrName/fileName
```

These examples show how the same server can be identified by an address or a local network name.

```
fmnet:/192.100.50.10/Test Target
fmnet:/FileMaker-Server.local/Test Target
```

Tip   A path specified by name will continue working even if the server address changes.

If the source database is hosted on the same server as the target, a relative path prefix can be used with the name of the file. Using this method will "future-proof" a database as it will continue to work even if the server address or name changes.

```
file:Test Target
```

Building Dynamic Paths

Unlike literal paths, a path can be specified dynamically so it can automatically change from one user's computer to the next. There are a few techniques for making dynamic paths: *using variables, using functions,* and *excluding file extensions.*

Using Variables in Paths

The *Specify File* dialog will accept a variable that specifies an entire path or a portion of a path. For example, the following three examples all work in the *Specify File* dialog.

```
fmnet:/$$ServerAddress/$$FileName
file:$PathToExport
$PathToImportFile
```

The first example uses two global variables to provide information about part of the path: the *server address* and *file name*. The second places the entire path into a local variable which is appended after the prefix. The third includes everything in the variable, including the prefix, so only the variable name is placed into the dialog. This last example introduces the idea of building an entire path in a variable instead of typing it as literal text into the *Specify File* dialog. There are a couple of benefits to doing so.

The most obvious benefit is that it becomes possible to generate dynamic paths instead of one entered as literal text. The *Set Variable* step allows a path to be generated using the full calculation interface allowing formulaic variation that would be impossible in the literal text entry provided by the *Specify File* dialog alone. Another benefit is the ability to confirm a valid path more easily before deploying a script and to troubleshoot problems with one later. When a script attempts to execute a step with an invalid path, it usually errors with a rather cryptic message. With a path in a variable, there are several options to view it while a script executes to confirm or troubleshoot it. A *Show Dialog* step (Chapter 25, "Showing Custom Dialogs") can be added as a troubleshooting step to display the variable for examination prior to the step that requires it. Alternatively, a variable can be monitored in the Data Viewer (Chapter 26, "Exploring the Data Viewer") during a *Pause/Resume Script* step added for troubleshooting purposes. However, the preferred modern way to troubleshoot a path in a variable is with the *Data Viewer* while using the *Script Debugger* (Chapter 26). Whichever method you use, simply looking at the path will usually reveal the cause of the error. As paths become more contextual and complexly assembled, being able to view the path prior to a step using it is indispensable.

Using Functions to Generate Contextual Paths

A *contextual path* is a path to a directory on the current user's computer. FileMaker provides several built-in functions to automatically generate a valid starting path which can be appended with folder and file names, placed in a variable, and used in any script step that uses the *Specify Path* dialog. They are indispensable whenever a database needs to access a local directory for importing, exporting, reading, writing, and more. It is especially important to use these when a hosted database needs to access a folder locally that will vary from user to user.

Note   See the "Chapter 24 – 02 Paths" example file.

These functions generate a path to a standard folder on the user's computer regardless of any name variations in the startup hard drive or user's folder.

```
Get ( SystemDrive )
// result = /Macintosh HD/
Get ( DesktopPath )
// result = /Macintosh HD/Users/karen_camacho/Desktop/
Get ( DocumentsPath )
// result = /Macintosh HD/Users/karen_camacho/Documents/
Get ( PreferencesPath )
// result = /Macintosh HD/Users/karen_camacho/Library/Preferences/
```

These two functions generate paths to the FileMaker application and the location of the current database file (when opened locally).

```
Get ( FileMakerPath )
// result = /Macintosh HD/Applications/

Get ( FilePath )
// result = file:/Macintosh HD/Users/karen_camacho/Desktop/Sandbox.fmp12
```

A *temporary folder* is an automatically generated hidden folder that only exists until FileMaker Pro is exited or quit. Since these are stored in an obscured directory generally hidden from the user's direct access, they are ideal for use as a staging location when exporting files prior to sending an email or storing transitory data files.

```
Get ( TemporaryPath )
// result = /Macintosh HD/var/folders/rt/n62fc5vd0hn7js2v4098/T/S10/
```

This formula demonstrates how to build a path to a file stored in a subfolder within the user's documents path where exported reports might be stored:

```
Get ( DocumentsPath ) & "Database Output/Reports/Monthly Finances.xlsx"
```

Excluding File Extensions

When a path targets a FileMaker database, the file extension is *completely optional*. Since this may change in a future version, it is a good idea to omit it when building a path, so the database can be easily updated later without having to find and edit every path. For example, the two paths below will locate the same file.

```
filemac:/Macintosh HD/Users/john_smith/Documents/Test Target
filemac:/Macintosh HD/Users/john_smith/Documents/Test Target.fmp12
```

Alternatively, store the current file extension as a global variable or in a custom function and append it to all paths. Then, if it changes in the future, you need only edit that one location to update all paths. This example assumes that a global variable named *$$Extension* is initialized when the database first opens using a Script Trigger (Chapter 27) or other means.

```
filemac:/Macintosh HD/Users/john_smith/Documents/Test Target$$Extension
```

Converting Paths

In version 19, two built-in functions were added to make it easier to convert between an *operating system path* format and a *FileMaker path.* This eliminates the now obsolete chore of programmatically parsing formulas and converting paths to accommodate a different format. Both functions accept two parameters: a *path* and a *format.* The format parameter for either can be one of three values indicating the respective source or target path format: *PosixPath, URLPath,* or *WinPath.*

```
ConvertToFileMakerPath ( path ; format )
ConvertFromFileMakerPath ( path ; format )
```

The *ConvertToFileMakerPath* function will transform an operating system path to one formatted for use with FileMaker script steps. It will add a prefix and drive identifier, as shown in the examples below. Here we use *PosixPath* to indicate that the source path is a POSIX style folder path.

```
ConvertToFileMakerPath ( "/Users/mmunro/Desktop/" ; PosixPath )
// result (macOS) = file:/Macintosh HD/Users/mmunro/Desktop/
// result (Windows) = file:/C:/Users/mmunro/Desktop/
```

The *ConvertFromFileMakerPath* function will transform a FileMaker path to one formatted for use in the operating system. It removes the prefix and drive identifier, as shown below.

```
ConvertFromFileMakerPath ( "file:/Macintosh HD/Users/mmunro/Desktop/" ;
PosixPath)
// result = /Users/mmunro/Desktop/
```

Performing Other Scripts

Sometimes it is desirable to have one script call another script. This allows a complex process to be broken down into digestible steps. It also helps eliminate redundancies by facilitating the design of certain scripts as shared utilities that can be executed by numerous other scripts. Scripts can even call themselves recursively to create complex iterative processes or to have one portion of a multifunction script run another portion of the same script.

Note   See the "Chapter 24 – 03 Perform Script" example file.

Using Perform Script

The *Perform Script* step allows one script to run another script. When added to a script, the step will appear with an *unknown* script assignment, as shown in Figure 24-20. The step has three active regions: *specified, script assignment,* and *parameter.*

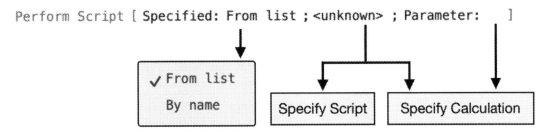

Figure 24-20. *The Perform Script step's options*

The *Specified* value indicates what type of reference to a script will be specified in the next section. This opens a menu with the following two choices:

- *From list* – Indicates that the next region will open a *Specify Script* dialog when clicked, assigning a script to the step by dynamic reference.

- *By name* – Indicates that the next region will open a *Specify Calculation* dialog when clicked, allowing a formula to generate a name.

Caution   A name generated with a formula is not dynamic and will not update if the target script name is changed!

The *script assignment* region of the step will open a *Specify Script* or *Specify Calculation* dialog depending on the first selection.

Clicking on the space after the *parameter* label will open another *Specify Calculation* dialog that is used to create a text value that will be passed to the script being called by the step (see "Exchanging Data Between Scripts" in this chapter).

Tip   Hold the Command (macOS) or Windows (Windows) key when clicking on a *Perform Script* step's target script to automatically open the assigned script in a new tab.

Exploring the Specify Script Dialog

The *Specify Script* dialog, shown in Figure 24-21, is used to select a script that will assign it to the *Perform Script* step, a layout button (Chapter 20, "Working with Button Controls"), a custom menu action (Chapter 23), or an interface event Script Trigger (Chapter 27). The assignment will be a dynamic reference to the script that will continue to work even if the name of the script changes. The dialog allows selection of a script from the current file or any external FileMaker data source defined in the database. To change files, click the menu at the top. The menu above the script list allows quick filtering to a single folder, and the search bar to its right allows a keyword search. An *Optional script parameter* can be defined to accompany the call to the selected script (see the next section). When assigning a script to a button or as an event trigger, this dialog includes the three buttons that allow adding, deleting, editing, or duplicating a script directly from the dialog.

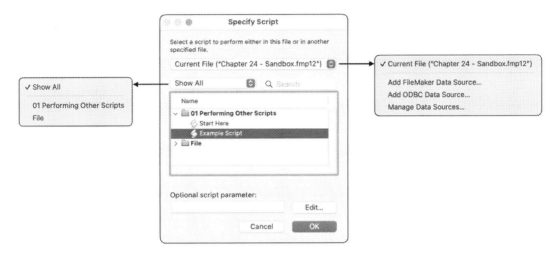

Figure 24-21. *Selecting a script for a button, script trigger, or script step*

Exchanging Data Between Scripts

Decades ago, global fields and global variables were used to "park" data prior to script calls to facilitate an archaic data exchange. One script sets the value of a global variable so that the other script it calls can access that information. Before that, some even used the clipboard for this purpose. However, these archaic methods are long obsolete and replaced with the use of parameters for data exchange between scripts. When a script performs another script, it can send along a parameter value which the receiving script uses as input. The receiving script can access that value with a built-in function and then return a result with another function. Let's step through the process of sending and receiving parameters and a result.

Sending Parameters

A *script parameter* is a text string sent to a script by a triggering object. Parameters are used to transmit any information that a script can use for any number of reasons. Instead of hard coding every field reference or other value inside a script, parameters allow the triggering object to push information to the script, allowing it to react to different information instead of performing a static function. A parameter can be anything: a single word, a sentence, a list of values, a field name, a field value, or a JSON object containing a complex array of key/value pairs as necessary. They can be typed as literal

values or constructed by a formula. To illustrate the use of parameters, create a script
that displays an incoming parameter in a dialog using the Show Custom Dialog script
step configured with this formula:

```
Get ( ScriptParameter )
```

Next create a button or a second script that uses the *Perform Script* step with a short
message typed into the *Optional script parameter* field. When the button is clicked or
script run, the targeted script should present a dialog displaying the message that was
sent as a parameter.

Note   See the "CH24-04 Sending Parameters" example file.

This is a simple demonstration of the process. An actual script can place the
parameter into a variable and then use it as raw material to use for various purposes,
instructions about which operations to perform, or anything else your solution may
require. A more complex parameter can push structured data to a script which will
require parsing to separate individual components.

Parsing a Parameter

A script parameter is always a singular text value. However, it can be constructed to
contain multiple values using a return-delimited value list, a reference to a repeating
field, or a JSON object. When receiving structured information representing multiple
components, a script will need to parse the values to deal with them separately. To
accommodate this, use one or more *Set Variable* or *Insert Calculated Result* steps
to parse the data, and park them into separate local or global variables. This can be
done with a *Let* statement and the *GetValue*, *GetRepetition*, or various JSON functions
depending on the structure of the incoming data.

Note   See the "CH24-05 Parsing Parameters" example file.

Parsing a Multi-Value Parameter

The following script example demonstrates four *Set Variable* steps in a script that access the parameter and then parse it into separate variables. For this example, we assume that it contains three return-delimited values, an *id, name,* and *status.* The first *Set Variable* step places the parameter into an $input variable. The next three steps all use the *GetValue* function to extract one of the three values which is placed into a local variable, *$id, $name,* and *$status.* From here on, the script can access the data from these variables.

```
Set Variable [ $input ; Value: Get ( ScriptParameter ) ]
Set Variable [ $id ; Value: GetValue ( $input ; 1 ) ]
Set Variable [ $name ; Value: GetValue ( $input ; 2 ) ]
Set Variable [ $status ; Value: GetValue ( $input ; 3 ) ]
```

Parsing a Multi-Value Parameter in One Step

Alternatively, the same parsing task can be performed by a single *Set Variable* step that uses a *Let* statement to place each value into a variable directly. In this case, the step's statement will be responsible for naming and setting all three variables, so the variable name in the step itself doesn't matter. To illustrate this, the step is configured to set a variable named *$null*, meaning the formula doesn't return a value.

```
Set Variable [ $null ; Value: <formula> ]
```

The formula for the step will be as follows:

```
Let ( [
    input = Get ( ScriptParameter ) ;
    $id = GetValue ( input ; 1 ) ;
    $name = GetValue ( input ; 2 ) ;
    $status = GetValue ( input ; 3 )
] ;
    ""
)
```

At the start of the variable declaration portion of the *Let* statement, the incoming parameter is captured and placed into an *input* statement variable. The next three variable declarations extract one of the three values which is placed into a local variable, *$id, $name,* and *$status.* From here on, the script can access the data from these variables.

> **Caution**   Using a return-delimited value list as a parameter is old-fashion and risks mismatch between a value and target variable. Use JSON to better manage complex, multi-value parameters!

Parsing Complex Parameters

While the two preceding examples parse a fixed number of three values contained in the parameter, it is possible to create more dynamic parsing functionality. If the number of values varies, a *While* function statement (Chapter 13) or *Loop* script step (Chapter 25) can be created to cycle through them dynamically. Also, a recursive custom function (Chapter 14) can step through each value, initializing it into a variable.

Parsing JSON into Variables

Using JSON (Chapter 14) as the parameter format allows the script to be expanded over time to accept additional values without breaking existing calls. A new key/value combination can be added to the JSON parameter without breaking an existing script that doesn't yet know how to parse that information.

A custom function named *json.split* with the following formula can quickly parse a script parameter into local variables. The function accepts one *json* parameter from which it extracts a list of keys using *JSONListKeys*. Each key's value is extracted from the *json* and into a *formula* variable is written a text-based *Let* statement. When that statement is run through the *Evaluate* function, it dynamically creates a variable with the name of the key containing its value. The example uses *SetRecursion* to limit the *While* function to ten iterations. However, this limit can be increased if required.

```
SetRecursion (
While (
[
        keys = JSONListKeys ( json ; "" ) ;
        result = ""
] ;
        keys ≠ "" ;
[
        key = GetValue ( keys ; 1 ) ;
```

```
        value = JSONGetElement ( json ; key ) ;
        formula =
                "Let ( $" & key & " = " &
                Quote ( value ) & " ; " & Quote ( "" ) & " )" ;
        null = Evaluate ( formula ) ;
        keys = RightValues ( keys ; ValueCount ( keys ) - 1 )
] ;
        ""

) ;
10 )
```

Any script accepting a single JSON Object as a parameter can include this step at the top to instantly convert all keys at the root level of the object into local variables:

```
Set Variable [ $null ; Value: json.split ( Get ( ScriptParameter ) ) ]
```

Sending and Receiving Script Results

A *script result* is a final value that a script sends when it is finished executing. Any script run by another script can send back a value using the *Exit Script* step. This step has a single *Text Result* calculation formula that generates the value to be returned as a result. Like an input parameter, a result can be a single value or complex data structure. This example shows a simple result returning the word "Success" to indicate to the calling script that the target script reached the end of its steps without failure.

```
Exit Script [ Text Result: "Success" ]
```

Note   See the "CH24-06 Sending Results" example file.

The script that called the other script can retrieve the result using the *Get (ScriptResult)* function. In this example, a script uses the *Perform Script* step to call an *Example Script* and then uses a *Show Custom Dialog* step to display a dialog containing the result from the other script.

```
Perform Script [ Specified: From list ; "Example Script" ; Parameter: ]
Show Custom Dialog [ Get ( ScriptResult ) ]
```

The result can also be placed into a variable and then uses later in the current script.

Tip   A script can have multiple exit points, each returning a different value from each to indicate points of failure or other information.

Using Perform Script on Server

When a database is hosted on a FileMaker Server (Chapter 32), scripts run with the *Perform Script* step will be run locally on the user's computer. Alternatively, a script can run on the database's host server using the *Perform Script On Server* (PSOS) step. The benefit of offloading a script to the host is that a complex script will be faster since the client and server don't need to exchange as much information across the network. Also, it can optionally run independently from the user's session, so they can move on to other work in the database simultaneously.

The step, shown in the example below, has the same parameters to *Perform Script* plus the option to *Wait for completion* which can be turned on or off. If turned on, the user's database will be locked up until the server finishes executing the script and returns a result. If off, the script will run independently and no longer interact with the user's computer. In this case, the user is free to continue working on data entry tasks or running other local scripts.

```
Perform Script on Server [ Specified: From list ; "Example Script" ;
Parameter:  ; Wait for completion: On ]
```

Before using this feature, it is important to realize that the context of the local computer's database window will not be known or accessible to the server when running the script. The server will perform the script as the current user but in a new session with any default layout or startup scripts run anew. Therefore, any contextual information about the user's current table, layout, record, found set, sort order, variables, or window will be completely unknown to the server when executing the script. If any of this information is required by the script being called, it must be included in a script parameter so the server can replicate the context before running. As a rule of thumb, if the target script is running a fully self-contained process, you need not worry about this issue. However, if it is running a process as an extension of the user's context, it will.

New scripts can be designed specifically to address this issue. When converting an existing script to run on the server, it may be necessary to split it into two: one script that loads the context information into a variable which will be sent as a script parameter that the other script will receive, reset the context on the server, and then perform its own steps. It is also possible to design a script that unifies the two and can run locally or on the server, depending on certain conditions. There are two things a script might need to know before trying to execute a script (another one or itself) on the server: if the database is hosted or running locally and if the script is running locally or on the server.

Determining a Database's Hosted Status

A script can check to see if a database is hosted or running locally and then use an *If* statement (Chapter 24, "Using Conditional Statements") to decide if it should run the other script locally or on the server. The following two nested functions will return the first word of the version of the host application.

```
LeftWords ( Get ( HostApplicationVersion ) ; 1 ) = "Server"
```

If the database is running locally, the *HostsApplicationVersion* function returns the version of the host applications, for example, "Server 21.1.1." The *LeftWords* function is used to parse the first word of that value which is compared to the literal text string "Server." So, the formula will return true (1) if the database is hosted and false (0) if it is running locally. Adding an *If* statement, a script can choose to perform another script on the server or locally depending on that result, as shown here:

```
If [ LeftWords ( Get ( HostApplicationVersion ) ; 1 ) = "Server" ]
    Perform Script On Server [ <script name> ]
Else
    Perform Script [ <script name> ]
End If
```

Determining a Script's Execution Status

Since a script can perform itself, it is possible to design any script to redirect its execution to the server if appropriate. This requires two things to be true. First, the database must be hosted on a server. Second, the script needs to determine if it is currently running locally (and should be redirected) or is already running on the server and should just continue running. The following formula will determine if both conditions are true.

```
LeftWords ( Get ( HostApplicationVersion ) ; 1 ) = "Server" and
not ( IsEmpty ( Get ( HostApplicationVersion ) ) )
```

That formula can be added as a custom function named *PerformScriptOnServer*. Then, any script that is designed to allow redirection to a server execution can use it in an *If* statement like the example below.

```
If [ PerformScriptOnServer ]
    # Add lines here to gather required context to pass as a parameter
    Perform Script On Server [ Specified: By name ; Get ( ScriptName ) ]
    Exit Script [ ]
End If
# Add lines here to perform whatever functions the script should perform
```

Caution   Running a script on the server takes a little practice to master, especially when passing and recreating a user's context.

Using Perform Script on Server with Callback

Introduced in version 20.1, the *Perform Script on Server with Callback* step runs a script on the database's host server without pausing. Once the local script has sent the request to the host server asking it to execute the target script, the user's database is free to continue other script steps or manual data entry work. Once the server completes performing the target script, it will "call back" and execute the specified local script responsible for handling results or notifying the user that the task is complete.

```
Perform Script on Server with Callback [
        Specified: From List ;
        "<Target Script>" ;
        Parameter: "" ;
        Callback script specified: From List ;
        "<Callback Script>" ;
        Parameter: "" ;
        State: Continue
]
```

The step has the following six parameters:

- *Specified* – Choose how the target script is specified: "From List" or "By Name."

- *Target script* – The script to be performed, either a reference selected from list or name entered in a *Specify Calculation* dialog.

- *Parameter* – An optional parameter to be sent to the target script.

- *Callback script specified* – Choose how the callback script is specified.

- *Callback script* – The script to be performed locally after the server has completed the target script, either a reference selected from list or name entered in a *Specify Calculation* dialog.

- *Parameter* – An optional parameter to be sent to the callback script.

- *State* – A menu of choices specifying how to handle a running script when the callback script is run: *Continue, Halt, Exit, Resume,* or *Pause*. This option was added in version 21 (2024).

Caution   When specifying a script by name, be sure to keep the reference dynamic to accommodate future name changes (Chapter 35, "Keeping Script Calls Dynamic")!

Choosing a Perform Script Option

Each of the three Perform Script four options has slightly different behaviors in respect to whether the local computer is busy during the server execution and the ability of the target script to return a result. These differences are illustrated in Table 24-1.

Table 24-1. *An overview of Perform Script options*

Step name	Target runs	Busy until complete	Receive result
Perform Script	Locally	Yes	Yes
Perform Script on Server	On Server	No	No
Perform Script on Server (Wait)	On Server	Yes	Yes
Perform Script on Server with Callback	On Server	No	Yes

The *Perform Script* step runs completely locally and keeps the local database busy during execution of the target script. Due to this, the initiating script can receive a result from the target script.

Tip   Use *Perform Script* for any script that is needed when the database is running locally!

The *Perform Script on Server* step will only keep the local database busy if configured to *Wait for Completion* of the target script. However, the initiating script can only receive a result if this option is on. So, the choice is fully offloading the process and freeing up the local computer and not receiving a result or keeping the local computer busy waiting for a result.

The *Perform Script on Server with Callback* step eliminates the need to choose. It immediately frees up the local database for other work while still providing the option to receive a result and perform following actions! The callback script can be a simple *Show Custom Dialog* step that notifies the user that the target script has completed or something more complex. If the target script begins a process that requires the user's attention to review or additional work, the callback script can steer the user back into the workflow. However, when doing this, consider a method that doesn't interrupt any other work the user may have started in the interim. For example, the callback script can open a new window with a message that the work is finished and ready for review with a button to start that process. Keeping this window non-modal allows the user to continue their other work and resume that process at their leisure.

Emphasizing the Importance of Context

As you design scripts, it is important to remember that *scripts are contextual*. Every script step executes within the context of the table occurrence assigned to the current layout displayed in the front window. A new record will be created in that table. A find request can be created which targets records in that table. Imports will bring records into that table, while exports will contain the current found set of records. The only field values that can be accessed or modified are those of the active record or records related to it. Any formula within a script step is also limited to the context of that layout.

The context starts as the layout active in the window when the script begins to run. However, a script can change layouts, perform finds, move to different records within the found set, or create new windows. Each of these actions changes the context for any remaining steps. A script that begins in one context can end in a different context after traversing many others in between. As the developer, you must keep track of which context will be active at each step and adjust the references to fields and other resources accordingly. FileMaker is generally good at helping by displaying relationships for the current layout when accessing fields and relationships in some areas of the development environment. However, it is possible to edit a script while viewing a layout other than the one it will operate in. So, care must be taken to keep straight which context a script will encounter at every step.

This challenge becomes more arduous as a database grows and becomes more complex. Scripts can run other scripts, and those scripts can run other scripts in a hierarchical "stack" of execution calls. Any script in the stack can change the context before handing control back to the original script. If you are keeping track of the context requirements of every script and intentionally designing scripts run by other scripts to account for this, it is easy to weave yourself into a convoluted web of confusion. If a step in a complex call stack attempts to access fields from a noncurrent context, it will cause errors and be confusing to users. It can also be disastrous if a step deletes a found set from the wrong context. Such errors can have real financial implications for your clients. When designing a complex mesh of interconnected scripts, be sure to do so with conscious intention and adequate care to manage context.

Identifying the Contextual Dependencies of Steps

Another aspect of the contextuality of scripts is that, although all steps operate contextually, they don't all have the same type of dependency. Some steps are *layout-table dependent* and access field values directly from the table of the layout's occurrence regardless of what is visible on the layout. Others are *layout-object dependent* and require direct interaction with something on the layout. This is because some steps target the schema directly and don't require a field present on the layout while others operate as a user would and require the target field to be present. A good rule of thumb is that a step may require a layout-object if it corresponds to a standard menu item. For example, *Set Field* isn't a menu item and doesn't require a field present on the layout to work. However, *Insert Text* does correspond to a menu item and requires the target field to be present.

Tip   To use a layout-object dependent step without the field displayed for users, put it in the offscreen developer area of the layout (Chapter 18, "Defining Layout Regions and Controls")!

Managing Scripting Errors

A *script error* is generated when a script attempts to perform an impossible action. An error can be caused by an incorrect or incomplete step configuration. It can also be caused by a step executing in the wrong context. FileMaker even generates an error when a scripted find doesn't find any matching records.

When an error occurs, a script may preset a dialog informing the user of the problem. The message can range from informative to vague, and, depending on their knowledge and the type of error that occurred, it may not make sense to a user. When a script attempts to set a field that is not accessible from the current context, the error message will say "This operation could not be completed because the target is not part of the related table." Since this is a programming error, a user may have no idea what this means or what to do to reach a resolution. Instead of relying on the default error messaging, scripts can capture errors and present more informative dialogs.

The *Set Error Capture* step can turn on or off an error capturing and suppression mechanism for the remainder of a script. When the parameter is turned On, the script will completely ignore any errors it encounters and continue processing until the script completes or until another step turns error capture back Off.

```
Set Error Capture [ On ]
```

Once errors are captured, the script will be silent when a problem occurs. So, it becomes your responsibility to detect problems at key points, notify the user with an informative message, and take alternative actions. The *Get (LastError)* function can be placed at key points in a script to determine if an error has occurred when the previous step is executed. The function will return a numeric value indicating either no error (0) or the number representing the error. An *If* step (Chapter 25) can take conditional action in the event an error is detected.

Note   See the "Chapter 24 – 07 Managing Errors" example file.

To illustrate this technique, the following example attempts to set a *Contact::Name Last* field. If this script is run from a Contact layout, there will be no error generated and no dialog presented. However, running it from a layout for a different table will generate an error and present a custom dialog. Depending on the error, its location, and other functions of the script, an *If* statement can include other steps to email a developer, perform alternative steps, halt completely, etc.

```
Set Error Capture [ On ]
Set Field [ "Contact::Name Last; "Smith" ]
If [ Get ( LastError ) ≠ 0 ]
    Show Custom Dialog [ <informative message here> ]
End If
```

The above example illustrates how to fcapture and then detect an error. However, it is impractical to add an error check after every step as shown. A carefully designed script may never need to check for errors like this and can capture errors just to silence an empty find result. However, there are situations where capturing errors is important. For example, steps that present users with a folder directory dialog will need to detect if the user clicks cancel and then exit the script (Chapter 24, "Get Folder Path").

Tip   For a complete list of errors, search for "FileMaker Pro error code reference guide" on Claris.com.

Summary

This chapter introduced scripting basics, including the script workspace and various step configuration interface options. We explored various formats for specifying file paths and discussed scripts running other scripts, passing parameters, receiving results, contextual awareness, and managing script errors. In the next chapter, we begin creating examples that perform common scripting tasks.

CHAPTER 25

Common Scripting Tasks

FileMaker includes a robust library of built-in steps that perform a wide variety of actions. In the last chapter, we touched on a couple of these in the introduction to scripting. Now, we can explore a handful of real-world examples to provide a foundation upon which to base your own exploration of the remaining script steps. This chapter covers the following topics:

- Performing basic functions
- Accessing folders and files
- Working with records
- Searching records
- Using conditional statements
- Showing custom dialogs
- Iterating with repeating statements
- Managing windows
- Using Insert from URL

Performing Basic Functions

Let's begin by exploring a few basic script steps that perform common functions: controlling the ability of users to abort a script, performing navigational context changes, and interacting with fields.

© Mark Conway Munro 2024
M. C. Munro, *Learn FileMaker Pro 2024*, https://doi.org/10.1007/979-8-8688-0835-7_25

Allowing User Abort

Any running script can be manually halted at any time by typing Esc (Windows) or a Period while holding the Command key (macOS). This ability can cause a lot of problems, especially with complex scripts. A cancelled, half-finished script can leave the user stranded on a staging layout not designed as an interface in the middle of a process that can't be restarted. A set of records may be half imported but not yet processed. Repeating the script could cause duplicates the second time around. Part of a found set may have been added to an unsent report in a now abandoned variable but also had fields changed so they don't show up in a find result if the script is repeated.

The *Allow User Abort* script step can avoid these and countless other catastrophes by denying a user's ability to halt a script. The step has one setting with a default value of on to allow interruption of the script and an option to turn it off to disable that ability. The step can be placed at the beginning of a script or anywhere in the workflow. It can be turned on and off as needed at different points in the workflow to only protect sensitive steps that must be completed. Once configured, all subsequent script steps in the current script will inherit that setting unless reversed by another instance of the step. The same is true if a parent script turns it off, where all other scripts performed by the parent will inherit that setting unless or until they explicitly change it. Similarly, if a subscript changes this setting, the parent script will inherit that setting when control is relinquished back to it.

```
Allow User Abort [ Off ]
```

The *Get (AllowAbortState)* function allows any formula to check the status of the abort state. This function returns 0 (false) if abort is disallowed and 1 (true) if it is allowed.

Caution   Don't turn off the ability to abort until a script has been adequately tested to avoid being locked into an endless loop or other situation that requires a force quit to escape a programming error!

Creating Navigation Scripts

Various steps can change a window's context by navigating to a different layout, record, or related record.

Go to Layout

The *Go to Layout* script step, shown in Figure 25-1, will switch the layout displayed in the current window to one specified by its settings. This can be used a single step on a button to quickly switch layouts or in a script that jumps between different layouts to collect information or perform tasks. The step has two active regions, *layout specifier* and *animation type*.

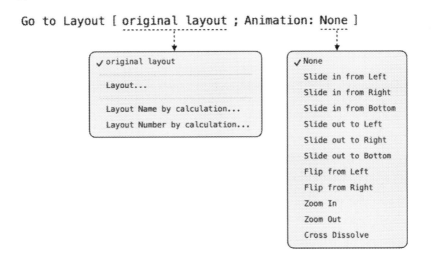

Figure 25-1. *The configuration options for the Go to Layout step*

The *layout specifier* region opens a menu of choices that are used to identify the *target layout*. The default selection will be *original layout* which instructs the script to navigate back to the layout that was active when the script started running. If this is the first instance of the step in a script, the result of this setting will be no change to the current layout. However, if a previous instance of the step in the same script changed layouts, this setting will automatically track and restore the user's starting layout. Choose the *Layout* option to open a *Specify Layout* dialog, and choose a reference to a specific target. The *Layout Name by calculation* and *Layout Number by calculation* options open the *Specify Calculation* dialog where you can enter a formula that determines the name or number of the target layout.

The *Animation* menu is used in FileMaker Go only. It specifies how the layout switch will be animated. This setting will be ignored when running the script on other platforms.

Go to Record/Request/Page

The *Go to Record/Request/Page* step, shown in Figure 25-2, navigates within the found set of a window. It will navigate to a specified item depending on the current Window mode, to a *record* (Browse), *find request* (Find), or *page* (Preview). This step can be assigned to buttons or performed by scripts. The step will have a second active region depending on the option selected on the first setting.

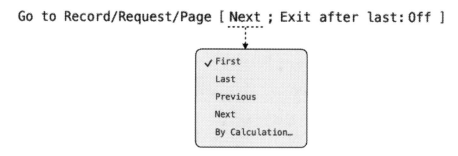

Figure 25-2. *The configuration options for the Go to Record/Request/Page step*

The *target specifier* opens a menu of options. These allow the step to jump directly to the *First* or *Last* item in the found set or to move one step to the *Previous* or *Next* item. The *By Calculation* option at the bottom opens a *Specify Calculation* dialog where a formula determines the number of the desired record, request, or page. When the target is *Previous* or *Next*, an additional *Exit after last* option appears, which can be toggled on or off. Turn this on to cause the step to automatically exit a *Loop* statement (described later in this chapter) after reaching the last available record in the direction indicated by the first parameter. When turned on, *Previous* will exit after reaching the first record/request/page, while *Next* will exit after reaching the last.

Go to Related Record

The *Go to Related Record* step navigates to one or more related records, performing multiple functions as a single step. Without this step, a user viewing a *Contact* record who wants to view the record for that contact's related parent *Company* in a new window would have to perform several manual steps: create a new window, change layouts, and perform a find. However, with this step, a button or script can quickly carry out the same task with a single action. After being added to a script, the entire step and the configuration icon button both open a *Go To Related Record Options* dialog, as shown in Figure 25-3.

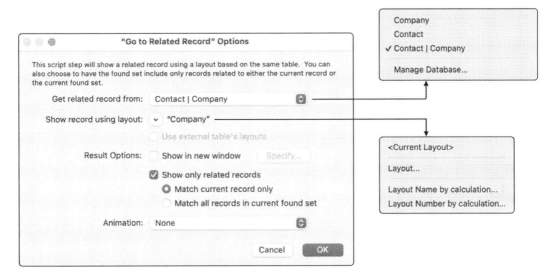

Figure 25-3. *The Go To Related Record step*

Note   See the "CH25-01 Go to Related" example file.

This example assumes a *Company* and *Contact* table, each with their own layout. A relationship connects the *Contact* occurrence to a new instance of *Company* named *Contact | Company*. A *Contact Company ID* field for the contact is connected to the *Record Primary Key* field in company.

To begin, open the *Get related record from* menu to see every table occurrence defined. The selection must point to the occurrence assigned to the layout on the other side of the relationship opposite that of the starting layout. Since the script will be executed while the user is looking at a *Contact* record and will navigate them to a related company, the *Contact | Company* occurrence is selected.

The *Show record using layout* menu has options identical to the *Go to Layout* script step. Select *Layout* to open a *Specify Layout* dialog and then select the *Company* layout. Alternatively, a *Specify Calculation* dialog can be opened to allow a formula to determine the layout name or number. The option to rename on the current layout is the default but shouldn't be used unless the target table is the same as the starting layout, as much be the case in a self-join relationship. If the target layout is in an external database, select the *Use external table's layouts* checkbox to instead show a list of layouts for the table from that external file.

The *Show in new window* checkbox and adjacent *Specify* button enable displaying the results in a new window instead of the starting window. These settings are identical to the *New Window* script step described later in this chapter.

The *Show only related records* option controls which records are included in the found set displayed in the target layout/window. When *disabled*, the step will attempt to preserve the found set already present in the target table. If the related record is present in that set, it will retain the set and drop the user on that record. If not, the step will find all records and take the user to the target record. When *enabled*, a different found set will be established in the target table depending on the radio button option selected. The *Match current record only* selection will result in a target found set of only the record(s) matching the related criteria for the starting record. This is like a one-to-one or *one-to-many* search, where the current starting record is used to find related records in the target table. The *Match all records in the current found set* option will result in a found set of every record in the target table that has a match to any record in the table of the starting layout's found set. This is the equivalent of a *many-to-many* search, where the entire current record set is used to find related records in the target table. The step, executed from a *Contact* record, will navigate to the one *Company* record that is assigned to that contact.

When the step is attached to a button placed in a portal row, it will navigate to the record clicked on within a found set of all the records that were displayed in the portal. For example, a *Company* layout with a portal of related *Contacts* can have a button that repeats for each row calling a reconfigured script that performs *Go to Related Records* through a different relationship. If there are five contacts displayed and the user clicks "John Smith," they will switch to the Contacts layout in a found set of the five contacts, viewing John's record. If they click "Karen Camacho" instead, they will switch layouts into a found set of the same five records but be viewing Karen's record.

Interacting with Fields

FileMaker has several steps that allow interactions with fields. These make possible moving focus into a field, changing the contents of a field, and resetting the field's defined serialization settings.

Go to Field

Three script steps control which field is in focus and are useful when creating scripts that assist a user during data entry tasks. They allow focus to shift to the next, previous, or a specific field.

The *Go to Next Field* and *Go to Previous Field* steps have no parameter options; they will simply move active focus to the next or previous field on the current layout based on the field tab order (Chapter 21, "Understanding Tab Order"). If a record is not yet open for editing and no field has focus, these steps will open the record and place focus in the first or last field in the tab order.

The *Go to Field* step, shown in Figure 25-4, moves focus to a specific field. After inserting into the script, double-click anywhere on the step to select a target field in a *Specify Field* dialog (Chapter 20, "Exploring the Specify Field Dialog"). The gear icon opens a panel with two options. Enable the *Select/perform* box to automatically select field contents, and/or open interface elements such as drop-down lists or calendars when entering the field. The *Go to target field* is an alternate way to specify the target field.

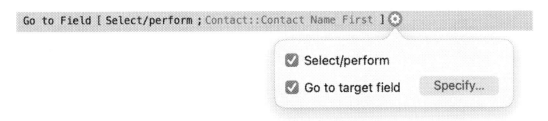

Figure 25-4. *The Go to Field step moves focus to a specific field*

Caution   The selected field must be present on the current layout, and the user must have access to enter it! If no target field is selected or the field is not accessible, the step will commit the record.

Set Field

The *Set Field* step will replace the current value of a field for the current record with a new value. The selected field must belong to the table of the current layout or in a related table occurrence. It doesn't need to be present on the layout since this step targets the schema directly. If no field is specified, the step will insert a value into a field if one on the layout has active focus. If no field is specified and no field has focus, the step will do nothing and silently generate a script error (102, Field is missing).

After inserting the step into a script, click the gear icon to open a configuration panel, as shown in Figure 25-5. The *Specify target field* option will open a *Specify Field* dialog and allow selection of a target field reference. Click the *Specify* button to open a *Specify Calculation* dialog, and define the value that will be placed into the field.

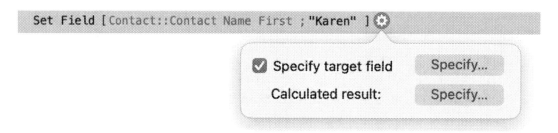

Figure 25-5. *The options for the Set Field step*

Once a field and a value are specified, they appear on the step line. From then on, those are active regions and can be clicked on directly to edit, providing a shortcut to the gear panel. The step can be configured to target a calculation or other non-modifiable field but will generate an error when executed. However, it is possible for this step to bypass a field's defined auto-enter restrictions that prohibit modification of its value during data entry (Chapter 8). So, be careful when choosing a target field.

Set Field by Name

The *Set Field by Name* step will change the value of a field specified by name. Like the *Set Field* step, this doesn't require a field to be present on the layout. However, unlike it, this step uses a formula to establish a text-based field reference instead of a dynamic one. The benefit is that the field targeted can vary from one execution to the next. So, a script can perform a similar function to a variety of different fields in the same or different tables. The major drawback is that the field reference will no longer update if a field name is changed in the schema (Chapter 35, "Keeping Field References Dynamic").

The options look the same as *Set Field*, except when you click to specify a target field, a *Specify Calculation* dialog opens and requires a formula to identify the field. The result must be text and include the name of a table occurrence and field. This example shows the step targeting the *Contact Name First* field.

```
Set Field By Name [ "Contact::Contact Name First" ; "Karen" ]
```

This example gets the name from a dynamic field reference rather than a literal text string so that it automatically updates if the field name changes.

```
Set Field By Name [ GetFieldName ( Contact::Contact Name First ) ;
"Karen" ]
```

Set Selection

The *Set Selection* step will select a range of text characters somewhere within a field present on the layout. It will target the field with active focus unless another target field is specified. The settings include specifying a target field, a start position and end position, as shown in Figure 25-6. Select *Go to target field* or click the adjacent *Specify* button to open a *Specify Field* dialog to choose a target field. Click the *Specify selection* button to open a *Set Selection* dialog, and enter two numeric values for *Start Position* and *End Position*. Each of these values can be entered as either a static number or a dynamic calculation that analyzes the field's content and selects a range of characters based on custom criteria. If the start and end position are the same value, the step will place the cursor at that position without a selection.

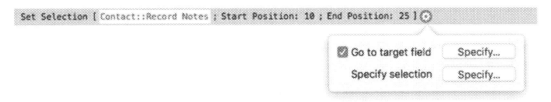

Figure 25-6. *The options for selecting text within a field*

Note   See the "Chapter 02 – Set Selection" example file.

The following script will insert a note placeholder prompt at the end of a *Contacts Notes* field.

```
Set Variable [ $placeholder ; Value: "[Type Note]" ]
Set Variable [ $note ; Value: Contact::Contact Notes ]
Set Field [ Contact::Contact Notes ; $note & "¶" & $placeholder
Set Selection [ Contact::Contact Notes ]
```

First, the "[Type Note]" prompt is stored in a *$placeholder* variable, and any existing notes are pulled from the field into a *$note* variable. Then, the *Set Field* step is used to set the value of the field to the existing notes, a paragraph, and the prompt. The *Set Selection* line is configured to target the notes field. Finally, the start and end values are entered in the *Specify Set Selection* dialog as shown in Figure 25-7. The *Start Position* is calculated by using the *Length* function to count the number of characters currently in the notes field minus the length of the placeholder prompt plus 1. The *End position* is just the total character count of the notes field. Since the prompt was inserted at the end, the script should select it and release control back to the user to begin typing over it.

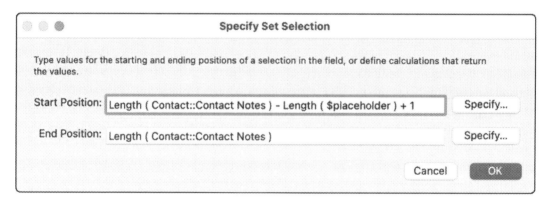

Figure 25-7. The options for selecting text within a field

Tip   To select the entire contents of the current field, use *Select All*.

Set Next Serial Value

The *Set Next Serial Value* step will update the next serial number value in a field's *Auto Enter* definitions (Chapter 8, "Field Options: Auto-Enter"). In most situations, this step won't be needed. For example, when users or scripts create new records, the field's *Next Value* setting is automatically incremented after a number is assigned. Any development or record migration tasks that require an update to the next serial number can be performed manually as a one time the change in field definitions. Most import records steps can be configured to automatically update this serial number definition (Chapter 5, "Setting Import Options"). However, in situations where a script automates a process that requires a serial number update, this step allows the setting change to be performed without human intervention. In that case, a script can identify the highest serial value currently in use and reset the field's next value.

Since this change is made to the field definition directly, the specified field does not have to be visible on the current layout. In fact, when resetting this to a static number without the need to look at existing records, this step can be run for any table from any context. However, in most cases, the script should be performed from a layout representing the table containing the field being reset.

Note   See the "CH25-03 Set Next Serial Value" example file.

The configuration options are like other steps that change field values. Click the gear icon to open the panel, and then select *a target field* and enter a *formula* for the result. Instead of setting the field value, the result of the formula will become the next serial number for new records. This example demonstrates how to reset the primary key's next serial number to one greater than the current highest value.

```
Show All Records
Unsort Records
Go to Record [ Last ]
Set Next Serial Value [ Record Primary ID ; Contact::Record Primary
ID + 1 ]
```

This script begins with the *Show All Records* step to ensure that we don't miss the highest value if it is outside the found set. Next, it runs the *Unsort Records* step since the primary keys are low to high when ordered chronologically as entered. If the last record in an unsorted list is not always the highest value, consider using a *Sort Records* step instead to sort the records by the serial field. The *Go to Record* step jumps to the last record which should now have the highest current value. Finally, the *Set Next Serial Value* targets the *Record Primary ID* field with the current value in that field for the current record plus one. Now, any new records created will be assigned the correct next serial number without any duplicates.

If the targeted serial number field is a text field with leading zeros, adding one will convert the result into a number without leading characters. To maintain a consistent number of characters in the field, the formula portion of the step will need to add a calculated number of zeros to the result. Assuming the field uses leading zeros to maintain six digits, the following formula ensures the appropriate result by adding six zeros to the left of the incremented id and then extracting six digits from the right. The result will always return the correct number of leading zeros regardless of how many digits make up the next serial value.

```
Right ( "000000" & ( Contact::Record Primary ID + 1 ) ; 6 )
// result = 000015
```

Accessing Folders and Files

Recent versions of FileMaker added and improved various script steps that can access folders and files. These steps allow a script to ask the user to choose a folder and to create, read, write, and delete text files.

Note   See the "CH25-04 Folders and Files" example file.

Get Folder Path

The *Get Folder Path* step, formerly named *Get Directory*, presents the user with a *Choose Folder* dialog. This allows a user to select any folder providing a script with a target location to be used by other steps that import, export, and save various resources. The step includes several configurable options accessed by clicking the gear icon, shown in Figure 25-8.

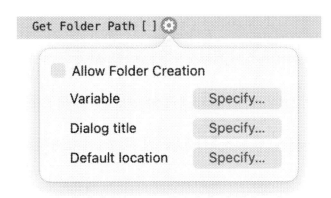

Figure 25-8. *The options for selecting a directory*

Select the *Allow Folder Creation* checkbox to enable a *New Folder* button in the *Choose Folder* dialog, making it possible for the user to create and select a new folder during the process of selecting a folder. The *Variable* button opens a limited *Set Variable Options* dialog that accepts only a name for a variable into which the selected folder path will be placed. The buttons by *Dialog title* and *Default location* both open their own *Specify Calculation* dialog allowing a formula to determine the dialog's title prompt and default starting folder path.

Caution   A variable is required, or the step will be ignored!

When this step executes, a dialog opens and waits for user to select a folder. Once they make a choice, the path to that folder is placed into the variable specified. The path may need to be converted to a FileMaker format (Chapter 24, "Converting Paths") or have a prefix added in order to work with other script steps.

The following example uses *Set Error Capture* to suppress an error message if the user clicks *Cancel* instead of selecting a folder. A *$defaultFolder* variable is set to contain the user computer's documents path. The *Get Folder Path* step is configured with that default path and a target variable named *$selectedFolder*. Next an *If* statement checks for a *LastError*. If the user cancels the dialog, the *Exit Script* step will stop the script from continuing. Otherwise, the user's folder selection in the *$selectedFolder* variable can be used later in the script.

```
Set Error Capture [ On ]
Set Variable [ $defaultFolder ; Value: Get ( DocumentsPath ) ]
Get Folder Path [ $selectedFolder ; $defaultFolder ]
If [ Get ( LastError ) = 1 ]
  Exit Script [ Text Result: "User Cancelled" ]
End if
```

Caution The dialog's appearance depends on the operating system. For example, macOS doesn't display the value specified as the *Dialog title*.

Manipulating Data Files

Since version 18, FileMaker has included a set of steps that allow a script to *create, close, delete, detect, open, read, rename,* and *write* data files on the user's computer.

Creating a Data File

The *Create Data File* step will create a new empty file that automatically replaces any preexisting file with the same name at a specified path. It has two settings, a *file path,* and has a *Create folders* option that can be turned on to automatically create any folders in the path specified that don't yet exist. Once created, a script can open the file and write to it.

The following example uses *Get Folder Path* to ask the user to select a target folder which it places into a *$selectedFolder* variable. Next, a *$filePath* variable is set to contain a path to a file in that folder named "Test.txt." Finally, the data file is created.

```
Get Folder Path [ $selectedFolder ]
Set Variable [ $filePath ; Value: "file:" & $selectedFolder & "Test.txt" ]
Create Data File [ "$filePath" ; Create folders: Off ]
```

This example adds two subfolders to the *$selectedFolder* path and has the *Create folders* options turned on. Because of this, it will create the file nested inside of the two folders within the selected folder.

```
Get Folder Path [ $selectedFolder ]
Set Variable [ $folderPath ; Value: $selectedFolder & "Subfolder/
Example/" ]
Set Variable [ $filePath ; Value: "file:" & $folderPath & "Test.txt" ]
Create Data File [ "$filePath" ; Create folders: On ]
```

Opening and Closing a Data File

The *Open Data File* step will open a data file at a path specified and assign it a unique File ID that will persist until the file is explicitly closed. This number acts as a reference pointer to the file and is required by other data file steps instead of a path, for example, the *Close Data File* step accepts only an ID that points to the file that should be closed, not a path. The step requires two settings: a *file path* of an existing file and a *Target* variable into which the automatic File ID assignment will be stored.

The following example assumes the *$filePath* variable contains a path to a data file created in the previous example. Using this path, it opens the file, places the File ID into a variable named *$fileID*, and then immediately uses that id to close the file.

```
Open Data File [ "$filePath" ; Target: $fileID ]
Close Data File [ File ID: $fileID ]
```

Caution   Failure to store the ID leaves a script no way to reference the file!

Confirming a File's Existence

When a referenced file does not exist, an error will be generated if a script attempts to open it. To avoid this, the *Get File Exists* step can first confirm the existence of a file and take an alternate course of action if it isn't found. The step accepts a *Source file* setting containing a path to a file. It will return a result of 1 (true) or 0 (false) into a *Target* field or variable. This example will check for the file on the desktop named "Test.txt" and put the Boolean result into a variable name *$fileExists*.

```
Set Variable [ $filePath ; "file:" & Get ( DesktopPath ) & "Test.txt"
Get File Exists [ "$filePath" ; Target: $fileExists ]
```

Reading a Data File

The *Read from Data File* step will read the contents of an open data file and place the content into a *Target* variable or field. It accepts four parameters, three accessible on a panel opened by clicking the gear icon.

- The *File ID* button opens a *Specify Calculation* dialog in which a formula must return a numeric file reference, typically the target result of the *Open Data File* step.

- The *Target* button opens a *Specify Target* dialog to allow the selection of a field or variable name into which the file's contents will be placed.

- The *Amount* button opens a *Specify Calculation* dialog in which a formula determines the number of bytes to read (leave blank for all).

- The *Read as* region of the step opens a menu with a choice of character encoding.

Building on the last example, this script opens a file specified in the *$filePath* variable, reads its contents as UTF-8 into a variable named *$fileContents*, and then closes the file. It first checks to see if a file named "Test.txt" is located on the desktop. If it exists, the steps inside the *If* statement open, read, and close the file.

```
Set Variable [ $filePath ; "file:" & Get ( DesktopPath ) & "Test.txt"
Get File Exists [ "$filePath" ; Target: $fileExists ]
If [ $fileExists ]
Open Data File [ "$filePath" ; Target: $fileID ]
Read from Data File [ File ID: $fileID ; Target: $fileContents ; Read
as: UTF-8 ]
Close Data File [ File ID: $fileID ]
End if
```

Writing to a Data File

The *Write to Data File* step will write data to an open file. It requires a *File ID* identifying the open file into which it should write and a *Data Source* with is a field or variable containing the text to be written. The *Write as* region has a menu for text encoding.

Finally, there is an option to *Append line feed* which automatically adds a line feed character after writing data. This example will overwrite an existing file on the desktop named "Test.txt," writing the current timestamp, a space, and the words "Hello, World."

```
Set Variable [ $filePath ; "file:" & Get ( DesktopPath ) & "Test.txt"
Set Variable [ $data ; Value: Get ( CurrentTimestamp ) & "Hello, World" ]
Create Data File [ "$filePath" ; Create folders: On ]
Open Data File [ "$filePath" ; Target: $fileID ]
Write to Data File [ File ID: $fileID ; Data source: $data ; Write
as: UTF-8 ]
Close Data File [ File ID: $fileID ]
```

Appending an Existing Data File

If a file already exists, it is possible to begin writing at the end of any existing data content instead of overwriting it. To do this, use the *Get File Size* and *Set Data File Position* steps to determine the number of bytes already in the file and to specify beginning the write after that point. The first of these accepts a file path and the file doesn't have to be opened. The second works the same as other steps, using the File ID identifying an open file.

This example demonstrates this technique, by appending the same file's contents with another timestamp and message. After this script executes, the file should contain two paragraphs, each with a different timestamp and different message.

```
Set Variable [ $filePath ; "file:" & Get ( DesktopPath ) & "Test.txt"
Set Variable [ $data ; Value: Get ( CurrentTimestamp ) & "Hello, Again" ]
Get File Size [ "$filePath" ; Target: $fileSize ]
Open Data File [ "$filePath" ; Target: $fileID ]
Set Data File Position [ File ID: $fileID ; New position: $fileSize ]
Write to Data File [ File ID: $fileID ; Data source: $data ; Write
as: UTF-8 ]
Close Data File [ File ID: $fileID ]
```

Alternatively, if the script reads from the file prior to writing, it sets the *Data File Position* to the end and will automatically begin writing after all existing data. This example removes the size and position steps and instead reads the data file to a *$null* target variable prior to writing the *$data* content.

```
Set Variable [ $filePath ; "file:" & Get ( DesktopPath ) & "Test.txt"
Set Variable [ $data ; Value: Get ( CurrentTimestamp ) & "Hello, Again" ]
Open Data File [ "$filePath" ; Target: $fileID ]
Read from Data File [ File ID: $fileID ; Target: $null ; Read as: UTF-8 ]
Write to Data File [ File ID: $fileID ; Data source: $data ; Write
as: UTF-8 ]
Close Data File [ File ID: $fileID ]
```

Working with Records

Numerous script steps perform interactions with records. The *New Record/Request* step will create a new record in the current window, while the *Duplicate Record/Request* step will create a duplicate of the current record. Both have no configurable options. The *Delete Record/Request* step will automatically delete the current record in the front window after presenting an optional confirmation dialog. Similarly, the *Delete All Records* step will delete every record in the found set after presenting an optional dialog. There are steps available to perform many of the record actions users can perform through the interface from the Records menu and toolbar options. Scripts can open, commit, copy, and revert records. There are steps for *Save Records as Excel*, *Save Records as PDF*, and *Save Records as Snapshot Link*. The *Truncate Table* step instantly deletes all records in a specified table, regardless of the current found set or the current layout context, and it does not perform the *Delete related records* function specified in any relationship (Chapter 9, "Relationship Options"). Most of these are easy enough to figure out with a little experimentation.

In addition, let's look at two steps used to move records in and out of a table: *Import Records* and *Export Records*.

Note   See the "CH25-05 Import and Export" example file.

Import Records

The *Import Records* step, shown in Figure 25-9, allows a script to import records into a table with or without human interaction.

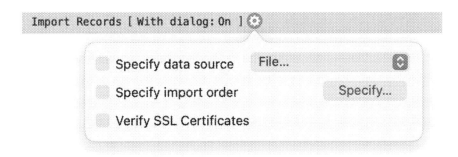

Figure 25-9. *The configuration options for Import Records*

The settings accessible on the configuration panel are identical to performing a manual import. Select the *Specify data source* checkbox to enter a path for the file to import. Similarly, the *Specify import order* checkbox and Specify button opens a dialog of the same name used to map import data to fields (Chapter 5, "Mapping Fields from Source to Target"). Enable *Verify SSL Certificates* when importing XML data from a server specified with a HTTP request. Back on the step itself, the *With dialog* option can be turned off to suppress dialogs when the step is performed, allowing a truly autonomous operation. However, if a data source and import order are left undefined, this setting will be ignored and the dialogs will appear to request the missing information from the user.

Like with a manual import, a script using this step can perform an *Add, Match,* or *Update* process. This example goes to a layout for a *Contacts* table, finds all records, deletes them, and imports new records from a spreadsheet file named "contacts.xlsx" in the same folder.

```
Go to Layout [ "Contacts - List" ; Animation: None ]
Show All Records
Delete all Records [ With dialog: Off]
Import Records [ With dialog: Off ; Table: Contact ; Source: "contacts.
xlsx" ; Worksheet: "Sheet1" ; Add: UTF-8 ]
```

Export Records

The *Export Record* step, shown in Figure 25-10, allows a script to automatically export records with or without human interaction. The Specify output file and *Specify export order* both open dialogs that, respectively, allow specification of a file path and field order. These interfaces are identical to those used for manual exports (Chapter 5,

"Exporting Records"). Two toggle options are found on the step itself. Like when importing, the *With dialog* can be turned off to suppress dialogs for autonomous operation, as long as both panel options are configured. When the *Create folders* option is turned on, the step will automatically create folders as needed to ensure every subfolder in the output path exists.

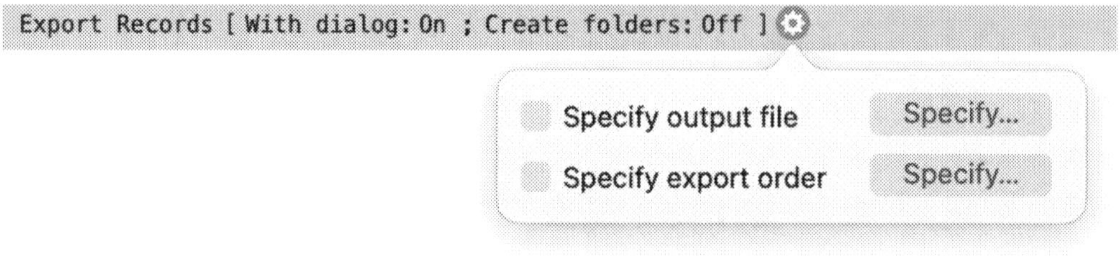

Figure 25-10. *The configuration options for Export Records*

This example finds all records in a *Contacts* table and exports them to a spreadsheet named "contacts.xlsx" in the same folder as the database.

```
Go to Layout [ "Contacts - List" ; Animation: None ]
Show All Records
Export Records [ With dialog: Off ; Create folders: Off ; "contacts.xlsx" ;
Add: UTF-16 ]
```

Searching Records

There are a handful of steps that can automate a change to the found set of records in the current window.

Note   See the "CH25-06 Searching" example file.

Performing a Scripted Quick Find

The *Perform Quick Find* step uses the text result of a formula as the criteria to perform a search within any field on the current layout that has *Quick Find* enabled (Chapter 19, "Behavior"). This is a scripted equivalent of a user typing a value into the toolbar search field and typing Enter. After inserting the step into a script, click the gear to open a *Specify Calculation* dialog. The text result of this formula will be the criteria for the search performed when the step executes.

```
Perform Quick Find [ "Smith" ]
```

Since the criteria is a formula, the value used can be typed directly into the step, pulled from a field, provided by a variable, or determined by a function (built-in or custom) or some combination of these. This is useful when a database is designed with a fully custom interface that hides and locks the toolbar but still requires the quick find functionality.

Searching with Find Mode

Scripts can create find requests and perform finds to create an automated process that mirrors what a user can do manually (Chapter 4, "Searching Records"). Steps can enter find mode, manage find requests, and perform a find.

Entering Find Mode

The *Enter Find Mode* step places the window into Find mode, giving the user or script steps an opportunity to enter find criteria in fields before performing a search.

```
Enter Find Mode [ Pause: On ]
```

The *Pause* setting can be toggled inline to pause the script immediately after entering Find mode. If turned on, the script will stop and wait for user input. It won't start up again until the user takes an action that initiates *Resume Script*. They can type Enter to continue the paused script, click a button configured to resume, or execute another script. If the *Pause* option is turned off, the script will enter Find mode and continue executing additional steps.

Clicking the gear icon on the step opens a *Specify Find Requests* dialog (Chapter 4, "Working with Saved Finds"). When used, the step will show the word "Restore" as shown below to indicate the fact that the find will start with the specified criteria restored.

```
Enter Find Mode [ Restore ; Pause: On ]
```

Regardless of the specification of find requests, once in Find mode, requests can be added, removed, or edited by other script steps or, if paused, by the user.

Managing Find Criteria and Requests

Once in Find mode, several steps manage find criteria and requests. Since a find request behaves like a record, any step that can modify the latter can modify the former. For example, the *Set Field* and *Set Field by Name* steps can set the value of a field for the current request like they do with records in Browse mode. Steps that *Insert*, *Clear*, *Paste*, and more can manipulate data in fields that are present on the layout. Similarly, steps that are used to manage records in Browse mode will manage requests in Find mode. For example, *New Record/Request* creates additional find requests, while *Delete Record/ Request* and *Duplicate Record/Requests* both target requests in Find Mode. *Omit record* also changes. Instead of removing a record from the current found set like it does in Browse, in Find mode it toggles the *Record Matching* choice for the current request between *Include* or *Omit* (Chapter 4, "Specifying a Matching Record Option"). With these steps, a script can construct a find request of any complexity.

For example, this script will enter Find mode and create three find request to find any *Company* record located in one of three states.

```
Enter Find Mode [ Pause : Off ]
Set Field [ Company::Company State ; "NY" ]
New Record/Request
Set Field [ Company::Company State ; "PA" ]
New Record/Request
Set Field [ Company::Company State ; "CA" ]
```

Notice that the script ends after setting up a find request without performing the find. This will leave the user in Find mode and require them to finish the process. This is fine if the intention of the script is to give the user a default find setup which they will finish and execute. However, the script can also perform the find it has constructed for a fully automated search.

Performing a Find

The *Perform Find* step can be used in one of two ways. When a script is in Find mode, it will perform the find and show the results in Browse mode as shown in this example.

```
Enter Find Mode [ Pause : Off ]
Set Field [ Company::Company State ; "NY" ]
Perform Find [ ]
```

Alternatively, the step can be used to instantly perform a find regardless of the current window mode. Clicking the gear icon on the step will open a *Specify Find Requests* dialog. With criteria entered, the step will display the word "Restore" to indicate that it is configured with the criteria required to produce find results. So, there is no need for other steps to enter find mode and set criteria.

```
Perform Find [ Restore ]
```

There is a lot of flexibility in how find criteria are entered when scripting the process. The first example above enters find, sets fields, and performs the find. The second example just performs the find with the criteria embedded. Alternatively, if the *Enter Find Mode* step restores criteria, there is no need to set fields between it and Perform Find.

```
Enter Find Mode [ Restore ; Pause: Off ]
Perform Find [ ]
```

Sometimes the complexity or variability of the criteria might lean toward using *Set Field* to enter all criteria. However, the choice between these three methods is completely up to you.

Using Other Find Steps

There are a variety of other steps available under the *Found Sets* category in the *Steps* pane. These mirror functions available to the user manually through the menus and toolbar icons (Chapter 4, "Searching Records"). The *Find Matching Records* step will immediately find records where the value in a specified field matches that field's value for the current record. The *Modify Last Find* step enters Find mode with the criteria requests for the last find performed restored. Finally, the *Constrain Found Set* and *Extend Found Set* steps perform functionality identical to the menu items of the same name.

Using Conditional Statements

A *conditional statement* is made up of one or more script steps that are only executed if a control condition is true. These are also known as *if-then statements*. A *control step* is a step whose sole purpose is controlling when other steps are executed. FileMaker has four control steps used to build conditional statements:

- *If* – Required at the start of a statement to define a formula that controls when the steps following it will be executed

- *Else If* – Optionally placed between an *If* and *End If* step to start a new group of conditional steps based on a new formula that controls when the steps following it will be executed

- *Else* – Optionally placed somewhere prior to an *End If* to denote a separate group of conditional steps that are performed only if all preceding conditions were false

- *End If* – Required to terminate the conditional statement previously started by an *If* step

---

Caution   Unlike the *If* and *Case* built-in functions used in formulas, these are steps used when building scripts!

The *If* and *Else If* steps each accepts one value, a formula entered by clicking the space between the brackets or the *fx button* icon, both shown in Figure 25-11. The formula entered must return a 1 (true) or 0 (false) value that determines if the steps that follow will be executed or not. As soon as one condition is true, the steps following it are executed and then control skip over any the other conditions to the *End if* step.

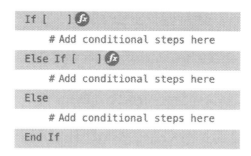

Figure 25-11. *The four control steps, two accepting a formula*

Let's work through some examples of varying complexity using an Invoice table with the following fields: *Invoice Date* and *Invoice Status*. The status is manually set to one of several possible values: *New, Sent,* and *Paid.* The evolving script example will be run once every 15 days and must decide which script to perform to handle the current record.

Note   See the "CH25-07 Conditional Statements" example file.

Creating a Single-Condition Statement

A *single-condition statement* contains one *If* step and an *End If* step controlling when the steps between them execute. This simple example below decides if the current invoice record should be emailed to a client or not by checking for an Invoice Status of "New." If this condition is true, it performs a script named "Email Invoice" and then sets the status field to "Sent."

```
If [ Invoice::Invoice Status = "New" ]
    Perform Script ["Email Invoice" ]
    Set Field [ Invoice::Invoice Status ; "Sent" ]
    Set Field [ Invoice::Invoice Date ; Get ( CurrentDate ) ]
End If
```

That ensures that an invoice already sent to a client isn't sent to a client again as a new invoice. However, it is currently ignoring invoices that have been sent but not paid. To handle additional conditions, we will need to expand the conditional statement.

Creating a Multiple-Condition Statement

A *multiple-condition statement* contains one *If* step and an *End If* step with one or more *Else If* steps between controlling which of two or more groups of steps will execute. The expanded example below runs one of three different scripts depending on the status and pushes the invoice further along in the collection cycle.

It begins by placing the value of the *Invoice Status* field into a *$status* variable to shorten the formulas and only access the record once. Then three conditions are checked, and one of the corresponding groups of two steps is executed if appropriate. If the invoice is unsent, it sent it and changes the status to "Sent." If it is sent, it performs the past due script and changes the status to "Past Due." If already past due, it performs a collections script and changes the status to "Delinquent."

```
Set Variable [ $status ; Value: Invoice::Invoice Status ]
If [ $status = "New" ]
```

```
     Perform Script ["Email Invoice" ]
     Set Field [ Invoice::Invoice Status ; "Sent" ]
     Set Field [ Invoice::Invoice Date ; Get ( CurrentDate ) ]
Else If [ $status = "Sent" ]
     Perform Script ["Email Invoice Past Due" ]
     Set Field [ Invoice::Invoice Status ; "Past Due" ]
Else If [ $status= "Past Due" ]
     Perform Script ["Email Invoice Collection Warning" ]
     Set Field [ Invoice::Invoice Status ; "Deliquent" ]
End If
```

Creating a Nested-Condition Statement

A *nested-condition statement* contains one or more conditional statements that are placed inside of another conditional statement. The hierarchy in the overall statement can be as complex as necessary. The example below has a conditional statement nested into the "Sent" condition to allow for three past due warnings based on the number of days since the invoice was sent. Assuming the script is performed every 15 days, a sent invoice will receive a past due email at 15 days, a second warning at 30 days, and a final warning at 45 days. After that, it will be marked as "Delinquent" and go to collections.

```
Set Variable [ $status ; Value:Invoice::Invoice Status ]
Set Variable [ $days ; Value:Get ( CurrentDate ) - Invoice::Invoice
Status ]
If [ $status = "New" ]
     Perform Script ["Email Invoice" ]
     Set Field [ Invoice::Invoice Status ; "Sent" ]
     Set Field [ Invoice::Invoice Date ; Get ( CurrentDate ) ]
Else If [ $status = "Sent" ]
   If [ $days < 16 ]
      Perform Script ["Email Invoice Past Due" ]
   Else If [ $days < 31 ]
      Perform Script ["Email Invoice Past Due Second Warning" ]
   Else
      Perform Script ["Email Invoice Past Due Final Warning" ]
      Set Field [ Invoice::Invoice Status ; "Past Due" ]
```

```
    End If
Else If [ $status= "Past Due" ]
    Perform Script ["Email Invoice Collection Warning" ]
    Set Field [ Invoice::Invoice Status ; "Delinquent" ]
End If
```

Since the formula of an *If* or *Else If* step can contain multiple clauses, the above could be written without nesting by having two conditions in the *Else If* steps for the "Sent" status.

```
Set Variable [ $status ; Value:Invoice::Invoice Status ]
Set Variable [ $days ; Value:Get ( CurrentDate ) - Invoice::Invoice
Status ]
If [ $status = "New" ]
    Perform Script ["Email Invoice" ]
    Set Field [ Invoice::Invoice Status ; "Sent" ]
    Set Field [ Invoice::Invoice Date ; Get ( CurrentDate ) ]
Else If [ $status = "Sent" and $days < 16 ]
    Perform Script ["Email Invoice Past Due" ]
Else If [ $status = "Sent" and $days < 31 ]
    Perform Script ["Email Invoice Past Due Second Warning" ]
Else If [ $status = "Sent"]
    Perform Script ["Email Invoice Past Due Final Warning" ]
    Set Field [ Invoice::Invoice Status ; "Past Due" ]
Else If [ $status= "Past Due" ]
    Perform Script ["Email Invoice Collection Warning" ]
    Set Field [ Invoice::Invoice Status ; "Delinquent" ]
End If
```

The example above will perform the exact same functionality as the previous without nesting, but with more verbose formulas. The choice between a flattened hierarchy like this or a nested one is up to you and can vary depending on the specific conditions and complexity of the statement.

Showing Custom Dialogs

In computer programming, a *dialog box* is a type of interface window used to facilitate an interaction between a user and a database. These are used to present information, warn a user about a problem, confirm a certain action, present a choice of action, request input, or provide some other messaging. FileMaker's *Show Custom Dialog* step is used to present a message to the user, allow them to make a choice from up to three buttons, and enter up to three pieces of text input. With the step added to a script, the gear icon opens a *Show Custom Dialog Options* dialog, which has two tabs: *General* and *Input Fields*.

Note   See the "CH25-08 Dialogs" example file.

Configuring a Dialog

To illustrate the various options for dialogs, let's create a script with a dialog-assisted creation of a *Company* record. Instead of relying on a user to enter a company name and website after creating a new record, our example will require these values to be entered as part of the record creation process controlled with a dialog.

Setting a Dialog's General Properties

The *General* tab of the *Show Custom Dialog Options* dialog, shown in Figure 25-12, is used to configure the messaging properties of a custom dialog.

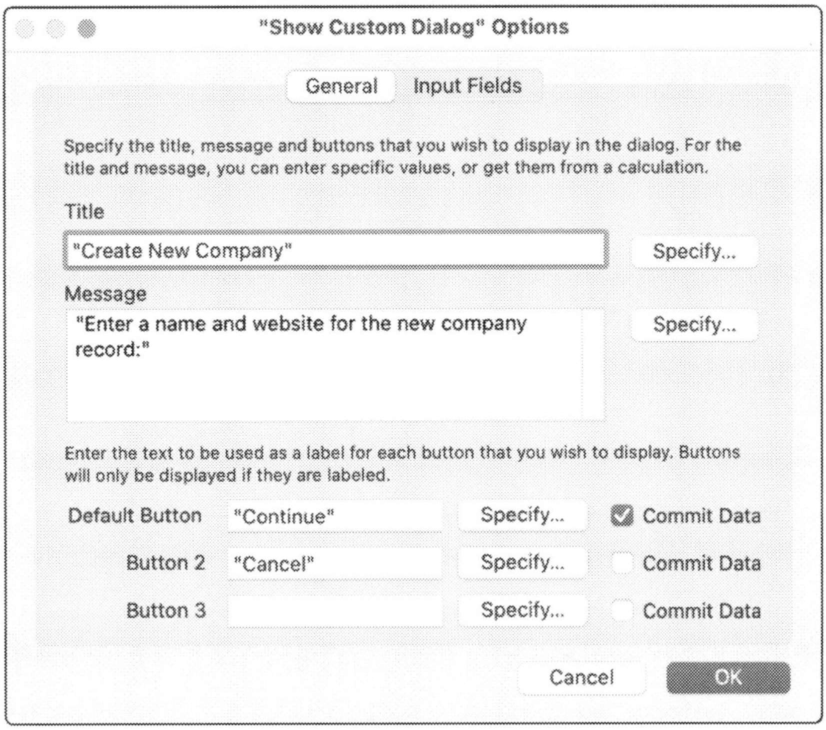

Figure 25-12. *The configuration of a dialog's messaging properties*

The *Title* and *Message* can each receive static text typed directly into their fields or from a formula entered by clicking the corresponding *Specify* buttons. These produce the values that appear in the title bar and body of the dialog and should clearly convey a message or request an action. In our example, the title identifies the process being undertaken, "Create New Company," while the message prompts them to enter some information.

A dialog can have up to three buttons, entered here in an order that will appear from right to left when the dialog is presented to the user. The *Default Button* will appear at the bottom right and be highlighted to indicate that it will respond to the user typing the Enter key. The other two will appear as normal buttons if a name is assigned.

The *Commit Data* checkboxes can be selected to cause a click on the corresponding button to commit the current record. This can be useful when the dialog requests information that is placed directly into fields as the user types.

The step configuration above will generate a dialog as shown in Figure 25-13. Next, we need to add input fields to allow the user to respond to the prompt.

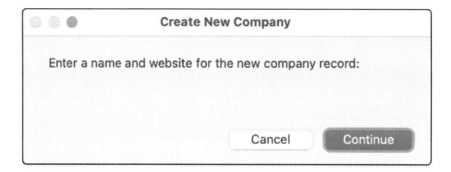

Figure 25-13. *The dialog presented to the user when the step is executed*

Caution   Dialogs do not automatically resize based on message length. Although users can resize, it is not obvious so keep messages concise to avoid missing information.

Setting a Dialog's Input Fields

The *Input Fields* tab of the *Show Custom Dialog Options* dialog, shown in Figure 25-14, is used to configure up to three input spaces which are each linked to either a target field or variable. This allows a dialog to receive input from the users in a controlled environment. In our example, we will request a name and website for the new company record we will be creating.

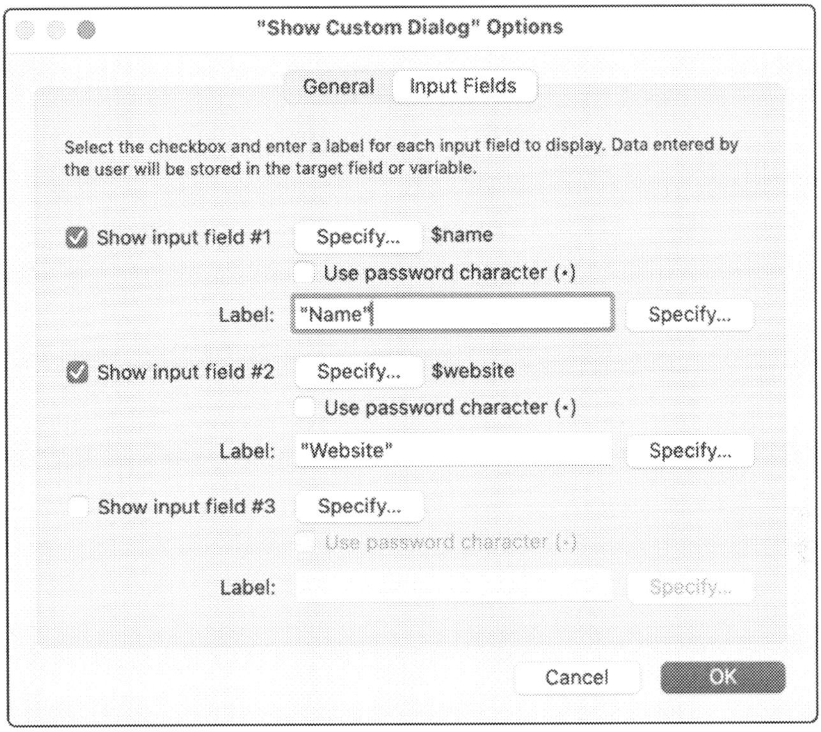

Figure 25-14. *The configuration of a dialog's input fields*

There are three sets of identical controls used to configure the field options for the dialog. To include a field in the dialog, enable the corresponding *Show* checkbox. Then click *Specify* to open a *Specify Target* dialog where you can select a field or enter a variable name. The target acts as both the source and destination of the text area in the dialog. When the dialog opens, any value in the target will be displayed in the input field as a default value. When the user edits that value, the target is immediately updated. In our example, we use variable names because we want to capture the user's input before creating a new record. That way, if the user cancels the dialog, we aren't left with an empty record!

The *Use password character* checkbox will render the field in the dialog as an obscured value, with each character appearing as a bullet point. Like the similar layout setting for fields (Chapter 20, "Concealed Edit Box"), this is a display feature only and does not alter or encrypt the text entered into the field. The value may still be visible on layouts unless the field is also configured to display as bullets. In any case, the script can access and manipulate the value like any other text string.

703

The *Label* field allows a field label to appear above the field in the dialog. By default, the field will be present on the dialog without a label. Enter a literal text value or click *Specify* to generate a label with a formula.

Then, repeat this for each additional input field if necessary. The configuration above will add fields to our example dialog, as shown in Figure 25-15.

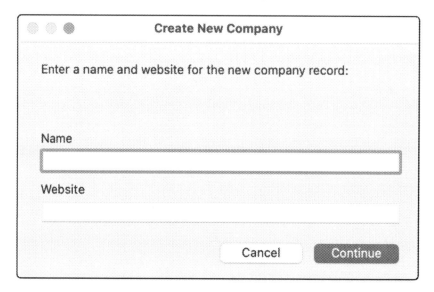

Figure 25-15. *The dialog presented to the user when the step is executed*

Tip   For dialogs with more button or fields, or to add pop-up menus or checkboxes, a custom layout can be opened in a "dialog" window using the *New Window* step (described later in this chapter).

Responding to User Actions

Now we are ready to add steps to detect the user's actions within the dialog and take actions based on their input.

Capturing a Dialog Button Click

When presented to the user, a dialog naturally pauses a script until they click a button to dismiss it. Once done, the script regains control and can access the index position of the button that was clicked. This is done using the *Get (LastMessageChoice)* function as shown in the example below. Here, the value is stored in a variable for later use:

```
Show Custom Dialog [ ]
Set Variable [ $button ; Get ( LastMessageChoice )
```

The value placed into the *$button* variable above will be a numeric index of the button clicked. If a dialog had three buttons defined – OK, Cancel, and Help – and the user clicks OK, the variable will be set to a value of 1. To convert the index number back into the name of the button, the following formula uses the *Choose* function (Chapter 13) to convert the index value to a text value.

```
Show Custom Dialog [ ]
Set Variable [ $index ; Get ( LastMessageChoice )
Set Variable [ $name ; Choose ( $index ; "" ; "OK" ; "Cancel" ; "Help" ) ]
```

In our example of creating a company record, the dialog offers two button choices – "Continue" and "Cancel" – which we will identify simply using their respective index position of 1 and 2 instead of converting them back to a name. Adding an If statement, we can exit the script for a "Cancel" selection and continue creating a record when they select "Continue," as shown here.

```
Show Custom Dialog [ ]
Set Variable [ $index ; Get ( LastMessageChoice )
If [ $index = 2 ]
    Exit Script [ ]
End If
New Record/Request
Set Field [ Company::Company Name ; $name ]
Set Field [ Company::Company Website ; $website ]
```

Confirming Dialog Input

A simple warning dialog may only have a single button and require no follow-up action. It informs the user of some fact and either carries on or exits the script. As we saw in the previous example, a dialog with button choices can take conditional action based on which button the user selected. However, a dialog would input fields that may require additional steps to confirm that the user has entered a value and take alternate actions if they fail to do so. In this example of a script named "Create Company," after the user clicks "Continue," the script will check that each field has a value. If they fail to enter a value in either field, the script will run itself again, until they either enter a value or click "Cancel."

```
Show Custom Dialog [ ]
Set Variable [ $index ; Get ( LastMessageChoice )
If [ $index = 2 ]
    Exit Script [ ]
End If
If [ $name = "" or $website = "" ]
    Perform Script [ Specified: From list ; "Create Company" ]
    Exit Script [ ]
End
New Record/Request
Set Field [ Company::Company Name ; $name ]
Set Field [ Company::Company Website ; $website ]
```

The input confirmation can be as sophisticated as required to confirm the data type requested. If a dialog requests a phone number, a formula can make sure the pattern of text entered matches a phone number and repeat the prompt if the user strays from it. Similarly, a formula can be written to confirm an email, website, or financial figure. FileMaker doesn't provide any automatic way to confirm the textual content format, so you will either need to write a custom formula or find a plug-in that has a function to detect the desired format.

When the confirmation steps occur in the middle of longer scripts, it may not be practical to run the entire script again from the top. In this case, consider using an iterative *Loop* statement (described later in this chapter) to keep repeating only the dialog portion of the script until a satisfactory entry is made.

Using Dialogs for Narrow Find Requests

The *Show Custom Dialog* step can be used to solicit a focused criteria from the user during a scripted find. When the search is limited to one to three target fields, a dialog can provide the interface into which the user enters criteria. This will save the user having to remember which fields they should be entering criteria into on a crowded layout. And, although you could design a small layout with just those fields to prompt the user for input, this eliminates the need to do so and keeps the process interface efficient. The dialog becomes the "layout" into which the user enters find criteria.

Note   See the "CH25-09 Narrow Find Dialog" example file.

In this example, a script that generates a report of paid invoices requires the user to enter a date range to identify which records should be included. After entering Find mode, the script sets the *Invoice Status* field to "Paid" since that is fixed criteria for the find. Then, it presents a dialog allowing the user to enter a date range directly into the *Invoice Date* field and waits for the user to enter a date range.

```
Go to Layout ["Invoice" ]
Set Error Capture [ On ]
Enter Find Mode [ Pause: Off ]
Set Field [ Invoice::Invoice Status ; "Paid" ]
Show Custom Dialog [
   "Search Paid Invoices" ;
   "Enter a date range (m/d/yyyy...m/d/yyyy):" ;
   Invoice::Invoice Date ]
Perform Find
```

Tip   Help users enter date ranges by inserting a default range into the target field or variable prior to the *Show Custom Dialog* step.

Iterating with Repeating Statements

A *repeating statement* is one or more steps of a script that are executed in sequence multiple times until a step exits the loop. FileMaker has three *control steps* that are used to construct repeating statements:

- *Loop* – Required to begin the statement, repeating all subsequent steps until a terminating step is executed

- *Exit Loop If* – Immediately terminates a loop when a formula entered is true, skipping to the step after the next *End Loop*

- *End Loop* – Required to mark the bottom termination point of the repeating statement where control returns to the start of the statement for the next iteration

---

Caution   The *End Loop* step doesn't end the looping process! Instead, it identifies the ending boundary of steps that will repeat.

Other steps placed inside the statement can also terminate the loop. For example, both *Exit Script* and *Halt Script* will stop an entire script, including any remaining iterations. These can be placed inside of an *If* conditional statement within the *Loop* statement to abruptly exit under specific conditions. Other methods of breaking a loop include the following:

- The *Exit after last* option of the *Next* or *Previous* option of a *Go to Record/Request/Page* and The *Go to Portal Row* steps.

- A user typing Esc (Windows) or Period with the Command key down (macOS), but only if *Allow User Abort* is "On."

Caution   If no step causes the loop to terminate, the statement will run endlessly until a force quit is performed or the FileMaker application runs out of memory!

Using Loop for Dialog Input Validation

In the previous section, we mentioned using an iterative loop for dialog input validation. Using a *Loop* statement, we can avoid having to repeatedly run the same script and can instead just repeat the dialog prompt until the user inputs the appropriate information. This has an added benefit of allowing us to change the dialog message content to emphasize the error made the first time through. In this example, a *$message* variable is set with the default prompt. Then, inside of a *Loop* step, the dialog is presented. After the dialog is dismissed, the *Exit Loop If* formula determines if the user entered the required values or not. If not, the *$message* prompt is changed, and the entire statement repeats. This continues until the user either enters valid information or cancels to exit the script.

Note   See the "CH25-08 Dialogs" file for this example.

```
Set Variable [ $message ; Value: "Enter a name for the new company:"  ]
Loop
   Show Custom Dialog [ "Create a New Company" ; $message ; $name ]
   If [ Get ( LastMessageChoice ) = 2 ]
     Exit Script
   End If
   Exit Loop If [$name ≠ "" ]
   Beep
   Set Variable [ $message ; Value: "You MUST enter a name for the new
company:"  ]
End Loop
New Record/Request
Set Field [ Company::Company Name ; $name ]
```

Using Loop to Step Through a Found Set

A script can "step" through a found set and repeat a sequence of steps, once for each record.

Note   See the "CH25-10 Loop Found Set" example file.

Performing Steps on Each Record

This example starts by navigating to the first record in a found set of *Invoice* records. Inside of a Loop statement, it performs another script named "Send Invoice" that sends an invoice to the customer for the current record. Then, a *Set Field* step changes the *Invoice Status* field from "New" to "Sent." Finally, it goes to the next record and repeats these steps until it reaches the last record of the found set and exits the loop.

```
Go to Record/Request/Page [ First ]
Loop
    Perform Script [ Specified: From list ; "Send Invoice" ; Parameter: ]
    Set Field [ Invoice::Invoice Status ; "Sent" ]
    Go to Record/Request/Page [ Next ; Exit after last: On ]
End Loop
```

Collecting Data from Each Record

This example loops through a found set of *Invoice* records and collects the value of several fields for each record. It uses an *Invoice Status Due* calculation field that determines if the invoice is open or past due and, if the latter, how many 15-day increments. Its formula below uses a *Let* statement to extract the status and date from fields, and then it determines how many days have passed since the invoice date. A *Case* statement generates a status value for the open invoice. If it is not sent, the result is an empty string. If the date is less then 15 days prior to the current date, the result is the word "Open" indicating that the invoice is due but not yet past due. Then, a series of 15-day increments is used to determine the overdue status before finally flagging the invoice as "Sent to Collections." The *Case* statement is wrapped in an *Upper* function to capitalize the entire result.

```
Let ( [
    status = Invoice Status ;
    days = Get ( CurrentDate ) - Invoice Date
] ;
    Upper (
    Case (
        status ≠ "Sent" ; "" ;
        days < 15 ; "Open" ;
```

```
        days < 30 ; "Over 15 Days" ;
        days < 45 ; "Over 30 Days" ;
        days < 60 ; "Over 14 Days" ;
        "Sent to Collections"
    )
    )
)
```

After sorting by *Invoice Status Due*, the script goes to the first record and then begins a *Loop* statement. A *Let* statement is used to append a *$body* variable with a line for the current record that includes the id, date, company, amount, and the status display. At the end of this script, the data collected is displayed in a dialog but could also be sent as an email or saved into a text file.

```
Sort Records [ Restore ; With dialog: Off ]
Go to Record/Request/Page [ First ]
Loop
    Set Variable [ $body ; $body &
        Invoice::Record Primary ID & " " &
        Invoice::Invoice Date & " " &
        Invoice::Invoice Company & " " &
        Invoice::Invoice Amount & " " &
        Invoice::Invoice Status Due & "¶" ]
    Go to Record/Request/Page [ Next ; Exit after last: On ]
End Loop
Show Custom Dialog [ "Invoice Report" ; $body ]
// result =
    000006 3/1/2024 Atlas Widgets 5000 SENT TO COLLECTIONS
    000007 3/15/2024 Long Haul Media 4950 OVER 45 DAYS
    000008 3/16/2024 Atlas Widgets 8750 OVER 45 DAYS
    000009 4/1/2024 Long Haul Media 3500 OVER 30 DAYS
    000010 4/1/2024 Fantastic Client 3750 OVER 30 DAYS
    000011 5/1/2024 Fantastic Client 6500 OPEN
```

Grouping Data with Subheadings

As the results of the preceding example grow, it becomes more difficult to discern the different status values. Instead of repeating a status for each invoice, we can consider creating groups of invoices with the status they share as a heading. The following example starts with the same found set of open invoices sorted by *Invoice Status Due*; this script uses a variable named *$lastStatus* to track the status value from the record in the last iteration. Anytime it encounters a new status value in the current record, it performs a conditional step to insert that status into to the *$body* variable with some extra paragraph returns to form the heading. Then it puts the status for the current record into the *$lastStatus* variable so that status will be ignored on each subsequent iteration until a different value is detected.

```
Set Variable [ $lastGroup ; "" ]
Go to Record/Request/Page [ First ]
Loop
   Set Variable [ $group ; Invoice::Invoice Status Overdue ]
   If [$group ≠ $lastGroup ]
      # Add header row
      Set Variable [ $body ; $body & Case ( $body ≠ "" ; "–¶" ) &
      $group & "¶" ]
      Set Variable [ $lastGroup ; $group]
   End If
   # Add body row
   Set Variable [ $body ; $ body &
   Invoice::Record ID & " " &
   Invoice::Invoice Date & " " &
   Invoice::Invoice Company Name & " " &
   Invoice::Invoice Amount & "¶" ]
   Go to Record/Request/Page [ Next ; Exit after last: On ]
End Loop
# Result =
   OPEN
   000011 5/1/2024 Fantastic Client 6500

   –

   OVER 30 DAYS
```

```
000009 4/1/2024 Long Haul Media 3500
000010 4/1/2024 Fantastic Client 3750
—

OVER 45 DAYS
000007 3/15/2024 Long Haul Media 4950
000008 3/16/2024 Atlas Widgets 8750
—

SENT TO COLLECTIONS
000006 3/1/2024 Atlas Widgets 5000
```

Looping Through Data

A *Loop* statement can also be used to "step" through data stored in a variable. Each iteration can perform operations on one paragraph of a return-delimited list of values or the data stored in one key of a JSON Object, working through them one by one until complete. There are different ways of controlling the process. One method involves setting up a couple of control variables to store a total count of values and the number of the current value which is incremented on each loop. The other method uses a reduction approach where the first value is extracted, processed, and removed from the source variable until nothing remains. Let's explore an example of each.

Both examples will build a series of find request using a list of states as the criteria. To find any *Contact* record with any one of the states in the list, we must enter Find mode and then create one request for each state listed.

Note   See the "CH25-11 Looping Through Data" example file.

Using Control Variables to Loop Data

A *control variable* is a value defined for the sole purpose of controlling how an iterative process operates. This is differentiated from a *data variable* that contains real information being manipulated by the process. The example below uses two control variables to step through data and create a find request for each state included. One will track the total item count and number of find requests required. The other will track the current item that should be extracted from the *$source* variable and to inform the script when it has reached the end of the list and should exit the loop.

713

```
Set Variable [ $source ; List ( "OH" ; "PA" ; "NY" ) ]
Set Variable [ $count ; ValueCount ( $source ) ]
Set Variable [ $current ; 1 ]
Enter Find Mode [ Pause : Off ]
Loop
   Set Field [ Contact::Contact State ; GetValue ( $source ; $current ) ]
   Set Variable [ $current ; $current + 1 ]
   Exit Loop If [ $current > $count ]
   New Record/Request
End Loop
Perform Find [ ]
```

A *$count* variable is set to contain the number of states in the $source variable using the *ValueCount* function to control how many loops will be performed. The *$current* variable is initially set to "1" to indicate a start on the first state in the list. This will be incremented by one each time we iterate through the list until it reaches the number in *$count*. After the *Enter Find Mode* step prepares the window for find criteria, the *Loop* statement begins. During each iteration, the *Set Field* uses the *GetValue* function to extract the state abbreviation in the list at the position indicated by *$current* and enters it into the *Contact Address State* field for the current find request. The *$current* variable is incremented by 1, and an *Exit Loop If* step checks to see if that number exceeds the *$count*. If not, it creates a *New Record/Request* and continues to the next iteration. If it does, the loop is exited and the script runs the *Perform Find* step.

Using the Reduction Method to Loop Data

This example creates the same set of find requests for states in a *$source* variable but does so with control variables. The *reduction method* of controlling a *Loop* statement involves extracting the first of a list of values and then removing it from the source so the next iteration can extract the first of the remaining list. In that case, the script knows to exit the process when the source variable is empty. This streamlines the statement by eliminating the need to have control variables but may slow down the script if the list is huge.

In the following example, *GetValue* always extracts the first state from *$source* and inserts it into the current request. Next, the *$source* variable is reset using the *ValueCount* and *RightValues* functions to remove the first value, leaving only the remaining values for future iterations. When the *$source* variable is empty, the *Exit Loop If* step terminates the loop and the find is performed.

```
Set Variable [ $source ; List ( "OH" ; "PA" ; "NY" ) ]
Enter Find Mode [ Pause : Off ]
Loop
   Set Field [ Contact::Contact State ; GetValue ( $source ; 1 ) ]
   Set Variable [ $source ; RightValues ( $source ; ValueCount
   ( $source ) - 1 ) ]
   Exit Loop If [ $source = "" ]
   New Record/Request
End Loop
Perform Find [ ]
```

Managing Windows

There are numerous steps that allow a script to resize, select, arrange, close, freeze, refresh, rename, scroll, and create windows. Many of these are relatively simple to use but should not be overlooked in their ability to control the interface.

The *Adjust Window* step changes the visibility or size of a window based on a selection from one of five options.

- *Resize to Fit* – Changes the dimensions of the window to the minimum size possible based on the layout content area within the confines of the current monitor dimensions

- *Maximize* – Resizes the window to the full size of the computer screen

- *Minimize* – Shrinks the window to an icon stored in the Dock (macOS) or taskbar (Windows)

- *Restore* – Returns a window to the size and position it was when the script started

- *Hide* – Removes the window from view, placing it into the *Window* ➤ *Show Window* menu from where it can be reopened by a user or script

The *Select Window* step will bring a specified window to the front, making it the currently active context. This is useful to reactivate a hidden window or to bring forward a window to be targeted for a specific task. The window can be referenced by name and can be associated with any open database, not just the one containing the script running the step.

The *Arrange all Windows* step will organize every open window one of four ways relative to each other: *Tile Horizontally, Tile Vertically, Cascade,* or *Bring All To Front.* The *Tile* options can open multiple windows evenly across the screen, while *Cascade* is useful to reset all windows back in view when some are displayed inaccessibly off-screen.

With the *Move/Resize Window* step, a script can adjust the *Height, Width, Distance from Top,* and *Distance from Left* dimensions for a specified window. This allows custom precise resizing and positioning of a window. For example, a new window can be moved exactly to the center of the screen with a fixed width and height matching the screen. It is even possible to move a window off-screen by setting the top and left distances to large negative numbers. This can be used to hide a *staging interface* from users until it is prepared and ready for interaction. They can still see the window under the *Windows* menu but won't see the preparation steps taken prior to moving it back in view. They can be locked out of accessing it by setting *Allow User Abort* to false until it is ready.

The *Freeze Window* step will halt all interface updates until either the script ends or the window is explicitly refreshed. Normally, changes to records and conditions will constantly refresh interface elements. These updates can be helpful to indicate to the. user that a process is working. However, a script performing lots of steps that impact the interface will slow performance. The freeze stops these updates from being displayed and will improve performance. However, the window will appear static which can mislead a user into thinking it has finished and is frozen to their interactions. So, consider switching to a "Stand by" layout, freezing the window, and then switching back to carry on with the scripted process. That way the user knows to wait until the interface returns to normal before attempting to interact.

The *Refresh Window* step will update the contents of the active window. This is useful to force an update during or after a script. It will update related record displays, reveal hidden objects when conditions change, and reactivate automatic interface updates by negating a *Freeze Window* step. This step has two options accessed through a gear icon panel. The *Flush cached join results* checkbox option will delete queries that cause related records to refresh. The *Flush cached external data* does the equivalent for external ODBC data source records which can be ignored when not using ODBC sources. Both settings will impact performance and shouldn't be selected if not relevant. For example, if the script didn't affect related records, the cache flush isn't needed and shouldn't be selected.

Other steps include *Close, Set Window Title,* or *Scroll Window.* But the game-changing power lies in the ability to create new windows.

Creating a New Window

A script can create new windows to satisfy any number of workflow requirements. A new window can open for specialized data entry tasks, including the following:

- Opening a related record without disrupting the user's location in a list in the current window

- Opening two records from the same table on the same layout for a side-by-side comparison

- Opening two records from different tables enabling the user to multitask

- Creating "light box"-style overlays on interface for quick option selection or entry tasks

- Presenting a small layout as a custom input soliciting dialog

- Preparing a hidden staging interface for an automated process

The *New Window* step creates an additional window. Window properties are configured in a *New Window Options* dialog shown in Figure 25-16. Once inserted into a script, double-click the step, or click on its gear icon to open the dialog. From here, you can specify the new window's style, name, layout, size, position, and options. Any of these settings that are not modified will inherit a default from the current window at the time the step executes.

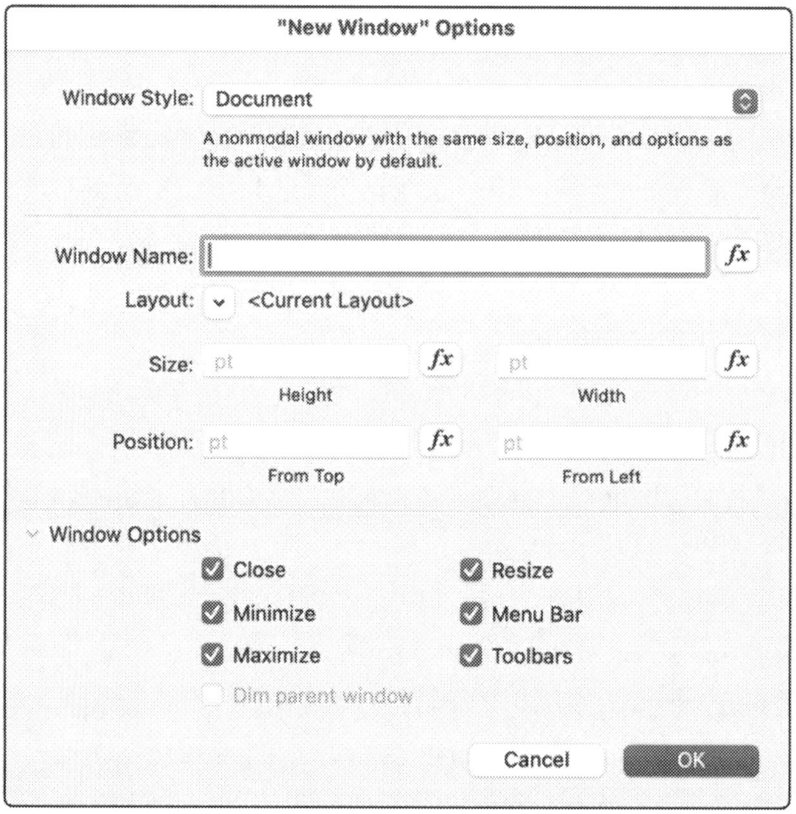

Figure 25-16. *The configuration options for creating a new window with a script*

Note   See the "CH25-12 New Window" example file.

Choosing a Window Style

The *Window Style* offers a selection of one of four types of windows. Any of these can be used for a variety of purposes, but some are more suited for specific functionality.

- *Document* – The default is a standard non-modal FileMaker window. These are ideal for general data entry work.

- *Floating document* – Is a non-modal window that remains in front of other windows. These can be used for displaying prompts, help guides, or control panels. These can be persistent but still allow other work performed in other windows.

- *Dialog* – Is a window that is modal to the application. These lock up every window, pausing for focused user input.

- *Card* – Is a window modal to and attached as an overlay on the active window. These lock up a single window and are a nice alternative to a full dialog window.

Note   A window is *modal* when it captures all input, forcing user interaction and/ or dismissal before resuming other work in the affected context.

Setting Window Name and Dimensions

The settings in the center of the *New Window Options* dialog are all optional. If not specified, the new window will always default these to the settings of the window active when the step is executed.

A *Window Name* can be entered in the text area or by clicking the *fx* button to generate one with a formula. If no name is specified, the new window will be named the same as the current window with a numeric suffix.

The *Layout* setting will open a *Specify Layout* dialog in which you can select any layout in the database as the target for display in the new window.

The *Size* settings control window *Height* and *Width* dimensions. The *Position* settings for *From Top* and *From Left* control the distance of the new window relative to the screen. Each of these can be typed directly into the field or determined with a formula by clicking the adjacent *fx* button. These can be used in conjunction with each other for precise centering or other alignments using built-in functions (Chapter 13, "Getting Window Dimensions").

Tip   A "staging" window can be created with large negative value for the *From Left* and *From Top* properties to "hide" a complex sequence of steps off-screen that would be visually distracting to a user if done in full view.

Configuring Window Options

The *Window Options* checkboxes control the properties of the new window. The *Close*, *Minimize*, *Maximize*, and *Resize* options enable the ability of a user to modify the window. If selected, a user can access these manual controls in the new window. The *Menubar* visibility can be visible or hidden (Windows only) as can the *Toolbars*. For *Card* windows only, the *Dim Parent Window* option will obscure the window behind the attached card window to help highlight its dimensions.

Caution   Opening a modal window without providing access to the close function or a button to close the window will trap the user and may require a force quit of the application to escape.

Building a Custom Dialog Window

One way to overcome the button and input field limitations of the *Show Custom Dialog* step is using the *New Window* step to open a custom layout designed as a dialog. In that case, since the dialog is really a layout displayed in a new window, it can contain any number of any type of layout objects formatted in any way required to accomplish the intended task. It can include lengthy instructions, any number of input fields configured with any control style, and way more than three buttons. A script can present the dialog in a new window of any size and pause for the user action before continuing. In this section, we create a simple dialog layout and script that opens it in a new window, enters Find mode, and pauses for the user to select a state in a pop-up menu. The layout will include four buttons to continue the script. Three will provide a choice of marketing email that would be sent to the found set for *Contacts* in the state selected and a fourth option to cancel the script.

Creating a Dialog Layout

Create a new layout named "Contact – Dialog Find" and assign it to the *Contact* table. Remove other default parts and shrink the *Body* part down to a desired dialog size, as shown in Figure 25-17. Add a text object for a heading and action prompt. Place the *Contact Address State* field formatted as pop-up menu assigned a value list of state abbreviations. Add four buttons along the bottom evenly spaced. Then configure their

Autosize settings in the *Position* tab of the *Inspector* pane to lock to the bottom right, so the window size can vary slightly without adversely affecting the appearance. Then, save the layout by returning to Browse mode. Next, create a script to use the dialog input to control its process.

Figure 25-17. *An example of a layout designed for use as a dialog*

Creating a Dialog Layout Script

A script that presents and responds to a custom dialog window can be configured in a variety of different ways depending on the options offered to the user. For example, one script can open a dialog window, pause for field input, and then respond to the user's click on a "Continue" button configured with a *Resume Script* step or a "Cancel" button configured to *Close Window* and *Halt Script*. However, when a dialog presents multiple buttons, the script needs a way to know which the user clicked. Remember, there is no function like *Get (LastMessageChoice)* used after a *Show Custom Dialog* step that indicates a button click on a layout. If each button resumes the paused script, the script has no way to know which the user selected. So, each button must be configured in a way that communicates to a script which choice was made. This can be done many ways, including the following:

- The script opens the dialog and stops. Each button calls a separate script that performs one function.

- The script opens the dialog and stops. Each button calls one script with a parameter indicating which button was pressed.

- The script opens the dialog and pauses. Each button sets a field or variable with a name indicating which was pressed and resumes the script.

Our example, shown in Figure 25-18, will be self-contained in a single script and use parameters to trigger different sections. It will open a dialog window, enter Find mode, and then pause for user input. The user should then select a state and click a button. If they click "Cancel" or type Enter, the script will skip over to the end and show a dialog indicating their choice. If they click a button but don't pick a state, it will play a sound and repeat the script from the top. If they click a button and have selected a state, it can then perform whatever steps are required on that found set. Let's look at the script line by line to see how it is structured.

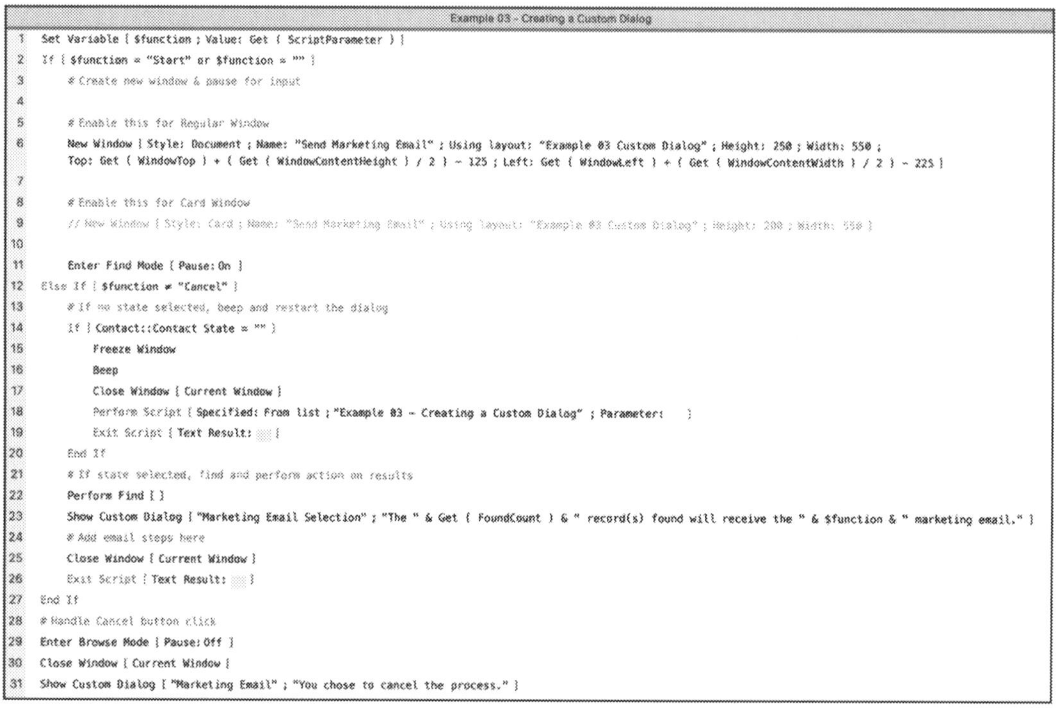

```
                                    Example 03 - Creating a Custom Dialog
1    Set Variable [ $function ; Value: Get ( ScriptParameter ) ]
2    If [ $function = "Start" or $function = "" ]
3        # Create new window & pause for input
4
5        # Enable this for Regular Window
6        New Window [ Style: Document ; Name: "Send Marketing Email" ; Using layout: "Example 03 Custom Dialog" ; Height: 250 ; Width: 550 ;
         Top: Get ( WindowTop ) + ( Get ( WindowContentHeight ) / 2 ) - 125 ; Left: Get ( WindowLeft ) + ( Get ( WindowContentWidth ) / 2 ) - 225 ]
7
8        # Enable this for Card Window
9        // New Window [ Style: Card ; Name: "Send Marketing Email" ; Using layout: "Example 03 Custom Dialog" ; Height: 200 ; Width: 550 ]
10
11       Enter Find Mode [ Pause: On ]
12   Else If [ $function = "Cancel" ]
13       # If no state selected, beep and restart the dialog
14       If [ Contact::Contact State = "" ]
15           Freeze Window
16           Beep
17           Close Window [ Current Window ]
18           Perform Script [ Specified: From list ; "Example 03 - Creating a Custom Dialog" ; Parameter:    ]
19           Exit Script [ Text Result:    ]
20       End If
21       # If state selected, find and perform action on results
22       Perform Find [ ]
23       Show Custom Dialog [ "Marketing Email Selection" ; "The " & Get ( FoundCount ) & " record(s) found will receive the " & $function & " marketing email." ]
24       # Add email steps here
25       Close Window [ Current Window ]
26       Exit Script [ Text Result:    ]
27   End If
28   # Handle Cancel button click
29   Enter Browse Mode [ Pause: Off ]
30   Close Window [ Current Window ]
31   Show Custom Dialog [ "Marketing Email" ; "You chose to cancel the process." ]
```

Figure 25-18. *The dialog script has conditions for each of five parameter values*

Tip   Run this script in the example file with *Script Debugger* turned on to walk through and analyze how it operates.

The script begins by placing the script parameter into a *$function* variable (Line 1). An *If* statement's first condition runs when the parameter is either empty or contains the word "Start." It opens the *New Window* to the dialog layout centered on the original window and then does *Enter Find Mode* with pause (Lines 2-11). When a user runs the script or clicks a button meant to start the process, the script knows this based on the parameter and opens the dialog. To get the new window to open centered over the current window, the *Left* and *Top* position formulas will be as shown below. In this case, the formula starts from the window's top and left positions on the screen. Then, it adds half of each of the of the window height and width, respectively, to establish the midpoint of the current window. Finally, it subtracts half of the new window's dimensions to achieve a proper centering of the new window over the old.

```
Get ( WindowTop ) + ( Get ( WindowContentHeight ) / 2 ) - 125 // Top
Get ( WindowLeft ) + ( Get ( WindowContentWidth ) / 2 ) - 225 // Left
```

Note   As we will see in the next section, Card windows auto-center and do not require Top/Left Window Position values.

Each button on the layout calls this same script but with a parameter matching its name. So, the next condition starting with the *Else If* step handles any button click that is not "Cancel" (Lines 12–26). A nested *If* statement confirms a selection in the *Contact State* field and, if empty, executes a *Freeze Window*, *Beep*, and Close Window before running *Perform Script* targeting the same script and then runs the *Exit Script* step (Lines 14–20). The user will perceive this as just a sound, but it completely resets the dialog and Find mode pause since their button click resumed the script and we need to wait for them to try again.

If they did select a state before the click, the *Perform Find* step isolates the found set of records (Line 22). Then a dialog informs how many records were found and which email function was selected (Line 23). This is optional and may be removed in favor of a *Loop* that sends an email for each record in the found set (not shown).

After that, the script runs the *Close Window* and *Exit Script* steps (Line 25–26). Since the find occurs within the dialog window, the found set only exists there, so we must perform the action process(es) before closing the window. Once closed, the user returns to their original window with the layout and found set they were viewing before starting this process.

Finally, at the bottom (Lines 29–31) we handle a "Cancel" button click or the user typing Enter on the keyboard. This runs the *Enter Browse Mode* and *Close Window* steps before an optional *Show Custom Dialog* which informs the user that they canceled the process.

Connecting the Dialog Buttons to the Script

Each button on the dialog layout should call the script with a parameter, as shown in Figure 25-19. Even though the script pauses after *Enter Find Mode*, these buttons need to be configured to *Exit Current Script* to restart the process correctly with the ability to restart the script if the user didn't select a state.

Figure 25-19. *Each button calls the script with a parameter and is set to exit the current script*

Introducing the Card Window

A *Card* is a modal window that appears as an overlay displayed on top of the current window's active layout. Unlike other window types, when a card is opened, the parent window's content becomes inactive and inaccessible. However, depending on the size of the card, the content may still be visible behind or around the card in an optionally diminished light. Unlike a *Dialog* window, which is modal to the application, a card is modal to a single window.

Cards are similar in appearance and behavior to modal windows found in other environments. For example, a macOS dialog can open as a "sheet," attached to the top of a window. Also, web pages often display various objects like advertisements or images in a similar "light box" format. In FileMaker, *Card* windows can be used for a variety of reasons like those other applications and countless more relative only to databases. A card can present navigation menus, custom toolbars, dialogs, wizards, custom help guides, expanded container field contents, print previews, and more. Anything you can display in a window can be presented on a card instead if desired.

Using formulas for size and position, a card window can appear centered in the window or attached to the top, left, bottom, or right. It can also be positioned next to the window. So, it can appear as a sidebar on either side, a macOS type "sheet," a tray opening to the side to expand the window, or any other type of familiar presentation display. Cards open a lot of new possibilities for creating dynamic interfaces that present robust options when needed, but keep them hidden away when not.

Tip   A card can be positioned anywhere on screen. However, because it is modally connected to the window, it should be positioned within the window bounds or at least attached to it.

Cards are particularly good for universal features access from any context in an interface design. Since they are just like windows and can display any layout, they have their own context which can be different from that of the parent window's active layout. So, a "Person Selection" interface can be designed on a card to pop open a list of contacts for selection and attachment to various contexts like *Company, Project, Invoice*, etc. Similarly, an "Email Template" list can be opened from anywhere and present a list of email templates filtered by whatever table the user was viewing. A Card window can open a layout with only a web viewer on it into which any script can quickly display html generated from any context. Any universal interface "service" you can imagine can pop out from anywhere in your solution to help reduce technical redundancy and facilitate resource sharing.

Converting the Custom Dialog Example to a Card

To create a card, simply select "Card" as the *Window Style* in the *New Window Options* dialog. As an example, let's convert the previous custom dialog window from the last section to be a card instead of a separate window. Start by opening the script and editing the *New Window* step options, as shown in Figure 25-20.

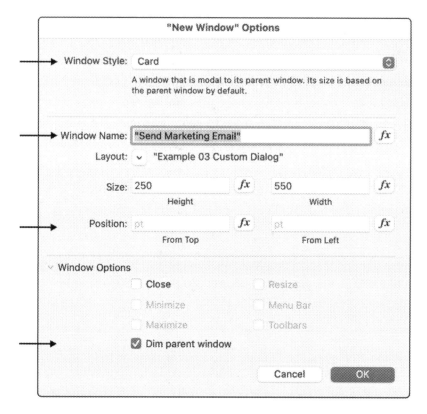

Figure 25-20. *The options when configuring a Card window*

After "Card" is selected from the *Window Style* menu, we will make a couple key changes to the configuration.

The *Window Name* will not be displayed on the card, but the name of a card window can sometimes be useful to identify the originating context and more. It can even be used to store information used by formulas in scripts or layout elements. For example, if multiple scripts open the same card window, a different name can be assigned by each so that a cleanup script or other formulas know which script started the process.

Cards are different than other window types that default to the original window dimensions if blank. If the *Size* values are left empty, the card will default to the actual dimensions of the target layout. But these can be modified to expand the layout to any size. Leave *Position* values blank to have the card centered in the parent window. For our example, these can all four be blank but can be changed to control precise locations within or beside the parent window.

The *Window Options* section changes dramatically for Card windows. The options for allowing resizing and toolbar/menu visibility are disabled because they aren't relevant to cards which can be resized or show a toolbar. The *Close* option remains and will display an "X" button on the upper left of the card to close it. This can be left disabled if the interface will provide the user with buttons for this function. The *Dim parent window* option becomes enabled and, if selected, will cast a shadow over any portion of the parent window's interface that is visible around the edges of the new window. This is a good option to select to avoid the user becoming confused and thinking visible controls behind the Card are live.

Once configured, run the script again to see the previous marketing email dialog opened as a Card.

Tip   A script run in a separate file can open a card layout, and it will appear in the originating database window and temporarily inherit all its properties.

Using Insert from URL

The *Insert from URL* step enters data results from a URL into a target field or variable. The command supports the http, https, ftp, ftps, and file protocols and includes cURL options. The step's panel includes options to specify various settings, as shown in Figure 25-21.

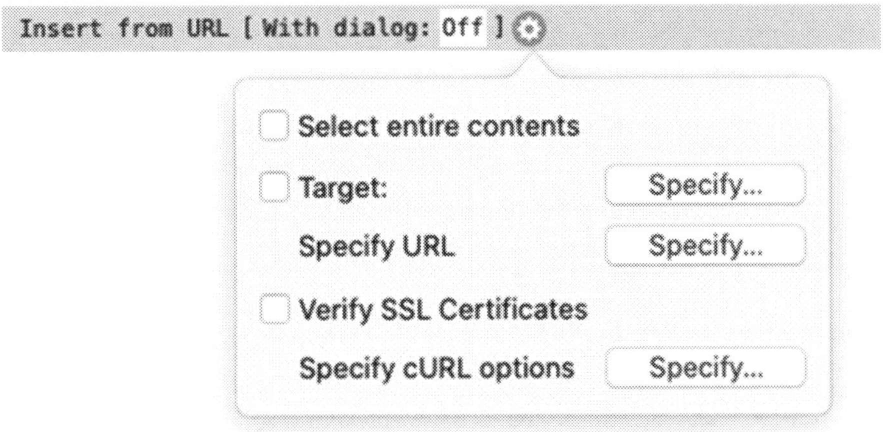

Figure 25-21. *The Insert from URL step's configuration panel*

Note   See the "CH25-13 Insert from URL" example file.

Downloading a File

This example will download a PDF file from a website and place it into a container field. After inserting the step into a script, click the gear icon and select the *Target* checkbox. In the *Specify Target* dialog that opens, select the field into which the downloaded file will be stored. Then, click to *Specify URL* and enter the URL of the file, like the PDF shown in Figure 25-22. Run the script and the file should appear in the container field.

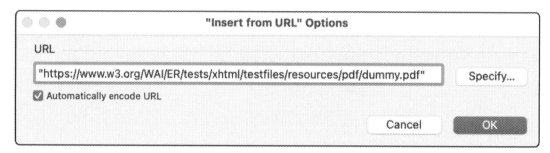

Figure 25-22.   *The Insert from URL step's configuration panel*

Caution   The container must be present on the layout, positioned on- or off-screen (Chapter 18, "Defining Layout Regions and Controls").

A URL for any public file can be replaced in the step to automatically download it instead. Clicking the Specify button in the options dialog allows the address to be constructed using a formula which can be used to download a different file into each record in a found set.

Accessing a Zip Code API

An *application programming interface* (API) is a mechanism that allows two software systems to communicate and exchange data. There are countless APIs available online, and the *Insert from URL* step can be used to interface with any of them. For example, a database can use the zip code lookup service from Datasheer, LLC (`https://www.zip-codes.com/zip-code-api.asp`). The site allows a URL to request a JSON object of information about any US zip code. You can register at the site for a free account (limited to 250 lookups/month) or purchase a variety of tiers up to 2 million lookups per month. This example uses a limited demo API key and can be run from a *Contact* layout after a zip code is entered into a field. The script starts by placing the site's API address and the current record's *Contact Zip* field value into a *$URL* variable.

```
Set Variable [ $URL ; Value: "https://api.zip-codes.com/ZipCodesAPI.
svc/1.0/QuickGetZipCodeDetails/" &
Contact::Contact Zip & "?key=DEMOAPIKEY" ]
```

Next, the *Insert from URL* step is configured with a *$Data* variable as the *Target* for results from the service. This step will ping the API using the *$URL* to request information for the specified zip code.

```
Insert from URL [ With dialog: Off ; Target: $Data ; $URL ]
```

Once executed, the *$Data* variable will contain a JSON object like the one shown here generated after the user enters "10039" into the *Contact Zip* field.

```
{
"city" : "New York",
"country" : "US",
"county" : "New York",
"postal_code" : "10039",
"state" : "New York",
"state_short" : "NY"
}
```

The final two *Set Field* steps place the *city* and *state* values parsed from the *$Data* result into the corresponding fields.

```
Set Field [ Contact::Contact City ; JSONGetElement ( $Data ; "City" ) ]
Set Field [ Contact::Contact State ; JSONGetElement ( $Data ; "State" ) ]
```

Tip   For the smoothest experience, use an *OnObjectValidate* script trigger (Chapter 27) to run this script after the user types into the *Contact Zip* field.

Using cURL Options

Client URL (cURL) is an open source, command-line tool for data transfer between different systems using the URL syntax. The technology greatly expands the functionality possible with website requests, sending a structured data object with the URL to the website. This offers a more secure method of data transfer with far greater structural flexibility. FileMaker's *Insert from URL* script step includes a button to *Specify cURL Options* when sending a request to a website that requires cURL parameters instead of embedding it directly in a URL. After entering the URL, click the *Specify* button and enter options, structured as required by the target website. For example, if a website requires authentication, the options might be formatted as shown in the following example. This example places a URL into one variable and cURL options in another and then uses these in the *Insert from URL* step which targets a *$Data* variable for the result.

```
Set Variable [ $URL ; Value: "https://www.example.com/" ]
Set Variable [ $Options ; Value: "--user name:password ]
Insert from URL [ With dialog: Off ; Target: $Data ; $URL ; cURL Options:
$Options ]
```

cURL can be used to push data to a web form as shown in the following example. A first name and last name are structured with field labels and included as the content of a data option which is then sent to a website's contact form.

```
Set Variable [ $URL ; Value: "https://www.example.com/contact.cgi" ]
Set Variable [ $Options ; Value: "--data \"firstname=Joe&lastname=
Smith\"" ]
Insert from URL [ With dialog: Off ; Target: $Data ; $URL ; cURL Options:
$Options ]
```

Summary

This chapter presented numerous examples of scripting tasks that can be used to automate activity within a database. In the next chapter, we will look at the built-in script debugging capabilities provided as part of FileMaker's advanced tools.

Debugging Scripts

A *software debugger* is an interactive tool used by developers to perform a controlled execution through a scripted process for analysis and troubleshooting purposes. A *debugging interface* provides control over the progress through lines of executing code alongside a live view of the interface being acted upon and the values stored in variables at each step. This allows developers to literally see how their code behaves line by line, greatly easing the task of evaluating performance and identifying the cause of problems. As a database grows more complex, a debugger quickly becomes an important tool for developers. FileMaker includes a *script debugger* that can easily move through a script's steps and follow a process through a hierarchy of interconnected scripts. In this chapter, we introduce basic script debugging and cover the following topics:

- Managing complexity with a debugger
- Opening the debugging interface
- Exploring debugging controls
- Setting custom breakpoints

> **Note** A debugger is used to troubleshoot code execution, not to identify problems when code fails to compile!

Managing Complexity with a Debugger

At first, debugging isn't a critical need. Troubleshooting a tiny script made up of a few steps is easy. When a problem is observed, you can mentally project what each step is doing and which is responsible for the error. An error message stating that "an operation could not be completed because the target is not part of the related table" is a little vague

© Mark Conway Munro 2024
M. C. Munro, *Learn FileMaker Pro 2024*, https://doi.org/10.1007/979-8-8688-0835-7_26

but clearly the result of a *Set Field* step improperly configured to change the value of a field in a table unrelated to the current layout's occurrence. If the script only contains one such step, the problem is easy to locate. The solution is to either choose the correct field in the correct table occurrence or to add a *Go to Layout* step at the beginning to ensure that the script is in the context required for the selected target field. Similarly, if a report prints out a blank page, it is likely a problem with the criteria set before a *Perform Find* step or the configuration of the *Print* step. Also, an endless loop is easy to find in a short script with only one *Loop* step which will likely be found missing an *Exit Loop If* step or to be using an incorrect condition formula to terminate the process. In all of these cases and many like them, debugging can be used but isn't essential. To fully appreciate the value of a script debugger, consider the challenges that arise when a database grows more complex.

Grappling with Script Length

Early scripts might be responsible for small processes that save users a little time. A simple script that finds, sorts, and prints records for a frequent report is easy to troubleshoot. However, as a database grows more complex, it will require longer scripts. Soon, scripts begin performing dozens or hundreds of steps. They change layouts, moving across multiple table contexts. They begin to include multiple conditional and iterative statements. For example, a script might build a complex set of find requests to generate a found set of active customers in one table, which are looped through to locate active projects for each from another table, which are looped through to find outstanding invoices for each project in a third table, which are sent to a list of email addresses from a fourth table, which are finally summarized in a variable and emailed to an internal accounting supervisor. The ability to step through a lengthy script to confirm its functionality is one of the benefits of debugging.

Seeing Hidden Processes

As scripts grow in size and intensity of task, techniques to hide the processing become desirable. For example, a script that loops through hundreds of records, setting fields, changing layouts, and more will constantly be refreshing the interface. This can become visually distracting to the user and negatively impact performance. To combat both problems, developers use the Freeze Window step at the start of a complex script.

But this makes it harder to know where in the scripted process a problem occurs. It is also a common practice to use the Set Error Capture to stop dialogs from popping up and interrupting a lengthy autonomous process. However, this makes it impossible to know where or even if an error occurs. When a problem occurs, it can be a challenge to decipher from an email of incorrect information sent to a customer by mistake what and where in hundreds of steps something went wrong. The ability to temporarily slow down a process, see what the script sees, and know what it knows at each step is another benefit of a debugger.

Facilitating Open-Ended Scripts

Adept programmers decrease redundancy by designing open-ended scripts that provide a universal generic service. A script that accepts parameters as input or has context adapting conditions can provide a flexible, general functionality that works from any table context to create powerful and efficient "services." These improve the structural efficiency and simplify certain development work, but they also increase complexity. An open-ended script, by its nature as a flexible and adaptive operations, is going to be more complex than it would be if it performs a hard-coded function. That makes it more difficult to troubleshoot when problems arise. A script accepting different input each time it runs will need to have that input reviewed when a problem occurs. A set of conditional values placed into variables are not easily viewed when a script executes. A debugger helps by allowing developers to observe variables in real time as they step through a script.

Identifying Script Calls

As an interface grows, the number of trigger points that call a script increases. At first, a dozen scripts might be accessible under the Scripts menu (Chapter 24, "Scripts Menu"). Some may be attached as a button action (Chapter 21, "Configuring a Button's Action"). As the interface becomes more sophisticated, scripts are called by custom menus (Chapter 23), interface Script Triggers (Chapter 27), external systems (Chapter 33), JavaScript functions in the HTML of a Web Viewer (Chapter 20), and more. Although the database design report (Chapter 31) provides information about where a script is called, there isn't an easy way to see this when designing interfaces. It is easy to forget that a script performing a fully automated process going to a certain layout designed for user tasks will trigger a script that performs steps that shouldn't be part of the process. Similarly, it is easy to connect a button to the wrong script or duplicate a button and forget to repoint it to a different script. A debugger can help you safely test a new button's target without running the whole script or to track down other problems by seeing everything that happens when a certain user action is taken.

Visualizing a Growing Call Stack

A *call stack* is a mechanism used by software to track the execution of processes being executed in a hierarchical cascade. Since only one process in a chain can be executing at a given moment, subsequent calls "stack up" in order from newer to old as new processes take over and previous ones wait to continue. In FileMaker, a call stack is formed or expanded when a script starts. If a script starts, executes its steps, and finishes, it will have formed a stack one level deep for the duration of that operation. If that script uses Perform Script (Chapter 24, "Performing Other Scripts") to call a second script, its adds a second call to the stack hierarchy. As it begins executing, the second script becomes active at the top of the stack while the first script waits below it. When the second script concludes operations, it is removed from the stack and control reverts back to the first script which continues executing.

When considered in conjunction with other challenges of a complex database design, it is easy to see how quickly one can get into trouble here. A button click configured to *Perform Script* creates a stack two levels deep. The button's operation is called by the user's click, and the button's action calls the script. If that script calls another script, it adds a new level. The user's click calls the button's action which calls the first script which calls the second script. Then, if the second script executes a *Go To Layout* step and opens a layout with an *OnRecordLoad* script trigger, the trigger runs a third script, adding another level to the stack. And that script might call other scripts. If that sounds confusing and difficult to visualize, consider that each script in a stack can change found sets, switch layouts, open multiple new windows, and create various unexpected context issues for other scripts in the stack. When a problem occurs during a dense call stack, it can be difficult to know which script caused the problem, not to mention knowing where, why, and under what interface conditions the problem occurred. Being able to visualize the entire call stack and see the current script's place in it is perhaps the primary service that a debugger provides.

Opening the Script Debugger

To access FileMaker's debugger, be sure that *Use Advanced Tools* preference is active (Chapter 2, "Preferences: General"). Once active, the debugger can be opened one of three ways, as shown in Figure 26-1.

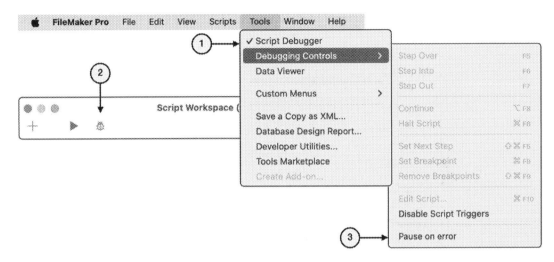

Figure 26-1. *The debugging options in the Tools menu and Script Workspace toolbar*

1. Select *Script Debugger* from the *Tools* menu to open the debugger window and initiate debugging in standby mode. Any script performed in the interface by any means will automatically open and pause in the debugger.

2. Click the *Debug the current script* button in the toolbar of the *Script Workspace*. This immediately opens and pauses the selected script in the debugger window.

3. Select the *Pause on Error* option in the *Debugging Controls* submenu of the *Tools* menu. When enabled with the debugger window closed, any script that encounters an error will open and pause in the debugger.

Once open and paused, you have control over how the process continues to execute.

Exploring the Script Debugger Window

The *Script Debugger* window, shown in Figure 26-2, is always open when debugging is active. The non-editable toolbar contains buttons for controlling the debugging process. The steps of the active script are listed in the middle with a green arrow label on the number of the paused step. Any steps with a manual breakpoint are similarly denoted with a blue arrow. The *Pause on error* checkbox below controls the setting that opens the debugger and pauses on any steps that generate an error during regular use, including those automatically suppressed with the *Set Error Capture* script step. At the bottom is the *Call Stack*, a hierarchy of nested script calls that are listed in execution order, from the current script back to the first script that started the currently active workflow.

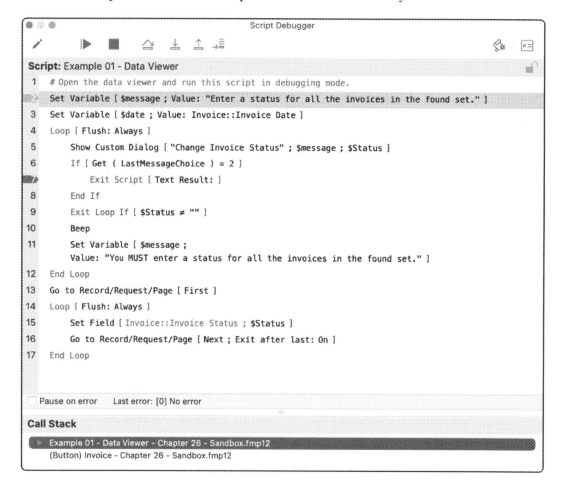

Figure 26-2. *The window used to debug scripts*

Note   See the "CH26-Sandbox" example file.

This script was called by a button action, as indicated by the *Call Stack* at the bottom. After the layout button was clicked, the debugger opened and showed the button's *Perform Script* action. The *Play* icon in the toolbar was clicked to bring us to the view. Each time a new script starts in the debugger, it pauses on the first step and freezes the interface in its current state. The seventh step has a manual breakpoint indicated by the blue arrow. This adds an additional forced pause at that step. The developer now has time to observe the state of the interface, review the current script steps, and decide the next option: continue running normally, stepping through the script line by line, opening the script to perform edits, or completely halting the entire script stack to make any required development changes.

Status Toolbar Items (Debugger Window)

The non-customizable status toolbar for the *Script Debugger* window, shown in Figure 26-3, provides control over the debugging process. These functions are also accessible through the *Debugging Controls* submenu of the *Tools* menu.

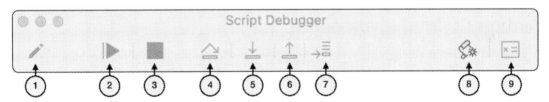

Figure 26-3. *The toolbar of the Script Debugger window*

1. *Edit script* – Open the paused script in the Script Workspace to perform edits while the execution is paused. Saving an edited script will halt debugging.

2. *Continue* – Continue running the paused script using default stepping/pausing options. It will run to until it encounters a step denoted as a manual breakpoint.

3. *Halt script* – Stops and closes all scripts in the entire stack.

4. *Step over* – Continue the current script, performing subscripts without debugging.

5. *Step into* – Continue the current script step by step, performing subscripts with debugging.

6. *Step out* – Continue the current script without pause until control is returned to the parent script, and then pause.

7. *Set next step* – Jump ahead to the selected step, skipping over the interim steps.

8. *Disable script triggers* – Toggle the enabled status of Script Triggers anywhere in the database file.

9. *Open data viewer* – Open the *Data Viewer* dialog (described later in this chapter).

Tip   The best way to learn the subtle difference between these options is to run any script and experiment.

Setting Custom Breakpoints

A *custom breakpoint* is a developer marked point in a script that forces a pause in the debugger. These are used to troubleshoot script problems more quickly without having to click step by step through every line of a lengthy script. Breakpoints allow you to stop a script at any arbitrary position and provides an opportunity to see the current layout context and review current values in key variables at a frozen moment in time. Breakpoints can be added to a script open in either the *Script Workspace* or *Script Debugger* window. To add a breakpoint, simply click the step number. A breakpoint is indicated when the number is illuminated in a blue arrow, as shown previously in Figure 26-2. Breakpoints can be removed individually by clicking the arrow icon. Select the *Remove Breakpoints* option from the *Debugger Controls* submenu of the *Tools* menu to remove all breakpoints from the current script paused in the debugger.

Exploring the Data Viewer

The *Data Viewer* is a dialog that gives developer access to observe values and test formulas on two tabs: *Current* and *Watch*. Although not exclusive to debugging a script, this dialog has features that expand when viewed in debugging mode.

Monitoring Current Values

The *Current* tab of the *Data Viewer* dialog displays a list of values, as shown in Figure 26-4. The values listed always includes all global variables and provides the easiest way for a developer to access these. During debugging, the list expands to include local variables and field values for any fields that are included in steps within the current script. A bullet appears next to a field if it is being accessed by the current step. This allows monitoring of these values while stepping through debugging the script.

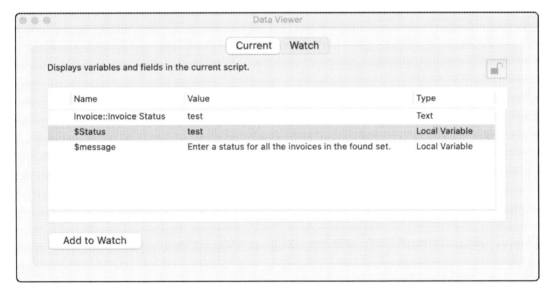

Figure 26-4. *The Current tab of the Data Viewer displays a list of values*

The list has three columns, showing each item's *Name, Value,* and *Type*. Click these headings to sort the list of values. Double-click a value to open it in a larger window. A variable is editable when opened – a field is never editable from this view. The *Add to Watch* button at the bottom will add the selected item to the *Watch* tab to allow selection and monitoring of subset of the values listed.

Watching Values

The *Watch* tab of the Data Viewer dialog is used to monitor values in a manually compiled list of expressions, as shown in Figure 26-5. Since the expression can be any formula, it allows an item to monitor a variable, field, or the result of a custom formula.

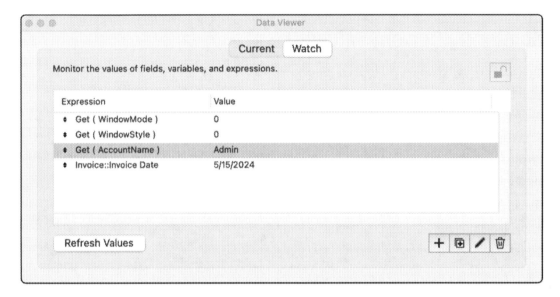

Figure 26-5. *The Watch tab of the Data Viewer displays a list of expressions and results*

The list has two columns showing each items *Expression* and *Value*. Click these headings to sort the list of values. On the lower right, four icon buttons provide the following control over what appears in the list:

- *Add expression* – Opens a *Specify Calculation* dialog to create a new item in the list.

- *Duplicate expression* – Creates a duplicate of the selected item which can be opened and customized.

- *Edit expression* – Opens the selected item into a *Specify Calculation* dialog for editing. An item can also be opened by double-clicking it in the list.

- *Delete expression* – Deletes the selected item(s) without a confirmation dialog.

The *Watch* tab provides a perfect "sandbox" for creating new formulas. The formula interacts with the current window's layout context and displays results in real time. So, a formula can be written and tested in its intended context before deploying it into a field, script, layout object, or custom function.

Summary

This chapter introduced the debugging capabilities of FileMaker and the *Data Viewer*. These provide an invaluable tool for troubleshooting databases with complex scripting and for developing new formulas. In the next chapter, we will learn how to trigger scripts in response to interface events.

CHAPTER 27

Using Script Triggers

A *script trigger* is a developer-defined connection between an *interface event* and a script. These are used to create dynamically responsive interfaces that can perform automated tasks based on a variety of user activity. Scripts used as the action for a button or custom menu must be manually performed by a user. That may be fine for tasks that are optional or require a conscious choice, but a non-optional critical business function may be overlooked and forgotten. In some cases, it can be inefficient and nonintuitive to require a user to perform extra clicks to initiate mandatory actions in the interface. Triggers allow an interface design to include dynamically responsive layouts that connect user events to custom scripts. Use them to automatically run a script when a file is first opened, a record is loaded, or a field is modified. FileMaker has over two dozen triggers for a variety of *file*, *layout*, and *object events*. Some events run the assigned script prior to the completion of the user action, allowing the script to execute custom steps and determine if the event should be performed to completion. Others run after the event, allowing the script to perform follow-up tasks. This chapter introduces script triggers, covering the following topics:

- Linking scripts to file events
- Linking scripts to layout events
- Linking scripts to object events
- Understanding event precedence
- Dealing with trigger exceptions

Tip Objects assigned a script trigger will optionally display a badge icon in Layout mode (Chapter 17, "View Menu").

743

© Mark Conway Munro 2024
M. C. Munro, *Learn FileMaker Pro 2024*, https://doi.org/10.1007/979-8-8688-0835-7_27

Linking Scripts to File Events

A *file event* occurs when a user opens or closes window, completes a transaction in a window, or changes the status of an AV file in a container field. To configure file event triggers, select the *File* ➤ *File Options* menu to access the *Script Triggers* tab of the *File Options* dialog, shown in Figure 27-1. This tab lists all the *file events* that can be linked to scripts. The event checkbox indicates an active event that is configured to trigger the script displayed in the second column. Below this is the Script Trigger Properties panel which shows details and options for the selected event. Click *Select* to specify the script that will be connected to that selected event.

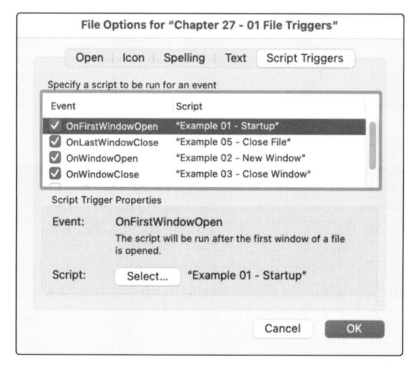

Figure 27-1. *The File Options dialog contains access to Script Trigger settings for file events*

There are six file events shown in Table 27-1. Each database is limited to one script for each event.

Table 27-1. *A summary of file events*

File event name	Script runs before event	Parameter option
OnFirstWindowOpen	–	–
OnFirstWindowClose	Yes	–
OnWindowOpen	–	–
OnWindowClose	Yes	–
OnWindowTransaction	Yes	Target field name
OnFileAVPlayerChange (iOS)	–	–

Note   See the "CH27-01 File Triggers" example file.

OnFirstWindowOpen

The *OnFirstWindowOpen* event occurs after the first window appears when a database file opens. This provides an opportunity for a database to run a startup script when opened. It can be used to perform interface setup functions prior to a user beginning work, including the following:

- Initialize global variables.

- Log the user's session start time.

- Locate a user's record of stored preferences.

- Restore the user's last window's size and position.

- Perform a default find and sort.

- Present a user with items that require their attention.

- Restore a user's last found set and current record.

The event only occurs when a database is opened by a user or by the *Open File* step run from a script in another file. It will not occur if the file opens automatically as a hidden window which happens when a table from the file is used in the relationship graph (Chapter 9). However, if a window opened this way is later selected from the *Windows* menu or brought to the front by some process, the event will trigger its script.

Tip   Navigation to a layout and hiding toolbars when a file opens can be configured without a trigger (Chapter 6, "File Options: Open").

OnLastWindowClose

The *OnLastWindowClose* event occurs before the last window is closed as a database shuts down. This provides an opportunity to run a shutdown script that performs a variety of tasks such as the following:

- Confirm the user intended to shut down.

- Confirm the user hasn't left any work half finished.

- Log the user's session end time.

- Store global variables into fields so they can persist into the next sessions.

- Store the user's last layout, found set, and current record.

- Store the last window size and location.

Since it is triggered before the event closes the window, the script has the opportunity to cancel the event by returning a false (0) value. For example, a script like the one shown below can confirm that the user actually intended to close the file and give them an option to cancel the event.

```
Show Custom Dialog [ "Really close the database?" ]
If [ Get ( LastMessageChoice ) = 1 ]
   Exit Script [ Text Result: 0 ]
End If
```

The *Show Custom Dialog* step is configured with the first (default) button named "Cancel" and the second named "Close." The *If* statement uses the *Get (LastMessageChoice)* function to detect which button was clicked. If the user clicked the first button to cancel, the *Exit Script* step returns a zero result which causes the triggering event to halt, thereby leaving the window and file open. If not, the script finishes with an implied true result and the event continues to close the file.

OnWindowOpen

The *OnWindowOpen* event occurs after any window first opens, either by a user selecting the *Window* ➤ *New Window* menu or a script running the *New Window* step. It is also triggered when a file previously opened hidden is brought forward for the first time. Like with the first window open for the file, this provides an opportunity to perform any configuration or setup routines for the new window.

When a database first opens, both the *OnFirstWindowOpen* and *OnWindowOpen* events will trigger scripts if configured. To avoid conflict, consider one of the following choices:

- Only use one or the other, not both.

- Use both, but avoid redundancy between their steps.

- Use both but add steps to suppress *OnWindowOpen* the first time.

To achieve the last option, add the steps below to the *OnWindowOpen* script which check the value in a global variable to see if it has run yet. When triggered after the first window opens, the variable would be empty, so the script can set its value and exit. If the variable has a value, it means the new window was created after the database has already been opened so the script can perform its other functions without conflict.

```
If [ $$RunOnWindowOpen = "" ]
        Set Variable [ $$RunOnWindowOpen ; 1 ]
        Exit Script [ ]
End If
// Add window open steps here
```

OnWindowClose

The *OnWindowClose* event occurs before a window is about to close. Like with the last window close, this provides an opportunity to perform last-minute validation functions or maintenance routines before dismissing the window. Since the script is triggered before the event, the script has the option to return a false (0) value, to cancel the event, and to allow the window to remain open.

When using both *OnlastWindowClose* and *OnWindowClose* in the same file, use the following script steps to skip the latter of these in favor of the former. This will exit the *OnWindowClose* script when there is only one window left open for the file.

```
If [ ValueCount ( WindowNames ( Get ( FileName ) ) ) = 1 ]
        Exit Script [ Text Result: 1 ]
End If
```

OnWindowTransaction

A *transaction* is temporary window state during which changes are stored until a commit or revert occurs. When a record is open for editing, a transaction is automatically opened until the record is committed. Steps introduced in version 19.6 allow scripts to explicitly open, commit, and revert a transaction. This allows a batch of changes queued up by a script to be committed or reverted all at once. The *OnWindowTransaction* trigger was added in version 20.1.

Note   Learn more about transactions in Chapter 36.

OnFileAVPlayerChange

The *OnFileAVPlayerChange* file event occurs after the playback state of a media file in a container field or URL is changed. For example, the event triggers when paused, played, or stopped or when the media stops upon reaching the end.

Caution   This event is only supported by FileMaker Go!

Linking Scripts to Layout Events

A *layout event* occurs when a user or script performs one of a variety of record, layout, and window actions. To configure layout event triggers, select the *Script Triggers* tab of the *Layout Setup* dialog (Chapter 18), shown in Figure 27-2. The controls for configuring event scripts are like the *File Options* dialog described previously, with one additional setting. The *Enable in* checkboxes control if the selected event will trigger scripts in Browse mode, Layout mode, or both.

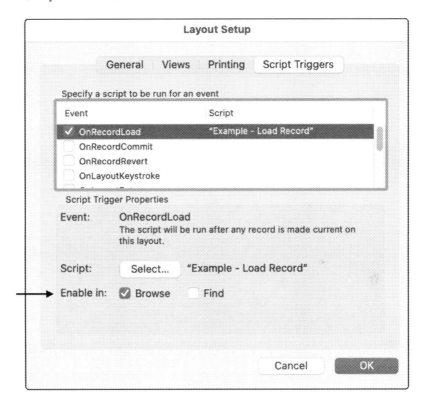

Figure 27-2. *The Layout Setup dialog is used to configure layout script triggers*

There are 12 layout events shown in Table 27-2. Each layout has its own separate list of these triggers.

Table 27-2. *A summary of layout events*

Layout event name	Script runs before event	Parameter Option
OnRecordLoad	–	Yes
OnRecordCommit	Yes	Yes
OnRecordRevert	Yes	Yes
OnLayoutKeystroke	Yes	Yes
OnLayoutEnter	–	Yes
OnLayoutExit	Yes	Yes
OnLayoutSizeChange	–	Yes
OnModeEnter	–	Yes
OnModeExit	Yes	Yes
OnViewChange	–	Yes
OnGestureTap	–	Yes
OnExternalCommandReceived	–	Yes

OnRecordLoad

The *OnRecordLoad* event occurs after a record becomes current which happens when any of the following occur from actions initiated by a user or script:

- Navigating to a different record within a found set

- Navigating to a different layout

- Creating a new record

- Deleting a record in a found set of more than one record and landing on a different record

- Creating a new window showing a table with one or more records

- Displaying search results

Note   See the "CH27–02 OnRecordLoad" example file.

The event provides an opportunity for a script to perform steps that prepare a window or the record it displays for data entry or other tasks. For example, a script can perform tasks like the following:

- Select the first row in a portal.

- Initialize some global variables that control how things appear.

- Capture and store the fact that a certain user looked at a record, forming an audit trail of activity.

- Update a web viewer with contents based on the current record.

Caution   If the script will visit another layout to create records or other actions, perform those steps in a new window to avoid re-triggering the event in an endless loop.

OnRecordCommit

The *OnRecordCommit* event occurs when a user or script commits a modified record. Any activity that causes a current record with unsaved changes to commit will trigger this event, including the following:

- A user explicitly committing a record by typing the Enter key or clicking outside of fields on the active record

- Navigating to a different record

- Creating, deleting, duplicating, or omitting records

- A script performing the *Commit Records/Requests* step

- Opening the *Manage Database* dialog or other developer dialogs

- Closing the window

- Closing the file

Note   See the "CH27–03 OnRecordCommit" example file.

The script is triggered when the commit process begins but before changes are saved, so it has the option to cancel the action by exiting with a false (0) value. This provides an opportunity to perform any post data entry steps. For example, the script can get a list of fields modified by the user using the *Get (ModifiedFields)* function and use this to perform actions such as the following:

- Handling advanced content validations that are too complicated to put into field definitions

- Performing automatic tasks in response to specific changes by the user

- Sending modification data to a log table to create an audit history of who changed what and when

OnRecordRevert

The *OnRecordRevert* event occurs before reverting a modified record to its previously committed state, caused by a user selecting the *Records* ➤ *Revert Record* menu or a script running the *Revert Record/Request* step. It provides an opportunity for a script to cancel the action by exiting with a false (0) value and/or to perform steps prior to reverting such as the following:

- Presenting a custom confirmation dialog to the user

- Undoing actions that won't be reversed as part of the automatic revert process

- Writing the event into a log table for an audit history of activity

---

Note   See the "CH27–04 OnRecordRevert" example file.

OnLayoutKeystroke

The *OnLayoutKeystroke* event occurs when any character is typed on the keyboard except those handled as functions by the operating system or FileMaker's active menu set. The event will trigger the assigned script for every keystroke, even when no field

752

has active focus. It also occurs before the keystroke is sent to FileMaker when a field is in focus. This provides an opportunity for a script to intercept one or more specific keystrokes and either suppress or reroute into a custom series of actions.

Limiting Keystrokes

Although impractical in most cases, the event can be used to create a layout that doesn't respond to any keystroke, including when a field is in focus. Simply assign the event to a script with only the *Exit Script* step returning a false result, as shown here:

```
Exit Script [ Text Result: 0 ]
```

> **Note**   See the "CH27–05 OnLayoutKeystroke (Limiting Keystrokes)" example file.

A more realistic use is to suppress the annoying dialog that appears when a user begins typing prior to entering a field. This script will only allow keystrokes when a field is active:

```
If [ Get ( ActiveFieldName ) = "" ]
      Exit Script [ Text Result: 0 ]
End If
```

Detecting Keystrokes with Built-In Functions

There are two trigger related built-in functions that can be used to detect the key and/or modifier key(s) typed by the user. The first simply returns a text string indicating the key the user just typed, as shown here:

```
Get ( TriggerKeystroke )
// Result = "t"
```

> **Note**   These functions also work with the *OnObjectKeystroke* event described later in this chapter.

The other function will return a number representing the modifier keys held while the keystroke was typed. This function is similar to the *Get (ActiveModifierKeys)* function which produces the same results but, in a general, does not trigger event context.

```
Get ( TriggerModifierKeys )
// Result = 4
```

The numbers returned by both *modifier key functions* are a sum of the following numbers combined based on which key(s) are held:

- Shift = 1

- Caps Lock = 2

- Control (macOS) and Ctrl (Windows) = 4

- Option (macOS) and Alt (Windows) = 8

- Command (macOS) = 16

Note   See the "CH27–06 OnLayoutKeystroke (Detecting Keystrokes)" example file.

For example, if the user types the number 1 while holding the macOS Control and Shift key down, the results will be as shown below. The modifier result is "5" because the Shift key (1) plus the Control key (4) equals 5.

```
Get ( TriggerKeystroke )
// Result = "1"
Get ( TriggerModifierKeys )
// Result = 5
```

Caution   All trigger specific functions only work within the targeted script, not as a parameter sent to the script from the object.

Performing a Script with a Key Combination

These functions can be used in an *OnLayoutKeystroke* to perform a script based on a key combination that is not present in the active menu set. The following example checks the key(s) typed and performs a script only when the user types "1" while holding down the macOS Control key. The script runs the *Perform Script* step and then uses the *Exit Script* with a result of 0 to halt the keystrokes. Any other keys typed are ignored by the script and continue into the active field.

```
If [ Get ( TriggerModifierKeys ) = 4 and Get ( TriggerKeystroke ) = "1" ]
    Perform Script [ ]
    Exit Script [ Text Result: 0 ]
End if
```

Closing a Card Window with the Escape Key

This example combines the trigger keystroke function with the *Code* function to close a Card window when the user types the Escape key, which is Code 27.

```
If [ Code ( Get ( TriggerKeystroke ) ) = "27" ]
    Close Window
    Exit Script [ Text Result: 0 ]
End if
```

If the above script is assigned to a layout that will be used as both a Document and Card window, be sure to check *Get (WindowStyle)* to confirm it is open as a Card before closing the window. This example will only close the window when the user types Escape while the layout is open as a Card.

```
If [ Get ( WindowStyle ) = 3 and Code ( Get ( TriggerKeystroke ) ) = "27" ]
    Close Window
    Exit Script [ Text Result: 0 ]
End if
```

OnLayoutEnter

The *OnLayoutEnter* layout event occurs after the active layout being browsed in a window changes. This event triggers the first time a layout is activated in a window, so it occurs when any of the following occur:

- The database opens the layout as the startup default.

- A user manually activates the layout by selecting it from the list of layouts in the menu bar or toolbar.

- A script activates the layout with a *Go To Layout* or *New Window* step.

- A developer changes from Layout mode to Browse mode.

Note   See the "CH27–07 OnLayoutEnter" example file.

The event operates like *OnRecordEnter* but, for the layout, provides an opportunity to perform steps that prepare a window for work performed on the specific layout. For example, a script can perform tasks like the following:

- Resizing and positioning the window based on the layout's design requirements

- Performing a default find and sort to show the user active records only

- Presenting the user a dialog of tasks to work on based on the layout's table

---

Caution   This is a user-based trigger, not a developer one. It triggers when a user first enters a layout in Browse or Find mode, not when a developer enters Layout mode!

OnLayoutExit

The *OnLayoutExit* layout event occurs before navigating away from the current layout. This event triggers whenever any of the following actions occur:

- A user manually selects a new layout.
- A script executes the *Go to Layout* script step.
- The window is about to close.

Note See the "CH27–08 OnLayoutExit" example file.

This event provides an opportunity for a script to cancel the action by exiting with a false (0) value after performing steps such as:

- Confirm the user intended to change layouts.
- Ensure that any work in the window has been completed.
- Close any extra windows that were opened in conjunction with work performed on the closing layout.
- Perform any automated cleanup or maintenance tasks associated with ending work in one module.
- Write the event into a log table for an audit history of activity.

OnLayoutSizeChange

The *OnLayoutSizeChange* event occurs after the window has changed size. This even occurs whenever any of the following activity occurs:

- A window is first opened.
- A window is resized.
- The window's toolbar or formatting bar is hidden or shown.
- An iOS device toggles between portrait and landscape.

This event provides an opportunity to perform actions related to window size. For example, a script triggered can automatically maintain the window in the center of the screen when resized or automatically enforce a minimum window size.

Centering a Window Automatically

A startup script triggered by the *OnFirstWindowOpen* event can center a window on screen to help focus the user on the tasks they will perform. However, if they resize the window, that perfect alignment will be knocked askew. The OnLayoutSizeChange event can be used to trigger a script that automatically recenters the window anytime its dimensions are altered by a user or script.

Note   See the "CH27–09 OnLayoutSizeChange (AutoCenter)" example file.

Connect the layout event to trigger a script with the following steps:

```
Set Variable [ $Left ; Value: Get ( ScreenWidth ) / 2 ) - Get
( WindowWidth ) / 2 ) ]
Set Variable [ $Top ; Value: Get ( ScreenHeight ) / 2 ) - Get
( WindowHeight ) / 2 ) ]
Move/Resize Window [ Current Window: Top: $Top ; Left : $Left ]
```

Since the script is triggered after the event occurs, as it executes, the current window dimensions will be the resized values. The script begins by calculating a new *$Left* and *$Top* variables for the window by taking half the screen measurement and subtracting half the window measurement in each respective dimension. Then the *Move/Resize Window* step is used to set the current window's *Top* and *Left* settings to those values. Once configured, each time the window's size changes, it will immediately move to a position that is perfectly centered on screen.

Enforcing a Minimum Window Size

Another good use for the *OnLayoutSizeChange* event is enforcing a minimum window size. Layout objects can be configured to automatically grow or move as a window resizes (Chapter 19, "Autosizing"). This keeps the interface looking good by avoiding empty space as a window increases in size. It works in reverse too but with a limit. If the window is resized to a dimension smaller than the actual layout content area, some objects will be out of view and the user will have to scroll to see them. A script trigger can easily check the new window size and increase it to a minimum for the layout.

Note   See the "CH27–10 OnLayoutSizeChange (Minimum Size)" example file.

Using Adjust Window to Enforce Minimum

There are two ways to accomplish this result. First, the *Adjust Window* step can be configured with the "Resize to Fit" option to automatically resize the window to fit all the layout contents in view, provided the layout is designed smaller than the screen size.

```
Adjust Window [ Resize to Fit ]
```

Using Move/Resize to Enforce Minimum

The other method allows the script to determine any minimum size, including a size larger than the defined layout content area if desired. The example below establishes a *$Height* and *$Width* variable that is first set to the corresponding dimension after resizing. Next, each is compared to a minimum value and, if lower, is replaced with the minimum. Finally, the Move/Resize Window step is used to set the *Height* and *Width* of the window to the number in the variable. So, if the window is below the minimum, it resizes to the minimum which is currently configured to be 800 x 1000. If the window is larger than the minimum, it maintains that current size.

```
Set Variable [ $Height ; Value: Get ( WindowHeight ) ]
Set Variable [ $Height ; Value: Case ( $Height < 800 ; 800 ; $Height ) ]
Set Variable [ $Width ; Value: Get ( WindowWidth ) ]
Set Variable [ $Width ; Value: Case ( $Width < 1000 ; 1000 ; $Width ) ]
Move/Resize Window [ Current Window ; Height: $Height ; Width: $Width ]
```

The four variable declarations are spelled out separately for clarity in print. However, these could be collapsed into a single *Set Variable* step that uses the following formula to set a *$Null* variable.

```
Let ( [
   Height = Get ( WindowHeight ) ;
   $Height = Case ( Height < 800 ; 800 ; Height ) ;
   Width = Get ( WindowWidth ) ;
   $Width = Case ( Width < 1000 ; 1000 ; Width )
] ;
   ""
)
```

Alternatively, the height and width of the formula can be embedded directly into the *Move/Resize Window* step to reduce the script to a single line. For example, the *Height* formula in the step could be as follows:

```
Let (
   Height = Get ( WindowHeight )
;
   Case ( Height < 800 ; 800 ; Height )
)
```

OnModeEnter

The *OnModeEnter* event occurs after a change to Browse, Find, or Preview mode (Chapter 3, "Defining Window Modes"). This provides an opportunity to prepare a window for specific activity such as the following:

- Setting up default criteria or opening a special layout when entering Find mode

- Checking for an empty found set when entering Browse mode and offering the user an option to *Find All* records or start a new find

- Adjusting print setup or resizing the window when entering Preview mode

---

Note   See the "CH27-11 OnModeEnter" example file.

Detecting the Current Window Mode

A formula can discover which current mode of the active window using this built-in function:

```
Get ( WindowMode ) // result = 0
```

The result will be a number representing the mode, as follows:

- 0 = Browse mode
- 1 = Find mode
- 2 = Preview mode

The formula below uses the *Choose* function (Chapter 15, "Choose") to translate the numeric value into text:

```
Choose ( Get ( WindowMode ) ; "Browse" ; "Find" ; "Preview" )
```

There are two additional results for special circumstances. If printing is in progress, the function will return a value of 3. If the formula is being evaluated from the Data Viewer instead of a field or layout object and the window is in layout mode, it will return a value of 4.

Caution   When a script runs while a window is in Layout mode, it will automatically switch to Browse mode and return a 0 value!

OnModeExit

The *OnModeExit* event occurs before changing the window's mode. It provides an opportunity for a script to cancel the action by exiting with a false (0) value and/or to perform steps prior to reverting such as the following:

- Ensuring the user has entered valid criteria prior to leaving Find mode

- Confirming the user hasn't left any work unfinished on the current record before leaving Browse mode

Since *the event* triggers a script before changing modes, there is no way to know which mode will become active. However, you can usually assume the target mode. For example, if exiting Find mode, it's almost guaranteed the mode being entered will be Browse mode.

OnViewChange

The *OnViewChange* event occurs after a window changes from one Content view to another (Chapter 3, "Defining Content Views"). It provides an opportunity for a script to perform specific tasks based on the view selected.

Detecting the Current Content View

A formula can discover which current Content view for the active window using this built-in function:

```
Get ( LayoutViewState ) // 0
```

The result will be a number representing the mode, as follows:

- 0 = Form
- 1 = List
- 2 = Table

The formula below uses the *Choose* function (Chapter 15, "Choose") to translate the numeric value into text:

```
Choose ( $View ; "Form" ; "List" ; "Table" ]
```

Changing to a View Specific Layout

A creative example of using the *OnViewChange* event, is to trigger a script that changes between one of three layouts in response to the user selecting a different view.

Note   See the "CH27-12 OnViewChange" example file.

The example *Contact* table has three layouts: *Contact List, Contact Form*, and *Contact Table*. Each of these is configured to allow a selection of all three *Content Views* even though they are each intended to be used for only one view. All three are configured to trigger the following script when the *OnViewChange* event occurs:

```
Set Variable [ $View ; Value: Get ( LayoutViewState ]
Set Variable [ $Name ; Value: Choose ( $View ; "Form" ; "List" ;
"Table" ) ]
Go to Layout [ Get ( LayoutTableName ) & " " & $Name )
If [ $Name = "List" ]
      View As [ View as List ]
Else If [ $Name = "Form" ]
      View As [ View as Form ]
Else If [ $Name = "Table" ]
      View As [ View as Table ]
End If
```

The script uses *Get (LayoutViewState)* to determine the new state selected by the user and then, with a *Choose* statement, converts this number into a name. So, if the user selects "List view," the *$View* variable will be set to "1" and then the *$Name* variable is set to "List." The *Go to Layout* step changes to a *Layout name by calculation* using a formula that gets the current layout's table name with the *Get (LayoutTableName)* function and appends the *$Name* after a space. So, if the user starts on the "Contact Form" layout and selects "List view," the script changes layouts to "Contact List." Then, an If statement is used to ensure that the Content view selected on the new layout is appropriate to its design.

Tip   Although it provides a good example, this approach is unconventional. It is more common for a form/list layout to allow one Content view each and a script to navigate between them.

OnGestureTap

The *OnGestureTap* event occurs when a tap gesture is performed on a layout. The event is triggered under the following conditions:

- FileMaker Go and Windows only (except Windows 7).

- Browse and Find modes only.

- Tap is not made in active web viewers or active edit boxes.

- Single tap is one, two, or three fingers (iOS).

- Double tap with one finger (iOS), which will trigger the event twice.

- Tap is with two fingers (Windows).

This provides an opportunity for a script to perform custom gesture specific actions or halt the gesture if necessary. The *Get (TriggerGestureInfo)* function returns the following list of values indicating details about the event:

- Literal text "Tap" indicates that a tap gesture occurred.

- The number of taps.

- The number of fingers used to tap.

- The document x coordinate location of the tap.

- The document y coordinate location of the tap.

- The object name of the layout element that was tapped.

OnExternalCommandReceived

The *OnExternalCommandReceived* event occurs when a user presses a button to control playback functions on an iOS device lock screen or on an external device, for example, play, pause, stop, next, and previous. The script is triggered after the event occurs, and it can use the *Get (TriggerExternalEvent)* function to gain information about the external event.

Linking Scripts to Object Events

An *object event* occurs when an action is performed to or within a layout object where user interaction is possible, unlike with text, line, and shape objects. To configure an object's event triggers, select the object in Layout mode and choose the *Set Script Triggers* option from one of the following locations:

- The *Format* menu

- The contextual menu for the object in the layout content area

- The contextual menu for the object in the *Objects* pane (Chapter 19, "Defining the Objects Tab")

- The *Popover Button Setup* dialog panel of a popover button or popover element of a button bar (Chapter 20, "Exploring the Popover Button Setup Options")

All of these will open a *Set Script Triggers* window for the object, as shown in Figure 27-3.

Figure 27-3. *The dialog used to configure an object's script triggers*

There are eight object events shown in Table 27-3. Each object has its own separate list of these triggers.

Table 27-3. *A summary of object events*

Object event name	Script runs before event	Parameter option
OnObjectEnter	–	Yes
OnObjectKeystroke	Yes	Yes
OnObjectModify	Yes	Yes
OnObjectValidate	Yes	Yes
OnObjectSave	After Save, Before Exit	Yes
OnObjectExit	Yes	Yes
OnPanelSwitch		Yes
OnObjectAVPlayerChange	–	Yes

OnObjectEnter

The *OnObjectEnter* event occurs after a layout object receives active focus when any of the following events occur:

- A user clicks to select or enter the object.

- A user tabs into the object (Chapter 21, "Understanding Tab Order").

- A script runs a step such as *Go to Object* or *Go to Next Field*.

The trigger works for most object types but appears more practical for objects you literally enter rather than simply select or click on. For example, clicking into a *field* or *portal row* and opening a *popover button* panel all work as expected. Each time you return to the same object, the trigger fires again. Meanwhile, objects like *buttons, button bars, tab controls, slide controls,* and *web viewers* do not. These may trigger the script the first time they are entered after a layout is loaded but tend to fail after that.

Caution   A popover button and its panel can each be assigned a separate script trigger for each event type. Use the *OnObjectEnter* trigger with the panel but not the button.

This trigger can be used in a variety of different ways, including the following:

- When entering a field, store the current contents in a variable to store as the "before" value in a change log table if the user modifies the field's contents when combined with an *OnObjectExit* event.

- When a popover button panel opens, a web viewer or other objects on the panel can be initialized or modified based on a variety of circumstances.

- When a portal row is selected, put the related record's *Record Primary ID* value into a local *Selected ID* field in the layout's table to form a new relationship used to display fields from the selected record outside the portal for expanded entry.

Displaying a Selected Portal Row's Fields

To demonstrate the last idea described above, create an example where a portal row selection will setup a second relationship for the selected related record and allow a user to view and edit fields in an expanded view below the portal.

Start by creating a *Company* and *Contact* table. Then create the following two relationships from the primary *Company* occurrence and two secondary *Contact* occurrences, as shown in Figure 27-4:

- *Company | Contact Portal* – This will be used as the portal's data source to list all contacts assigned the company's *Record Primary ID* as their *Contact Company ID*.

- Company | Contact Selected – This will link a single contact to the company and allow all its fields to be displayed and edited below the portal when a row is selected. The trigger will enter the contact's *Record Primary ID* into the *Selected Contact ID* to establish this connection.

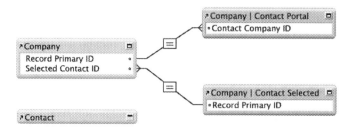

Figure 27-4. *The relationship setup for a portal listing all company contacts and a single selected contact*

The portal row's *OnObjectEntry* event is configured to trigger a script with the following one step.

```
Set Field [
        Company::Selected Contact ID ;
        Company | Contact Portal::Record Primary ID
]
```

Then, any fields from the *Contact* table using the *Company | Contact Selected* occurrence can be placed on the *Company* layout below the portal. When the user selects a portal row, these fields will display values for that row's record and allow editing.

Note   See the "CH27-13 OnObjectEntry (Portal Selection)" file for a working example with more detail.

OnObjectKeystroke

The *OnObjectKeystroke* event occurs when any character is typed on the keyboard, while an object has focus except those handled as functions by the operating system or FileMaker's active menu set. Both keystroke events – *OnLayoutKeystroke* and *OnObjectKeystroke* – are similar but with one difference. They both trigger before the keystroke's completion and can each intercept the event by using the *Exit Script* step with a false (0) result. Both can access the *Get (TriggerKeystroke)* and *Get (TriggerModifierKeys)* functions to determine which key code caused the event and if any modifier keys were being held at the time. The only difference is that the *OnLayoutKeystroke* event occurs with or without an object in focus, while *OnObjectKeystroke* requires an object being entered first.

Caution   Both *TriggerKeystroke* and *TriggerModifierKeys* only work within the targeted script, not as a parameter sent to the script from the object.

OnObjectModify

The *OnObjectModify* event occurs after the value of an object has changed. The event only occurs in response to interface-related actions to an object with focus, including the following:

- Typing a keystroke

- Selecting a value from a field formatted with a value list-based control style (Chapter 20, "Configuring a Field's Control Style")

- Modifying a value using the *Cut*, *Paste*, or *Clear* functions

- Modifying a value using drag and drop

- Changing a value with an interface-related script step like *Insert Text*

- Changing the active panel on a *tab control* or *slide control*

Running a Script After a Pop-Up Menu Selection

The *OnObjectModify* event provides a valuable ability to add a scripted action to any field configured with a value list-based control style. For example, when a user selects an item from a field's pop-up menu, a script runs in response to it. The script can take an action appropriate to the menu item selected. There are two primary ways to use this technique:

- Add a scripted action to an existing data entry field. For example, when a user changes the value in an *Invoice Status* field from "New" to "Sent," that entry action can immediately run a script to send the invoice to the client.

- Add a control field to a layout containing a menu of script actions. For example, an *Actions Menu* field is added the heading of a layout with a menu of ten scripted actions the user can select. Here the field isn't used for data entry, but to provide an alternative consolidated access to a bunch of scripts. The field should be a global field to avoid conflict between users.

Note   See the "CH27-14 OnObjectModify (Field Selection)" example file.

This technique works best with a value list control style because the entry modification is a single action entry into the field. Unlike typing character by character where the final data entry takes place over a sequence of events, when selecting a value from a pop-up menu, radio button, or checkbox set, the selected value is immediately entered all at once after the click.

Refreshing Portal Filter Results During Typing

The *OnObjectModify* event can also be useful with edit box fields. Previously we explored a technique of allowing the value entered in a field to be used as criteria for filtering portal records (Chapter 20, "Filtering Portal Records"). The example there involved a filter field using a pop-up menu control style. That example worked find because a selection immediately causes the portal filtering formula to reevaluate and update results. But what if we wanted to change this setup as follows:

- The filter field is a freeform edit box the user can type into.

- The portal filtering criteria include partial text matches to values in any one of multiple fields.

- The results update after each character is typed so the user sees results in real time.

The first two points could be achieved without a script trigger. But the user would have to type an entire search term into the field and then exit the field before the portal results were updated. Using the *OnObjectKeystroke* event, we can achieve all three objectives and create a dynamical portal that filters as the user types each keystroke.

Note   See the "CH27-15 OnObjectModify (Portal Filter)" example file.

The conversion of the example from Chapter 20 is straightforward. Change the *Portal Filter* field's control style from pop-up menu to edit box and then add an *OnObjectModify* trigger to run a script with the following steps:

```
Commit Records/Requests [ With dialog: Off ]
Refresh Portal [ Object Name: "contacts" ]
Go to Field [ Company::Portal Filter ]
```

Then, the portal's filter records formula can be updated to use *PatternCount* function to detect partial text matches in several fields, as shown here:

```
Let ( [
 criteria = Company::Portal Filter
] ;
 criteria = "" or
 PatternCount ( Company | Contact::Contact Name First ; criteria ) > 0 or
 PatternCount ( Company | Contact::Contact Name Last ; criteria ) > 0 or
 PatternCount ( Company | Contact::Contact Address City ; criteria ) > 0 or
 PatternCount ( Company | Contact::Contact Address State ; criteria ) > 0
)
```

Now, the visible rows in the portal will refresh as the user types each character into the *Portal Filter* field.

OnObjectValidate

The *OnObjectValidate* event occurs when the value of a modified object is about to be validated. This happens as a record is being committed or focus is about to shift to another object, but prior to the object's change in value being saved and the object exited. The event provides an opportunity for the script to validate the change to the object, perform additional actions, and/or halt the event by returning a false (0) result.

Note   See "Understanding Event Precedence" later in this chapter to see an overview of event order as an object is exited and a record is committed.

OnObjectSave

The *OnObjectSave* event occurs after a modified object has been validated and saved but before being exited. The triggered script can halt the object exit step by returning a false (0) result, but the validated and saved value will remain.

OnObjectExit

The *OnObjectExit* event occurs anytime an object is about to lose active focus regardless of any modifications. This happens when the user or a script moves focus to another object, portal row, or field repetition. It also occurs when any action that causes a record to commit occurs. The script is triggered before exiting the object so it can halt the process if necessary.

OnPanelSwitch

The *OnPanelSwitch* event occurs before the current active view of a tab control or slide control changes to a selected inactive view. This event provides an opportunity for a script to cancel the action by exiting with a false (0) value before the view change occurs.

Identifying Panel Views

The built-in *GetLayoutObjectAttribute* function includes an *isFrontPanel* option to identify which view of a tab or slide control is currently active. If each view is assigned an *object name* (Chapter 21, "Naming Objects"), the function can be used to determine which is active. The following formula and results assume that a tab control has three tabs, assigned names, and that the second tab is currently active:

```
GetLayoutObjectAttribute ( "tab1" ; "isFrontPanel" ) // result = 0
GetLayoutObjectAttribute ( "tab2" ; "isFrontPanel" ) // result = 1
GetLayoutObjectAttribute ( "tab3" ; "isFrontPanel" ) // result = 0
```

That function works fine for determining which tab is active in the interface during general use. However, during an *OnPanelSwitch* event, there are two other functions specifically designed to identify the current, starting tab, and the target tab.

Note   See the "CH27-16 OnPanelSwitch" example file.

The *TriggerCurrentPanel* function returns the *number* and *display name* of the view being switched from. The *TriggerTargetPanel* function returns the same values for the view that is about to become active. So, if the second tab is active and the user clicks the third tab, the script, the functions will return the following results:

```
Get ( TriggerCurrentPanel )    // result = "2¶tab2"
Get ( TriggerTargetPanel )     // result = "3¶tab3"
```

Caution   These two functions can only be used in the script called by the event trigger, but not as parameters sent from the trigger.

The *GetValue* function can be used to extract the numeric index, from the two results:

```
GetValue ( Get ( TriggerCurrentPanel ) ; 1 ) // result = 2
GetValue ( Get ( TriggerTargetPanel ) ; 1 ) // result = 3
```

The name on the second paragraph of the raw results returned by these functions is the *Object name* assigned the tab in the *Inspector* pane and not the name displayed on the tab label! However, the number value can be converted with the *Choose* function to the label name. For example, if the tabs are labeled *Address*, *Emails,* and *Phone Numbers,* the following formula will set a *$start* and *$end* local variable with the label name of each:

```
Let ( [
 start = Get ( TriggerCurrentPanel ) ;
 start = GetValue ( start ; 1 ) ;
 $start = Choose ( start ; "" ; "Address" ; "Emails" ; "Phone Numbers" ) ;
 target = Get ( TriggerTargetPanel );
 target = GetValue ( target ; 1 ) ;
```

```
$target = Choose ( target ; "" ; "Address" ; "Emails" ; "Phone Numbers" )
];
  ""
)
```

During the moment of flux between the switch from the current to the target panel, the triggered script can use these functions to perform different tasks based on the start and end panes and halt the switch if necessary. For example, it can check fields on the current panel to determine if any work is left incomplete and force the user to finish before allowing them to go to the next panel.

OnObjectAVPlayerChange

The *OnObjectAVPlayerChange* event occurs after media in an object change state. For example, the event will trigger a script when a user pauses, plays, or stops a video in a field or when the video stops upon reaching the end. This event is only supported by FileMaker Go on iOS devices.

Understanding Event Precedence

Some interface actions will trigger a series of multiple events that FileMaker executes in a specific order of precedence. The choice of where your script intercepts the action depends on the kind of action intended and whether the option to cancel the event is important.

Opening a Database File

When opening a database file, the events in Table 27-4 will be trigger scripts in the order shown.

Table 27-4. *The order of events when a database file is first opened*

Order	Event name	Script runs before event
1	*OnFirstWindowOpen*	–
2	*OnWindowOpen*	–
3	*OnLayoutEnter*	–
4	*OnModeEnter*	–
5	*OnRecordLoad*	–

Caution   The file's setting to *Switch to layout* when opening occurs prior to any script triggering events (Chapter 6, "File Options: Open").

Exiting a Field with Unsaved Changes

When a user exits a field with unsaved changes by tabbing to the next field, the events in Table 27-5 will trigger scripts in the order shown.

Table 27-5. *The order of events when tabbing out of a field with unsaved changes*

Order	Event name	Script runs before event
1	*OnObjectKeystroke*	Yes
2	*OnLayoutKeystroke*	Yes
3	*OnObjectValidate*	Yes
4	*OnObjectSave*	After Save, Before Exit
5	*OnObjectExit*	Yes

Note   If the user clicks into another field instead of tabbing, the first two events do not occur.

Committing a Record with Unsaved Changes

When committing a record with unsaved changes, the events in Table 27-6 will trigger scripts in the order shown.

Table 27-6. *The order of events when committing a record with unsaved changes*

Order	Event name	Script runs before event
1	OnObjectValidate	Yes
2	OnObjectSave	After Save, Before Exit
3	OnObjectExit	Yes
4	OnRecordCommit	Yes

Changing Layouts

When changing layouts, the events in Table 27-7 will trigger scripts in the order shown.

Table 27-7. *The order of events when changing layouts*

Order	Event name	Script runs before event
1	OnLayoutExit	Yes
2	OnLayoutEnter	–
3	OnRecordLoad	–

Note   When changing layouts in a window from a record with unsaved changes, the entire record commit sequence will be performed first followed by the changing layout sequence.

Opening a New Window

When opening a new window, the events in Table 27-8 will trigger scripts in the order shown.

Table 27-8. *The order of events when opening a new window*

Order	Event name	Script runs before event
1	*OnWindowOpen*	–
2	*OnLayoutEnter*	–
3	*OnModeEnter*	–
4	*OnRecordLoad*	–
5	*OnLayoutSizeChange*	–

Dealing with Trigger Exceptions

It is important to remember that script triggers are interface-related actions. Consequently, there are numerous operations that will not initiate a triggering event. Keep these exceptions in mind when designing a scripted workflow, and develop a work around to accommodate any required actions that may not be triggered. The following activity will not generate a script triggering event:

- Field changes caused by their schema definitions don't trigger. For example, a calculation field refresh or text inserted by an auto-enter calculation will not trigger.

- Field changes by script steps that modify fields directly do not trigger scripts. For example, *Set Field* or *Set Field By Name* does not trigger while the *Insert Text* step will.

777

- A change to a field on one layout without assigned script triggers will change the displayed value on another layout but will not trigger a script there.

- Actions that perform bulk actions directly to table data do not trigger. For example, *Import Records, Export Records, Replace Field Contents,* and *Relookup Field Contents* don't trigger.

- Field changes made through the *Show Custom Dialog* step's input fields will not trigger.

- Changes made by *Spelling* and *Find/Replace* functions used manually or with scripts will not trigger.

- The *OnObjectKeystroke* and *OnLayoutKeystroke* will not trigger when the active object is a web viewer.

When non-triggering steps can't be avoided, consider adding steps to a script to force the trigger script for the relevant objects to run or add steps to explicitly perform the desired functionality. Alternatively, don't use script triggers excessively, especially in situations where they aren't absolutely required and may create unnecessary complexities when excluded by these exceptions.

Summary

This chapter continued the discussion of scripting, focusing on how interface events can trigger scripts. In the next chapter, we will explore how plug-ins can extend the built-in functions and script steps available.

Extending Features with Plug-ins

A *plug-in* is a software extension package that extends the capabilities of FileMaker by adding new functions and/or script steps. Some even go as far as modifying the development interface with new features. Plug-ins for FileMaker are available from third-party vendors, which means they involve an added expense and logistical considerations to install and maintain them over time. However, the features they provide would be difficult or impossible to achieve using only built-in tools. This chapter covers plug-in concepts including the following:

- Finding plug-ins
- Installing plug-ins
- Accessing plug-ins

Finding Plug-ins

Plug-ins for FileMaker can be found from a variety of different vendors. Start by searching the Claris Marketplace (marketplace.claris.com), and take a look at some other prominent offerings directly available from the developer website.

MonkeyBread Software

The MBS plug-in from Monkey Bread Software (monkeybreadsoftware.com) boasts over 6,500 functions. The impressive feature list includes enhancements to the *Script Workspace*, connectivity features, OS integration, and content editing. Some highlights include the following:

- Syntax coloring.

- Search in scripts, lists, or relationships.

- CURL for up-/downloads, send/receive e-mail.

- Accessing scanners.

- Access to Address book, Calendars, and Reminders.

- Window management functions.

- Send user notifications.

- Control printers.

- Convert images, draw, and annotate.

- Create, edit, or merge PDF documents.

- Generate and recognize barcodes.

- Read and write Excel files.

- Fill Word files.

Productive Computing

The Productive Computing plug-in offerings (productivecomputing.com) include the following:

- *Address Book Manipulator* – Enables bidirectional data flow between a database and the macOS Contacts application

- *iCal Manipulator* – Enables bidirectional data flow between a database and the macOS Calendar application

- *Biometric Fingerprint Reader* – Adds the ability to incorporate fingerprint security and script control options to a database

Prometheus Systems Consulting

Prometheus Systems Consulting sells dozens of plug-ins (360works.com), including the following:

- *360Works Email* – Send and receive email messages within a database. Supports SMTP, POP, and IMAP.

- *360Works Plastic* – Enables credit card processing within a database. Supports both Authorize.net and Verisign/PayPal Payflow.

- *360Works Web Services Manager* – Publishes your custom FileMaker scripts as XML Web Services that can be accessed by SOAP (Simple Object Access Protocol)–compatible software.

Troi Automatisering

Troi Automatisering offers several plug-ins (troi.com), including the following:

- *Troi Dialog* – Create dynamic, feature-rich dialogs.

- *Troi Encryptor* – Generate passwords and save them in the keychain.

- *Troi File* – Access files and folders outside FileMaker, zip and unzip files and folders, search directories, and more.

Installing Plug-ins

Any computer accessing a database using plug-in functions must have the plug-in installed locally. However, installation resources can be embedded in and installed from a database file, either in a separate installer database or directly within a database solution. Some plug-in vendors deliver plug-ins embedded inside of an installer database, and you can add storage and installation resources to a hosted database to streamline the process.

To prepare a database to install a plug-in, create a container field for each plug-in installer. This may require more than one if the database is used in a cross-platform workflow of different operating systems. Create a script that uses the *Install Plug-in File* step to handle the installation. The following example stores a list of installed plug-ins into a variable named *$installed* and then uses the *PatternCount* function to determine if the Troi File Plug-in needs to be installed or updated. If so, it uses *Get (SystemPlatform)* to determine if it should install the macOS or Windows plug-in.

```
Set Variable [ $installed ; Value : Get ( InstalledFMPlugins ) ]
If [ PatternCount ( $installed ; "Troi File Plug-in;15.0.0" ) = "" ]
   If [ Get ( SystemPlatform ) = 1 ]
      Install Plug-in File [ Resources::Troi_File.fmplugin ]
   Else
      Install Plug-in File [ Resources::Troi_File.fmx]
   End if
End if
```

To ensure that each user's computer has the proper installation, the script can run automatically as part of a script triggered at database launch by an *OnFirstWindowOpen* event (Chapter 29). The script can be expanded to check for errors to confirm that the installation process was successful and warn the user to contact a database administrator if a problem was detected. For example, the script will fail if the preference to *Allow Solutions to Install Files* is not enabled. The *Plug-ins* tab of the *Application* preferences dialog, shown in Figure 28-1, lists every plug-in installed on the local computer. From here, you can manually confirm installation and enable, disable, and configure a plug-in.

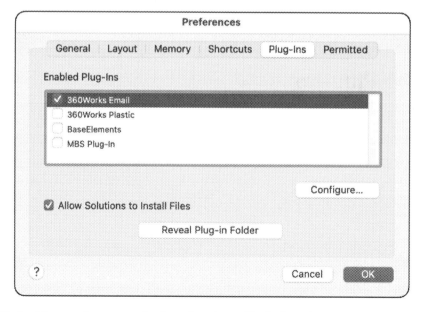

Figure 28-1. *The preference tab showing installed plug-ins*

Accessing Plug-in Functions

Once installed, a plug-in's functions will appear as a new category in either the *Functions* pane of *Specify Calculation* dialogs or the *Steps* pane of the *Script Workspace*. Some plug-ins appear in both lists, as shown in Figure 28-2. From here, plug-in functions can be easily inserted into formulas (Chapter 12) and scripts (Chapter 24) like built-in functions and steps.

Figure 28-2. *Plug-ins appear in the Steps pane of the Script Workspace (back) and/or in the Functions pane of the Specify Calculation window (front)*

Summary

This chapter presented the basic process for finding, installing, and accessing plug-ins. In the next chapter, we explore the options for managing database security.

PART VI

Deploying and Maintaining Solutions

After a database is developed, it's time to secure and deploy it into the workflow. Throughout the entire process from design to development to deployment, there are skills required to maintain healthy files and tools available to help analyze and modify them. These chapters cover the basics of securing, deploying, analyzing, and keeping a solution free of corruption:

CHAPTER 29

Managing Database Security

In the modern age of global network connectivity, news of data breaches, leaked information, and malicious exploitation should make clear the need to secure access to database content. However, database security doesn't end at avoiding unauthorized access by nefarious outsiders. Restrictions on the content authorized users can create, view, modify, and use are equally important. Further, restricting user access to the structural design of a database can help stop careless or malicious alterations to the schema, interface, and script functions. Even minor accidental changes to a formula or script can be catastrophic to a company's workflow and may result in severe financial consequences. Only those with adequate technical skills and competent knowledge of business logistics should be authorized to act as a developer. FileMaker's credentialing features offer an array of choices for how to secure a file and limit who can do what. This chapter explores these features, covering the following topics:

- Exposing default security limits
- Defining user accounts
- Exploring privilege sets
- Managing external file access
- Extending credentials in formulas

© Mark Conway Munro 2024
M. C. Munro, *Learn FileMaker Pro 2024*, https://doi.org/10.1007/979-8-8688-0835-7_29

Exposing Default Security Limits

Every database begins with *default credentials* that are configured to be unobtrusive and allow instant access to the full content and structure of the file. Anyone who can see the file in a directory or shared using peer-to-peer networking can open it without any login dialog and will have full access to everything. This default state is considered "unlocked" although there is a default full access "Admin" account with no password which is auto-entered when the file opens (Chapter 6, "File Options: Open"), so it appears as accessible as any document file. This may be acceptable for a personal database used as a document file on a local computer or opened by small teams on a secure internal network where security isn't a concern. However, in most cases, credentialing is highly recommended to protect sensitive content and structural programming. When hosting a database with FileMaker Server or FileMaker Cloud, it is required.

Caution   When a file is configured to auto-enter a *Full Access* account or if no password is assigned it, FileMaker Server and FileMaker Cloud will refuse to host it.

A database's *account credentials* define who can open a file and what actions their privileges allow. FileMaker's only requirement is that a database has at least two accounts defined: one active full access development account and another guest account that provides read-only access. Every new database is created with both. The "Admin" account with no password assigned is the default full access account. A second account named "[Guest]" allows a user to open the file without entering a username or password but with severely limited privileges. This account cannot be deleted but is disabled by default. When enabled, a *Sign-in As Guest* option appears in the login dialog.

The first step to securing a database is to deselect the auto-entry of the default account. This will present the user with the login dialog and requires them to enter the account name (still without a password). But to create a more secure platform, a password should be assigned to that account, and it should be limited to developers only. Then, additional user accounts and privilege sets should be defined for others.

Defining User Accounts

Credential settings are defined in the *Manage Security* dialog, shown in Figure 29-1. This dialog is opened by selecting the *Manage* ➤ *Security* under the *File* menu.

Figure 29-1. *The dialog used to manage credentials to limit access to a database*

The central list shows the accounts defined in the file for the selected authentication method, defaulting to *FileMaker File or External Server* with the only two default accounts shown. The *Authenticate via* menu toggles the account list by the selected authentication method. FileMaker supports the following account types:

- *FileMaker File* – An account that is stored inside the database file and internally authenticated. These can be used on hosted files but is the only option for local, nonhosted files.

- *External Server* – An account relies on an external user group stored on the host computer or a centrally managed authentication server, such as *Apple Open Directory* or *Windows Active Directory*.

- *Claris ID* – An account that references a FileMaker Cloud user or group name. The FileMaker application must be signed into a cloud account to see this option. This is the only type able to access databases hosted by Claris.

- *Apple ID* – An account that relies on a user signing into their Apple account.

- *Open Authorization* – An account that relies on one of the following providers to handle authentication of a user or group: Amazon, Google, Microsoft Azure, or custom OAuth service.

Adding a Password to the Default Account

To begin securing a database, add a password to the default account. Select the "Admin" account in the list to open the *account settings panel* on the right, shown in Figure 29-2. In this panel, you can edit the *Account Name*, enter a *Description*, and change other settings. To edit the *Password*, click the pencil icon to open a *Set Password* dialog and enter a new password. A password can be any length and may include any characters. However, to ensure compatibility with WebDirect, they should be limited to ASCII characters that don't contain accented or non-Roman characters. They are case-sensitive, so be aware of Shift-lock. The entry dialog provides a *password quality rating* that ranges from "weak" to "moderate" to "strong."

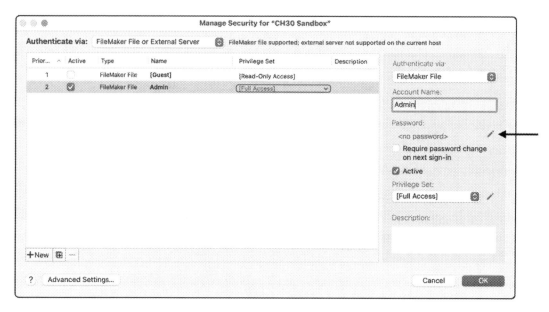

Figure 29-2. *The settings panel for a selected account, showing the change password button*

When closing the *Manage Security* dialog after entering a new password, FileMaker will present a *Verify Access* dialog to ensure that you know an account name and password that has full access privileges. This helps to ensure that you don't lose access to the file. Be sure to write down the password you enter so that you don't forget it! The next time the database file is opened, a sign-in dialog will prompt entry of credentials. The *Account Name* will default to the computer's name and doesn't necessarily indicate an acceptable account for access. Enter the credentials and click *Sign In* to regain access.

Note   Use the "Admin" account to open the "Chapter 29 Sandbox" file with "Password" as the password.

Creating a FileMaker File Account

A *FileMaker File* account defines sign-in credentials and privileges for a user that will be stored internally and can be used to access the file even when not hosted on a server. To begin, open the *Manage Security* dialog and follow the steps shown in Figure 29-3.

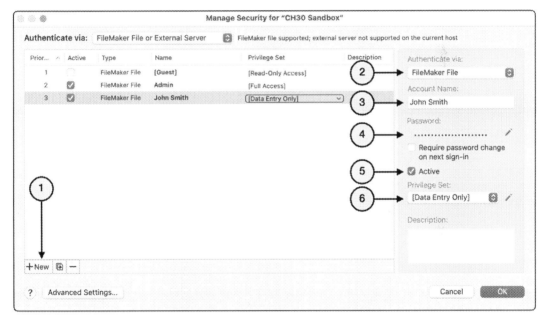

Figure 29-3. *The process for configuring an internal account*

1. Click the *New* button to add a new account to the list. The account will be selected and ready to configure in the panel.

2. Confirm that the authentication option is *FileMaker File*.

3. Enter an account name, for example, "John Smith."

4. Click the pencil icon to enter a password. To force a user to change their password to something private, check the *Require password change on next sign-in* box.

5. Make sure the *Active* checkbox is selected. The credentials will not work if unchecked.

6. Select a *Privilege Set* to determine the permissions granted to the user (discussed later in this chapter).

Close the Manage Security dialog and the database. Then, sign in under the new account to experience the database as a user with reduced privileges.

Using External Authentication

When a database is hosted on a FileMaker Server, both the database and the server can be configured for *external authentication*. An *External Server* account is defined in the database with the name of a user account group managed externally on the host computer or a centrally managed authentication server, such as *Apple Open Directory* or *Windows Active Directory*. When a user enters credentials that don't match a *FileMaker File* account, the following sequence occurs:

- The host FileMaker Server sends the credentials to the external authentication server.

- If authenticated, a list of the user's assigned group names is returned to FileMaker Server.

- The first group with the same name as an *External Server* account in the database determines their account entry and privileges.

So, the user must have a valid account on the external server, assigned to a user group which matches an account in the database. For example, assume three FileMaker databases, each configured with an *External Server* account named "FMP_Staff" and hosted on a FileMaker server. When an employee named "Harold Jones" is hired, the IT department adds a user record for him on their authentication server with a password of "THX1138" and assigns him to a user group named "FMP_Staff" which has six other employees as members. Now, without any modification to the three FileMaker databases and without any account inside them in his name or password, Harold can enter his credentials to gain access to each of them under the privilege set assigned to the "FMP_Staff" account. If Harold's employment is later terminated, IT can simply disable his active directory account, and he loses access to all three FileMaker databases and any other systems associated with that account.

> **Caution**   External authentication only works when a database is hosted by a FileMaker Server. You must retain at least one full access *FileMaker File* account for offline use.

Creating an External Server Account

To create a new *External Server* account, open the *Manage Security* dialog, and follow the steps shown in Figure 29-4.

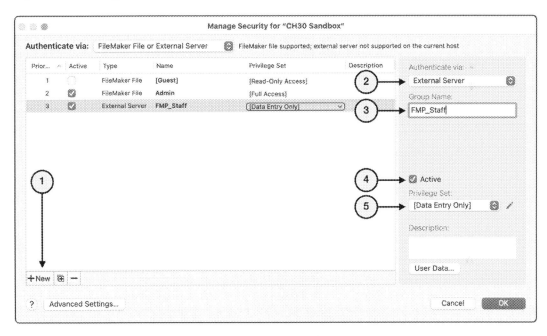

Figure 29-4. *The process for configuring an external account*

1. Click the *New* button to add a new account to the list.

2. Select *External Server* as the authentication method.

3. Enter a *Group Name* that is defined on the authentication server, remembering that these are case-sensitive.

4. Make sure the *Active* checkbox is selected. The credentials will not work if unchecked.

5. Select a *Privilege Set* to determine the permissions granted to any user who signs in as a member of that group.

Creating a User and Group (macOS)

Every user that will access the database using external authentication must have a user account on the host computer (or authentication server) that is a member of a group defined in the database. To begin, create a group following these steps:

1. Open *System Settings* and select the "Users & Groups" section.

2. Click the *Add Group* button.

3. Enter your computer admin credentials to make the change.

4. Enter a name for the group, for example, "FMP_Staff."

5. Click the *Create Group* button.

6. Open the group info panel.

7. Activate users to make them members of the group.

Tip   On macOS, user accounts can be created as *Sharing Only* to avoid creating unnecessary directories and resources.

Enabling FileMaker Server External Authentication

Users can only log in using an external account when the database is hosted on a FileMaker Server configured to allow authentication from external accounts. To confirm this for FileMaker Server 2024 (21), follow these steps:

1. Open and sign into the *Admin Console* (Chapter 32).

2. Click the *Administration* tab along the top.

3. Click on *External Authentication* in the sidebar.

4. Under the *Database Sign In* heading, enable *External Server Accounts*.

Exploring Privilege Sets

A *privilege set* is a collection of permissions defining a level of access to data, layout, and other features. Once defined, a privilege set can be assigned to one or more user accounts to establish their abilities within the database. To view, create, and edit privilege sets, open the *Manage Security* dialog, and click the *Advanced Settings* button. This will open an *Advanced Security Settings* dialog, shown in Figure 29-5. Click the *Privilege Sets* tab to view the list of defined sets.

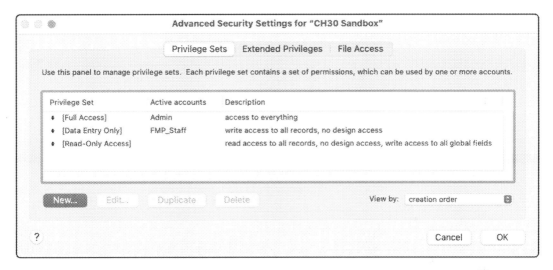

Figure 29-5. *The dialog used to define sets of access privileges for user accounts*

Using Default Privilege Sets

Every database will have three default privilege sets, each of these has a square bracket around their names. These are non-editable except for the ability to enable and disable extended privileges.

- *Full Access* – Allows unrestricted access to every available feature and all content. This should be reserved for developers only. FileMaker requires at least one account that uses this set.

- *Data Entry Only* – Provides limited access for data entry work. Users can create, edit, and delete records in every table. They can use but not structurally alter layouts, scripts, and value lists. They can print and export. They are automatically disconnected from a server when idle, and they can change their own account password.

- *Read-only access* – Similar to the preceding but more restricted with no access to modify content or structure in any way.

If these defaults do not provide adequate levels for a project, create custom sets for more control.

Creating Custom Privilege Sets

To create a new privilege set, open the *Advanced Security Settings* dialog, click on *Privilege Sets* tab, and click the *New* button. This will open a new empty set in the *Edit Privilege Set* dialog, shown in Figure 29-6. By default, a new set allows almost no access.

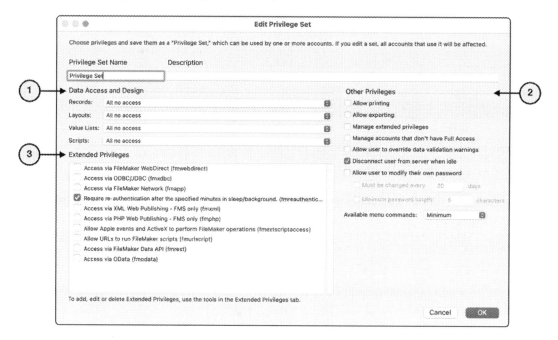

Figure 29-6. *The dialog used to edit permissions for a privilege set*

Enter a name and optional description at the top. Then begin enabling the desired permissions which are grouped into three categories:

1. *Data access and design* – Allows access by resource type

2. *Other privilege* – A mixture of miscellaneous features

3. *Extended privileges* – Enables specific capabilities with ten default options that can be expanded

---

Caution   A custom privilege set cannot grant developer access to modify the structural schema (table, fields, and relationships). Only the default, non-editable *Full Access* set allows these.

Configuring Data Access and Design Settings

The first set of privilege settings control data access and design permissions. These govern the actions users can perform by resource type: *Records, Layouts, Value Lists*, and *Scripts*. Each has a menu of options that control access to all entities within its class, plus an option to assign custom privileges to individual objects.

Controlling Record Access

The *Records* pop-up menu of the *Edit Privilege Set* dialog offers five options that control what users can do with records:

- *Create, edit, and delete in all tables.*

- *Create and edit in all tables.*

- *View only in all tables.*

- *All no access.*

- *Custom privileges.*

The first four are self-descriptive and apply to records in every table. If the privilege set does not require granular control for individual objects, select one of these. Alternatively, to configure specific objects, select the *Custom Privileges* option to open the *Custom Record Privileges* dialog, shown in Figure 29-7. Every table in the database is listed here with an extra row at the bottom that defines default privilege settings for any new table that is created in the future. Below the list are five pop-up menus for specifying the *View*, *Edit*, *Create*, *Delete*, and *Field Access* permissions for the selected table(s) in the list above.

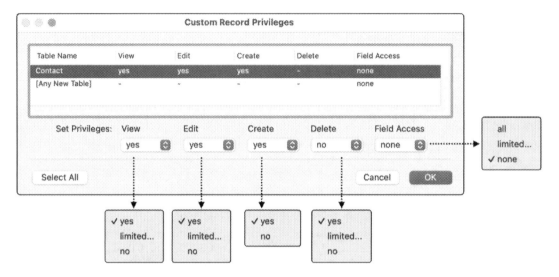

Figure 29-7. *The dialog used to control permissions for record access per table*

Note   See the "Chapter 29-01 Record Access" example file.

The settings available across all five pop-up menus are similar with only a few minor differences. The first four have a "yes" and "no" option that does the same thing: enable or disable the function for the selected table. For example, to allow creation of records in the selected table(s), select "yes" under the *Create* menu. Three of these four also have a "limited" option that opens a *Specify Calculation* dialog, so a formula can provide more finely tuned control over access to the function. For example, a formula can allow deletion of a record only when a field has a certain value or on a certain day of the week. The *Edit* menu is disabled when the *View* option is set to not allow access, since you can't grant permission to edit something that the user can't view.

The *Field Access* menu options are slightly different than the other four. Although they perform similar functionality, they are named to relate to fields instead of functions. Choose "all" to allow editing access to all fields and "none" to restrict access. Select "limited" to open a *Custom Field Privileges* dialog, shown in Figure 29-8. This dialog allows each field to have a setting of either *modifiable, view only,* or *no access.* It also includes an option that defines default settings for any new fields added to the table in the future.

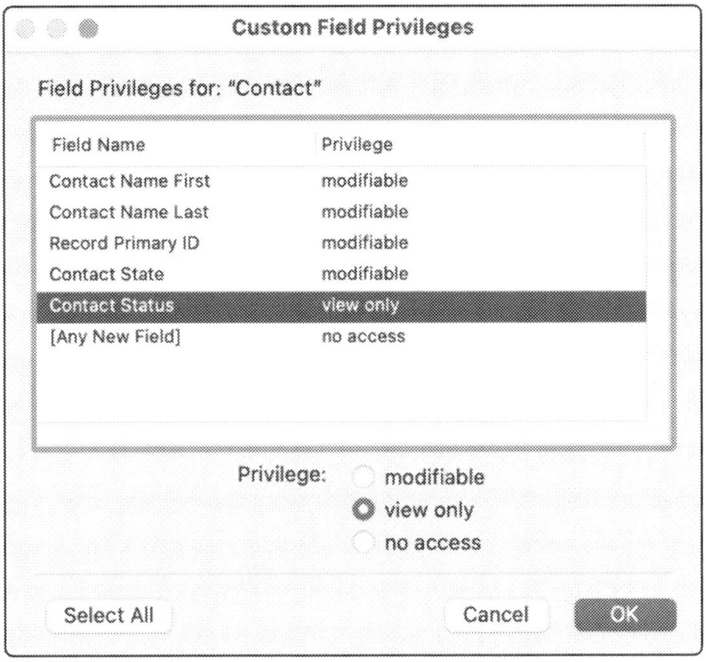

Figure 29-8. *The dialog used to control the privileges of individual fields for a table*

Controlling Layout Access

The *Layouts* pop-up menu of the *Edit Privilege Set* dialog offers four options that control what a user can do with layouts:

- *All modifiable*

- *All view only*

- *All no access*

- *Custom privileges*

Caution   If a user can't view a layout, neither can a script that runs during their session, unless it is configured to run with full access.

Like the options for Records, the first three options above apply to all layouts in the file. To enable or disable individual layouts, choose the *Custom Privileges* option to open the *Custom Layout Privileges* dialog, shown in Figure 29-9.

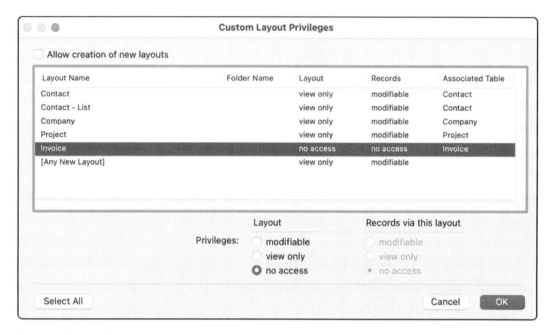

Figure 29-9. *The dialog used to control permissions by layout*

Enable the *Allow creation of new layouts* checkbox at the top corner to allow users to create new layouts. Every layout in the database is listed with an option at the bottom that defines the default privilege settings for any new layout that is created in the future. Below the list are two sets of privilege options for the selected layout(s). The *Layout* options offer three levels of permission for the selected table(s):

- *Modifiable – Enter Layout mode and design layouts.*

- *View only – View and interact with layouts in Browse mode without any design options.*

- *No access – No access to view, interact or edit layouts.*

The *Records via this layout* radio buttons control the permission for record interactions when a layout is viewable or modifiable. This allows you to grant layout-by-layout control over field interactions beyond the previously discussed record settings that apply to every layout.

Note   See the "Chapter 29-02 Layout Access" example file.

Controlling Value List Access

The *Value List* pop-up menu of the *Edit Privilege Set* dialog offers four options that control what users can do with value lists. These work like the settings for layout access.

- *All modifiable*
- *All view only*
- *All no access*
- *Custom privileges*

Controlling Script Access

The *Scripts* pop-up menu of the *Edit Privilege Set* dialog offers four options that control what users can do with scripts. These work like the settings for layout access.

- *All modifiable*
- *All executable only*
- *All no access*
- *Custom privileges*

Enabling Other Privilege Settings

On the right side of the *Edit Privilege Set* dialog are *Other Privileges*, seen previously in Figure 29-6. The functionality enabled by most of these features should be fairly obvious by their phrasing. However, a few are worth mentioning.

The *Allow exporting* option enables a variety of data output functions including exporting records, saving records as an Excel file, copying all records in the found set, and saving a copy of records. It also controls the ability of external scripts to access and extract record information. For example, AppleScript on macOS will not be able to get field values if this setting is disabled.

When the *Allow user to override data validation warnings* option is enabled, users will have the option to override any field validation warning dialog, including those that are not explicitly defined to allow it (Chapter 8, "Field Options: Validation").

The *Allow user to modify their own password* enables the *File ➤ Change Password* menu item. The adjacent checkboxes allow scheduling of a forced password change at regular intervals and control a minimum length for any new passwords they select.

The selection from the *Available menu commands* pop-up menu controls the menus available. While access to menus can be influenced by other permissions granted to the privilege set and by the presence of custom menus (Chapter 23), this option specifies a blanket category of commands they can access. Choose "All" to grant access to the entire active menu bar. Limit them to basic editing functions by choosing "Editing Only." Select "Minimum" to severely restrict them to menus for only the most basic functions such as open, close, and create database files, window functions, perform scripts, preferences, and help.

Caution   The menu setting for new privilege sets defaults to minimal which provides almost no enabled functions! Be sure to change this when creating new accounts.

Enabling Extended Privileges

An *extended privilege* is a keyword-based permission setting that can be assigned to one or more privilege sets. These enable access to one specific type of functionality. FileMaker includes several extended privileges that are fixed to specific functions, mostly various types of inbound networking and scripting access. The *Extended Privileges* section of the *Edit Privilege Set* dialog seen previously in Figure 29-6 includes a list of additional privileges that can be enabled or disabled as needed.

Some extended privileges grant the ability of users to sign in via specific methods.

- *fmwebdirect* – Allows access to a server-hosted database from a web browser

- *fmapp* – Allows access to the file from the FileMaker Pro and FileMaker Go apps

Others provide protocol-specific access to a server-hosted database by external systems. These also assume network sharing and/or server configuration for these specific services.

- *fmxdbc* – Allows incoming access with ODBC/JDBC

- *fmxml* – Allows XML web publishing access

- *fmphp* – Allows PHP web publishing access

- *fmrest* – Allows access from a *Representational State Transfer* (RESTful) web service via the *FileMaker Data API*

Two others provide scripted access.

- *fmextscriptaccess* – Allows access with AppleScript (macOS) and ActiveX (Windows)

- *fmurlscript* – Allows triggering a database script from a URL (Chapter 33, "Accessing a Database with FileMaker URL")

All these default extended privileges can be enabled or disabled for each account. Custom extended privileges can be defined to control custom features in your database (discussed later in this chapter).

Managing External File Access

Using *Data Sources*, any database can seamlessly access resources in other files (Chapter 9, "Managing Data Sources"). Tables from one data source can be added to the relationship graph in another and become the context of layouts or the data source of portals. Records from that table can be created, edited, and deleted in the source file. Scripts can be performed, value lists shared. Creating a multi-file solution is as easy as adding one file as the data source in another and having the correct credentials. Although not necessarily applicable to most solutions, this ease of use creates a potential security risk for more sensitive data storage.

FileMaker defaults to a middle ground between ease of use and security. For a database to access resources in another, credentials authorizing a full access privilege set are the only requirement. To modify this level of security, open the *File Access* tab of the *Advanced Security Settings* dialog, shown in Figure 29-10.

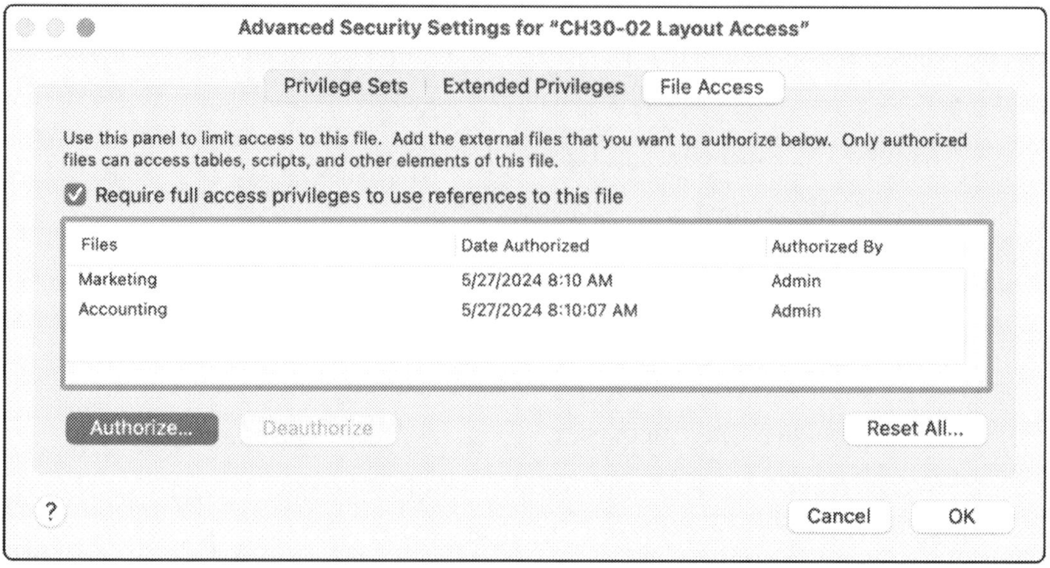

Figure 29-10. *The File Access tab authorizes external file access to the current database*

To accommodate totally unrestricted external access to this database, uncheck the *Require full access privileges* checkbox. Once done, all restrictions are removed, and any FileMaker database can access resources without entering credentials. This removal of all restrictions is not recommended even for files that require a minimum level of protection.

To tighten the restrictions, leave the box checked and use this interface to explicitly authorize which file(s) can access resources in the current database. If any files are listed, those are the only files able to access resources unless further authorizations are performed.

Click *Authorize* to add files that are not currently open and accessing resources. This adds the file to the list but also assigns it a unique ID so that it can't be switched with another file of the same name at the same location and bypass the authorization process. To remove authorization for a file, select it and click *Deauthorize*.

The *Reset All* button reassigns IDs for the files listed and requires them to be reauthorized. Use this to ensure unique identifiers if a duplicate or clone of a file should be granted access along with the original.

Extending Credentials in Formulas

The security options are adequate for limiting access to the file and various built-in capabilities. They even extended down into custom structural elements, permitting granular control over fields, layouts, value lists, and scripts. However, that reach is limited and can't extended deeper. By the nature of a custom application design tool, it is impractical for the credentialing interface to offer control of individual custom layout objects, conditional formula statements, custom menu visibility, and more. For example, a privilege set can control a layout's view-ability but has no options to limit access to the various individual objects it contains. Similarly, a set can limit a script to certain users but has no option to control individual steps within it. Although it can't reach further down into custom resources, a formula can access credential information and exert more detailed customization and restrictions. There is some risk of doing this, but those can be abated with another feature: *custom extended privileges*. Let's review the various options to use credentials in formulas and weigh the pros and cons of each.

Accessing Credentials from Formulas

Three built-in functions can identify the user's account name, privilege set, and, when using an external authentication method, account group. These can be used in any formula.

```
Get ( AccountName )                  // result = Harold Jones
Get ( AccountPrivilegeSetName )      // result = [Data Entry Only]
Get ( AccountGroupName )             // result = FMP_Staff
```

Limiting Access to Features by Account Name

To limit a feature to individual users by account name, use the built-in function and specify the account(s) who should or should not have access. For example, to hide a layout object from Harold Jones and Rashida Fields, use the formula below as the object's *Hide objects when* setting (Chapter 21, "Hiding Objects").

```
Get ( AccountName ) = "Harold Jones" or
Get ( AccountName ) = "Rashida Fields"
```

If, instead, an object should be hidden from everyone except Harold and Rashida, simply change from equals to not equals and change "or" to "and," as shown below.

```
Get ( AccountName ) ≠ "Harold Jones" and
Get ( AccountName ) ≠ "Rashida Fields"
```

This technique can be used anywhere a formula is accepted. A script can use an *If* statement to conditionally limit the execution of a group of individual steps for a specific user. For example, if an invoice report script is executable by many users but has a section that generates a sensitive financial report that should only execute when the script is run by the Chief Financial Officer, the account name can be used to determine if the steps should execute or not. Below, four steps are conditional and will only execute if the current user is Rashida.

```
If [ Get ( AccountName ) = "Rashida Fields" ]
    Go to Layout [ "Invoice - Special Report" ; Animation: None ]
    Sort Records [ Restore ; With dialog: Off ]
    Print [ With dialog: On ]
    Go to Layout [ Original Layout ; Animation: None ]
End if
```

This technique provides a simple way to limit a feature by account name but is not ideal since the names used as literal text will not dynamically update when accounts are changed. Extensive use of names in calculations creates a potential nightmare. Any change to the company workforce may require changes to employee names used in dozens, hundreds, or thousands of different formulas. Even something as simple as a coworker marrying and changing her last name can require a lot of work in a complex database. In a large organization with high turnover, locating and changing all uses of a username in formulas could become a full-time job. Embedding literal names in formulas isn't a good practice.

Caution   Account names used in formulas do not update when credentials change! Avoid excessive use of this technique.

Limiting Access to Features by Account Privilege Set

Instead of using account names in formulas to limit access to key features, consider using a privilege set name. This avoids having to change formulas when new accounts are added, renamed, or deleted. As the accounts assigned to a privilege set change, the formulas continue working. For example, if Harold Jones and Rashida Fields both work in the accounting department, their accounts can be assigned an "Accounting" privilege set. Then, our previous example for hiding layout objects can be changed to the formula below.

```
Get ( AccountPrivilegeSetName ) = "Accounting"
```

Similarly, our script's conditional steps can be limited by department rather than account name.

```
If [ Get ( AccountPrivilegeSetName ) = "Accounting" ]
   Go to Layout [ "Invoice - Special Report" ; Animation: None ]
   Sort Records [ Restore ; With dialog: Off ]
   Print [ With dialog: On ]
   Go to Layout [ Original Layout ; Animation: None ]
End if
```

Since neither of their names are included in the formula, a name change, promotion, expansion of the accounting department, or termination won't require a change to these or any other formulas using the privilege set. User accounts can be shuffled, renamed, or deleted, and the formulas keep working. If Rashida is promoted and her account assigned to the "Marketing" privilege set, the steps shown above no longer execute when she runs the script. If Linda Camacho is hired and added to the "Accounting" set, she immediately has access to those steps, objects, and other conditional formula-controlled features using that set.

The conditional features can be as complex as required. Another script may control which layout a user navigates too based on their department. The script below uses a sequence of *If* and *Else If* script steps to target a department-specific home menu layout. First, it places the privilege set name for the current user into a *$set* variable. Then it uses this to determine which *Go to Layout* step should be performed, each targeting a different layout.

```
Set Variable [ $set ; Value: Get ( AccountPrivilegeSet ) ]
If [ $set = "human resources" ]
   Go to Layout [ "Home HR" ; Animation: None ]
Else If [ [ $set = "sales" ]
   Go to Layout [ "Home Sales" ; Animation: None ]
Else If [ [ $set = "production" ]
   Go to Layout [ "Home Production" ; Animation: None ]
End if
```

This approach is far better than using account names but still has risks. First, the privilege set name is used as literal text in formulas and won't update if that name changes in the future. That risk can be avoided by carefully planning names and never changing them. However, that's not always possible and it's not the only risk.

Caution   Using privilege set names in formulas may have similar risks as account names! At least consider the option to use a *custom extended privilege* where appropriate.

Another problem is that roles and responsibilities may shift within a company workflow. If this happens, the tasks assigned to different privilege sets might need to be shuffled around which creates the same problem we saw when using account names. Also, since each user can be assigned only a single privilege set, it may be difficult to figure out how many sets to create to properly group large groups of functional conditions. You can end up in a situation where each set is used by only one person, defeating the purpose of using sets instead of accounts.

Using credentials in formulas does extend the ability of security settings beyond the *Manage Security* dialog and can have valid uses. But excessive use in a complex database used by a growing company can prove to be labor-intensive to maintain. What may begin as simple ad hoc exceptions added to a few dozen formulas for one user or group can quickly grow and eventually burden a developer with the chore of keeping track hundreds or thousands of credential exceptions lost and forgotten in the dark corners of a crowded interface design. Fortunately, FileMaker has an amazing capability that can solve this problem: *custom extended privileges*.

Leveraging Custom Extended Privileges

A *custom extended privilege* is a developer-named, keyword-based "feature permission" that can be named in formulas to create conditional features while being dynamically assignable to users through privilege sets. This eliminates the need to use account and privilege set names in formulas by conceptually reversing the interaction between the credentialing system and formula conditions. Rather than extending credential information "down" into formulas, a custom extended privilege can be thought of as extending a custom feature name used in formulas "up" into the credentialing system. Once created, the permission can be easily enabled and disabled in one or more privilege sets, making them adaptable to future changes to a company's personnel.

Note   See the "CH29-03 Custom Extended Privilege" example file.

Creating a Custom Extended Privilege

Open the *Manage Security* dialog, click the *Advanced Settings* button, and then select the *Extended Privileges* tab, shown in Figure 29-11. This lists all built-in and custom extended privileges defined in the file. From here you can create, edit, and delete extended privileges, including built-in choices.

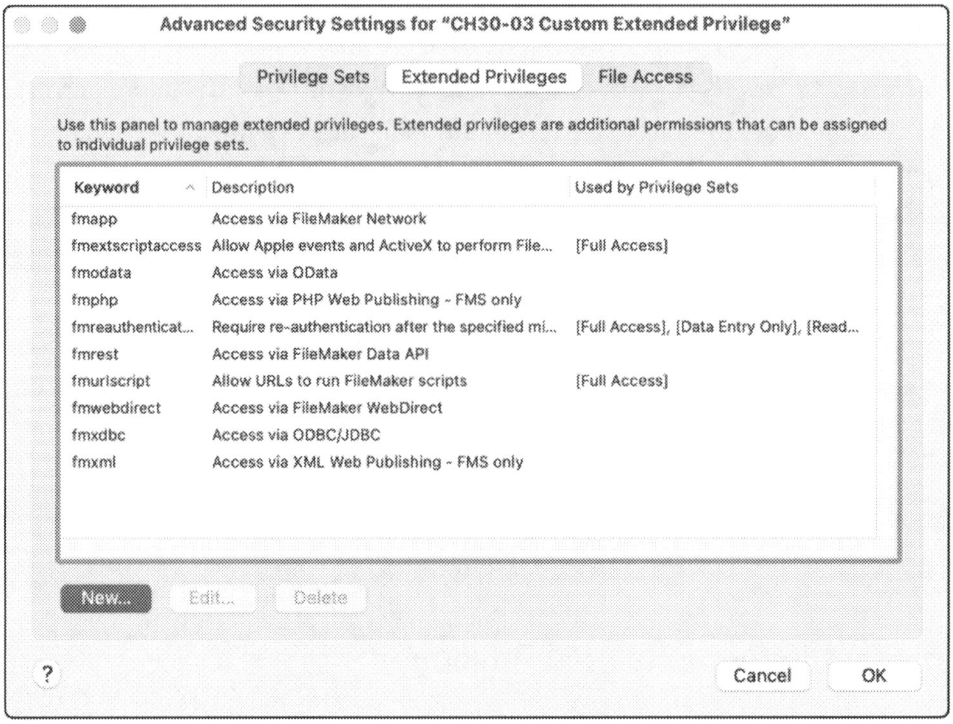

Figure 29-11. *The interface for managing extended privilege*

To create a new extended privilege, start by identifying a set of features and/ or objects that you want to make conditional based on a user's privilege set. For the sake of simple illustration, let's create one that controls a user's ability to approve an *Invoice* record by clicking a button on a layout. The button will need to be conditionally hidden, so unauthorized users can't see or click it. To begin, choose a name for the new privilege. The name should be a short keyword made up of two or more words that is unique and clearly indicates the function(s) it will control. For this example, a name like "InvoiceApproval" will describe the capability we are defining in our example.

Once a keyword is chosen, click the *New* button to create a new extended privilege, and open it in an *Edit Extended Privilege* dialog, shown in Figure 29-12. Type the name of the custom privilege in the *Keyword* field and enter a *Description*. The *Access* list shows all privilege sets with a checkbox indicating those with permission to access this custom privilege. For this example, only a full access developer will have the ability to see the button.

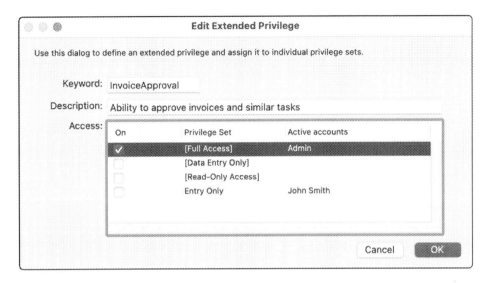

Figure 29-12. *The dialog used to create and edit custom extended privileges*

Assigning a Custom Extended Privilege to a Set

After closing the *Edit Extended Privilege* dialog, the custom privilege will be accessible from any privilege set as a checkbox in the list of extended privileges, as shown in Figure 29-13. It can also be enabled or disabled for the privilege set from here.

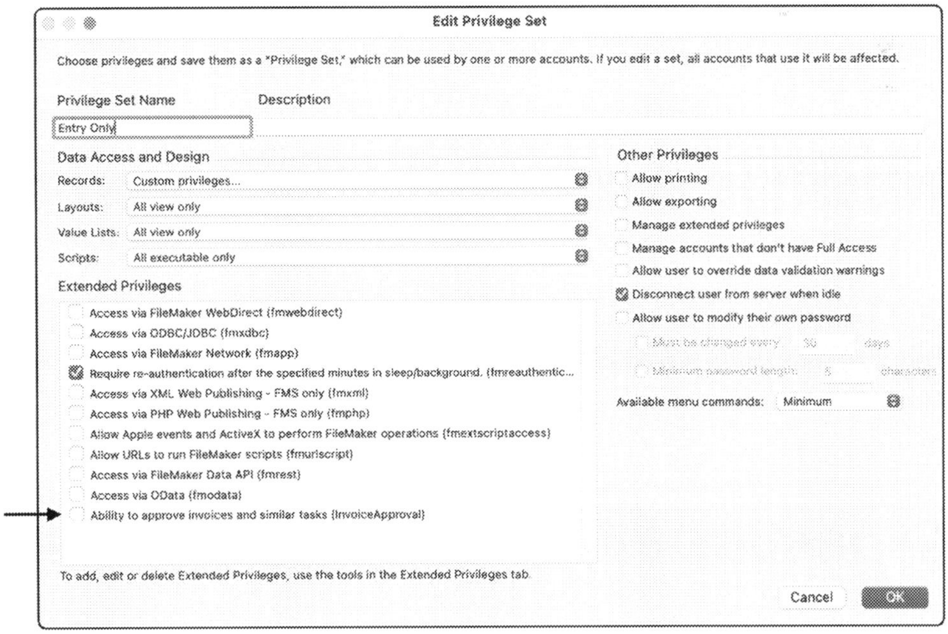

Figure 29-13. *The new extended privilege enabled on a privilege set*

Limiting Access to Features with a Custom Extended Privilege

Once configured, the "InvoiceApproval" extended privilege can be used in any formula to manage a conditional feature. In our example, the following will be used as the *Hide object when* formula to hide it when the user's privilege set does not have the privilege enabled.

```
FilterValues ( Get ( AccountExtendedPrivileges ) ; "InvoiceApproval" ) = ""
```

The *Get (AccountExtendedPrivileges)* function returns a list of the names of all enabled extended privileges for the current account's assigned privilege set. Then it checks that the list includes "InvoiceApproval" using the *FilterValues* function (Chapter 13, "Manipulating Values"). If not, the formula returns true (1) causing the button to hide.

Summary

This chapter explored the credential options for securing a database. In the next chapter, we will explore the developer tools for analyzing and modifying files.

CHAPTER 30

Using Developer Tools

In addition to the *Script Debugging* (Chapter 26) and *Custom Menus* (Chapter 23), the Tools menu includes a few additional features. This chapter explores these remaining tools, covering the following topics:

- Saving a database as XML

- Generating a database design report

- Exploring developer utilities

- Accessing the Tools Marketplace

- Creating a custom add-on

Save a Database as XML

The *Save a Copy as XML* feature exports a representation of the current database file as an XML file. The file includes most of the raw structural details about the file's schema, layouts, scripts, and more, but does not include any record content. These files can be used for a variety of uses such as the following:

- Store a schematic of a database for documentation purposes.

- Compare versions of a database to generate a change log.

- Identify the user account and timestamp of various resources.

- Extract lists of and details about structural resources.

- Review structural elements while troubleshooting issues.

The export can be initiated by selecting the *Save a Copy as XML* item from the *Tools* menu or running a script that uses step of the same name. The step can be executed only by users with full access and has two parameters. Click the *Window name* to open a

M. C. Munro, *Learn FileMaker Pro 2024*, https://doi.org/10.1007/979-8-8688-0835-7_30

Specify Calculation dialog, and enter or generate the name of the window of an open file. Click the *Destination file* to open a *Specify File* dialog, and enter a name or file path in which to save the XML file. Both must be configured, or the step will fail with an error.

```
Save a Copy as XML [ Window name: "Sandbox" ; Destination file: "db.xml" ]
```

The XML file is not easily human-readable, as shown in Figure 30-1. However, its structural format is ideal for detailed technical analysis or running through an XML analysis software. The format may change over time in future versions as the FileMaker format evolves, so any comparisons should be performed on two files generated from the same version. For more technical detail, use *Save a Copy as XML*. For a more readable report on a database structure, use a design report.

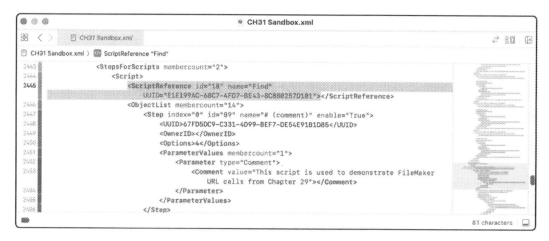

Figure 30-1. *A glimpse of an XML file detailing a script's structure*

Caution   The XML file generated will reveal sensitive details about the database. Keep it safe to avoid unauthorized access!

Generating a Database Design Report

A *database design report* (DDR) is a detailed report of a database file structure, listing every table in the database with optional information about other resources. These reports can be saved as a HTML or XML file and can be used to perform the following development tasks:

- Troubleshoot structural problems by locating missing references, broken relationships, and more.

- Find obsolete elements to help maintain a clean structure.

- Locate interface elements still pointing to an old script or custom functions.

- Glimpse statistics about component counts and usage.

- Save a structural snapshot of a database at a certain point in time, which can be compared to a later structure to identify changes.

- View in a web browser or import into a DDR analysis tool.

Generating a Design Report

To generate a design report, open a database and select the *Tools* ➤ *Database Design Report* menu. This will open the *Database Design Report* dialog, shown in Figure 30-2.

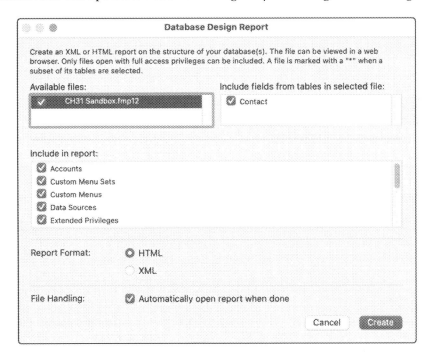

Figure 30-2. *The dialog used to create a database design report*

The following three areas of the dialog allow selection of which information to include in the report:

- *Available files* – Select from one or more open database files.

- *Include fields from tables* – Select one or more tables from the currently selected file.

- *Include in report* – Select which resources from this scrolling list.

The *Report Format* option at the bottom controls the file format of report to be generated. Use HTML to easily read report and XML if importing into an analysis software tool. Then, click *Create* to choose a save location and generate the report.

Exploring an HTML Design Report

A design report saved in the HTML format will produce a collection of web pages, as shown in Figure 30-3.

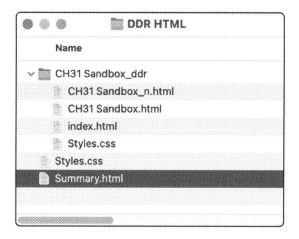

Figure 30-3. *The results of a design report saved as HTML*

The *Summary.html* contains a navigable overview of each included database with a columnar summary of objects. The *Styles.css* files contain style information for these reports, one for the summary and one for pages inside of each database folder. Each database included in the report will be represented by a folder, in this case only a single folder for the *CH30 Sandbox* database. Inside each database folder, an *Index.html* page contains a complex table structure with navigable sidebar detailing every object and lots of detailed information about them. This can be opened directly or through the summary page. The other two html files contain sidebar navigation and body panels that are displayed in the index file. To view the report, open either the *Summary.html* or *index.html* file. The details include hyperlinks and are searchable.

Exploring an XML Design Report

A design report saved in the XML format will produce two files, as shown in Figure 30-4.

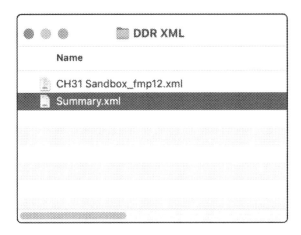

Figure 30-4. *The results of a design report saved as XML*

The *Summary.xml* file contains a summary of each included files showing a count of resources like the HTML style report. A detail file for each database is included with structural details like the results produced by the *Save a Copy as XML* function.

Introducing Professional DDR Tools

Several companies offer products that import an XML design report and present the material in an easier to read interface that is more functional than the HTML pages provided by FileMaker. Developers who build complex databases that require a lot of analysis will appreciate the improved viewing experience of these products. Some of the most popular include the following:

- *BaseElements* – `www.baseelements.com`
- *FM Perception* – `www.fmperception.com`
- *InspectorPro* – `www.beezwax.net`

Exploring Developer Utilities

FileMaker includes a set of utilities that can perform the following processes on a batch of files like renaming, removing admin access, enabling kiosk mode, adding extensions, and encryption functions. To explore these features, select *Developer Utilities* from the *Tools* menu to open a window of the same name, as shown in Figure 30-5.

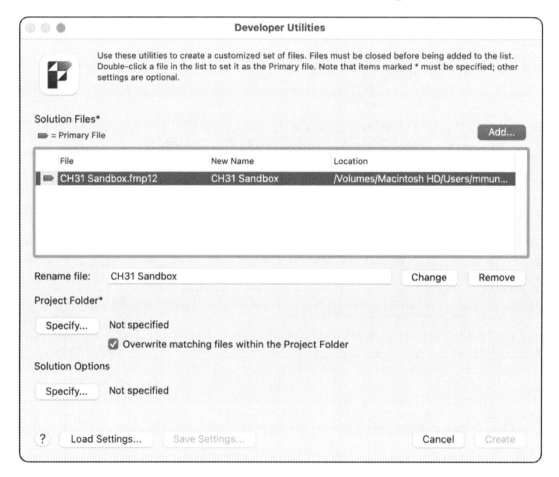

Figure 30-5. *The dialog containing various developer utility functions*

Once the dialog is open, click the *Add* button to place one or more closed files into the *Solution Files* list. These will be batch-manipulated by the options selected below. Within the list, a red arrow designates one file as "primary" which is used by the *Kiosk* option to denote which database contains the starting "home" interface. Below the list are controls for renaming files, selecting an output folder where modified files will be saved, and configuring optional actions to be performed.

Renaming Files

The *Rename file* option is the recommended method for renaming databases that are part of a multi-file solution since it will not only change the file but also update all external file references to it within all other files in the list. To request a name change, select a file above and type a new name in the text area provided. The name should be entered without an extension. Once entered, click the *Change* button to save the rename request. The modified name will be queued into the *New Name* column of the file list. These will not take effect until a *Project Folder* is specified for outputting the renamed files and the *Create* button is clicked.

Tip   Name changes can be performed with one or more solution options configured in the interface.

Specifying a Project Folder

The utility dialog always creates modified copies of the files into a specified *Project Folder*. Before you can rename files or perform other solution options, click the *Specify* button and select a folder for this output. Check the box to automatically overwrite any files with the same name that exists in the selected folder.

Caution   Always use an empty folder so the modified files don't replace originals in case of a mistake or if something goes wrong!

Specifying Solution Options

This *Specify* button under *Solution Options* opens a *Specify Solution Options* dialog containing a list of the following utility functions that can alter the structure of the files:

- Remove admin access from files permanently.

- Enable kiosk mode for non-admin accounts.

- Databases must have a FileMaker file extension.

- Create error log for any processing errors.

- Enable database encryption (or re-encrypt files).

- Remove database encryption.

One or more of these can be selected and configured for inclusion in the batch process to be performed. After selecting the desired options, click *OK* to close the *Specify Solution Options* dialog to return to the *Developer Utilities* dialog.

Removing Admin Access from Files

Select the *Remove admin access from files permanently* checkbox to save copies of the files with all admin access removed from every user account and most design and structural elements rendered read-only. This essentially prevents anyone from acting as a developer within the file while allowing normal data entry and other uses to continue unabated. While this can be a useful method to secure a file for sale as a product or distribution as a demo, it should be used with caution and while retaining a safe unmodified backup file. After completion, there will be no way to modify tables, fields, relationships, or scripts.

Caution   The removal of admin access is irreversible! Always maintain redundant backups of your files.

Enabling Kiosk Mode

The *Enable Kiosk mode for non-admin accounts* option will force the files to open in full screen mode with no menu bar available for all non-admin users. As its name implies, this is a great option for creating touch kiosks where you don't want to allow users access to anything except the interface controls you make accessible on layouts. The database must have at least one non-admin user account defined, which must be used to open in kiosk mode. Once in kiosk mode, a user's only ability to navigate within the file or to close the file will be through the controls you provide on layouts. There will be no menu bar, and even access to operating system functions such as force quit or toggle applications will be completely disabled. You must add a button somewhere to allow the database to be closed. However, be sure to include some sort of authentication process to exclude regular users from quitting the solution and accessing the underlying operating system.

Caution   If you don't provide a button on the layout that will quit the application or close the database, the *only* option will be to perform a hard restart of the computer that may lead to file damage.

Requiring a FileMaker File Extension

Select the *Databases must have a FileMaker file extension* option to automatically add a missing file extension to any file during the process.

Creating an Error Log of Errors

Select the *Create Error log for any processing errors* option to generate a log file of any errors occurring while processing other utility functions. This is optional with any other function but is required when using encryption options and will be selected by default. Once selected, click the *Specify* button to specify a name and location other than the default which is "Logfile.txt" in the Project Folder.

Exploring Encryption Features

FileMaker includes several encryption features throughout the development environment that can be employed to protect data. Container fields using managed external storage (Chapter 10) can be configured to use *Secure storage* which automatically encrypts stored files. Various built-in functions provide *Base64* and *Crypt* options for encoding/decoding and encrypting/decrypting data that is stored in fields or exchanged with other systems. SSL Encryption certificates installed on a host computer protect data when in transit between client and server; these are encouraged by FileMaker Server and required by FileMaker Cloud.

In addition to those features, the *Developer Utilities* dialog includes two options for encrypting and decrypting files. The first of these employs *encryption at rest* protection of the entire database file by adding a layer of protection beyond the standard credentialing for normal access. An encrypted database is structurally modified to protect it from unauthorized access, tampering, or analysis while stored on disk, for example, if someone acquires a stolen backup or archive copy of the database. This is the opposite of *encryption in transit* provided by SSL certificates to protect data being transferred between a host and client.

Enabling Database Encryption (or Re-encrypt Files)

The *Enable Database Encryption* option will structurally alter the files encrypting them with a password you define. Once completed, this key must be entered when interacting with the file in a directory. This happens when

- Opening a file from a local directory, the key must be entered in addition to standard credentials.

- Opening and sharing a file on a FileMaker host computer, the key must be entered.

Caution   Be sure to keep encryption keys safely stored since there is no possibility of recovery!

For a file hosted on a FileMaker Server, encryption is optional. FileMaker Cloud requires encryption and will automatically encrypt an unencrypted file when uploaded. Once hosted, only standard credentials are required for a user access.

To encrypt the selected file(s), select the option in the *Specify Solution Options* dialog, and configure the settings below, shown in Figure 30-6.

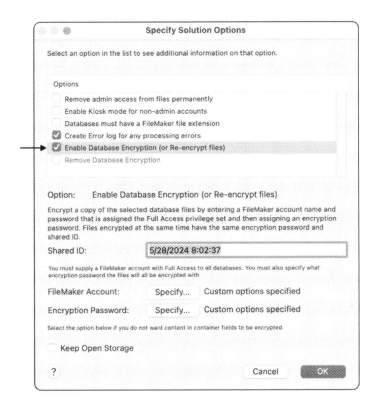

Figure 30-6. *The settings required when enabling encryption*

The *Shared ID* text field contains a case-sensitive string of up to 32 characters and is used to link all the database files in a multi-file solution. When one file is opened and the encryption password entered, other files that were encrypted using the same identifier will not ask for that password when opened through the first file. So, a solution made up of multiple files should always be encrypted at the same time or, at least, the same identifying value. The default is a date and time, but this can be modified to contain any value.

To encrypt the file(s), you must enter credentials for a *FileMaker Account* that is assigned a full access privilege set. Click *Specify* to enter those credentials. Then, click the *Specify* button to enter an *Encryption Password*. This opens the *Database Encryption Password* dialog, shown in Figure 30-7. Here you enter and confirm a password that will be used as the key during encryption and will be required prior when opening a file locally or hosting it on a server. The dialog will rate the quality of the password and allow you to enter a *Password Hint*.

Figure 30-7. *The settings required when enabling encryption*

Back on the *Specify Solution Options* dialog, select the *Keep Open Storage* checkbox to maintain externally stored container files in an unencrypted state if desired. Leave this unchecked to automatically encrypt all container field content, including fields configured to use *Open storage* (Chapter 10, "Defining a Field's External Storage Directory").

Once finished, close the *Specify Solution Options* dialog to return to the *Developer Utilities* dialog. Then, click *Create* to run the utility and create encrypted copies of the files in the specified *Project Folder*.

Now, two dialogs will appear when opening the encrypted file(s) created by this process. First an *Open Encrypted Database* prompt requires entry of the encryption password. After that is successfully confirmed, a standard login prompt for user account credentials appears. When opening an encrypted file for hosting on a server, only the first of these will appear. Users accessing the file across the network see only the prompt for account credentials.

Tip   When encrypting a multi-file solution, be sure to use the same full access credentials and encryption password for every database.

Removing Database Encryption

The *Remove Database Encryption* option will save a copy of the files in an unencrypted state, restoring normal operating behavior and access methods. Select the option in the *Specify Solution Options* dialog, and enter the required settings, shown in Figure 30-8. Type the *Encryption Password* for the file(s) to prove that you have access to modify the files. Then, click the *Specify* button to enter a *FileMaker Account* with full access. Both should be the same in all the selected files. After entering these, close the *Specify Solution Options* dialog to return to the *Developer Utilities* dialog. Then, click *Create* to run the utility. The decrypted files will appear in the specified *Project Folder*.

Figure 30-8. *The settings required to remove file encryption*

Accessing the Tools Marketplace

Select *Tools Marketplace* from the *Tools* menu to open the Claris Marketplace web page. The site contains a collection of developer tools and products created by Claris Partners and includes a growing number of items, such as the following:

- Project templates and starter solutions

- Specialty tools and feature modules for users or developers

- Plug-ins that add functions, script steps, or custom features

- Add-ons that expand the default capabilities of a database with JavaScript-enabled features

Access the marketplace directly by visiting marketplace.claris.com.

Creating a Custom Add-On

The *Tools* menu also includes a *Create Add-On* menu item. A specially designed database can be saved as an Add-On template to provide a specific reusable feature which can be inserted into other databases. There are specific requirements for designing a file for this purpose. Consult the document from Claris titled "Creating an add-on in Claris FileMaker Pro" to learn more.

Summary

This chapter discussed advanced features accessible through the FileMaker Pro application's Tools menu. In the next chapter, we review methods and practices for maintaining healthy files and recovering should problems arise.

CHAPTER 31

Maintaining Healthy Files

A FileMaker database is a type of document. However, unlike normal documents, the process of saving is completely automated and out of the reach of human action. Each time a modified record is committed (Chapter 4, "Closing a Record"), changes made in a file are automatically saved, so there is no need to explicitly perform a save function. Changes will be written back to the file without any action required, either directly in the local computer or through the network by the host computer. Users can modify records, and developers can modify structural elements with confidence that the work will be written to disk. However, things can go wrong! So, it's important to know how to avoid, identify, and remedy problems to maintain healthy files. This chapter discusses some of the problems that can occur and how to help ensure they don't end in tragedy.

- Avoiding design and training deficiencies
- Controlling a file size
- Optimizing performance
- Identifying and avoiding file damage
- Exploring maintenance functions
- Troubleshooting a damaged file

Avoiding Design and Training Deficiencies

An overwhelming number of database accidents are the result of user confusion caused by a combination of inadequate training, poor interface design, and/or careless scripting. A few problems that arise often involve users overwriting records, forgetting to commit, deleting carelessly, or misidentifying a found set. Consider these while designing your solution and prior to deploying it.

© Mark Conway Munro 2024
M. C. Munro, *Learn FileMaker Pro 2024*, https://doi.org/10.1007/979-8-8688-0835-7_31

Overwriting an Existing Record

Overwriting existing content is a more common problem than you might think and occurs for a variety of different reasons.

Avoiding Inadequate User Training

People lacking general computer experience or specific database knowledge often do not intuitively grasp that they need to create a new record prior to typing data. Some assume that the window is like a web form that is used for entry but sends the data elsewhere for saving, and they type over the last entry. Whatever the assumption, there are two ways to avoid this problem. One is to add a prominent interface button that is clearly labeled for creating a new record. This at least helps inform the user of the fact that records must be created. The other, perhaps most important thing is explicit training to ensure that everyone understands the need to create a new record before typing information for a new entry.

Caution   Developers sometimes overlook the need for user training. A good design can help reduce the need but isn't a substitute for it.

Clarifying a Duplicate Record

Another cause of overwriting data occurs when a user tries and fails to duplicate a record and begin editing the original. The problem here is that the built-in function doesn't produce any visual differences between the original and duplicate record. The record count in the toolbar will increase, and if a field containing an auto-entered, unique record identifier is present on the layout, it will contain a different value. Otherwise, the duplicate record will appear indistinguishable from the original. If the user mistypes a key command or misses clicking a button and doesn't actually produce a duplicate, they may accidentally begin typing over the original. Training can help them know where to look to visually confirm a new record has been created. However, a better way to avoid this is to use a method that clearly indicates that a duplicate record has been created and is ready for data entry.

Using Auto-Enter to Clear Fields

The easiest way to clear a field when duplicating a record is to check the auto-enter *Data* checkbox and leave the entry value blank (Chapter 8, "Field Options: Auto-Enter"). Another way to indicate a duplicate record is to clear key fields using an *auto-enter calculation*. The formula below clears the field value when duplicating using the *Evaluate* function.

```
Evaluate ( "" ; Record Primary ID )
```

Note   See the "CH31-01 Clear with Auto-Enter" example file.

The function accepts two parameters:

- *Expression* – A formula statement that to be executed

- *Fields* – A list of field references that, when modified, cause the expression to be evaluated

In the example, the *expression* is an empty string because we want the field to clear. Using *Record Primary ID* as the triggering field works because it is only assigned a new value when the record is duplicated. Use this formula as the *Calculated* value in the field's *Auto-Enter* options, and turn off the *Do not replace existing value of field* checkbox.

Using a Script to Denote a Duplicate Record

For even more control, replace the default *Duplicate* function with your own script to more overtly modify the record and interact with the user like the one shown below.

Note   See the "CH31-02 Duplicate with Script" example file to compare the built-in menu function with a button executing a custom script.

```
Duplicate Record/Request
Set Field [ Company::Company Name ; Company::Company Name & " COPY" ]
Set Field [ Company::Company Website ; "" ]
Show Custom Dialog [ "Duplication Complete" ]
```

The script starts by creating a duplicate record. It then adds the word "Copy" after the value in the *Company Name* field to help inform the user that they are looking at a duplicate and not the original record. It also clears out the *Company Website* field since we know that will need to be modified. Finally, it displays a dialog informing the user that the process has been performed. Users will become accustomed to seeing these overt indicators and, in their absence, be more likely to realize that they failed to create a duplicate.

Tip   Connect the script to a custom menu (Chapter 23) to completely override the default *Duplicate* function in the menu bar.

Highlighting Fields with Conditional Formatting

Another way to clearly inform the user they are looking at a duplicate record is to highlight fields with format changes (Chapter 21, "Conditional Formatting"). If the duplication script adds the word "Copy" to a key field, that fact can be used to highlight one or more fields with a colorful background or other visual indicators. Doing this reinforces that the duplicate was created and that work needs to be performed.

Note   See the "CH31-03 Highlight Conditionally" example file.

The *Company Name* field's condition can be configured as shown in Figure 31-1. Since we are checking the content of the field being formatted, use the *Value is* and *containing* conditions to check for the existence of the word "COPY" in the field. If true, the selected *Fill Color* will apply. Other fields, like Company Website, can be highlighted using a *Formula is* condition with this code:

```
PatternCount ( Company::Company Name ; " COPY" ) > 0
```

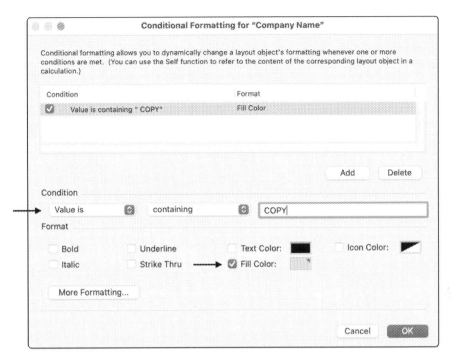

Figure 31-1. *The conditional formatting to highlight the Company Name field red*

This reinforces to the user that they are looking at a duplicate of the original company's record. Once the name on the duplicate is modified, all the formatting highlights will disappear.

Confusing Browse and Find Modes

Another mistake new users make is confusing Browse and Find modes, then inadvertently editing an actual record thinking they are entering search criteria. Since both modes operate on the same layout design, it is easy to see how it might be confusing at first. The changes to the menu and toolbar in Find mode can easily be overlooked, and a find request appears very similar to a regular record. For many versions, FileMaker has displayed helpful indicators like a little magnifying glass icon that appears in every field in Find mode. Adding your own visual indicators to a layout can help further emphasize a successful switch in modes. Layout objects can hide or change formatting to avoid the problem of confusing Browse mode for Find mode.

The reverse happens when a user confuses Find mode for Browse mode. Find mode can look very much like a new empty record waiting for data entry. A user may begin creating record after record without realizing they are creating find requests that will disappear when they return to Browse mode. FileMaker has a "circuit breaker" dialog that appears after several find requests are created, reminding the user they are in Find mode.

Adding custom visual indicators between the two modes will help with both problems. Use one of the formulas below to hide, conditionally format, or change labels on various objects to assist the user in distinguishing which mode there are in.

```
Get ( WindowMode ) = 0 // indicates Browse Mode
Get ( WindowMode ) = 1 // indicates Find Mode
```

Caution   Don't allow developer bias to assume users will have your insider knowledge! A skilled developer can test an interface design from the perspective of a new user and preemptively identify points of confusion before they become a disaster.

Forgetting to Commit a Record

At the completion of a data entry task, an edited record must be committed for it to be saved and released for access by others. This happens automatically when a user navigates to another record or closes a file. They can also manually commit a record (Chapter 4, "Closing a Record"). If they leave a record open after a data entry task, it creates an annoyance for other users waiting to see, access, or edit the data. It can also cause conflicts for themselves if they try to access the open record in a second window on their own computer. Leaving records with uncommitted changes may even be dangerous and cause file damage if the application crashes, is force quit, or loses its network connection. Encourage users to commit records promptly after making changes, and consider using conditional layout elements to visually indicate when a record has active focus with changes that require committing.

Deleting Records Carelessly

Accidental record deletion can be the result of either the inexperience of new users or the overconfidence of experienced users. The delete confirmation dialog contains a minimalistic generic message that assumes the user is aware of the context. It does not adequately indicate which specific record(s) are about to be deleted, and this can be a major problem when the user has lost track of window context or isn't paying attention. This is especially confusing on a List view when a user mistakenly assumes the record they are looking at is the record selected. Also, when using multiple windows, they may think they are deleting a record in one window when they are really in another. Ironically, this problem can more often affect experienced users. While a new user may nervously read a dialog message and proceed with caution, an experienced user can become sloppy and click through a dialog with an unwarranted overconfidence. Record deletion is not something the *Undo* command can reverse, so the only way to retrieve deleted records is to re-import them from a backup copy of the database. So, consider a few options to help avoid this problem.

A custom menu can override the delete functions and present a customized, informative warning dialog that clearly articulates which record is going to be deleted by including key identifying fields (Chapter 23, "Overriding a Menu Item Function"). Adding a second confirmation dialog can also help avoid accidents, especially when deleting a large found set. It is a little more inconvenient but can avoid the greater inconvenience of erroneous deletions. Alternatively, a custom dialog can require a user to type a word or phrase, providing an explicit confirmation of intent before a script continues with the deletion request. Also, consider placing strict limits on how many records can be deleted at once to avoid mistakes that wipe out an entire table's contents by having a custom script deny the request and present the record count in an informative dialog. Finally, account privileges (Chapter 29, "Controlling Record Access") can completely restrict the ability to delete for users who aren't authorized.

Misidentifying a Found Set

When a user does not identify a found set, they may accidentally perform one of several functions that affect more records than they intend. If a user thinks the found set contains 10 records when it really contains 10,000, performing functions like *Delete All Records*, *Replace Field Contents*, or *Find/Replace* can create a disaster. Make sure that users understand what a found set is and how to confirm it prior to using these functions in a minimum requirement. Going further, create more informative dialogs with custom menus (Chapter 23), and require the user to enter some text as a confirmation of the action they are performing. For example, force them to enter the word "Delete" when confirming a single record delete, or enter the number of records when deleting the found set. Also, completely disable these features for users who don't require them with account privileges (Chapter 29).

The same problem can occur due to developer error when creating scripts. A poorly designed script that runs automatically or a script made accessible to a user at the wrong moment can perform these same functions with even greater rapidity than humans, and the damage may not be immediately apparent. Take extra care to ensure that a script can only run in the appropriate context and that it has built-in conditional statements to ensure it won't wipe out important data!

Tip   Don't assume users know when a button or menu item is safe to click. Make an interface "bulletproof" by hiding access to objects and scripts that are not applicable!

Controlling File Size

Everything added to a database will increase the size of the file. Creating new tables, fields, layouts, and scripts increases file size. Entering hundreds, thousands, or millions of records increases file size. Indexed fields with large amounts of text and container fields with large files inserted both increase file size. This is a natural process and doesn't pose an immediate problem, especially since FileMaker limits databases to the amount of disk space available with a technical maximum of 8 terabytes. However, it is still a good idea to follow the adage "less is more" and design a database to be as efficient as possible both in its structure and content. Files with a large and convoluted structural design can be slower and confusing to developers and may be prone to other problems. There are two primary issues that can make a file larger than it needs to be: inefficient design and fragmentation.

Designing Efficiently

One way to maintain a slim file size and keep things operating efficiently is to design efficiently. This can be achieved using various techniques that are worth keeping in mind when creating a solution.

Using External Storage

One of the easiest ways to keep a file size under control is to use external storage for container fields (Chapter 10, "Storing a Reference to an External File"). When a container field stores images or files internally, the database size will increase by the size of the item stored. This can make a huge impact on file size, especially when storing hundreds or thousands of large images. If the database is hosted on a server (or used locally but doesn't need to be a self-contained file), using external container storage is recommended and will greatly reduce the size of the database. The user won't see a difference since FileMaker manages displaying files as if they were internal.

Limiting Field Indexes

Field indexes can also cause a rapid increase in the size of a file (Chapter 8, "Field Options: Storage"). This is especially true when lengthy notes fields are indexed. Indexing is important for certain functions and shouldn't be avoided. However, to the extent possible, try to minimize field indexes. Fields that won't be used in finds, sorts, or relationships don't need to be indexed at all and can have their *indexing* field option set to "None." Some fields that are used for these functions can be indexed using the "Minimal" setting which creates a smaller index of values. Using these settings where possible can help reduce the additional size burden imposed by indexes.

Avoiding Graphical Overload

A graphically rich interface design can improve the user experience and create a more professional front end to your system. However, inserting actual graphics into layouts can increase the size of the file and the length of time it takes to load and draw layouts. So, try to find a balance between a visually stunning display and a practical, efficient design by considering a few basic guidelines:

- Always use FileMaker's built-in layout objects instead of custom graphics where possible. For example, use a button object with native styling applied instead of a fancy custom graphic.

- When using custom icons on buttons, import them as SVG files into the file's icon library (Chapter 20, "Using an Icon Label"). Do not paste them directly on a layout as graphic overlays.

- Any custom graphics placed directly on the layout should be optimized for screen use, using lower resolution especially if they are not on print layouts.

FileMaker maintains a hidden database of layout graphical content and will only store one version when an identical image is used on multiple layouts. However, any variation between the images on each layout results in a separate entry and increases file size.

Tip   Before bringing in a custom graphic, be sure you are fully informed about all the style options available natively.

Creating an Open-Ended Design

Another way to keep a database slim is using a more sophisticated structural and interface design to avoid redundancy in tables, layouts, and scripts. This involves designing open-ended, dynamic resources that can be used more broadly and with variable features and functions. Although this is an advanced topic that could be its own book, here are a few ideas for creating a more efficient design with resource sharing:

- A commonly used formula or a group of similar formulas can be moved into a single custom function to avoid repeating the same code (Chapter 15).

- A table designed to store notes related to Contact records and a table storing notes related to a Project record could be combined into one shared table with a field indicating the parent type to which the note belongs.

- Consider "normalizing" excessively "wide" tables. If a table normally uses 10 fields, but a seldom used lengthy form adds an additional 90 fields, consider pairing off the additional 90 fields into a separate table. Otherwise, it will end up pre-allocating space for all 100 fields, whether needed or not, multiplied by the number of records.

- Design layouts to provide global functionality, accessed from anywhere. For example, don't create multiple relationships to a commonly related *Company* table. Instead open a Card window to provide quick access to the data directly from anywhere (Chapter 25, "Managing Windows").

- Use parameters to provide input for scripts designed to process different information and perform multiple variations on a single operational function to avoid creating numerous scripts for each function.

- Scripts can also be designed to be contextually aware and provide a common operation from anywhere. For example, a single delete record script can present a detailed confirmation dialog for any table.

Note   Although structural redundancy doesn't enormously impact file size, an open-ended design can help a little while also making a solution more versatile and efficient for developers.

Dividing into Separate Files

Another way to reduce a bloated file is to divide resources into a multi-file solution. Technically, this doesn't reduce the size of a solution – it divides it into separate smaller files. Further, dividing a file into separate databases can create some complexity and redundancy. However, splitting a huge file into several smaller files can be beneficial and is worth considering.

FileMaker employs a "full-stack" file architecture capable of containing multiple back-end data tables and front-end interface resources in a single document file. Keeping everything together in a single file is the intuitive choice and can be workable for most situations. However, consider the following different options for dividing resources across multiple files:

- *Separate modules* – Two or more files, each containing data and interface for one or more tables grouped by some criteria. For example, a solution may have a module for each: accounting, sales, and operations.

- *Data separation* – Two files, one containing all data tables and the other containing all interface resources. The data tables are pulled into the front-end file's relationship graph and used as if they were internal.

- *Distributed data* – One file for all interface resources and two or more files containing one group of data tables.

- *Combination* – A combination of some integrated full-stack modules and others using some degree of data separation. This happen when integrating third-party modules into your existing solution.

Although the topic of a *data separation* or *distributed data* models is enormously complex and should be its own chapter or even an entire book, there are a few key details and benefits to that approach worth at least mentioning. First, the ideal configuration involves the following files:

- A single file dedicated to only interface related functionality

- One or more files containing only data tables

A few pros and cons of this are as follows:

- Pro – It avoids the need for redundancies in multiple interface files found with separate modules. All layouts can share custom functions, value lists, scripts, and more.

- Pro – The graph for schema related relationships can be kept separate from interface related relationships. When comingled in a single file, it can become difficult to tell them apart, and that can cause confusion as the solution evolves. Separation keeps the data file relationships to only those needed for calculations, auto-enter calculations, and create and delete settings, greatly enhancing performance and stability when a record is created or deleted.

- Pro – A corrupted data file can be swapped out for a recovered one without affecting the interface. The same is true of replacing a corrupted interface file, and it just works with the data files.

- Con – Custom functions that are used by interface and schema need to be added and updated in both files causing a redundancy, albeit a minor one.

- Con – Opening the *Manage Database* dialog for the layout you are viewing requires that you first open the data file in which it resides.

Avoiding Fragmentation

Another way to control file size is to perform periodic file maintenance. As records are created and deleted through the course of normal data entry, empty space can accumulate within the file. This can also happen as developers add and remove resources. Over time, this artificially inflates the file's size and may impact performance and stability. Saving the file as a compacted copy (described later in this chapter) will safely recreate the file, fitting as much data into each block as possible to reclaim unused space by removing the bloat of empty "ghost" blocks.

Optimizing Performance

The structural design of a database can impact performance and its health. A good design will perform well, allowing users and scripts to do their work without delay. Changes are made, records are found, and scripts are run fast and cleanly. A poor design can drag a file to a halt, presenting users with the dreaded spinning "busy" cursor and may even cause them to hastily force quit the file. A bad design can cause simple processes to drag on so long that it overloads the application's memory and may even cause crashing. All of these can lead to corruption and worse problems. Consider a few good practices that will help optimize the performance of your solution!

Optimizing the Schema

These are a few ways to keep your tables, fields, relationships, and custom functions healthy and happy:

- Use more auto-enter calculations and less calculation fields.

- Keep calculation field formulas local and indexed as much as possible.

- Avoid SQL queries in calculation fields, especially those used on multi-record views.

- Organize relationships into lean, separated *table occurrence groups* instead of *hub-and-spoke monoliths* (Chapter 9, "Using Table Occurrences"). Limit relationship "hops" to 2 or 3 away from a primary table.

- Use *While* loops (Chapter 13) and recursion (Chapter 15) sparingly in formulas and custom functions. When doing so, be sure to carefully construct them to avoid unnecessary iteration and protect them with the *setRecursion* function (Chapter 15, "Controlling Recursion Limits").

Optimizing the Interface

Layouts can range from simple, streamlined views to graphically rich, complex interfaces. However, here are a few principles to be mindful of to help ensure efficient performance:

- Perform sorts on local fields and not through a relationship if possible.

- On multi-record List views and portals, minimize the overall number of objects. Especially avoid objects involving complex functionality, for example, lots of related fields or items performing SQL queries will slow down large lists.

- Avoid excessive hide and conditional formatting, especially in List views and portals.

- On a Form layout, try to minimize the number of advanced controls such as portals and panels.

- Divide complex layouts into multiple less complex layouts with easy navigation buttons to quickly toggle between them.

- Minimize the use of objects with shadows, semitransparent colors, gradients, or large graphics.

- Minimize the number of unstored calculations in fields, especially in lists.

- Use script triggers (Chapter 27) sparingly, and avoid connecting simple interface events with complex scripts that might create long lag times that interfere with a user's ability to work.

- Use themes and styles for object formatting (Chapter 22).

Optimizing the Scripts

Scripts can perform simple tasks or complex automated processes. Consider these tips to keep things running smoothly, especially for more complex scripts:

- Use the *Freeze Window* command to halt unnecessary interface refreshing during complex scripts.

- Create an empty "Automation" staging layout with no script triggers for each table for script use.

- Avoid performing scripts on layouts with script triggers.

- Offload slow scripts to the host computer with *Perform Script on Server* (Chapter 24, "Performing Other Scripts").

- Set a variable to the time at the start and end of a script, and calculate how long it takes to run and test different methods of doing the same thing (Chapter 13, "Calculating Time Elapsed").

- Run complex scripts through the debugger to check for any unexpected activity that might slow things down (Chapter 26).

Identifying and Avoiding File Damage

Any digital file has some risk of becoming damaged. Since databases are typically accessed by many users simultaneously across a network and are continually reading from and writing to disk, they can be more vulnerable and at greater risk of data loss. Developers should be aware of what can cause damage, how to avoid it, ways to detect it, and the correct approach to repair it.

Caution   File damage can range from a minor problem that initially goes unnoticed to a catastrophic inability to open the file!

Detecting File Damage

There are several indications of file damage. Some can be false positives and require that other causes be ruled out first before jumping to a conclusion. Others are clearly indications of damage.

Distinguishing False Positives from Real Damage

The following are symptoms of damage that require ruling out other causes first:

- A field displaying a question mark instead of data can be evidence of corruption especially when it appears on every field. However, a calculation returning the wrong data type or an inadequate field width on a layout can also produce a question mark!

- Records appearing blank may indicate corruption. Other causes can be not realizing some records are omitted from the found set or fields being positioned so they don't render properly in a List view or portal.

- Records missing may indicate corruption. But first make sure a user didn't accidentally delete them!

- Weird search results may indicate index corruption. First adjust the settings or recreate indices by turning off indexing on a field and turning it back on. Also, rule out problematic script design, inexperienced users, broken relationships, and networking issues which can all create results mistaken for corruption.

Identifying Clear Signs of Damage

Other symptoms clearly indicate damage, including the following:

- A database performing a consistency check when opened indicates the file wasn't closed properly and could have damage.

- A repeated or random consistency check, especially without a crash event or force quit preceding it, could indicate lingering damage.

- The FileMaker application randomly crashing when working in the database may be an operating system or networking issue, but it can also indicate corruption in the database.

- Finally, sometimes, a dialog will simply inform that the file is damaged, can't be opened, or should be recovered.

Avoiding File Damage

The best ways to avoid file damage is to share properly across a network, make sure that files are closed properly, and maintain hardware and software.

Share Properly

When sharing a database with others, never place it in a directory that can be accessed by more than one person at a time. This includes a folder on a shared server volume or any type of cloud storage, for example, Dropbox, Google Drive, etc. If two users open the same database file directly from a folder, it is guaranteed to become corrupted. Instead, use FileMaker's *peer-to-peer sharing*, or host the file on a FileMaker Server to ensure proper multiuser read/write management and greater protection from user crashes. Also, when opening a database on the host server directly for maintenance or testing, take extra care to open it through the host access interface and not directly from the folder where it is stored (Chapter 32, "Opening a Hosted Database"). If you are certain that the files are not actively hosted (Chapter 32, "Managing Database Files"), it is safe to open them directly. However, make sure all the files are closed before rehosting them!

Close Files Properly

Most file damage occurs when a database was improperly closed. This can result in the loss of data, corrupted data, and/or structural flaws. FileMaker (including FileMaker Server) makes considerable use of caching. Even if a record is committed and saved within the database, the changes exist in temporary memory storage until a later time when FileMaker flushes that cache to disk. So, while the file is open, the copy on the drive is considered incomplete. Only during the close process does FileMaker fully assemble and write the entire file to disk. The proper close method is to close all database windows or to quit the FileMaker application by selecting the *File* ➤ *Quit Application* menu. Some ways a database may be improperly closed include the following:

- Computer power is interrupted, resulting in abrupt shutdown of an open database.

- A system-wide crash that also crashes FileMaker.

- A glitch that causes FileMaker to unexpectedly quit.

- If the network connection is dropped due to the user's computer going to sleep while a hosted database is open.

- A hasty force quit of the application with databases open when a user mistakes a spinning cursor during a lengthy script process for a crash.

- A force quit is required to stop a faulty script endlessly looping with abort capability turned off.

- A force quit required to stop runaway recursion.

- Trying to directly open or make a copy of a database from a folder when actively hosted by FileMaker Server.

Tip Databases hosted on a FileMaker Server are cushioned from user computer crashes and force quit damage. Files run locally are more vulnerable!

Maintain Hardware and Software

Always maintain stable and up-to-date hardware and software, paying close attention to these details:

- Don't rush to upgrade anything. Perform extensive testing on a safe copy of your database prior to upgrading hardware or software.

- Avoid beta software for live production use.

- Keep host and user operating systems up to date.

- Keep the FileMaker application up to date, including all interim bug fix releases.

- Use an adequate uninterruptable power supply and surge protector on all computers to avoid sudden shutdowns in the event of a power loss, especially a database server.

- Run any recommended hardware maintenance using a disk utility program, and don't let computers get outdated to the point of risking failure.

- Don't allow the host computer to run out of disk space.

- Use fast, modern hardware and networking equipment with adequate cabling.

- Perform regular database maintenance.

Tip   Consider using FileMaker Cloud which handles most hardware and software maintenance functions automatically.

Exploring Maintenance Functions

There are several functions available to help maintain database integrity and troubleshoot file damage. Each must be performed locally, so files hosted on a network must be taken offline and manipulated directly in a copy of the FileMaker Pro desktop application. These functions are *Save a copy as, Consistency check,* and *Recover.*

Tip   Always make regular backups of your databases and preserve an extra development copy of major structural changes. If damage occurs, the safest action is to revert to a recent backup or recover data from the damaged file and import it into a reliable backup.

Saving a Copy As

The *Save a Copy As* function, accessible under the *File* menu or as a script step, will create a new copy of an open database as one of these four types selectable in the save file dialog: *Copy, Compacted, Clone,* or *Self-Contained.*

Choose the *Copy* option to save the database as an identical copy of itself without any changes. This is identical to the *Save As* function in most applications and can also be done by duplicating a closed file using the operating system file duplication command. It doesn't have any diagnostic function; it simply makes a copy.

Choose the *Compacted copy (smaller)* option to save an optimized copy of the database with empty space removed, resulting in a smaller file size. Used periodically, this can maintain the health of a file, especially if a lot of content is deleted from a file or lots of structural changes have occurred.

Choose the *Clone (no records)* option to save a copy of the database's structure only. This will include tables, fields, relationships, page setup options, field definitions, custom functions, layouts, scripts, and more, without any records. This can be used when troubleshooting a problem as it quickly isolates a file's structure from its content.

Choose the *Self-contained copy (single file)* option to save a copy with external container data (Chapter 10) embedded back into the file's container fields, making it fully self-contained. This doesn't have any diagnostic function but can be helpful in consolidating container data from a variety of different locations for relocating or when transporting the file for some reason.

Performing a Consistency Check

A *consistency check* is a process that will read every block that makes up a file, verify the internal structure of each block, and confirm it is properly linked to other blocks. This process does not read the data within blocks, check the file schema, or check higher-level structures as those functions are only performed by the full *Recover* process. Each time a database opens, FileMaker checks the file and automatically performs a consistency check if it detects that the file has been improperly closed. A manual consistency check can be performed on any closed file as a troubleshooting step when damage is suspected. Launch the FileMaker Pro application and select the *File ➤ Recover* menu. In the file selection dialog, shown in Figure 31-2, select the file suspected of damage. Instead of clicking the *Select* button, which would begin the full *Recover* process, click the *Check Consistency* button.

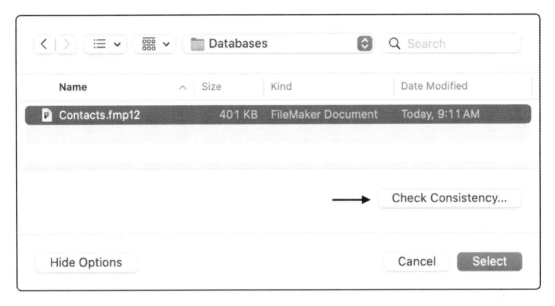

Figure 31-2. *Use the check consistency button instead of performing a full recovery*

FileMaker will immediately check the file and report the results in both a dialog and "Recover.log" file. If no problems have been reported, the file is probably safe to continue using. If damage is reported, it may recommend performing the recovery process. After the consistency check is complete, the file selection dialog remains open so you can choose to recover the file, perform a consistency check on a different file, or cancel.

Recovering a File

When a database is damaged or acting buggy, the *Recover* function can be used to rebuild a new copy of the file and regain access to its contents. This process is aggressive and will do whatever is necessary to restore access to a file! It will rebuild the file block by block and attempt to correct any corruption. However, if an object can't be repaired, it may be deleted. Because of its aggressive nature, the function should be used as a diagnostic or emergency data recovery tool and not for regular maintenance.

To perform the recovery process, launch the FileMaker Pro application, and select the *File* ➤ *Recover* menu. In the file selection dialog, locate the damaged file, and click the *Select* button. In the *Save* dialog, enter a name, select a location to save a recovered copy of the file, and optionally specify advanced options (described in the next section). Then click *Save* to begin the recovery process.

FileMaker will rebuild the file to the specified save location and report the results. Based on the information provided, you can determine if the recovered copy of the file is safe for use or if you should transfer the content into a previously saved backup copy. If no stable backup is available, it is possible to meticulously review the recovery log to see what type of structural objects are reported as corrupt and then systematically delete resources and repeat the recovery process over and over until you isolate the corrupt resources. Then, each corrupted item can be deleted and recreated in the original file and the process repeated until the recovery process reports the file has no problems. However, preserving safe backups is the best practice.

Caution   Recovering a file clears any file-based Script Trigger and other settings in *File Options*! Be sure to reset them.

Advanced Recovery Options

The *Advanced Recover Options* dialog, shown in Figure 31-3, can be opened during the *Recover* process to control which processes are performed. In the Save dialog that opens, select the *Use Advanced Options* checkbox, or click the adjacent *Specify* button to open this dialog.

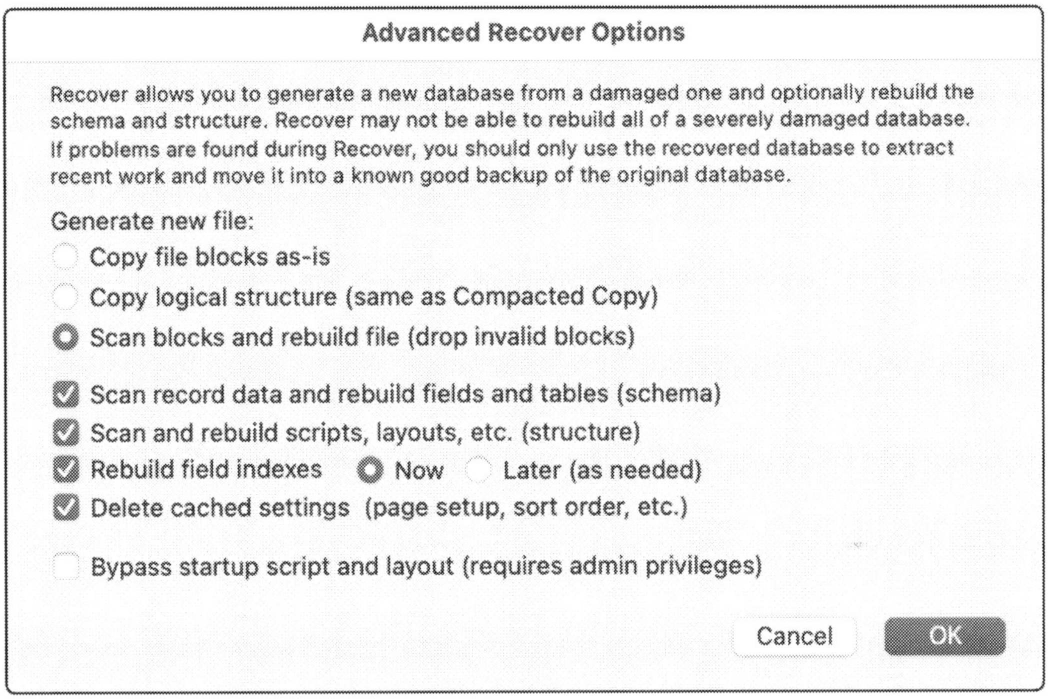

Advanced Recover Options

Recover allows you to generate a new database from a damaged one and optionally rebuild the schema and structure. Recover may not be able to rebuild all of a severely damaged database. If problems are found during Recover, you should only use the recovered database to extract recent work and move it into a known good backup of the original database.

Generate new file:
- ○ Copy file blocks as-is
- ○ Copy logical structure (same as Compacted Copy)
- ◉ Scan blocks and rebuild file (drop invalid blocks)

- ☑ Scan record data and rebuild fields and tables (schema)
- ☑ Scan and rebuild scripts, layouts, etc. (structure)
- ☑ Rebuild field indexes   ◉ Now   ○ Later (as needed)
- ☑ Delete cached settings (page setup, sort order, etc.)

- ☐ Bypass startup script and layout (requires admin privileges)

Cancel   OK

Figure 31-3. *The advanced options for recovery a file*

The *Generate new file* section controls which of three ways a new file will be created during the recovery process. Select *Copy file blocks as-is* to copy all file blocks exactly as they exist in the source file. The resulting file may still include damaged blocks. This is the equivalent of just saving a copy of the current file. Select *Copy logical structure* to copy all data in the source file without checking the blocks, but it will rebuild the tree structure. The resulting file may still include damaged blocks. This is the equivalent of saving a compacted copy of the current file. Finally, select *Scan blocks and rebuild file (drop invalid blocks)* to completely rebuild the file, including only undamaged and non-duplicate blocks. The resulting file may be structurally unsound and may only be suitable for data extraction into a reliable backup copy. This choice is the full recovery process and default selection.

The checkboxes below control the following optional functions during recovery:

- *Scan Record Data and Rebuild Fields and Tables (schema)* – Rebuilds the file's database schema (tables, fields, and relationships), removing fields or records found to be at invalid locations within the file, and recreates missing fields and table definitions.

- *Scan and Rebuild Scripts, Layouts, etc. (structure)* – Rebuilds the file's structure (layouts, scripts, themes).

- *Rebuild Field Index* – Clears indexes with a choice of when to rebuild them. Rebuilding now takes longer but is done before anyone uses the file. Rebuilding later forces indexes to be rebuilt as needed when users search or perform other functions. See Chapter 8 for more on field indexing.

- *Delete Cached Settings* – Removes settings for last choices made when printing, importing/exporting, sorting, finding, etc.

- *Bypass Startup Script and Layout* – Disables script triggers (Chapter 27) and the file's default layout, opening to a newly created blank recovery layout instead.

Troubleshooting a Damaged File

When a file explicitly reports damage and won't open, you have no choice but to recover and usually will need to extract the data into a reliable backup of the structure. However, when a file opens but exhibits severe intermittent crashing, there are several steps required to safely locate the damage, determine the best course of action, and transfer records into a good structure.

Locating Damage

The first troubleshooting step involves locating the damage by determining if it is in the database structure or record data. Depending on what you find, your recovery option and choice of file for future use may vary.

Checking the Database Structure

To determine if the database structure is damaged, follow these steps:

- Create a troubleshooting copy of the original file, naming it something unique, for example, "Broken Database."

- Isolate the structure by making a copy without any record data. Open the "Broken Database" file, and perform the *Save a Copy as* command, selecting the *Clone (no records)* option and naming it "Broken Database Structure." Then close the "Broken Database" file.

- Next, compact the "Broken Database Structure" file to preemptively fix any minor issues that might get in the way of troubleshooting. Open it, and perform the *Save a Copy as* command, selecting *compacted copy (smaller)* option and naming it "Broken Database Structure Compacted." Then close the file.

- To diagnose the structure, *Recover* the "Broken Database Structure Compacted" using default recovery settings (uncheck advanced options) and saving it as "Broken Database Structure Recovered."

At the end of this process, you should have a folder with the five files shown in Figure 31-4. Open the "Recover.log" file and check to see if any damage is reported.

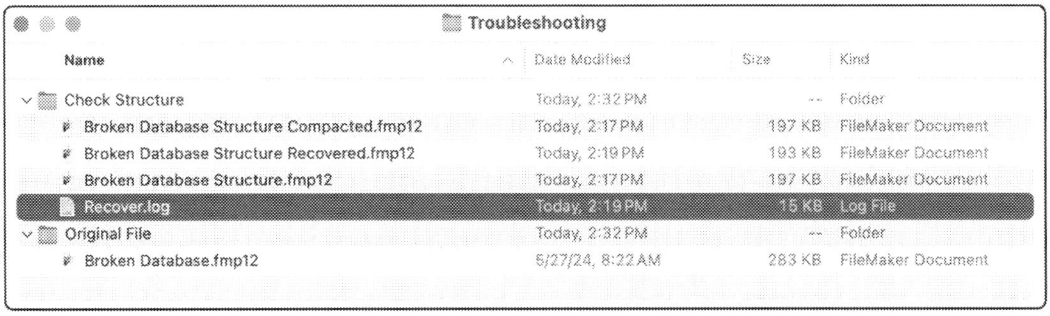

Figure 31-4. *The files prepared for troubleshooting the file structure*

If damage is found, you may be able to skip checking the record data. Instead recover the original "Broken Database" file, and transfer record data from that into a reliable backup structure. Ideally this is a preserved clone of a backup from a time prior to the introduction of corruption. If the corruption has been lingering awhile and you do not have access to such a file, you can use the recovered file generated previously as the structure. However, keep in mind that the recovery process may result in renamed or deleted objects that could not be recovered, so some work to remedy these may be required. For example, a field might be renamed "Recovered Field," or a "Recovered Blob" or "Recovered Library" table occurrence can appear in the relationship graph and may or may not indicate corruption or data loss. Any "Recovered Blobs" are *binary large objects* that are usually recovered layout objects from that hidden graphical content database which can be deleted.

Caution   If the FileMaker recovery report explicitly states that a file is not safe for use, using it anyway is not recommended.

Checking the Record Data

If damage to the file structure has been ruled out or if you want to check both, follow these steps to determine if the record data is damaged:

1. Open the "Broken Database" troubleshooting copy, and perform the *Save a Copy* as command, selecting *compacted copy (smaller)* option and naming it "Broken Database Records Compacted." Then close the file.

2. Recover the "Broken Database Records Compacted" using default recovery settings by unchecking the advanced options and naming it "Broken Database Records Recovered."

At the end of this process, you should have a folder with the five files shown in Figure 31-5. Open the "Recover.log" file and check to see if any damage is reported.

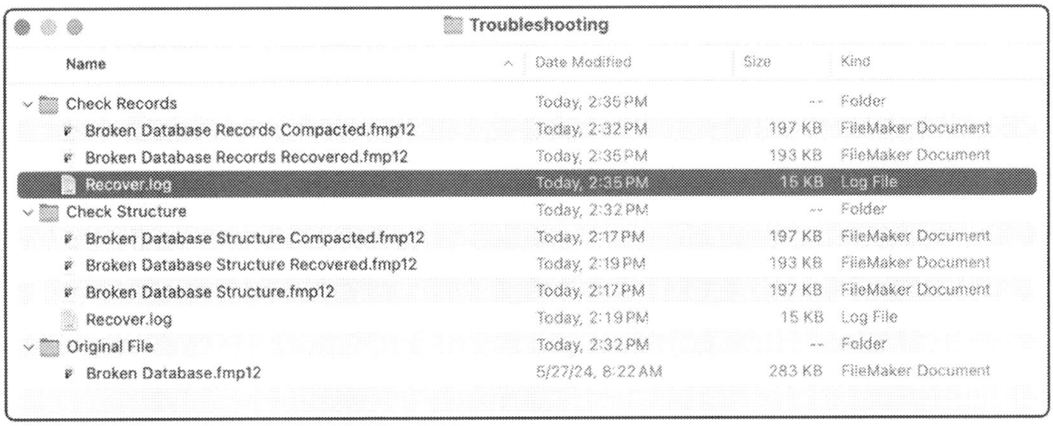

Figure 31-5. *The various files prepared for troubleshooting the file records*

Determining the Best Course of Action

If no damage is reported in both the file structure and record data, you can try to use the recovered file at the conclusion of the record data check. If random crashes or other problems continue to occur, consider transferring the record data into a safe structure anyway. If the structure or record data reported damage, immediately transfer the record data to safe structure.

Transferring Records into a Good Structure

To move record data from the recovered file into a reliable structure, follow these steps:

1. Make a copy of either the recovered file from the conclusion of the record data check (the "Broken Database Records Recovered" file) or the original troubleshooting copy.

2. Open the file.

3. Perform a *Find All* to confirm a found set of all records.

4. Export all records using the *Excel Workbooks (.xlsx)* type option. Be sure to check the *Use field names as column names in first row* option in the *Excel Options* dialog. In the *Export Options* dialog, take care to select all fields from the *Current Table* and not just the ones visible on the current layout, which is the default option.

Caution   Exporting to a non-FileMaker format guarantees the data is cleanly separated from any structural corruption. However, container fields are not supported and can't be exported this way. Those must be manually restored in the new database. You may attempt to export these to the FileMaker format instead but then need to double-check to confirm that no corruption follows the data in the transfer.

5. Repeat steps 3 and 4 for every table in the database.

6. Identify a stable copy of the database structure. Ideally use a clone that was created from a time prior to the corruption event. If that is not available, use a recovered copy (like the "Broken Database Structure Recovered" from the previous process) if the database structure is no longer reporting damage.

7. Import the records from the spreadsheet(s) into each table of the safe structure.

Summary

This chapter explored how to keep files healthy and procedures to troubleshoot file damage. In the next chapter, we discuss deploying a solution.

Deploying a Solution

After completing the development phase, it is time to deploy the database into the target workflow. There are two primary choices: deploying to a local device (a computer folder or iOS device) or sharing on a network from a host server. Each option has different benefits, and the choice affects who can access the file, how, and from where. Each product in the FileMaker family has different capabilities for deployment and access (Chapter 1, "Reviewing the Product Line"). In this chapter, we explore these options, introducing specific topics related to deploying and accessing a solution, including the following:

- Deploying to a local device
- Sharing databases on a network
- Hosting with FileMaker Server
- Hosting with FileMaker Cloud
- Hosting with Ottomatic by Proof+Geist
- Using WebDirect

Deploying to a Local Device

A solution designed for personal use can be deployed to a local device, either to a folder directory on a user's computer or to an individual iOS device.

Deploying to a Folder Directory

The easiest deployment method is to a folder directory on a user's computer. Once copied there, the FileMaker Pro desktop application can open and use the database. This provides a lot of convenience, since the database can be closed and moved to

855

M. C. Munro, *Learn FileMaker Pro 2024*, https://doi.org/10.1007/979-8-8688-0835-7_32

another folder or duplicated for reuse as easily as one would with a word processing or spreadsheet document. While this is an easy and useful option for a single user, opportunities for sharing are limited.

- Physically sharing by sending a copy to coworkers is an option. However, each person will have a separate copy of the file without the benefits of collaborative, simultaneous use.

- Placing the database into a folder on a networked file server would allow others to access the file. However, this is not recommended for reasons discussed later in this chapter.

- Using services like Dropbox or Google Drive may corrupt files when syncing even with only a single user accessing the file.

- The FileMaker Pro desktop app can act as a micro-server and safely share a file opened from a local folder with *peer-to-peer sharing* (described later in this chapter). However, that is limited to five simultaneous connections by other users with access limited to FileMaker products and intended for development testing only.

If sharing the database with others isn't an important consideration, using a database from a local folder is a suitable option. Just make sure the file is closed before moving it to another folder, and keep it in a folder that other users can't access.

Caution   If FileMaker crashes or is force quit, a local database can become corrupt. Although typically recoverable, there is a risk of data loss. For added safety, use FileMaker Server instead.

Deploying to an iOS Device

A database can be deployed directly onto an iPhone or iPad and then accessed by the device user with the free FileMaker Go iOS application. Since the database is physically stored on the device, this provides the benefit of portability. The user can access the database anywhere they have their device, even when not connected to a cellular or wireless network. Once deployed to an iOS device, use of the file is limited to data entry related tasks with no option to structurally alter the file. Also, there is no option to share a database from the device for simultaneous workgroup access, so each device has an isolated copy of the file. However, this option is perfect for convenient single-user access to a database designed for smaller screens.

Tip   It is possible to open a file hosted on a FileMaker Server on an iOS device if that device has access to the host network.

To install, start by downloading the *Claris FileMaker Go 2024* app onto the device. Then, connect the device to a computer and copy the database from a folder into the *FileMaker Go* folder in the device's *Files* tab. On macOS Sonoma (14.4), this is done by following these steps, as shown in Figure 32-1:

1. Open a new Finder window and make the sidebar visible.

2. Select the target iOS device under the *Locations* sidebar group.

3. Select the *Files* tab. Then drag the database file into the *FileMaker Go* folder.

Note   Four sample databases will be automatically installed into the folder. These can be deleted from the *Files* tab if desired.

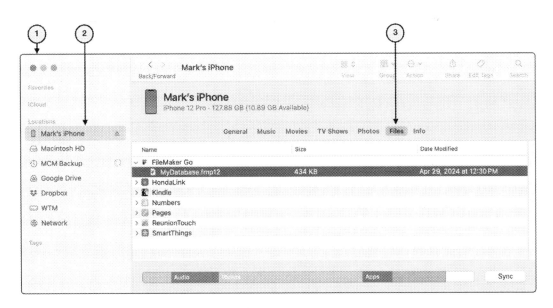

Figure 32-1.   *The macOS Sonoma (14.4) window for configuring an iPhone*

Once installed on the device, launch the FileMaker Go app. Tap on the *My Apps* tab at the bottom, and then tap the *On My iPhone location,* as shown in Figure 32-2. The next screen will display a list of databases installed on the device. Tap to open the desired database to open.

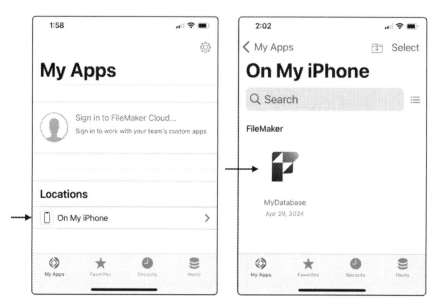

Figure 32-2. *The FileMaker Go app's access to databases installed on an iPhone*

The FileMaker Go app can also access databases shared on a network. Select *Hosts* and choose a FileMaker Server from those available on the local network, or enter an address for a remote server.

Sharing Databases on a Network

The most common deployment involves sharing databases across a computer network. This enables every member of a team to access and work in the file simultaneously. However, it is important to make clear that sharing a database on a network is not the same as sharing a document file in a shared server folder. A database file is a document, and it can be placed in a shared directory on a file server accessible by multiple people. If more than one user opens the file at the same time, each copy of FileMaker will begin reading and writing to the file as data entry tasks are performed. This will result in file corruption and data loss! If this happens, the file must be run through the Recovery process and may be damaged beyond repair (Chapter 31, "Troubleshooting a Damaged File").

Caution   Never share a database file on a shared folder directory!

The proper method of sharing a database across a network is through a share-enabled version of FileMaker software acting as a host service. This can be done using *peer-to-peer sharing* with the FileMaker Pro desktop app, a dedicated server running FileMaker Server, or FileMaker Cloud. In either scenario, the folder containing the databases is not shared. Instead, the folder is safely located on the host computer but "hidden" behind the host software which manages all connections and coordinates conflict-free read/write processes, as illustrated in Figure 32-3.

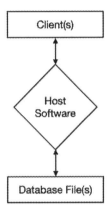

Figure 32-3. *A database with client access managed by host software*

Once the host is actively serving up a database, users can gain access to a variety of different ways depending on the exact configuration.

- Select the *File ➤ Hosts ➤ Show Hosts* menu in the desktop application or click *Hosts* in an *Open File* dialog to see a dialog listing favorite and local hosts.

- Select the *Hosts* tab in the FileMaker Go iOS app lists the same.

- When configured for WebDirect, users can access databases from the host through a web browser, for example, http://127.0.0.1/fmi/webd.

- Files hosted on FileMaker Server or FileMaker Cloud can be configured to allow incoming connections using ODBC/JBDC and Representational State Transfer (REST) with the FileMaker API.

Understanding Collaborative Limitations

Sharing a database allows simultaneous access by users and developers. However, there are several limitations automatically enforced to avoid conflicts between users working in the same hosted file. The following list of actions are each limited to a single user at a time. The first three can be undertaken at the same time if the users are each modifying a different record, layout, or script. The remaining development actions are limited to a single user at a time within the respective developer dialog, that is, one user can edit value lists, and at the same time another is editing schema since they are done in different dialogs.

- Editing the *same* record

- Modifying the *same* layout

- Modifying the *same* script

- Modifying *any* database schema: tables, fields, and relationships

- Modifying *any* value list

- Modifying *any* data source

- Modifying *any* security access privileges

Configuring Network Settings

To share a file, use the *FileMaker Network Settings* dialog, shown in Figure 32-4. Open this by selecting the *Share with FileMaker Clients* option from the *File* ➤ *Sharing* submenu or using the toolbar's *Share* menu.

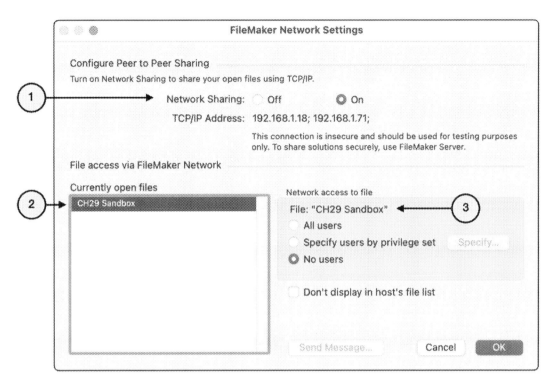

Figure 32-4. *The dialog used to configure database network sharing*

This dialog serves two purposes. The top enables the local application to accept incoming peer-to-peer connections, while the bottom configures network access for individual files. Follow these steps depending on your needs:

1. Turn *Network Sharing* on only if the local FileMaker Client application will host files on the network using *peer-to-peer sharing.*

2. Select an open database to configure its ability to accept incoming connections wherever it is hosted.

3. Select the user account(s) that can be used for incoming connections, either "All users" or specify one or more groups of users by privilege set.

Caution   FileMaker will not host a database lacking adequate account credentials (Chapter 29)!

The *Don't display in host's file list* checkbox option can be selected for background data files that are shared but shouldn't be opened directly by the user. Enabling this will cause the database to be invisible to the user in the host's menu of available files but still be opened by other files that use resources within it.

Configuring Peer-to-Peer Sharing

The *peer-to-peer sharing* option allows a user to share up to 125 databases with their copy of the FileMaker Pro desktop application and act as host for up to five concurrent remote client connections. Since the peer host is running a client version of the software, both the host and other connected users can perform data entry and development tasks in the files, depending on their access privileges. The top half of *FileMaker Network Settings* dialog is used to enable peer sharing for the client's local application. The *Network Sharing* setting can be turned on or off here. Once turned on, the *TCP/IP Address* of the computer will be displayed which users can use to find the host. A warning also appears here about peer sharing not being a secure network protocol since only FileMaker Server and FileMaker Cloud have options for the Secure Sockets Layer (SSL) certification that enables secure transfer across a network. While not adequate for large workgroups or where security is important, this method can be workable for sharing a database with a small group of colleagues. However, it is intended for development testing.

Setting File Access via FileMaker Network

The bottom half of the *FileMaker Network Settings* dialog includes a list of databases open locally and allows network access settings to be configured in the adjacent panel. These settings control client access to the file when it is hosted by FileMaker Server, FileMaker Cloud, or a peer-enabled copy of the FileMaker Pro desktop application. With a file selected, choose which users can connect to the selected file from another workstation. Select *All Users* to allow any user who enters valid credentials to access the selected file. Select *Specify users by privilege set* to limit access to specific privilege sets you select. The default selection for a new file is *No users* which will deny all access to the file until the setting is changed. The *Don't display in Launch Center* checkbox will hide the database in the *Hosts* open database dialog. A user must manually enter the name and address of the file to open it directly. This setting can be used to increase security or exclude from the list of available files any background data files without interfaces that open automatically when another database using its tables opens.

Note   Similar dialogs accessed from the *File ➤ Sharing* menu are used to configure the database's ODBC/JDBC and WebDirect settings.

Opening a Hosted Database

To open a hosted file with the FileMaker Pro desktop application, select the *File ➤ Hosts ➤ Show Hosts* menu, or click the *Hosts* button on the *Open File* dialog. This opens a *Hosts* dialog, shown in Figure 32-5, which provides access to files from host computers instead of from local folder directories. The sidebar contains three collapsible groups:

- *Claris ID* – Used to access databases hosted on a FileMaker Cloud account. Cloud-hosted files can also be opened from the *My Apps* section of the *Launch Center*.

- *Favorites* – Access files saved as favorites by right-clicking the file in another group and choosing *Add to Favorites* from the contextual menu.

- *Local* – Access a local peer or local FileMaker Server (as shown).

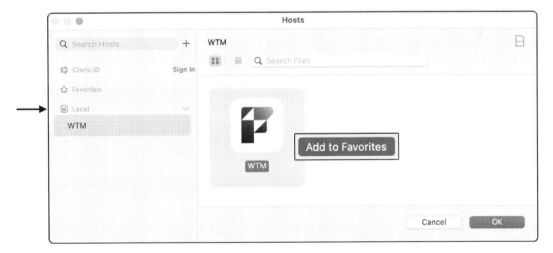

Figure 32-5. *The Host dialog provides access to files shared by other computers*

Hosting with FileMaker Server

FileMaker Server is a fast, reliable, and scalable software package that securely shares database files across a network. The server has powerful features and benefits including the following:

- Reliable, full-time serving of databases to users of any of the FileMaker product line running on macOS, Windows, or iOS.

- Multiple, flexible licensing options that can be mixed and matched to suit the needs of your individual team members.

- Share databases on the Web without web programming using *FileMaker WebDirect,* or use *Custom Web Publishing* to create data-driven websites with PHP or XML.

- Use *Open Database Connectivity* (ODBC) and *Java Database Connectivity* (JDBC) to share hosted database with remote systems.

- Monitor and manage the server locally or remotely using either the *Admin Console* web interface or the *fmsadmin* command-line tools.

- Automate administration tasks with automatic database backups and scheduled scripts.

- Scripts can be designed to offload tasks from the client's software to run on the server using the *Perform Script On Server* step (Chapter 24).

Note   For more information beyond the hosting basics described in this chapter, consult the FileMaker Server product support section located at `https://www`
`.claris.com/resources/documentation/`.

Preparing a Host Computer

There are important considerations when choosing a computer for a server host. The computer should have a fast processor, plenty of RAM, and a solid-state hard drive. Connect it to a network using a wired, high-speed, dedicated network connection, and ideally assign it a static IP address. To allow for priority use of the processor, hard disk, and network capacity, dedicate the computer exclusively for hosting databases. To avoid corruption, the folder containing live hosted databases should not be backed up directly by the OS or third-party software. Instead, use FileMaker Server's built-in scheduled backup feature, and then make additional copies of those backups to other drives. Also, disable screen savers and energy-saving hibernation features in favor of monitor dimming. Turn off indexing services such as the macOS Spotlight feature, and don't use antivirus software scans.

Tip   Check the Claris website for current minimum hardware requirements for a server and other server recommendations.

Defining Installed Resources

FileMaker Server is loaded onto a computer using a standard software installer. However, it isn't a traditional application and will not appear in the computer's Applications folder. Instead, the following resources will be installed:

- *Database server* – Hosts the databases, sharing them with FileMaker Pro and FileMaker Go clients.

- *Web publishing engine* – Handles the optional WebDirect services, managing traffic between a Web Server and the Database Server.

- *Web server* – macOS uses its own copy of the Apache web server. On Windows, the Internet Information Services is enabled during installation and used as the web server.

- *PHP engine* – Used to route calls for the FileMaker API to the Web Publishing Engine.

- *Admin console* – Accessed through a web browser on the server or a client computer; this is used to configure and administer the server.

- *Command-line interface executable* – The *fmsadmin* commands are used to administer the server through a command-line interface.

- *User account* – Specifies an account under which the server will run. The default choice on macOS is a new *fmserver* user created by the installer and, on Windows, the Local System. A custom account can be specified instead, if desired.

- *User group* – A new user group called *fmsadmin* is created and must be assigned to hosted database files.

Accessing the Admin Console

The *Admin Console* is a web-based interface used to administer and monitor the server. After installation of the server software package, a bookmark to the local host will be found on the computer's desktop. The console can also be accessed manually at the following address:

```
http://localhost:16001/admin-console
```

To access the console remotely, replace the localhost with the server address.

```
https://10.0.1.20:16000/admin-console
https://10.0.1.20/admin-console
```

When the console page opens and requests authentication, enter the administrator's name and password you defined during installation. Server administration controls are organized across seven tabbed pages:

- *Dashboard* – Summarizes server details, status, and performance information

- *Databases* – Lists all installed databases and connected clients, with controls to manage databases and communicate with or disconnect clients

- *Backups* – Used to schedule and view backups

- *Configuration* – Contains general settings, clients, folders, scheduled scripts, notifications, certificates, and logging

- *Connectors* – Contains settings for WebDirect, Web Publishing, FileMaker Data API, Plug-ins, and ODBC/JDBC connections

- *Administration* – Contains license, admin password, and external authentication settings

- *Logs* – Used to view logs and configure log settings

Uploading Files to a FileMaker Server

Database files can be added to the server by manually moving them into the *Databases folder* or uploading them from a client computer through the FileMaker Pro desktop application.

Moving the File into the Databases Folder

The server keeps hosted files in a *Databases* subfolder of the *FileMaker Server* folder. If installed into the default location, this folder will be in one of two locations depending on the operating system. It will be found in the *Library* folder on macOS or in the *Program Files* folder on Windows, both shown below.

```
/Library/FileMaker Server/Data/Databases
[drive]:\Program Files\FileMaker\FileMaker Server\Data\Databases\
```

To manually install files, simply drag them into the *Databases* folder. However, when adding files this way, they may need to be reassigned to the *fmserver* user and *fmsadmin* group.

Caution   If databases are actively hosted by the server, do not interact with them directly in the folder! Removing, replacing, or directly opening them with the FileMaker Pro desktop application will cause major corruption. Confirm files are not actively hosted before performing any of these functions.

Uploading a File from a Client Computer

A database file created on a client computer can be uploaded directly to a server through the FileMaker Pro desktop application. For FileMaker Cloud servers, this is the only method available for uploading a file to the server. Open the *Upload to Host* dialog by selecting the *Upload to Host* option from the *Sharing* submenu or the *Sharing* icon menu in the toolbar. The dialog is like the *Hosts* dialog with a sidebar for selecting a host, as shown in Figure 32-6. Once selected, sign in to the host to begin adding databases.

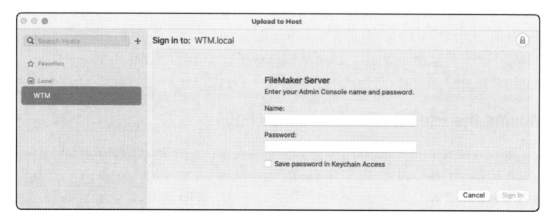

Figure 32-6. *The sign-in dialog is used to upload to a host*

After entering admin credentials for the selected host, the dialog shows an empty list waiting for database uploads. Drag databases into the list or click the *Browse* button to select them through a dialog. As databases are added, FileMaker runs a consistency check to determine the health of the file and checks to see if it has adequate security for hosting, as shown in Figure 32-7. In the example, two uploads are in the list. The first has failed to pass the authentication requirements and is not eligible to upload. The second has passed and is ready. Enable the checkbox next to each approved file to include it in the upload. The checkbox at the bottom of the dialog will cause files to automatically open on the server after the upload is complete.

Figure 32-7. *The dialog showing database file(s) to be uploaded*

Managing Database Files

To manage hosted databases, log in to the *Admin Console* and click the *Databases* tab. A drop-down menu next to each database in the list contains the following commands:

- *Open* – Opens the database, hosting it for network access. This will require entry of a password if the file is encrypted.

- *Close* – Close and cease hosting the database.

- *Download* – Download a copy of a closed database to the local hard drive. In macOS, this feature will not work if pop-up windows are blocked by the browser preferences!

- *Remove* – Remove a closed database from the list, and move it into a special subfolder in the *Databases* folder that is not available for hosting.

- *Verify* – Close, verify, and reopen a database.

- *Clear the encryption passwords* – Remove the saved encryption password from the selected database file(s).

Tip   A similar menu at the top of the database list mirrors these options but with commands that affect all databases.

Restarting a Server Computer

When the server is actively hosting files, it may be actively communicating with clients, be holding recent changes in cache, or be in the middle of writing those changes to disk. A file can become corrupt if the server process is force quit or hardware is abruptly forced to shut down. To avoid damage, it is important to avoid certain risks and properly close databases. Always use an adequate uninterruptible power supply (UPS) device on the server to ensure it can sustain power interruptions. Also, it is a good practice to close all databases in the *Admin Console* prior to shutting down a computer. Never force quit the application or perform a hard reboot of the computer without first closing files unless necessary due to a major crash or malfunction.

Using the Command-Line Interface

The *fmsadmin* command-line tool allows administration of the server using the Terminal app (macOS) or the command prompt (Windows). These commands are automatically installed in the following platform-specific folder(s):

```
macOS = /Library/FileMaker Server/Database Server/bin/fmsadmin
macOS (symbolic link) = /usr/bin/fmsadmin
Windows = [drive]:\Program Files\FileMaker\FileMaker Server\Database
Server\fmsadmin.exe
```

Formatting a fmsadmin Command

The formula for a command is as follows:

```
fmsadmin <command> <options>
```

For example, to get a list of all hosted databases, type the following command into the Terminal and type Enter:

```
fmsadmin list files
```

Certain functions require authentication and will prompt you to enter the server administrator user name and password. Optionally, you can include credential information with the command to avoid the secondary prompt. Simply add them as shown in the pattern and example here:

```
fmsadmin <command> -u <user> -p <password>
fmsadmin list files -u Admin -p J56TF3
```

Available fmsadmin Commands

The *fmsadmin* tool contains the following commands, each with various options available:

- *autorestart* – Get or set the auto-restart feature of the server.

- *backup* – Back up one database or every database in a folder.

- *clearkey* – Remove saved database encryption passwords.

- *close* – Close one or more databases.

- *certificate* – Manage SSL certificates.

- *disable* – Disable schedules or statistics logging.

- *disconnect* – Disconnect one or more clients.

- *enable* – Enable schedules or statistics logging.

- *help* – Get help with available commands.

- *list* – List clients, databases, plug-ins, or schedules.

- *open* – Start hosting databases.

- *pause* – Temporarily stop the database server.

- *remove* – Move files out of the Databases folder.

- *resetpw* – Reset the admin user password.

- *restart* – Restart the server, adminserver, FMSE, WPE, or XDBC process.

- *resume* – End a temporary pause of the database server.

- *run* – Run a schedule.

- *send* - Send a message to connected users.
- *standby* - Manage standby server connections, roles, and updates.
- *start* - Start the server, adminserver, FMSE, WPE, or XDBC process.
- *status* - Get the status of clients or databases.
- *stop* - Stop the server, adminserver, FMSE, WPE, or XDBC process.
- *verify* - Check the consistency of databases.

Getting Detailed Command Help

To get more information about a command and its options, type "help" followed by the name of the command. For example, use the prompt below to return a help page for the close command, as shown in Figure 32-8.

```
fmsadmin help close
```

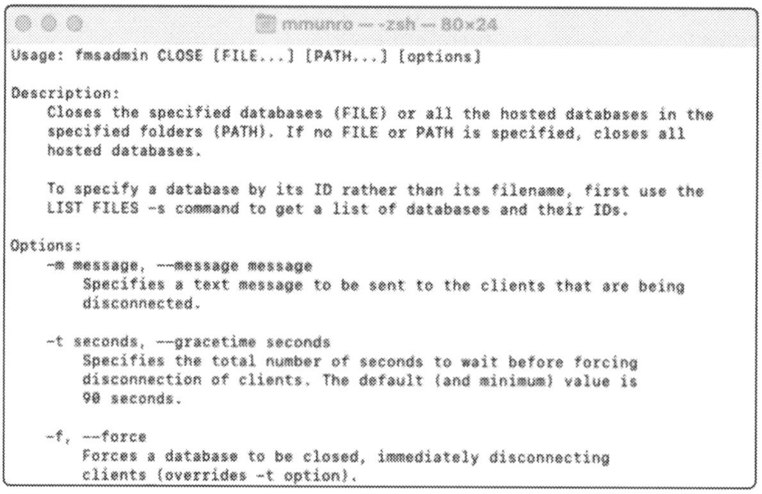

```
Usage: fmsadmin CLOSE [FILE...] [PATH...] [options]

Description:
    Closes the specified databases (FILE) or all the hosted databases in the
    specified folders (PATH). If no FILE or PATH is specified, closes all
    hosted databases.

    To specify a database by its ID rather than its filename, first use the
    LIST FILES -s command to get a list of databases and their IDs.

Options:
    -m message, --message message
        Specifies a text message to be sent to the clients that are being
        disconnected.

    -t seconds, --gracetime seconds
        Specifies the total number of seconds to wait before forcing
        disconnection of clients. The default (and minimum) value is
        90 seconds.

    -f, --force
        Forces a database to be closed, immediately disconnecting
        clients (overrides -t option).
```

Figure 32-8. *An example of the command help request*

Hosting with FileMaker Cloud

FileMaker Cloud is a service by Claris that provides reliable access to Cloud-hosted databases. While the use and configuration interface are nearly identical as those described earlier for FileMaker Server, there are some important differences with Cloud.

The hardware is managed by Claris, so you don't need to be concerned with hardware or energy costs. There is no way to access the folder structure directly, so interactions with the server and databases can only be performed through the *Admin Console*. To protect your information, all databases must be encrypted when uploaded to the cloud. Various maintenance tasks such as daily backups, software upgrades, automatic restarts during nonbusiness hours, and other maintenance tasks are or can be performed automatically. Another benefit is that Claris provides round the clock support options.

Note   For more information about Claris hosting your database solution, visit www.claris.com/filemaker/cloud/.

Hosting with Ottomatic by Proof+Geist

FileMaker Server hosting by third parties is also an option. One notable service is the *Ottomatic platform* by Proof+Geist. It is a one-stop shop for FileMaker developers and users to host, manage, deploy, and connect FileMaker apps to the world. It is the only SOC II certified FileMaker hosting and application platform that goes far beyond traditional hosting services. It is globally available, packed with powerful features and backed by a world-class support team. Try Ottomatic and get automated application updates, developer environments, and powerful FileMaker extensions that can help make your applications soar. Other key features and capabilities include the following:

- Manage both cloud and on-premise servers with a unified cloud console.

- View server stats and adjust server settings.

- Download backups and other files stored on the server.

- Start, stop, and restart FileMaker Server and related services with *OttoFMS*.

- Deploy solutions and schedule deployments with *OttoDeploy*.

- Migrate FileMaker data.

- Receive data from web services and applications with webhooks.

- Configure custom OAuth solutions.

- Create custom integrations and automations with the Developer API.

- Access comprehensive logs for enhanced debugging and monitoring capabilities.

- A human support team augmented by advanced automated server monitoring to help keep you up and running.

- SOC2 Certified with Service Level Agreement (SLA) and custom support options available.

To learn more about the Ottomatic platform, visit the following:
`https://www.ottomatic.cloud/learn-filemaker-pro-book`

Using WebDirect

FileMaker WebDirect brings a custom database to the web browser without requiring a knowledge of advanced web technologies. With the configuration of a few settings, any database can be easily made available to users through a web browser. All the web programming required to present the database in a web front end is handled automatically by FileMaker Server or FileMaker Cloud. Layouts are automatically rendered in the browser, and, except for certain incompatible script steps and the ability to easily work in multiple windows, most functionality is identical to that on a desktop or iOS device.

Preparing for WebDirect

Before sharing with WebDirect, be sure to exhaustively test the interface to ensure it functions as expected. Although WebDirect does an impressive job of rendering a FileMaker layout into a web page, there are some features that either aren't supported or will not work as expected in WebDirect. Keep these in mind when designing a layout that will be deployed on the Web.

- *Browser tabs* - The entire WebDirect interface loads inside a single tab of the browser. If the user tries to open WebDirect in a separate tab, they will be creating an additional session.

- *Multiple windows* – Like with FileMaker Client, WebDirect allows multiple windows in a session but calls them virtual windows because they load within the singular browser tab. When a window is created and selected, the entire WebDirect interface shifts to reflect the selected window. It is possible to create, select, and close virtual windows. It is not possible to resize nor reposition virtual windows.

- *Custom menus* – WebDirect does not support custom menus.

- *Text styling* – Various features like highlighting, paragraph text styles, and tab stops are not supported. Rich text is limited and can't be applied during data entry, and editing a field in WebDirect will remove any existing formatting.

- *Graphic effects* – Gradients, drop shadows, or opacity settings might not display as intended.

- *Keyboard shortcuts* – Shortcuts or key commands like those involving the Command key on macOS or the Control key on Windows are not supported.

- *Layered objects* – A mouse click will not pass through one item and target an item layered beneath it like it does in FileMaker.

- *Script steps* – Any steps encountered that are incompatible with WebDirect will be skipped over as the script continues to run. The client's file system can't be accessed by scripts, so users need to select files to import or insert, and any exported files will be downloaded to the web browser's default downloads folder.

- *Script triggers* – A few event triggers may not behave as expected. For example, *OnLayoutKeystroke* may not capture all keystrokes while *OnObjectEnter* and *OnObjectExit* may not trigger under certain conditions.

- *Value lists* – A list with lots of items will not scroll smoothly like on the desktop. The user must click through "pages" of items. Either limit items in lists or use other methods such as a Card window opening a tall radio button control style or a web viewer connected to a script that inserts a selected value.

- *Web viewers* – Using complex JavaScript or interactive features like drag and drop or certain media content might not function correctly.

To learn more about the various considerations when developing for WebDirect, visit the Claris WebDirect guide:

`https://help.claris.com/en/webdirect-guide/content/index.html`

Caution   Always carefully test a new solution on each target platform prior to deploying it into a production workflow!

Configuring a Database for WebDirect

To configure a database for WebDirect access, select "Configure for FileMaker WebDirect" from the *File* ➤ *Sharing* menu. This opens the FileMaker WebDirect Settings dialog, shown in Figure 32-9.

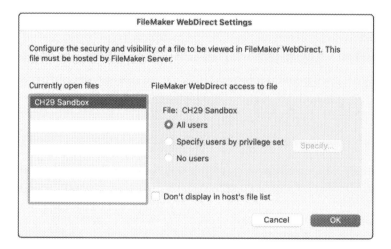

Figure 32-9. *The dialog used to enable WebDirect access to a file*

To configure a file for WebDirect, follow these steps:

- If more than one database is open, select the desired file from the list of open files.

- Select the user account(s) that can be used for incoming connections, either "All users," or specify one or more groups of users by privilege set.

The privilege sets selected will automatically have the *fmwebdirect* extended privilege activated which is a requirement for users assigned to that set to access the database through a web browser. This extended setting can also be turned on or off by opening the *Manage Security* dialog and editing privilege sets (Chapter 29, "Exploring Privilege Sets").

The *Don't display in host's file list* checkbox option can be selected for background data files that are shared but shouldn't be opened directly by the user. Enabling this will cause the database to be invisible to the user in the host's menu of available files but still be opened by other files that use resources within it.

Configuring a Server for WebDirect

The host server must also be configured so that WebDirect is enabled, as shown in Figure 32-10.

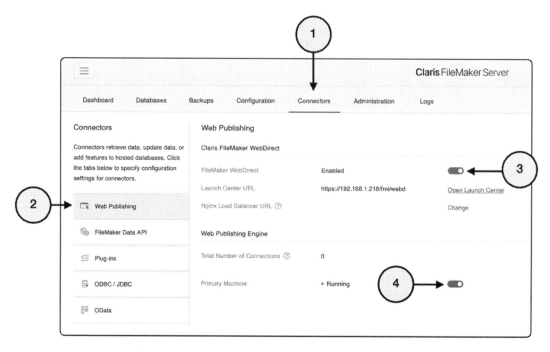

Figure 32-10. *Configuring the host server for WebDirect*

Sign in to the Admin Console and follow these steps:

1. Select the "Connectors" tab.

2. Select *Web Publishing* in the sidebar.

3. Click to enable *FileMaker WebDirect*.

4. Click to enable the *Web Publishing Engine*.

When activating the *Web Publishing Engine*, FileMaker Server may require you to download and install a Java Development Kit. Follow the instructions presented to accurately select, download, and install this required software.

Accessing a Database in the Browser

Once configured and hosted, users should be able to access databases by opening the *Launch Center URL* listed in the *Admin Console*. In the example shown, the address is as follows:

```
https://192.168.1.218/fmi/webd
```

Open the link in a browser to access the menu of databases with WebDirect sharing enabled, as shown in Figure 32-11. Select a file from the available list and enter account credentials in the *Sign in* screen.

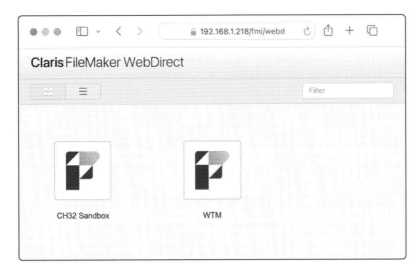

Figure 32-11. *The Launch Center showing a list of hosted files configured for WebDirect access*

Status Toolbar (WebDirect)

When the database opens, the content area will look almost identical to the experience in the desktop application. However, the menu and toolbar are transformed completely, condensed into a set of controls and menus shown in Figure 32-12.

- Menus are accessed by clicking the drop-down arrow on the left and then clicking through the hierarchy of commands.

- The navigation display looks similar except for the record count area opening a panel with controls for sliding through the found set and a menu for the *Show All Records*, *Show Omitted Only*, and *Omit Record* commands.

- Three icons after this provide access to the New Record (+), *Delete Record* (-), and *Sort* functions.

- The magnifying glass icon next to the *QuickFind* control opens a panel menu for access to the *Enter Find Mode* and *Repeat Last Find* commands.

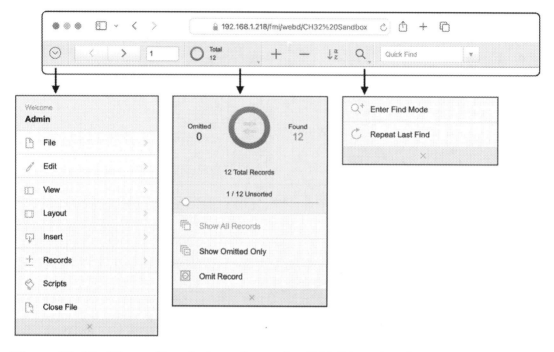

Figure 32-12. *The toolbar design when using WebDirect in a browser*

Caution   A user's access to a database via the web counts against the number of connections granted by the FileMaker Server license agreement! Be sure to purchase enough to cover all connections.

Summary

This chapter introduced the methods of solution deployment and various ways to access databases. In the next chapter, we explore some methods of exchanging data with external systems.

Interfacing External Systems

As a modern development platform, FileMaker can be integrated with external systems using a wide range of technologies. Users can easily use and share *snapshot link* files that provide bookmarking capabilities, instantly opening a database and taking the user to a specific context. A *FileMaker URL* can be embedded in a web page or emailed to automatically open and perform a script. Custom AppleScripts can be written on macOS to automate database tasks and create integrated workflows with other scriptable applications. A database can reach out to connect to ODBC and JDBC databases or become an ODBC data source for external systems. The *FileMaker Data API* offers a modern way to integrate databases with web services and external applications using the *Representational State Transfer* (REST) architecture. These are some of the options discussed in this chapter as we explore the following topics:

- Sharing bookmarks with snapshot links

- Accessing a database with FileMaker URL

- Automating FileMaker with AppleScript

- Connecting to an ODBC Database

- Connecting with the FileMaker Data API

Sharing Bookmarks with Snapshot Links

A *snapshot link* is an XML file that stores information about a record or a found set of records which can be used to recreate a previously existing found set. They act like a sharable bookmark, referencing a specific context and found set of records within a

M. C. Munro, *Learn FileMaker Pro 2024*, https://doi.org/10.1007/979-8-8688-0835-7_33

database. Opening a snapshot link file will automatically open the database, navigate to the layout, and restore the found set of records, thereby recreating the same context a user was viewing at the time they saved the snapshot. These files can be stored in folders and sent to coworkers, allowing users to exchange lists of records with other users. For example, a client folder on a company file server can store a snapshot link file that instantly opens the database to a list view of contacts for that company.

Note See the "CH33-01 Snapshot Link" example folder.

To generate a snapshot link, select the *File ➤ Save/Send Records As ➤ Snapshot Link* menu. This will open a *Save Records* dialog with snapshot configuration options, shown in Figure 33-1. Enter a name and choose a save location for the link. The *Save* menu contains two options: *Current record* or *Records being browsed*. The optional *After saving* checkbox can be used to create an email with the snapshot attached. A script can use the *Send Records as Snapshot Link* step which contains the same configuration dialog to automate snapshot link generation. Once the file is saved, change layouts and/or the found set of records, and then double-click the saved snapshot to see it recreates the previous context.

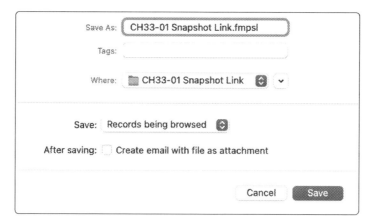

Figure 33-1. *The dialog used to configure and save a snapshot link*

Caution For the snapshot link to work, the database must be hosted in a location accessible by everyone at the same path or address, ideally hosted on a FileMaker Server.

Accessing a Database with FileMaker URL

The *FileMaker URL* Internet protocol is automatically registered during the FileMaker Pro client application install and allows specially formatted URLs to open a database and run a script. As long as a user account's privilege set is explicitly granted permission to the *fmurlscript* extended privilege (Chapter 29), a URL can target the database using any of the following methods:

- *From a Web Browser* – Type or paste a URL into a web browser and the command will be routed to FileMaker.

- *From a Web Page* — Use a *href* tag to create a link in a custom web page loaded into a web browser. It can also be placed in a web viewer on a layout in a database, although the new *FileMaker.PerformScript* JavaScript function is a better option for internal calls from HTML to FileMaker (Chapter 20, "Calling a FileMaker Script with JavaScript").

- *From a FileMaker Script* – Use the *Open URL* script step to trigger other scripts in a database from a calculated address. However, the *Perform Script* step now has a better option to run a script by a calculated name (Chapter 24, "Performing Other Scripts").

- *From External Applications and Scripts* – Programming languages such as AppleScript can instruct the FileMaker application to run the URL.

Note   See examples in the "CH33-02 FileMaker URL" example folder.

Formatting a Basic FMP URL

The address must include a *prefix*, *address*, and *file name*.

```
<prefix>://<address>/<file><extension>
```

The inclusion of an extension is optional. Starting with version 18, the *prefix* can include a version number to specify a version if many are installed. Without a version specified, the URL should route to the last installed version. An *address* is always required to open a database. To reference a file that is already open, use a dollar symbol ($) as the address. For example, to refer to an open *Contacts* database, the address would be formatted as shown in the following examples:

```
fmp://$/Contacts.fmp12
fmp18://$/Contacts.fmp12
fmp21://$/Contacts.fmp12
```

If the target database is stored in the user's local *Documents* folder, use a tilde as the address as shown in the following example which will automatically open the database:

```
fmp19://~/Contacts.fmp12
```

All URLs must be *percent encoded* except when using the *Open URL* script step within FileMaker. For example, a database named "Learn FileMaker" would require the space changed to "%20" as shown in the following example:

```
fmp://$/Learn%20FileMaker.fmp12
```

Tip   When building a URL in a FileMaker calculation, use the *GetAsURLEncoded* function to automatically handle encoding.

Addressing a Hosted Database

To use the FMP URL to access a database hosted on a network server, include the address to a host computer. For example, if a Contacts database was hosted, the URL can be formatted with an IPv4 address, IPv6 address, or a DNS name as shown in these three examples:

```
FMP://10.1.0.10/Contacts.fmp12
FMP://[2001:0db8:0a0b:12f0:0000:0000:0000:0001]/Contacts.fmp12
FMP://filemaker-server.local/Contacts.fmp12
```

Including Access Credentials

To bypass the database's account credential dialog and achieve a seamless operation, an account and password can be specified in the URL. These can be added as colon-delimited values ahead of the address separated by an "@" sign. For example, a database with an account named "admin" that has a password of "58Jt234" can be opened without a password dialog using the address shown in the following example:

```
FMP://admin:58Jt234@10.1.0.10/Contacts.fmp12
```

Caution   Saving credential information in a URL is a security risk! Limit this to internal web access and/or low-risk databases.

Including a Script Name

The URL can also instruct FileMaker to run a script in the database. Add a question mark after the database name, then "script=" and a URL encoded script name. For example, the following will confirm a *Contacts* database is open from the specified host computer, and then run a script named "Find":

```
FMP://10.1.0.10/Contacts.fmp12?script=Find
```

For brevity, the account credentials are excluded in the above example and will be in other examples in this section. However, these can be included to ensure the database opens without a dialog requesting that information. When the script runs, it will be executed with the privileges and limitations of the user account used to sign into the database.

Adding a Script Parameter

When targeting a script that accepts parameters, the URL can include a param value by appending it after the script name and an ampersand. For example, instead of always searching for the same criteria, the *Find* script from the previous example can be designed to accept a parameter and use that value as some or all of the criteria for the search. Each of these examples will run the same script but provide a different status value to find records that have "Active" or "Hold" in a status field.

```
FMP://10.1.0.10/Contacts.fmp12?script=Find&param=Active
FMP://10.1.0.10/Contacts.fmp12?script=Find&param=Hold
```

Adding Script Variables

The URL can go even farther and initialize local variables within the script by adding an ampersand and the name and value of the variables, following the pattern shown here:

```
FMP://<address>/<database>?<script>&param=<Parameter>&<$variable>=<value>
```

This example initializes a variable specifying a state name for the find script:

```
FMP://10.1.0.10/Contacts.fmp12?script=Find&param=Active&$State=TX
```

Automating FileMaker with AppleScript

External scripting languages can control a FileMaker database. On macOS, *AppleScript* is an *Open Scripting Architecture* (OSA) compliant language that can communicate with and control applications (https://goo.gl/i7Olnx). Back in 1994 when the language was first introduced as a part of the Macintosh System 7.5, FileMaker was one of the first scriptable applications. Since then, support for the language has continued to provide a great option for automating database functions and integrating it into workflows with other applications. If a user account's privilege set is explicitly granted permission to the *fmextscriptaccess* extended privilege (Chapter 29), an AppleScript will be able to control application and database actions.

Note   See examples in the "CH33-03 AppleScript" folder.

Defining the Tell FileMaker Statement

AppleScripts are written using the *Script Editor* application located in the *Utilities* subfolder of the *Applications* folder of every macOS computer. Event instructions are sent to an application using a *tell statement* that points to the application and encloses the object references and commands.

```
tell application "FileMaker Pro"
    <commands>
end tell
```

Opening FileMaker's Script Dictionary

Every scriptable macOS application has a script dictionary which can be opened by dropping the application onto the *Script Editor* application or by launching the editor and selecting the *File ➤ Open Directory* menu. This opens a window exposing the dictionary of objects and commands available for controlling the application, as shown in Figure 33-2.

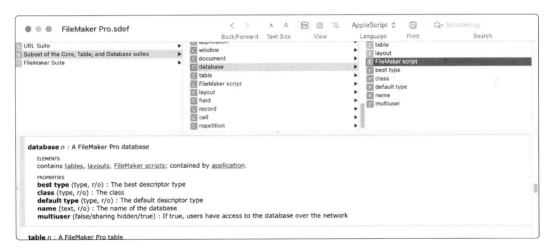

Figure 33-2.   *The FileMaker Pro AppleScript dictionary window*

Caution   FileMaker's script commands use three different words to describe a database window: *database*, *document*, and *window*. Each of these can be used interchangeably but may have a slightly different effect.

Scripting Basic Tasks

As a brief introduction to automating FileMaker with scripts, this section presents a few simple examples of opening a database, activating an open database, changing layouts, performing a find, and counting records. These can be expanded with other functions to create complex scripted workflows that perform vastly more complex actions. They can also be woven with script commands sent to other applications to create powerful inter-application data transfer solutions.

Note   FileMaker also includes a script step called "Perform AppleScript" that allows AppleScript commands to be embedded in a database script that sends commands to other applications.

Opening a Database

AppleScript can open a database from any folder using the *open file* command. This example sets the value of three variables to the path to a database, an account name, and password. These are used to instruct FileMaker to open the file:

```
set pathToDatabase to "Macintosh HD:Users:mmunro:CH33-03 AppleScript.fmp12"
set textAccount to "Admin"
set textPassword to ""
tell application "FileMaker Pro"
    open file pathToDatabase with passwords textPassword for Accounts
    textAccount
end tell
```

To open a hosted database, the *getURL* command will accept a FileMaker URL described earlier in this chapter.

```
tell application "FileMaker Pro"
   getURL "fmp://Admin:58Jt-234@10.0.1.20/CH33-03%20AppleScript.fmp12"
end tell
```

Caution   Including database credential information in an AppleScript document is a security risk! Keep your script files in a safe location.

Activating an Open Database

To bring an open database to the front of the document window stack, this example checks if the document exists and then uses the *show* command to activate the database:

```
set nameDatabase to "CH33-03 AppleScript"
tell application "FileMaker Pro"
   if (document nameDatabase exists) = true then
      show document nameDatabase
   end if
end tell
```

Changing Layouts

This example activates a layout named "Contact List" using the *show* command:

```
tell application "FileMaker Pro"
   tell document "CH33-03 AppleScript"
      show layout "Contact List"
   end tell
end tell
```

Showing All Records

To perform the *Show All Records* command, use the *show* command with a reference of *every record*.

```
tell application "FileMaker Pro"
   tell database "CH33-03 AppleScript"
      tell table "Contact"
         show every record
      end tell
   end tell
end tell
```

Finding Records Based on a Field Value

This example appends a *whose* clause to the *show* command to search based on a specific value within one field.

```
set nameTable to "Contact"
set nameField to "Contact State"
set textToFind to "NY"
tell application "FileMaker Pro"
   tell database "CH33-03 AppleScript"
      tell table nameTable
         show every record whose cell nameField of table nameTable contains
         textToFind
      end tell
   end tell
end tell
```

A *whose* clause can be appended with various operators for matching data in the field, including *contains, does not contain, is equal to,* and *is not equal to.* Further, clauses can be grouped with others to form compound search criteria, as shown in these examples:

```
show every record whose cell nameField of table nameTable contains value1
show every record whose cell nameField of table nameTable is equal to value2
show every record whose cell nameField of table nameTable is not equal
to value3
```

Counting Records in the Found Set

To count the records in the found set of the current window, a *tell window* statement is required to refer to the context displayed, regardless of the layout or table.

```
tell application "FileMaker Pro"
   tell window "CH33-03 AppleScript"
      return the number of every record
   end tell
end tell
```

Counting Every Record in a Table

To count the total records in the table regardless of the current window's layout, use a *tell database* statement.

```
tell application "FileMaker Pro"
   tell database "CH33-03 AppleScript"
      return the number of every record of table "Contact"
   end tell
end tell
```

Connecting to an ODBC Database

Open Database Connectivity (ODBC) is a standard application programming interface (API) that provides client applications a common language for interacting with other database systems. Developed in the early 1990s by Microsoft and Simba Technologies, it quickly became a standard for database access to data in other systems. Later, it was used by Sun Microsystems as the basis for their *Java Database Connectivity* (JDBC), which is a similar API for accessing systems written in the Java language. FileMaker can act as an *ODBC client application,* supporting connections from a database out to external SQL data sources such as those from Oracle, Microsoft SQL, and MySQL. Once connected, tables from the external database can be added to the FileMaker database. These "shadow tables" act like a native FileMaker table with a few exceptions. FileMaker can also accommodate incoming connections, allowing a database to be used as an ODBC and JDBC data source by external systems. This section covers the basics of adding an ODBC table to a FileMaker relationship graph and setting up FileMaker as an ODBC data source.

Caution   ODBC connections are not required to connect two FileMaker databases!

Installing an ODBC Driver (macOS)

FileMaker can use both ODBC and JDBC to communicate with an external data source. On a Macintosh computer, it is necessary to install software to establish a connection. Once installed and configured, FileMaker connects to the *Driver Manager* application which accesses a *Client Driver* configuration to connect to the *ODBC Data Source*, as illustrated in Figure 33-3. This process must be performed on a computer hosting a database that will be used as an ODBC client, accessing a remote ODBC data source, and on a FileMaker Server when it hosts databases acting as an ODBC data source for external systems.

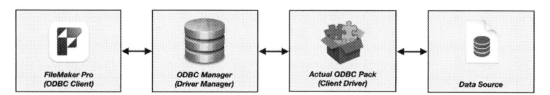

Figure 33-3. *Connecting a FileMaker database to an ODBC data source on a Macintosh computer*

The process for connecting a macOS computer and FileMaker database to an external ODBC data source is as follows:

1. Install ODBC Resources (Drive Manager and Client Drivers).

2. Configure an ODBC Driver.

3. Connect a FileMaker database to the ODBC client driver.

4. Insert and use ODBC tables in the FileMaker database.

Installing ODBC Resources

First, start by downloading and installing the freeware *ODBC Manager application* onto the host computer, by following these steps:

1. Download the "ODBC Manager" disk image from `www.odbcmanager.net`.

2. Locate the "ODBC_Manager_Installer.dmg" file in your *Downloads* folder and launch it.

3. The "ODBC Manager" disk image will appear on your desktop and should open in a window.

4. Double-click the "ODBC Manager.pkg" file to launch the installer.

5. Step through the installer panels to complete the installation.

Once finished, the *ODBC Manager* application should be in your *Utilities* subfolder of the *Applications* folder.

Installing the ODBC Driver

Next, download and install the *ODBC Driver Pack* from Actual Technologies, by following these steps:

1. Download the "Actual ODBC Pack" disk image, available at `www.actualtech.com/download.php`.

2. Locate the "Actual_ODBC_Pack.dmg" file in your *Downloads* folder and launch it.

3. The "Actual ODBC Pack" disk image will appear on your desktop and should open in a window.

4. Double-click the "Actual ODBC Pack.pkg" file to launch the installer.

5. Step through the installer panels to complete the installation.

Note   The driver is a fully functional demo, limited to display only the first three rows resulting from any query. Purchase a license key from Actual Technologies web store to remove this limit.

Configuring an ODBC Driver

Next, add and configure a driver for the specific database to which a connection will be made. Begin by opening the *ODBC Manager* application, shown in Figure 33-4.

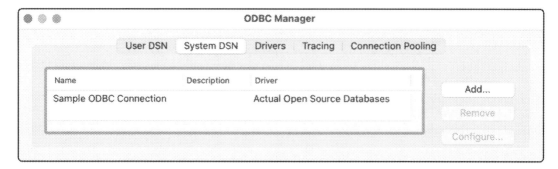

Figure 33-4. *The ODBC Manager with a single connection*

Then follow these steps:

1. Click the *System DSN* tab.

2. Click the *Add* button.

3. In the panel that opens, choose a driver appropriate for the target database: *Actual access, Actual open source databases, Actual oracle,* or *Actual SQL server.*

4. Enter settings into the multi-panel driver specific configuration dialog. These vary but generally include the server address, database name, user name, and password.

5. Click the *Done* button to close the configuration dialog.

6. The final panel of the configuration dialog allows you to test the connection.

7. Quit the *ODBC Manager* application.

Connecting FileMaker as an ODBC Client

Now, with installed and configured ODBC resources, it is time to connect a FileMaker database to the driver. This is done by setting up an *external data source* in the database and then adding table(s) from the external ODBC source into the FileMaker relationship graph.

Setting Up External Data Source

Select the *File* ➤ *Manage* ➤ *External Data Sources* menu item to open the *Manage External Data Source* dialog, shown in Figure 33-5. From here, you can create, edit, and delete references to external databases.

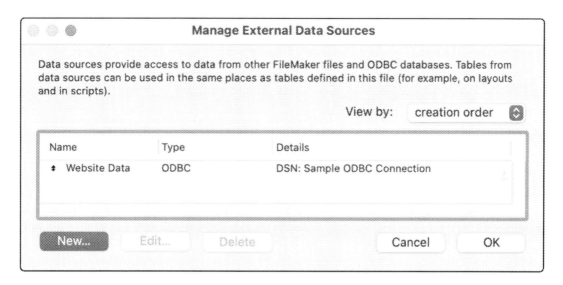

Figure 33-5. *The dialog to manage external data sources*

To add a new external source like the one shown, click the *New* button to open the *Edit Data Source* dialog. At first, the dialog will ask for a *File Path List* because the *Type* is set to "FileMaker." Once you select "ODBC" instead, the dialog will change, as shown in Figure 33-6.

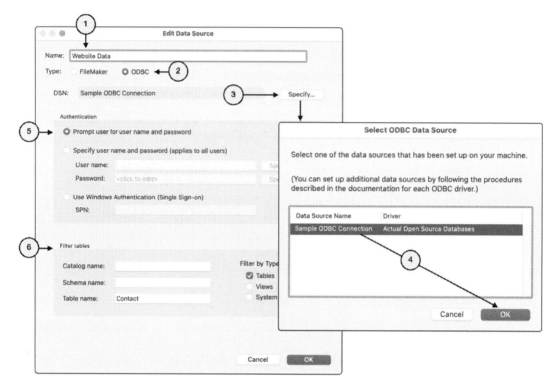

Figure 33-6. *The process for setting up an external data source*

Follow these steps to configure a connection to the ODBC driver:

1. *Name* – Enter a unique name for the data source for use within FileMaker. This doesn't have to match the actual ODBC database but it can.

2. *Type* – Select "ODBC" radio button. The dialog will transform to accommodate authentication and filter table options.

3. *DSN* – Click the *Specify* button to select the System DSN configured previously.

4. *Select ODBC data source* – Select the desired data source from the list defined earlier, and then click to close the dialog.

5. *Authentication options* – Optionally indicate how a user name and password should be entered at the user level when a database attempts to access the data source. For the smoothest user experience, enter the user name and password directly here so the user doesn't have to repeat that process with each new access.

6. *Filter tables* – Optionally add filtering criteria to control which
    tables are displayed when a connection is made. This can be
    helpful when a database has many tables, and you need to limit
    which are available within FileMaker to avoid failures. When
    finished, click to close the dialog.

Adding an ODBC Table to Relationship Graph

Adding an ODBC Table to a FileMaker database is a little different than with a regular
native table. Instead of adding it to the *Tables* tab of the *Manage Database* dialog and
it automatically appearing in the relationship graph (Chapter 9), a new ODBC table is
manually added to the graph which automatically adds it back into the table list. To do
this, open the *Manage Database* dialog and click the *Relationships* tab. Then follow these
steps shown in Figure 33-7:

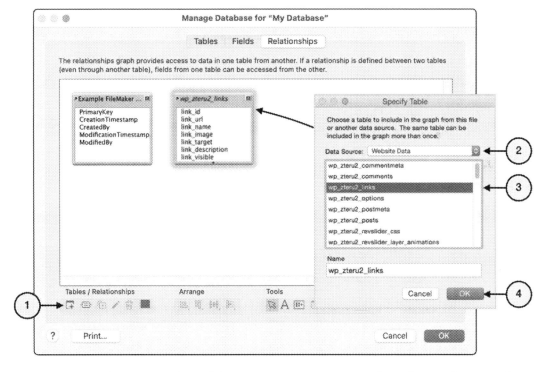

Figure 33-7. *The process for adding an ODBC source to the relationship graph*

1. Click the *Add Occurrence* button.

2. In the *Specify Table* dialog that opens, select the ODBC database in the *Data Source* menu.

3. Select the table from the list.

4. Click to add the table to the occurrence graph and list of tables.

Comparing an ODBC Shadow Table

When an ODBC table is added to the relationship graph, FileMaker automatically creates a "shadow table" in the *Tables* tab. This is an internal representation that mirrors the external table. These appear in the list on the *Tables* tab with italic formatting. Although this brings the external table into the database and allows interactions like a native FileMaker table, there are a few notable differences, including the following:

- *Schema lock* – The structure of the external data source is not available for modification from within FileMaker. The shadow table in FileMaker allows some modification, but this does not affect the remote table!

- *Deleting fields* – Fields can be deleted from the shadow table to help thin out the amount of data queried, but the fields remain in the remote table.

- *Modifying fields* – Auto-Enter settings (Chapter 8) for fields can be customized for the shadow table.

- *Adding supplemental fields* – Fields can be added to the shadow table but are limited to unstored calculations and summary fields and are not added to the remote table.

- *Data types* – When the remote table has separate data types for certain information that are handled as a single data type by FileMaker (e.g., integers and floating-point data instead of just number fields), a calculation may be required to convert data into a FileMaker data type.

- *Data entry limitations* – When the amount of data for certain field types is limited, FileMaker will try to respect these limits to avoid problems, but special care may be required.

- *Data updates* – Automatic refreshes of record changes in the external table are less frequent across the network than changes to native FileMaker tables. Use the *Refresh Window* script step to force an update and ensure that the data displayed is current.

- *Record locking* – Unlike native tables, records open for editing are not locked, so users can be editing the same record simultaneously. A warning dialog will alert users if the record had been modified since they began editing and give them the ability to stop to avoid overwriting the other user's changes.

- *Indexing* – FileMaker can't index SQL fields, so searches in external tables should be limited to those fields already indexed by the remote table to avoid long delays.

Tip   For more information, locate the "Claris FileMaker ODBC and JDBC Guide" online.

Setting Up FileMaker as an ODBC Data Source

A database can be configured as an ODBC or JDBC data source for incoming connections when hosted by the following:

- FileMaker Pro – Allowing up to five local connections from a system on the same computer

- FileMaker Server – Allows unrestricted connections from local or remote systems

---

Caution   FileMaker Cloud does not support using a database as an ODBC data source!

Configuring the Database

To allow a database to act as a data source and receive incoming connections, select
"Enable ODBC/JDBC" from the *File* ➤ *Sharing* menu. This opens the ODBC/JDBC
Settings dialog, shown in Figure 33-8.

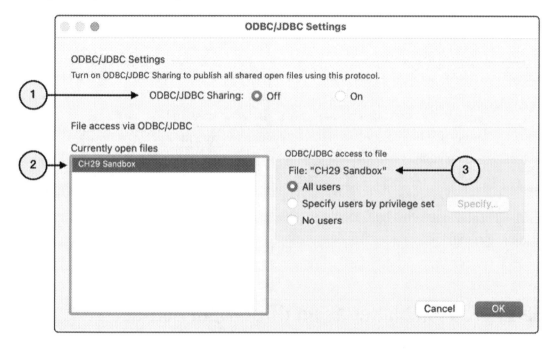

Figure 33-8. *The dialog for configuring ODBC/JDBC Sharing*

Like the configuration dialog for *FileMaker Network Settings* (Chapter 20,
"Configuring Network Settings"), this dialog serves two purposes. The top enables the
local application to accept incoming connections, while the bottom configures ODBC
access for individual files. Follow these steps depending on your needs:

1. Turn *ODBC/JDBC Sharing* on only if the local FileMaker Pro
    client application will host a file that needs to accept incoming
    connections.

2. Select an open database to configure its ability to accept incoming
    connections wherever it is hosted.

3. Select the user account(s) that can be used for incoming
    connections, either "All users" or specify one or more groups of
    users by privilege set.

The privilege sets selected will automatically have the *fmxdbc* extended privilege activated which is a requirement for users assigned to that set to accommodate incoming ODBC/JDBC connections. This extended setting can also be turned on or off by opening the *Manage Security* dialog and editing privilege sets (Chapter 29, "Exploring Privilege Sets").

Configuring the Server

When hosting databases on a FileMaker Server, the settings must be enabled to accept incoming ODBC/JDBC connections, as shown in Figure 33-9.

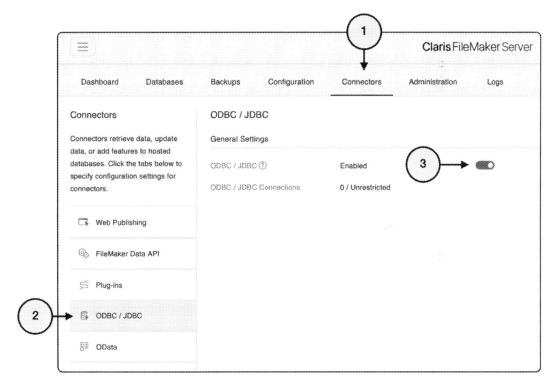

Figure 33-9. *The server console settings to enable incoming ODBC/JDBC connections*

Sign into the Admin Console and follow these steps:

1. Select the "Connectors" tab.

2. Select *ODBC/JDBC* in the sidebar.

3. Click to enable incoming access.

Learning More

For more information about using FileMaker with ODBC/JDBC, including lots of technical detail, visit the following:

`https://help.claris.com/en/odbc-jdbc-guide.pdf`

Connecting with the FileMaker Data API

The *FileMaker Data API* (Data API) is a *Representational State Transfer* (REST) conforming API architecture that facilitates data exchange between external systems and databases hosted by FileMaker Server or FileMaker Cloud. The Data API is used for a variety of connections including the following:

- *Integrating with web applications* – Integrates real-time access and updates, allowing a web application to display and modify FileMaker data.

- *Data analytics* – Reporting tools can access and integrate data in data analysis and visualization tools more advanced than those available in FileMaker.

- *Business process automation* – External systems can trigger actions in FileMaker and pull/push updated information to keep systems synchronized.

- *Third-party integration* – CRM systems, email platforms, and payment gateways can be integrated with FileMaker to streamline operations and reduce manual data entry.

How It Works

Once a database and server are configured to allowing incoming API requests, external REST API client applications can find, create, edit, duplicate, and delete records in a hosted database. It is like the reverse of FileMaker sending requests to external APIs (Chapter 25, "Using Insert from URL"). Instead, a request is sent to FileMaker as illustrated in Figure 33-10. A REST API client sends a FileMaker Data API call in the form of an HTTPS request to a web server over port 443. This request is routed through the *FileMaker Web Server* to the *FileMaker Data API Engine*. The URL and JSON of the HTTPS request is converted and sent to the *Database Server*, which accesses the database, performs the specified action(s), and sends a result back to the engine, to the web server, and finally to the requesting client application.

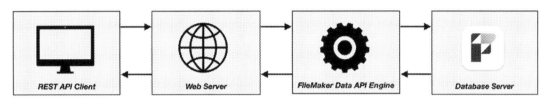

Figure 33-10. *The REST API data workflow from a requesting client to the database server and back*

Preparing for the FileMaker Data API

To use the FileMaker Data API, both the database and its host server must be configured to allow such a connection.

Preparing a Database

A target database can be a new file dedicated for use with the API or an existing solution with resources added for incoming access. If using an existing database, Claris recommends creating a layout exclusively for the API to establish a context and limit what resources incoming commands can access. At minimum, the database must have one account using a privilege set with the *fmrest* extended privilege enabled (Chapter 29, "Enabling Extended Privileges"). Without this setting enabled, the incoming request will not be granted permission to access the database. Ideally, create one account dedicated to the API instead of using a user account. This allows you to further limit which fields, layouts, and scripts the incoming request can access.

Configuring the Server

The host server must also be configured to allow API access, following the steps shown in Figure 33-11.

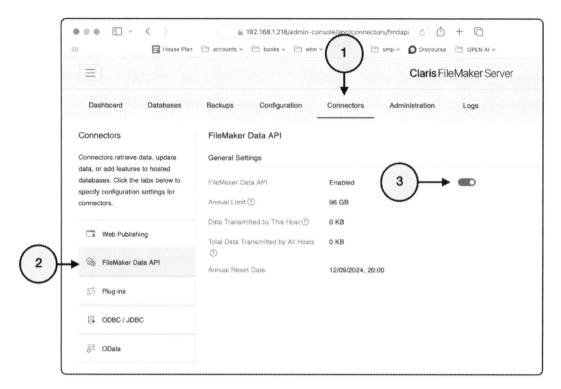

Figure 33-11. *The server console settings to enable incoming FileMaker Data API connections*

Sign into the Admin Console and follow these steps:

1. Select the "Connectors" tab.

2. Select *FileMaker Data API* in the sidebar.

3. Click to enable the service.

Formatting an API Request

Once a database is configured to allow incoming API request, the external system will need to get an authentication token from the FileMaker Server and then format an HTTP request for the action they wish to perform.

Getting an Authentication Token

An *authentication token* for FileMaker Data API access is issued in response to a database access request that contains valid credential information for signing into a database with the *fmrest* privilege enabled. The server domain address, database name, account name, and account password must be specified in the request.

```
POST /fmi/data/vLatest/databases/CompanyReports/sessions HTTP/1.1
Host: serverDomain.com
Content-Type: application/json
{
     "fmDataSource": [
          {
               "database": "CompanyReports",
               "username": "account_name",
               "password": "account_password"
          }
     ]
}
```

If the request passes authentication, the response will be a JSON Object containing a token which can be used in future API calls.

```
{
     "response": {
          "token": "12c7j8c2zqtd864b9d00e2d89f6a2e6a",
          "expiration": "2024-07-31T12:34:56Z"
     },
     "messages": [{
          "code": "0",
          "message": "OK"
     } ]
}
```

Caution   Remember that a token will expire after a period of inactivity, or the expiration date specified. After that, you will need to request a new token!

Running a Script

Once a token is obtained, an HTTP request like the following can run a script named "RunReport" from a *Reports* layout in a *CompanyReports* database with a report type specified as a script parameter:

```
POST /fmi/data/vLatest/databases/CompanyReports/layouts/Report/
script/RunReport HTTP/1.1
Host: serverDomain.com
Authorization: Bearer 12c7j8c2zqtd864b9d00e2d89f6a2e6a
Content-Type: application/json

{
    "script.param": "reportType=YTD"
}
```

After the script runs, a JSON Object will be returned to the calling process. This will contain various bits of information and include a *scriptResult* containing the information returned from the script via the *Exit Script* step.

```
{ "response":
{
        "scriptResult": "Successfully generated report",
        "scriptError": "0",
        "scriptResult.data":
                {
                "reportId":"55613",
                "recordCount": 56 }
                },
"messages": [ { "code": "0", "message": "OK" } ]
}
```

Learning More

Running a script is just one of the functions the FileMaker Data API can perform. For more information about what it can do and how it works, including lots of technical detail, visit the following:

https://help.claris.com/en/data-api-guide/content/index.html

Summary

This chapter explored many options for connecting external systems for data exchange. In the next chapter, we begin an exploration of more advanced topics, starting with building a summary report.

PART VII

Exploring Advanced Topics

After learning the basics and gaining experience building custom databases, eventually, you'll begin venturing into more advanced areas. These chapters begin an exploration of some more advanced topics to start that journey, covering the following topics:

Building a Summary Report

A *summary report* is a complex List view that organizes records into one or more summarizing groups and can include group and grand totals. Groupings are defined with *sub-summary parts* added to the layout which are assigned a sort field. When records are sorted by that field, they are treated as a group and a summarization part is inserted above or below them to display headings, divider lines, totals, and more. For example, a list of *Contacts* can be grouped by state and include a count of how many reside in each. A list of *Products* can be grouped by manufacture and include a count and total cost. The report can include as many group levels as needed. In this chapter, we will build a report of *Invoice* records that are summarized first by year and then, within each, by month. A total of invoice amounts will be included by month and year, with a grand total at the end.

- Planning the layout
- Adding group fields to the Invoice table
- Creating the report layout
- Refining the layout's formatting

Note   See the "CH34-01 Summary Report" example file.

Planning the Layout

To create a report layout that summarizes records by year and month, with a group information both above and below, the records will require six layout parts, as illustrated in Figure 34-1.

911

M. C. Munro, *Learn FileMaker Pro 2024*, https://doi.org/10.1007/979-8-8688-0835-7_34

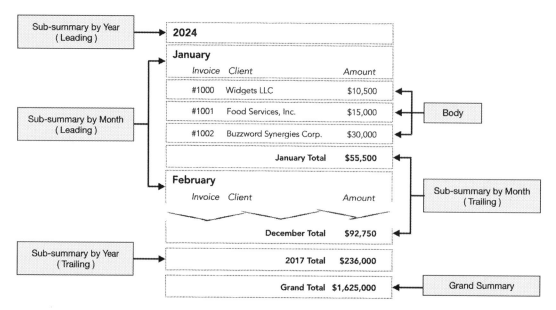

Figure 34-1. *An illustration of an invoice report summarizing sales by year and month*

Grouping by Year

The report starts with a part that will display the year for a group of records below it. The part is defined as a *Sub-summary when sorted by (Leading)* and configured with a sort field of *Invoice Year.* If the records are sorted first by *Invoice Year,* this part will appear before each group of records whenever a new year is detected. The only object shown is the year field formatted in a large font and made bold, so it stands out as a heading. To prepare for this part, we will need the following field:

- *Invoice year* – Extracts the year number from the *Invoice Date* to be displayed on the part and used as the summarizing sort field.

Tip   Add icons, lines, background color, or other graphical elements to indicate the part is a group divider.

Grouping by Month

Next, another part is defined as a *Sub-summary when sorted by (Leading)*, using the *Invoice Month* sort field. So, when records are sorted secondly by *Invoice Month*, this part will appear before each group of records whenever a new month is detected. The labels for column headings are placed in this summary part, so they will appear above each group of individual records whenever a new month begins.

Although the *month name* is displayed on the layout, for the months to be arranged chronologically, the actual sort and layout part must be based on a *month number* instead of name. To prepare for this, we will need two fields:

- *Invoice month name* – Extracts the month name from the *Invoice Date* for display in the part

- *Invoice month number* – Extracts the month number from the *Invoice Date* for use as the summarizing sort field

Displaying the Records

In the center, we will have a *Body* part which will contain all the existing invoice number, client, and amount fields. When rendered as a sorted list, this part will repeat once for every record in the found set but be displayed in sorted groups based on the enclosing sub-summary parts. So, January 2024 has one group of three records (shown), while other months like February will have their own group of records repeating the Body part (not shown).

No additional fields will be required for this part beyond those that would already exist in an *Invoice* table.

Showing Subtotals and Grand Totals

Two additional *Sub-summary when sorted by (Trailing)* will be placed below the Body. The first will be configured with *Invoice Month* as its sort field, and the second will use *Invoice Year*. These operate the same as the corresponding leading parts but appear after each sorted group of records. In this example, these are used to display subtotal of the *Invoice Total* field for a found set that precedes them. So, after the January 2024 record group, the first sub-summary will display the total for those invoices. This will be repeated for each month until reaching the end of the year where the second sub-summary appears with the total for the entire year. Then, the report will continue for additional years.

Finally, at the bottom is a *Grand Summary (Trailing)* part which will provide a space for displaying a grand total of all the records included in the entire report. To prepare for all three trailing summary parts, we will need the following field:

- *Invoice total summary* – A summary field that totals the *Invoice Total* field

In all three summary parts displaying a total, the same *Invoice Total Summary* field can be used. Each part will automatically summarize the values for the records in the group it subsumes. Although not shown in the illustration, an *Invoice Count Summary* field could be added to a summary part to display the number of records in each group.

Adding Group Fields to the Invoice Table

Before creating the report layout, add the additional fields required by the plan. For this example, the fields shown in Figure 34-2 are required:

Field Name	Type ∧	Options / Comments (Click to toggle)
✦ Invoice Company Name	Text	
✦ Invoice Number	Text	Auto-enter Serial
✦ Invoice Amount	Number	
✦ Invoice Date	Date	Indexed
✦ Invoice Month	Calculation	= Month (Invoice Date)
✦ Invoice Month Name	Calculation	= MonthName (Invoice Date)
✦ Invoice Year	Calculation	= Year (Invoice Date)
✦ Invoice Amount Summary	Summary	= Total of Invoice Amount
✦ Invoice Count Summary	Summary	= Count of Invoice Number

Figure 34-2. *The field definitions for an Invoice table required for the report*

The first four entry fields are typical in an Invoice table: company, number, amount, and date. The three calculation fields convert the date into a month number, month name, and year number using the formulas shown. These will be used to sort records and display values in summary parts. The two summary fields will be used to display the total count and the total dollar amount of invoices in the various sub-summary and trailing grand summary parts.

Creating the Report Layout

Finally, it is time to create the report summary layout. Enter Layout mode and select *New Layout/Report* from the *Layout* menu. In the New Layout/Report dialog, perform the steps shown in Figure 34-3.

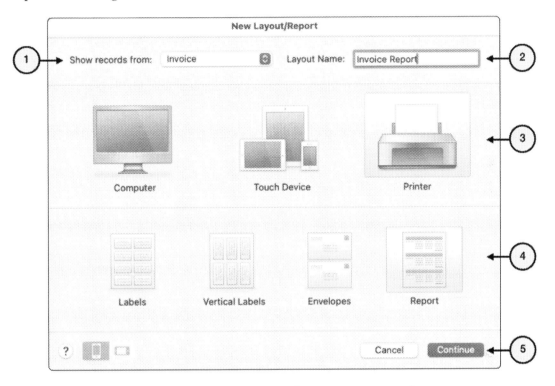

Figure 34-3. *The steps to start the process of creating a report layout*

1. Select the *Invoice* table.

2. Enter *a Layout Name* of "Invoice Report."

3. Click the *Printer* icon.

4. Click the *Report* icon.

5. Click the *Continue* button.

   This will begin a sequence of up to eight dialogs that step through options to preconfigure parts, content, summarization, sorting, and more.

Tip   Although somewhat laborious and abstract, use these dialogs to build your first summary report. After that, you may find it easier to manually configure one from scratch.

Dialog 1: Include Subtotals and Grand Totals

The first report configuration dialog will appear with two options, shown in Figure 34-4. The checkboxes provide the option to *Include subtotals* and to *Include grand totals*. Select both options to include these parts and to ensure that the *Specify Subtotals* and *Specify Grand Totals* (dialogs 6 and 7) are included in the configuration process. Click *Next* to continue.

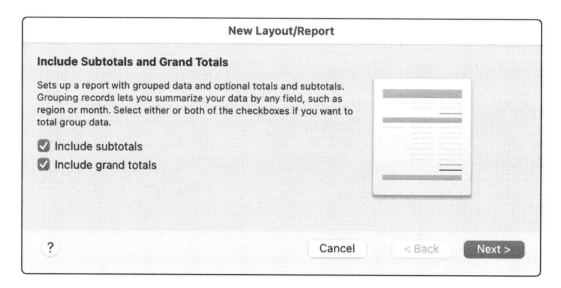

Figure 34-4. The first of eight report configuration dialogs

Dialog 2: Specify Fields

The second dialog specifies the fields that will be placed on the report, as shown in Figure 34-5. While fields can be added after the layout is created, selecting certain fields now makes them available for summarization options in subsequent dialogs. Add fields from the list on the left to the right, by double-clicking or using the *Move* buttons. Fields

916

can be dragged within the available list to determine their default order across the new layout. In our example, we include the number, date, customer, amount, year, and month, all from the *Invoice* table.

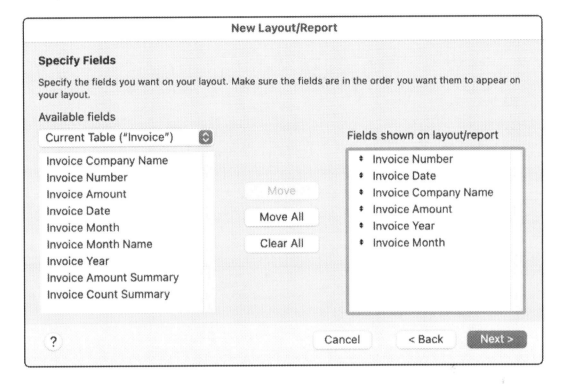

Figure 34-5. *The second of eight report configuration dialogs*

Tip   Include fields from a related table by selecting a table occurrence in the menu above the *Available fields* list.

Dialog 3: Organize Records by Category

The third report dialog specifies sort fields that organize records and act as grouping criteria for the report's sub-summaries, shown in Figure 34-6. The fields added in the previous dialog are displayed in Report fields list (left) and can be added to and enabled in the *Report categories* list (right). Each selected field will be included as a summarizing category for groups of sorted records. Enable the checkbox to include the field in both the sub-summary layout part and the body of the report. In our example, the *Invoice Year* and *Invoice Month* fields are both added as categories and checked because they will be used to summarize groups of records.

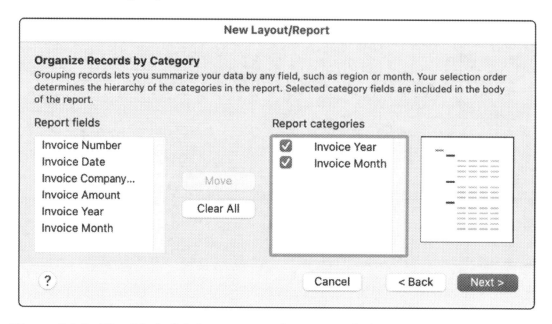

Figure 34-6. *The third of eight report configuration dialogs*

Dialog 4: Sort

The fourth report dialog is used to specify a sort order, as shown in Figure 34-7. This dialog contains an interface like the standard *Sort Records* dialog (Chapter 4, "Sorting Records in the Found Set"). Any fields added as *Report categories* in the previous dialog will automatically appear locked at the top of the *Sort order*. Having been selected to summarize groups, they are required in the sort order. Additional fields can be added below these to further sort records in the body of the report. These should be added in the order matching the desired look of the report. In our example, we will also sort by *Invoice D*ate, so the records appear in chronological order within each month.

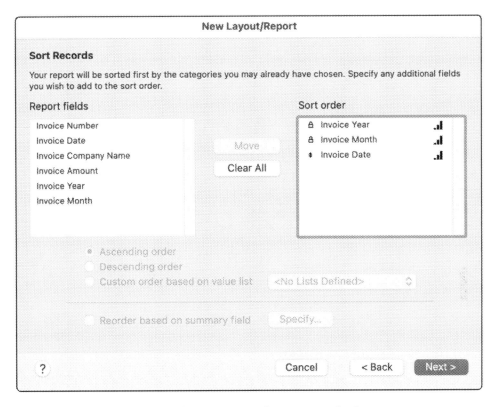

Figure 34-7. *The fourth of eight report configuration dialogs*

Dialog 5: Specify Subtotals

The fifth report dialog will only appear if the *Specify subtotals* checkbox was selected in the first dialog. This allows the addition of one or more summary fields that will be displayed above or below groups of records on a sub-summary part that groups by the selected field. To add a field, follow the steps shown in Figure 34-8:

1. Click the *Specify* button. This will open a *Specify field* dialog in which the only selection choices are summary fields. Select *Invoice Amount Summary* and click OK. This will add the selected field next to the *Specify* button but not yet add it to the list below.

2. Select a *Category to summary by* of "Invoice Year" and choose "Below record group" in the *Subtotal placement* menu.

3. Click *Add Subtotal* to add this field to the list below.

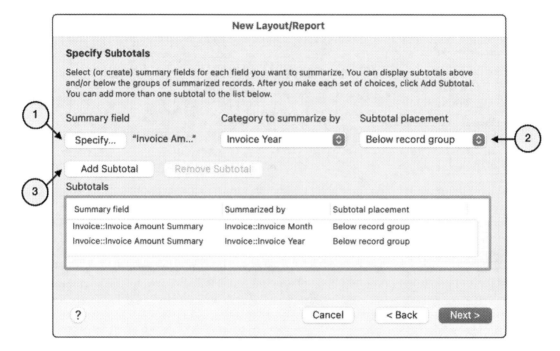

Figure 34-8. *The fifth of eight report configuration dialogs*

Repeat those steps again, except choose "Invoice Month" as the *Category to summarize by*.

Dialog 6: Specify Grand Totals

The sixth report dialog will only appear if the *Specify grand totals* checkbox was selected in the first dialog. This works like the previous dialog but uses summary fields to display a grand total of all records on the report. To add a field, follow the steps shown in Figure 34-9:

1. Click the *Specify* button. This will open a *Specify field* dialog in which the only selection choices are summary fields. Select *Invoice Amount Summary* and click OK. This will add the selected field next to the *Specify* button but not yet add it to the list below.

2. Select a Grand total placement of "End of report."

3. Click *Add Grand Total* to add this field to the list below.

Figure 34-9. *The sixth of eight report configuration dialogs*

Dialog 7: Header and Footer Information

The seventh report dialog, shown in Figure 34-10, allows selection of optional placeholders for standard information automatically placed in six different locations on the layout. Each pop-up menu contains the same choices: *Page Number, Current Date, Layout Name, Large Custom Text, Small Custom Text,* and *Logo.*

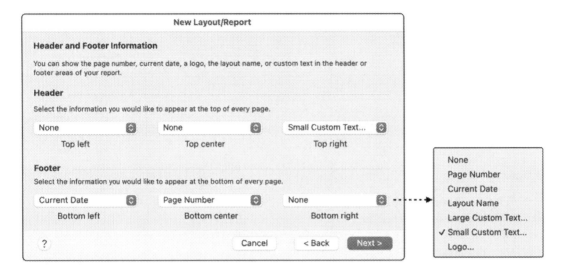

Figure 34-10. *The seventh step is used to select standard header and footer info*

Dialog 8: Create a Script

The eighth and final dialog offers the option to automatically create a script for the new report layout. Without a script, a user is required to manually perform a find, navigate to the report layout, sort records, and print or preview the report. Scripts can be manually created to perform these steps (Chapters 24–28). This last dialog, shown in Figure 34-11, offers the convenience of an automatic head start.

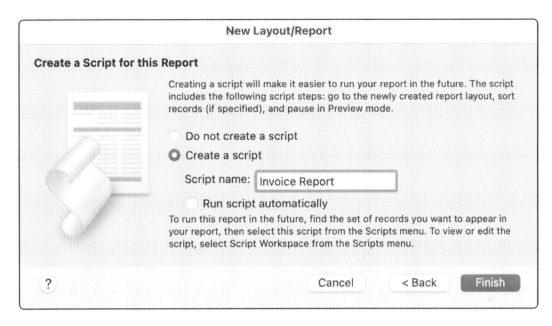

Figure 34-11. *The eighth and final report configuration dialog*

Click the *Create a Script* option, and enter a custom *Script name* or keep the default one based on the layout name entered at the beginning of the process. Select the *Run script automatically* checkbox to assign an *OnLayoutEnter* script trigger (Chapter 27) that will run the script whenever a user navigates to the new layout. Then click the *Finish* button to create the new layout and script.

The script created will include two or three steps, automatically configured depending on other options in this process. It will always include steps to *Enter Browse Mode* and *Go to Layout*. If sort fields were specified in the fourth dialog, it will include a step to *Sort Records by* the field(s) selected. Once created, the script can be further customized as needed. For example, as configured, it assumes the report should include every record in the found set. However, a step can be added to find a set of records based on the current date, week, month, or year or using other criteria including that solicited from a user.

Refining the Layout's Formatting

Once a report layout is created, it will usually require cleanup and customization. The example in Figure 34-12 shows the layout based on the options selected in the preceding example. The exact appearance may vary depending on the layout theme used in the database.

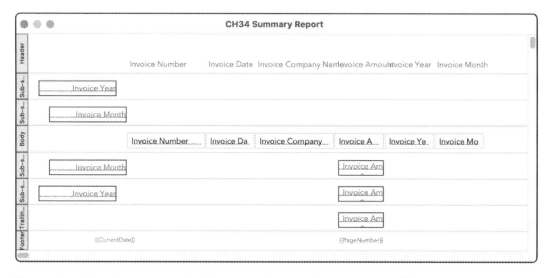

Figure 34-12. *An automatically created report layout typically requires refinement*

Consider performing the following tasks to prepare the layout for use:

- Add a text for a report heading, company name, address, etc.

- Shrink the height of parts to tighten the design and save space.

- Format backgrounds and labels as needed to create the stylistic needs of the report.

- If a logo was included, the size and position might require adjustment.

- The field labels for the body fields automatically added at the top can be moved into a sub-summary just above the body, so they are repeated directly above each group of fields by month.

- Also, the field labels automatically show the full name of the field and may overlap and include naming prefixes and may require editing.

Once finished, the report may look closer to the one in the example file, as shown in Figure 34-13.

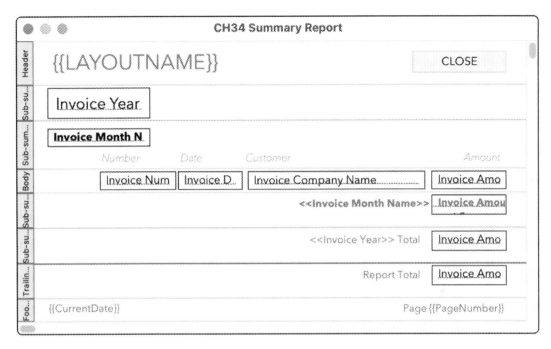

Figure 34-13. *The report layout with a cleaned up design*

Now, run the script to see the report sorted and sub-summarized in Browse mode, as shown in Figure 34-14.

Figure 34-14. *The report, sorted and ready for printing*

Summary

This chapter introduced the steps required to create a complex report with sub-summaries and group totals. In the next chapter, we discuss the importance of keeping object references dynamic and practices for using text-based references in a way to maintain dynamic updates when names change.

Keeping Object References Dynamic

An *object reference* is a software link to an object used by another object. A field used in a formula's statement, a layout used in a *Go to Layout* script step, and a script run from another script with the *Perform Script* step are all object references. As a modern software title, FileMaker utilizes *dynamic object references* where the links are established by object ID instead of by name. This ensures link integrity if an object's name changes or, where possible, if another object is created with the same name. For ease of use, developers establish object links by name through a programming interface that hides the ID-based connection. However, some FileMaker functions and script steps allow developers to specify objects by name for added flexibility. This creates *static object references* that execute by name and will not update when a target object's name changes. When using these functions, developers must choose between never renaming objects for fear of breaking links or meticulously finding and updating any such reference to a renamed object. Alternatively, there are custom techniques that allow a formula to use an object name that was derived from a dynamic reference. This chapter explores the topic of object references, covering the following topics:

- Understanding where choice exists
- Deriving names from dynamic references

Understanding Where Choice Exists

Object references are used throughout the development environment in FileMaker. These can be categorized into three types: dynamic, static, or a combination of the two. This chapter is primarily focused on the latter, references where there is a choice between dynamic or static. But take a moment to consider each.

© Mark Conway Munro 2024
M. C. Munro, *Learn FileMaker Pro 2024*, https://doi.org/10.1007/979-8-8688-0835-7_35

Identifying Dynamic Only References

A *dynamic only reference* is a link to an object where there is no choice other than to establish a dynamic ID-based link to a target object. If an object is selected by clicking it in a developer dialog, it will generate a dynamic reference. Some areas where an object choice is always dynamic include the following:

- A field used as a *Looked-up value* for another field

- A field choice in the *Edit Relationship* dialog

- A field choice in the *Specify Fields for Value List* dialog

- A field choice in a *Sort Records* dialog

- A field choice in a *Specify Find Request* dialog

- A field selected in a *Specify Target* dialog for numerous script steps

- A field selected in a *Replace Field Contents* dialog

- A value list selected as the data source for a field object's *Control style*

- An object selected in a *Custom Privileges* dialog for a *Privilege Set*

- A custom function inserted into a formula (unless typed in the text parameter of the *Evaluate* function)

All of these will continue to work even if the targeted resource's name is changed.

Identifying Static Only References

A *static only reference* is a link to an object where the only choice is to refer to the object by name.

Using Name-Based Script Steps

If an object is specified by typing the name assigned it in the *Inspector* pane into, it is a static only reference. These include the following script steps that require an *Object name* to identify the target object on a layout: *Go to Object*, *Refresh Object*, and *Set Web Viewer*. These are not a huge cause for concern for a few reasons:

- The name used by them is typically assigned to an object for the sole purpose of the reference. In other words, a web viewer doesn't require a name unless a script step is going to push HTML to it.

- The reference tends to be used on a one object instance to one script step basis. So, there aren't likely to be multiple references to the same object.

- They can be mediated with thoughtful naming standards that are more resistant to change over time.

- If name changes are required, the number of areas requiring a change will tend to be limited.

Using Name-Based Design Functions

There are several built-in functions that only accept object names. For example, many *design functions* accept a file, table, layout, script, or value list name. These don't have an interface driven choice to select an object or insert an ID, so they are technically considered static only references. The fact that these are typically only used in more advanced solutions that demand custom functionality to become aware of the structural design makes them also not much of a concern. However, there are ways to access the ID for use in formulas and convert it back to a name in real time as the formula is executed (discussed later in this chapter).

Naming Variables

One item worth mentioning is the fact that variables names are always static! A local or global variable is established with a *Let* statement, *While* statement, or *Set Variable* script step using a developer assigned name. Once defined, a variable can be referenced from numerous formulas, and all those references are static. So, if a name change is made to a widely used variable, it is the developer's responsibility to locate and update them all!

Tip   Choose the name for variable wisely, especially those used frequently.

Identifying Static or Dynamic References

There are several areas where a formula or action can be configured to use either a static or dynamic reference, including the following:

- A field reference in formulas can be entered as references or a literal text string. Some built-in functions use text-based references, and others use dynamic references. Others convert back and forth between the two.

- The *Go to Layout* script step's target layout can be a dynamic reference specified through a *Specify Layout* dialog, or a layout name, or number specified by a formula.

- In the *Set Field* and *Set Field by Name* script steps, the former uses a dynamic reference to target a field, and the latter uses a text-based name generated by a formula.

- The *Perform Script* and *Perform Script by Name* script steps.

These areas where a choice exists are worth a closer look. It is important to consider the pros and cons of each. If choosing a static reference, there are methods to do so while remaining associated with a dynamic reference and avoiding broken links.

Deriving Names from Dynamic References

The best choice is to always use dynamic references wherever possible. When a need arises to use a text-based reference, try using a technique in the rest of this chapter that demonstrates how to safely use *static references* that are derived from *dynamic ones*. This approach provides the best of both worlds: the programmatic flexibility of static references but used in a way that still traces back to a dynamic reference. Let's work through some examples of keeping references to fields, layouts, scripts, and value lists dynamic.

Keeping Field References Dynamic

Fields are the most common object type in a database. They are used extensively throughout a database's schema, interface, and scripts. Since they also tend to be renamed more often than other resources as a database evolves, it is crucial to keep all field references dynamic!

Maintaining Dynamic References to Standard Fields

A *standard field* is a field added to multiple tables with the same name that stores a frequently used type of information.

These can be FileMaker's default fields (Chapter 8, "Exploring Default Fields") or developer created fields (Chapter 8, "Creating Your Own Standard Fields"). For example, every table in the database will have a default standard field containing a primary key, e.g., "Record Primary ID" in our example files. Depending on the specific database, most or all tables may also have a custom *Record Title* and *Record Status* as custom standards.

Other smaller groups of tables may share similarly named fields when they all connect to a frequently related table. A *Company ID* field will present in any table that requires a relationship to a *Company* record. These include *Contact*, *Project*, and *Invoice*. They each may also have a *Company Name* field that automatically stores the related record's name.

Any open-ended formula or script designed to perform a common function or action using a standard field from several different layout contexts can easily tempt the use of static references. Let's work through some examples to illustrate the various options available.

Extracting a Company Name Dynamically

For this example, we will assume that four tables all have a *Company Name* field. Depending on the current layout, one of these four field references will produce a value:

```
Company::Company Name
Contact::Company Name
Project::Company Name
Invoice::Company Name
```

If an open-ended custom function needs to extract the value from any of these standardized *Company Name* fields from the current record regardless of the layout, there are several ways to accomplish this.

Making the Table Occurrence Static with Dynamic Field References

In this example, a *Let* statement puts the table name for the current layout into a *tableName* variable and uses a *Case* statement to access a different field depending on that value.

931

```
Let ( [
    tableName = Get ( LayoutTableName )
] ;
    Case (
        tableName = "Company" ; Company::Company Name ;
        tableName = "Contact" ; Contact::Company Name ;
        tableName = "Project" ; Project::Company Name ;
        tableName = "Invoice" ; Invoice::Company Name
    )
)
```

This keeps all the field references dynamic, but the table occurrence names are static, literally typed in quotes. This involves risk should any of the following events occur:

- *Renaming* – Although it may happen infrequently, should any of the table names change in the future, the formula will require a manual update or it will fail.

- *Expansion* – Any new table added to the database with a *Company Name* field that will use this function will need to be manually added to the formula, e.g., *Product, Staff,* or *Vendor*.

So, we have simply replaced the redundancy of having to duplicate a fully dynamic formula in each table with a non-flexible repetition within a single formula. Therefore, this approach doesn't achieve our objective of keeping references dynamic.

Making the Table Occurrence Dynamic with a Static Field Name

The next example simply reverses the problem, dynamically accessing the name of the layout's table using a built-in function but then using a static field name.

```
Get ( LayoutTableName ) & "::Company Name"
```

This is more concise and has the flexibility to automatically expand to any new table added later without requiring a manual edit. However, using a static field name retains some risk if the name changes. It might be fine to use this approach for a field you are certain will never change, but when dealing with an evolving database, that assumption may come back to haunt you. If you or another developer decides to change the *Company Name* field in all the tables to "companyName" or Company_Name," this formula will fail if not updated. So, again, this fails to achieve our objective of keeping references dynamic.

Using Fully Dynamic References

The best approach is to keep both the *table occurrence* and the *field name* dynamic in an open-ended formula that can access the field of the same name from multiple layout contexts, demonstrated in this example.

```
Let ( [
    reference = GetFieldName ( Company::Company Name ) ;
    fieldName = GetValue ( Substitute ( reference ; "::" ; "¶" ) ; 2 )
] ;
    GetField ( Get ( LayoutTableName ) & "::" & fieldName )
)
```

Note   See the "CH35-01 Extract Company Name" example file.

Used as the formula for a custom function or in a step of an open-ended script, the formula above will successfully extract the value from a "Company Name" field from any layout for any table that has such a field. It will automatically update if any of the table occurrence names change or if the standard field name is changed in all the tables. The *Let* statement performs the following:

1. A *reference* variable is set to contain a static, text-based reference to the *Company Name* field derived dynamically from that field in the *Company* table using the *GetFieldName* function which returns "Company::Company Name."

2. The *Substitute* and *GetValue* functions are used to extract the name from the *reference* variable and placed into a *fieldname* variable by converting the colons in the text-based reference into a paragraph return and extracting the second value, which returns "Company Name."

3. The *GetField* function's parameter includes the current layout's table name concatenated with two colons and the *fieldName* to form a new, dynamically generated text reference to the field based on the current table, e.g., "Invoice::Company Name," "Project::Company Name," or any of the other layouts. When this is evaluated, the result will be the contents of the referenced field.

This technique can be used to dynamically extract any standard field from any table in a database without concern about future name changes or the addition of new tables. The only requirement is that the target field name must be standardized across all tables.

Finding Records by Company ID Dynamically

Another example can be found where an open-ended script needs to perform a find using a standard field. For example, assume a *Company ID* field is used in four tables, each forming a relational link to a *Company* record. The scripted process to follow needs to be able to find records related to a specific company in of these tables. Starting with a $companyID variable, it will search for matching records in a "Company ID" field in whichever table is currently active.

Note   For illustrative purposes, these examples show a static value placed in a *CompanyID* variable. A script could load this from the *company* record prior to changing layouts to perform a search.

Making the Table Occurrence Static with Dynamic Field References

This first attempt uses a verbose If statement with static table occurrence names, as shown here:

```
Set Variable [ $companyID ; Value: "000001" ]
Set Variable [ $tableName ; Value: Get ( LayoutTableName ) ]

Enter Find Mode [ Pause: Off ]
If [ $tableName = "Contact" ]
     Set Field [ Contact::Company ID ; $companyID ]
Else If [ $tableName = "Project" ]
```

```
        Set Field [ Project::Company ID ; $companyID ]
Else If [ $tableName = "Invoice" ]
        Set Field [ Invoice::Company ID ; $companyID ]
Else If [ $tableName = "Vendor" ]
        Set Field [ Vendor::Company ID ; $companyID ]
Else If
Perform Find []
```

While this maintains dynamic references to the individual *Company ID* fields, the table names used in the *If* statement are in quotes and, therefore, literal non-dynamic text. Further, it is also verbose and would require additional clauses added if additional tables with a *Company ID* field were added later.

Using Fully Dynamic References

The *Set Field By Name* step can compress the script by replacing all the separate *Set Field* steps in the previous example. If it uses text-based field reference derived from dynamic ones, as shown in the formula below, it solves the problems with the previous example by keeping the field reference dynamic and being able to expand when additional tables are added with a *Company ID* field.

```
Let ( [
   reference = GetFieldName ( Contact::Company ID ) ;
   fieldName = GetValue ( Substitute ( reference ; "::" ; "¶" ) ; 2 )
] ;
   Get ( LayoutTableName ) & "::" & fieldName
)
```

The *reference* variable is set to a text-based reference using a dynamic reference to the *Company ID* field in the *Contact* table. Since we are accessing a standardized field name, we just need to point to any one instance of the field that we know exists to extract the name dynamically. The script could have used any of the other tables, like *Projects* or *Invoices*. However, unlike the example extracting a company name, we can't use the Company table for this because it doesn't have a *Company ID* field, since it is the primary record.

Also different from the extraction of the company name, here the *Let* statement's formula does not use *GetField* to convert the text-based reference into a live one. This is because the *Set Field By Name* step expects a text-based field reference and would see the result of *GetField* as the value in the field instead of the text reference to the field.

Note   See the "CH25-02 Find Company ID" example file.

With the formula above used to set the value of a *$field* variable, we can now compress the original script down to this, and it will work in any non-company table with a field named "Company ID."

```
Set Variable [ $CompanyID ; Value: "000001" ]
Set Variable [ $field ; <see formula above> ]
Enter Find Mode [ Pause: Off ]
Set Field By Name [ $field ; $companyID ]
Perform Find []
```

Keeping Fields Dynamic in SQL Queries

One of the most frequent places text-based references are used is when writing SQL Queries (Chapter 16, "Creating SQL Queries"). The *Select* statement is written as text and requires a field name and table name specified. For example, this will select the *Company Name* field from every record in the *Company* table.

```
ExecuteSQL ("SELECT \"Company Name\" FROM Company" ; "" ; "" )
```

Both the table name and field name are typed as literal text strings, so a name change to either will break the formula wherever this is used. A database utilizing a large quantity of SQL queries with text-based references will create a worst-case scenario for name changes. You would either spend hours locating and modifying the text-based names during off hours or just tolerate resources whose names you have outgrown. Instead, consider deriving the text components for all SQL queries from dynamic references, so name changes don't break all the formulas using them. The following example demonstrates the technique:

```
Let ( [
    reference = GetFieldName ( Company::Company Name ) ;
    reference = Substitute ( reference ; "::" ; "¶" ) ;
    tableName = Quote ( GetValue ( reference ; 1 ) ) ;
    fieldName = Quote ( GetValue ( reference ; 2 ) )
] ;
    ExecuteSQL ("SELECT " & fieldName & " FROM " & tableName ; "" ; "" )
)
```

936

Note   See the "CH35-03 Dynamic SQL Query" example file.

The *Let* statement converts a dynamic field reference into a string and places it into the *reference* variable. The *Substitute* function replaces the colons with a paragraph return and updates the *reference* variable. Next, the *GetValue* function extracts the first and second paragraph from the reference variable and places them into the *tableName* and *fieldName* variables, respectively. The *Quote* function wraps each of these in quotations to protect against spaces in the names. From there, those variables are used to construct the text for the SELECT statement which becomes a parameter for the *ExecuteSQL* function. When structured this way, any changes to the table or field name will automatically be updated and the query will continue to function as expected without modification.

Keeping Layout References Dynamic

Another common function in a database is navigation. Users can manually change layouts through the default interface. However, scripts can assist in this while performing other actions along the way. Fully automatized workflow processes also change layouts constantly as the jump around finding and using records for a variety of purposes. The *Go to Layout* has four options for targeting a layout:

- *Original layout* – Select this to automatically return to the layout that was current at the start of the script.

- *Layout* – Select this to reference a layout in the *Specify Layout* dialog.

- *Layout name by calculation* – Select this to enter a formula that generates a text result containing the name of the layout.

- *Layout number by calculation* – Select this to enter a formula that generates a text result containing the number of the layout.

The first two options are dynamic and won't be affected by name changes. The last two use static values resulting from a formula and will be affected by name changes or order, respectively. The need to use these doesn't arise too often, but, when it does, there are a few techniques to consider.

Returning to the Last Layout by Name

Unlike with fields, FileMaker doesn't provide a simple method of converting a dynamic layout reference into text. The *Get (LayoutName)* or *Get (LayoutNumber)* function does return the name or ordered number of the current layout. These can be used to record the current layout name and use that value to return to it later should a text-based name be desired. For example, a navigational system involving several "home" layouts where the user should return to the one they viewed last when they click a main menu button will need to navigate to one of a batch of layouts depending on which the user last visited. A script navigating away from a home layout can record the current layout name in a global variable.

```
Set Variable [ $$LastHome ; Get ( LayoutName ) ]
```

Later, when they click a "home" button, the script step can navigate by name, using the value in the variable.

```
Go to Layout [ $$LastHome ; Animation: None ]
```

This can also be used to record the user's last layout name in a settings file and return them to it the next time they log in. The only risk is if the layout name changes between the time of recording the name and the attempt to return to the layout.

Creating a Layout ID to Name Converter

For solutions that require greater variability in targeting layouts, create a function that can convert a layout name to ID and vice versa. For example, a custom function named *GetLayout* with a *target* parameter and the following code:

```
While (
[
        file = Get ( FileName ) ;
        names = LayoutNames ( file ) ;
        ids = LayoutIDs ( file ) ;
        result = ""
] ;
        ids ≠ "" and result = "" ;
[
        currentName =  GetValue ( names ; 1 ) ;
```

```
        currentID = GetValue ( ids ; 1 ) ;
        result =
                Case (
                        currentName = target ; currentID ;
                        currentID = target ; currentName ;
                        result
                ) ;
        names = RightValues ( names ; ValueCount ( names ) - 1 ) ;
        ids = RightValues ( ids ; ValueCount ( ids ) - 1 )

] ;

        result
)
```

Note   See the "CH35-04 GetLayout Function" example file.

The function can be called with either a layout name or ID as the *target* parameter, and it will return the opposite, as shown in the two examples below. Use the first in the *Data Viewer* to determine the ID of the desired layout during development. The second would be used in formulas where a layout is targeted by name.

```
GetLayout ( "Contact" )        // result = 13
GetLayout ( "13" )             // result = Contact
```

Since the FileMaker assigned IDs for layouts don't change, this allows you to get the ID for a layout during development and to store or use it as a literal value in a script. Then, when a script is ready to navigate to the layout, the ID can be passed to the function to convert it to the current name of that layout to use that name in the *Go to Layout* step.

```
Go to Layout [ GetLayout ( "13" ); Animation: None ]
```

Using this formula, it is completely safe to use the *Layout name by calculation* option since the unchanging IDs used in the formula would always be converted to the current name at runtime.

Keeping Script Calls Dynamic

The *Perform Script* and *Perform Script on Server* both have a "by name" option which allows a target script to be identified with a text-based name determined by a formula. Like with layouts, using this option involves the same risks but can be abated in much the same way.

Targeting the Current Script

The *Get (ScriptName)* function will return the name of the script currently running. This offers a limited option to store the name in a variable or field and run it later by name. But it would be at risk for name changes between the time that name is stored and when the script is again called. Worse, it doesn't help a script target another script by name.

Creating a Script ID to Name Converter

For solutions that require greater variability in targeting scripts by name, create a function that can convert a script name to ID and vice versa. Create a new custom function named *GetScript* with a parameter of *target*. Then, add the same code from the *GetLayout* function, except to change the two design functions to *ScriptNames* and *ScriptIDs*.

```
While (
[

        file = Get ( FileName ) ;
        names = ScriptNames ( file ) ;
        ids = ScriptIDs ( file ) ;
        result = ""
] ;
        ids ≠ "" and result = "" ;
[

        currentName =  GetValue ( names ; 1 ) ;
        currentID = GetValue ( ids ; 1 ) ;
        result =
                Case (
                        currentName = target ; currentID ;
                        currentID = target ; currentName ;
```

```
                        · result
            ) ;
    names = RightValues ( names ; ValueCount ( names ) - 1 ) ;
    ids = RightValues ( ids ; ValueCount ( ids ) - 1 )

] ;

    result
)
```

Note   See the "CH35-05 GetScript Function" example file.

The function can be called with either a script name or ID as the target parameter, and it will return the opposite, as shown in these examples. Use the first in the *Data Viewer* to determine the ID of the desired script during development. The second would be used in formulas where a script is targeted by name.

```
GetScript ( "Target Script" )         // result = 10
GetScript ( "10" )                    // result = Target Script
```

Now a script can be performed by name using a formula while remaining dynamic. Since the name-determining formula only contains the ID which is converted to the corresponding script's current name at runtime, the formula will be immune to name changes.

```
Perform Script [ Specified: by name ; GetScript ( "10" ) ; Parameter : ]
```

Keeping Calls from JavaScript Dynamic

Web viewers can use the *FileMaker.PerformScript* function to run a script (Chapter 20, "Calling a FileMaker Script with JavaScript"). However, in the HTML code, script names tend to be entered as a literal text string. If that name ever changes, the web viewer's button will no longer work until it is manually updated by a developer. Using the *GetScript* function created in the previous example, the HTML generating formula can be modified to dynamically update to the script's current name and be immune to future name changes.

Note   See the "CH35-06 JavaScript" example file.

The HTML code formula in this example uses the custom *GetScript* function to translate a script ID into the current name, guaranteeing that a future name change doesn't break the code.

```
"data:text/html,
<html>
<head>
</head>
<body>
<h1>Test FMP Script</h1>
<button onclick=\"runScript()\">Test FMP Script</button>
<script>
    function runScript() {
        FileMaker.PerformScript ( \"" & GetScript ( "10" ) & "\", \"Hello,
        World!\" );
    }
</script>
</body>
</html>"
```

Keeping Value List Calls Dynamic

There are no interface elements or script steps that refer to a value list by name. However, the *ValueListItems* function uses a text-based name to return the items of a value list and is venerable to future name changes. Fortunately, like with layouts and scripts, a custom function can be written to allow value list IDs to be used in formulas and converted back to names at runtime. This keeps all formulas accessing value list items from breaking in the event of a value list name change.

Creating a Value List ID to Name Converter

Create a new custom function named *GetValueList* with a parameter of *target*. Then, add the same code from the preceding *GetLayout* or *GetScript* function, except to change the two design functions to use *ValueListNames* and *ValueListIDs*.

```
While (
[
        file = Get ( FileName ) ;
        names = ValueListNames ( file ) ;
        ids = ValueLIstIDs ( file ) ;
        result = ""
] ;
        ids ≠ "" and result = "" ;
[
        currentName =  GetValue ( names ; 1 ) ;
        currentID = GetValue ( ids ; 1 ) ;
        result =
                Case (
                        currentName = target ; currentID ;
                        currentID = target ; currentName ;
                        result
                ) ;
        names = RightValues ( names ; ValueCount ( names ) - 1 ) ;
        ids = RightValues ( ids ; ValueCount ( ids ) - 1 )
] ;
        result
)
```

Note   See the "CH35-07 GetValueList Function" example file.

The function can be called with either a value list name or ID as the target parameter, and it will return the opposite, as shown in these examples. Use the first in the *Data Viewer* to determine the ID of the desired list during development. The second would be used in formulas where a value list is targeted by name.

```
GetValueList ( "Address States" )        // result = 7
GetValueList ( "7" )                      // result = "Address States"
```

Since formulas would only store the ID and that would be converted to the corresponding value lists current name at runtime, the formula will be immune to name changes. For example, this formula will return the items in the "Address States" value list, even if that list is renamed in the future.

```
ValueListItems ( Get ( FileName ) ; GetValueList ( 7 ))
```

Summary

This chapter explored the issue of keeping dynamic object references, with various techniques for embracing the programmatic variability of static text-based references in a safe way that still traces back to dynamic references and avoids breaking links when object names change. In the next chapter, we explore using transactions to manage a batch of changes as a unified event.

Using Transactions

A *transaction* is a temporary window state during which record changes are held in a queue and then executed together as a single operation, either all committed or all reverted. By holding a batch of potential changes, a transaction avoids problems of rolling back actions performed earlier if an error occurs later in the process or if some other programmatic change of course is required. It can also increase the speed of certain actions since the work exists in a virtual space until committed. Implicitly, transactions have existed in FileMaker for some time. When a user begins editing a record, an implicit transaction opens and begins collecting field edits. Those changes are held until the record is closed by an action that either commits or reverts the record. This implicit transaction is limited in scope to changes made on a single record with no formal way to apply the concept to wider batches. Over the years, developers concocted methods to overcome this limitation, but they were still limited and difficult to implement. Recently, Claris introduced new functions and script steps that both simplify and broaden the scope of transactions. Now, a script can explicitly open a transaction and perform changes or pause while the user acts. The transaction will persist in an open state until it is either committed or reverted by the script, an error, or interface action. These expand transactions from an *implicit record-based scope* to an *explicit window-based scope* that is fully controlled by custom scripts. This chapter covers the following topics:

- Introducing transactions
- Managing window transactions
- Detecting an Open Transaction State
- Creating a Transaction Enabled Dialog
- Using the *OnWindowTransaction* trigger

© Mark Conway Munro 2024
M. C. Munro, *Learn FileMaker Pro 2024*, https://doi.org/10.1007/979-8-8688-0835-7_36

Introducing Transactions

A *database transaction* is a group of operations performed on a database that are treated as a single, indivisible unit that can be executed or reverted together. FileMaker has two types of transactions: *record-based* and *window-based*.

Defining a Record Transaction

A *record transaction* is an editing session that persists only while one record is open for editing. The transaction is opened when one of the following events occur:

- A user or script makes a first edit to a field on a record or in related records in a portal.

- A script executes the *Open Record* step.

- A new record is created.

This type of transaction has existed in FileMaker for a long time and is primarily used to isolate a record during an editing session to avoid conflicts between users. During the transaction, the record is locked so other users can't edit it and can't see the edits being made by the transaction owner. The transaction is closed when any of the following events occur:

- The user commits the record by clicking the layout background or reverts it by selecting *Revert Record* from the *Records* menu.

- A script executes the *Commit Record* or *Revert Record* steps.

- A user or script creates or navigates to another record within the window.

- A user or script changes layouts within the window.

- A developer dialog is opened.

- The window or file is closed.

The default behavior for an interrupted record-based transaction is to commit the record. For example, if a user edits several fields and closes the file, the changes made are saved unless a *Script Trigger* (Chapter 27) intervenes and reverts the record before the event.

Defining a Window Transaction

A *window transaction* is an editing session that persists within a window for the duration of the script that initiates it, or until it is committed, reverted, or interrupted. These transactions can collect events for any number of records across numerous layouts for different tables. This makes it ideal for databases that manage data used in accounting, invoicing, financial workflows, or anywhere multiple records need to be created or modified all at once as a batch, or not at all. It includes the ability to roll back the entire batch of changes in the event of an error, user cancelation, or some other interruption. It also maintains record locks on any edited record until the transaction completes to avoid other users seeing partial results or accidentally causing an interruption to a complex process by interacting with them. Some developers have reported speed improvements when wrapping an *Import Records* or *Loop* statements inside of a transaction.

A window transaction begins when a script executes the *Open Transaction* step, which was introduced in version 19.6.1. Once opened, the transaction will collect any record actions performed within the window. These can be performed by the script, subscripts performed by the script, or, if usings a *Pause* step, by input performed by the user. Although changes are only being recorded for later implementation, to a user performing entry tasks, it will appear like any other work in the database. A new or duplicated record appears in the found set – a deleted one disappears. Field edits can be made to multiple records and appear to commit. The user or script can change layouts and perform actions across multiple records.

Tip   Records functions in the menu and toolbar will be disabled when a script pauses. Add buttons to the layout to give users access to create, duplicate, or delete records during the transaction.

A transaction ends when it is either committed or reverted. This can be done by the script with a statement terminating *Close Transaction* step or a *Revert Transaction* step (discussed later in this chapter). There are also many actions that will cause an active transaction to automatically commit or revert.

A window transaction will *automatically commit and end* when any of the following occur:

- The script changes the layout window using the *New Window, Close Window,* or *Select Window* steps.

- The *Manage Database, Manage Container,* or *Manage Data Source* developer dialogs are opened.

- The *Save a Copy* as or *Re-Login* actions or script steps are performed.

- The file is closed.

A window transaction will *automatically revert and end* when any of these occur:

- A field configured to always validate has a value entered that does not match the validation options.

- The script performs the *Revert Transaction* step.

- The script is canceled, including by the Script Debugger.

- The script performs the *Halt Script* step within a transaction.

- The script encounters any privilege error restricting field, record, or table access.

When a window-based transaction is reverted, all the changes made during the session are lost.

Caution   When pausing during a transaction for user input, limit access to actions within the interface to avoid them accidentally doing loads of regular work in a transaction without realizing it!

Managing Window Transactions

Using window-based transactions requires a script to be configured with at least two steps to open and commit the transaction. Within that, any number of steps can be added to perform data entry tasks, pause for user input, capture errors, and revert. Let's walk through the basics of the various steps involved.

Opening a Transaction

A transaction is initiated with the *Open Transaction* step. When adding this step to a script, it will automatically insert a terminating *Commit Transaction* step with it. Since a transaction only persists during the execution of the script that initiates it, the *Commit Transaction* step is required to terminate the statement.

```
Open Transaction
        // Add steps here
Commit Transaction
```

Anything added between those two steps will be performed within the transaction and not be committed until the termination of the statement.

Note   See the "CH36-01 Opening a Transaction" example file.

In the example below, a script creates a new *Contact* record for each name listed in a variable. Regardless of the number of names in the list, all the records will be created in the transaction queue during the execution of the *Loop* statement. Once that finishes and the transaction commits, all the records will be created at once.

```
Set Variable [ $names ; "John Doe¶Karen Smith¶Frank Camacho" ]
Set Variable [ $count ; ValueCount ( $names ) ]
Set Variable [ $current ; ValueCount ( $names ) ]
Open Transaction [ ]
        Loop
                New Record/Request
                Set Field [ Contact::Name ; GetValue ( $names ; $current )
                Set Variable [ $current ; $current + 1 ]
                Exit Loop If [ $current > $count ]
        End Loop
Commit Transaction
```

Note   There is a limit of one transaction active at a time so nested *Open Transaction* steps will be ignored.

Reverting a Transaction

The biggest reason to use window transactions is for the script to have the option to rollback all the changes made should the circumstances warrant it. This is accomplished using the *Revert Transaction* step.

```
Revert Transaction [ ]
```

When placed in a script without any parameter options specified, it will immediately end the transaction and revert all the changes made. This can be placed inside of an *If* statement to make it conditional, as shown here:

```
Show Custom Dialog [ "Records are ready. Commit or Revert?" ]
If [ Get ( LastMessageChoice ) = 2 ]
      Revert Transaction [ ]
End If
```

Note   See the "CH36-02 Reverting a Transaction" example file.

However, the step also has its own built-in parameter for establishing the condition(s) under which it should revert and the ability to generate a custom error, as shown in Figure 36-1.

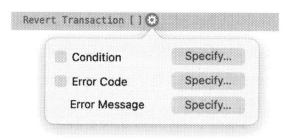

Figure 36-1. The configurable options for the Revert Transaction script step

The following options each opens a *Specify Calculation* dialog to allow a formula to control one option:

- *Condition* – Enter a formula that returns a Boolean to control if the step executes and revert the current transaction or not.

- *Error code* – Enter a formula to generate a custom error number if the *Condition* is true.

- *Error message* – Enter a formula to generate a custom error message if the *Condition* is true.

Instead of using an *If* statement to conditionally execute the revert step, this can be performed inline using the *Condition* formula.

```
Show Custom Dialog [ "Records are ready. Commit or Revert?" ]
Revert Transaction [ Condition: Get ( LastMessageChoice )= 2 ]
```

Tip   When records created in a transaction are reverted, sequential Primary IDs assigned them will be skipped over for future records. Use UUID for primary keys instead, and assign any sequential values at the end of the transaction process to ensure continuity.

Performing Subscripts

If a script uses the *Perform Script* step to run a subscript from within a transaction, all the steps in that script are executed as part of the parent script's transaction. Since FileMaker forbids nested transactions, any transaction steps in the subscript will simply be ignored. The subscript can include its own transaction steps that control a transaction when run directly. However, when run as a subscript within a parent script's transactions, new transaction steps will be ignored. As of version 21 (2024), a *Revert Transaction* in a subscript will end the parent transaction and revert all changes. Prior to that, this step would also have been ignored.

Caution   Keep careful track of all the steps in a multi-script transaction sequence. If the parent script reverts the transaction, changes performed by any of the subscripts will be lost!

To illustrate using subscripts, use the last two examples to create two scripts that will create contact records from a name list with a revert option. However, the record creation *Loop* will be handled by a subscript. A script named "Parent" will perform the following steps, handling establishing the name list, passing it to the subscript named "Create," and then presenting the user with an option to commit or revert.

```
Set Variable [ $names ; "John Doe¶Karen Smith¶Frank Camacho" ]
Open Transaction [ ]
  Perform Script [ Specified: From list ; "Create" ; Parameter: $names ]
  Show Custom Dialog [ "Records are ready. Commit or Revert?" ]
  Revert Transaction [ Condition: Get ( LastMessageChoice )= 2 ]
Commit Transaction
```

Note   See the "CH36-03 Performing Sub-scripts" example file.

The second script named "Create" will perform the steps below. It establishes the $names variable by accessing the script parameter from the parent script.

```
Set Variable [ $names ; Get ( ScriptParameter ) ]
Set Variable [ $count ; ValueCount ( $names ) ]
Set Variable [ $current ; ValueCount ( $names ) ]
Loop
      New Record/Request
      Set Field [ Contact::Name ; GetValue ( $names ; $current )
      Set Variable [ $current ; $current + 1 ]
      Exit Loop If [ $current > $count ]
End Loop
```

Everything in this script will be subsumed under the transaction established in the parent. If the user chooses to revert there, none of the records created in the subscript will exist.

Dealing with Errors

One of the primary reasons to use transactions is the ability to revert a batch of changes in the event of an error. The *Get (LastError)* function (Chapter 24, "Managing Scripting Errors") can be placed at strategic locations within a transaction statement to detect errors and take a corrective course of action. The function can be used in a *Set Variable* step to record the fact of an error for later action or in the *Condition* formula of a *Revert Transaction* step to immediately stop the transaction. The *Get (LastErrorLocation)* function, added in version 19.6.1, returns the script name, step name, and line number when an error occurs on the preceding step. This is helpful when reporting an error as it allows a developer to pinpoint the location, especially when the error occurs in a subscript.

To illustrate the basics of detecting and reacting to errors, let's create an example where a parent script opens a transaction and then runs a subscript that creates a record and fills in a field. However, to force an error, the subscript uses the *Set Field By Name* and targets a nonexistent field, as shown here:

```
New Record/Request
Set Field By Name [ "Not a Field" ; "Hello, World" ]
```

The parent script will perform the following steps:

```
Set Error Capture [ On ]
Open Transaction [ ]
     Perform Script [ Specified: From list ; "Create" ; Parameter: "" ]
     Set Variable [ $errorNumber ; Value: Get ( LastError ) ]
     Revert Transaction [ Condition: $errorNumber ≠ 0 ]
Commit Transaction
If [ $errorNumber ≠ 0 ]
     Show Custom Dialog [ "Error" ; "Error code: " & $errorNumber ]
End If
```

Note   See the "CH36-04 Detecting Errors" example file.

To include details about the location of the error within the subscript, change the *Set Variable* step to set a *$null* variable with the following formula:

```
Let ( [
        $errorNumber = Get ( LastError ) ;
        $errorLocation = Get ( LastErrorLocation )
] ;
        ""

)
```

Then, set the Show Custom Dialog setup to display the following formula:

```
"Error Code: " & $errorNumber & ":¶" & $errorLocation
```

Detecting an Open Transaction State

A *Get* function added in version 19.6.1 provides an opportunity for a formula to detect if a window has an open transaction. The function will return a Boolean result, true (1) if the window has a transaction currently open and false (0) if not.

```
Get ( TransactionOpenState )
```

This can be used to set controls over interface and script operations. For example,

- A *Hide* formula (Chapter 19, "Behavior") can disable layout objects when pausing for user input during a transaction.

- A button bar segment, tab panel, or other object's name can change during a transaction.

- Steps in a subscript can be conditionally performed if a parent script has an open transaction.

Caution   Add a *Refresh Window* step after opening a transaction to ensure that layout elements update their hide behavior and names.

Creating a Transaction Enabled Dialog

Let's create an example of a window used as a dialog that solicits information about a new Company record, including a related Contact, but has a "Cancel" option.

Note   See the "CH36-05 Dialog Example" example file.

Setting up the Tables

This example assumes a *Company* and *Contact* table exist with a minimum set of fields:

- In the *Company* table: *PrimaryKey*, *Company Name*, and *Company Website*

- In the *Contact* table: *Company ID*, *Contact Email*, *Contact Name*, *Contact Title*

Creating the Relationship

In the relationship graph, both tables have a primary occurrence. A secondary occurrence of the *Contact* table is related to the primary *Company* occurrence, as shown in Figure 36-2.

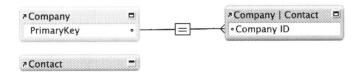

Figure 36-2. *The relationship graph showing the requirements for the example*

The relationship settings should at least have the *Allow creation go records in this table via the relationship* option turned on for the *Contact* side, as shown in Figure 36-3.

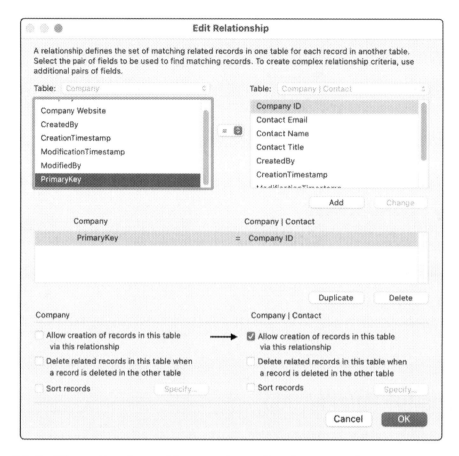

Figure 36-3. *The option to enable record creation in a portal*

Designing the Dialog Layout

A layout for the *Company* table must be created. In the example, this is named "Company Creation Dialog" and designed as shown in Figure 36-4.

Figure 36-4. *The layout that will be used as a dialog for creating new company records*

The layout includes the following components:

- A heading and prompt for user action.

- The name and website fields for the *Company* table. These two have a *Placeholder* formula of "required" indicating to the user that they must enter a value to continue.

- The *Contact Name* field in the portal also has *Placeholder* formula of "[New Contact]," so the user understands that the persistent empty row is used to enter a new record.

Writing the Scripts

The dialog feature will require two scripts, one to initiate the "New Company" dialog and another to handle a *Cancel* button click.

Creating a "New Company" Script

A script named "New Company" will be responsible for initiating the process of requesting information from the user about a new company record. It will perform the following steps:

```
# Open new window centered
Set Variable [ $width ; Value: 650 ]
Set Variable [ $height ; 550 ]
Set Variable [ $left ; Value: ( Get(ScreenWidth)/2 ) - ( $width/2 )]
Set Variable [ $top ; Value: ( Get(ScreenHeight)/2 ) - ( $height/2 )]
New Window [ Style: Document ; Name: "New Company" ]

#Wait for user input
Allow User Abort [ Off ]
Open Transaction [ ]
       New Record/Request
       Loop [ Flush: Always ]
              Pause/Resume Script [ Indefinitely ]
              Set Variable [ $close ; Value:
                     Company::Company Name ≠ "" and
                     Company::Company Website ≠ "" and
                     Count ( Contact::PrimaryKey ) > 0
              Exit Loop If [ $close ]
              Beep
       End Loop
Commit Transaction
Close Window [ Current Window ]
```

The first part of the script sets up values to center a window on screen and then uses them with *New Windows* step to create a "dialog" open to the layout. This part must be performed outside of the *Open Transaction* since opening a new window would end an active transaction.

The second part begins with *Allow User Abort* set to "off" to make sure a user can't stop the script using key commands or the *Cancel* button in the toolbar. Then it opens a transaction for these remaining steps:

- *New Record/Request* – Makes a new record in the *Company* table.

- *Loop* – Begins a loop which will be used to keep the user in the dialog if they fail to enter required fields.

- *Pause/Resume Script* – Waits for user input.

- *Set Variable* – After the user types Enter or clicks the "Create" button on the dialog to resume the script, a *$close* variable is set to a Boolean result indicating if the three requirements are fulfilled.

- *Exit Loop If* – Exits the loop only if the *$close* variable is true.

- *Beep* – If the loop was not exited, the computer makes an alert sound and repeats

- *End Loop* – Marks the end of the Loop statement.

- *Close Window* – If the loop, the window is closed.

- *Commit Transaction* – Terminates the transaction statement.

Notice that there is no *Revert Transaction* step used in this technique. That is because we are relying on a *Cancel* button to perform a script that closes the window which immediately reverts the transaction.

Caution   The Close Window step must fall outside of the transaction, or it will automatically revert!

Creating a "Cancel Button" Script

A script named "Cancel Button" will contain two steps. First it turns error capture on to suppress any error messages and then closes the current window.

```
Set Error Capture [ On ]
Close Window [ Current Window ]
```

Connecting the Buttons to the Scripts

The two buttons are configured as shown in Figure 36-5:

- The *Create* button action is a *Single Step*, set to *Pause/Resume Script*. Since the layout opens in a paused state, clicking this button will resume the script.

- The *Cancel* button action is a *Perform Script*, targeting the "Cancel Button" script. The *Options* setting is set to "Exit Current Script."

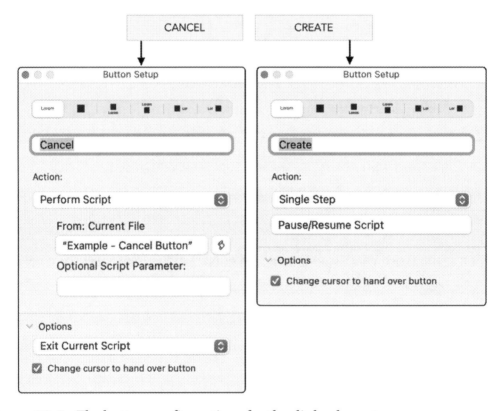

Figure 36-5. *The button configurations for the dialog layout*

Using the Feature

A button placed on any other layout can target the "New Company" script to start the process. The dialog will open and pause for user input and stay open until they either enter all required values or click "Cancel." If they cancel, the transaction is reverted automatically, and new records will remain.

Using the OnWindowTransaction Trigger

In version 20.1, a new Script Trigger for file events (Chapter 27, "Linking Scripts to File Events") was added for reacting to a committed transaction. The *OnWindowTransaction* event occurs before a window commits a transaction. It triggers the assigned script and includes a JSON Object script parameter containing details about every operation that was completed within the transaction. The JSON contains a hierarchy of keys starting with the file name and base table name where each change occurred. These contain a JSON Array of the records affected, each containing an array with three values:

- *Operation* – Identifies the record action taken: *New, Modified, Deleted.*

- *Record ID* – FileMaker's numeric identification number for the affected record (not a field value).

- *Optional field value* – The contents of an optional field can be specified in the *File Options* dialog, shown in Figure 36-6. This allows you to include your own *Record Primary ID* field or other data in the JSON that the script will use to process the transaction. If the field specified exists in the current layout's table, its contents are included. If it doesn't exist or is left blank, this array position will contain an empty string.

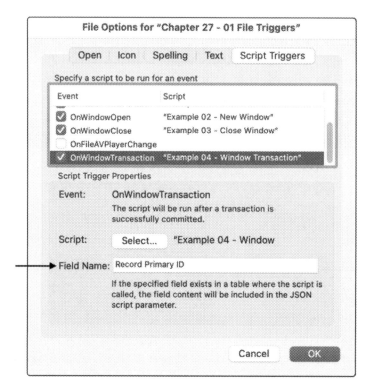

Figure 36-6. *The optional field name whose contents will be inserted into the JSON parameter*

Here is an example of the JSON contents after a record creation transaction:

```
{
    "CH27-01 File Triggers" :
    {
        "Contact" :
        [
            [
                "New",
                24,
                "000034"
            ]
        ]
    }
}
```

Note   See the "CH27-01 File Triggers" file for this example of a *record transaction*. See the "Ch36-06 OnWindowTransaction" file for an example of a *window transaction*.

The script can parse and use the transaction information as needed. To demonstrate this, the following example shows the extraction of transaction data from a single record change parsed and turned into a sentence.

```
Let ( [
    json = Get ( ScriptParameter ) ;
    file = JSONListKeys ( json ; "" ) ;
    table = JSONListKeys ( json ; file ) ;
    tableKey = file & "." & table ;
    tableJSON = JSONGetElement ( json ; tableKey ) ;
    operation = JSONGetElement ( json ; tableKey & "[0].[0]" ) ;
    id = JSONGetElement ( json ; tableKey & "[0].[1]" ) ;
    Other = JSONGetElement ( json ; tableKey & "[0].[2]" )
] ;
    "A " & Quote ( operation ) &
    " transaction was detected. It affected record " &
    id & Case ( Other ≠ "" ; " (" & Other & ")" ) &
    " in the " & Quote ( table ) & " table of the " &
    Quote ( file ) & " file."
)
```

When the above formula is placed into a *Show Custom Dialog* step, the message shown in Figure 36-7 will be displayed. Of course, this is for demonstration purposes only. A more practical script might parse the JSON information and use it to record the event in a log table or perform a set of steps depending on the operation performed. For example, a new record creation can be followed by steps that create certain related records.

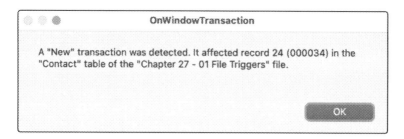

Figure 36-7. *A sentence built from the transaction's JSON information*

According to the documentation, the script is triggered before this event and can return a false (0) value, to cancel the event. However, the actual effects of doing so are unclear since nothing changes with respect to a new, modified, or deleted record.

Summary

This chapter introduced the concept of window-based transactions to perform a sequence of tasks as a single unit of work. In the next chapter, we introduce machine learning capabilities for macOS computers.

CHAPTER 37

Using Core Machine Learning (macOS)

Core Machine Learning (Core ML) is a macOS framework developed by Apple, Inc. that simplifies the integration of artificial intelligence (AI) features into applications. A *machine learning model* is a computational algorithm that is trained to identify patterns or make decisions about a previously unseen dataset. FileMaker gained support for Core ML image and text processing models in version 19.0. This chapter explores the basics of using machine learning in a database, covering the following topics:

- Getting started with Core ML
- Creating a field for a model
- Finding a model
- Creating fields for input and output
- Writing a script to classify images
- Running the script
- Adjusting the result parameters
- Parsing the results

Getting Started with Core ML

Core ML works by comparing a source item against an ML Model file and generating results based on probabilities in a process as shown in Figure 37-1. First, a developer locates or creates a model file that is "trained" to perform a specific function. This file is stored in a container field. Then, a script loads it using the *Configure Machine*

965

© Mark Conway Munro 2024
M. C. Munro, *Learn FileMaker Pro 2024*, https://doi.org/10.1007/979-8-8688-0835-7_37

Learning Model step, and the *ComputeModel* function is used to instruct the model to evaluate a piece of source material. Depending on the model's design, the JSON result predicts something about the input. For example, an *image processing model* can make predictions about the subject of the photo, in this case, predicting with 32% certainty that the source material is a "tabby cat."

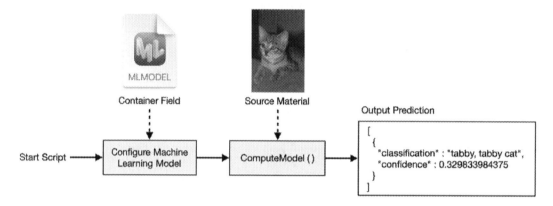

Figure 37-1. *An overview of a Core ML setup in FileMaker*

Note   See the "CH37-01 CoreML" example file.

Creating a Field for a Model

The only structural requirement for using Core ML is that a database must have access to a *machine learning model* file in a container field. Where that field exists and how it is accessed can vary depending on how many other models will be used or how it will be accessed. If a database requires access to a single model, primarily from one table context, consider adding a global field to that table. However, if the database requires several models or if they are used from a variety of different contexts, consider creating a dedicated "Model" table as a library of models. This can be set up in different ways, including the following:

- A single record with one global field for each model. These will be accessible from any context but must be loaded when the database is not hosted.

- One record for each model stored in a single non-global field. This makes it possible to update the model, while the file is hosted but requires the script to navigate to the table and find the model it needs.

For now, while working in a test sandbox, simply create a global container field named "CoreML Model" and place it on a layout.

Tip   Remember that global field content must be set locally, before the database is hosted!

Finding a Model

The next step is to find a Core ML model file. There are numerous free and paid options online. However, remember that FileMaker is currently limited to text and image models. There are several good examples available for free on Apple's site:

`https://developer.apple.com/machine-learning/models/`

To follow along with the example, download the "MobileNetV2.mlmodel" file and drag it into the container field.

Creating Fields for Input and Output

The source image or text sent to a model for processing can be provided by a field or variable. The same is true for the target location for the JSON result. In the example, we will create two fields:

- *Image* – A container field that will contain an image for evaluation

- *CoreML Result JSON* – A text field into which we will place the results

Writing a Script to Classify Images

To classify an image in a field, a script must perform these steps:

- Use the *Configure Machine Learning Model* step to load the CoreML Model from the container, and configure it for image processing.

- Use the *ComputeModel* function to send an image to the model for processing.

- Put the results somewhere. In our example, these will be placed into a field.

- Optionally, unload the model from memory using the *Configure Machine Learning Model* step.

This script performs those actions:

```
Set Variable [ $modelName ; Value: Substitute ( GetContainerAttribute
( Sandbox::CoreML Model ; "Filename" ) ; ".mlmodel" ; "" ) ]
Configure Machine Learning Model [ Operation: Vision ; Name: $modelName ;
From: Sandbox::CoreML Model ]
Set Variable [ $result ; Value: ComputeModel( $modelName ; "image";
Sandbox::Image ) ]
Set Field [ Sandbox::CoarML Result JSON ; Case ( $result ≠ "" ;
JSONFormatElements ( $result ) ) ]
Configure Machine Learning Model [ Operation: Unload ; Name: $modelName ]
```

Since these steps are rather crowded with parameters, let's walk through each step by step and perform a closer inspection!

Step 1: Getting the Model File Name

Later, a step and function will require the name of the model file, which can be typed as a literal text string. However, to avoid typos and make experimentation with different models easier, the first line of our example will parse the actual name of the file in the container field, and place it into a *$modelName* variable.

```
Set Variable [ $modelName ; Value: Substitute ( GetContainerAttribute
( Sandbox::CoreML Model ; "Filename" ) ; ".mlmodel" ; "" ) ]
```

The *Value* formula uses the *GetContainerAttribute* function (Chapter 13, "Working with Containers") to extract the file name of the model. This is nested within a *Substitute* function that replaces the ".mlmodel" file extension with an empty string to isolate the name.

Step 2: Configuring the Model

The second step uses the *Configure Machine Learning Model* step to load and configure the model file into memory.

```
Configure Machine Learning Model [ Operation: Vision ; Name: $modelName ;
From: Sandbox::CoreML Model ]
```

The step has three parameters:

- *Operation* – This opens a menu of the following choices:

    - *Unload* – Releases the model from memory

    - *Vision* – Specifies that the model processes images

    - *General* – Specifies that the model processes text

- *Name* – The name of the model file without an extension. This value can be provided by a literal text string, a field, or a variable.

- *From* – A selected container field with the model file being configured.

In the example, we select "Vision," provide the *$modelName*, and point to the container field holding the model file.

Step 3: Evaluating the Source

Once the model is configured in memory, any formula can use the *ComputeModel* function to evaluate an image. The function requires the following three parameters:

```
ComputeModel( $modelName ; "image"; Sandbox::Image )
```

- *modelName* – The name of a model file (without extension) that is currently loaded in memory.

- *parameterName* – A text string specifying the name of an input parameter expected by the model. In the example, this is set to "image."

- *value* – A value provided as input for the model. Since the example is sending an image for evaluation, this is set to a container field.

In the example script, a *Set Variable* step captures the result in a variable, as shown here:

```
Set Variable [ $result ; Value: ComputeModel( $modelName ; "image";
Sandbox::Image ) ]
```

Note   Additional *parameterName* and *value* parameters can be added when needed.

Step 4: Placing the Results

The results of the process can be used in any way required by the script being written. The example places this into a field for review and experimentation. A *Case* statement confirms a *$result* value and converts it to a readable format using *JSONFormElements*.

```
Set Field [ Sandbox::CoarML Result JSON ; Case ( $result ≠ "" ;
JSONFormatElements ( $result ) ) ]
```

Step 5: Unloading the Model

The model can remain loaded in memory if needed. However, when only processing intermittently, this can be released by selecting "Unload" as the *Operation* and providing the name of the model.

```
Configure Machine Learning Model [ Operation: Unload ; Name: $modelName ]
```

Running the Script

Once written, run the script to see the result. If configured properly, the image in the container field of the current record should be processed by the model file and the result dropped into a field. Those results will be a JSON Array of objects with a *classification* and *confidence* value, as shown here:

```
[
        {
                "classification" : "tabby, tabby cat",
                "confidence" : 0.329833984375
        },
        {
                "classification" : "Egyptian cat",
                "confidence" : 0.2205810546875
        },
        {
                "classification" : "tiger cat",
                "confidence" : 0.16845703125
        },
        {
                "classification" : "lynx, catamount",
                "confidence" : 0.00521087646484375
        }
]
```

The results are ranked in order by a percentage of confidence about the prediction. In this case, the top result informs that the model thinks the image is of a "tabby cat" with a 32% level of confidence. Below this, we see numerous additional results that quickly become ridiculous. For example, the same image was reported as possibly being a ping-pong ball, telephone, lipstick, remote control, and more, albeit all with less than 1% confidence.

Adjusting the Result Parameters

When processing images with a "Vision" model, the *ComputeModel* has two optional parameters that control the results:

- *confidenceLowerLimit* – Specify a value between 0.0 and 1.0 that indicates the lowest limit of confidence to include in the results.

- *returnAtLeastOne* – A Boolean indicating if a result should be included even when they are all excluded by the confidence limit.

Setting a Confidence Limit

A minimum confidence level can be specified by adding a label parameter and a value parameter to the *ComputeModel* function. Add a "confidenceLowerLimit" text parameter to inform the function that a minimum confidence percentage number is provided in the next parameter. The formula shown below will limit results to only those with a confidence level of 20% or higher.

```
ComputeModel( $modelName ; "image"; Sandbox::Image );
"confidenceLowerLimit" ; .2 ]
// result =
[
    {
        "classification" : "tabby, tabby cat",
        "confidence" : 0.329833984375
    },
    {
        "classification" : "Egyptian cat",
        "confidence" : 0.2205810546875
    }
]
```

Balancing the Limit with a Guaranteed Result

Setting the minimum confidence level too high may return no results. Since you can't be certain of how well a model will do from one image to the next, it can be tempting to set the threshold drastically low. However, an additional "returnAtLeastOne" parameter can be used instead to ensure that we always receive at least one result, even if all results fall below the minimum. This example shows a limit of 75% but returns one result with 32% confidence since we specified True for this parameter.

```
ComputeModel( $modelName ; "image"; Sandbox::Image );
"confidenceLowerLimit" ; .75 ; "returnAtLeastOne" ; True ]
// result =
[
    {
        "classification" : "tabby, tabby cat",
        "confidence" : 0.329833984375
    }
]
```

Parsing the Results

The JSON result in a field or variable can be parsed as needed. The formula below demonstrates a *While* statement looping through the JSON and building a list of every classification keyword in the same order of confidence.

```
While (
[
    json = CoreML Result JSON ;
    result = ""
] ;
    json ≠ "[]" and json ≠ "" ;
[
    current = JSONGetElement ( json ; "[0].classification" ) ;
    result = List ( result ; Substitute ( current ; ", " ; "¶" ) ) ;
```

```
        json = JSONDeleteElement ( json ; "[0]" )
] ;
        result
)
```

Summary

This chapter explored using *Core Machine Learning* (Core ML) models in a database and worked through an example of classifying an image. In the next chapter, we introduce how to leverage artificial intelligence in your databases.

CHAPTER 38

Leveraging Artificial Intelligence

Artificial intelligence (AI) is a type of software automation that uses sophisticated algorithms to perform complex tasks that would normally require human intelligence. The emergence of technologies like ChatGPT from OpenAI and its ability to simulate human intelligence have sparked a widespread interest, opening a new dimension of what is possible with computers. In recent years, FileMaker has gained new capabilities that facilitate the integration of AI features in a database. In version 19, the *Insert from URL* script step (Chapter 25, "Using Insert from URL") gained *Client for URLs* (cURL) options to communicate with a wide variety of APIs, including AI systems like ChatGPT. That version also gained *Core Machine Learning* (CoreML) support, enabling developers to automate image and text related tasks (Chapter 37). In version 21 (2024), Claris introduced additional capabilities, including the ability to more easily link a database to an OpenAI account for use with some new AI related functions and script steps. Using these features, a database can use AI to generate, parse, process, or evaluate content in endless different ways. This chapter introduces the subject of artificial intelligence and how to integrate it into a database, exploring the following topics:

- Introducing large language models
- Accessing the OpenAI API
- Performing completions
- Performing a semantic find

© Mark Conway Munro 2024
M. C. Munro, *Learn FileMaker Pro 2024*, https://doi.org/10.1007/979-8-8688-0835-7_38

Introducing Large Language Models

A *large language model* (LLM) is an advanced artificial intelligence system designed to understand and generate humanlike text in response to prompts. They are a type of machine learning model trained on vast amounts of textual data to establish a statistical foundation from which a wide range of natural language processing tasks become possible. The scale of these models is staggering, typically measured in billions of parameters. Similarly, the data used to train them is diverse and extensive, drawing from articles, books, websites, and various other sources of information. From this training, LLMs learn language patterns and acquire an understanding of conversational context. Once trained, they use probabilities to formulate content that can answer questions, translate languages, summarize text, identify sentiment, generate content, and engage in realistic conversational interactions with humans.

Using a browser, users can access and interact with OpenAI's LLMs, such as the various iterations of GPT. With carefully worded prompts, they can use the service to perform various tasks in a familiar browser interface. However, the OpenAI API provides an endpoint for direct access to the same LLMs by third party computer software, including FileMaker Pro. With an API key and a carefully engineered JSON prompt, scripts can instruct an OpenAI model to perform a task. The results will be returned to the script for further processing. This provides developers the ability to leverage AI directly in their custom databases.

Although each model works differently, they generally receive a prompt and predict what should follow logically from it. In the conversational model like GPTs, a completion is performed. A model can be instructed to adopt a specific role which sets its behavior in responding. For example, it can act as user, assistant, expert in a field, a system, etc. The role can range from very specific to a general sense of how to act. The prompt can also include details about the expected format of the response.

Accessing the OpenAI API

The *OpenAI API* offers a robust set of features designed to empower developers with advanced natural language processing capabilities. By integrating the API, you can harness the power of language models to generate humanlike text, translate languages, summarize content, and more. Opening an account is straightforward: simply visit the OpenAI website, sign up with your email, and follow the verification steps.

```
https://openai.com
```

Once registered, you can create API keys from the dashboard. A *project key* is a unique identifier associated with a specific project or application within your OpenAI account. It acts as a secure credential that authorizes your application's requests to the API, ensuring that only authenticated and approved projects can access the OpenAI services. To create a project key, log in to your OpenAI account, navigate to the API keys section, and generate a new key for your project. This key should be kept confidential and included in your application's code to authenticate API requests, allowing you to manage and monitor usage specific to that project. This is an pseudo-example of the format of a project API key you will generate and use in your project.

```
sk-12345678abcdef1234567890abcdef12
```

To use the API, you will need to purchase tokens. Tokens are the units of computation used by the API, with each API call consuming a certain number based on the request's complexity and length. To purchase tokens, log in to your OpenAI account and navigate to the billing section. Choose a pricing plan that fits your needs, enter your payment information, and complete the transaction. Your account will then be credited with tokens, which you can monitor and manage through the OpenAI dashboard. This system ensures you only pay for what you use, offering flexibility and control over your usage and expenses.

Once you have a key and token access, it is time to begin building database features that tap into the power of artificial intelligence!

Surveying OpenAI Models and Features

The models and features accessible through the OpenAI API at the time of this book's publication are as follows:

- *GPT-4o* – The latest and most advanced model, capable of understanding complex tasks and generating humanlike text with high accuracy and coherence

- *GPT-4o mini* – Versatile text generation and comprehension, balancing cost and faster performance

- *GPT-4* – The legacy model which is superseded by the two above

- *DALL-E* – Image generation from textual descriptions, enabling creative visual content generation

- *Whisper* – Automatic speech recognition (ASR) for transcribing spoken language

- *Embeddings* – Converting text into numerical vectors for semantic understanding and various downstream tasks

---

Caution   The GPT product line is continually evolving. Always check OpenAI's website for the latest version information. Be sure to experiment with different models as the results may vary slightly.

Each model enables a spectrum of applications, ranging from answering questions, parsing complex data, writing code, generating multimedia content, and more. As an introduction to integrating AI into a FileMaker database, we will work through an example of using *Insert from URL* script step to interact with the GPT model and then explore the embedding process that enables the new *Perform Semantic Search* step.

The features offered by an API model are called *capabilities*. In this chapter, we will focus on two of OpenAI's capabilities: *completions* and *embeddings*.

Performing Completions

A *completion* is text generated by a large language model in response to an input prompt. A model predicts the appropriate response based on the input it is given. In its simplest form, a completion is like an auto-complete process, where the computer tries to guess the next word in a sentence based on what has already been typed. For example, if the prompt is "Once upon a," a model will predict that the intention is a stock phrase used to introduce a folktale narrative and suggest as the next word "time."

However, completions with powerful models like those accessible through OpenAI's API can be far more sophisticated. Instead of simply providing the next logical word in a sentence, they can answer questions on virtually any subject. They can also generate new content, albeit content derived from the materials used to train it. With careful prompt engineering, they can perform much more complex tasks, including the following:

- Proofread written material, confirming accuracy or editing content by acting as an editor in a specific industry or genre.

- Generate code snippets in any programming language to solve specific computational requirements.

- Perform complex parsing tasks and return content in a specified format such as JSON or other structured arrangements.

More complex completion prompts can include lengthy instructions about the role the assistant should adopt, the desired tasks, and the output requirements. They can also include a sequence of mock conversational exchanges between a pseudo user and assistant showing before and after examples relevant to the input, task, and output expectations. This real-time "training" allows the model to use contextual examples to better understand the request and provide more accurate results.

To demonstrate how to use completions, we will create two examples. The first will answer a simple prompt from a user or developer to get the city and state associated with a zip code. The second will parse contact information from any text and return it as a JSON Object.

Sending a Zip Code Lookup Prompt

To illustrate the process, we will begin with a simple example that sends a prompt to OpenAI's *chat completion model* that displays the result in a field. Although the prompt generated will be from a field and can take a variety of different forms, our examples will focus on providing a US postal code and requesting access the associated city and state.

Note   See the "CH38-01 Zip Code" example file.

Configuring Demonstration Fields

The example file has two input fields:

- *OpenAI API Key* – Enter an OpenAI project key and make sure your account has a credit card approving a budget amount authorized. In a production environment, you should hide this key from users by placing it in a custom function, a script step, or a field not easily accessible on layouts.

- *Input* – This field will accept the text of the prompt to be sent to the model for processing. In a production environment, input for a prompt could be provided by users through the interface or typed literally by developers.

The example file also has three fields to display the prompt generated for the API, the raw response, and the result parsed from the response. These are not required in a typical production system. Here they assist in visualizing the components for educational and troubleshooting purposes.

Writing the Script

A script is required to create the prompt, configure cURL options, execute the *Insert from URL* step, and handle results.

Loading Some Variables

Begin by loading the API key and URL for the completion model into variables.

```
Set Variable [ $apikey : Value: Sandbox::OpenAI API Key ]
Set Variable [ $url : Value: "https://api.openai.com/v1/chat/completions" ]
```

Building the Prompt

When using ChatGPT in a web browser, a user can simply type a message and send it. Accessing the model directly from an application requires a little more information. The prompt is a JSON Object containing two primary keys: *model* and *messages*. The *model* is a string that specifies which system we are targeting with the prompt, in this case "gtp-4." The *message* key must contain an array of one or more objects, each with a key for *role* and *content*. The *role* indicates the role for the content and can be system, assistant, or user. To build our first simple example, we include a single array object containing the *Input* field as the content and indicate this as from a user.

```
JSONSetElement ( "" ;
      [ "model" ; "gpt-4" ; JSONString ];
      [ "messages.[0].role" ; "user" ; JSONString ] ;
      [ "messages.[0].content" ; Sandbox::Input ; JSONString ]
)
```

Caution   A "user" role indicates any message not from the API. It can be text directly from a human user but also content generated by a database script. Prompts can include pseudo-conversations between a pseudo user and assistant (see the next section's example).

If the *Input* field contains "city and state for 11208," the prompt generated by the formula above will be the following JSON places into a *$prompt* variable. This will instruct the model that a user is requesting the city and state for 11208.

```
{
    "messages" :
    [
        {
            "content" : "city and state for 11208",
            "role" : "user"
        }
    ],
    "model" : "gpt-4"
}
```

Configuring cURL Options

The cURL options will vary from one API to another. In our example, we must specify a *content-type* and *authorization* headers, with *data* combined into a full command as shown below. This is the formula used to generate a value for a *$curl* variable.

```
"-H \"Content-Type: application/json\"
-H \"Authorization: Bearer " &  $apikey & "\"" &
" -d @$prompt"
```

Tip   Instead of writing the options in a formula with escaped quotes, use the *Insert Text* script step to insert it into a variable. The text will be easier to read and compare against API documentation. Then, use *Set Variable* to substitute any merge fields like @APIKey.

The use of quotations is very deliberate here and may be confusing to first-time developers. The *$apikey* is placed outside of quotations, to concatenate its value instead of its name with the rest of the authorization header text. However, the *$prompt* is placed inside of quotations which seems counterintuitive but is required to ensure proper formatting of the curl command. The actual result of the formula, and the value placed into the *$curl* variable, is shown below. When this is used as the *cURL options* parameter for the *Insert for URL* script step, it automatically handles pulling and including the value from *$prompt* variable.

```
-H "Content-Type: application/json" -H "Authorization: Bearer 3d84fetc" -d
@$prompt
```

Executing Insert from URL

Now we can assemble these parts and send the request to the API using the Insert from URL script step, configured as shown below. This calls the URL of the OpenAI completion model stored in the *$url* variable, includes the options from the *$curl* variable, and targets the *$response* variable for the results.

```
Insert from URL [ Select ; With dialog: Off ; Target: $response ; $url ;
cURL Options: $curl ]
```

Handling the Result

After the *Insert from URL* step executes, the $response variable will contain whatever results were generated. If unsuccessful, any error message or information will be found in the variable. If successful, the result will be a JSON Object containing a variety of information about the request and processing. This includes various metadata about the transaction, token usage, and an array named "choices." The first item here will contain a message object with the *content* and *role* of the result. Using *JSONGetElement* with a key path, we can extract the result as follows:

```
JSONGetElement ( $response ; "choices.[0].message.content" )
// result = Brooklyn, New York
```

Refining the Prompt for a Structure Response

To make this example a more practical method of extracting a zip code, we can refine the prompt to indicate that we are seeking a structure response. To request the results as JSON, the prompt would be rewritten as follows:

```
"city and state for 11208 as JSON"
```

Now, the result will be a JSON Object with a *city* and *state* key. A script can easily parse these and enter them into fields in a manner like the example using a dedicated postal code lookup service (Chapter 25, "Accessing a Zip Code API"). This method can be an alternative for that service.

```
{
    "city": "Brooklyn",
    "state": "NY"
}
```

Note   The result expectations included in a prompt can be as specific as needed and can include an example of the JSON format desired.

Parsing Contact Information from Text

A completion task offloaded to an LLM like OpenAI can be far more sophisticated than simply finding an answer to a simple question like the preceding zip code lookup. A complex prompt can include a pseudo-conversation between a hypothetical user and an AI assistant to provide before and after examples of source material and response expectations to help inform the assistant how to handle the next, actual prompt. To illustrate this, let's work through an example of instructing OpenAI to parse contact information from any text sent. This would allow a script to transform the body of an email into a JSON Object with contact information which can then be parsed and entered into table of people.

Note   See the "CH38-01 Parse Address" example file.

Building a Complex Prompt

The prompt for a complex task is structurally identical to the simple zip code lookup in the previous section. The difference is that we will include a more complex message array that establishes a role for the assistant, more clearly identifies the task, provides result expectations, and includes an array of messages that act as an example.

Establishing the System's Role, Task, and Result

The first item in the *message array* must establish a system role. The "Role" key will have a value of "System," and the "Content" key will explain how the assistant should act and provide details about the task it must perform and the format for the results:

Act as a mailing list data entry employee parsing text. You will parse some text, looking for a mailing address and returning it in JSON. *Only* respond with the JSON object, with *no* additional explanation or details. Include missing values in the JSON as empty strings. The following is the JSON schema to use to respond:

```
{
        "$schema":"http://json-schema.org/draft-07/schema#",
        "type":"object",
        "properties": {
                "Name":"The name of the person",
                "Street":"The street portion of the address" ,
                "City":"The name of the city",
                "State":"The abbreviation of the state",
                "Zip":"The postal code for the address",
                "Phone":"A work or home phone number",
                "Email":"An email address",
                "Web":"A website address"
        }
}
```

Expanding the Message Array

Depending on the nature of the task and the amount of variation in the input to be provided, the above might suffice as the entire prompt. However, with more complexity or to address specific erroneous results, it is a good idea to provide at least a couple of before and after examples. This is done by including additional elements in the *message array* that alternate between a fabricated user prompt and hypothetical response from the assistant. Below is one example of a simple set of prompt-response examples.

First, we add an object to the array showing a possible prompt from a user. This has contact information embedded in a simple paragraph made of two sentences.

```
{
"content" : "My name is Gerald Franklin. I live at 10 Fantasy Lane,
Pittsburgh, PA 15106\r",
"role" : "user"
}
```

Next, we provide the assistant response we would expect from the above user prompt.

```
{
"content" : "{\r  "Name": "Gerald Franklin" ; \r  "Street": "10 Fantasy
Lane" ; \r  "City": "Pittsburgh" ; \r  "State": "PA" ; \r  "Zip":
"15106"\r}",
"role" : "assistant"
}
```

The number of additional examples you provide can vary based on the complexity of the task and how well the model responds. The example file shows four different examples added to the message array before the new prompt is added which contains the actual data we want to be processed. At this point the pattern of the *messages* key of the JSON in the *$messages* variable will be as follows:

```
[
{ "role" : "system", "content" : "<describe, role, task and result>" },
{ "role" : "user", "content" : "<example prompt 1>" },
{ "role" : "assistant", "content" : "<example response 1>" },
{ "role" : "user", "content" : "<example prompt 2>" },
{ "role" : "assistant", "content" : "<example response 2>" },
{ "role" : "user", "content" : "<example prompt 3>" },
{ "role" : "assistant", "content" : "<example response 3>" },
```

```
{ "role" : "user", "content" : "<example prompt 4>" },
{ "role" : "assistant", "content" : "<example response 4>" },
{ "role" : "user", "content" : "<actual prompt of text to process>" }
]
```

Tip   The larger the prompt, the greater the token cost incurred for processing! Start with a short description and fewer examples, then add to it as your testing reveals the need for more specificity.

Once the prompt is created, the cURL options and setup of *Insert from URL* script step are identical to the zip code lookup example. Now, any paragraph containing contact information can be processed to produce a result. The example file shows this text being inserted for processing:

If you have any questions or need further information, please feel free to contact Jane Doe. You can reach her at her office phone number, (555) 123-4567, or via email at jane.doe@example.com. Additionally, you can send correspondence to her office address at 123 Maple Street, Suite 400, Springfield, IL 62701. Jane is available Monday through Friday from 9 AM to 5 PM, and she looks forward to assisting you. http://www.wtmedia.com

The result should be a JSON Object with all the contact information parsed out of the input and ready for a script to create a new record. The paragraph above, should produce this result:

```
{
  "Name": "Jane Doe",
  "Street": "123 Maple Street, Suite 400",
  "City": "Springfield",
  "State": "IL",
  "Zip": "62701",
  "Phone": "(555) 123-4567",
  "Email": "jane.doe@example.com",
  "Web": "http://www.wtmedia.com"
}
```

Performing a Semantic Find with Embeddings

A *semantic find* is a type of search that improves accuracy of results by attempting to understand the intent and contextual meaning of the search terms instead of performing a simple keyword match. It uses *natural language processing* (NLP), *machine learning*, and *artificial intelligence* (AI) to comprehend the context, the relationships between words, and the searcher's intent. This enhances the user experience by allowing criteria to be expressed in a natural and conversational manner without the need to conform strictly to a field and keyword format. Popular examples of semantic searching include virtual assistants like Siri, Alexa, Google Assistant which attempt to convert a spoken prompt into an intelligent result. In version 21 (2024), FileMaker gained new functions and scripts steps that utilize OpenAI's service to create embeddings and use them to perform semantic finds in a database. The following is an overview of setting up a semantic find in a database:

- Create a paid OpenAI API account (described earlier in this chapter).

- Create a container field in the target search table to store embeddings.

- Create and Store Embeddings – Create a script that uses the *Configure AI Account* and *Insert Embedding* script steps to create semantic search vectors that will be used later when performing a find.

- Perform Semantic Find – Create a script that solicits a search phrase from a user, then uses the *Configure AI Account* and *Perform Semantic Find* script steps to search records based on semantic matches between the search phrase and stored embeddings.

Note   See the "Chapter 38-03 Semantic Find" example file.

Using Embeddings

An *embedding* is a numerical representation of data that capture and store the semantic meaning of words, phrases, or entire documents as vectors, encoding details of the text. These are crucial in a semantic search, enabling a system to understand and compare the meaning of textual content. By storing the semantic meaning of some text, a search engine can understand the context in which words are used, beyond mere keyword matching. Some examples of this are:

- Distinguishing between the different meanings of a word like "bank," in various contexts such as the bank of a river, a savings bank.

- Understanding that a search for "medical results" should include mentions of "blood tests" or "x-rays" even when the words "medical" and "results" are not present in the text.

- Match results of a formal technical term like "automobile" to a search using a colloquial term "car."

Preparing Data for Embedding

To create an embedding, you will need to identify which fields contain data that should be included in the search. For example, a record containing movie reviews may have a title, category and description field to be included while metadata fields like creation date or user are typically not required. Once identified, you will need to combine the fields into a single value to send for embedding. This concatenation can be done in a variable by the script creating the embedding or preprocessed in a calculation field. The example file uses a calculation field named "Embedding Data" that combines into a single value a static "type" value and three fields: *Movie Title, Movie Category*, and *Movie Description.*

```
"Type: Movie." &
"Title: " & Movie Title & ". " &
"Category: " & Movie Category & ". " &
"Description: " & Movie Description
```

Note   The static *Type* field helps inform a context of movie records. A database containing records for books, music and movies, would use a field value instead of this static one.

Field labels like those shown above are optional, although including these may provide some additional context to inform the embedding process. Whatever the content included, consider pre-processing it as needed to ensure an optimal embedding process. The text should be as concise as possible, devoid of unnecessary white space, special characters, or other extraneous content that does not contribute important meaning. Although the embedding model can accommodate large amounts of text, try to keep the detail as short as possible to ensure faster processing times and keep token costs lower. However, don't sacrifice important context or meaningful text for those considerations.

Using the Configure AI Account Script Step

In version 21 (2024), the *Configure AI Account* script step was added to automatically connect a script to an artificial intelligence account. With this step, a script can be easily connected to an account without worrying about complex cURL options.

```
Configure AI Account [ Account Name: "myAccount" ; Model Provider: OpenAI ;
API key: "sk-proj-Pjt3F6COMA4o..." ]
```

The step has the following three parameters:

- *Account name* – A name assigned to the AI account you are configuring which will be used in other script steps and functions to be called. This is a name you choose for your script, not something related to the model provider.

- *Model provider* – Select either "OpenAI" or "Custom." If choosing the latter, an additional parameter must define an endpoint URL for the model provider.

- *API key* – An authorization key or project token that grants access to the model provider's services.

Caution   This step must be performed prior to running the *Insert Embedding* or *Perform Semantic Search* steps or prior to using some of the new AI functions related to these tasks.

Using Insert Embedding for the Current Record

The *Insert Embedding* script step added in version 21 (2024) enters a file containing a vector representation of input text into a container field or variable. The file is generated by the model service specified and previously configured. This shows an example script configuring an OpenAI account and then inserting an embedding.

```
Configure AI Account [
        Account Name: "myAccount" ;
        Model Provider: OpenAI ;
        API key: "sk-proj-Pjt3F6COMA4o…"
        ]
Insert Embedding [
        Account Name: "myAccount" ;
        Embedding Model: "text-embedding-3-small" ;
        Input: Sandbox::Embedding Data ;
        Target: Sandbox::Embedding
        ]
```

The step has the following four parameters:

- *Account name* – A text value containing the name of the model provider account to be accessed as established in the preceding *Configure AI Account* step

- *Embedding model* – The name of the model that will be used to generate embedding vectors, based on the options available from the account provider, for example, "text-embedding-3-small" is an OpenAI model

- *Input* – A field reference or variable containing the text data to be sent to the model for embedding

- *Target* – A reference to a container field or variable that will receive the embedding result

Once configured and saved, run the script. An embedding file should appear in the *Sandbox::Embedding* field.

Tip   Use a Script Trigger (Chapter 27) to automatically insert a new embedding whenever the input fields are modified.

Using Insert Embedding for the Found Set

Alternatively, embeddings can be created for every record in the current found set with the *Insert Embeddings in Found Set* step. The step is almost identical to the version for the current record, with a couple of notable differences:

- A *Target Field* must be specified instead of a *Target*. In other words, there is no option to put the results into a variable since one will be created for each record.

- A *Replace Target Contents* option enables or disables generating embeddings for records that already have a file in place.

- A *Parameters* option can contain a JSON Object specifying limits on size, number, and frequency of requests that are sent to the model.

Specifying Parameters

The optional *Parameters* option's JSON Object can contain the following keys to set limits on the embedding process:

```
{
    "MaxRecPerCall" : 60,
    "MaxRetryPerWorker" : 15,
    "MaxWaitPerRetry" : 250000,
    "TruncateTokenLimit" : 1500,
    "TruncateEnabled" : 1
}
```

- *MaxRecPerCall* – Sets the maximum number of records that will be processed with each call to the API model. The default of 20 can be set from 1 and 500.

- *MaxRetryPerWorker* – Sets the maximum number of API call failures allowed. The default of 5 can be set from 1 to 100.

- *MaxWaitPerRetry* – Sets the maximum number of milliseconds to wait between OpenAI API calls. If exceeded due to too many requests per minute, the script step generates an error. The default of 60,000 can be set from 20 to 3,600,000.

- *TruncateTokenLimit* – Sets a limit on the number of tokens worth of input to accept from the Source Field. The default of 8,185 can be set from 0 to 8,192.

- *TruncateEnabled* – A Boolean indicating if the token limit should be enabled or not. The default is 1 (true).

Using the Perform Semantic Find Step

The *Perform Semantic Find* script step will find records matching a natural language query string by comparing it to embeddings. The step has the following parameter options:

- *Query by* – Select the type of query to perform: "Natural language" (text) or embedding "Vector data."

- *Record set* – Select to search "All records" or "Current found set."

- *Target field* – A reference to a field, either a text field of embedding vectors or a container field storing an embedding file.

- *Return count* – A number indicating records to return as the result set; leave empty for the default of 10.

- *Cosine similarity condition* – Select how data should be compared to the *Cosine similarity value.* Choices include *greater than, less than, equal to,* etc.

- *Cosine similarity value* – Enter a number indicating the threshold to determine semantic similarity, ranging from -1 (dissimilar) and 1 (similar).

When the *Query by* parameter is set to "Natural language" as in our example, these additional parameters are available:

- *Account name* – A text value containing the name of the model provider account to be accessed as established in a preceding *Configure AI Account* step

- *Embedding model* – The name of the model that was used to generate the embedding vectors in the *Target field*

- Text – A text value containing a search query which will be compared to the embedding vectors to find similarity and produce results

Creating a Semantic Find Script

Creating a semantic find script involves three basic steps: configuring an AI account, gathering the search query, and performing the find. In this example, a *Show Custom Dialog* step is used to request a query string from the user which is placed into a *$search* variable and then sent to an OpenAI account for processing.

```
Configure AI Account [
      Account Name: "myAccount" ;
      Model Provider: OpenAI ;
      API key: "sk-proj-Pjt3F6COMA4o…"
      ]
Show Custom Dialog [ "Search for" ; "Enter a search query." ; $search ]
Perform Semantic Find [
      Query by: Natural language ;
      Account Name:"myAccount" ;
      Embedding Model: "text-embedding-3-small" ;
      Text: $search ;
      Record set: All records ;
      Target field: Sandbox::Embedding ;
      Cosine similarity contion: greater than or equal to ;
      Embedding similarity value: .3
      ]
```

When the script is run, a dialog will appear asking the user to enter a search query. This can be a short sentence describing the type of records they want to find. For example, they can enter "Space movies" or "Movies with romance" and find the results in the table that have a semantic match to that, even if those keywords are not present in the fields.

Tip   See the online documentation for more information about additional AI related functions and script steps introduced in version 21 (2024).

Summary

This chapter introduced FileMaker's ability to interact with artificial intelligence APIs like the OpenAI API.

Index

A

© Mark Conway Munro 2024
M. C. Munro, *Learn FileMaker Pro 2024*, https://doi.org/10.1007/979-8-8688-0835-7

C

D

H

I

K

L

M

N

P

Printed in the United States
by Baker & Taylor Publisher Services